Image and Video Forensics

Image and Video Forensics

Editors

Irene Amerini
Gianmarco Baldini
Francesco Leotta

MDPI • Basel • Beijing • Wuhan • Barcelona • Belgrade • Manchester • Tokyo • Cluj • Tianjin

Editors
Irene Amerini
Sapienza University of Rome
Italy

Gianmarco Baldini
European Commission, Joint
Research Centre
Italy

Francesco Leotta
Sapienza University of Rome
Italy

Editorial Office
MDPI
St. Alban-Anlage 66
4052 Basel, Switzerland

This is a reprint of articles from the Special Issue published online in the open access journal *Journal of Imaging* (ISSN 2313-433X) (available at: https://www.mdpi.com/journal/jimaging/special_issues/image_video_forensics).

For citation purposes, cite each article independently as indicated on the article page online and as indicated below:

LastName, A.A.; LastName, B.B.; LastName, C.C. Article Title. *Journal Name* **Year**, *Volume Number*, Page Range.

ISBN 978-3-0365-2806-9 (Hbk)
ISBN 978-3-0365-2807-6 (PDF)

© 2021 by the authors. Articles in this book are Open Access and distributed under the Creative Commons Attribution (CC BY) license, which allows users to download, copy and build upon published articles, as long as the author and publisher are properly credited, which ensures maximum dissemination and a wider impact of our publications.

The book as a whole is distributed by MDPI under the terms and conditions of the Creative Commons license CC BY-NC-ND.

Contents

About the Editors vii

Irene Amerini, Gianmarco Baldini and Francesco Leotta
Image and Video Forensics
Reprinted from: *J. Imaging* 2021, 7, 242, doi:10.3390/jimaging7110242 1

Yohanna Rodriguez-Ortega, Dora M. Ballesteros and Diego Renza
Copy-Move Forgery Detection (CMFD) Using Deep Learning for Image and Video Forensics
Reprinted from: *J. Imaging* 2021, 7, 59, doi:10.3390/jimaging7030059 5

Yasmin M. Alsakar, Nagham E. Mekky and Noha A. Hikal
Detecting and Locating Passive Video Forgery Based on Low Computational Complexity Third-Order Tensor Representation
Reprinted from: *J. Imaging* 2021, 7, 47, doi:10.3390/jimaging7030047 21

Sara Ferreira, Mário Antunes, Manuel E. Correia
Exposing Manipulated Photos and Videos in Digital Forensics Analysis
Reprinted from: *J. Imaging* 2021, 7, 102, doi:10.3390/jimaging7070102 47

Marina Gardella, Pablo Musé, Jean-Michel Morel and Miguel Colom
Forgery Detection in Digital Images by Multi-Scale Noise Estimation
Reprinted from: *J. Imaging* 2021, 7, 119, doi:10.3390/jimaging7070119 71

Stephanie Autherith and Cecilia Pasquini
Detecting Morphing Attacks through Face Geometry Features
Reprinted from: *J. Imaging* 2020, 6, 115, doi:10.3390/jimaging6110115 87

Dennis Siegel, Christian Kraetzer, Stefan Seidlitz and Jana Dittmann
Media Forensics Considerations on DeepFake Detection with Hand-Crafted Features
Reprinted from: *J. Imaging* 2021, 7, 108, doi:10.3390/jimaging7070108 105

Oliver Giudice, Luca Guarnera and Sebastiano Battiato
Fighting Deepfakes by Detecting GAN DCT Anomalies
Reprinted from: *J. Imaging* 2021, 7, 128, doi:10.3390/jimaging7080128 135

Federico Marcon, Cecilia Pasquini and Giulia Boato
Detection of Manipulated Face Videos over Social Networks: A Large-Scale Study
Reprinted from: *J. Imaging* 2021, 7, 193, doi:10.3390/jimaging7100193 153

Lars de Roos and Zeno Geradts
Factors that Influence PRNU-Based Camera-Identification via Videos
Reprinted from: *J. Imaging* 2021, 7, 8, doi:10.3390/jimaging7010008 169

Pasquale Ferrara, Rudolf Haraksim and Laurent Beslay
Performance Evaluation of Source Camera Attribution by Using Likelihood Ratio Methods
Reprinted from: *J. Imaging* 2021, 7, 116, doi:10.3390/jimaging7070116 185

Davide Dal Cortivo, Sara Mandelli, Paolo Bestagini and Stefano Tubaro
CNN-Based Multi-Modal Camera Model Identification on Video Sequences
Reprinted from: *J. Imaging* 2021, 7, 135, doi:10.3390/jimaging7080135 203

Anselmo Ferreira, Ehsan Nowroozi and Mauro Barni
VIPPrint: Validating Synthetic Image Detection and Source Linking Methods on a Large Scale Dataset of Printed Documents
Reprinted from: *J. Imaging* **2021**, *7*, 50, doi:10.3390/jimaging7030050 223

Luca Maiano, Irene Amerini, Lorenzo Ricciardi Celsi and Aris Anagnostopoulos
Identification of Social-Media Platform of Videos through the Use of Shared Features
Reprinted from: *J. Imaging* **2021**, *7*, 140, doi:10.3390/jimaging7080140 247

Rahimeh Rouhi, Flavio Bertini, Danilo Montesi
No Matter What Images You Share, You Can Probably Be Fingerprinted Anyway
Reprinted from: *J. Imaging* **2021**, *7*, 33, doi:10.3390/jimaging7020033 263

Slim Hamdi, Samir Bouindour, Hichem Snoussi, Tian Wang and Mohamed Abid
End-to-End Deep One-Class Learning for Anomaly Detection in UAV Video Stream
Reprinted from: *J. Imaging* **2021**, *7*, 90, doi:10.3390/jimaging7050090 283

Georgios Karantaidis, and Constantine Kotropoulos
An Automated Approach for Electric Network Frequency Estimation in Static and Non-Static Digital Video Recordings
Reprinted from: *J. Imaging* **2021**, *7*, 202, doi:10.3390/jimaging7100202 299

Zuheng Ming, Muriel Visani, Muhammad Muzzamil Luqman and Jean-Christophe Burie
A Survey on Anti-Spoofing Methods for Facial Recognition with RGB Cameras of Generic Consumer Devices
Reprinted from: *J. Imaging* **2020**, *6*, 139, doi:10.3390/jimaging6120139 319

Ivan Castillo Camacho and Kai Wang
A Comprehensive Review of Deep-Learning-Based Methods for Image Forensics
Reprinted from: *J. Imaging* **2021**, *7*, 69, doi:10.3390/jimaging7040069 375

About the Editors

Irene Amerini is Assistant Professor at Department of Computer, Control, and Management Engineering Antonio Ruberti, Sapienza University of Rome, Italy. In 2018, she obtained a Visiting Research Fellowship at the School of Computing and Mathematics, Charles Sturt University (AU) offered by the Australian Government—Department of Education and Training through the Endeavour Scholarship and Fellowship program. In 2010, she spent part of her PhD course at the Digital Data Embedding Laboratory, Department of Electrical and Computer Engineering, Binghamton University (U.S.). She received her Ph.D. in computer engineering, multimedia, and telecommunication from the University of Florence in 2011. Her research interests are focused on multimedia forensics and deep learning for image and video analysis. She is member of the IEEE Information Forensics and Security Technical Committee, EURASIP TAC Biometrics, Data Forensics and Security, and of the IAPR TC6–Computational Forensics Committee. She is a Guest Editor of several international journals and Associate Editor of the following journals: Journal of Information Security and Applications, IEEE ACCESS and Journal of Electronic Imaging.

Gianmarco Baldini is currently a Senior Researcher/Project Manager in the Joint Research Centre of the European Commission. He received his Laurea degree in Electronic Engineering from the University of Rome, Italy, in 1993, and his PhD in computer science at the University of Insubria, Italy, in 2019. He has worked in the R&D departments in the field of wireless communications in Italy, Ireland, and the U.S.A. before joining the European Commission, Joint Research Centre (JRC) in 2007. In the JRC, he has worked in wireless communications, security, positioning, and machine learning, and he has contributed to the formulation of European policies in the areas of radio frequency spectrum, road transportation, and cybersecurity. He is currently working on the European Radio Frequency spectrum policy and wireless communication technologies including 5G, energy efficiency of wireless networks, and the application of machine learning/artificial intelligence to wireless communications.

Francesco Leotta is an Assistant Professor at DIAG in Engineering in Computer Science at Sapienza. He received his Ph.D. in Engineering in Computer Science from Sapienza University in 2014. His research concerns algorithmic, methodological, experimental, and practical aspects of different areas of information systems, including ubiquitous computing, human–computer (and robot) interaction, and digital humanities. Such topics are challenged in the application domains of smart spaces, smart manufacturing, and cultural heritage. He has co-authored more than 50 peer-reviewed scientific papers on the above research topics. He has been/is actively involved in many projects at the international (EU FP7 and H2020 programmes) and national level. He is also very active in the organization of conferences, with scientific and organizational roles. He regularly serves as reviewer for top-ranked conferences and journals in the above mentioned research topics.

Editorial

Image and Video Forensics

Irene Amerini [1,*], Gianmarco Baldini [2] and Francesco Leotta [1]

1. Department of Computer, Control and Management Engineering A. Ruberti, Sapienza University of Rome, 00185 Rome, Italy; leotta@diag.uniroma1.it
2. European Commission, Joint Research Centre, 21027 Ispra, Italy; gianmarco.baldini@ec.europa.eu
* Correspondence: amerini@diag.uniroma1.it

Citation: Amerini, I.; Baldini, G.; Leotta, F. Image and Video Forensics. *J. Imaging* **2021**, *7*, 242. https://doi.org/10.3390/jimaging7110242

Received: 11 November 2021
Accepted: 11 November 2021
Published: 17 November 2021

Publisher's Note: MDPI stays neutral with regard to jurisdictional claims in published maps and institutional affiliations.

Copyright: © 2021 by the authors. Licensee MDPI, Basel, Switzerland. This article is an open access article distributed under the terms and conditions of the Creative Commons Attribution (CC BY) license (https://creativecommons.org/licenses/by/4.0/).

Nowadays, images and videos have become the main modalities of information being exchanged in everyday life, and their pervasiveness has led the image forensics community to question their reliability, integrity, confidentiality, and security more and more. Multimedia contents are generated in many different ways through the use of consumer electronics and high-quality digital imaging devices, such as smartphones, digital cameras, tablets, wearable sensors, and other Internet of Things (IoT) devices. The ever-increasing convenience of image acquisition has facilitated instant distribution and sharing of digital images on digital social platforms, determining a great amount of the exchanged data. Moreover, the pervasiveness of powerful image editing tools has allowed the manipulation of digital images for malicious or criminal ends, up to the creation of synthesized images and videos with the use of deep learning techniques. In all cases (e.g., forensic investigations, fake news debunking, information warfare, and mitigation of cyberattacks), where images and videos serve as critical demonstrative evidence, forensic technologies that help to determine the origin, authenticity of sources, and integrity of multimedia content become essential tools. In response to these needs, the multimedia forensics community has produced major research efforts regarding visual content authentication.

The call for papers for the Special Issue "Image and Video Forensics" was opened to anyone wishing to present advancements in state of the art, innovative research and ongoing projects on multimedia forensics and content verification to tackle new and serious challenges in ensuring media authenticity. This Special Issue solicited contributions from researchers in diverse areas such as image processing, artificial intelligence, computer vision and multimedia forensics.

This Special Issue received several submissions, which underwent a rigorous peer review process. After the review process, 18 articles (16 research papers and 2 review articles) were selected based on the ratings and comments. The published articles cover various applications of image and video forensics research, focusing on different branches such as forgery detection, deepfake detection, source identification and anomaly detection, and develop and apply a range of techniques, from image processing to computer vision, based on handcrafted features and/or deep learning.

The issue of media content authenticity verification has been taken into account from different points of view, considering traditional manipulation as well as more recent threats such as deepfakes. Rodriguez-Ortega et al. [1] presented a copy-move forgery detection technique based on a deep learning model to overcome the problem of generalization among different datasets. Alsakar et al. [2] focused instead on the analysis and identification of forgery in videos based on low computational complexity third-order tensor representation. Two types of forgery have been considered: insertion and deletion for static and dynamic videos. Ferreira S. et al. [3] exploited a support vector machine (SVM) classifier to distinguish between genuine and fake multimedia files, which may indicate the presence of deepfake content. This method was integrated as new modules in the widely used digital forensics application Autopsy. In their contribution, they proposed the extraction of a set of simple features resulting from the application of a discrete Fourier transform (DFT) to digital photos and video frames. Gardella et al. [4] focused on noise inconsistency in order to assess the authenticity of a digital image. To this end, they presented a multi-scale approach suitable for studying the highly correlated noise present in JPEG-compressed images. A noise level function was estimated for each image block and then compared with the noise level of the whole image. In the article proposed by Autherith and Pasquini [5], the detection of morphing attacks on digital faces was considered. To facilitate and improve this investigation they proposed the analysis of the locations of facial landmarks identified in two images, with the goal of capturing inconsistencies in facial geometry introduced by the morphing process.

Other contributions have addressed the problem of deepfake detection. Siegel et al. [6] tackled this issue, discussing if hand-crafted features could be used as an alternative to the learned features obtained through a deep learning algorithm. The proposed method made use of three sets of hand-crafted features and three different fusion strategies to implement DeepFake detection, demonstrating a similar generalization behavior to neural network-based methods.

Similarly to [6], Giudice et al. [7] focused their attention on deepfake image detection. To this end, they presented a new pipeline able to detect the GAN (generative adversarial network)-specific frequencies representing a unique fingerprint of the different generative architectures. By employing discrete cosine transformation (DCT), anomalous frequencies were detected and, in particular, the β statistics inferred by the AC coefficients distribution were used to recognize the different GAN engines that generated the data. Finally, Marcon et al. [8] addressed the problem of detecting manipulated videos of faces shared on social media platforms. In their contribution, a large scale performance evaluation was carried out involving general purpose deep networks and state-of-the-art manipulated data. The presented results confirmed that a performance drop was observed in every case where unseen shared data were tested by networks trained on non-shared data, finally concluding that fine-tuning operations can mitigate this problem.

Together with forgery detection, many challenging problems are faced by the multimedia forensics research community, such as source camera identification, the task of linking a particular digital image with its source device, social media identification, establishing the social network provenance of a certain image, as well as recovering from digital evidences the processing steps applied to the data, starting from the acquisition procedure up to tracking the spread and evolution of multiple images. De Roos and Geradts [9] investigated different factors, such as resolution, length of the video and compression, that influence camera video identification based on PRNU (photo response non-uniformity noise). To this end, Ferrara et al. [10] presented a new approach for the performance evaluation of source camera attribution by using likelihood ratio methods obtained from the PRNU similarity scores. Dal Cortivo et al. [11] investigated the camera model identification on video proposing a CNN (Convolutional Neural Network) based method jointly exploit audio and visual information. Ferreira A. et al. [12] focused their contribution on validating synthetic image detection and source linking methods on a new large scale dataset of printed documents.

The research community has recently shown an ambition to scale multimedia forensics analysis to real-world open systems. To this end, Maiano et al. [13] presented a method for assessing the social media platform of provenance of a video sequence, considering the interrelation among features captured from videos as well as those shared by images. Rouhi et al. [14] compared different classification-based methods to achieve both smartphone identification and user profile linking within social networks.

Other contributions to this special session have addressed the problem of anomaly detection in unmanned aerial vehicle (UAV) video streams. Hamdi et al. [15] proposed an end-to-end architecture capable of generating optical flow images from original UAV images and extracting compact spatio-temporal characteristics for anomaly detection purposes. Karantaidis et al. [16] investigated the challenging problem of electric network frequency (ENF) estimation in static and non-static digital video recordings, designing an automated approach based on simple linear iterative clustering via the exploitation of areas with similar characteristics.

Finally, to conclude, two review articles have contributed to the success of this special issue. The first one is a comprehensive survey on anti-spoofing methods for facial recognition with Red Green Blue (RGB) cameras of generic consumer devices by Ming et al. [17]. The second one, by Castillo Camacho and Wang [18], covers the topic of deep learning-based methods for image forensics, reviewing methods dealing with forgery detection and source identification with an overview of adversarial forensics and of the main dataset used.

Funding: This research received no external funding.

Acknowledgments: We express our sincere gratitude to the authors for their contributions, to the reviewers for their efforts in reviewing the manuscripts, and to the editorial staff of the MDPI Journal of Imaging for their endless support in making this Special Issue possible. We hope it will benefit the scientific community and increase the interest in this exciting area of research, providing new perspectives for the development of proper security enhancement approaches for image and video-related applications.

Conflicts of Interest: The authors declare no conflict of interest.

References

1. Rodriguez-Ortega, Y.; Ballesteros, D.; Renza, D. Copy-Move Forgery Detection (CMFD) Using Deep Learning for Image and Video Forensics. *J. Imaging* **2021**, *7*, 59. [CrossRef]
2. Alsakar, Y.; Mekky, N.; Hikal, N. Detecting and Locating Passive Video Forgery Based on Low Computational Complexity Third-Order Tensor Representation. *J. Imaging* **2021**, *7*, 47. [CrossRef] [PubMed]
3. Ferreira, S.; Antunes, M.; Correia, M. Exposing Manipulated Photos and Videos in Digital Forensics Analysis. *J. Imaging* **2021**, *7*, 102. [CrossRef]
4. Gardella, M.; Musé, P.; Morel, J.; Colom, M. Forgery Detection in Digital Images by Multi-Scale Noise Estimation. *J. Imaging* **2021**, *7*, 119. [CrossRef]
5. Autherith, S.; Pasquini, C. Detecting Morphing Attacks through Face Geometry Features. *J. Imaging* **2020**, *6*, 115. [CrossRef] [PubMed]
6. Siegel, D.; Kraetzer, C.; Seidlitz, S.; Dittmann, J. Media Forensics Considerations on DeepFake Detection with Hand-Crafted Features. *J. Imaging* **2021**, *7*, 108. [CrossRef]
7. Giudice, O.; Guarnera, L.; Battiato, S. Fighting Deepfakes by Detecting GAN DCT Anomalies. *J. Imaging* **2021**, *7*, 128. [CrossRef] [PubMed]
8. Marcon, F.; Pasquini, C.; Boato, G. Detection of Manipulated Face Videos over Social Networks: A Large-Scale Study. *J. Imaging* **2021**, *7*, 193. [CrossRef] [PubMed]
9. De Roos, L.; Geradts, Z. Factors that Influence PRNU-Based Camera-Identification via Videos. *J. Imaging* **2021**, *7*, 8. [CrossRef]
10. Ferrara, P.; Haraksim, R.; Beslay, L. Performance Evaluation of Source Camera Attribution by Using Likelihood Ratio Methods. *J. Imaging* **2021**, *7*, 116. [CrossRef]
11. Dal Cortivo, D.; Mandelli, S.; Bestagini, P.; Tubaro, S. CNN-Based Multi Modal Camera Model Identification on Video Sequences. *J. Imaging* **2021**, *7*, 135. [CrossRef] [PubMed]
12. Ferreira, A.; Nowroozi, E.; Barni, M. VIPPrint: Validating Synthetic Image Detection and Source Linking Methods on a Large Scale Dataset of Printed Documents. *J. Imaging* **2021**, *7*, 50. [CrossRef] [PubMed]
13. Maiano, L.; Amerini, I.; Ricciardi Celsi, L.; Anagnostopoulos, A. Identification of Social-Media Platform of Videos through the Use of Shared Features. *J. Imaging* **2021**, *7*, 140. [CrossRef] [PubMed]
14. Rouhi, R.; Bertini, F.; Montesi, D. No Matter What Images You Share, You Can Probably Be Fingerprinted Anyway. *J. Imaging* **2021**, *7*, 33. [CrossRef]
15. Hamdi, S.; Bouindour, S.; Snoussi, H.; Wang, T.; Abid, M. End-to-End Deep One-Class Learning for Anomaly Detection in UAV Video Stream. *J. Imaging* **2021**, *7*, 90. [CrossRef]
16. Karantaidis, G.; Kotropoulos, C. An Automated Approach for Electric Network Frequency Estimation in Static and Non-Static Digital Video Recordings. *J. Imaging* **2021**, *7*, 202. [CrossRef] [PubMed]
17. Ming, Z.; Visani, M.; Luqman, M.; Burie, J. A Survey on Anti-Spoofing Methods for Facial Recognition with RGB Cameras of Generic Consumer Devices. *J. Imaging* **2020**, *6*, 139. [CrossRef]
18. Castillo Camacho, I.; Wang, K. A Comprehensive Review of Deep-Learning-Based Methods for Image Forensics. *J. Imaging* **2021**, *7*, 69. [CrossRef] [PubMed]

Article

Copy-Move Forgery Detection (CMFD) Using Deep Learning for Image and Video Forensics

Yohanna Rodriguez-Ortega [†], Dora M. Ballesteros [*,†] and Diego Renza [†]

Faculty of Engineering, Universidad Militar Nueva Granada, Bogotá 110111, Colombia; est.yohanna.rodrig@unimilitar.edu.co (Y.R.-O.); diego.renza@unimilitar.edu.co (D.R.)
* Correspondence: dora.ballesteros@unimilitar.edu.co; Tel.: +57-1-650-0000
† These authors contributed equally to this work.

Abstract: With the exponential growth of high-quality fake images in social networks and media, it is necessary to develop recognition algorithms for this type of content. One of the most common types of image and video editing consists of duplicating areas of the image, known as the copy-move technique. Traditional image processing approaches manually look for patterns related to the duplicated content, limiting their use in mass data classification. In contrast, approaches based on deep learning have shown better performance and promising results, but they present generalization problems with a high dependence on training data and the need for appropriate selection of hyperparameters. To overcome this, we propose two approaches that use deep learning, a model by a custom architecture and a model by transfer learning. In each case, the impact of the depth of the network is analyzed in terms of precision (P), recall (R) and F1 score. Additionally, the problem of generalization is addressed with images from eight different open access datasets. Finally, the models are compared in terms of evaluation metrics, and training and inference times. The model by transfer learning of VGG-16 achieves metrics about 10% higher than the model by a custom architecture, however, it requires approximately twice as much inference time as the latter.

Keywords: copy-move forgery detection; computer vision; deep learning; fake image; transfer learning; VGG

Citation: Rodriguez-Ortega, Y.; Ballesteros, D.M.; Renza, D. Copy-Move Forgery Detection (CMFD) Using Deep Learning for Image and Video Forensics. *J. Imaging* **2021**, *7*, 59. https://doi.org/10.3390/jimaging7030059

Academic Editor: Irene Amerini

Received: 16 February 2021
Accepted: 16 March 2021
Published: 20 March 2021

Publisher's Note: MDPI stays neutral with regard to jurisdictional claims in published maps and institutional affiliations.

Copyright: © 2021 by the authors. Licensee MDPI, Basel, Switzerland. This article is an open access article distributed under the terms and conditions of the Creative Commons Attribution (CC BY) license (https://creativecommons.org/licenses/by/4.0/).

1. Introduction

In recent years, the expansion of Internet services and the proliferation and strengthening of social platforms such as Facebook, Instagram and Reddit have had a significant impact on the amount of content circulating in digital media. According to the International Telecommunication Union (ITU), at the end of 2019, 53.6% of the world's population uses the Internet, which means that approximately 4.1 billion people have access not only to this technology, but also to different tools available online [1]. Although in most cases the content shared is original or has only been manipulated for entertainment purposes, in other cases the manipulation may be intentional for disinformation purposes, with political and forensic repercussions, for example, using the fake content as digital evidence in a criminal investigation.

Image or video manipulation refers to any action that can be performed on a digital content using software editing tools (e.g., Adobe Photoshop, GIMP, PIXLR) or artificial intelligence. In particular, the copy-move technique copies a part of an image and then pastes it into the same image [2]. As editing tools advance, the quality of the fake images increases and they appear to the human eye as original images. In addition, post-processing manipulations, such as JPEG compression, brightness changes, or equalization, can reduce the traces left by manipulation and make it more difficult to detect [3].

The copy-move forgery detection (CMFD) includes hand-crafted and deep learning-based methods [2]. The former is mainly divided into block-based, keypoint-based and hybrid approach. The second uses custom architectures from scratch or fine-tuned models of pre-trained architectures such as VGG-16 [4]. Block-based approaches use different types of features extraction, for example, Fourier transform, DCT (Discrete Cosine Transform) [5,6] or Tetrolet transform [7]. One of their concerns is the reduction of performance when the copied object is rotated or resized, as the detection of counterfeiting is done through a matching process [8]. On the other hand, keypoint-based approaches such as SIFT (Scale Invariant Feature Transform) [9] and SURF (Speed-UP Robust Features) [10] are more robust to rotation and lighting variations but they have several challenges to overcome such as detecting counterfeits in regions of uniform intensity, natural duplicate objects detected as fake duplicate objects, and dependence on actual key points in the image [6]. A hybrid approach provided more stable results in terms of precision (P), recall (R) and $F1$ score, but only for a single data set [11].

Recent approaches use Convolutional Neural Network (CNN) for feature extraction and classification [12,13]. For example, a custom CNN with nine convolutional layers and a fully connected (FC) layer was proposed in [14]. The architecture was trained separately with CASIA v1 and CASIA v2 datasets, obtaining an accuracy of 98.04% and 97.83%, respectively. A similar work used a custom model with six convolutional layers and three FC layers, with batch normalization in all the convolutional layers, and dropout in the FC layers (except the last one); using the CoMoFoD dataset, the internal validation of this model reached an accuracy of 95.97% [15]. A less deep custom architecture uses only two convolutional layers and two FC layers [16]. The authors trained and validated the model with one, two and three datasets obtaining $F1$ scores of 90%, 94% and 95%, respectively. Although they address the problem of generalization, their mixed datasets are unbalanced, one with a ratio of 2:1 for fake and original images, and the other with a ratio of 2:3. Finally, a data-driven local descriptor with CNN obtained $F1$ scores between 0.5 and 0.7 for the CoMoFoD dataset [17].

Complementary to custom designs with CNNs, a second group of CNN-based approaches use transfer learning (TL). In this case, pre-trained models are used even for feature extraction or by means of fine-tuning. For example, a pre-trained AlexNet model is followed by a feature comparison block and a post-processing stage which provides $F1$ score of 93% for the GRIP dataset [18]. In other case, VGG-16 has been used as a feature extractor up to the last pooling layer [19]. Experiments were conducted with the MICC-F220 dataset reporting precision of 98%, recall of 89.5%, $F1$ score of 92% and accuracy of 95%.

Although there are many proposals that have addressed the problem of CMFD, concerns and challenges remain as listed below:

- Most classification models using deep learning have been trained and validated with a unique dataset, limiting their use to other kind of tampered images. In other words, they have not addressed the problem of generalization;
- The CNN models trained with various datasets did not use class-balanced data, so they could be biased to a particular class;
- Most methods did not report image prediction times, so it is not possible to know if they are suitable in applications that require real time or massive data analysis;
- The deep learning-based works have used a single design strategy, either custom or by transfer learning, but, to our knowledge, no work has compared the two approaches for the same dataset.

According to the above, this research makes a contribution in the following aspects:

- Two models of CMFD based on deep learning are proposed, one corresponding to custom design and the other by transfer learning. Additionally, the dependence of the depth of the network on the performance of the classifier is evaluated.
- The generalization problem is addressed by training and validating the proposed models with data from eight public datasets. Also, external validation results are also compared when the architecture is trained on a single dataset.
- Finally, the inference time of the custom model is compared with that of the VGG-16 based model.

The rest of the paper is organized as follows—Section 2 presents the proposed architectures by custom design and transfer learning. Section 3 describes the experimental tests and the models selected for each design strategy. Section 4 presents the results for the generalization problem, as well as the comparison between the proposed models in terms of performance metrics and inference times. Section 5 discusses the results. Finally, Section 6 summarises the work.

2. Proposed Architectures for CMFD

We propose two approaches for CMFD. The first uses a custom design and the second uses transfer learning. Both design strategies are based on CNNs. In the following, we will explain each case.

2.1. Architectures by Custom Design

In this design strategy, we considered that the features that allow us to identify whether an image is original or has been manipulated with the copy-move technique are not found in very deep layers, since high-level features such as shape are not useful to solve this kind of problem. This is supported by previous studies, which state that in terms of network depth, the number of convolutional layers plus the number of *FC* layers, should not exceed 10 layers [14–16]. In our design, we propose five architectures with different depths, up to five convolutional layers (*conv*) with two *FC* layers. Figure 1 shows the proposed architectures, where each block specifies the type of layer (i.e., *conv*, pooling (*pool*) or *FC*), the number of filters and the size of the kernel. For example, *block1_conv*, 32, (3 × 3) is the first convolutional layer with 32 filters and kernel size of (3 × 3).

In all cases, the input image is resized to 400 × 400 × 3. The first convolutional layer has 32 filters of (3 × 3) size, with the Leaky_ReLU activation function using alpha = 0.09. In this layer, the padding is fixed as same, and the stride is 1 pixel. Its output is a feature map of 400 × 400 × 32, which has the same height *(H)* and width *(W)* of the input image, and the number of channels is equal to the number of filters. Next, the MaxPooling layer reduces the size of the input, that is, the feature map, in terms of *H* and *W*, but preserving the number of channels, according to Equation (1):

$$H_o \times W_o = \lceil (H + 2p - k + 1)/s \rceil \times \lceil (W + 2p - k + 1)/s \rceil, \qquad (1)$$

where $\lceil . \rceil$ is the ceiling function, k is the kernel size, s is the stride, p is the padding, H_o is the height of the output, and W_o is the weight of the output. With $H = 400$, $W = 400$, $p = 0$, $k = 3$ and $s = 3$, the output is $H_o \times W_o = \lceil (400 - 3 + 1)/3 \rceil \times \lceil (400 - 3 + 1)/3 \rceil = 133 \times 133$.

Hence, the difference between the architectures is the number of convolutional layers. The second architecture has two *conv+pool* layers; the third architecture has three *conv+pool* layers; and so on. All convolutional layers have padding equal to *same* so the *H* and *W* values of the input feature maps are preserved. Except for the first MaxPooling layer, these blocks work with $k = 2$. The last two layers are fully-connected with 1028 and 2 units, respectively. Leaky_ReLU is used up to the penultimate layer, while softmax is used in the last layer.

Table 1 summarizes the hyperparameters of the five architectures by custom design. This table consists of four parts: the first part corresponds to the convolutional layers (from *block1_conv* to *block5_pool*); the second part corresponds to the *FC1* layer; the third part corresponds to the *FC2* layer; and the last part consolidates the five architectures.

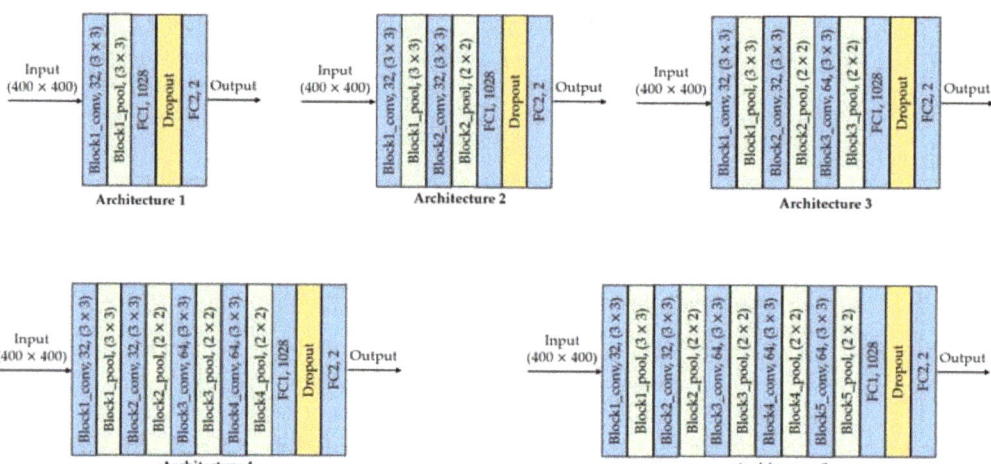

Figure 1. Architectures by custom design: *conv* is the convolutional layer, *pool* is pooling layer, *FC* is the fully-connected layer.

Table 1. Hyperparameters of the proposed architectures by custom design: k is the kernel size, s is stride, p is padding.

Layer	No. of Filters or Neurons	k	s	p	Output Shape	Trainable Parameters
Input	–	–	–	–	(400, 400, 3)	0
block1_conv	32	3	1	same	(400, 400, 32)	896
block1_pool	32	3	3	0	(133, 133, 32)	0
block2_conv	32	3	1	same	(133, 133, 32)	9248
block2_pool	32	2	2	0	(66, 66, 32)	0
block3_conv	64	3	1	same	(66, 66, 64)	18,496
block3_pool	64	2	2	0	(33, 33, 64)	0
block4_conv	64	3	1	same	(33, 33, 64)	36,928
block4_pool	64	2	2	0	(16, 16, 64)	0
block5_conv	64	3	1	same	(16, 16, 64)	36,928
block5_pool	64	2	2	0	(8, 8, 64)	0
FC1 (architecture 1)	1028	–	–	–	–	581,898,372
FC1 (architecture 2)	1028	–	–	–	–	143,296,004
FC1 (architecture 3)	1028	–	–	–	–	71,648,516
FC1 (architecture 4)	1028	–	–	–	–	16,843,780
FC1 (architecture 5)	1028	–	–	–	–	4,211,716
FC2	2	–	–	–	–	2058
Architecture 1	–	–	–	–	–	581,901,326
Architecture 2	–	–	–	–	–	143,308,206
Architecture 3	–	–	–	–	–	71,679,214
Architecture 4	–	–	–	–	–	16,911,406
Architecture 5	–	–	–	–	–	4,316,270

Regarding activation function, Leaky_ReLU is chosen to avoid the dying ReLU problem. The alpha value (α) is fixed to 0.09 for convolutional layers, and 0.1 for the first *FC* layer. This activation function is calculated according to Equation (2).

$$f(x) = max\{\alpha x, x\}, \qquad (2)$$

where $f(x)$ is the output of the activation function, and x is the input. Unlike the ReLU function, negative values are allowed at the output.

The second group of hyperparameters are related to the training stage. We have selected the following attributes: 80 epochs, categorical cross-entropy as loss function,

SGD as the optimizer with a learning rate of 0.001 and a decay of 0.0001. Finally, with the purpose of reducing overfitting, we apply two strategies, dropout of 0.3 in the next-to-last layer, and image augmentation with horizontal and vertical flip.

2.2. Architectures by Transfer Learning (TL)

VGG-16 is one of the widely known models for image classification, which was trained with the sub-set of 1000 classes for the ImageNet Challenge [20]. The VGG architecture was proposed by the Visual Geometry Group of the University of Oxford and it is characterized by a stack of convolutional layers that precede a MaxPooling layer [21]. It has 3×3 and 1×1 filters, with a stride fixed to 1 pixel, and it includes 13 convolutional layers and 3 *FC* layers. Compared to the proposed architectures by custom design, VGG-16 differs in the depth of the network, in the number of filters in the convolutional layers, in the activation function, and also in the number of convolutional layers stacked before the pooling layer.

We have selected the pre-trained model VGG-16 for the following reasons:

- It is a sequential architecture as the proposed one, then we can compare the performance of the custom model with the model by transfer learning for the same type of architecture and analyze whether the features learned from a pre-trained model are useful for this type of classification problem;
- In recent work, some models by transfer learning with VGG-16 have been shown to be useful for identifying fake images from different types of manipulations such as copy-move [19] and colorization [12];
- Although VGG-16 is an architecture with a larger number of parameters and higher inference times than other architectures such as Inception or ResNet, it can be pruned for real-time applications without performance degradation [22].

Regarding transfer learning, there are several choices of using pre-trained models, one of them replaces part of the layers of the original architecture and preserves the others [13]. For instance, VGG-16 architecture can be preserved up to *block4_pool* layer and then add fully-connected layers with a different number of outputs. The new architecture will have pre-trained (frozen) parameters corresponding to those of the layers *block1_conv1* to *block4_pool*, and trainable parameters corresponding to the new *FC* layers.

In our case, we tested the performance of four different architectures from VGG-16, that is, different frozen points. Figure 2 shows the architectures with this design strategy and Table 2 shows their corresponding hyperparameters. The first part corresponds to the architecture that was transferred from VGG-16 with its pre-trained parameters. The second part corresponds to the *FC1* layer which depends on the frozen point. The third part is the *FC2* layer. The last part is the total number of parameters for each of the four architectures, which includes the pre-trained parameters and the trainable parameters (i.e., *FC1* + *FC2*). In all cases, the input image size is $300 \times 300 \times 3$.

On the other hand, to illustrate the features learned by the VGG 16 pre-trained model, we have selected the *block4_pool* layer to display one of its feature maps. Figure 3 shows the example for the filter 60. Similar patterns are detected in the feature maps for the two flowers, that is, a green and yellow semi-circle appears in the corresponding areas that have flowers. This type of pattern allows the classifier to make the decision on the originality of the image.

Finally, to train the transfer-learning based model, the same hyperparameters defined for the custom architecture are selected: 80 epochs, categorical cross-entropy as loss function, SGD as the optimizer with a learning rate of 0.001 and a decay of 0.0001. However, in this case, the dropout value is 0.45.

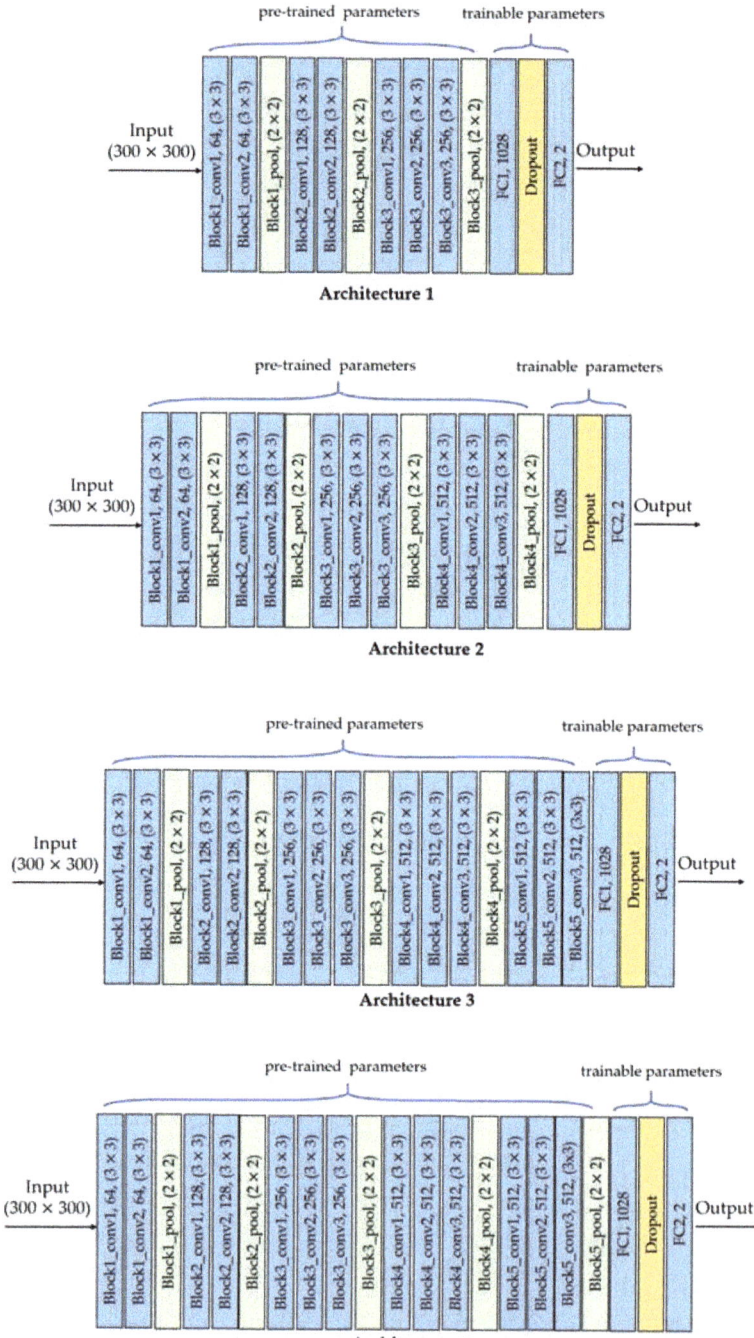

Figure 2. Architectures by TL: *conv* is convolutional layer, *pool* is pooling layer, *FC* is fully-connected layer.

Table 2. Hyperparameters of the architectures by transfer learning: *k* is the kernel size, *s* is stride, *p* is padding.

Layer	No. of Filters or Neurons	k	s	p	Output Shape	Trainable Parameters
Input	–	–	–	–	(400, 400, 3)	0
block1_conv1	64	3	1	same	(300, 300, 64)	1792
block1_conv2	64	3	1	same	(300, 300, 64)	36,928
block1_pool	64	2	2	0	(150, 150, 64)	0
block2_conv1	128	3	1	same	(150, 150, 128)	73,856
block2_conv2	128	3	1	same	(150, 150, 128)	147,584
block2_pool	128	2	2	0	(75, 75, 128)	0
block3_conv1	256	3	1	same	(75, 75, 256)	295,168
block3_conv2	256	3	1	same	(75, 75, 256)	590,080
block3_conv3	256	3	1	same	(75, 75, 256)	590,080
block3_pool	256	2	2	0	(37, 37, 256)	0
block4_conv1	512	3	1	same	(37, 37, 512)	1,180,160
block4_conv2	512	3	1	same	(37, 37, 512)	2,359,808
block4_conv3	512	3	1	same	(37, 37, 512)	2,359,808
block4_pool	512	2	2	0	(18, 18, 512)	0
block5_conv1	512	3	1	same	(18, 18, 512)	2,359,808
block5_conv2	512	3	1	same	(18, 18, 512)	2,359,808
block5_conv3	512	3	1	same	(18, 18, 512)	2,359,808
block5_pool	512	2	2	0	(9, 9, 512)	0
FC1 (architecture 1)	1028	–	–	–	–	360,278,020
FC1 (architecture 2)	1028	–	–	–	–	170,533,892
FC1 (architecture 3)	1028	–	–	–	–	170,533,892
FC1 (architecture 4)	1028	–	–	–	–	42,634,244
FC2	2	–	–	–	–	2058
Architecture 1	–	–	–	–	–	362,015,566
Architecture 2	–	–	–	–	–	178,171,214
Architecture 3	–	–	–	–	–	185,250,638
Architecture 4	–	–	–	–	–	57,348,932

Figure 3. Example of feature maps for the *block4_pool* of the pre-trained VGG-16 model: (**a**) original image, (**b**) fake image with copy-move, (**c**) output of the filter 60 for the original image, (**d**) output of the filter 60 for the fake image. The source of (**a**,**b**) is [23] with permission of the authors.

3. Experimental Tests

Bearing in mind that one of the purposes of this research was to address the problem of generalization, it is mandatory to consider several datasets for model training. Then, a unified dataset should have diversity in image size, format, color space and editing quality, that is, whether the manipulation is perceptible or not. This is done by unifying several datasets, some of which have been widely used in the literature, while others are new. Specifically, we have selected eight datasets, as follows: Coverage, CG-1050 v1, CG-1050 v2, MICC-F220, MICC-F2000, Copy-move Forgery Dataset (CMFD), CASIA v1 and CASIA v2. Table 3 shows the characteristics of each dataset.

The unified dataset contains images in JPEG, BMP and TIF formats, color and grayscale images, different sizes of the copied object and different orientation. They were split in training, validation, and testing (60%, 20% and 20%, respectively). Additionally, all images were converted to JPEG format, to train the model using images with a lossy compression format. Table 4 shows the number of fake and original images taken from each dataset.

Table 3. Characteristics of the selected datasets.

Dataset	Grayscale	Color	TIFF	JPEG	BMP	Original	Fake
COVERAGE [24]		x	x			x	x
CG-1050 v1 [25]	x	x		x		x	x
CG-1050 v2 [26]	x	x		x		x	x
MICC-F220 [27]		x		x			x
MICC-F2000 [27]		x		x		x	x
CMFD dataset [23]		x			x	x	x
CASIA v1 [28]		x		x			x
CASIA v2 [28]		x		x			x

Table 4. Unified dataset: number of images taken from single datasets.

Dataset	Fake	Original
COVERAGE	100	99
CG-1050-V1	331	100
CG-1050-V2	328	1044
MICC-F220	29	0
MICC-F2000	700	346
CMFD	383	50
CASIA V1	370	0
CASIA V2	706	0

It was necessary to add original images since some datasets only contained fake images. Table 5 shows the final distribution of the unified dataset, including 1308 original images obtained from a personal repository.

Table 5. Distribution of the unified dataset: training, validation, and test.

Dataset	Training	Validation	Test
Fake	1765	590	592
Original	1766	590	591

As shown in Table 5, the unified dataset is balanced by class, so that the models are not biased towards a particular class.

3.1. Comparison Metrics

To compare the performance of the classifier, we use three metrics that are suitable for balanced datasets, such as the unified dataset, corresponding to precision (P), recall

(R) and F1 score. Precision measures the ratio of images predicted as fake that belong to that class. Recall gives the ratio of fake images that are correctly classified. Finally, the F1 score is the harmonic mean between precision and recall. These metrics are obtained using Equations (3)–(5):

$$P = \frac{TP}{TP + FP}, \quad (3)$$

$$R = \frac{TP}{TP + FN}, \quad (4)$$

$$F1 = 2 \times \frac{P \times R}{P + R}, \quad (5)$$

where *TP* is the number of True Positives, *FP* is the number of False Positives and *FN* is the number of False Negatives. The class fake is the positive class while the class original is the negative class.

In addition, we use accuracy (*acc*) to compare our results with some of the state-of-the-art proposals. This metric is obtained with Equation (6):

$$acc = \frac{TP + TN}{TP + FP + TN + FN}, \quad (6)$$

The four metrics range between 0 and 1, their ideal value is 1 and the worst is 0.

3.2. Impact of the Depth for the Custom Architecture

To assess how architecture depth affects model performance, we trained the five custom-designed architectures of Figure 1. As shown in Figure 4, model performance decreased as depth increased, the F1 scores are very similar between layers *block4_pool* and *block5_pool* with a very low overfitting. The impact of the depth of the architecture was also analyzed in terms of external validation with the test dataset, that is, using images unknown to the trained model. Figure 5 shows the behavior of F1 score, precision and recall by varying the number of convolutional layers. According to the results, *block2_pool* and *block4_pool* have the lowest variation in their metrics (P, R, F1), which means a better balance between precision and recall, however, the highest scores correspond to *block4_pool*.

Considering the above results, the proposed model by custom design was obtained from the architecture 4, that is, up to *block4_pool* with two *FC* layers.

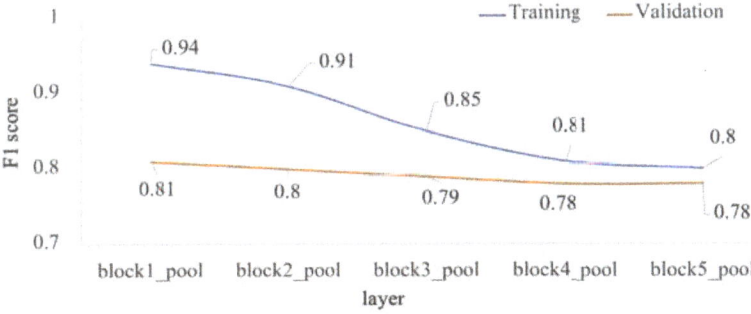

Figure 4. Impact of the depth for the custom architecture in terms of F1 score: training vs validation. The *x*-axis corresponds to the last layer before the *FC1* layer, and the *y*-axis is the *F1* score.

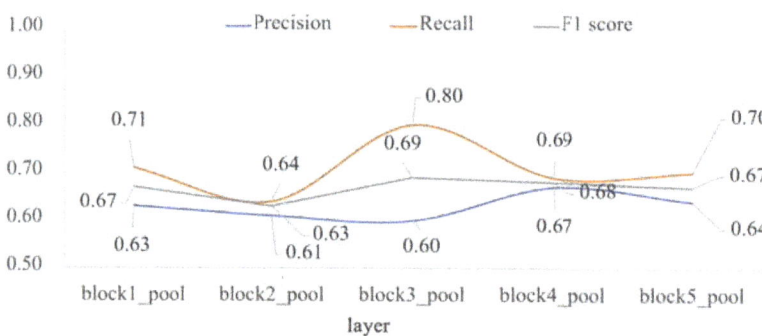

Figure 5. Impact of the depth for the custom architecture in terms of *P*, *R* and *F1* score: external test. The *x*-axis corresponds to the last layer before the *FC1* layer, and the *y*-axis are the evaluated metrics.

3.3. Impact of the Depth for the Architecture by Transfer Learning

In the second approach, the four architectures in Figure 2 were evaluated, as it is shown in Figure 6. Each architecture corresponds to a specific freezing point of the pre-trained VGG-16 model: *block3_pool*, *block4_pool*, *block5_conv3* and *block5_pool*. The worst metrics were obtained for the most superficial freezing layer, where the metrics for training and validation did not exceed 0.5. Using deeper freezing points, the *F1* score in training exceeded 0.9 for *block4_pool* and *block5_pool* and 0.8 for *block5_conv3*. In validation, the *F1* score presented values of 0.83, 0.81 and 0.81 for *block4_pool*, *block5_conv3* and *block5_pool*, respectively. In summary, the *F1* score did not increase when increasing the network freezing point beyond the *block4_pool* layer.

Finally, the four models by transfer learning were validated with the test dataset. Figure 7 shows the results in terms of *F1* score. For the *block3_pool* layer, the best metric is precision, but for the *block5_conv3* layer the best metric is recall. The good balance between precision and recall is found in *block4_pool* layer in which *P*, *R*, and *F1* score are very close among them. This layer is a breaking point in the performance of the classifier. As the freezing point gets deeper, the performance metrics decrease, being lower than 0.71 for the *block5_pool* layer.

Therefore, the proposed model by transfer learning was obtained from the architecture 2, that is, up to *block4_pool* from VGG-16, plus two new *FC* layers.

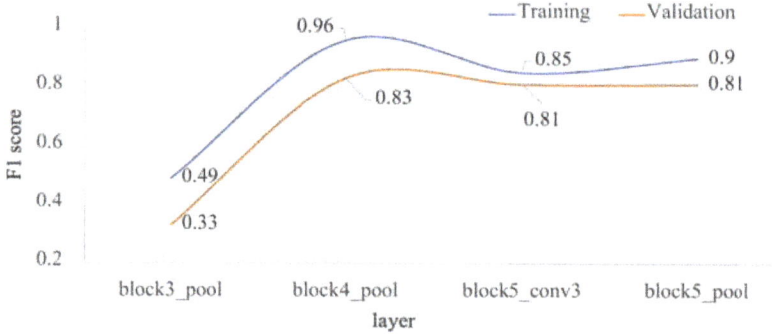

Figure 6. Impact of the depth for the architecture by transfer learning using VGG-16, in terms of *F1* score: training vs. validation. The *x*-axis corresponds to the selected last layer of VGG-16, and the *y*-axis is the *F1* score.

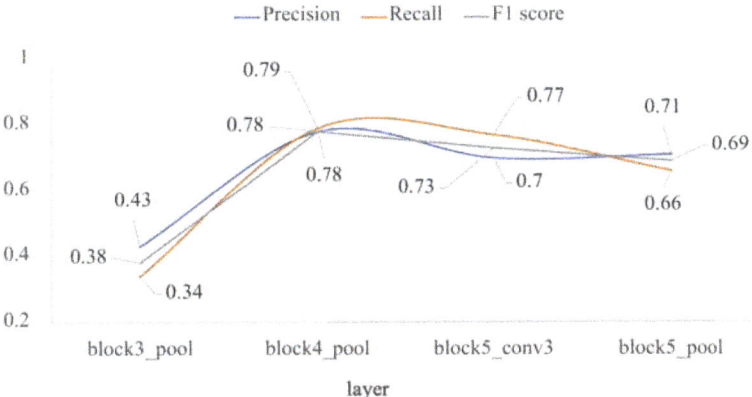

Figure 7. Impact of the depth for the architecture by transfer learning using VGG-16, in terms of *P*, *R* and *F1*: external test. The *x*-axis corresponds to the selected last layer of VGG-16, and the *y*-axis are the evaluated metrics.

4. Results

Considering that the TL-based model obtained better performance metrics than the custom-designed model (i.e., 0.78 vs 0.68 for *F1* score), the TL-based model is selected for the generalization tests in Sections 4.1 and 4.2. In addition, both models are compared in terms of performance, training and inference times, in Section 4.3.

4.1. Training with a Single Dataset

In this section we trained the architecture 2 of the TL-based strategy with six different datasets, (i.e., CASIA v1, CASIA v2, CG-1050 v1, CG-1050 v2, Copy-move forgery dataset (CMFD) and MICC-F2000), obtaining six different models. Figure 8 shows the results in terms of *F1* score for training and validation. It should be noted that, for the datasets of CASIA v1, MICC-F2000 and CG-1050 v1, *F1* scores are very close to each other for training and validation, and close to 1; while for CASIA v2 and CMFD, the values are higher than 0.9. Only, for the CG-1050 v2 dataset, the validation value is distant from the training one. In summary, the same architecture is able to obtain high scores for different datasets when the model is validated with data similar to those used in the training stage.

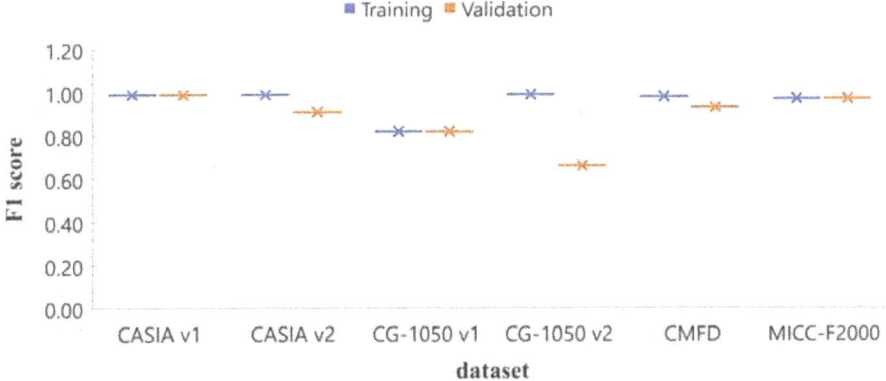

Figure 8. Comparison in terms of *F1* score with a single dataset (training vs. validation). The *x*-axis corresponds to the model trained with the specific dataset, and the *y*-axis is the *F1* score.

The next step is to compare the results with those reported in the literature with a single dataset. Table 6 shows either the *acc* or the *F1* score for some works, divided in three groups: CASIA (v1, v2), CMFD and MICC (F2000, F220, F600). For the copy-move forgery dataset (CMDF) group, the results were very similar between them. For the CASIA group, similar results are found for custom CNN and by transfer learning models. For the MICC group, deep learning-based methods outperform hand-crafted based methods. However, it is not clear whether the classifiers are biased to one class, as few papers report all four metrics: *acc*, *P*, *R* and *F1*. For instance, in [29] the authors reported a precision of 89.0% and recall of 100%, which implies that these metrics are not balanced, and specifically, the classifier is slightly biased to the positive class.

Thus, our proposed TL-based model exceeds most of the results reported by other works, in two of the three groups of this comparison. It should be noted that transfer learning with VGG-16 had already been used for the same classification task (i.e., ref [19]) up to the *block5_pool* layer, but its results in terms of *F1* score are lower than those of our work. This is because after the *block4_pool* layer the performance decreases, as is reported in Figure 7.

Table 6. Comparison between state-of-the-art approaches in terms of accuracy (acc) and *F1* score for the datasets: CASIA (v1, v2), CMFD and MICC (F2000, F220, F600). The higher the better.

Method/Year/Reference	CASIA	CMFD	MICC	acc	F1
CNN (9 *conv* layers)/2016/[14]	x			98.0%	
Our–VGG-16 based/2020	x			98.0%	99.0%
Keypoint clustering/2020/[30]		x			93.8%
Our–VGG-16 based/2020		x		94.0%	93.0%
VGG-16 based (*block5_pool*)/2019/[19]			x	95.0%	92.0%
CNN (6 *conv* layers)/2020/[31]			x	99.5%	
CNN (3 *conv* layers, dual branch)/2021/[29]			x	96.0%	94.0%
Hand-crafted (feature point)/2016/[32]			x		74.0%
Hand-crafted (hybrid feature extraction)/2020/[11]			x		93.0%
Our–VGG-16 based/2020			x	97.0%	97.0%

4.2. Adressing the Problem of Generalization

We evaluate the generalization capacity when the architecture by transfer learning is trained with a single dataset versus several datasets. We test the six models trained with a single dataset (Section 4.1) against the unified dataset, and we compare their results with the selected model of Section 3.3. Figure 9 shows a radar plot in which each vertex of the triangle corresponds to *P* (up), *R* (down, right) and *F1* score (down, left). The best model is the one whose curve is the most external, without biasing any of the metrics.

As shown in Figure 9, the outermost curve corresponds to the model trained with the unified dataset, in which there is an adequate balance between *P* and *R*, and therefore the three values (*P*, *R* and *F1* score) are very similar between them. The second place is occupied by the model trained with CASIA v2 in which again the metrics are balanced but are lower than in the first case. One of the worst curves was found with the model trained with CMFD dataset, in which *R* is high but *P* is low. This means that few fake images are labelled as original, but many original images are labelled as fake.

According to the above, not only the results for individual datasets are important to know the quality of the model, but also the generalization results. An architecture trained and evaluated on a single dataset can achieve high *F1* score values, but it is no guarantee of high performance for new images.

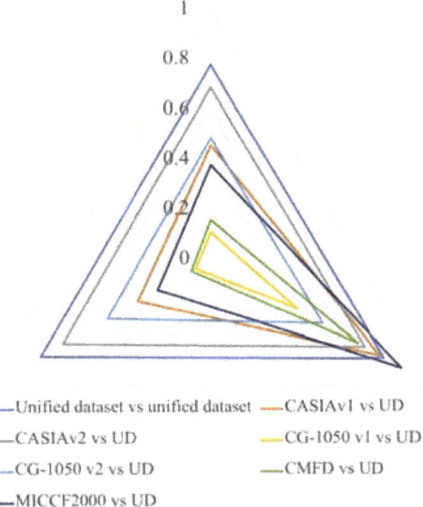

Figure 9. Ability of generalization: single dataset vs. unified dataset (UD). The triangle represents P (up), R (down, right) and $F1$ score (down, left).

4.3. Custom Model vs. Vgg-16 Based Model

In this last test section, we compare the two proposed models in terms of performance (Table 7), number of parameters (Table 8) and training and inference times (Table 9).

In terms of performance, the model by transfer learning shows higher scores in all four statistics. However, in both models, there is a high trade-off between accuracy and recall, and therefore, the amount of misclassifications is similar for the two classes (original and fake).

Table 7. Comparison of the two proposed models in terms of *acc*, *P*, *R* and *F1* score.

Model	acc	P	R	F1
Model by custom design	0.68	0.67	0.69	0.68
Model by transfer learning	0.78	0.78	0.79	0.78

In the second comparison, all parameters are trainable in the custom architectures, while only the *FC* layer parameters are trainable in the architectures by transfer learning. In the first case, architecture 4 from Table 1 was selected, while in the second case, architecture 2 from Table 2 was selected. As shown in Table 8, the total number of parameters of the second approach is much higher than the former.

Table 8. Comparison of the two proposed models in terms of number of parameters.

Model	Parameters	Trainable	Non-Trainable
Model by custom design	16,911,406	16,91,406	0
Model by transfer learning	178,171,214	170,535,950	7,635,264

On the other hand, in terms of training and inference times (Table 9), the model by custom architecture uses about 65% of that of the transfer-learning-based.

Table 9. Comparison of the two proposed models in terms of training and validation times, *h* is hours, *sec* is seconds.

Model	Training Time (h)	Inference Time by Image (sec)
Model by custom design	1.8	0.0354
Model by transfer learning	2.8	0.0532

In summary, the model by the custom architecture has a lower number of parameters than the model by transfer learning, with less inference time, but with a lower success rate in the classification.

5. Discussion

This research addressed the generalization problem, where models trained with a single dataset can show very high results with similar data, but their performance decreases significantly with data dissimilar to that of the training stage. In most papers, copy forgery detection models have been trained and validated (internally) with a single dataset or with datasets from the same "family", for example, CASIA (v1 and v2) or MICC (2000, F220 F600), but not with data from multiple and highly diverse datasets.

Fitting the model for single datasets is not a very difficult task, as presented in Figure 8, where the same architecture was used to train six single models with high results in five of the six cases. However, in a real scenario, the trained models must classify images dissimilar to those used in the training stage, and then, models trained with a single data set do not perform adequately, as was shown in Figure 9. For instance, the model trained with the CMFD dataset obtained *F1* scores close to 1 when evaluated with images from the same dataset, but its performance decreased when tested with images from other datasets showing high recall and very low precision.

For this reason, to approach a real scenario, we used a unified dataset from different individual datasets, some of which have already been used in other works and others are new, with a high diversity as summarized in Table 3. Obtaining a trained model with high precision and recall, and a proper balance between these two metrics was not an easy task, so it was necessary to evaluate several hyperparameters. After several adjustments of the hyperparameters (both related to the architecture as well as the training stage) we obtained two promising models, which are presented in this paper.

It is worth noting that the task of copy-move forgery detection is not yet solved, because every day in social networks new high quality manipulated images are found, which could be classified not only by an algorithm but by human beings as originals.

6. Conclusions

In this paper we proposed two deep learning-based models, a custom model and a TL-based model, to evaluate its effectiveness in the CMFD task. Additionally, we address the generalization problem when the architecture is trained only with one dataset but tested with several datasets versus the approach trained with a large dataset. Finally, we evaluate not only the performance of the proposed models but their training and inference times. According to our results, the custom architecture with few convolutional layers have greater generalization problems than those with more layers; however, in the VGG-16 pre-trained model it was found that when using a freezing point beyond the *block4_pool* layer the classifier results get worse. Additionally, it was found that models trained with a single dataset tend to classify images into a single class (original or fake), such that P and R metrics are not balanced (one high and one low). The best balance between these metrics was obtained when the weights of the pre-trained VGG-16 model were frozen in the *block4_pool* layer and the unified dataset was used. Besides, the improved performance in classifying original and fake images in the VGG-16 based model has a direct relationship with the inference time, which is almost double that of the custom model.

Future work may consider extending the training dataset, assessing the impact of other hyperparameters on classifier performance and a hybrid approach mixing an image pre-processing stage using domain transformation (e.g., DFT, DCT, and DWT) with feature extraction based on deep learning.

Author Contributions: Conceptualization, D.M.B. and D.R.; methodology, Y.R.-O. and D.M.B. and D.R.; software, Y.R.-O. and D.M.B.; validation, Y.R.-O.; formal analysis, D.M.B.; investigation, D.M.B. and D.R.; data curation, Y.R.-O.; writing—original draft preparation, Y.R.-O. and D.M.B.; writing—review and editing, D.R.; visualization, D.M.B.; supervision, D.M.B. and D.R. All authors have read and agreed to the published version of the manuscript.

Funding: This research was funded by "Vicerrectoría de Investigaciones—Universidad Militar Nueva Granada", grant number IMP-ING-2936 of 2019–2021.

Institutional Review Board Statement: Not applicable.

Informed Consent Statement: Not applicable.

Data Availability Statement: The data CG-1050 used in this study are openly available in [25,26].

Conflicts of Interest: The authors declare no conflict of interest.

Abbreviations

The following abbreviations are used in this manuscript:

acc	Accuracy
CNN	Convolutional Neural Network
CMFD	Copy-Move Forgery Detection
conv	Convolutional layer
DCT	Discrete Cosine Transform
DFT	Discrete Fourier Transform
DWT	Discrete Wavelet Transform
FC	Fully-Connected
P	Precison
pool	Pooling layer
R	Recall
SIFT	Scale Invariant Feature Transform
SURF	Speed-Up Robust Features

References

1. ITU. Statistics. Available online: https://www.itu.int/en/ITU-D/Statistics/Pages/stat/default.aspx (accessed on 4 December 2020).
2. Thakur, R.; Rohilla, R. Recent Advances in Digital Image Manipulation Detection Techniques: A brief Review. *Forensic Sci. Int.* **2020**, *312*, 110311. [CrossRef]
3. Abd Warif, N.B.; Wahab, A.W.A.; Idris, M.Y.I.; Ramli, R.; Salleh, R.; Shamshirband, S.; Choo, K.K.R. Copy-move forgery detection: survey, challenges and future directions. *J. Netw. Comput. Appl.* **2016**, *75*, 259–278. [CrossRef]
4. Ferreira, W.D.; Ferreira, C.B.; da Cruz Júnior, G.; Soares, F. A review of digital image forensics. *Comput. Electr. Eng.* **2020**, *85*, 106685. [CrossRef]
5. Dua, S.; Singh, J.; Parthasarathy, H. Detection and localization of forgery using statistics of DCT and Fourier components. *Signal Process. Image Commun.* **2020**, *82*, 115778. [CrossRef]
6. Gani, G.; Qadir, F. A robust copy-move forgery detection technique based on discrete cosine transform and cellular automata. *J. Inf. Secur. Appl.* **2020**, *54*, 102510. [CrossRef]
7. Meena, K.B.; Tyagi, V. A copy-move image forgery detection technique based on tetrolet transform. *J. Inf. Secur. Appl.* **2020**, *52*, 102481. [CrossRef]
8. Sharma, S.; Ghanekar, U. A hybrid technique to discriminate Natural Images, Computer Generated Graphics Images, Spliced, Copy Move tampered images and Authentic images by using features and ELM classifier. *Optik* **2018**, *172*, 470–483. [CrossRef]
9. Alberry, H.A.; Hegazy, A.A.; Salama, G.I. A fast SIFT based method for copy move forgery detection. *Future Comput. Inform. J.* **2018**, *3*, 159–165. [CrossRef]
10. Badr, A.; Youssif, A.; Wafi, M. A Robust Copy-Move Forgery Detection In Digital Image Forensics Using SURF. In Proceedings of the 2020 8th International Symposium on Digital Forensics and Security (ISDFS), Beirut, Lebanon, 1–2 June 2020; pp. 1–6.

11. Tinnathi, S.; Sudhavani, G. An Efficient Copy Move Forgery Detection Using Adaptive Watershed Segmentation with AGSO and Hybrid Feature Extraction. *J. Vis. Commun. Image Represent.* **2020**, *74*, 102966. [CrossRef]
12. Ulloa, C.; Ballesteros, D.M.; Renza, D. Video Forensics: Identifying Colorized Images Using Deep Learning. *Appl. Sci.* **2021**, *11*, 476. [CrossRef]
13. Pachón, C.; Ballesteros, D.M.; Renza, D. Fake Banknote Recognition Using Deep Learning. *Appl. Sci.* **2021**, *11*, 1281. [CrossRef]
14. Rao, Y.; Ni, J. A deep learning approach to detection of splicing and copy-move forgeries in images. In Proceedings of the 2016 IEEE International Workshop on Information Forensics and Security (WIFS), Abu Dhabi, United Arab Emirates, 4–7 December 2016; pp. 1–6.
15. Thakur, R.; Rohilla, R. Copy-Move Forgery Detection using Residuals and Convolutional Neural Network Framework: A Novel Approach. In Proceedings of the 2019 2nd International Conference on Power Energy, Environment and Intelligent Control (PEEIC), Greater Noida, India, 18–19 October 2019; pp. 561–564.
16. Kumar, S.; Gupta, S.K. A Robust Copy Move Forgery Classification Using End to End Convolution Neural Network. In Proceedings of the 2020 8th International Conference on Reliability, Infocom Technologies and Optimization (Trends and Future Directions) (ICRITO), Noida, India, 4–5 June 2020; pp. 253–258.
17. Liu, Y.; Guan, Q.; Zhao, X. Copy-move forgery detection based on convolutional kernel network. *Multimed. Tools Appl.* **2018**, *77*, 18269–18293. [CrossRef]
18. Muzaffer, G.; Ulutas, G. A new deep learning-based method to detection of copy-move forgery in digital images. In Proceedings of the 2019 Scientific Meeting on Electrical-Electronics & Biomedical Engineering and Computer Science (EBBT), Istanbul, Turkey, 24–26 April 2019; pp. 1–4.
19. Agarwal, R.; Verma, O.P. An efficient copy move forgery detection using deep learning feature extraction and matching algorithm. *Multimed. Tools Appl.* **2019**, *79*, 1–22. [CrossRef]
20. Russakovsky, O.; Deng, J.; Su, H.; Krause, J.; Satheesh, S.; Ma, S.; Huang, Z.; Karpathy, A.; Khosla, A.; Bernstein, M.; et al. Imagenet large scale visual recognition challenge. *Int. J. Comput. Vis.* **2015**, *115*, 211–252. [CrossRef]
21. Simonyan, K.; Zisserman, A. Very deep convolutional networks for large-scale image recognition. *arXiv* **2014**, arXiv:1409.1556.
22. He, Y.; Zhang, X.; Sun, J. Channel pruning for accelerating very deep neural networks. In Proceedings of the IEEE International Conference on Computer Vision, Venice, Italy, 22–29 October 2017; pp. 1389–1397.
23. Ardizzone, E.; Bruno, A.; Mazzola, G. Copy–move forgery detection by matching triangles of keypoints. *IEEE Trans. Inf. Forensics Secur.* **2015**, *10*, 2084–2094. [CrossRef]
24. Wen, B.; Zhu, Y.; Subramanian, R.; Ng, T.T.; Shen, X.; Winkler, S. COVERAGE—A novel database for copy-move forgery detection. In Proceedings of the 2016 IEEE International Conference on Image Processing (ICIP), Phoenix, AZ, USA, 25–28 September 2016; pp. 161–165.
25. Castro, M.; Ballesteros, D.M.; Renza, D. A dataset of 1050-tampered color and grayscale images (CG-1050). *Data Brief* **2020**, *28*, 104864. [CrossRef]
26. Castro, M.; Ballesteros, D.M.; Renza, D. CG-1050 v2: Original and Tampered Images. 2019. Available online: https://data.mendeley.com/datasets/28xhc4kyfp/1 (accessed on 17 December 2020).
27. Amerini, I.; Ballan, L.; Caldelli, R.; Del Bimbo, A.; Serra, G. A sift-based forensic method for copy–move attack detection and transformation recovery. *IEEE Trans. Inf. Forensics Secur.* **2011**, *6*, 1099–1110. [CrossRef]
28. Dong, J.; Wang, W.; Tan, T. Casia image tampering detection evaluation database. In Proceedings of the 2013 IEEE China Summit and International Conference on Signal and Information Processing, Beijing, China, 6–10 July 2013; pp. 422–426.
29. Goel, N.; Kaur, S.; Bala, R. Dual branch convolutional neural network for copy move forgery detection. *IET Image Process.* **2021**, *15*, 656–665. [CrossRef]
30. Chen, H.; Yang, X.; Lyu, Y. Copy-move forgery detection based on keypoint clustering and similar neighborhood search algorithm. *IEEE Access* **2020**, *8*, 36863–36875. [CrossRef]
31. Elaskily, M.A.; Elnemr, H.A.; Sedik, A.; Dessouky, M.M.; El Banby, G.M.; Elshakankiry, O.A.; Khalaf, A.A.; Aslan, H.K.; Faragallah, O.S.; Abd El-Samie, F.E. A novel deep learning framework for copy-moveforgery detection in images. *Multimed. Tools Appl.* **2020**, *79*, 19167–19192. [CrossRef]
32. Yu, L.; Han, Q.; Niu, X. Feature point-based copy-move forgery detection: covering the non-textured areas. *Multimed. Tools Appl.* **2016**, *75*, 1159–1176. [CrossRef]

Article

Detecting and Locating Passive Video Forgery Based on Low Computational Complexity Third-Order Tensor Representation

Yasmin M. Alsakar *, Nagham E. Mekky and Noha A. Hikal

Department of Information Technology, Faculty of Computers and Information Science, Mansoura University, Mansoura 35516, Egypt; nagham@mans.edu.eg (N.E.M.); dr_nahikal@mans.edu.eg (N.A.H.)
* Correspondence: yasminmahmoud@mans.edu.eg; Tel.: +20-10-6695-3844

Abstract: Great attention is paid to detecting video forgeries nowadays, especially with the widespread sharing of videos over social media and websites. Many video editing software programs are available and perform well in tampering with video contents or even creating fake videos. Forgery affects video integrity and authenticity and has serious implications. For example, digital videos for security and surveillance purposes are used as evidence in courts. In this paper, a newly developed passive video forgery scheme is introduced and discussed. The developed scheme is based on representing highly correlated video data with a low computational complexity third-order tensor tube-fiber mode. An arbitrary number of core tensors is selected to detect and locate two serious types of forgeries which are: insertion and deletion. These tensor data are orthogonally transformed to achieve more data reductions and to provide good features to trace forgery along the whole video. Experimental results and comparisons show the superiority of the proposed scheme with a precision value of up to 99% in detecting and locating both types of attacks for static as well as dynamic videos, quick-moving foreground items (single or multiple), zooming in and zooming out datasets which are rarely tested by previous works. Moreover, the proposed scheme offers a reduction in time and a linear computational complexity. Based on the used computer's configurations, an average time of 35 s. is needed to detect and locate 40 forged frames out of 300 frames.

Keywords: inter-frame forgery; digital forensics; correlation; SVD; Harris; GLCM; Tensor; video forensic

Citation: Alsakar, Y.M.; Mekky, N.E.; Hikal, N.A. Detecting and Locating Passive Video Forgery Based on Low Computational Complexity Third-Order Tensor Representation. *J. Imaging* **2021**, *7*, 47. https://doi.org/10.3390/jimaging7030047

Academic Editor: Irene Amerini

Received: 10 February 2021
Accepted: 1 March 2021
Published: 5 March 2021

Publisher's Note: MDPI stays neutral with regard to jurisdictional claims in published maps and institutional affiliations.

Copyright: © 2021 by the authors. Licensee MDPI, Basel, Switzerland. This article is an open access article distributed under the terms and conditions of the Creative Commons Attribution (CC BY) license (https://creativecommons.org/licenses/by/4.0/).

1. Introduction

Recently, recording videos using digital cameras, smartphones, and surveillance camcorders has become very easy and has been performed for many reasons in our everyday activities. Millions of videos are available every day, either uploaded over different internet sites or shared among social media. However, any video is easy to create or forge due to the widespread use of software video editing applications. Any editing video software can be used to tamper with videos such as Adobe Video Editor, Photoshop, Premiere by Adobe, and Windows Movie Maker, which are really good methods to easily edit video content, as anyone can edit the video files as it will be similar to the original content. These software applications have made forgery identification very difficult and have led to serious issues. Recently, detecting forged videos has gained great interest and has become a trending research topic compared to video authentication but authenticating the video contents may be unavailable all the time [1,2].

Digital video consists of a large group of sequential images, also known as frames, displayed in rapid succession to create the illusion of motion. Any malicious tampering in video content that alters its visual meaning is considered video forgery. Fast transition between scenes can be easily distinguished from forgery [3]. Video Forgery is categorized into three types regarding its operations domain. The first type is intra-frame forgery, also called a copy-move attack, this happens in the spatial domain, where certain objects are copied and pasted from one region to another within the same frames [4]. The second type is spatiotemporal domain forgery, called a region splicing attack, which occurs when some objects are copied from some frames and pasted onto other frames [5]. The last type is inter-frame, which occurs in the temporal domain if some frames are deleted from the original video (frame deletion), inserted from another video (frame insertion), or duplicated from the same video (frame duplication) [6]. In actuality, the first two types can be easily observed by the human eye, since the movement of forged objects through frames mostly fails to achieve smooth transitions. Inter-frame forgeries have gained researchers' interest due to their great implications and detecting challenges.

Video forgery detecting methods are categorized into active and passive methods [7]. Active methods are based on analyzing certain types of embedded authentication information inside the original video, such as watermarks or digital signatures. This information is reviewed and checked to prove the correctness of the videos. Fake videos are those that failed in the authentication process. However, most of the videos are not protected by authentication information. Therefore, passive approaches have become necessary as they are more flexible, robust and effective. Passive methods trace video frames searching for signs of forgery, such as: insertion, duplication, deletion, and replacement of frames into original videos. Moreover, passive methods can detect different types of forgeries and localize them.

Throughout the state-of-the-art methods, passive approaches work on video frames one-by-one in the spatial domain to detect signs of forgery. They compare all successive video frame features and depend on spatial correlation measures to prove the discontinuity of frame sequences. These features limit passive approaches performance in terms of detection time and accuracy, especially in the case of large video sizes with a low content variation. Recently, tensor data representation has been considered a trend computational approach to deal with large videos, it provides greater model fitting stability, easier to read and saves time [8].

The offered approach in this paper develops a new inter-frame forgery passive approach that has high efficiency in respect to the achieved detection accuracy at minimum computational complexity. The main idea is as follows:

- The method is based on comparing a limited number of orthogonal-features extracted from third-order tensor video decomposition;
- First, the whole video sequence is geometrically constructed into sub-groups, and each sub-group is mathematically decomposed into a group of third-order tensors. Then, instead of comparing all the frame/feature correlations, a group of arbitrarily chosen core sub-groups is orthogonally transformed to obtain essential features to trace along the tube fibers. Moreover, if a forgery is detected, these features can be used to localize the forged frames with high accuracy;
- The novelty of this paper is the great accuracy in detecting inter-frame forgeries. Hence, the geometric construction of successive video frames into third-order tensor tube fiber mode offers a great reduction in the number of pixels needed to trace forgeries;
- Checking one or two core sub-groups/third-order tensors of a limited number of pixels in the orthogonal domain is enough to detect frame discontinuities, compared with classic passive methods that examine the entire frame sequences. Additionally, this construction encapsulates the spatial and temporal features of successive frames into 2D matrices which can be manipulated and tested easily with high accuracy and less computational complexity.

The following paper structure is outlined as follows: Section 2 discusses the related work on passive video forgery methods. Section 3 introduces a comprehensive analysis of the proposed method. Section 4 presents the experimental investigation results of the proposed method. A comparison and analysis of the results are given in Section 5. Finally, in Section 6, the conclusions and future directions are introduced.

2. Related Work

Many important research developments have been made around digital video forensics. In this section, a summary of related research on passive approaches is introduced. Passive approaches trace video frames searching for three types of forgery: multiple/double compression, region tampering, and inter-frame video forgery. This proposed paper mainly considers the inter-frame forgery type in detail.

Inter-frame video forgeries occur by inserting, deleting and duplicating frames in a video. Many studies that worked on inter-frame types faced problems such as accuracy and complexity of detecting and locating. Previous studies worked by comparing successive frames and found that they required a long time for video forgery detecting and locating regardless of forgery type. The most commonly used techniques in the studies were handcrafted methods [9] that depend on different methods of manual extraction of features from video frames. There are many methods for extracting various types of features from video frames. Forgery has been identified according to the stability of the characteristics detected for the specific problem such as frame duplication, frame deletion, frame insertion–deletion and insertion–deletion–duplication. Inter-frame forgery case-related research is introduced in the following sections.

In the case of frame duplication detection, Yang et al. [10] solved frame duplication forgeries using an effective two-stage method. It calculated the similarities using the correlation coefficient between Singular Value Decomposition (SVD) features extracted from each frame. Singh et al. [11] identified duplicated frames from video by extracting nine characteristics for each frame and then lexicographical sorting was carried out to group similar frames. Between these characteristics, Root Mean Square Error (RMSE) was calculated. To recognize the duplicated frames, the correlation between frames was calculated.

For the frame deletion cases, Liu et al. [12] detected frame deletion by analysis of its time and frequency domain features and measuring the periodicity of the Sequence of Average Residual of P-frames (SARP) of videos with frames deleted, SARP results were represented in spikes at certain positions in the Discrete-Time Fourier Transform (DTFT) spectrum. YU et al. [13] detected frame deletion by presenting two features to measure the prediction residual variation magnitude and intramacro block number.

For the case of frame deletion and insertion, Wang et al. [14] depended on computing the consistency of correlation coefficients of gray values (CoGVs) and then fed them into Support Vector Machine (SVM) to classify forged and original videos. Zhang et al. [15] proposed a sequence to detect frame deletion and insertion using two steps, In the first step, the correlation was calculated for Local Binary Patterns (LBPs) of every frame and in the second step, abnormal point detection was applied using the Chebyshev inequality twice. Aghamaleki and Behrad [16] identified frame insertion or deletion, mathematically analyzing the quantization error traces of P-frame residual errors. An algorithm was then proposed to classify rich areas of quantization-error in the P-frame. A wavelet-based algorithm was addressed to enrich the quantization error traces in the frequency domain. These interpreted and spatially limited residual errors are used to detect video forgery in the temporal domain.

For the case of frame deletion, insertion and duplication cases, Bakas et al. [6] detected frame duplication insertion and deletion in videos. They extracted outlier frames using correlation and then used finer levels to eliminate false positives from the first level. Zhao et al. [17] focused on similarity analysis and passive blind forensics scheme for shots of videos was analyzed to identify inter-frame type forgeries. This method consisted of two parts: Hue-Saturation-Value (HSV) color histogram comparison and Speeded Up Robust Features (SURF) feature extraction together with the Fast Library for Approximate Nearest Neighbors (FLANN) double-checking matching. Qiong et al. [18] detected inter-frame forgery based on the histogram of oriented gradients (HOG) and motion energy image (MOI).

Some studies tended to use deep learning methods in forgery detecting and locating but faced problems such as low accuracy, only detected forgery and some of them were forced to use labeled training sets as they used supervised learning. Long et al. [19] detected and localized frame duplicated frames in videos using a coarse-to-fine deep Convolution Neural Network (CNN) framework. This paper used the Siamese network with the ReSnet network to identify duplicated frames. Bakas and Naskar [20] detected frame insertion, duplication and deletion using a 3D convolutional neural network that used another CNN layer, which was used for temporal information extraction from videos. Li et al. [21] extracted features and localized abnormal points. In the extracting feature phase, the 2-D phase congruency of each frame was detected, since it was a good image characteristic. Then, the correlation between the neighboring frames was determined. In the second phase, the abnormal points were identified using a clustering algorithm (k-means). The normal and abnormal points were clustered into two categories.

The first video forgery type is multiple/double compression which occurs when a video is to be manipulated in compressed format [22,23]. The second type is region tampering which occurred by copying and pasting small parts of the frame at another location [24–26]. There is little attraction to the researchers for first and second types of inter-frame video forgeries. Table 1 summarizes the forgery type, feature method used, strengths and limitations of previously discussed studies.

Table 1. Video forgery detecting methods.

References	Forgery Type	Feature Method Used	Strengths	Limitations
[10]	Frame duplication	Similarity between SVD features vector of each frame.	High accuracy in detecting forgery	Failed in detecting other types of forgery such as insertion or reshuffling.
[11]	Frame duplication	Correlation between the successive frames.	Detected and localized frame duplication in higher accuracy.	Failed when frame duplication was performed in a different order.
[12]	Frame deletion	Sequence of average residual of P-frames (SARP) and its time- and frequency-domain features.	Was very effective with the detecting.	Worked with fixed GOP only.
[13]	Frame deletion	Magnitude variation in prediction residual and intra macro blocks number.	Worked stably under various configurations.	Failed if the number of deleted frames was very small.
[14]	Frame insertion and deletion.	Correlation coefficients of gray values.	Efficient in classifying original videos and forgeries.	Worked with still background datasets.
[15]	Frame insertion and deletion.	Quotients of correlation coefficients between (LBPs) coded frames.	High detecting accuracy and low computational complexity.	Detected only if forgeries exist but cannot distinguish frame insertion and deletion.
[16]	Frame insertion and deletion.	Quantization error in residual errors of P-MB in P frames.	Effective detecting.	Not suitable for videos with a low compression ratio.
[6]	Frame insertion, deletion and duplication.	Correlation between the Haralick coded frame.	Worked efficiently for static as well as dynamic videos.	Not able to detect other types of forgery such as frame reshuffling and replacement.
[17]	Frame insertion, deletion and duplication.	HSV color histogram comparison and SURF.	Was efficient and accurate in terms of forgery identification and locating.	Failed to detect inter-frame video with many shots.
[18]	Frame insertion, deletion and duplication.	HOG and MOI.	Was efficient in insertion and duplication.	Failed to detect frame deletion in silent scenes.
[19]	Frame duplication.	An I3D network and a Siamese network were used.	Detected frame duplication in an effective method.	Compression might decrease the accuracy and failed to detect frame deletion forgery.
[20]	Frame insertion, deletion and duplication.	(3D-CNN) is used for detecting the inter-frame video forgery.	Detected inter-frame video forgeries for static as well as dynamic single-shot videos.	Failed in localization of forgeries and detecting of multiple video shot forgeries.

Table 1. Cont.

References	Forgery Type	Feature Method Used	Strengths	Limitations
[21]	Frame insertion, deletion and duplication.	Correlation between 2-D phase congruency of successive frames.	Localized the tampered positions efficiently.	Failed in distinguishing whether the inserted frames are copied from the same video or not.
[22]	Multiple/double compression	Pixel estimation and double compression statistics.	High detection accuracies.	Failed in localization forged frames.
[23]	Multiple/double compression	Number of different coefficients between I frames of the singly and doubly compressed MPEG-2 videos.	Effective in double compression detection with same bit rate.	Performance depends on proper selection of recompression bitrate.
[24]	Region tampering	Motion residuals.	High accuracy.	Failed in forgery localization.
[25]	Region tampering	Zernike moments and 3D patch match.	Effective in forgery detecting and locating regions.	Accuracy was very low.
[26]	Region tampering	Optical flow coefficient is computed for each part.	Detected copy/move forgery effectively.	Detection failed in videos with a high amount of motion.

According to the previous problems, the main challenge is the manipulation of large videos. The tensor structure provides an excellent method for representing many kinds of highly correlated data such as videos. It is used in many applications as in [27–29]. Cheng et al. [8] discussed tensor data decomposition and its great influence on dimension reduction. Tensor data are routinely encountered in many fields such as genomics, image processing, finance and chemometrics. In Kountchev et al. [30] the advantages of third-order tensors and their application in video representation in multi-dimensional order were discussed. A third-order tensor was used to reduce the computational complexity. A new three-Dimensional Inverse Spectrum Pyramid (3D-ISP) approach was proposed for hierarchical third-order tensor decomposition. The tensors were transformed into 3D WalshHadamard spectrum space forms (WHT) that provided high dimensionality reduction.

3. Proposed Method

The proposed method undergoes passive approaches for the detecting and locating of inter-frame video forgeries. However, instead of spatially comparing the whole pixel correlation through all successive frames, a group of tracing orthogonal features [31,32] is extracted from a third-order tensor representation of tube fiber geometrical frame construction and compared with its successive groups. Third-order tensor video construction, as depicted in Figure 1, is a representation of high dimensionality data with a multiway array structure. The three-way arrays of a third-order tensor are not called row vector and column vectors but are called tensor fibers. The tensor fiber is a one-way array with at least one subscript fixed. The fibers of a third-order tensor are vertical, horizontal and depth fibers that can be represented in three different modes. The vertical fibers of the third-order tensor are called column fibers (the column subscript is fixed) and the horizontal fibers are also known as row fibers (the row subscript is fixed). The depth is also called tube fiber (the row and column subscripts are fixed).

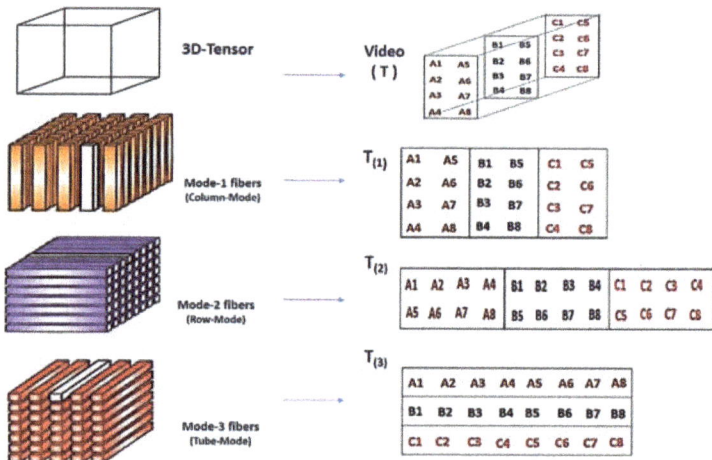

Figure 1. Third-order tensor construction and unfolding matrices.

In the proposed method, mode-3 fibers are used. Since tube fibers preserve the continuity of the spatial and temporal video scene together with its correlation characteristics, in addition, the tracing features extracted from third-order tensor representation achieve high dimensionality reduction and exact continuity measure [8].

The methodology of the proposed approach is illustrated in Figure 2. It consists of three successive phases: (i) Third-order tensor decomposition, (ii) Forgery detecting and (iii) Forgery locating. The next subsections present detailed explanations for each phase.

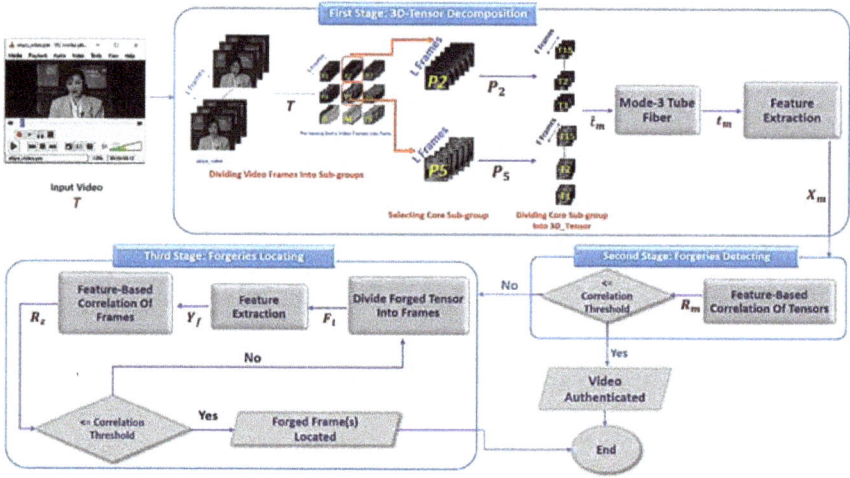

Figure 2. The proposed methodology.

3.1. First Phase: 3D-Tensor Decomposition

This phase is used to geometrically construct a third-order video tensor representation. As mentioned earlier, the main contribution in this phase is the great accuracy and reduction in computations, especially when dealing with large videos. Table 2 indicates the abbreviation list of variables used in this paper. The steps are given in details as follows.

Table 2. List of Symbol abbreviations.

Symbol	Description	Symbol	Description
T	The input video.	U and V^T	Unitary matrix.
L	Total number of all video frames.	X_m	SVD feature matrix of every 3D-tensor of the selected P_n.
$H \times W$	Total number of rows and columns.	Q	Total number of 3D-tensor feature vectors of selected Pn.
P_n	nth sub-group of a total number of N sub-groups consisting the whole T.	R_m	Correlation between the successive 3D-tensors of the selected P_n.
$\tilde{t}_m$	mth 3D-tensors of a total number of M tensors consisting P.	S_f	SVD matrix of each frame in 3D-tensor of the selected P_n.
I	Frame matrix of each P_n.	Y_f	SVD feature matrix of every frame of the 3D-tensor.
t_x, t_y	Partial derivatives of the pixel intensity with coordinates (x,y) in horizontal and vertical direction.	B	Total number of each frame feature vectors of the selected P_n.
$Corn$	Harris corner response.	R_z	Correlation values between successive frames of 3D-tensors.
$\{(x_c, y_c)\}$	All Harris corner points.	F	Number of frames of forged 3d-tensors.

3.1.1. Tube Fibers Representation

Consider an input video T consisting of L frames, each has a dimension of $H \times W$ pixels, where H and W represent the total number of rows and columns, respectively. The video sequence T is divided into equal sub-groups P each of length equals L frames, each sub-group P is represented by a number of third-order tensors (mode-3 (tube fiber)) that is used to represent the flow of video data, which is a vector defined by fixing the first two indices (row and column, respectively) and varying the third index (number of frames), Here the 3D tensor is not represented by all frames, but the core P of the video frames that are always changed in the video. Practically, only one core sub-group P is chosen for 3D tensor representation to test video authenticity. Now, the mathematical expression that describes the above explanation is Equation (1):

$$T = \bigcup_{n=1}^{N} P_n \qquad (1)$$

where P_n is the nth sub-group P, and N is total number of sub-groups of the input video. After dividing the video into sub-groups, core sub-groups are selected to be represented by several 3D tensors $\tilde{t}_m$, as Equation (2):

$$P_n = \bigcup_{M} \tilde{t}_m(i,j,k) : i = \{0,1,2,\ldots h\}, j = \{0,1,2,\ldots w\}, k = \{0,1,2,\ldots F\} \qquad (2)$$

where $F < L$, is the total number of frames of each 3D-tensor $\tilde{t}_m$, as F decreases the accuracy of detecting forged frames increases, and vice versa. However, for the proposed techniques, it should not decrease by 10 frames or increase by 30 frames to get high detection accuracy, low computational complexity and to help in locating inter-frame forgeries as will be seen in the experimental results section. Finally, w and h are the selected number of columns and rows t_m, where: $h < H$, and $w < W$ and $m = \{1,2,\ldots,M\}$, M is the number of all 3D tensors.

Referring to Figure 1, each $\tilde{t}_m$ is represented mathematically by a mode-3 tube 2D matrix as Equation (3):

$$t_m = I(F, h, w) = \begin{bmatrix} I_1(1,1) \ldots I_1(h,1) I_1(1,2) \ldots I_1(1,w) \ldots I_1(h,w) \\ I_2(1,1) \ldots I_2(h,1) I_2(1,2) \ldots I_2(1,w) \ldots I_2(h,w) \\ \vdots \\ I_F(1,1) \ldots I_F(h,1) I_F(1,2) \ldots I_F(1,w) \ldots I_F(h,w) \end{bmatrix} \quad (3)$$

For example, if a total video container matrix T has dimensions of (192 × 192 pixels) × 300 frames, it can be divided into a total of nine P sub-groups, each with dimensions of (64 × 64 pixels) × 300 frame. The most important sub-groups can be chosen to be divided into a group of third-order tensors which are represented as a 2D matrix as in Equation (3) with dimensions of 20 × 4096 pixels. Here, it can be noted that the dimensions division process is arbitrary and corresponds to the nature of the scene of the suspected video.

3.1.2. Feature Extraction

Feature extraction is an important step for reducing data dimensionality, computational time and complexity. Each 2D matrix t_m is processed for feature extraction. There are many feature extraction methods used in forgery detecting and locating. Based on the previous studies, the three most effective methods used for extracting good features to trace are: Harris [33,34], Gray Level Co-occurrence Matrix (GLCM) [6] and Singular Value Decomposition (SVD) [22], In this paper, each of which is applied for 2D matrix, tested and compared to obtain the best combination.

Harris Feature Extraction

In this step, Harris feature extraction is applied for each 2D matrix t_m as in Equation (3). Different detectors of the interest points were suggested and used based on the application field. The Harris detector, which is the fast, robust and rotation invariant, is commonly used in many computer vision applications that use the autocorrelation function to determine locations where the signal changes in one or two directions occur as in [33]. The concept behind the algorithm for Harris corners is that the intensity of the image will change significantly in several corner directions, while the intensity of the image will change significantly in a corner some direction along the edge and this phenomenon can be formulated by studying the changes in intensity resulting from local window shifts. The intensity of the image can change greatly around a corner point when the window is rotated in an arbitrary direction. At approximately an edge point, the intensity of the image will greatly change when the window is rotated in the perpendicular direction. Following this theory, the Harris detector uses a second-order moment matrix as the basis of its corner decisions. Unless otherwise specified, all corner points and edge points identified by the Harris corner detector refer to Harris corner interest points as in [34].

Harris feature extraction is applied for each tensor t_m included in each core sub-group P. Therefore, the autocorrelation matrix M for a given third-order tensor t_m at point (x, y) can be calculated as in Equation (4):

$$M(x,y) = \sum_{x,y} W(x,y) \begin{bmatrix} t_x^2(x,y) & t_x t_y(x,y) \\ t_x t_y(x,y) & t_y^2(x,y) \end{bmatrix} \quad (4)$$

where t_x and t_y are pixel intensity respective derivatives in the x and y directions at point (x, y). That is,

$$t_x = t \otimes [-1, 0, 1] \approx \partial t / \partial x \quad (5)$$

$$t_y = t \otimes [-1, 0, 1]^T \approx \partial t / \partial y. \quad (6)$$

where the operator $\otimes$ represents convolution. The off-diagonal entries are the product of t_x and t_y, while the diagonal entries are the squares of the respective derivatives and t is the element of t_m. $W(x, y)$ can be uniform in the weighting function, but is more generally an isotropic and σ represents standard deviation. Circular Gaussian as in Equation (7):

$$W(x,y) = g(x,y,\sigma) = \frac{1}{2\pi\sigma^2} \exp\left(-\frac{x^2+y^2}{2\sigma^2}\right) \tag{7}$$

This gives greater weight to those values close to a local region's center. Let α and β be the $M(x, y)$ eigenvalues. These values provide a quantitative description of how the measure of autocorrelation changes its main curvatures in spatially. The image regions can be split into three groups according to the autocorrelation matrix eigenvalues: plain regions, edges, and corners. Note that the $\sigma\beta$ product is sensitive to corners, while the $\sigma + \beta$ sum is sensitive to both edges and corners. In addition, the trace and the determinant of a general diagonalizable matrix agree with the product and the sum of its eigenvalues:

$$Tr(M(x,y)) = \alpha + \beta = t_x^2(x,y) + t_y^2(x,y) \tag{8}$$

$$Det(M(x,y)) = \alpha\beta = t_x^2(x,y) \cdot t_y^2(x,y) - (t_x t_y(x,y))^2 \tag{9}$$

Using $Tr(M(x, y))$ and $Det(M(x, y))$ to determine the corner response is attractive because it prevents the need for explicit decomposition of the $M(x, y)$ eigenvalue. The corner response is calculated using Equation (10):

$$Corn(x,y) = Det(M(x,y)) - K \cdot Tr^2(M(x,y)) = \sigma\beta - K \cdot (\sigma+\beta)^2 \tag{10}$$

where K is an empirically selected scalar value out of the range value (0.04, ..., 0.16). Corner points have high positive eigenvalues and thus a large response to the Harris measure. Thus, corner points that are greater than a specified threshold are recognized as local maxima of the Harris measure response:

$$\{(x_c, y_c)\} = \{(x_c, y_c) | Corn(x_c, y_c) > Corn(x_i, y_i), \forall\, Corn(x_i, y_i) \in W(x_c, y_c), Corn(x_c, y_c) > t_{th}\} \tag{11}$$

where $\{(x_c, y_c)\}$ is the corner point set, $Corn(x_c, y_c)$ is the Harris measure response computed at point (x, y), $W(x_c, y_c)$ is an 8-neighbor set centered around point (x_c, y_c) and t_{th} is a specified threshold. Obviously, the number of Harris corner points identified depends on the threshold t_{th} [34].

GLCM Feature Extraction

Another different method for feature extraction is applied to improve the results of the Harris feature. Each sub-tube matrix p is processed for GLCM feature extraction. The Gray Level Co-occurrence Matrix (GLCM) is a method of texture feature extraction that is used effectively in various problems of image processing, such as segmentation, image recognition, classification, retrieval and texture analysis as in [6]. The GLCM method is used for feature extraction from video frames after which these texture features are subjected to correlation. GLCM is a statistical measurement of a second order (between two pixels or two pixels subgroups in an image). The non-normalized frequencies of co-occurrence can be interpreted as a function of angle and distance as follows. Four GLCMs for $\theta = 90°$ are constructed. Ninety degrees as video frames are arranged in tube tensor as Equation (12).

$$t_{90°,d}(a,b) = |\{((k,l),(m,n)): |k-m| = d, l = n\}| \tag{12}$$

where (k, l) and (m, n) express the locations of pixels with gray levels a and b. a, b represent the gray levels of pixel within a frame window separated by distance d and $|\{\cdots\}|$ represents set cardinality.

SVD Feature Extraction

Due to the nature of motions in video scenes, the required features must satisfy certain specifications. These features must provide stability, scaling properties and rotation invariance, to help trace those features through entire sub-tubes. SVD is a matrix factorization that has algebraic and geometric invariant properties. It has the ability to extract unique features for an image, which form a steady representation of image blocks. It has proven a great performance results in different applications [22,35].

SVD feature extraction is the method of robust and accurate decomposition of the orthogonal matrix. It is becoming increasingly common in the field of signal processing because of conceptual SVD and stability reasons. Image processing is an attractive algebraic transformation.

In a minimally square sense, the SVD is the ideal matrix decomposition that stores the full signal energy into as few coefficients as possible. It is an effective and stable method of dividing the matrix into a set of linearly independent components, each with a contribution of its energy. It is a numerical method used in numerical analysis to diagonalize matrices. Due to its endless advantages such as maximum energy packing which is usually used in compression, ability to manipulate the image based on two distinctive subspaces of data and noise subspaces, it is an attractive algebraic transformation for image processing, which is commonly used in noise filtering and is also utilized in watermarking applications.

In this paper, the SVD algorithm is deployed to third-order tensor. For each t_m, a singular value obtains the feature vectors of each part via SVD, which is given by Equation (13):

$$t_m = U X_m V^T \tag{13}$$

U and V^T are the unitary matrices, and X_m is the singular value of t_m which is a diagonal matrix. The one-dimensional vector is formed from the diagonal elements of t_m, and the vector can be expressed as $X_m = \{x_{m1}, \ldots, x_{mQ}\}$. X_m a feature vector of t_m.

3.2. Second Phase: Forgery Detecting

3.2.1. Features-Based Correlation of Tensors

Here, the autocorrelation between consecutive tensors features is calculated. For example, after extracting SVD feature vector X_m for each mode-3 tube 2 D- matrix, the correlation coefficient between every two consecutive feature vectors is calculated using the standard Pearson correlation [36] as in Equation (14):

$$R_m = \frac{\sum_t (x_m(t) - \overline{x_m}) \times (x_{m+1}(t) - \overline{x_{m+1}})}{\sqrt{\sum_t (x_m(t) - \overline{x_m})^2 \times \sum_t (x_{m+1}(t) - \overline{x_{m+1}})^2}} \tag{14}$$

where R_m is the correlation between each two consecutive feature vectors of t_m and $t_m + 1$ tensors. Here, $X_m(t)$ is the mth SVD feature of the t_m tensor and $\overline{X_m}$ represents the average of all SVD features of the mth tensor. This is repeated for all chosen P of the input video. For example, if a video consists of 300 frames, it is divided into several P according to its size, the chosen core P are divided into tensors and so be 15 tensors, each of which contains 20 frames. The correlation is calculated between every consecutive pairs of these 15 tensors to get 14 correlation values. These values are statistically averaged to get an average value of the correlation among tensors. Hence, a threshold value is calculated based on the obtained statistics and is used to detect video forgery. Thresholds vary in correspondence to the nature of each video. Using Chebyshev's inequality [37], this threshold is computed as follow:

$$Threshold = \mu - m \cdot \sigma \tag{15}$$

where μ and σ are the mean and the standard deviation, respectively, of correlation distribution R_i values of the total adjacent m tensors. Their mathematical representations are as follows:

$$\mu = \frac{\sum_{i=1}^{m-1} R_i}{m-1} \qquad (16)$$

$$\sigma = \sqrt{\frac{\sum_{i=1}^{m-1}(R_i - \mu)^2}{m-1}} \qquad (17)$$

For unknown data distribution, the lower bound for the threshold within a group of adjacent tensors can be determined by applying Chebyshev's inequality. The correlation value computed from Equation (14) is compared with the computed threshold to define the type of forgery as insertion or deletion. Algorithm 1 illustrates the procedure of detecting.

Algorithm 1 Forgery Type Determination.

Input: Correlation values R_m where m = 1: M and *Threshold*. (14)–(15)
Output: Forgery type.
1. **Begin**
2.   for R_m where m = 1: M **do**
3.   if R_m & R_{m+1} <= *Threshold* **then**
4.   Forgery type is insertion
5.   else if R_m <= *Threshold* **then**
6.   Divide tensors with suspected values into Sub-Frames.
7.   if two suspected points are found **then**
8.   Forgery type is insertion
9.   else
10.   Forgery type is deletion
11.   end
12.   else
13.   No forgery (video is original)
14.   end
15.   end
16. end

3.2.2. Insertion Forgery Detecting

For more illustrations, let us consider a practical implementation for Algorithm 1. The tensor correlation distribution analysis of the original foreman video dataset is shown in Figure 3a. The video consists of 300 frames and is divided into 15 tensors and each tensor contains 20 frames. Figure 3b depicts the frame insertion forgery correlation distribution analysis after inserting 40 frames from external video starting as mentioned earlier. Now, considering Figure 3b, the two abnormal tensors-correlation drops comparing with the threshold value, (Algorithm 1—step 7) represent the start and the end forged tensors, respectively. These two abnormal points correspond to point 5 (which indicates correlation between the 5th and 6th tensors) and point 7 (which indicates correlation between the 7th and 8th tensors). This verifies that there are forged frames in tensors number 5, 6, and 7 respectively.

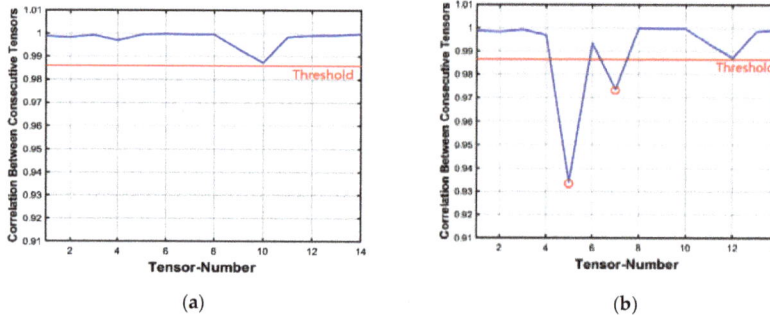

Figure 3. Inter-tensor correlation distribution analysis. (**a**) Original video Inter-tensor correlation distribution and (**b**) Forged video Inter-tensor correlation distribution (Insertion attack).

3.2.3. Deletion Forgery Detecting

To detect the frame deletion forgery case, the proposed method is applied to the forged dataset. For testing, we made 50 forged datasets for the deletion case. The correlation distribution analysis for the foreman dataset is shown in Figure 4a. Recall that the original video consists of 300 frames divided into 15 tensors at each part and each tensor contains 20 frames. Figure 4b indicates the frame deletion forgeries correlation distribution analysis in the forged video, 30 frames deleted from this video starting from frame number 100 ended at frame number 130. As presented in Figure 4b, one abnormal point is found at 5 (Algorithm 1—step 10) which indicates a correlation between the 5th and 6th tensors. This shows that there is a forgery attack in tensors 5, 6, and 7.

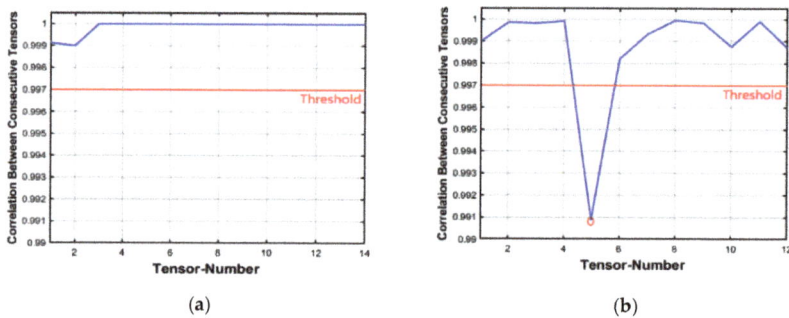

Figure 4. Inter-tensor correlation distribution analysis. (**a**) Original video Inter-tensor correlation distribution and (**b**) Forged video Inter-tensor correlation distribution (Deletion attack).

3.3. Third Phase: Forgery Locating

Recalling the proposed methodology, Figure 2, this phase is applied only if the video is detected as forged. The purpose of this phase is to locate the forged frames. Next, its steps are explained in detail.

3.3.1. Tensors Analysis

In the case of detecting forgery between two consecutive tensors, one tensor before and one tensor after are invoked, all these tensors are analyzed as frames (in our example

20 frames per tensor) to locate forgery in the video. The extracted frames are denoted by F_i ($i = 1, 2, \ldots, F$). The feature vectors of each frame via SVD are obtained, which are given by:

$$S_f = U Y_f V^T \quad (18)$$

S_f is SVD matrix of each frame in 3D-tensor, $Y_f = \{Y_{f1}, \ldots, Y_{fB}\}$ is one-dimensional vector as a feature of f_i and Y_{f1} and Y_{fB} are first and last feature values.

3.3.2. Features-Based Correlation of Frames

After calculating singular values for each sub-frame in selected forged tensors, the correlation coefficient between every two consecutive sub-frames is computed. According to the correlation values, the threshold is determined to localize the forgery in the video. The same equation is applied in but between every consecutive frame as:

$$R_z = \frac{\sum\limits_f (Y_z(f) - \overline{Y_z}) \times (Y_{z+1}(f) - \overline{Y_{z+1}})}{\sqrt{\sum\limits_t (Y_z(f) - \overline{Y_z})^2 \times \sum\limits_t (Y_{z+1}(f) - \overline{Y_{z+1}})^2}} \quad (19)$$

where R_z denotes the correlation between the fth and $(f + 1)$th subframes, $Y_z(f)$ refers to the zth SVD feature of the zth Sub-frames, and $\overline{Y_z}$ refers to all SVD features means of the zth sub-frames. For example, if forgery is detected in tensors 5, 6 and 7, then these tensors are divided into frames from 100 to 160 and correlation is calculated between these frames to locate the position of forgery. According to the correlation values, the threshold is determined using the same Chebyshev's inequality [37] except that the mean and the standard deviation Equations (16)–(17) are calculated for the internal frames in each $\tilde{t}_m$. The same procedure is used to localize the forgery in the video.

3.3.3. Locating Forgeries

Insertion Forgeries

Forgeries are simply localized from abnormal values in the inter tensor correlation distribution. However, for locating refinement, an inter-frame correlation distribution is applied. The distribution analysis for the foreman original video is shown in Figure 5a, which indicates that the correlation between frames is very high. Figure 5b shows the frame insertion forgeries correlation distribution analysis in the foreman video sequence. Forty frames from a foreign video were inserted starting at frame number 101 and ending at frame number 140 and two abnormal points were detected: the first point indicated the first inserted frame and the other indicated the last inserted frame. This is the final step in which we can localize the forged inserted frames.

Deletion Forgeries

Figure 5c shows the frame deletion forgeries inter-frame correlation distribution analysis in the video sequence. More analysis is performed starting from frame number 60 to frame number 160 and the results in the localization of 30 missing frames starting from frame number 111 were deleted. This is the final step in which we can localize the forged deleted frames. Algorithm 2 illustrates the proposed scheme of inter-tensor and inter-frame correlation to localize the insertion and deletion forgeries in videos.

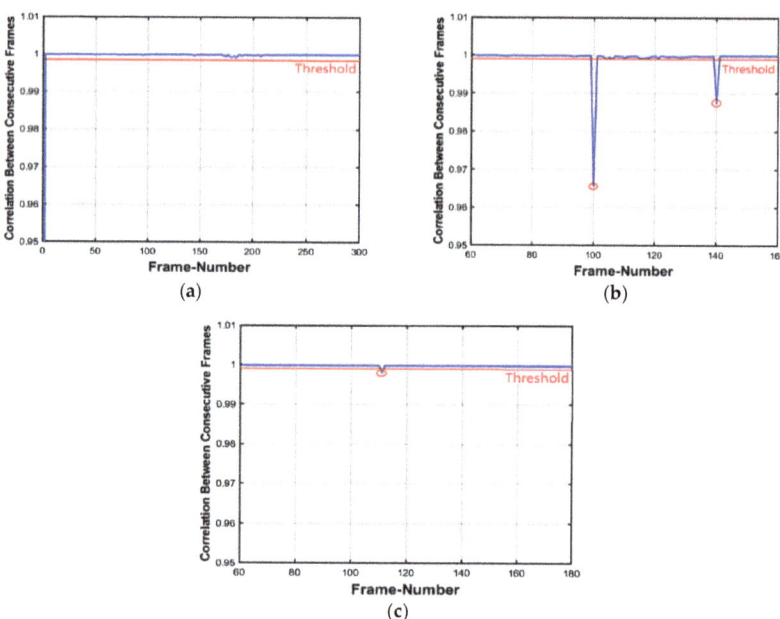

Figure 5. Inter-frame of foreman video sequence Correlation distribution: (**a**) Original video and (**b**) Forged video (Insertion attack) (**c**) Forged video (Deletion attack).

Algorithm 2 Forgery Location Determination.

Input: Correlation values R_m where $m = 1: M$, *Threshold*, t which is tensor number.
Output: Number of inserted or deleted Forged frames.

1. begin
2.   for R_m where m = 1:M **do**
3.   if Forgery is detected at R_m & R_{m+1} **then**
4.   Forgery type is insertion.
5.   Divide tensors whose numbers are t − 1, t, t + 1, t + 2 into frames (from s to n).
6.   Compute correlation between every two consecutive frames in R_z.
7.   for R_z where z = 1:n-1 **do**
8.   if Two suspected values are found **then**
9.   Forgery location determined
10.   end
11.   else if forgery is detected at R_m **then**
12.   Repeat steps 5, 6.
13.   if two suspected values are found **then**
14.   Forgery type is insertion and forgery determined
15.   else if one suspected value is found **then**
16.   Forgery type is deletion and forgery determined
17.   end
18.   else
19.   No forgery
20.   end
21.   end
22. end

4. Experimental Results and Discussion

To evaluate the performance of the proposed scheme, a MATLAB computer simulation program (R2018a, MathWorks, Natick, MA, USA) was developed for testing and validating several experiments. The computer configuration used in these experiments is described as follows: CPU: Intel(R) core (TM) i7-9750H CPU @2.60 GHZ (Lenovo, Beijing, China); Memory size: 16 GB RAM; OS: Microsoft Windows 10 (Microsoft, Redmond, WA, USA); the Coding: MATLAB R2018a;. The next subsections explain the tested dataset, the standard evaluation parameters. Finally, comparisons and discussion are introduced.

4.1. Tested Dataset Description

Experiments on the proposed scheme are performed with a standard dataset consisting of eighteen video clips with a frame rate of 30 frames per second (fps), from the TRACE library, where each YUV sequence is either in Quarter Common Intermediate Format (QCIF) which is (176 × 144) format or Intermediate Format (CIF) which is (352 × 288) format [38]. The tested dataset contains videos with static backgrounds, slow-motion backgrounds, fast-moving (single or multiple) foreground objects, zoom in and zoom out. Table 3 summarizes the characteristics of the tested datasets.

Table 3. Tested dataset characteristics.

NO.	Dataset Name	Length	Frame Rate	Format	Resolution
1	Akyio	300	30 fps	YUV	176 × 144
2	Hall Monitor	300	30 fps	YUV	176 × 144
3	Paris	1065	30 fps	YUV	352 × 288
4	Suzie	150	30 fps	YUV	176 × 144
5	Flower	250	30 fps	YUV	352 × 288
6	Miss America	150	30 fps	YUV	352 × 288
7	Waterfall	260	30 fps	YUV	352 × 288
8	Container	300	30 fps	YUV	352 × 288
9	Salesman	449	30 fps	YUV	176 × 144
10	Claire	494	30 fps	YUV	176 × 144
11	Bus	150	30 fps	YUV	352 × 288
12	Foreman	300	30 fps	YUV	176 × 144
13	Tempete	260	30 fps	YUV	352 × 288
14	Coastguard	300	30 fps	YUV	176 × 144
15	Carphone	382	30 fps	YUV	176 × 144
16	Mobile	300	30 fps	YUV	176 × 144
17	Mother and Daughter	300	30 fps	YUV	176 × 144
18	News	300	30 fps	YUV	176 × 144

Manual forgeries are performed for frame insertion and deletion attacks on the above dataset. Videos are made using the ffmpeg tool which provides command-line or programmatic access to video and audio processing. The original video is first decomposed into individual frames, and then the forgery is performed by inserting or removing frames. In this paper, both forgery attack experiments are tested against small and large numbers of forged frames to test the robustness of the proposed scheme. Forged videos are created starting with 10 forged frames up to 50 frames. Forged videos are created using the Audio Video Interleave (AVI) extension in MATLAB R2018a and eventually, the forged videos are translated into the .YUV extension.

4.2. Evaluation Standards

To evaluate the validity of the scheme, three performance indices are considered: precision, recall and F1 score [39–41] which are computed as follows:

$$Precision = \frac{TP}{TP + FP} \qquad (20)$$

$$Recall = \frac{TP}{TP + FN} \qquad (21)$$

$$F1\ score = \frac{2 \times Precision \times Recall}{Precision \times Recall} \tag{22}$$

where TP is the true positive number which means that the forged video was detected as forged, TN is the true negative number which means that the original video was detected as original, FP is the number of false positive which means that the original video was detected as forged and FN is the number of false negatives which means that forged videos were detected as the original.

4.3. Computational Complexity Analysis

The proposed technique offers a great advantage of speeding up the detecting and locating process since it offers a great opportunity for parallel processing for different tensors at the same time instead of consecutive frame processing compared with state-of-the-art methods. This advantage has a great influence on the total time needed for forgery detecting and locating as will be discussed later. However, tensor size is linearly proportional to the number of computations.

Table 4 illustrates the relation between tensor size and the total number of operations needed in the detecting and locating process. Through our simulation, 20 frames in every tensor are selected as it has a great reduction in the total number of operations while providing high detection accuracy. This relation also is graphically illustrated in Figure 6. The total number of operations per tensor is calculated using the MATLAB R2018a counting operations function. Compared with state-of-the-art methods, most of them calculate the correlation between the whole frame's pixels/frame's features of different frames along the video sequence. However, no previous data about computational complexity was mentioned before in state-of-the-art methods since it mainly depends on the programmer's skills. It can be obviously seen that the proposed tensor structure is proven to provide a high reduction in the total number computations since a limited number of tensors of small size are needed for detecting and locating process instead of dealing with whole sequences and the entire frames/features.

Table 4. The relation between number of operations and tensor size.

Tensor Size	Number of Operations		
	F = 20 frames/tensor	F = 30 frames/tensor	F = 40 frames/tensor
F × 16 × 16	5136	7696	10,256
F × 32 × 32	20,512	30,752	40,992
F × 64 × 64	81,984	122,944	163,904
F × 100 × 100	200,100	300,100	400,100
F × 128 × 128	327,808	491,648	655,488

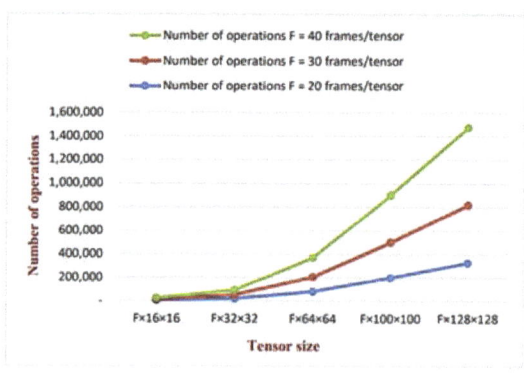

Figure 6. The increase in total number of operations against the increase in tensor size.

5. Comparisons and Discussion

In this section, the proposed scheme is applied to the eighteen datasets depicted in Table 3, and their forged versions. Tested against two types of forgery: insertion and deletion. The comparison results of applying three methods of feature extraction: Harris feature extraction, GLCM feature extraction and SVD, on a maximum of hundred forged videos for insertion and deletion cases, are introduced and discussed. Each of them influences the results as introduced in the following subsections.

5.1. Insertion Forgery

For testing forgery attack detecting and locating, several experiments were conducted to trace the performance accuracy of the proposed scheme against the increase/decrease in the number of forged frames. Table 5 shows and compares the precision of the detecting and locating phases. The proposed scheme shows a noticeable enhancement when applying the SVD feature extraction method. Precision up to 96% in the detection phase is reached and 99% in localization capability. These results reflect the stability, scaling property and geometric invariance property of the SVD feature extraction method.

As shown in Table 5, the greater the number of frames inserted from the external video, the faster the forgery position is determined because this increase of forged frames causes a significant change in the content of the video. The charts in Figure 7a,b visually summarize the results of Table 5. It visually points out the superiority of the SVD feature extraction method in both detecting and locating phases, and it has the best results in terms of precision, recall and F1 score. For more robust investigations, the proposed scheme is tested against the increase in the number of frames inserted into the original videos.

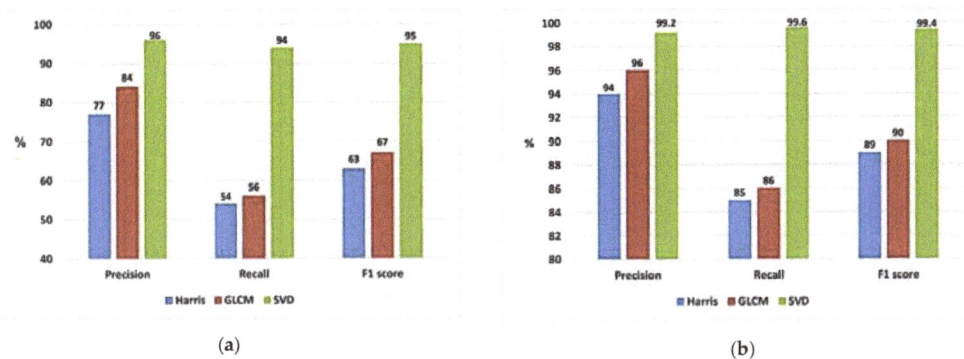

Figure 7. Performance chart of three different feature extraction techniques used for insertion forgery cases. (**a**) Insertion detecting phase and (**b**) Insertion locating phase.

Figure 8 shows the detecting and locating results for five different videos under different numbers of inserted frames. The left side of this figure shows the inter tensor correlation figures that detect the existence of forgery and at this level, there are almost two or sometimes one abnormal value that expresses insertion forgery while the right side accurately localizes the number of inserted foreign frames. This right side indicates that two abnormal values indicate the start and the end of forgery in videos.

Table 5. Insertion detecting and locating performance measures of the proposed scheme for three different feature extraction methods.

No	Detecting Stage									Locating Stage								
	HARRIS			GLCM			SVD			HARRIS			GLCM			SVD		
	Precision (%)	Recall (%)	F1 Score (%)	Precision (%)	Recall (%)	F1 Score (%)	Precision (%)	Recall (%)	F1 Score (%)	Precision (%)	Recall (%)	F1 Score (%)	Precision (%)	Recall (%)	F1 Score (%)	Precision (%)	Recall (%)	F1 Score (%)
10	77	54	63	84	56	67	96	94	95	90	81	85	96	82	88	98	98	98
20	77	54	63	84	56	67	96	94	95	93	84	88	96	87	91	98	100	99
30	77	54	63	84	56	67	96	94	95	96	87	91	96	87	91	100	100	100
40	77	54	63	84	56	67	96	94	95	96	87	91	96	87	91	100	100	100
50	77	54	63	84	56	67	96	94	95	96	87	91	96	87	91	100	100	100
Avg.	77	54	63	84	56	67	96	94	95	94	85	89	96	86	90	99.2	99.6	99.4

5.2. Deletion Forgery

The proposed scheme is tested and evaluated against the detecting and locating of deletion forgeries with different cases of deleted numbers of frames. As mentioned before, the SVD feature extraction method is used in deletion attacks as it achieves efficient results in insertion attacks. Table 6 shows the results of detecting and locating these different cases. It is very difficult to detect and localize deletion forgeries for fewer than 10 frames in the video as the changes in it are very small. However, the proposed scheme shows large robustness in detecting and locating against the increase in the number of deleted frames (up to 50 frames). Precision up to 92% in the detecting phase is reached and 98.4% in the locating phase. Figure 9 illustrates results for five different videos under different numbers of deleted frames. The left side of this figure shows the inter-tensor correlation figures that detect the deletion forgery existence and in this, there is only one abnormal point that always indicates the forgery, while the right side accurately localizes the position of the deleted forged frames and in this right level there is only one point that indicates the position of the forgery.

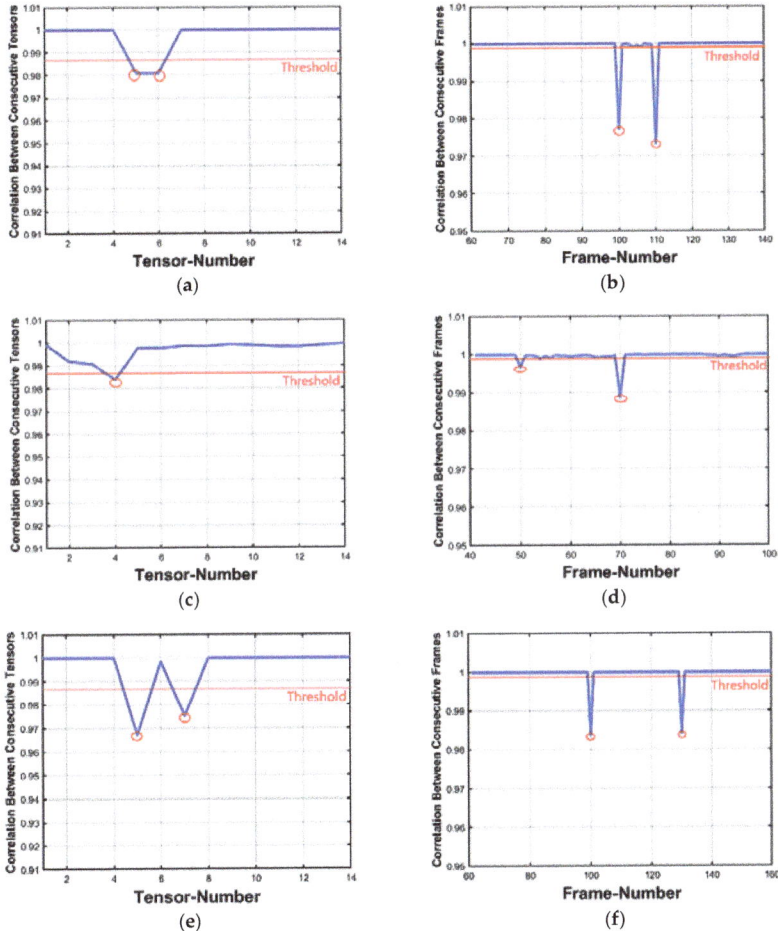

Figure 8. Cont.

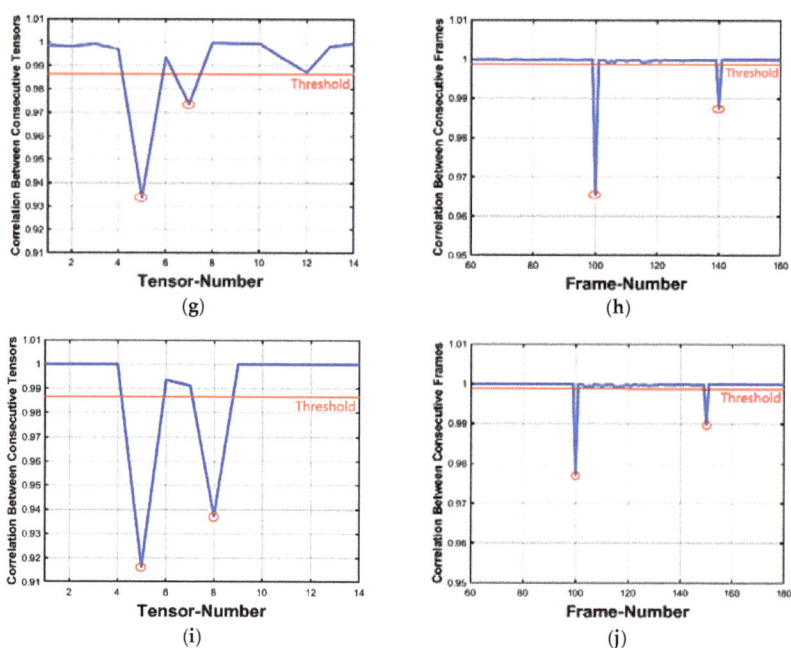

Figure 8. (**a,c,e,g,i**) insertion forgery detecting and (**b,d,f,h,j**) insertion forgery locating of 10, 20, 30, 40 and 50 forged frames respectively.

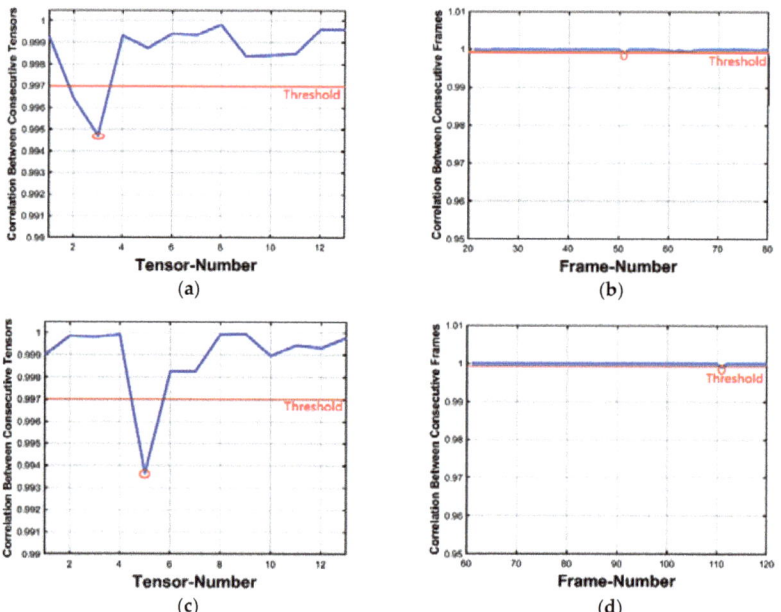

Figure 9. *Cont.*

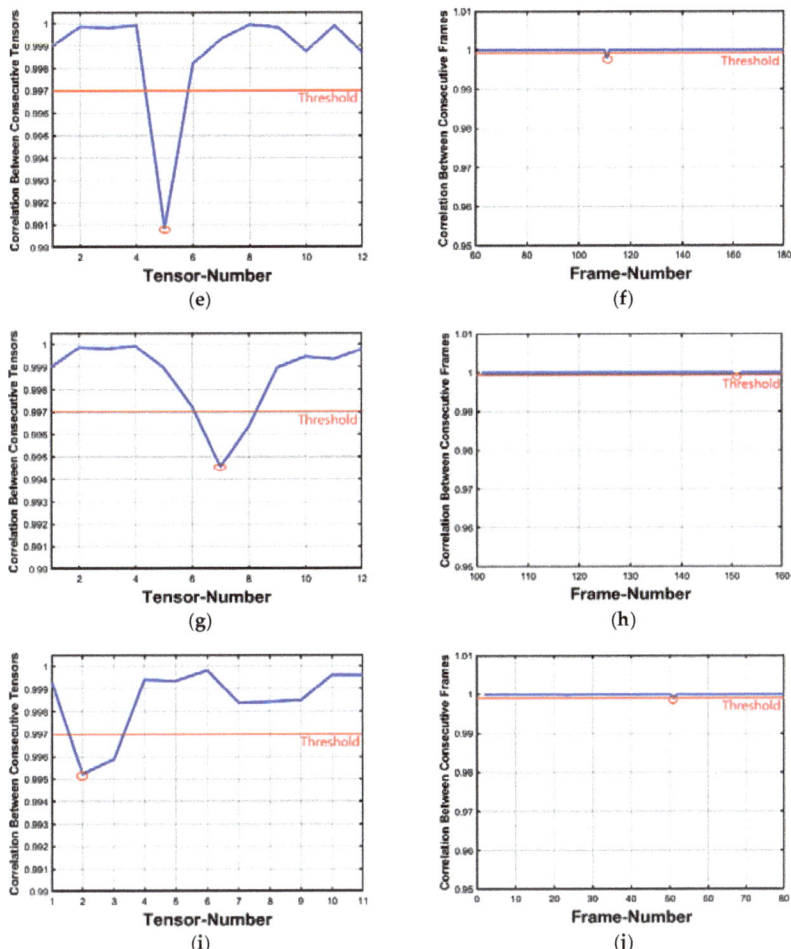

Figure 9. (a,c,e,g,i) deletion forgery detecting and (b,d,f,h,j) deletion forgery locating of 10, 20, 30, 40 and 50 forged frames respectively.

Table 6. Deletion forgery detecting and locating. Results based on SVD-tensor features.

No. of Forged Frames	Detecting			Locating		
	Precision (%)	Recall (%)	F1 Score (%)	Precision (%)	Recall (%)	F1 Score (%)
<10	None	None	None	None	None	none
10	92	90	91	98	96	97
20	92	90	91	98	98	98
30	92	90	91	98	98	98
40	92	90	91	98	98	98
50	92	90	91	100	100	100
Avg.	92	90	91	98.4	98	98.2

5.3. Comparison with State-of-the-Art

Comparison with the state-of-the-art is provided in order to compare the proposed scheme performance with different methods. We tested all methods on the same dataset. Table 7 summarizes the comparative results for both types of forgery among the recent techniques and the proposed one. The overall precision, recall and F1 score of the proposed methods are 99%, 95% and 96% respectively which shows superiority compared with published methods. Figure 10 illustrates these results.

Table 7. Performance comparison between proposed approach and other related methods.

Methods	Attacks Types	Precision (%)	Recall (%)	F1 Score (%)
Ref. [16]	Insertion, Deletion	89	86	87
Ref. [15]	Insertion, Deletion	95	92	93
Ref. [13]	Deletion	72	66	69
Ref. [6]	Insertion, Deletion	85	89	87
Ref. [18]	Insertion, Deletion and Duplication	98	99	98
Proposed	Insertion, Deletion	99	99	99

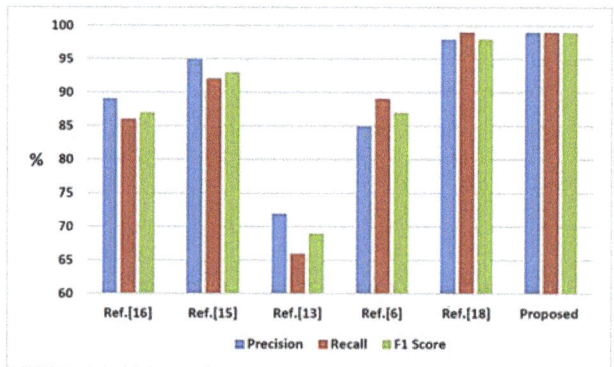

Figure 10. Performance chart of proposed approach compared with other related methods.

The method proposed by Yu et al. [13] detected and localized frame deletion forgeries only. The scheme proposed by Aghamaleki and Behrad [16] is applicable to frame insertion and deletion forgery in low accuracy. Zhang et al. [15]'s scheme can detect frame insertion/deletion video forgeries for still background videos. Bakas et al. [6] proposed a method that can detect frame insertion, deletion and duplication forgeries for still background, as well as dynamic background videos but the comparison was performed with insertion and deletion results. The scheme proposed by Qiong et al. [18] is for insertion, deletion and duplication cases but it took many computations and failed in detecting frame deletion in silent scenes.

The proposed method of this paper can detect insertion and deletion forgeries for a still background as well as dynamic background videos. The proposed method offers high accuracy in respect of the achieved precision at a minimum number of features compared with previous works.

Recalling that the proposed tensor geometric structure provides a high reduction in computational time due to the small size of tensors and the possibility of processing tensors in a parallel manner rather than the consecutive approaches used in the state-of-the-art. However, it is difficult to compare experimental time with the state-of-the-art methods although they used the same dataset since different computer configurations together with different programmers' skills are deployed. In this paper, based on the previously mentioned computer configurations used in these experiments, the average computation time per tensor is less than 2.2 s. Third-order tensor representation together with a good feature extraction method offered this great reduction. Considering the average computations time for previous methods [6,17,42], although different computer configurations were used, the proposed method clearly outperforms these methods, since a limited number of tensors is used in the investigation process rather than the other methods that exploit the whole frame's pixels/frame's features. Table 8 illustrates the total time needed for forged frames detecting and locating. It can be noted that as the number of inserted forged frames increases, the total time increases since more computations for tensors are needed, while as the number of deleted frames increases, the total time decreases since the number of frames decreases.

Table 8. Total time needed for Detecting and locating passive forgery.

Video	Original Length	Forgery Operation	Tampered Length	Total Time (Seconds)
1	300	10 frames inserted in 101:110	310	39.42
2	300	20 frames inserted in 50:70	320	39.49
3	250	30 frames inserted in 101:130	280	38.24
4	300	40 frames inserted in 100:140	340	39.89
5	382	50 frames inserted in 221:270	432	40.97
6	449	20 frames inserted in 201:220	469	41.40
7	300	50 frames inserted in 101:150	350	40.01
8	1065	30 frames inserted in 50:80	1086	46.24
9	300	40 frames inserted in 170:210	340	39.75
10	300	10 frames deleted in 50:59	290	27.46
11	300	20 frames deleted in 50:69	280	26.45
12	260	30 frames deleted in 160:190	230	23.89
13	449	40 frames deleted in 360:400	409	29.02
14	300	40 frames deleted in 200:240	260	25.22
15	150	10 frames deleted in 60:79	140	22.02
16	300	20 frames deleted in 100:119	280	26.44
17	250	30 frames deleted in 160:190	220	23.42
18	300	40 frames deleted in 170:210	260	25.36

6. Conclusions

Videos are linear groups of highly correlated data that consume time and computational complexity. Recently, the most common methods for video compression represents such data on the basis of a geometric tensor representation. This paper proposed a low computational complexity scheme based on tensor representation and orthogonal tracing feature algorithms for detecting and locating insertion and deletion forgery in videos. Three different common tracing features were tested, evaluated, and compared to choose the outperforming one. Experiments and comparisons showed the superiority of SVD tube-fiber tensor construction in detecting and locating these two types of video forgeries. Different datasets of different characteristics were examined, and the proposed scheme was tested against the increase in the forged frame number. The proposed method performed efficiently for static as well as dynamic videos, quick-moving foreground items (single or multiple), zooming in and zooming out datasets. Experimental results showed that the proposed approach obtains effective accuracy with a high precision value of up to 99% and a reduction in time and computational complexity. Future research in this direction is still open, and it will include enhancing the detecting and locating process for more types of attacks.

Author Contributions: Conceptualization, Y.M.A., N.E.M. and N.A.H.; methodology, Y.M.A., N.E.M. and N.A.H.; software, Y.M.A., N.E.M. and N.A.H.; validation, Y.M.A., N.E.M. and N.A.H.; formal analysis, Y.M.A., N.E.M. and N.A.H.; investigation, Y.M.A., N.E.M. and N.A.H.; resources, Y.M.A., N.E.M. and N.A.H.; data curation, Y.M.A., N.E.M. and N.A.H.; writing—original draft preparation, Y.M.A., N.E.M. and N.A.H.; writing—review and editing, Y.M.A., N.E.M. and N.A.H.; visualization, Y.M.A., N.E.M. and N.A.H.; supervision, N.E.M. and N.A.H.; project administration, N.E.M. and N.A.H. All authors have read and agreed to the published version of the manuscript.

Funding: This research received no external funding.

Institutional Review Board Statement: Not applicable.

Informed Consent Statement: Not applicable.

Data Availability Statement: Not applicable.

Acknowledgments: The authors thank Department of Information Technology, Faculty of Computers and Information Science, Mansoura University.

Conflicts of Interest: The authors declare no conflict of interest.

References

1. Li, Z.; Zhang, Z.; Guo, S.; Wang, J. Video inter-frame forgery identification based on the consistency of quotient of MSSIM. *Secur. Commun. Netw.* **2016**, *9*, 4548–4556. [CrossRef]
2. Sencar, H.T.; Memon, N. Overview of state-of-the-art in digital image forensics. In *Algorithms, Architectures and Information Systems Security*; World Scientific: Singapore, 2009; pp. 325–347.
3. Abdulhussain, S.H.; Al-Haddad, S.A.R.; Saripan, M.I.; Mahmmod, B.M.; Hussien, A.J.I.A. Fast Temporal Video Segmentation Based on Krawtchouk-Tchebichef Moments. *IEEE Access* **2020**, *8*, 72347–72359. [CrossRef]
4. Mehta, V.; Jaiswal, A.K.; Srivastava, R. Copy-Move Image Forgery Detection Using DCT and ORB Feature Set. In Proceedings of the International Conference on Futuristic Trends in Networks and Computing Technologies, Chandigarh, India, 22–23 November 2013; Springer: Singapore, 2019; pp. 532–544.
5. Kobayashi, M.; Okabe, T.; Sato, Y. Detecting forgery from static-scene video based on inconsistency in noise level functions. *IEEE Trans. Inf. Forensics Secur.* **2010**, *5*, 883–892. [CrossRef]
6. Bakas, J.; Naskar, R.; Dixit, R. Detection and localization of inter-frame video forgeries based on inconsistency in correlation distribution between Haralick coded frames. *Multimed. Tools Appl.* **2019**, *78*, 4905–4935. [CrossRef]
7. Sitara, K.; Mehtre, B.M. Digital video tampering detection: An overview of passive techniques. *Digit. Investig.* **2016**, *18*, 8–22. [CrossRef]
8. Cheng, Y.H.; Huang, T.M.; Huang, S.Y. Tensor decomposition for dimension reduction. *Comput. Stat.* **2020**, *12*, e1482. [CrossRef]
9. Nanni, L.; Ghidoni, S.; Brahnam, S. Handcrafted vs. non-handcrafted features for computer vision classification. *Pattern Recognit.* **2017**, *71*, 158–172. [CrossRef]
10. Yang, J.; Huang, T.; Su, L. Using similarity analysis to detect frame duplication forgery in videos. *Multimed. Tools Appl.* **2016**, *75*, 1793–1811. [CrossRef]
11. Singh, V.K.; Pant, P.; Tripathi, R.C. Detection of frame duplication type of forgery in digital video using sub-block based features. In Proceedings of the International Conference on Digital Forensics and Cyber Crime, Seoul, Korea, 6–8 October 2015; Springer: Cham, Switzerland, 2015; pp. 29–38.
12. Liu, H.; Li, S.; Bian, S. Detecting frame deletion in H. 264 video. In Proceedings of the International Conference on Information Security Practice and Experience, Fuzhou, China, 5–8 May 2014; Springer: Cham, Switzerland, 2014; pp. 262–270.
13. Yu, L.; Wang, H.; Han, Q.; Niu, X.; Yiu, S.-M.; Fang, J.; Wang, Z. Exposing frame deletion by detecting abrupt changes in video streams. *Neurocomputing* **2016**, *205*, 84–91. [CrossRef]
14. Wang, Q.; Li, Z.; Zhang, Z.; Ma, Q.J. Video inter-frame forgery identification based on consistency of correlation coefficients of gray values. *J. Comput. Commun.* **2014**, *2*, 51. [CrossRef]
15. Zhang, Z.; Hou, J.; Ma, Q.; Li, Z. Efficient video frame insertion and deletion detection based on inconsistency of correlations between local binary pattern coded frames. *Secur. Commun. Netw.* **2015**, *8*, 311–320. [CrossRef]
16. Aghamaleki, J.A.; Behrad, A. Inter-frame video forgery detection and localization using intrinsic effects of double compression on quantization errors of video coding. *Signal Process. Image Commun.* **2016**, *47*, 289–302. [CrossRef]
17. Zhao, D.-N.; Wang, R.-K.; Lu, Z.-M. Inter-frame passive-blind forgery detection for video shot based on similarity analysis. *Multimed. Tools Appl.* **2018**, *77*, 25389–25408. [CrossRef]
18. Fadl, S.; Han, Q.; Qiong, L. Exposing video inter-frame forgery via histogram of oriented gradients and motion energy image. *Multidimens. Syst. Signal Process.* **2020**, *31*, 1365–1384. [CrossRef]
19. Long, C.; Basharat, A.; Hoogs, A. A Coarse-to-fine Deep Convolutional Neural Network Framework for Frame Duplication Detection and Localization in Video Forgery. CVPR Workshops 2019. pp. 1–10. Available online: http://www.chengjianglong.com/publications/CopyPaste.pdf (accessed on 10 February 2021).
20. Bakas, J.; Naskar, R. A Digital Forensic Technique for Inter–Frame Video Forgery Detection Based on 3D CNN. In Proceedings of the International Conference on Information Systems Security, Bangalore, India, 17–19 December 2014; Springer: Cham, Switzerland, 2018; pp. 304–317.
21. Li, Q.; Wang, R.; Xu, D. An Inter-Frame Forgery Detection Algorithm for Surveillance Video. *Information* **2018**, *9*, 301. [CrossRef]
22. Subramanyam, A.V.; Emmanuel, S. Pixel estimation based video forgery detection. In Proceedings of the 2013 IEEE International Conference on Acoustics, Speech and Signal Processing, Vancouver, BC, Canada, 26–31 May 2013; pp. 3038–3042.
23. Huang, Z.; Huang, F.; Huang, J. Detection of double compression with the same bit rate in MPEG-2 videos. In Proceedings of the 2014 IEEE China Summit & International Conference on Signal and Information Processing (ChinaSIP), Xi'an, China, 9–13 July 2014; pp. 306–309.
24. Chen, S.; Tan, S.; Li, B.; Huang, J. Automatic detection of object-based forgery in advanced video. *IEEE Trans. Circuits Syst. Video Technol.* **2015**, *26*, 2138–2151. [CrossRef]

25. D'Amiano, L.; Cozzolino, D.; Poggi, G.; Verdoliva, L. Video forgery detection and localization based on 3D patchmatch. In Proceedings of the 2015 IEEE International Conference on Multimedia & Expo Workshops (ICMEW), Torino, Italy, 29 June–3 July 2015; pp. 1–6.
26. Bidokhti, A.; Ghaemmaghami, S. Detection of regional copy/move forgery in MPEG videos using optical flow. In Proceedings of the 2015 The International Symposium on Artificial Intelligence and Signal Processing (AISP), Mashhad, Iran, 3–5 March 2015; pp. 13–17.
27. Kountchev, R.; Anwar, S.; Kountcheva, R.; Milanova, M. Face Recognition in Home Security System Using Tensor Decomposition Based on Radix-(2×2) Hierarchical SVD. In *Multimodal Pattern Recognition of Social Signals in Human-Computer-Interaction*; Schwenker, F., Scherer, S., Eds.; Springer International Publishing: Cham, Switzerland, 2017; pp. 48–59.
28. Kountchev, R.K.; Iantovics, B.L.; Kountcheva, R.A. Hierarchical third-order tensor decomposition through inverse difference pyramid based on the three-dimensional Walsh–Hadamard transform with app.lications in data mining. *Data Min. Knowl. Discov.* **2020**, *10*, e1314.
29. Kountchev, R.K.; Mironov, R.P.; Kountcheva, R.A. Hierarchical Cubical Tensor Decomposition through Low Complexity Orthogonal Transforms. *Symmetry* **2020**, *12*, 864. [CrossRef]
30. Kountchev, R.; Kountcheva, R. Low Computational Complexity Third-Order Tensor Representation Through Inverse Spectrum Pyramid. In *Advances in 3D Image and Graphics Representation, Analysis, Computing and Information Technology*; Springer: Singapore, 2020; pp. 61–76.
31. Abdulhussain, S.H.; Mahmmod, B.M.; Saripan, M.I.; Al-Haddad, S.; Jassim, W.A.J. A new hybrid form of krawtchouk and tchebichef polynomials: Design and application. *J. Math. Imaging Vis.* **2019**, *61*, 555–570. [CrossRef]
32. Mahmmod, B.M.; Abdul-Hadi, A.M.; Abdulhussain, S.H.; Hussien, A.J. On computational aspects of Krawtchouk polynomials for high orders. *J. Imaging* **2020**, *6*, 81. [CrossRef]
33. Shivakumar, B.; Baboo, S.S. Automated forensic method for copy-move forgery detection based on Harris interest points and SIFT descriptors. *Int. J. Comput. Appl.* **2011**, *27*, 9–17.
34. Chen, L.; Lu, W.; Ni, J.; Sun, W.; Huang, J. Region duplication detection based on Harris corner points and step sector statistics. *J. Vis. Commun. Image Represent.* **2013**, *24*, 244–254. [CrossRef]
35. Van Loan, C.F. Generalizing the singular value decomposition. *J. Numer. Anal.* **1976**, *13*, 76–83. [CrossRef]
36. Sedgwick, P.J.B. Pearson's correlation coefficient. *BMJ* **2012**, *345*, e4483. [CrossRef]
37. Amidan, B.G.; Ferryman, T.A.; Cooley, S.K. Data outlier detection using the Chebyshev theorem. In Proceedings of the 2005 IEEE Aerospace Conference, Big Sky, MT, USA, 5–12 March 2005; IEEE: Big Sky, MT, USA, 2005; pp. 3814–3819.
38. Pulipaka, A.; Seeling, P.; Reisslein, M.; Karam, L.J. Traffic and statistical multiplexing characterization of 3-D video representation formats. *IEEE Trans. Broadcasting* **2013**, *59*, 382–389. [CrossRef]
39. Su, Y.; Nie, W.; Zhang, C. A frame tampering detection algorithm for MPEG videos. In Proceedings of the 2011 6th IEEE Joint International Information Technology and Artificial Intelligence Conference, Chongqing, China, 20–22 August 2015; IEEE: Chongqing, China, 2011; pp. 461–464.
40. Mizher, M.A.; Ang, M.C.; Mazhar, A.A.; Mizher, M.A. A review of video falsifying techniques and video forgery detection techniques. *Int. J. Electron. Secur. Digit. Forensics* **2017**, *9*, 191–208. [CrossRef]
41. Shanableh, T. Detection of frame deletion for digital video forensics. *Digit. Investig.* **2013**, *10*, 350–360. [CrossRef]
42. Liu, Y.; Huang, T. Exposing video inter-frame forgery by Zernike opponent chromaticity moments and coarseness analysis. *Multimed. Syst.* **2017**, *23*, 223–238. [CrossRef]

Article

Exposing Manipulated Photos and Videos in Digital Forensics Analysis

Sara Ferreira [1,*], Mário Antunes [2,3,*] and Manuel E. Correia [1,3]

1. Department of Computer Science, Faculty of Sciences, University of Porto, 4169-007 Porto, Portugal; mdcorrei@fc.up.pt
2. Computer Science and Communication Research Centre (CIIC), School of Technology and Management, Polytechnic of Leiria, 2411-901 Leiria, Portugal
3. INESC TEC, CRACS, 4200-465 Porto, Portugal
* Correspondence: sara.ferreira@fc.up.pt (S.F.); mario.antunes@ipleiria.pt (M.A.)

Citation: Ferreira, S.; Antunes, M.; Correia, M.E. Exposing Manipulated Photos and Videos in Digital Forensics Analysis. *J. Imaging* 2021, 7, 102. https://doi.org/10.3390/jimaging7070102

Academic Editors: Irene Amerini, Gianmarco Baldini and Francesco Leotta

Received: 22 April 2021
Accepted: 21 June 2021
Published: 24 June 2021

Publisher's Note: MDPI stays neutral with regard to jurisdictional claims in published maps and institutional affiliations.

Copyright: © 2021 by the authors. Licensee MDPI, Basel, Switzerland. This article is an open access article distributed under the terms and conditions of the Creative Commons Attribution (CC BY) license (https://creativecommons.org/licenses/by/4.0/).

Abstract: Tampered multimedia content is being increasingly used in a broad range of cybercrime activities. The spread of fake news, misinformation, digital kidnapping, and ransomware-related crimes are amongst the most recurrent crimes in which manipulated digital photos and videos are the perpetrating and disseminating medium. Criminal investigation has been challenged in applying machine learning techniques to automatically distinguish between fake and genuine seized photos and videos. Despite the pertinent need for manual validation, easy-to-use platforms for digital forensics are essential to automate and facilitate the detection of tampered content and to help criminal investigators with their work. This paper presents a machine learning Support Vector Machines (SVM) based method to distinguish between genuine and fake multimedia files, namely digital photos and videos, which may indicate the presence of deepfake content. The method was implemented in Python and integrated as new modules in the widely used digital forensics application Autopsy. The implemented approach extracts a set of simple features resulting from the application of a Discrete Fourier Transform (DFT) to digital photos and video frames. The model was evaluated with a large dataset of classified multimedia files containing both legitimate and fake photos and frames extracted from videos. Regarding deepfake detection in videos, the Celeb-DFv1 dataset was used, featuring 590 original videos collected from YouTube, and covering different subjects. The results obtained with the 5-fold cross-validation outperformed those SVM-based methods documented in the literature, by achieving an average F1-score of 99.53%, 79.55%, and 89.10% , respectively for photos, videos, and a mixture of both types of content. A benchmark with state-of-the-art methods was also done, by comparing the proposed SVM method with deep learning approaches, namely Convolutional Neural Networks (CNN). Despite CNN having outperformed the proposed DFT-SVM compound method, the competitiveness of the results attained by DFT-SVM and the substantially reduced processing time make it appropriate to be implemented and embedded into Autopsy modules, by predicting the level of fakeness calculated for each analyzed multimedia file.

Keywords: digital forensics; cybersecurity; multimedia content manipulation; deepfake; convolutional neural networks; support vector machines; discrete fourier transform

1. Introduction

Cybercrime has challenged national security systems all over the world, and, in the last five years, there has been an increase of 67% in the incidence of security breaches worldwide [1], with malicious activities like phishing, ransomware, and cryptojacking being the most popular threats to cybersecurity [2–4]. In a broad sense, malicious actors are taking advantage of human and technical vulnerabilities, to steal and acquire illicit benefits from victims. The widespread global reach of cyberattacks, their level of impact, sophistication, and dire consequences for society can be analyzed within several distinct dimensions, namely economic disruption, psychological disorder, and other threats to national defense [5,6]. The pandemic we are all currently enduring has also raised a global awareness about how dependent we now are on the Internet to carry on a semblance of normal life. Activities we took for granted in our daily lives, like working, reading, talking, studying, and shopping, are now highly dependent on digital services. This creates a perfect context for an increase in online fraud and other criminal activities in cyberspace [7,8].

Defacing and deepfakes take advantage of multimedia content manipulation techniques to tamper digital photos and videos. They can inflict severe reputational and other kinds of damages on their victims. These cyberthreats use hyper-realistic videos that apply Artificial Intelligence (AI) techniques to change what someone says and does [9]. Coupled with the reach and speed of social media, convincing deepfakes can quickly reach millions of people, negatively impact society in general and create real havoc on the lives of its victims. A deepfake attack may have different motivations. Fake news [10], revenge porn [11], and digital kidnapping, usually involving under-aged or otherwise vulnerable victims [12], associated with ransomware blackmailing, are among the most relevant forms of deepfaking attacks that can create havoc on the lives of its victims.

Digital forensics analysis is carried out mainly by the criminal investigation police. It embodies techniques and procedures for the collection, preservation, and analysis of digital evidence that may exist in electronic equipment [13]. Digital forensics techniques are essential to investigating crimes that are committed with computers (e.g., phishing and bank fraud), as well as those carried on against individuals, where evidence may reside on a computer (e.g., money laundering and child exploitation) [14].

When conducted manually, solely by the means of a human operator, digital forensics can be very time-consuming and highly inefficient in terms of identifying and collecting complete and meaningful digital evidence of cybercrimes [15]—in a process akin to the proverbial "search of a needle in a Haystack". Moreover, the manual analysis of multimedia content, for the identification of manipulated videos or photos, often results in the misclassification of files.

Effective forensic tools are essential, as they have the ability to reconstruct evidence left by cybercriminals when they perpetrate a cyberattack [16]. However, there exists an increasing number of highly sophisticated tools that make life much easier for cybercriminals to carry out complex and highly effective digital attacks. The criminal investigator is thus faced with a very difficult challenge in trying to keep up with these cyber-criminal operational advantages [17]. Autopsy (https://www.autopsy.com/ (accessed on 22 June 2021)) is a digital forensic tool that helps to level out this field. It is open-source and widely used by criminal investigators to analyze and identify digital evidence and artifacts of suspicious and anomalous activities. It incorporates a wide range of native modules to process digital objects, including images (on raw disks), and also provides a highly effective framework that allows the community to develop more modules for otherwise more specialized forensic tasks.

Machine Learning (ML) has boosted the automated detection and classification of digital artifacts for forensics investigative tools. Existing ML techniques to detect manipulated photos and videos [18] are seldom not fully integrated into forensic applications. Therefore, ML-based Autopsy modules, capable of detecting deepfakes are relevant and will most certainly be very much appreciated by the investigative authorities. The good results already observed by the reported ML methods for deepfake detection have not yet been fully translated into substantial gains for cybercrime investigation, as those methods have not often been incorporated into the most popular state-of-the-art digital forensics tools [19].

This paper describes the deployment and development of a standalone application to detect both digital photos as well as videos that have been manipulated and may be part of a deepfake attack. The application was further deployed as two separate modules for Autopsy, namely one to detect manipulated digital photos and other manipulated videos. The standalone application and the Python modules developed for Autopsy incorporate an

SVM-based model [20] to detect discrepancies in photos and video frames, namely splicing and copy–move anomalies. It works by extracting a set of fifty features calculated by a Discrete Fourier Transform (DFT), applied to the input files that are then further processed by an SVM-based method. These Autopsy modules were tested with a classified dataset of about 40,000 photos and 800 videos, composed of both faces and objects, where it is possible to find examples of slicing and copy–move manipulations. One part of this dataset consists of frames from deepfake videos that are part of the Celeb-DFv1 dataset [21]. The results obtained prove that Support Vector Machines (SVM) -based methods can attain very good precision on the detection of both tampered photos and videos. Regarding photos, we have achieved a mean precision of 99.6% and a F1-score of 99.5%, with a 5-fold cross-validation. Manipulated video detection achieved a mean precision of 74.4% and a F1-score of 79.5%. When processing photos and videos altogether, a mean precision of 81.1% and an F1-score of 87.9% were obtained.

The contributions of this paper can be outlined as follows:

- A labeled dataset composed of about 40,000 multimedia files. It incorporates state-of-the-art datasets of both normal examples and those subjected to some kind of manipulation, namely splicing, copy–move and deepfaking.
- An SVM-based model to process multimedia files and to detect those that were digitally manipulated. The model processes a set of simple features extracted by applying a DFT method to the input file. The tests were performed on the newly created dataset.
- The development of two ready-to-use Autopsy modules. One to detect the fakeness level of digital photos and the other to detect the fakeness level of input video files. The Autopsy modules take advantage of the SVM-based model implemented as a standalone application and have been made available in the following GitHub repository: https://github.com/saraferreirascf/Photo-and-video-manipulations-detector (accessed on 22 June 2021). The datasets are also available in the GitHub link, and the modules are ready to be installed and used in Autopsy.

The remainder of this paper is organized as follows. Section 2 describes the most up-to-date methods used to detect multimedia content manipulation, followed by a comprehensive description of the main fundamentals and methods behind the subject of deepfake detection. Section 3 explains digital forensics and characterizes some key concepts behind the Autopsy forensics tool, namely the set of existing available ingest modules. Section 4 depicts the overall architecture and the multimedia files process pipeline, delineating the overall benchmark process of the deepfake multimedia dataset. The experimental setup environment and the datasets processed by our experiments are described in Section 5. Section 6 presents the performance metrics used, the results obtained followed by their corresponding analysis. Finally, Section 7 states the main conclusions and delineates some future work.

2. Literature Review and State of the Art

This section describes some of the fundamentals behind digital forensics and multimedia manipulation techniques. It also surveys some of the most relevant and popular ML techniques that can be used to detect fake multimedia content.

2.1. Multimedia Manipulation Techniques

Digital photos and video manipulation is a very appealing and highly effective medium to spread misinformation. There are three popular main types of manipulation that can be applied to a multimedia file, namely copy–move, splicing, and deepfake. Despite the similarity of the overall final result, as it consists mainly of manipulating objects, faces, or voices in multimedia files, the methods to produce and further enhance the manipulation and then the ML techniques employed to detect these manipulations are very distinct and can be highly challenging for a fully automated detection system.

There are two good examples of how copy–move manipulation can be used to great effect to spread fake information and wrest the original photo from its context. Nearly a decade ago, Iran was accused of doctoring a photo of its missile tests. The photo depicted in Figure 1 was released on Iran's Revolutionary Guards official website, which claimed that four missiles were heading skyward simultaneously [22], when in fact only three missiles were launched. More recently, in July 2017, a fake image of Russian President Vladimir Putin was distributed on social media related to his meeting with US President Donald Trump during the 2017 G20 summit. This fake image garnered several thousand likes and retweets [23].

(a) Original photo.   (b) Manipulated photo.

Figure 1. An example [24,25] of a copy–move manipulation technique.

This manipulation technique consists of copying or moving parts of a photo to another place in the same photo. The goal is to give the illusion of having more elements in the photo than those that are really there. The main reason behind the increase of copy–move manipulation is the simplicity of the method. Textured areas such as grass, foliage, gravel, or fabric with irregular patterns, are ideal for this purpose because the copied areas will probably blend into the background and the human eye will not be able to easily discern any suspicious artifacts. As the copied parts came from the same digital photo, their noise, color palette, dynamic range, and other important properties will be compatible with the rest of the photo. This type of manipulation is difficult to detect by methods that look for statistical measurements' incompatibilities in different regions of the photo [26].

Splicing (Figure 2) consists of superimposing different regions of two photos, with deepfake being the most relevant consequence. It is an artificial and automated manipulation of media, usually made by employing AI techniques, in which a person's face in an existing photo or video is swiped by someone else's face. This manipulation is often used as an initial step of photo-montage, which is very popular in digital photo content editing. The splicing tampered image could be used in news reports, photography contests, key proof in academic papers, and so on, which could bring negative impacts.

As a result, it is an important issue to develop reliable splicing detection methods. In the forgery process, the manually introduced transitions of edges and corners are different from those in the legitimate photos. The differences are commonly described by the inconsistency and abnormality, and they are used for splicing detection [27].

The term "deepfake" is the combination of "deep learning" and "fake" [9]. In general, deepfake is achieved by manipulating realistic videos with the aim to depict people saying or doing things that did not happen. This kind of manipulation is usually difficult to detect, as it uses real footage to make it the closest thing to reality. Figure 3 depicts two frames extracted from two videos, one being legitimate (Figure 3b,c) and the other manipulated (Figure 3a,d). As can be seen in Figure 3a in comparison with Figure 3c, the eyes seem a little foggy and are looking in opposite directions. If someone without knowledge of the real frame was looking at the manipulated one, they might think it was a cross-eyed person and not notice that it was a deepfake. In Figure 3d, similarly to Figure 3b, the face is a little foggy and even blurry, and the quality is not compatible with the rest of the photo. In some cases, when comparing two photos, it is easy to see which is the deepfake, but having access only to the manipulated image, with the naked eye, it is not so perceptible that the photo has been manipulated, further demonstrating the importance of creating modules to identify this type of manipulation.

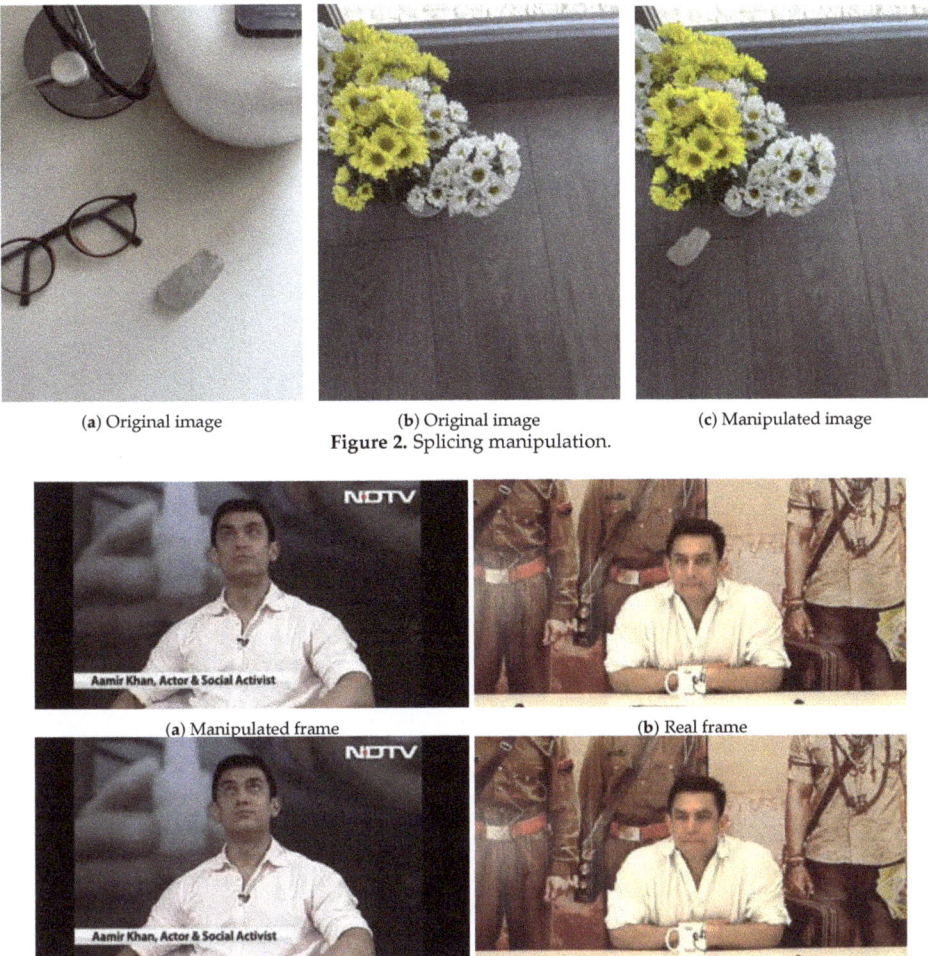

(a) Original image (b) Original image (c) Manipulated image

Figure 2. Splicing manipulation.

(a) Manipulated frame (b) Real frame

(c) Real frame (d) Manipulated frame

Figure 3. Comparison between fake and real frames in deepfake videos. These frames were extracted from videos in the Celeb-DFv1 dataset [21].

While deepfake of photos and videos is not new and can be observed in a lot of digital content, it has leveraged powerful machine learning and AI techniques to improve content manipulation [28]. The most common ML methods used to improve deepfakes are based on deep learning and involve training generative neural network architectures, such as auto-encoders or Generative Adversarial Networks (GANs) [29]. By using GANs, two Artificial Neural Networks (ANN) work together to create a real-looking media. The first neural network, usually called "the generator", tries to create new samples that are good enough to trick the second network training with a dataset containing real photos. In conclusion, a GAN can look at thousands of photos of a person and produce a new portrait that approximates those photos without being an exact copy of any one of them. Deepfake has garnered widespread attention, as it has been used in digital campaigns of spreading fake news. This manipulation technique is also responsible for digital kidnap, revenge porn, and financial fraud [30,31].

2.2. Techniques Used to Detect Multimedia Manipulation

Bearing in mind that the use of deepfake in digital crimes is a growing problem and has a great impact on today's society, some algorithms were developed to tackle this type of manipulation, namely Difference of Gaussian (DoG) and Oriented Rotated Brief (ORB). DoG and ORB are two widely used techniques to automatically detect copy–move manipulation in photos. This method was suggested by Niyishaka et al. [32] and comprises three steps: corners detection with Sobel algorithm [33]; features extraction with DoG and ORB [32,34]; and, finally, features correspondence. This method combines detection techniques based on blocks and key points in a single model. A match is found between two points of interest if the distance is less than a predetermined threshold.

Unmasking deepfake with DFT and ML is a method described in [20]. It is based on a classical frequency domain analysis with DFT, followed by a classification based on ML techniques, namely by using Support Vector Machines (SVM). The frequency characteristics of a photo are analyzed in a space defined by a Fourier transform, namely by using a spectral decomposition of the input data, which indicates how the signal's energy is distributed over a range of frequencies. Mathematically, DFT decomposes a discrete signal into sinusoidal components of various frequencies ranging from 0 (constant frequency, corresponding to the image mean value) up to the maximum of the admissible frequency, given by the spatial resolution. The frequency–domain representation of a signal carrying information about the signal's amplitude and phase at each frequency is computed as described in (1):

$$X_{k,l} = \sum_{n=0}^{N-1} \sum_{0}^{M-1} x_{n,m} \cdot e^{(-\frac{i2\pi}{N}k_n)} \cdot e^{(-\frac{-i2\pi}{M}l_m)} \quad (1)$$

After applying a Fourier Transform to a photo, the returned values are represented in a new domain but within the same dimensionality. The output still contains 2D information, to which an azimuthal average is applied to compute a robust 1D representation of the DFT power spectrum. At this point, each frequency component is the radial average from the 2D spectrum previously calculated. In this case, the number of extracted features (frequency component) is a value chosen, taking into account computational time and classification scores. In the experiments made, fifty features were extracted from each photo. Figure 4b depicts the bidimensional representation of the DFT power spectrum of the photo depicted in Figure 4a. The resulting unidimensional array, containing the fifty selected features, is illustrated in Figure 4c.

After the features extraction, Support Vector Machines (SVM) is used to create a model based on a training dataset with manipulated and genuine photos. The model is then applied to a test dataset, to identify an optimal separating hyperplane that maximizes the margin between both classes (details described in Section 2.3).

Castillo and Yang [35] present a comprehensive review of the state-of-the-art deep learning-based methods for image forensics, both photos and videos. An exhaustive set of methods are introduced for a set of problems, namely median filtering, double JPEG, contrast enhancement, and general-purpose image processing operations. The performance obtained with the methods described, using distinct input features and datasets, is far above 90% accuracy.

One of the most impressive forms of ANN architecture is the Convolutional Neural Network (CNN) [36]. CNN is a deep learning algorithm which takes as input an input image, assigns importance (learning weights and biases) to various aspects and objects present in the image, and has the ability to differentiate one from the other. This type of neural network is comprised of neurons that self-optimize through learning. Each neuron receives an input and performs an operation, such as a scalar product followed by a nonlinear function [37].

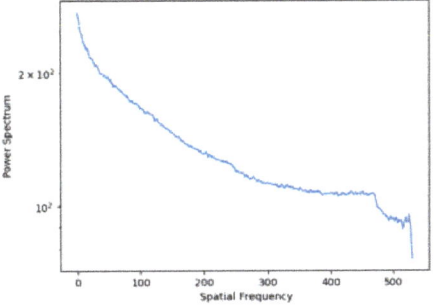

(a) Photo being tested. This frame was extracted from a video in the Celeb-DFv1 dataset [21]

(b) DFT power spectrum

```
[1.         0.84224635 0.78570679 0.75473273 0.71715572 0.69231963
 0.67016791 0.65023157 0.63120031 0.61437809 0.59388545 0.58517916
 0.56403071 0.54422546 0.53295873 0.51479493 0.50410594 0.49511568
 0.4845871  0.47045922 0.46812872 0.46119489 0.45625843 0.43764557
 0.43271859 0.41981565 0.41594143 0.41101351 0.41115967 0.40293237
 0.4003339  0.40234623 0.39866122 0.39430526 0.39588078 0.39216254
 0.38928573 0.39037718 0.38334375 0.3876251  0.3903337  0.38917909
 0.38776943 0.38989556 0.36038236 0.34553551 0.34024391 0.33761494
 0.34297509 0.27801506]
```

(c) Features vector

Figure 4. Photo features extraction by using Discrete Fourier Transform (DFT).

The method described by Jafar et al. [38] applies a deep learning and CNN approach to detect a deepfake by using DFT in previously extracted mouth features (DFT-MF). Deepfake video extraction is completed by the moviePy tool and takes into account the occurrences of certain words. By using the identified face landmarks, the frames in which the person has his mouth closed are removed. In this method, a standard of two words per second and five words as a sentence indicator are defined. If the video has more than fifty fake frames, it is considered deepfake.

Recurrent Neural Networks (RNN) is a type of ANN that can have an internal memory to process sequences of inputs along the way in the net. This network allows previous outputs to be used as inputs while having hidden states. RNN models are mostly used in the fields of natural language processing and speech recognition [39]. CNN and RNN methods have been fully efficient to deal with the recognition of tampered images and videos [40]. Several authors have applied mixed CNN-RNN based architectures to detect anomalies in videos and recognize facial expression [41–43].

In short, the concept of a Generative Adversarial Network (GAN) is that two networks are trained to compete with one another. The "generator" network is trained to produce artificial photos that are indistinguishable from a given dataset of real photos, whereas the "discriminator" is trained to correctly classify all photos as being either real or coming from the generator (forged photos). In response to the development of GANs, the forensics investigators have begun to develop methods to detect whether or not a given image was generated by a network trained in a GAN framework [44].

Yang et al. [40] present an exhaustive survey of deep learning-based image forensics. A wide set of sources are presented, namely source camera identification, recaptured image forensic, computer graphics image forensics, GAN-generated image detection, and source social network identification. A vast number of detection methods were surveyed, each one using different network architectures and depth. The results are expressive and reveal the good performance obtained by deep learning-based approaches to tackle with image forensics.

In [45], a method is described to extract and analyze the similarity between audio (speech) and visual (face) modalities from within the same video. Effective cues corresponding to perceived emotion from the two modalities within a video are extracted and compared, to infer whether the input video is real or fake. To train the model, a real video is passed along with its deepfake through the network and obtains modality and perceived emotion embedding vectors for the face and speech of the subject. These embedding vectors are used to compute the triplet loss function to minimize the similarity between the modalities from the fake video and maximize the similarity between modalities for the real video. This method obtained an Area Under Curve (AUC) score of 84.4% on the DFDC dataset [46] and 96.6% on the DeepFake-TIMIT Dataset (https://www.idiap.ch/dataset/deepfaketimit (accessed on 22 June 2021)).

Despite the significant results attained with deep learning based methods, feature extraction and classifier methods, like DFT and SVM, respectively, have produced competitive results and can be well integrated into off-the-shelf forensic tools like Autopsy.

2.3. Support Vector Machines (SVM)

SVM is a supervised learning classifier based on Vapnik's Statistical Learning Theory and Structural Minimization Principle [47]. It is included in a set of kernel-based learning methods, in which the problem is addressed by mapping the data to a larger dimensional space. This mapping may not be linear, and the function that allows this mapping is called a kernel [48]. SVM introduced the concept of a kernel method for pattern analysis into machine learning scenarios [49], in which data are mapped into a high-dimensional feature space where each point represents a feature of the input data. This mapping is carried out by using a function ϕ (2), which is denominated by kernel function and where data are mapped into some feature space F via a nonlinear mapping, as depicted in Figure 5. Although it does not involve any computations in high-dimensional space, with the use of kernels, all computations needed are performed directly in input space [48].

$$\Phi : \mathbf{R}^N \to F \tag{2}$$

The linear hyperplane (in the feature space) that separates both classes is then selected. It only requires the evaluation of a kernel function and involves only the processing of dot products (3):

$$k(\mathbf{x}, \mathbf{y}) := (\Phi(\mathbf{x}), \Phi(\mathbf{y})). \tag{3}$$

Omitting details that can be found elsewhere [47], when using SVM for classification of data into two distinct classes, the overall idea is to find the optimal hyperplane between the positive and negative examples, which is defined as the one giving the maximum margin between the training examples that are closest to it. Figure 5 depicts the overall idea behind SVM. Support Vectors (SV) are the examples that lie closest to the separating hyperplane, and once this hyperplane is found, new examples can be classified simply by determining on which side of the hyperplane they fall. By using these support vectors, the margin of the classifier is maximized, and, by eliminating the support vectors, the position of the hyperplane changes.

SVM aims to maximize the margin between the data points and the hyperplane. The loss function that helps maximize the margin is hinge loss:

$$c(x, y, f(x)) = (1 - y * f(x)) \tag{4}$$

The Regularization Parameter tells the SVM optimization how much it wants to avoid misclassification of each training example. If C is high, the optimization will choose a smaller margin hyperplane, so the misclassification rate of the training data will be low. In the opposite direction, if C is low, then the margin will be large, even if there are classification errors of the training data. The cost is 0 if the predicted value and the current value are of the same sign. If they are not, the loss value is calculated. A smoothing parameter is also added to the cost function, to balance margin maximization and loss. After adding the smoothing parameter, the cost function looks like (5):

$$min_w \lambda ||w||^2 + \sum_{i=1}^{n}(1 - y_i <x_i, w>) \qquad (5)$$

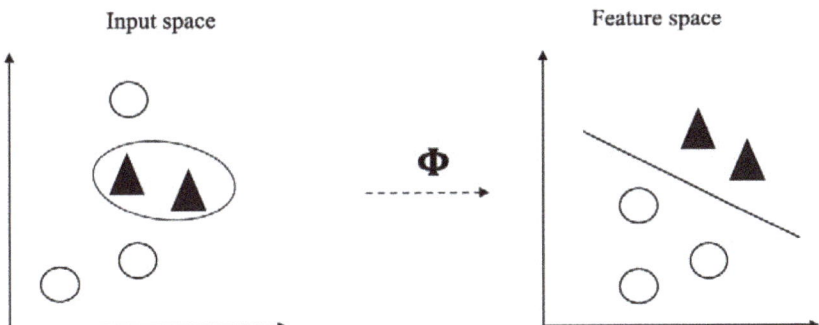

Figure 5. Mapping the training data nonlinearly into a higher-dimensional feature space, and constructing a linear separating hyperplane in the feature space.

A learning algorithm usually tries to learn the most common features (what differentiates one class from another) of a class and classification is based on the learned representative features (so classification is based on the differences between classes). SVM works the other way around, as it finds the most similar examples between classes, represented by the support vectors.

SVM models have been applied as learning classifiers to distinguish between original and tampered photos and videos. In [50], an SVM classifier is used to detect re-sampled images. The method is based on examining normalized energy density present within varying size windows in the second derivative of the frequency domain and exploits this characteristic mentioned to derive a 19-dimensional feature vector that is used to train the SVM classifiers. SVM is also used in the methods described previously in Section 2.2 [20,32].

3. Digital Forensics

Digital forensics has gained a growing interest in the criminal ecosystem (e.g., attorneys, prosecutors, trial, criminal police), as the number of cybercrimes and crimes using electronic equipment has increased in the past several years. Nowadays, the vast majority of crimes, ranging from the most traditional like murder or assault, to cybercrime, takes advantage of electronic devices connected to the Internet. This shift in the modus operandi has direct implications on the increasing number of equipment (e.g., PC, laptops, external storage devices, mobile phones, among others) seized by the police in the scope of a process, and consequently on the methodology adopted to analyze those devices.

Criminal police have been challenged to implement emergent methodologies to accelerate the analysis process, and, at the same time, to automatically extract, analyze, and preserve the digital evidence being collected in electronic equipment, namely disks, smartphones, and other devices with storage capacity. These tools embody techniques and procedures to produce a sustained reconstruction of events, to help digital forensics' investigators build a list of evidence that may dictate information about the suspect's innocence or guilt. The manual analysis by the criminal investigation team is still needed but oriented towards specific artifacts previously selected by the digital forensics tools and not necessarily in repetitive and tiresome tasks.

The protection of digital forensics information, and preservation of digital evidence, is achieved by establishing strict guidelines and procedures, namely detailed instructions about authorized rights to retrieve digital evidence, how to properly prepare systems for evidence retrieval, where to store any recovered evidence, and how to document these activities to guarantee data authenticity and integrity [51].

Figure 6 depicts the overall procedure to extract and analyze electronic devices, namely those with storage capabilities. The device is plugged into a write blocker, to prevent any write operation that may be done inadvertently. Then, by using a program to extract a raw image of the storage device, such as Forensic ToolKit (FTK, https://accessdata.com/ (accessed on 22 June 2021)), a E01 format image file is produced. Taking the E01 file as input, the digital forensics analysis starts, by using adequate tools, such as Autopsy Digital Forensics (https://www.autopsy.com/ (accessed on 22 June 2021)) or EnCase Forensic Software (https://security.opentext.com/encase-forensic (accessed on 22 June 2021)). The output produced is a list of artifacts that are worth investigating and which digital evidence has to be preserved to be accepted in court.

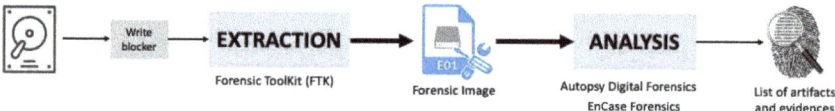

Figure 6. Overall procedure to extract and analyze electronic devices.

Autopsy is a widely used digital forensics tool to analyze a raw image file previously extracted from the electronic device. It is open-source and has distinct and well-appreciated visualization features to help the criminal investigator to assertively search the most relevant artifacts. Autopsy has the following key concepts:

- A case is defined in the Autopsy as a container with one or more data sources. Only one case can be opened at a time and is mandatory to start a digital forensics investigation in Autopsy.
- Data source is the term used to refer to raw disk images and logical files that are added to a case.
- Autopsy maintains a central SQlite or PostgreSQL database where all metadata files and results analysis are stored.
- After the data source analysis, the results are being gradually posted into a blackboard in the form of artifacts.

Data source analysis is made through available modules. The main reason to consider writing a module for Autopsy instead of a stand-alone tool is that Autopsy handles several data input types and ways to display the results to the user, which is an advantage as many forensic investigators do not have prior knowledge of programming [52].

Autopsy takes advantage of built-in modules and allows the community to develop new ones that may be based on already existing ones. These modules can be written in Java or Python (in this case, Autopsy uses Jython, to enable Python). There are four types of modules in Autopsy, namely ingest, report, content viewers, and result viewers.

Ingest modules, depicted in Figure 7, are executed when a new data source is added to a case. They are called "File Ingest Modules" and are executed to examine the contents of a group of files in the data source. For example, "Data Source Ingest" modules are executed once for each image or set of logical files, to analyze artifacts.

Report modules are typically executed after a user has examined the results. The purpose of this module is to execute analysis and report the results obtained. Content viewers are graphical and focus on displaying a file in a specific form. They can be used, for example, to view a file in hexadecimal format. Finally, result viewers show information about a set of files. They are used, for example, to view a set of files in a table.

Some modules like File Type Identification, Email Parser, and Encryption Detection are available through Autopsy as illustrated in Figure 7. For example, the File Type Identification module identifies files based on their internal signatures and does not rely on file extensions. The Email Parser module identifies MBOX, EML, and PST format files based on file signatures, extracting the e-mails from them, and adding the results to the blackboard artifact for each message. The Encryption Detection module searches for files that could be encrypted using both a general entropy calculation and more specialized tests for certain file types. It is also possible to use modules developed by the third-parties. In [53], the authors present a module to successfully recover messages exchanged between TikTok users through the app communication channels. It is also possible to obtain the list of TikTok contacts of a user's account, photos linked to the app, and TikTok videos watched by the user's smartphone. Another example is described in the module described in [54], which allows forensic investigators to collect the needed information about Cortana, the new voice-activated personal digital assistant of the Windows 10 operating system.

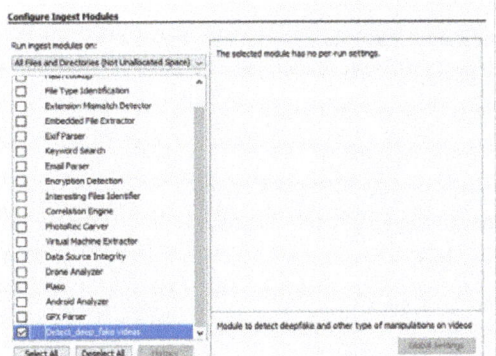 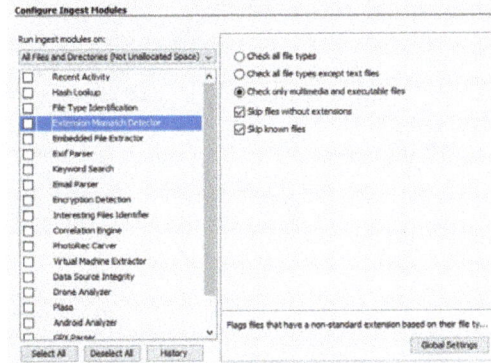

(a) Example of a module without per-run settings (b) Example of a module with per-run settings

Figure 7. List of modules available in the Autopsy tool.

XRY mobile forensics tool from MSAB (https://www.msab.com/products/xry/ (accessed on 22 June 2021)) is an intuitive and efficient software for Windows. It allows a fast and secure high-quality data extraction from mobile devices while maintaining the integrity of the evidence. XRY allows a rapid logical and physical extraction of files, and its file format maintains secure and accountable evidence at all times, with complete forensic auditing and protection of evidence from the moment the extraction begins.

Cellebrite (https://www.cellebrite.com/en/home/ (accessed on 22 June 2021)) is an Israeli toolset used for the collection, analysis, and management of digital data. It is a competitor of XRY for mobile device extraction and analysis, providing a wide set of features to extract data from digital devices.

EnCase from Opentext Security (https://security.opentext.com/encase-forensic (accessed on 22 June 2021)) has several products designed for forensics, security analytic, and e-discovery use. Encase is traditionally used in forensics to recover evidence from seized hard drives and support mobile devices' extraction and analysis. It allows the investigator to conduct an in-depth analysis of user files to collect evidence such as documents, pictures, Internet history, and Windows Registry information, among other features.

Forensic ToolKit (FTK) from AccessData (https://accessdata.com/products-services/forensic-toolkit-ftk (accessed on 22 June 2021)) is an open-source tool that provides real-world capabilities that help forensics' digital investigation teams separate critical data from trivial details and protect digital information while complying with digital regulations. This tool can be used by both criminal police and the private sector to perform complete forensic examinations of a computer. It includes customizable filters that allow the examiner to inspect thousands of files, including locating emails purportedly excluded from a computer; this feature is compatible with Outlook, AOL, Outlook Express, Netscape, Earthlink, Yahoo, Hotmail, Eudora, and MSN email.

The use of digital forensics tools is crucial to automate the extraction and analysis of electronic devices in the context of digital forensics. Autopsy has been widely used in forensics analysis and third-party modules have a positive impact on implementing additional and specific features. In the scope of this paper, two ingest modules were developed to detect deepfake digital photos and videos, respectively. The modules are described in Section 4 and are ready to be incorporated into the Autopsy forensics tool.

4. Architecture

This section describes the architecture that was deployed to process input videos and to classify them as being genuine or manipulated. It also describes the Autopsy module developed to classify videos in a digital forensics context and the dataset created for this context.

4.1. General Architecture

The overall architecture of the standalone application developed to classify photos and videos is depicted in Figure 8. It has three main building blocks: pre-processing, processing, and results analysis.

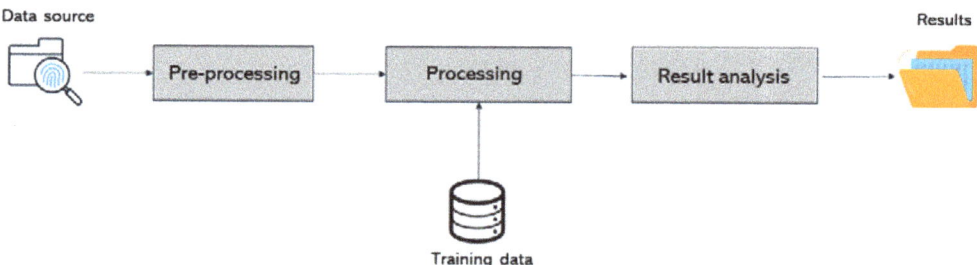

Figure 8. Overall architecture of the standalone application and Autopsy modules.

To obtain a functional deepfake detection system using Discrete Fourier Transform and Machine Learning, it is necessary for a first step to obtain the input data to feed the classification model, which will be used to classify each image as manipulated (deepfake) or legitimate.

Pre-processing is depicted in Figure 9 and consists initially of taking three to four frames per second from the input videos. This was achieved by creating a Python script, and all the frames extracted are added to the final dataset. By having all the photos in the dataset, the features' extraction is made by applying the DFT method described in Section 2.2 [20]. The output is a labeled input datasets for both training and testing. The preprocessing phase reads the photos through the OpenCV library and further extracts their features [20]. Using this method, exactly fifty features were obtained for each photo that were then loaded into a new file with the corresponding label (0 for fake photos and 1 for the genuine ones). At the end of the preprocessing phase, a fully labeled dataset is available and ready to feed the SVM model.

The processing phase, depicted in Figure 10, corresponds to the SVM processing. In a first step, the following parameters were chosen: the RBF (Radial basis function) kernel and a regularization parameter of 6.37. This choice took into account the best practices adopted for similar experiments and the comparison with other parameters.

The implementation of SVM processing was made through the scikit-learn library for Python 3.9. With the generated data ready to be classified and the SVM model created, the results analysis phase follows and is depicted in Figure 11.

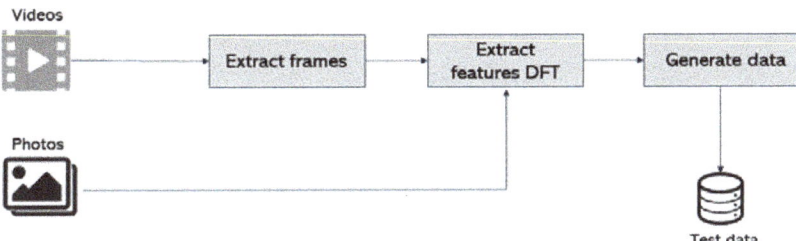

Figure 9. Pre-processing phase.

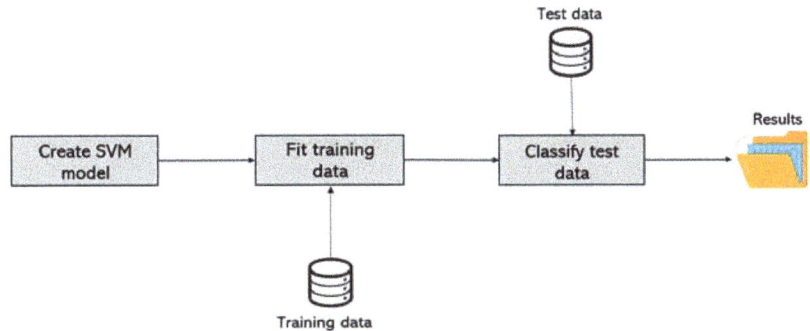

Figure 10. Processing phase.

Figure 11. Results analysis phase.

The model created by SVM at the processing phase is then used to get a prediction for each photo in the testing dataset. The tests were carried out with a 5-fold cross-validation, by splitting the dataset into ten equal parts and using nine for training and one for testing. The dataset is balanced, regarding the number of fake and genuine photos and videos.

For each SVM model evaluation, the results obtained include the confusion matrix, precision, recall and F1-score; and the calculated prediction that allows us to deduce the probability of an image has been manipulated.

4.2. Autopsy Module Architecture

As stated before, Autopsy is among the most used digital forensics applications and is open to the integration of third-party modules. Autopsy processes the input data and shows the results by using report modules.

Autopsy uses Jython in new modules development, to enable Python scripting. Jython is converted into Java byte code and runs on the JVM. As it is limited to Python 2.7, to overcome this limitation and the fact that some libraries used by the SVM classification method did not work with Python 2.7, three Python executables were created: one to extract frames from videos; another to process photo's features; and the third one to create the SVM model and to classify the photos.

The data source ingest module that runs against a data source added to the Autopsy, was developed, and its architecture is similar to Figure 12. To start this analysis, it is necessary to create a new "case" inside Autopsy and add one data source to it. An example of a data source is a disk image. Then, the module starts by extracting each video within the data source added to the Autopsy case and saves them in a temporary directory. Only videos with the extension ".mp4" were considered in the processing.

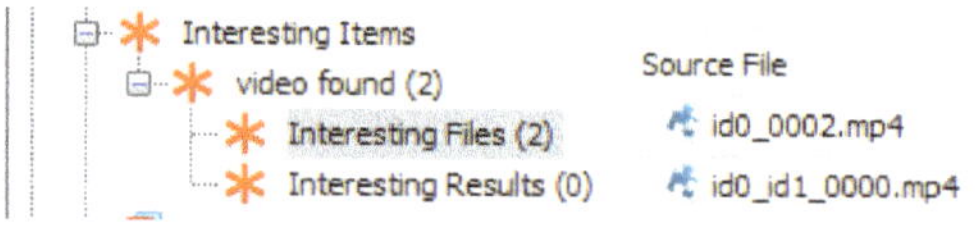

(a) Artifacts found   (b) Video files found

Figure 12. Videos found in data source—Autopsy module.

For each video stored in the temporary directory, the first script is performed where three to four frames per second (depending on the original number of frames per second and the video duration) will be extracted and saved. The second executable then extracts the features from each frame stored and outputs obtained and, with the training file already created and distributed with the module, feeds the last Python executable, which creates the SVM classifier. The artifacts with the classification results are calculated and posted in the Autopsy blackboard, which are further displayed to the user.

The model outputs a prediction of fakeness, as depicted in Figure 13. In the case of classifying if a video is manipulated or not, if a third or more of the frames of a video are classified as fake, it is considered that it is likely to be deepfake.

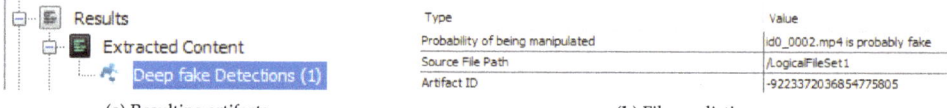

(a) Resulting artifacts   (b) File prediction

Figure 13. Artifacts with final classification—Autopsy module.

The standalone application architecture matches the Autopsy data source ingest module (Figure 7). The standalone application was developed before the Autopsy module, which gave the possibility to develop and test the method while disregarding the needed compatibility with the Python libraries and with the strict format that is required by Autopsy for the development of new modules.

5. Datasets

A dataset containing both people's faces and objects was created to train and test the SVM-based classification model. The dataset used in [20] is a compilation of photos available in the CelebA-HQ dataset [55], Flickr-Faces-HQ dataset [56], "100 K Faces project" (https://generated.photos/ (accessed on 22 June 2021)) and "this person does not exist" project (https://thispersondoesnotexist.com/ (accessed on 22 June 2021)). Table 1 itemizes the datasets collected and used in the experiments.

Some complexity was added to the dataset, by including objects and others people's faces, being possible to detect other types of manipulations aside from deepfake. The COVERAGE dataset [57] is a copy–move forgery database with similar but genuine objects that contains 97 legitimate photos and 97 manipulated ones. The Columbia Uncompressed Image Splicing Detection Evaluation Dataset [58] was also added, which consists of high-resolution images, 183 authentic (taken using just one camera and not manipulated), and 180 spliced photos. An additional 14 legitimate and 14 fake ad hoc photos were also added, containing splicing and copy–move manipulations. For the video, Celeb-DF [21] was used to provide fake and real videos to train the model. This dataset contains 795 fake videos and 158 real ones extracted from Youtube. To combine these videos with the rest of the dataset, three frames per second were extracted from each video being treated as a photo thenceforth. In total, 6201 frames were extracted from real videos and 31,551 from fake ones.

Table 1. Composition of the dataset.

Name	Fake	Real
CelebA-HQ dataset	-	10,000
Flickr-Faces-HQ dataset	-	10,000
"100 K Facesproject"	10,000	-
"this person does not exist"	10,000	-
COVERAGE dataset	97	97
Columbia Image Splicing Dataset	180	183
Created by us	14	14
Celeb-DFv1	795	158
	21,086	20,452

To use these photos to train and test our model, the dataset must be balanced. To achieve that, if at some point we have more real photos than fake ones, we only use the minimum between them. To be more specific, as we have 31,551 fake photos extracted from videos and 6201 real photos, we will only use 6201 photos from the fake ones, with 12,402 photos extracted from videos in total. Adding up all datasets containing only photos, we have 20,291 fake photos and 20,294 real ones. Putting it all together, the new dataset used in this paper is balanced and has 52,990 photos divided into two classes: 26,495 genuine (or real) photos and 26,495 that were manipulated. Table 2 specifies the composition of the datasets tested, namely for photos and videos. For each dataset, the number of examples used for training and testing is also indicated. The results presented in Section 6 were validated through a 5-fold cross-validation methodology. That is, each dataset was equally divided into five parts, each one being tested against the model trained with the remaining four parts.

Table 2. Composition of the training and testing datasets.

	Training	Testing
Photos	32,464	8116
Videos	9920	2480
Photos and Videos	42,384	10,596

The Autopsy modules are optimized for Autopsy version 4.15.0 and were developed in Python version 3.9. The experiments were carried on in a PC with Windows 10, 8 GB RAM and AMD Ryzen 5 2600.

6. Results Analysis

This section describes the results obtained from the experiments and the corresponding analysis. The experiments were validated by a 5-fold cross-validation approach, for the dataset created described in Section 5. Evaluation metrics are described in Section 6.1, and the analysis of the results is presented in Section 6.2. Finally, Section 6.3 describes the results obtained with the benchmark of DFT-SVM and a CNN-based model.

6.1. Evaluation Metrics

The metrics used to evaluate the results were Precision (P), Recall (R), and F1-score, which can be calculated through the well-known and documented confusion matrix depicted in Table 3 [59].

Table 3. Confusion matrix.

	Positive	Negative
Positive	TP	FP
Negative	FN	TN

In the confusion matrix, each row represents the instances in a predicted class, while each column represents the instances in an actual class. The positive class refers to the manipulated photos, while the negative class represents the original and unmanipulated ones. True Positives (TP) represent the events where the model has correctly predicted the positive class, while True Negatives (TN) are the events correctly predicted as negative, that is, genuine photos. False Positives (FP) and False Negatives (FN) evaluate the events that were incorrectly predicted by the model, namely those that correspond to legitimate photos classified as manipulated and those manipulated that were classified as genuine, respectively.

Precision and Recall correlate the metrics described above. Precision measures the percentage of examples identified as true that are genuine and correspond to real photos or videos. Precision is calculated by (6):

$$P = \frac{TP}{(TP+FP)} \qquad (6)$$

Recall is the percentage of manipulated images that we could find of the total number of manipulated images. Recall corresponds to the following (7):

$$R = \frac{TP}{(TP+FN)} \qquad (7)$$

F1-score is a harmonic mean between Precision and Recall. The range for F1-score is between [0, 1] and measures the preciseness and robustness of the classifier—that is, the number of instances that were correctly classified and those that were misclassified, respectively. F1 measure is calculated by (8):

$$F1 = 2 * \frac{P*R}{(P+R)} \qquad (8)$$

Accuracy (9) is calculated by the ratio between the correctly classified examples (real and fake photos and videos) and the total number of examples (correctly and incorrectly classified):

$$A = \frac{TP+TN}{(TP+TN+FP+FN)} \qquad (9)$$

6.2. Results with DFT-SVM

Table 4 describes the results obtained with a 5-fold cross-validation to the dataset of digital photos. The table highlights the partial results obtained in each split, namely the number of FP, FN, TP, and TP, as well as the calculated values for P, R, F1, and accuracy. The corresponding mean scores obtained with the 5-fold cross-validation are also indicated.

The mean value obtained for accuracy (A) is 99.51%, which surpasses the result of 93.52% achieved in [32]. The number of incorrectly classified examples, namely false positives and false negatives, is low, having a mean value of 14 and 25.8, respectively.

The results attained with a 5-fold cross-validation processing for the dataset of videos are presented in Table 5. The mean values for F1-score and accuracy are 79.55% and 77.94%, respectively. Regarding misclassified examples, the average values for FP and FN are, respectively, 365 and 180 for a total amount of 2480 examples.

Table 4. Results obtained with 5-fold cross-validation against the dataset of photos.

	TP	TN	FP	FN	Precision	Recall	F1-Score	Accuracy
Split 1	3999	4070	20	27	0.9950	0.9933	0.99941	0.9942
Split 2	4089	3986	17	24	0.9958	0.9942	0.9950	0.9949
Split 3	4091	3983	11	31	0.9973	0.9925	0.9949	0.9948
Split 4	3972	4111	11	22	0.9972	0.9945	0.9959	0.9960
Split 5	4010	4070	11	25	0.9973	0.9938	0.9955	0.9952
Mean	4032.2	4044	14	25.8	0.9965	0.9941	0.9953	0.9951

Table 5. Results obtained with 5-fold cross-validation against the dataset of videos.

	TP	TN	FP	FN	Precision	Recall	F1-Score	Accuracy
Split 1	1092	891	307	190	0.7746	0.8474	0.8093	0.7996
Split 2	1054	862	385	179	0.7324	0.8548	0.7889	0.7726
Split 3	1066	883	351	180	0.7523	0.8555	0.8006	0.7859
Split 4	1033	884	385	178	0.7285	0.8530	0.7858	0.7730
Split 5	1055	855	397	173	0.7266	0.8591	0.7873	0.7702
Mean	1060	865	365	180	0.7438	0.8548	0.7955	0.7794

Considering that videos are composed of a set of photos, a third experiment was made to accommodate both multimedia content types. Table 6 presents the results obtained with the whole dataset composed of 52,990 examples, applying a 5-fold cross-validation.

Table 6. Results obtained with 5-fold cross-validation against the dataset of photos and videos.

	TP	TN	FP	FN	Precision	Recall	F1-Score	Accuracy
Split 1	5319	4016	1192	71	0.8169	0.9868	0.8939	0.8808
Split 2	5216	4104	1221	57	0.8103	0.9992	0.8909	0.8974
Split 3	5228	4055	1248	67	0.8073	0.9873	0.8883	0.8770
Split 4	5201	4137	1203	57	0.8121	0.9891	0.8819	0.8815
Split 5	5211	4101	1218	68	0.8105	0.9871	0.8902	0.8787
Mean	5235	4082.6	1216.4	64	0.8114	0.9879	0.8910	0.8792

It is possible to observe that the mean values for precision, recall, and F1-score are respectively 81.14%, 98.79%, and 89.10%. The calculated mean accuracy is 87.92%, and the overall results outperform those attained and documented in [20]. We can conclude that we obtained very satisfactory results considering the work already developed and available in the literature for SVM-based methods, despite using a dataset with more diversity on manipulation types. The results could be even better with an even more diverse training dataset and preserving the same quality of photos.

The Receiver Operating Characteristic (ROC) curve is a versatile and well-adopted technique to graphically show the performance of a binary classifier. It plots the probability of detection (TPR) versus the probability that a false alarm (FPR) may happen, at different classification thresholds. Figure 14a depicts the ROC curve for video classification, where it is possible to observe its high performance, as the fake videos classifier gives a curve closer to the top-left corner.

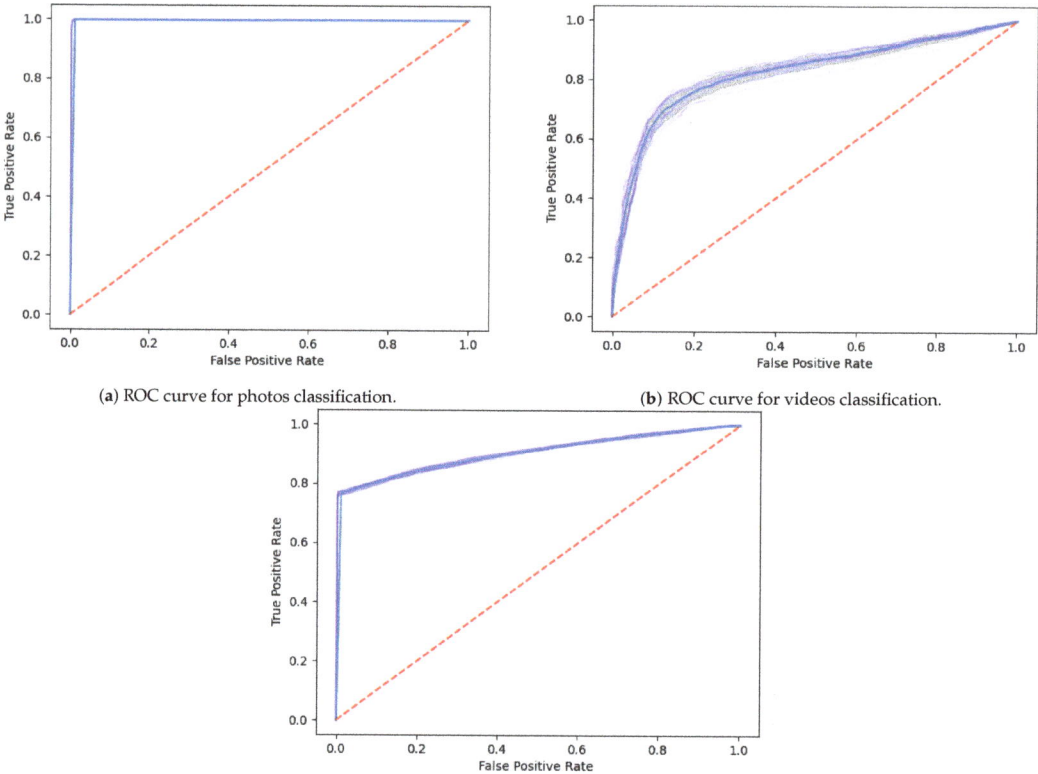

(a) ROC curve for photos classification.
(b) ROC curve for videos classification.
(c) ROC curve for photos and videos classification.

Figure 14. Receiver Operating Characteristic (ROC) curves calculated for photos and videos processing.

Figure 14b illustrates the ROC curve related to the processing of the whole dataset, with photos and videos. It is also possible to observe the good performance of the classifier, in which the curve is pushed to the upper left corner of the graphic.

6.3. Benchmark with CNN-Based Methods

The SVM method proposed in this paper was compared with a CNN-based method, to benchmark both methods in terms of classification performance and processing time. CNNs are comprised of three types of layers: convolutional layers, pooling layers, and fully-connected layer [37]. The CNN created to benchmark with an SVM model consists of a convolutional layer with relu, following a pooling layer, another convolutional layer with relu, another pooling layer followed by a flatten layer to pass the multidimensional input to one dimension, and ending with two dense layers (fully-connected layers), one with relu and one with softmax. The CCN architecture was built on the top of Tensorflow (https://www.tensorflow.org/ (accessed on 22 June 2021)), being a neural network library Keras used to create the training and testing datasets.

Table 7 depicts the results obtained with the benchmarking of the videos dataset processing, namely the comparison of the results obtained with the DFT-SVM and CNN based methods.

Table 7. Benchmark videos.

	Precision	Recall	F1-Score	Accuracy
DFT with SVM	0.7438	0.8548	0.7955	0.7794
CNN	0.8820	0.8045	0.8415	0.8387

Regarding videos processing, when comparing with previously documented experiments, it is possible to note that, using the Celeb-DF dataset as part of the input dataset, the results outperform those obtained by [38], which uses DFT with Mouth Features (MF) to extract features and a CNN-based method to classify the videos. The reported accuracy was 71.25%.

Table 8 describes the results obtained with the benchmarking of the photos dataset processing, namely the comparison of the results obtained with the DFT-SVM and CNN based methods. It is possible to observe that the results obtained are similar to those reported by the authors in [20], by applying the same DFT-SVM method, but with a restricted dataset.

Table 8. Benchmark photos.

	Precision	Recall	F1-score	Accuracy
DFT with SVM	0.9965	0.9941	0.9953	0.9951
CNN	0.9970	0.9966	0.9968	0.9967

Regarding the processing times, CNN and SVM based methods possess quite distinct realities. Table 9 depicts the observed time spent by SVM and CNN based methods, under the same hardware setup, for processing the aggregated dataset proposed in Section 5. The values indicated in Table 9 are only related to the testing processing time, and do not include the preprocessing phase and features extraction. It is possible to observe that the processing time consumed by the CNN-based model is considerably higher than that spent by the SVM-based method, for both photo and video processing.

Table 9. Processing time spent for videos and photos, in the format hh:mm:ss.

	Photos	Videos
DFT with SVM	00:00:51	00:02:00
CNN	06:36:00	02:40:00

Deep learning based methods have been widely used, and are considered state-of-the-art cutting edge in what image and video forensics are about [35,40]. However, the features extraction methods and the overall functioning of deep learning based models, such as CNN and RNN, are time-consuming to process, and less flexible to be embedded into standalone off-the-shelf digital forensics tools, like Autopsy. Regarding the DFT-SVM compound method, the results achieved with the dataset proposed in this paper are competitive with the CNN model for both photos and videos, with a significantly lower processing time. The trade-off between the processing time and the evaluation performance obtained by DFT-SVM method [20] should thus be taken in account in the development of forensic tools to support and help criminal investigator's digital forensics daily routine.

By observing the available Autopsy third-party modules listing (https://github.com/sleuthkit/autopsy_addon_modules (accessed on 22 June 2021)), and also the modules developed by the Autopsy's community (https://www.osdfcon.org/ (accessed on 22 June 2021)), to the best of the authors' knowledge, there is not yet a registered and ready-to-use Autopsy module designed and developed to detect deepfake and digitally manipulated photos and videos in a forensics context.

7. Conclusions and Future Work

This paper described the development of an application to detect tampered multimedia content. An SVM-based method was implemented in a standalone application, to process the previously extracted features obtained by a DFT calculation in each multimedia file. Two modules for Autopsy digital forensics tool were developed, namely a module to detect tampered photos and another one to identify deepfake videos. The fundamentals behind digital forensics, SVM, and DFT were described. The most relevant and up-to-date literature review related to digital forensics on multimedia content was made, namely the survey on deep learning-based methods applied to photos and videos forensics.

The deliverables obtained with this research, namely the ready-to-use Autopsy modules, give a helping hand to digital forensics investigators and leverage the use of ML techniques to fight cybercrime activities that involve multimedia files. The overall architecture and development take advantage of two well-known and documented techniques to deal with feature extraction in multimedia content and to automatically detect from learning classifier models, respectively, the Discrete Fourier Transform (DFT) technique to extract features from photos, and SVM to classify files. Both techniques were incorporated in the developed standalone application, which was further integrated as two separated Autopsy modules. The dataset proposed in [20] was extended with different sources, mainly to accommodate deepfake videos. The final dataset has about 53,000 photos, enriched with faces and objects, where it is possible to find examples of deepfake, splicing, and copy–move manipulations. Some of the photos are frames extracted from deepfake videos.

The results were presented in three distinct dimensions: the classification performance obtained with a 5-fold cross-validation for photos and videos processing; the benchmark between SVM and CNN-based methods using the dataset proposed in this paper; and the processing time of SVM and CNN-based methods. The results obtained with SVM were promising and in line with previous ones documented in the literature for the same method [20]. It was possible to achieve a mean F1-score of around 99.5% for manipulated photos detection and 78.4% for deepfake video detection. Deep learning methods, namely CNN-based, outperformed those achieved by SVM, however with a considerably higher processing time. Strictly concerned with daily-routine digital forensic interest, despite the better results obtained with CNN-based methods, the trade-off with the processing time benefits the use of the SVM method with the features extracted by DFT.

By analyzing the misclassified photos and video frames, a possible cause could be related to the low resolution of the photos. A richer dataset with heterogeneous examples regarding the resolution of the photos would improve the overall results obtained. The optimal number of features that should be extracted from the photos, and its impact in computational time, is also worth investigating. An ensemble of learning classifiers, composed of both deep learning and SVM based methods, could benefit both the performance obtained and the processing time. A net model for forensic detection using CNN, eventually using a different architecture, is also worth investigating and implementing.

Besides the well-accepted implementation in Autopsy modules, an emergent subject that may benefit from the developed architecture is the detection of fake news and the spread of hate speech in social networks. The low processing time and the high performance obtained with the DFT-SVM method make it eligible to be incorporated as a plugin that may be used easily, and in real time, to detect the fakeness level of multimedia content spread in social networks.

Author Contributions: Conceptualization, S.F., M.A., M.E.C.; Data curation, S.F., M.A.; Formal analysis, S.F., M.A., M.E.C.; Funding acquisition, M.E.C.; Investigation, S.F., M.A., M.E.C.; Methodology, S.F., M.A.; Software, S.F.; Supervision, M.A., M.E.C.; Validation, M.A., M.E.C.; Visualization, S.F.; Writing—original draft: S.F., M.A., M.E.C.; Writing—Review and Editing; S.F., M.A., M.E.C. All authors have read and agreed to the published version of the manuscript.

Funding: This work is financed by National Funds through the Portuguese funding agency, FCT—Fundação para a Ciência e a Tecnologia, within project UIDB/50014/2020.

Institutional Review Board Statement: Not applicable.

Informed Consent Statement: Not applicable.

Data Availability Statement: Data is publicly available under an MIT license, at the following GitHub repository: https://github.com/saraferreirascf/Photo-and-video-manipulations-detector.

Acknowledgments: The authors acknowledge the facilities provided by INESC TEC, Faculty of Sciences, and University of Porto, for the support to this research. This work is financed by National Funds through the Portuguese funding agency, FCT - Fundação para a Ciência e a Tecnologia, within project UIDB/50014/2020.

Conflicts of Interest: The authors declare no conflict of interest.

Abbreviations

The following abbreviations are used in this manuscript:

A	Accuracy
AI	Artificial Intelligence
ANN	Artificial Neural Networks
AUC	Area Under Curve
CNN	Convolutional Neural Networks
DFT	Discrete Fourier Transformation
DoG	Difference of Gaussian
FTK	Forensic Tool Kit
FN	False Negative
FP	False Positive
GAN	Generative Adversarial Network
ML	Machine Learning
ORB	Oriented Rotated Brief
PST	Personal Storage Table
P	Precision
R	Recall
RNN	Recurrent Neural Network
ROC	Receiver Operating Characteristic
SV	Support Vector
SVM	Support Vector Machines
TN	True Negative
TP	True Positive

References

1. Accenture/Ponemon Institute: The Cost of Cybercrime. *Netw. Secur.* **2019**, *2019*, 4. [CrossRef]
2. Roškot, M.; Wanasika, I.; Kroupova, Z.K. Cybercrime in Europe: Surprising results of an expensive lapse. *J. Bus. Strategy* **2020**. [CrossRef]
3. Kertysova, K.; Frinking, E.; van den Dool, K.; Maričić, A.; Bhattacharyya, K. *Cybersecurity: Ensuring Awareness and Resilience of the Private Sector Across Europe in Face of Mounting Cyber Risks-Study*; Technical Report; European Economic and Social Committee: 2018. Available online: https://www.eesc.europa.eu/en/our-work/publications-other-work/publications/cybersecurity-ensuring-awareness-and-resilience-private-sector-across-europe-face-mounting-cyber-risks-study (accessed on 22 June 2021).
4. ENISA Threat Landscape—2020. Available online: https://www.enisa.europa.eu/topics/threat-risk-management/threats-and-trends/ (accessed on 16 March 2021).
5. Anderson, R.; Moore, T. The economics of information security. *Science* **2006**, *314*, 610–613. [CrossRef]
6. Bada, M.; Nurse, J.R. The social and psychological impact of cyberattacks. In *Emerging Cyber Threats and Cognitive Vulnerabilities*; Academic Press: Amsterdam, The Netherlands, 2020; pp. 73–92.
7. Lallie, H.S.; Shepherd, L.A.; Nurse, J.R.; Erola, A.; Epiphaniou, G.; Maple, C.; Bellekens, X. Cyber Security in the Age of COVID-19: A Timeline and Analysis of Cyber-Crime and Cyber-Attacks during the Pandemic. *Comput. Secur.* **2021**, 102248. [CrossRef]
8. Alheneidi, H.; AlSumait, L.; AlSumait, D.; Smith, A.P. Loneliness and Problematic Internet Use during COVID-19 Lock-Down. *Behav. Sci.* **2021**, *11*, 5. [CrossRef] [PubMed]
9. Westerlund, M. The emergence of deepfake technology: A review. *Technol. Innov. Manag. Rev.* **2019**, *9*, 40–53. [CrossRef]

10. Botha, J.; Pieterse, H. Fake News and Deepfakes: A Dangerous Threat for 21st Century Information Security. In Proceedings of the International Conference on Cyber Warfare and Security, Norfolk, VA, USA, 12–13 March 2020; Academic Conferences International Limited: Reading, UK, 2020 ; pp. 57–66 .
11. Harris, D. Deepfakes: False pornography is here and the law cannot protect you. *Duke L. Tech. Rev.* **2018**, *17*, 99.
12. Spivak, R. Deepfakes: The Newest Way to Commit One of the Oldest Crimes. *Geo. L. Tech. Rev.* **2019**, *3*, 339–340.
13. Soltani, S.; Seno, S.A.H. A survey on digital evidence collection and analysis. In Proceedings of the 2017 7th International Conference on Computer and Knowledge Engineering (ICCKE), Mashhad, Iran, 26–27 October 2017; pp. 247–253. [CrossRef]
14. Garfinkel, S.L. Digital forensics research: The next 10 years. *Digit. Investig.* **2010**, *7*, S64–S73. [CrossRef]
15. Casey, E. The chequered past and risky future of digital forensics. *Aust. J. Forensic Sci.* **2019**, *51*, 649–664. [CrossRef]
16. Horsman, G. Tool testing and reliability issues in the field of digital forensics. *Digit. Investig.* **2019**, *28*, 163–175. [CrossRef]
17. Raghavan, S. Digital forensic research: Current state of the art. *CSI Trans. ICT* **2013**, *1*, 91–114. [CrossRef]
18. Tolosana, R.; Vera-Rodriguez, R.; Fierrez, J.; Morales, A.; Ortega-Garcia, J. Deepfakes and beyond: A survey of face manipulation and fake detection. *Inf. Fusion* **2020**, *64*, 131–148. [CrossRef]
19. Bhatt, P.; Rughani, P.H. Machine learning forensics: A new branch of digital forensics. *Int. J. Adv. Res. Comput. Sci.* **2017**, *8*, 47–66 . [CrossRef]
20. Durall, R.; Keuper, M.; Pfreundt, F.J.; Keuper, J. Unmasking deepfakes with simple features. *arXiv* **2019**, arXiv:1911.00686.
21. Li, Y.; Yang, X.; Sun, P.; Qi, H.; Lyu, S. Celeb-df: A large-scale challenging dataset for deepfake forensics. In Proceedings of the IEEE/CVF Conference on Computer Vision and Pattern Recognition, Seattle, WA, USA, 13–19 June 2020 ; pp. 3207–3216.
22. Hadhazy, A. Is That Iranian Missile Photo a Fake? 2008. Available online: https://www.scientificamerican.com/article/is-that-iranian-missile/ (accessed on 11 march 2021).
23. Tait, A. How a Badly Faked Photo of Vladimir Putin Took Over Twitter. 2017. Available online: https://www.newstatesman.com/science-tech/social-media/2017/07/how-badly-faked-photo-vladimir-putin-took-over-twitter (accessed on 11 March 2021).
24. Iran 'Faked Missile Test Image'. Available online: http://news.bbc.co.uk/2/hi/middle_east/7500917.stm (accessed on 22 June 2021).
25. In an Iranian Image, a Missile Too Many. Available online: https://thelede.blogs.nytimes.com/2008/07/10/in-an-iranian-image-a-missile-too-many/ (accessed on 22 June 2021).
26. Fridrich, A.J.; Soukal, B.D.; Lukáš, A.J. Detection of copy–move forgery in digital images. In Proceedings of the Digital Forensic Research Workshop, Cleveland, Ohio, USA, 6–8 August 2003 ; Citeseer: Pennsylvania, PA, USA, 2003. .
27. Xu, B.; Liu, G.; Dai, Y. Detecting image splicing using merged features in chroma space. *Sci. World J.* **2014**, *2014*. [CrossRef]
28. Kietzmann, J.; Lee, L.W.; McCarthy, I.P.; Kietzmann, T.C. Deepfakes: Trick or treat? *Bus. Horizons* **2020**, *63*, 135–146. [CrossRef]
29. Nguyen, T.T.; Nguyen, C.M.; Nguyen, D.T.; Nguyen, D.T.; Nahavandi, S. Deep learning for deepfakes creation and detection. *arXiv* **2019**, arXiv:1909.11573.
30. Christian, J. Experts Fear Face Swapping Tech Could Start an International Showdown. 2018. Available online: https://theoutline.com/post/3179/deepfake-videos-are-freaking-experts-out (accessed on 22 June 2016).
31. Roose, K. Here, Come the Fake Videos, Too, 2018. Available online: https://www.nytimes.com/2018/03/04/technology/fake-videos-deepfakes.html (accessed on 22 June 2016).
32. Niyishaka, P.; Bhagvati, C. Digital image forensics technique for copy–move forgery detection using dog and orb. In Proceedings of the International Conference on Computer Vision and Graphics, Madrid, Spain, 17–19 July 2018 ; Springer: Berlin/Heidelberg, Germany, 2018; pp. 472–483.
33. Vincent, O.R.; Folorunso, O. A descriptive algorithm for sobel image edge detection. In Proceedings of the Informing Science & IT Education Conference (InSITE), Macon, GA, USA, 12–15 June 2009 ; Informing Science Institute California: Santa Rosa, CA, USA, 2009 ; Volume 40, pp. 97–107.
34. Rublee, E.; Rabaud, V.; Konolige, K.; Bradski, G. ORB: An efficient alternative to SIFT or SURF. In Proceedings of the 2011 International Conference on Computer Vision, Barcelona, Spain, 6–13 November 2011 ; IEEE: Piscataway, NJ, USA, 2011; pp. 2564–2571.
35. Castillo Camacho, I.; Wang, K. A Comprehensive Review of Deep-Learning-Based Methods for Image Forensics. *J. Imaging* **2021**, *7*, 69. [CrossRef]
36. Diallo, B.; Urruty, T.; Bourdon, P.; Fernandez-Maloigne, C. Robust forgery detection for compressed images using CNN supervision. *Forensic Sci. Int. Rep.* **2020**, *2*, 100112. [CrossRef]
37. O'Shea, K.; Nash, R. An introduction to convolutional neural networks. *arXiv* **2015**, arXiv:1511.08458.
38. Jafar, M.T.; Ababneh, M.; Al-Zoube, M.; Elhassan, A. Forensics and Analysis of Deepfake Videos. In Proceedings of the 2020 11th International Conference on Information and Communication Systems (ICICS), Copenhagen, Denmark 24–27 August 2020 ; IEEE: Piscataway, NJ, USA, 2020; pp. 053–058.
39. Amidi, A.; Amidi, S. CS 230—Recurrent Neural Networks Cheatsheet. Available online: https://stanford.edu/~shervine/teaching/cs-230/cheatsheet-recurrent-neural-networks (accessed on 14 June 2021).
40. Yang, P.; Baracchi, D.; Ni, R.; Zhao, Y.; Argenti, F.; Piva, A. A survey of deep learning-based source image forensics. *J. Imaging* **2020**, *6*, 9. [CrossRef]

41. Martinez, B.; Valstar, M.F.; Jiang, B.; Pantic, M. Automatic analysis of facial actions: A survey. *IEEE Trans. Affect. Comput.* **2017**, *10*, 325–347. [CrossRef]
42. He, J.; Li, D.; Yang, B.; Cao, S.; Sun, B.; Yu, L. Multi view facial action unit detection based on CNN and BLSTM-RNN. In Proceedings of the 2017 12th IEEE International Conference on Automatic Face & Gesture Recognition (FG 2017), Washington, DC, USA, 30 May–3 June 2017; IEEE: Piscataway, NJ, USA, 2017; pp. 848–853.
43. Zhi, R.; Liu, M.; Zhang, D. A comprehensive survey on automatic facial action unit analysis. *Vis. Comput.* **2020**, *36*, 1067–1093. [CrossRef]
44. McCloskey, S.; Albright, M. Detecting gan-generated imagery using color cues. *arXiv* **2018**, arXiv:1812.08247.
45. Mittal, T.; Bhattacharya, U.; Chandra, R.; Bera, A.; Manocha, D. Emotions Don't Lie: A Deepfake Detection Method Using Audio-Visual Affective Cues. 2020. Available online: https://arxiv.org/abs/2003.06711 (accessed on 22 June 2020).
46. Dolhansky, B.; Howes, R.; Pflaum, B.; Baram, N.; Ferrer, C.C. The deepfake detection challenge (dfdc) dataset. *arXiv* **2020**, arXiv:2006.07397.
47. Vapnik, V. *The Nature of Statistical Learning Theory*; Springer Science & Business Media: Berlin/Heidelberg, Germany, 2013.
48. Hearst, M.A.; Dumais, S.T.; Osuna, E.; Platt, J.; Scholkopf, B. Support vector machines. *IEEE Intell. Syst. Their Appl.* **1998**, *13*, 18–28. [CrossRef]
49. Boser, B.E.; Guyon, I.M.; Vapnik, V.N. A training algorithm for optimal margin classifiers. In Proceedings of the Fifth Annual Workshop on Computational Learning Theory, Pittsburgh, PA, USA, 27–29 July 1992 ; pp. 144–152.
50. Feng, X.; Cox, I.J.; Doërr, G. An energy-based method for the forensic detection of re-sampled images. In Proceedings of the 2011 IEEE International Conference on Multimedia and Expo, Barcelona, Spain, 11–15 July 2011; IEEE: Piscataway, NJ, USA, 2011; pp. 1–6.
51. 5 Steps for Conducting Computer Forensics Investigations | Norwich University Online. Available online: https://online.norwich.edu/academic-programs/resources/5-steps-for-conducting-computer-forensics-investigations (accessed on 8 April 2021).
52. Technology, B. Why Write Modules? Available online: https://www.sleuthkit.org/autopsy/docs/api-docs/4.1/platform_page.html (accessed on 22 June 2016).
53. Domingues, P.; Nogueira, R.; Francisco, J.C.; Frade, M. Post-Mortem Digital Forensic Artifacts of TikTok Android App. In Proceedings of the 15th International Conference on Availability, Reliability and Security (ARES '20), Dublin, Ireland, 25–28 August 2020 ; Association for Computing Machinery: New York, NY, USA, 2020. [CrossRef]
54. Sabernick III, B.A. Development of an autopsy forensics module for cortana artifacts analysis. *Int. J. Comput. Sci. Inf. Secur.* **2016**, *14*, 111.
55. Karras, T.; Aila, T.; Laine, S.; Lehtinen, J. Progressive growing of gans for improved quality, stability, and variation. *arXiv* **2017**, arXiv:1710.10196.
56. Karras, T.; Laine, S.; Aila, T. A style-based generator architecture for generative adversarial networks. In Proceedings of the IEEE/CVF Conference on Computer Vision and Pattern Recognition, Long Beach, CA, USA, 16–20 June 2019 ; pp. 4401–4410.
57. Wen, B.; Zhu, Y.; Subramanian, R.; Ng, T.T.; Shen, X.; Winkler, S. COVERAGE—A novel database for copy–move forgery detection. In Proceedings of the 2016 IEEE International Conference on Image Processing (ICIP), Phoenix, AZ, USA, 25–28 September 2016 ; IEEE: Piscataway, NJ, USA, 2016; pp. 161–165.
58. Hsu, Y.F.; Chang, S.F. Detecting image splicing using geometry invariants and camera characteristics consistency. In Proceedings of the 2006 IEEE International Conference on Multimedia and Expo, Toronto, ON, Canada, 9–12 July 2006; IEEE: Piscataway, NJ, USA, 2006; pp. 549–552.
59. Shung, K.P. Accuracy, Precision, Recall or F1? 2018. Available online: https://towardsdatascience.com/accuracy-precision-recall-or-f1-331fb37c5cb9 (accessed on 8 April 2021).

Article

Forgery Detection in Digital Images by Multi-Scale Noise Estimation

Marina Gardella [1,*], Pablo Musé [2], Jean-Michel Morel [1] and Miguel Colom [1,*]

[1] Centre Borelli, ENS Paris-Saclay, Université Paris-Saclay, CNRS, 91190 Gif-sur-Yvette, France; jean-michel.morel@ens-paris-saclay.fr

[2] IIE, Facultad de Ingeniería, Universidad de la República, Montevideo 11300, Uruguay; pmuse@fing.edu.uy

* Correspondence: marina.gardella@ens-paris-saclay.fr (M.G.); miguel.colom-barco@ens-paris-saclay.fr (M.C.)

Abstract: A complex processing chain is applied from the moment a raw image is acquired until the final image is obtained. This process transforms the originally Poisson-distributed noise into a complex noise model. Noise inconsistency analysis is a rich source for forgery detection, as forged regions have likely undergone a different processing pipeline or out-camera processing. We propose a multi-scale approach, which is shown to be suitable for analyzing the highly correlated noise present in JPEG-compressed images. We estimate a noise curve for each image block, in each color channel and at each scale. We then compare each noise curve to its corresponding noise curve obtained from the whole image by counting the percentage of bins of the local noise curve that are below the global one. This procedure yields crucial detection cues since many forgeries create a local noise deficit. Our method is shown to be competitive with the state of the art. It outperforms all other methods when evaluated using the MCC score, or on forged regions large enough and for colorization attacks, regardless of the evaluation metric.

Keywords: blind estimation; forged image detection; heatmap; JPEG; noise level function

Citation: Gardella, M.; Musé, P.; Morel, J.-M.; Colom, M. Forgery Detection in Digital Images by Multi-Scale Noise Estimation. *J. Imaging* **2021**, *7*, 119. https://doi.org/10.3390/jimaging7070119

Academic Editors: Irene Amerini, Gianmarco Baldini and Francesco Leotta

Received: 31 May 2021
Accepted: 6 July 2021
Published: 17 July 2021

Publisher's Note: MDPI stays neutral with regard to jurisdictional claims in published maps and institutional affiliations.

Copyright: © 2021 by the authors. Licensee MDPI, Basel, Switzerland. This article is an open access article distributed under the terms and conditions of the Creative Commons Attribution (CC BY) license (https://creativecommons.org/licenses/by/4.0/).

1. Introduction

An escalating number of falsified images are being shared on the web and feeding fake news. Indeed, the popularization of digital devices as well as the development of user-friendly manipulation software have resulted in an increase in the traffic of manipulated content. The credibility of images is under question, and therefore, methods relying on scientific evidence are required to assess the authenticity of images.

Two different approaches have emerged to address this issue. On the one hand, techniques such as digital image watermarking prevent image forgery by embedding data at the moment of digitization. Such data can be detected or extracted later to authenticate the image [1]. Although these methods provide reliable authentication, they are limited to specifically equipped cameras.

On the other hand, passive methods that do not depend on prior knowledge have also been developed. These methods rely on the fact that image forgery techniques leave specific traces that can be detected as local inconsistencies in the image statistics [2,3]. Most classic methods aim to detect specific cues such as misalignment of the Bayer pattern or perturbations in the demosaicing traces [4–6], differences in the camera response function [7,8], or inconsistencies in the JPEG-compression grid or quality [9–12].

Recent deep-learning models have been developed to tackle the task of forgery detection [13]. These methods can be trained to detect specific falsification techniques such as splicing [14,15], copy-move [16,17] and inpainting [18,19], or to detect general attacks [20–22]. The main challenge shared by these methods is the construction of adequate training datasets ensuring good results on new real-world examples.

As first suggested by [3], noise residuals can provide substantial cues for detecting forgeries. Indeed, the initial Poisson noise [23] is transformed by multiple operations specific to each image formation process [24], leading to the final JPEG image. Hence, detecting noise inconsistencies is a rich source of forgery evidence. The use of noise residuals has evolved over time. Early methods [25,26] directly search inconsistencies in this residual whereas more recent algorithms use it as an input for further feature extraction [27,28]. Accurately estimating the residual noise traces after the complex set of transformations of the camera's processing chain is the main challenge of this class of algorithms.

With these considerations in mind, we propose a noise-based method built on non-parametric multi-scale noise estimation [29]. The multi-scale approach has been shown to effectively deal with the correlations introduced by the demosaicing and JPEG-compression processes [30] and stands out as a suitable framework for noise inconsistency analysis.

The rest of the article is organized as follows. Section 2 reviews the image forgery detection techniques based on noise inspection. The proposed method is described in Section 3. Section 4 presents experimental results in addition to a comparison with other state-of-the-art techniques. The main conclusions are summarized in Section 5, where future work directions are also highlighted.

2. Related Work

The residual noise observable in images depends on the in-camera processing pipeline. It can therefore reveal the presence of tampered regions by detecting local inconsistencies in the noise statistics that are incompatible with a unique camera processing chain. Such inconsistencies can be produced by the forgery or its post-processing.

The most outstanding source of non-uniform noise is the photo-response non-uniformity (PRNU) which is caused by small differences in the way sensors react to the light source. PRNU-based forensics methods, such as [31–33], are mostly used for source camera identification. However, since PRNU varies across the image itself, it can also provide evidence of a local manipulation. The main limitation is that PRNU-based detection methods require access to a certain number of (untampered) images taken with the same camera, to accurately estimate the PRNU pattern.

Blind noise-based detection methods usually estimate noise variance locally to detect suspicious regions and then apply a classification criterion to locate forgeries. In [25], the noise variance is estimated in blocks using a median absolute deviation (MAD) estimator in the wavelet domain. Classification is performed using homogeneous noise standard deviation criteria. In turn, Ke et al. [34] proposes noise level estimation using principal component analysis (PCA) [35]. K-means is then applied to group image blocks into two clusters. A similar approach can be found in [36]. A different method was introduced in [37], where block-wise noise estimation is based on the observation that the kurtosis values across different band-passed filter channels are constant [38]. The method concludes by segmenting the image into regions with significantly different noise variances by k-means. In [39], the image is segmented using the simple linear iterative clustering (SLIC) algorithm. Then, for each region, five filters are used to extract noise. The computed noise features are then used for classification, which is performed by energy-based graph cut.

The aforementioned methods estimate a single and constant noise level, namely an additive white Gaussian noise (AWGN) model. However, this hypothesis does not hold in realistic scenarios since noise levels depend on the image intensity [40]. More recent methods consider this fact and estimate a noise level function (NLF) rather than a single noise level. In [41], the authors proposed to jointly estimate the NLF and the camera response function (CRF) by segmenting the image into edge and non-edge regions. Noise level functions are then compared and an empirical threshold is fixed in order to detect salient curves. The methods introduced in [42,43] instead analyze a histogram based on the noise density function at the local level in order to reveal suspicious areas. The method proposed in [44] computes an NLF-based on Wiener filtering. Local noise levels in regions with a certain brightness are assumed to follow a Poisson distribution, according to which, the larger the distance to the NLF, the higher the probability of forgery. On the other hand, the approach developed in [45] consists of estimating a noise level function that depends on the local sharpness rather than on the intensity.

Recently, forgery detection methods based on deep learning and feature modeling have been developed. The method reported in [27] proposes using noise residuals to extract local features and compute their co-occurrence histograms, which are then classified in two classes using the expectation–maximization algorithm. More recently, the same authors presented a novel CNN-based method for noise residual extraction [28]. A similar approach can be found in [46]. On the other hand, Zhou et al. [47] proposed a two-stream CNN, one for the detection of tampering artifacts and the other to leverage noise features. Deep learning-based methods are more general than previously described ones. A major limitation of these methods is that they require large training datasets, which are not always available. Furthermore, their performance generally remains dataset dependent.

3. The Proposed Method

We propose a new method for JPEG-compressed image forgery detection based on multi-scale noise estimation. The method addresses the fact that, after going through the complete camera processing pipeline, noise is not only signal-dependent but also frequency-dependent. In particular, after demosaicing, noise becomes spatially correlated, and furthermore, the quantization of the DCT coefficients during JPEG-compression differently affects the noise at each frequency. In this context, multi-scale noise estimation is the most suitable approach since it enables capturing noise at medium and low frequencies.

Let I be an image with C color channels. We first split the image into $W \times W$ blocks with $1/2$ overlap, extending the image in the borders by mirroring if necessary. We will refer to these blocks as macroblocks.

For each color channel, we estimate the global image noise curve as well as the local noise curves for each macroblock using an adaptation of the technique [29], described in Appendix A. For each channel, we compare the global noise curve with the ones locally obtained by computing the number of bins of the local noise curve that are below the global noise curve. By doing so, we obtained a heatmap for each channel that shows, for each macroblock, the percentage of bins in its noise curve whose count is below the global estimation. The information contained in the C obtained heatmaps is then combined by taking their geometric mean. As a result, we obtain a single heatmap.

For non-forged images, we expect the macroblocks to show similar noise levels functions as the one computed for the whole image. However, noise estimation is highly affected by image content. Indeed, noise overestimation is expected to happen in textured regions [48]. As a consequence, local noise curves computed over textured areas may be above the global one, even if no tampering has been performed. To prevent this kind of macroblock being perceived as suspicious, we only consider the number of bins below the global noise curve. Indeed, the global noise curve provides a lower bound for local noise curves since the noise estimation algorithm [29] has more samples from which to choose the adequate ones to estimate noise. Therefore, local noise curves that are below the global one are suspected to correspond to a different source. Figure 1 depicts the previously described situation. Indeed, we can observe that the non-forged macroblock shows higher noise levels than the global image, even though it is not tampered. On the other hand, the manipulated macroblock exhibits lower noise levels.

The next step consists of repeating the previously described process but replacing the image I and the macroblocks by their down-scaled version. To this aim, let S be the operator that tessellates the image into sets of 2×2 pixels blocks, and replaces each block by the average of the four pixels. We define $S_n(I)$ as the n-th scale of an image I obtained by applying n times the operator S to the image I. This procedure allows noise curves to show the noise contained in lower frequencies and can provide further evidence of tampering that could be hidden under strong JPEG-compression.

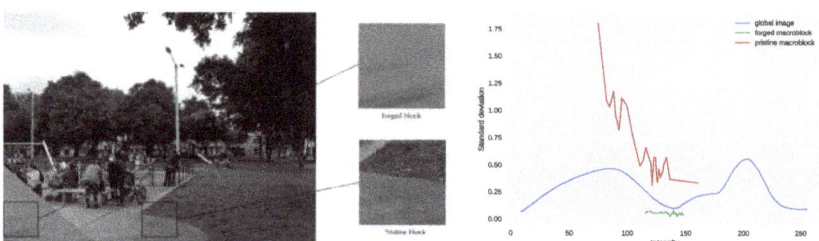

Figure 1. Estimated noise curves for the global image and for two macroblocks—one of which is contained in the manipulated region and the other is coming from the non-manipulated part of the image.

By iterating the process at successive scales, we obtain one heatmap per scale which shows the geometric mean of the percentages obtained at each channel. Each of these heatmaps may provide useful information to detect tampering since they account for noise contained at different frequencies. The sum of the heatmaps obtained at the different scales is computed and then normalized in the $[0, 255]$ interval. To obtain the final heatmap, for each pixel we compute the average of the values of each macroblock containing it.

The residual noise present in images having undergone demosaicing and JPEG-compression is correlated and therefore creates medium-sized noise spots. This may cause the blocks of size 8×8 used for noise estimation to fit inside these spots, thus causing noise underestimation. Again, estimating noise in sub-sampled versions of the image enables these spots to fit inside the scanning blocks and to accurately measure low-frequency noise. We propose repeating the sub-scaling process until reaching $S_2(I)$, as suggested in [30].

Further scales could be also considered. However, the most relevant information is already retrieved at S_2. Furthermore, the macroblock's size would become critically small and unfit to estimate noise curves: if the original macroblocks are sized $W \times W$ in S_0, in S_1 they will be of size $(W/2) \times (W/2)$, and in S_2 of size $(W/4) \times (W/4)$. Indeed, as shown in Appendix B, the best performance for the proposed method is achieved when considering macroblocks of size $W = 256$. In this context, the macroblocks are sized 128×128 in S_1 and 64×64 in S_2.

Figure 2 shows the pipeline of the proposed method, from the moment that the algorithm is fed with the input image until the final heatmap is delivered. Additionally, a summarized version of the proposed method is given below.

Given a suspect image and the parameters for the method (macroblock side, stride and number of scales), the proposed algorithm goes as follows:

1. Open the suspect image.
2. Get a list of all macroblocks according to the given macroblock size and the considered stride.
3. For each scale and each color channel, estimate the global NLF of the image and compare it to NLF computed at each macroblock. We are interested in the percentage of histogram bins below the global curve.
4. To obtain the final result of the algorithm, the heatmaps obtained at each of the scales are combined.

Please refer to Algorithm 1 for a detailed pseudo-code description. The actual source code is available at (accessed on 31 May 2021) https://github.com/marigardella/PB_Forgery_Detection, together with the instructions and requirements to run the method. Further implementation details are given in Appendix C.

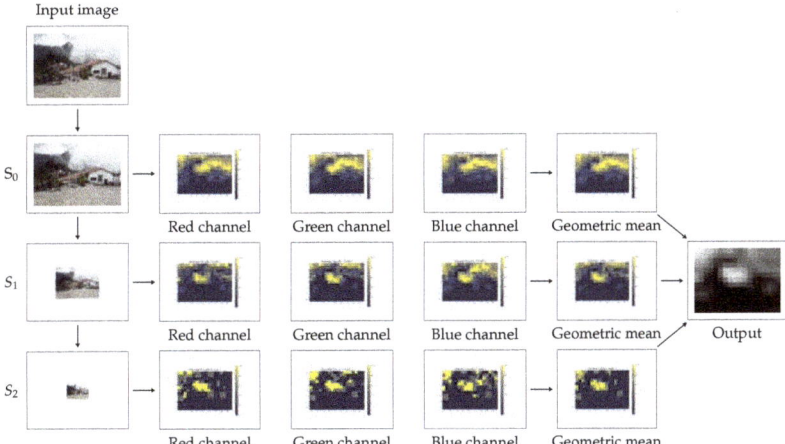

Figure 2. Complete pipeline of the method: successive scales are extracted from the input image. At each scale, one heatmap per color channel is computed and then combined according to their geometric mean. Finally, the obtained heatmaps at each scale are summed and normalized to produce the final output.

Algorithm 1 Pseudo-code for the proposed method

Input: image I of shape $N_x \times N_y$ with C color channels.
Parameters: $W = 256$ macroblock side, $S = 0.5$ stride, num_scales = 3 number of scales.
1: $M_x = \lfloor N_x/(W \times S) \rfloor - 1$. ▷ horizontal number of macroblocks
2: $M_y = \lfloor N_y/(W \times S) \rfloor - 1$. ▷ vertical number of macroblocks
3: macroblocks_list ← list of all $W \times W$ macroblocks with S stride.
4: **for** each scale s **do**
5:     **for** each channel c **do**
6:         $I_s^c \leftarrow$ get image in scale s and channel c.
7:         $f_{I_s^c} \leftarrow$ noise curve estimation for I_s^c using [29] as described in A.
8:         $H^c \leftarrow$ zeros($M_x \times M_y$).
9:         **for** each macroblock in macroblocks_list **do**
10:             $M_s^c \leftarrow$ get macroblock in scale s and channel c.
11:             $f_{M_s^c} \leftarrow$ noise curve estimation for M_s^c using [29] as described in A.
12:             $H^c[M_s^c] \leftarrow$ percentage of bins of $f_{M_s^c}$ below $f_{I_s^c}$.
13:         **end for**
14:     **end for**
15:     $H_s \leftarrow$ geometric mean of the heatmaps H^c.
16: **end for**
17: $H_{\text{aux}} \leftarrow$ sum and normalization of heatmaps H_s.
18: $H \leftarrow$ compute for each pixel the average of H_{aux} for each macroblock containing it.
19: **return** H.

4. Experimental Results

We conducted two experiments. First, we evaluated the relevance of the multi-scale approach by comparing the results obtained using a single scale ($S_0(I)$), two sub-scales ($S_0(I)$ and $S_1(I)$) and three sub-scales ($S_0(I)$, $S_1(I)$ and $S_2(I)$). Second, we compared our method with state-of-the-art forgery-detection algorithms based on noise analysis.

Datasets

All experiments were conducted on the CG-1050 database [49] which contains four datasets, each one corresponding to a different forgery technique: colorization, copy-move, splicing and retouching. The total number of forged images is 1050. This database is varied in nature, including images captured in 10 different places. The size of the images is 3456 × 4608 or 4608 × 3456 pixels. The database includes both RGB and grayscale images, all of which are JPEG-compressed. The estimated JPEG-quality [50] for each dataset is shown in Table 1.

Table 1. Average JPEG-quality and range for each of the datasets.

	Retouching	Colorization	Splicing	Copy-Move
Average JPEG-quality	86.9	86.8	87.3	86.8
JPEG-quality range	[71,88]	[71,88]	[71,88]	[71,88]

Forgery masks were constructed by computing the absolute difference between the original image and the forged one in each channel. To avoid pixels whose values had changed due to global manipulations rather than tampering, the difference from one image to another was thresholded. Only pixels whose value varied more than this threshold for at least one channel were kept. Masks were then further refined in order to prevent isolated pixels from being regarded as forged. The thresholds used were 15 for the copy-move, colorization and splicing datasets and 10 for the retouching one.

The distribution of the mask's size on each of the four datasets is shown in Figure 3.

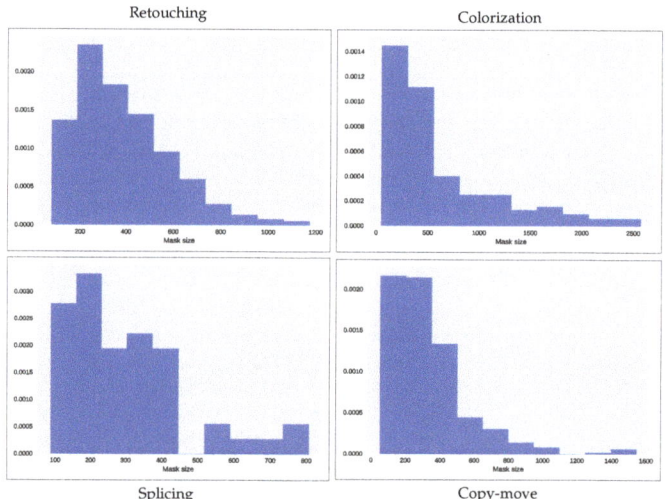

Figure 3. Distribution of the forgery size in each of the datasets considered. The forgery size is shown as the square root of the mask size, which represents the side of its equivalent square.

Evaluation Measures

Forgery localization is a particular case of binary classification. Indeed, there are two possible classes for each pixel: forged (positive) or non-forged (negative). Performance measures are usually based on the confusion matrix [51], which has four values, each one corresponding to the four possible combinations of predicted and actual classes, as shown in Figure 4.

		Predicted class	
		Positive	Negative
Actual class	Positive	True positive	False negative
	Negative	False positive	True negative

Figure 4. Confusion matrix: rows represent the actual classes while columns represent the prediction. The matrix has four possible values, corresponding to the four possible combinations of predicted and actual classes.

Three metrics based on these four quantities are proposed in order to compare the results obtained in both experiments. Namely, we evaluated the results using the IoU, the F1 and the MCC scores, defined as

$$\text{MCC} = \frac{\text{TP} \times \text{TN} - \text{FP} \times \text{FN}}{\sqrt{(\text{TP} + \text{FP}) \times (\text{TP} + \text{FN}) \times (\text{TN} + \text{FP}) \times (\text{TN} + \text{FN})}},$$

$$\text{IoU} = \frac{\text{TP}}{\text{TP} + \text{FN} + \text{FP}},$$

$$\text{F1} = \frac{2\text{TP}}{2\text{TP} + \text{FN} + \text{FP}}.$$

where TP stands for true positive, TN for true negative, FN for false negative and FP for false positive.

These metrics are designed to evaluate binary-estimated masks. However, all of the methods analyzed in this paper propose continuous heatmaps rather than binary masks. To adapt the metrics to the continuous setting, we used their weighted version. In this approach, the value of a heatmap H at each pixel x is regarded as the probability of forgery of the pixel. Therefore, we define the weighted true positives, weighted true negatives, weighted false negatives and weighted false positives as:

$$\text{TP}_w = \sum_x H(x) \times M(x),$$

$$\text{TN}_w = \sum_x (1 - H(x)) \times (1 - M(x)),$$

$$\text{FN}_w = \sum_x H(x) \times (1 - M(x)),$$

$$\text{FP}_w = \sum_x (1 - H(x)) \times M(x),$$

respectively, where H is the output heatmap normalized between 0 and 1, and M is the ground-truth binary mask where pixels with a value of 1 are forged. Then, the weighted version of the IoU, F1 and MCC scores are obtained replacing TP, TN, FN and FP with their weighted versions. It is important to point out that for some of the methods, the output is a two-sided heatmap (meaning that suspicious regions can appear in lighter or darker colors). Taking this into consideration, both the output heatmap and the inverted one are evaluated and only the highest score is kept.

4.1. Relevance of the Multi-Scale Approach

We first examined the pertinence of a multi-scale scheme. For this purpose, we computed the results obtained when considering one single scale $S_0(I)$ (which would correspond to the input image), using two scales $S_0(I)$ and $S_1(I)$, and using three scales $S_0(I), S_1(I)$ and $S_2(I)$. The scores obtained for each of these settings are shown in Table 2.

Table 2. MCC, IoU and F1 scores for our method with one scale (PB1), two scales (PB2) and three scales (PB3).

	MCC			
	Retouching	Colorization	Splicing	Copy-Move
PB1	0.0672	0.0958	0.0276	**0.0380**
PB2	0.0848	0.1066	0.0310	0.0377
PB3	**0.0915**	**0.1108**	**0.0316**	0.0362

	IoU			
	Retouching	Colorization	Splicing	Copy-Move
PB1	0.0242	0.0721	0.0112	0.0148
PB2	0.0284	0.0756	0.0122	**0.0149**
PB3	**0.0300**	**0.0761**	**0.0123**	0.0145

	F1			
	Retouching	Colorization	Splicing	Copy-Move
PB1	0.0454	0.1122	0.0216	0.0281
PB2	0.0529	0.1175	0.0234	**0.0282**
PB3	**0.0557**	**0.1192**	**0.0236**	0.0276

We can observe that using multiple scales leads to better results compared to a single one. Indeed, in all four datasets, the scores obtained by PB2 and PB3 are better than those obtained by PB1 for the three metrics. Regarding the number of scales yielding a better performance, the use of three scales obtains the best scores for the retouching, colorization and splicing datasets, whereas the use of two scales achieves a better performance in the copy-move dataset. However, the results obtained for the copy-move dataset are poor for the three variants of the method, and furthermore, they have very similar scores. We conclude that the use of three scales, $S_0(I)$, $S_1(I)$ and $S_2(I)$, gives the best performance among the evaluated alternatives. In fact, given that JPEG-compression is applied in 8×8 blocks without overlap, it is at S_2 that the most accurate noise estimation is achieved since we are able to capture noise contained in lower frequencies, which is less affected by the quantization of the DCT coefficients.

4.2. Comparison with State-of-the-Art Methods

In order to assess the performance of our method, we compared the results obtained on the CG-1050 dataset with those delivered by state-of-the-art noise-based methods: Splicebuster [27], Noiseprint [28], Mahdian [25], Pan [26], Zeng [36], Zhu [45] and Median [52]. For each algorithm, we used a publicly available implementation [53]. Table 3 lists all the evaluated methods as well as their reference article and the link to the source code used for the comparison.

Table 3. State-of-the-art methods used for the comparison as well as their reference and link to source code.

Method	Ref.	Source Code
Mahdian	[25]	https://github.com/MKLab-ITI/image-forensics (accessed on 31 May 2021)
Pan	[26]	https://github.com/MKLab-ITI/image-forensics (accessed on 31 May 2021)
Zeng	[36]	https://github.com/MKLab-ITI/image-forensics (accessed on 31 May 2021)
Median	[52]	https://github.com/MKLab-ITI/image-forensics (accessed on 31 May 2021)
Splicebuster	[27]	http://www.grip.unina.it/research/83-multimedia_forensics (accessed on 31 May 2021)
Noiseprint	[28]	http://www.grip.unina.it/research/83-multimedia_forensics (accessed on 31 May 2021)
Zhu	[45]	https://github.com/marigardella/Zhu_2018 (accessed on 31 May 2021)

The obtained results are given in Table 4. We observe that Splicebuster outperforms the rest of the methods in the retouching and splicing datasets regardless of the metric.

Table 4. Results of the evaluated methods measured by the average weighted IoU, F1 and MCC scores for each dataset that maximized the score.

	MCC				
	Retouching	Colorization	Splicing	Copy-Move	Average Ranking
PB3	0.0915 (2)	**0.1108** (1)	0.0316 (2)	**0.0362** (1)	1.5
Splicebuster	**0.1176** (1)	0.0535 (4)	**0.0502** (1)	0.0233 (4)	2.5
Mahdian	0.0434 (6)	0.0566 (3)	0.0247 (4)	0.0257(3)	4
Pan	0.0513 (4)	0.0681 (2)	0.0282 (3)	0.0306 (2)	2.75
Noiseprint	0.0558 (3)	0.0361 (6)	0.0182 (6)	0.0177 (6)	5.25
Median	0.0479 (5)	0.0469 (5)	0.0204 (5)	0.0195 (5)	5
Zeng	0.0180 (7)	0.0262 (7)	0.0119 (8)	0.0117 (8)	7.5
Zhu	0.0147 (8)	0.0201 (8)	0.0180 (7)	0.0123 (7)	7.5
	IoU				
	Retouching	Colorization	Splicing	Copy-Move	Average Ranking
PB3	0.0300 (3)	**0.0761** (1)	0.0123 (2)	0.0145 (2)	2
Splicebuster	**0.0600** (1)	0.0577 (2)	**0.0242** (1)	**0.0166** (1)	1.25
Mahdian	0.0168 (5)	0.0548 (4)	0.0102 (5)	0.0131(5)	4.75
Pan	0.0198 (4)	0.0576 (3)	0.0109 (4)	0.0138 (4)	3.75
Noiseprint	0.0312 (2)	0.0450 (7)	0.0114 (3)	0.0142 (2)	3.5
Median	0.0163 (6)	0.0513 (5)	0.0095 (7)	0.0123(6)	6
Zeng	0.0136 (7)	0.0441 (8)	0.0084 (8)	0.0114 (8)	7.75
Zhu	0.0129 (8)	0.0453 (6)	0.0102 (5)	0.0116(7)	6.5
	F1				
	Retouching	Colorization	Splicing	Copy-Move	Average Ranking
PB3	0.0557 (3)	**0.1192** (1)	0.0236 (2)	0.0276 (2)	2
Splicebuster	**0.1081** (1)	0.0965 (2)	**0.0448** (1)	**0.0314** (1)	1.25
Mahdian	0.0324 (5)	0.0902 (4)	0.0199 (6)	0.0250(5)	5
Pan	0.0380 (4)	0.0946 (3)	0.0211 (4)	0.0264 (4)	3.75
Noiseprint	0.0588 (2)	0.0778 (7)	0.0222 (3)	0.0271 (3)	3.75
Median	0.0315 (6)	0.0857 (5)	0.0185 (7)	0.0236 (6)	6
Zeng	0.0264 (7)	0.0765 (8)	0.0165 (8)	0.0220 (8)	7.75
Zhu	0.0250 (8)	0.0779 (6)	0.0200 (5)	0.0224(7)	6.5

Our method ranks first for colorization attacks for all the three metrics considered. This forgery technique shows the relevance of considering noise curves instead of single noise levels. Indeed, when changing the color in a region of the image, noise levels are not necessarily perturbed. However, those noise levels will not be consistent with the new intensity but with the original. Estimating noise curves as the proposed method does enables detecting this kind of inconsistency which only appears when considering intensity-dependent noise models.

Regarding the copy-move dataset, Splicebuster delivers the best results when considering the F1 and IoU scores. However, our approach obtains the best MCC score.

The average ranking shows that Splicebuster outperforms the rest of the methods when considering both the F1 and IoU scores, followed by our method. Nevertheless, our method achieves the best average ranking when considering the MCC score, followed by Splicebuster.

Noiseprint stands out as the third best performing method for the IoU and F1 scores. It even ranks second for retouching and copy-move attacks when considering these scores. However, it shows a poor performance for the colorization dataset. This can be explained by the fact that the camera signature is left unchanged when performing this kind of manipulation.

The Pan and Mahdian methods are middle-ranked, showing better results when considering the MCC score. Finally, Median, Zeng and Zhu show the worst performance of all the considered methods regardless of the metric considered.

All of the evaluated methods have different resolutions which may affect their performance when forgeries are too small. To analyze the effects of the size of the forgeries, we computed the average score as a function of the forgery size. Figure 5 shows the average score obtained by each method when setting different lower bounds for the forgery size in each of the datasets considered.

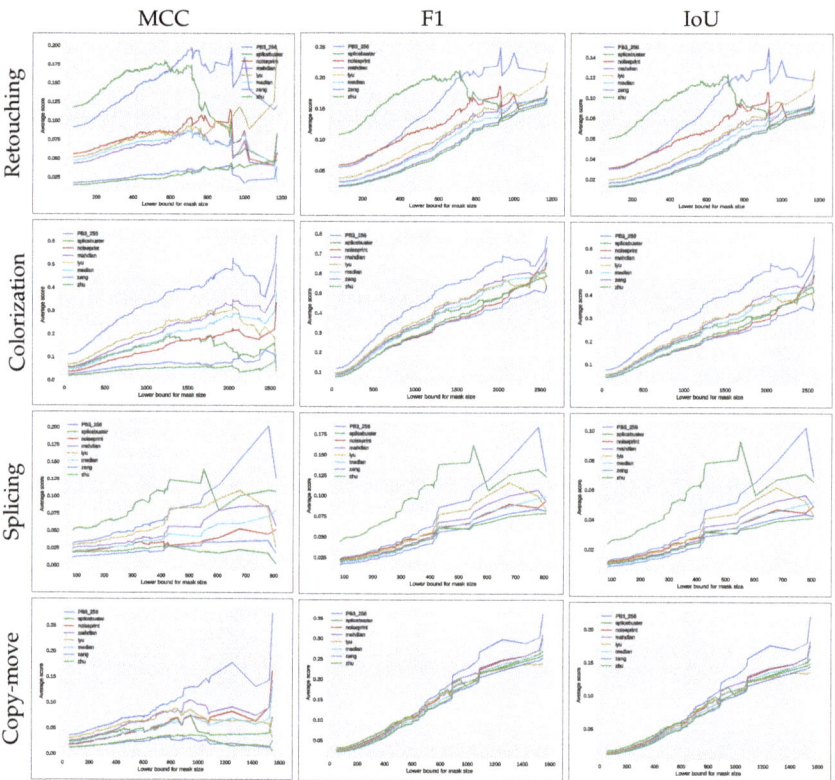

Figure 5. Average weighted MCC (**left**), IoU (**middle**) and F1 (**right**) scores obtained by each method as a function of the lower bound for the forgery size, in each of the datasets considered. Forgery size is shown as the square root of the mask size, which represents the side of its equivalent square.

The results suggest that our method outperforms the state-of-the-art approaches when considering large forgeries in all the datasets regardless of the considered score. The fact that it does not perform that well when considering small manipulations is a direct consequence of the size of the macroblocks. Indeed, for our method to provide reliable detection, the tampered region should be at least of the size of one of the tested macroblocks. In contrast, the performance of Splicebuster decreases as we consider larger forgeries. This is partially expected since the Gaussian-uniform model used in this method is better suited for small forgeries, as suggested by their authors in the original paper [27].

For further evaluation, we used the visual inspection of the results obtained by the proposed method and state-of-the-art approaches. Figure 6 shows examples of the outputs obtained by these methods for the colorization and retouching attacks, respectively, as well as for the corresponding original untampered images.

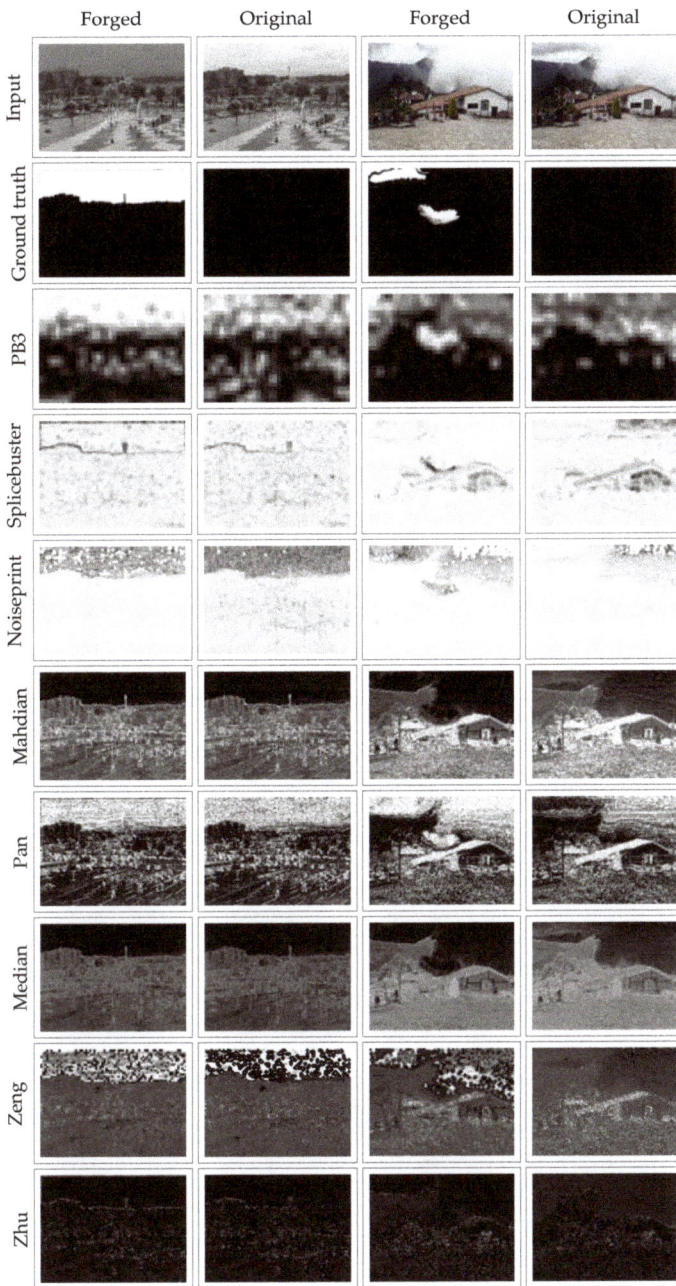

Figure 6. Results obtained for examples where colorization (**first column**) and retouching (**third column**) were performed, as well as for their corresponding original images (**second and fourth columns**). On the successive rows, the results obtained by each of the approaches for these images.

For the colorization attack shown in Figure 6, we can observe that, for all of the approaches except ours, the heatmap obtained when applying the method to the forged and original images are very similar. None of these methods is able to distinguish the tampered region by detecting the traces of the forgery. Instead, the proposed method provides a significant difference between the forged and pristine image; we observe that the forgery clearly stands out while for the pristine image, the values of the heatmap in that area are moderated.

In the case of retouching, we observe that all of the methods point out the forged region or at least part of it as suspicious. However, several interpretation problems arise. When analyzing the results provided by Splicebuster, we can notice that the heatmap corresponding to the tampered image precisely points to the border of part of the forgery. However, when considering the pristine image, there are several areas of the heatmap showing the same values, even if they are not tampered. The Noiseprint results better localize the forgery even though false alarms are present in the pristine image. Mahdian, Pan, Median, Zeng and Zhu methods show a further drawback: in the heatmap corresponding to the manipulated image, the forged regions stand out at the same level as other non-tampered parts of the image. The interpretation of the heatmaps is left to the user who has to decide whether the regions detected as suspicious should be considered forged or discarded. On the other hand, our method is able to localize the forgery when applied to the tampered image while showing no extreme values for the pristine one, making it easier for users to interpret.

5. Conclusions, Limitations and Future Research

In the fight against disinformation, the use of objective methods able to detect manipulated multimedia content becomes crucial. Providing such tools is the aim of the digital forensics research community, and in particular, of the present work. We believe that image forgery detection is a key resource to fight fake news.

JPEG images are broadly used and clearly stand out as one of the most popular image formats. From the acquired raw image to the final JPEG format delivered by the camera, a complex processing chain is applied. Along this process, the originally Poisson-distributed noise undergoes several transformations, resulting in a complex noise structure in the JPEG image whose model does not match the AWGN hypothesis. Noise inconsistency analysis is a rich resource for forgery detection given that forged regions are likely to have undergone a different processing pipeline or an out-of-camera manipulation. However, noise-based methods require accurately dealing with the changes induced by the successive steps of the camera processing chain.

In the present paper, we proposed a method that can correctly deal with the complex noise residuals observable in the JPEG image. The proposed method implements a multi-scale approach which has shown to be suitable for analyzing the highly correlated noise present in JPEG-compressed images.

Our comparative results show that our method outperforms state-of-the-art approaches when evaluating the results with the MCC score. For colorization attacks, our method performs best, regardless of the metric. In addition, when the size of the forgeries is large enough, our method shows the best performance in all the datasets, for all three considered metrics.

Nevertheless, the proposed method has its own limitations, mainly related to too-small and too-large forgeries. Indeed, if the forgery is too small with respect to the macroblock's size, the method is likely to miss it. On the other hand, if the forgery is comparatively too large, the global noise curve may be distorted by the tampered region. The method is also by construction unable to detect a pure internal copy-move. Indeed, such a manipulation leaves the noise model unaltered. As a final negative note, the method cannot detect splicing when the forged region has more noise than the background image.

Future work includes refining the noise estimation step to use smaller macroblocks and thus improving the localization capabilities of our method.

Author Contributions: Conceptualization, M.G., P.M., J.-M.M. and M.C.; methodology, M.G., P.M., J.-M.M. and M.C.; software, M.G. and M.C.; validation, M.G.; formal analysis, M.G., P.M., J.-M.M. and M.C.; investigation, M.G.; resources, M.C.; data curation, M.G. and M.C.; writing—original draft preparation, M.G., P.M., J.-M.M. and M.C.; writing—review and editing, M.G., P.M., J.-M.M. and M.C.; visualization, M.G.; supervision, P.M., J.-M.M. and M.C.; project administration, P.M., J.-M.M. and M.C.; funding acquisition, M.G., J.-M.M. and M.C. All authors have read and agreed to the published version of the manuscript.

Funding: This work was supported by the Paris Region Ph.D. grant from Région Île-de-France, the International Fact-Checking Network (IFCN) and Agence France Presse (AFP) through the Enhancing Visual Forensics (Envisu4) project, the DGA Defals challenge n° ANR-16-DEFA-0004-01, MENRT and Fondation Mathématique Jacques Hadamard.

Institutional Review Board Statement: Not applicable.

Informed Consent Statement: Not applicable.

Data Availability Statement: Images from the CG-1050 database [49] were used in this article. The full database and documentation can be downloaded from https://data.mendeley.com/datasets/dk84bmnyw9/2 (accessed on 31 May 2021). The source codes for Splicebuster [27] and Noiseprint [28] methods are available at http://www.grip.unina.it/research/83-multimedia_forensics (accessed on 31 May 2021). The source codes for Pan [26], Mahdian [25], Median [52] and Zeng [36] algorithms are available at https://github.com/MKLab-ITI/image-forensics/blob/master/matlab_toolbox (accessed on 31 May 2021). The implementation of the Zhu [45] method is available at https://github.com/marigardella/Zhu_2018 (accessed on 31 May 2021). Finally, the source code for the proposed method is available at https://github.com/marigardella/PB_Forgery_Detection (accessed on 31 May 2021).

Conflicts of Interest: The authors declare no conflict of interest. The funders had no role in the design of the study; in the collection, analyses, or interpretation of data; in the writing of the manuscript, or in the decision to publish the result.

Abbreviations

The following abbreviations are used in this manuscript:

JPEG	Joint Photographic Experts Group
PRNU	Photo-Response Non-Uniformity
MAD	Median Absolute Deviation
PCA	Principal Component Analysis
SLIC	Simple Linear Iterative Clustering
AWGN	Additive White Gaussian Noise
NLF	Noise Level Function
CRF	Camera Response Function
CNN	Convolutional Neural Network
DCT	Discrete Cosine Transform
MCC	Matthews' Correlation Coefficient
IoU	Intersection Over Union
TP	True Positive
TN	True Negative
FP	False Positive
FN	False Negative

Appendix A. Adaptation of Ponomarenko's Noise Estimation Method

The proposed method is an adaptation of Ponomarenko's noise estimation method [29]. We set the default number of samples per bin to 10,000 instead of 40,000 as the original article suggests. In this way, we obtain enough bins to build the NLF of macroblocks. Additionally, the number of filtering iterations that are applied to filter the noise curve is set to 0 for the macroblocks' noise curves, while it is set to 5 for the global noise curve, as suggested by the original article. Since the NLF filtering is intended to reduce the peaks caused by textures, by doing so, the macroblocks' estimated noise curves can be regarded as a conservative upper bound of the actual noise curve.

Appendix B. Optimal Macroblock Size

The main parameter of the proposed method is W, the size of the macroblocks where local noise curves are computed. The larger this size, the more accurate the NLF estimation. However, the size of the macroblocks directly affects the precision with which forgeries are located. As shown in Figure 5, the performance of the method relies on the macroblocks' size.

In order to evaluate the capabilities of the method, we carried out an analysis of such performance depending on the size of the macroblocks. We tested three possible values for W: 512, 384 and 256. The results, presented in Table A1, suggest that the best performance is achieved for $W = 256$. Indeed, for the retouching, colorization and copy-move datasets, the best scores are obtained when considering macroblocks of size 256×256. On the other hand, when considering the splicing dataset, macroblocks of size 512×512 yield a better IoU score. However, the difference is very small and when considering other metrics, $W = 256$ achieves higher scores.

Table A1. MCC, IoU and F1 and scores for our method with one scale (PB1), two scales (PB2) and three scales (PB3) and considering different macroblock sizes: 512, 384 and 256.

	MCC			
	Retouching	Colorization	Splicing	Copy-Move
PB1_512	0.0585	0.0770	0.0246	0.0316
PB2_512	0.0729	0.0830	0.0268	0.0321
PB3_512	0.0804	0.0901	0.0291	0.0320
PB1_384	0.0625	0.0838	0.0242	0.0348
PB2_384	0.0789	0.0924	0.0284	0.0350
PB3_384	0.0869	0.1015	0.0289	0.0344
PB1_256	0.0672	0.0958	0.0276	**0.0380**
PB2_256	0.0848	0.1066	0.0310	0.0377
PB3_256	**0.0915**	**0.1108**	**0.0316**	0.0362
	IoU			
	Retouching	Colorization	Splicing	Copy-Move
PB1_512	0.0226	0.0650	0.0113	0.0141
PB2_512	0.0262	0.0673	0.0120	0.0144
PB3_512	0.0278	0.0691	**0.0124**	0.0142
PB1_384	0.0234	0.0679	0.0110	0.0145
PB2_384	0.0274	0.0708	0.0120	0.0146
PB3_384	0.0289	0.0730	0.0122	0.0144
PB1_256	0.0242	0.0721	0.0112	0.0148
PB2_256	0.0284	0.0756	0.0122	**0.0149**
PB3_256	**0.0300**	**0.0761**	0.0123	0.0145
	F1			
	Retouching	Colorization	Splicing	Copy-Move
PB1_512	0.0428	0.1032	0.0215	0.0268
PB2_512	0.0492	0.1067	0.0229	0.0272
PB3_512	0.0520	0.1099	0.0235	0.0270
PB1_384	0.0441	0.1068	0.0211	0.0275
PB2_384	0.0512	0.1112	0.0229	0.0277
PB3_384	0.0540	0.1151	0.0232	0.0274
PB1_256	0.0454	0.1122	0.0216	0.0281
PB2_256	0.0529	0.1175	0.0234	**0.0282**
PB3_256	**0.0557**	**0.1192**	**0.0236**	0.0276

Appendix C. Implementation Details

The main code is written in Python. The implementation of [29] used in the algorithm is written in C++. The source code for the proposed method was run in an AMD EPYC 7371 server with 16 cores (32 with hyperthreading), at 2.2 GHz clock rate and with 125 Gb of RAM. The run-time employed by the method to analyze an image of size 4608×3456 is 2 min and 22 s.

References

1. Singh, N.; Jain, M.; Sharma, S. A Survey of Digital Watermarking Techniques. *Int. J. Mod. Commun. Technol. Res.* **2013**, *1*, 6.
2. Farid, H. Digital doctoring: How to tell the real from the fake. *Significance* **2006**, *3*, 162–166. [CrossRef]
3. Popescu, A.C.; Farid, H. Statistical Tools for Digital Forensics. In *Information Hiding, Proceedings of the 6th International Workshop, IH 2004, Toronto, ON, Canada, 23–25 May 2004, Selected Papers*; Springer: Berlin, Germany, 2005; pp. 128–147.
4. Choi, C.H.; Choi, J.H.; Lee, H.K. CFA Pattern Identification of Digital Cameras Using Intermediate Value Counting. In Proceedings of the Thirteenth ACM Multimedia Workshop on Multimedia and Security, MM&Sec '11, Buffalo, NY, USA, 29–30 September 2011; Association for Computing Machinery: New York, NY, USA, 2011; pp. 21–26. [CrossRef]
5. Shin, H.J.; Jeon, J.J.; Eom, I.K. Color filter array pattern identification using variance of color difference image. *J. Electron. Imaging* **2017**, *26*, 043015. [CrossRef]
6. Bammey, Q.; Gioi, R.G.v.; Morel, J.M. An Adaptive Neural Network for Unsupervised Mosaic Consistency Analysis in Image Forensics. In Proceedings of the IEEE/CVF Conference on Computer Vision and Pattern Recognition (CVPR), Seattle, WA, USA, 14–19 June 2020.
7. Lin, Z.; Wang, R.; Tang, X.; Shum, H.Y. *Detecting Doctored Images Using Camera Response Normality and Consistency*; Association for Computing Machinery, Inc.: New York, NY, USA, 2005.
8. Hsu, Y.F.; Chang, S.F. Image Splicing Detection Using Camera Response Function Consistency and Automatic Segmentation. In Proceedings of the International Conference on Multimedia and Expo, Beijing, China, 2–5 July 2007.
9. Ye, S.; Sun, Q.; Chang, E.C. Detecting digital image forgeries by measuring inconsistencies of blocking artifact. In Proceedings of the 2007 IEEE International Conference on Multimedia and Expo, Beijing, China, 2–5 July 2007; pp. 12–15.
10. Bianchi, T.; De Rosa, A.; Piva, A. Improved DCT coefficient analysis for forgery localization in JPEG images. In Proceedings of the 2011 IEEE International Conference on Acoustics, Speech and Signal Processing (ICASSP), Prague, Czech Republic, 22–27 May 2011; pp. 2444–2447.
11. Krawetz, N.; Solutions, H.F. A picture's worth. *Hacker Factor Solut.* **2007**, *6*, 2.
12. Nikoukhah, T.; Anger, J.; Ehret, T.; Colom, M.; Morel, J.M.; Grompone von Gioi, R. JPEG grid detection based on the number of DCT zeros and its application to automatic and localized forgery detection. In Proceedings of the IEEE Conference on Computer Vision and Pattern Recognition Workshops, Long Beach, CA, USA, 16–17 June 2019; pp. 110–118.
13. Castillo Camacho, I.; Wang, K. A Comprehensive Review of Deep-Learning-Based Methods for Image Forensics. *J. Imaging* **2021**, *7*, 69. [CrossRef]
14. Rao, Y.; Ni, J.; Zhao, H. Deep Learning Local Descriptor for Image Splicing Detection and Localization. *IEEE Access* **2020**, *8*, 25611–25625. [CrossRef]
15. Bi, X.; Wei, Y.; Xiao, B.; Li, W. RRU-Net: The Ringed Residual U-Net for Image Splicing Forgery Detection. In Proceedings of the 2019 IEEE/CVF Conference on Computer Vision and Pattern Recognition Workshops (CVPRW), Long Beach, CA, USA, 16–17 June 2019; pp. 30–39.
16. Rodriguez-Ortega, Y.; Ballesteros, D.M.; Renza, D. Copy-Move Forgery Detection (CMFD) Using Deep Learning for Image and Video Forensics. *J. Imaging* **2021**, *7*, 59. [CrossRef]
17. Liu, Y.; Guan, Q.; Zhao, X. Copy-move Forgery Detection based on Convolutional Kernel Network. *Multimed. Tools Appl.* **2018**, *77*, 18269–18293. [CrossRef]
18. Li, H.; Huang, J. Localization of Deep Inpainting Using High-Pass Fully Convolutional Network. In Proceedings of the IEEE/CVF International Conference on Computer Vision (ICCV), Seoul, Korea, 27–28 October 2019.
19. Wang, X.; Niu, S.; Wang, H. Image Inpainting Detection Based on Multi-task Deep Learning Network. *IETE Tech. Rev.* **2021**, *38*, 149–157. [CrossRef]
20. Wu, Y.; AbdAlmageed, W.; Natarajan, P. ManTra-Net: Manipulation Tracing Network for Detection and Localization of Image Forgeries with Anomalous Features. In Proceedings of the IEEE/CVF Conference on Computer Vision and Pattern Recognition (CVPR), Long Beach, CA, USA, 16–20 June 2019.
21. Jianbo S.; Malik, J. Normalized cuts and image segmentation. *IEEE Trans. Pattern Anal. Mach. Intell.* **2000**, *22*, 888–905. [CrossRef]
22. Huh, M.; Liu, A.; Owens, A.; Efros, A.A. Fighting Fake News: Image Splice Detection via Learned Self-Consistency. In Proceedings of the European Conference on Computer Vision (ECCV), Munich, Germany, 8–14 September 2018.
23. Foi, A.; Trimeche, M.; Katkovnik, V.; Egiazarian, K. Practical Poissonian–Gaussian Noise Modeling and Fitting for Single-Image Raw-Data. *IEEE Trans. Image Process. Publ. IEEE Signal Process. Soc.* **2008**, *17*, 1737–1754. [CrossRef]
24. Colom, M. Multiscale Noise Estimation and Removal for Digital Images. Ph.D. Thesis, Universitat de les Illes Balears, Balearic Islands, Spain, 2014.

25. Mahdian, B.; Saic, S. Using noise inconsistencies for blind image forensics *Image Vis. Comput.* **2009**, *27*, 1497–1503. [CrossRef]
26. Pan, X.; Zhang, X.; Lyu, S. Exposing Image Forgery with Blind Noise Estimation. In Proceedings of the Thirteenth ACM Multimedia Workshop on Multimedia and Security, MM&Sec '11, Buffalo, NY, USA, 29–30 September 2011; Association for Computing Machinery: New York, NY, USA, 2011; pp. 15–20. [CrossRef]
27. Cozzolino, D.; Poggi, G.; Verdoliva, L. Splicebuster: A New Blind Image Splicing Detector. In Proceedings of the 2015 IEEE International Workshop on Information Forensics and Security (WIFS), Rome, Italy, 16–19 Novenber 2015. [CrossRef]
28. Cozzolino, D.; Verdoliva, L. Noiseprint: A CNN-based camera model fingerprint. *arXiv* **2018**, arXiv:1808.08396. Available online: https://arxiv.org/abs/1808.08396 (accessed on 1 July 2021).
29. Colom, M.; Buades, A. Analysis and Extension of the Ponomarenko et al. Method, Estimating a Noise Curve from a Single Image. *Image Process. On Line* **2013**, *3*, 173–197. [CrossRef]
30. Colom, M.; Lebrun, M.; Buades, A.; Morel, J. Nonparametric Multiscale Blind Estimation of Intensity-Frequency-Dependent Noise. *IEEE Trans. Image Process.* **2015**, *24*, 3162–3175. [CrossRef] [PubMed]
31. Lukás, J.; Fridrich, J.; Goljan, M. Digital Camera Identification From Sensor Pattern Noise. *IEEE Trans. Inf. Forensics Secur.* **2006**, *1*, 205–214. [CrossRef]
32. Chen, M.; Fridrich, J.; Goljan, M.; Lukáš, J. Determining image origin and integrity using sensor noise. *IEEE Trans. Inf. Forensics Secur.* **2008**, *3*, 74–90. [CrossRef]
33. Korus, P.; Huang, J. Multi-scale Analysis Strategies in PRNU-based Tampering Localization. *IEEE Trans. Inf. Forensics Secur.* **2017**, *12*, 809–824. [CrossRef]
34. Ke, Y.; Zhang, Q.; Min, W.; Zhang, S. Detecting image forgery based on noise estimation. *Int. J. Multimed. Ubiquitous Eng.* **2014**, *9*, 325–336. [CrossRef]
35. Pyatykh, S.; Hesser, J.; Zheng, L. Image noise level estimation by principal component analysis. *IEEE Trans. Image Process.* **2012**, *22*, 687–699. [CrossRef]
36. Zeng, H.; Zhan, Y.; Kang, X.; Lin, X. Image splicing localization using PCA-based noise level estimation. *Multimed. Tools Appl.* **2017**, *76*, 4783–4799. [CrossRef]
37. Lyu, S.; Pan, X.; Zhang, X. Exposing Region Splicing Forgeries with Blind Local Noise Estimation. *Int. J. Comput. Vision* **2014**, *110*, 202–221. [CrossRef]
38. Zoran, D.; Weiss, Y. Scale invariance and noise innature image. In Proceedings of the IEEE International Conference on Computer Vision, Kyoto, Japan, 29 September–2 October 2009.
39. Liu, B.; Pun, C.M. Splicing forgery exposure in digital image by detecting noise discrepancies. *Int. J. Comput. Commun. Eng.* **2015**, *4*, 33. [CrossRef]
40. Liu, C.; Szeliski, R.; Kang, S.B.; Zitnick, C.; Freeman, W. Automatic Estimation and Removal of Noise from a Single Image. *IEEE Trans. Pattern Anal. Mach. Intell.* **2008**, *30*, 299–314. [CrossRef]
41. Yao, H.; Wang, S.; Zhang, X.; Qin, C.; Wang, J. Detecting image splicing based on noise level inconsistency. *Multimed. Tools Appl.* **2017**, *76*, 12457–12479. [CrossRef]
42. Julliand, T.; Nozick, V.; Talbot, H. Automatic image splicing detection based on noise density analysis in raw images. In Proceedings of the International Conference on Advanced Concepts for Intelligent Vision Systems, Lecce, Italy, 24–27 October 2016; Springer: Berlin, Germany, 2016; pp. 126–134.
43. Julliand, T.; Nozick, V.; Echizen, I.; Talbot, H. Using The Noise Density Down Projection To Expose Splicing in JPEG Images. 2017. Available online: https://hal.archives-ouvertes.fr/hal-01589761 (accessed on 1 July 2021)
44. Pun, C.M.; Liu, B.; Yuan, X. Multi-scale Noise Estimation for Image Splicing Forgery Detection. *J. Vis. Commun. Image Represent.* **2016**, *38*, 195–206. [CrossRef]
45. Zhu, N.; Li, Z. Blind image splicing detection via noise level function. *Signal Process. Image Commun.* **2018**, *68*, 181–192. [CrossRef]
46. Mayer, O.; Bayar, B.; Stamm, M.C. Learning unified deep-features for multiple forensic tasks. In Proceedings of the 6th ACM Workshop on Information Hiding and Multimedia Security, Innsbruck, Austria, 20–22 June 2018; pp. 79–84.
47. Zhou, P.; Han, X.; Morariu, V.I.; Davis, L.S. Learning rich features for image manipulation detection. In Proceedings of the IEEE Conference on Computer Vision and Pattern Recognition, Salt Lake City, UT, USA, 18–23 June 2018; pp. 1053–1061.
48. Liu, C.; Freeman, W.T.; Szeliski, R.; Kang, S.B. Noise Estimation from a Single Image. In Proceedings of the 2006 IEEE Computer Society Conference on Computer Vision and Pattern Recognition—Volume 1, CVPR '06, New York, NY, USA, 17–22 June 2006; IEEE Computer Society: Washington, WA, USA, 2006; pp. 901–908. [CrossRef]
49. Castro, M.; Ballesteros, D.M.; Renza, D. A dataset of 1050-tampered color and grayscale images (CG-1050). *Data Brief* **2020**, *28*, 104864. [CrossRef] [PubMed]
50. Krawetz, N. A Picture's Worth . . . Digital Image Analysis and Forensics Version 2. *Hacker Factor Solut.* **2007**, *6*, 2.
51. Stehman, S.V. Selecting and interpreting measures of thematic classification accuracy. *Remote. Sens. Environ.* **1997**, *62*, 77–89. [CrossRef]
52. Wagner, J. Noise Analysis for Image Forensics. Available online: https://29a.ch/2015/08/21/noise-analysis-for-image-forensics (accessed on 30 May 2021).
53. Zampoglou, M.; Papadopoulos, S.; Kompatsiaris, Y. Large-scale evaluation of splicing localization algorithms for web images. *Multimed. Tools Appl.* **2017**, *76*, 4801–4834. [CrossRef]

Article

Detecting Morphing Attacks through Face Geometry Features

Stephanie Autherith [1] and Cecilia Pasquini [2,*]

1. Department of Computer Science, University of Innsbruck, Technikerstraße 21A, 6020 Innsbruck, Austria; stephanie.autherith@uibk.ac.at
2. Department of Information Engineering and Computer Science, University of Trento, Via Sommarive 9, 38123 Trento, Italy
* Correspondence: cecilia.pasquini@unitn.it

Received: 19 September 2020; Accepted: 21 October 2020; Published: 29 October 2020

Abstract: Face-morphing operations allow for the generation of digital faces that simultaneously carry the characteristics of two different subjects. It has been demonstrated that morphed faces strongly challenge face-verification systems, as they typically match two different identities. This poses serious security issues in machine-assisted border control applications and calls for techniques to automatically detect whether morphing operations have been previously applied on passport photos. While many proposed approaches analyze the suspect passport photo only, our work operates in a differential scenario, i.e., when the passport photo is analyzed in conjunction with the probe image of the subject acquired at border control to verify that they correspond to the same identity. To this purpose, in this study, we analyze the locations of biologically meaningful facial landmarks identified in the two images, with the goal of capturing inconsistencies in the facial geometry introduced by the morphing process. We report the results of extensive experiments performed on images of various sources and under different experimental settings showing that landmark locations detected through automated algorithms contain discriminative information for identifying pairs with morphed passport photos. Sensitivity of supervised classifiers to different compositions on the training and testing sets are also explored, together with the performance of different derived feature transformations.

Keywords: face morphing; forensics detection; face landmarks; automatic border control

1. Introduction

Automated face recognition and verification are widely studied problems in computer vision, for which accurate solutions have been developed and commercialized [1,2]. As a result, they are used in security contexts as means for person authentication, thus representing an alternative to more traditional schemes based on passwords and PINs (Personal Identification Number) and to other biometric traits like fingerprints. This includes applications such as face-based authentication in mobile devices and automated border controls (ABC) through passport photos [3].

In the ABC scenario, face information is used for identity verification starting from electronic Machine Readable Travel Documents (eMRTD). To this end, a live probe image of the subject physically present at border control is acquired and compared with the image stored in his/her eMRTD via face verification (FV) algorithms, which provide a binary output indicating whether the two images depict the same subject. In order to aid both algorithmic and human FV, photos in eMRTD must fulfil restrictive quality standards, as specified by the International Standard Organization (ISO) and the International Civil

Aviation Organization (ICAO) guidelines. In particular, the face must be straight looking, acquired in frontal position, and not covered by hair or clothes.

Facilitated by these requirements, advanced FV algorithms can typically perform identity verification rapidly and accurately, but their effectiveness can be compromised if the images stored in eMRTDs contain alterations. A relevant case is represented by face images resulting from morphing operations [4], i.e., when two images of different subjects are blended together through geometric operations. In this case, FV algorithms are led to detect a match between the morphed image of the eMRTD and probe images from both subjects, as we illustrate in Figure 1.

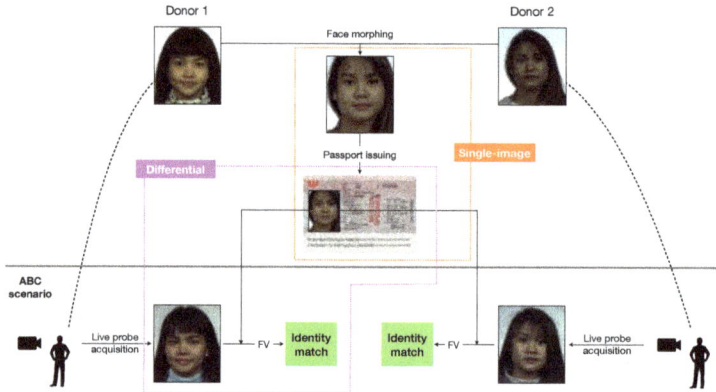

Figure 1. Illustration of a morphing attack against face verification (FV)-based automated border control (ABC) systems (examples are taken from the dataset in [5]): the area of analysis of single-image and differential approaches is highlighted.

In many countries, the image stored in the eMRTD is provided by the citizen during the passport application process, either in printed format or via web-platforms. This offers opportunities for an attacker to introduce altered visual information to be used to their advantage. In this context, a *morphing attack* would allow the same passport containing a morphed photo to be used by two different subjects, potentially including citizens with known criminal records for which border crossing would be forbidden. This kind of attack is particularly insidious as humans can be deceived as well with good probability, as it is shown in [6]. Moreover, it does not require physical forgeries of passports.

In order to contrast possible frauds exploiting these vulnerabilities, techniques for the detection of morphing attacks have been proposed in recent years.

The majority of them focuses on a *single-image* scenario, i.e., they analyse the photo in the eMRTD looking for traces of morphing operations. This includes inhomogeneities in texture patterns, camera fingerprints and compression traces, or visual artefacts like ghost shadows or illumination patterns. An advantage of this class of techniques is that they operate on eMRTD information only and could in principle reveal anomalies before the actual ABC context or even directly during the passport application process, thus enabling an early prevention of morphing attacks. However, they typically suffer from generalization issues due to the high variability of pre- and postprocessing operations which should be expected in real world scenarios [7]. In fact, as widely investigated in the field of image forensics, steps like compression [8], printing/scanning operations [9], resizing [10], and aspect ratio correction might be applied to the photo under investigation with highly diverse parameters and in turn introduce further subtle distortions and artifacts, which can have a strong impact on the (typically weak) morphing traces in the image signal [11,12].

Another interesting yet less explored approach is to consider a *differential* scenario, where the morphing detection is performed with the identity verification process at border control. In this case, the eMRTD photo and the live probe image can be jointly analyzed; thus, the decision is based on an *image pair*. While less timely than the single-image case in detecting anomalies, differential detection can leverage the additional information given by the acquired probe image.

In our work, we address this differential scenario and focus on the use of geometric face features to determine whether the image pair actually contains photos of the same subject or the reference eMRTD image depicts a morphed face. The rationale behind this choice is to capture the geometric inconsistencies between the morphed face and the genuine subject's face that are unavoidably introduced in the morphing process. In fact, the morphing operation impacts the 2D face geometry, while its role has been only marginally investigated in the literature for morphing detection [13,14]. We fill this gap by developing and assessing the effectiveness of binary detectors based on the location of facial landmarks detected in both faces, the eMRTD photo, and the live probe. Those detectors are intended to be applied at ABC on top of the FV algorithm in cases where it detects an identity match between the two faces, since morphing attacks steer the FV decisions towards a positive match.

We can summarize our contributions as follows:

- We conduct an extensive experimental campaign to assess the effectiveness of landmark-based geometric features for the pairs. This includes adopting different training/testing conditions to encourage a sufficiently high variability between training and testing sets in terms of source datasets and subject characteristics and to better assess the generalization abilities of the detectors. A corpus of images belonging to different source datasets has been constructed, which represents a wider and more diverse benchmark with respect to previous studies in this direction [13,14].
- We identify the more relevant face areas for morphing detection through an ablation study on semantically related groups of landmarks, thus gaining insights on the face locations where more discriminative patterns can be found.
- We compare the performance of different transformations of the full set of facial landmarks, including feature representations previously proposed the literature [13,14] and geometric features stemming from findings in facial anthropometry.
- We evaluate the effect of noise sources that can typically affect the image pairs in realistic scenarios, revealing that the performance of the proposed detectors against unseen processing in the training tests are largely preserved. This confirms the advantage of geometric-based method of being stable against common image alterations, as opposed to texture-based approaches.

The manuscript is organized as follows: Section 2 reports an overview of existing approaches for face morphing creation and detection; in Section 3, we illustrate the detection framework and feature representations adopted; Section 4 fully reports the outcomes of the experimental tests we conducted; and Section 5 concludes the paper.

2. Related Work

We illustrate how morphed faces are created (Section 2.1) and then give an overview of the detection techniques proposed in the literature, differentiating between single-image (Section 2.2) and differential (Section 2.3) approaches.

2.1. Creation of Morphed Faces

Face morphing consists of merging together two images depicting two different subjects (called *donors*) into one *morphed* face image, which contains characteristics of both subjects. This process generally involves several rule-based procedures and, although variants can be devised [15], we refer to the work in [6] and visually summarize the main steps in Figure 2.

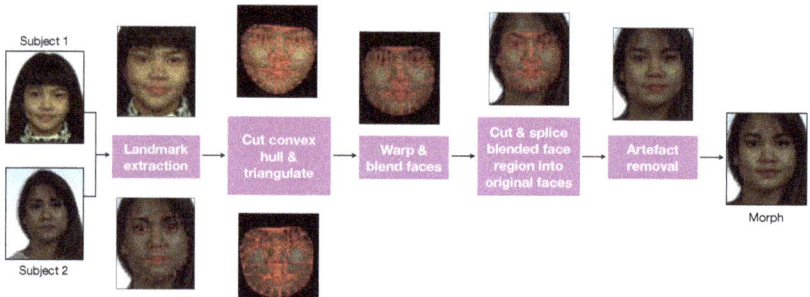

Figure 2. Visualization of the morphing process.

Firstly, facial landmarks are detected in both images and linearly blended with a factor which is commonly set to 0.5 [6], so to obtain intermediate landmarks, which are subsequently triangulated. Then, both images are warped to be aligned to the intermediate landmarks and joined together again through cross-dissolving. This can be done on the entire image or by operating only on the convex hull of the landmark set to ease seamless alterations. Additional manual operations can then be applied to remove visual artifacts. Also, visually plausible morphs are generally possible provided that the subjects are depicted in a frontal pose and share similar characteristics, including the same gender.

While some tools are available online [16], obtaining high-quality full-face morphs that do not contain evident visual artefacts and that could then be used for potential attacks is highly time-consuming or requires specific software, generally proprietary [17] or not publicly available [6].

Given the impressive results obtained for other visual tasks, in [18], the authors attempt to use Generative Adversarial Models (GAN) to systematically create morphed faces, although generated images have a fairly low resolution. A follow-up study has been reported in [19], where a higher quality is reached, thus highlighting the potential advantages and promising outcomes of this approach.

2.2. Single-Image Detectors

The methods developed to detect morphing attacks on the reference eMRTD photo mostly rely on pattern recognition techniques used in image processing and image forensics. In fact, the key idea is to detect traces in the image signal of the operations involved in the morphing creation process.

Several approaches explored the effectiveness of texture and keypoint descriptors in detecting anomalies within the passport photo [20–22]. This includes Local Binary Patterns (LBP) [23], Binarized Statistical Image Features (BSIF), and Weighted Local Magnitude Patterns, also combined with other handcrafted features used in computer vision such as Scale Invariant Feature Transform (SIFT), Speeded Up Robust Features (SURF) [24], and Histogram of Oriented Gradients (HOG) [20].

Other methodologies resort to techniques originating from image forensics for the detection of local image modifications. To this purpose, a possible approach is to analyse the Photo Response Non-Uniformity (PRNU), which is an imperceptible spatial noise pattern caused by inaccuracies in the sensor manufacturing process. Every acquiring sensor has a characteristic PRNU, and alterations due to morphing can be revealed through its estimation [25,26]. Similarly, local modifications imply diversified compression histories within the same picture, which can be captured by analyzing proper statistical artifacts [15,27]. Also, traces of alterations can be found through modeling light reflection and light sources in different faces areas, observing whether they are physically consistent [28].

Recently, deep features have also been used for morphing detection, either by training or fine-tuning known architectures [29,30] or by using pretrained models as feature extractors . The advantage of neural networks is that they can in principle detect different kind of artifacts, although large datasets with high variance are necessary for training them successfully.

2.3. Differential Detectors

Differential detectors are less explored with respect to single-image methods, and few approaches appear so far in the literature.

One direction is explored by the work in [31,32], where the authors develop a pipeline to reverse the morphing process and to retrieve two face images starting from the one stored in the eMRTD. A morphing attack is detected if one of the two resulting face strongly matches the probe image.

Then, the works in [13,14] firstly combine information from facial landmarks detected in both images, and are further defined in Section 3.2, as they are considered as baselines in our tests. Therefore, the *directed distances* proposed in [13] constitute a transformation aimed at exposing shifting patterns in the landmark geometry. Those geometric artefacts are introduced by the warping step specifically in the morphing process. The features in [14] instead comprise *distances and angle differences* computed between landmarks of two face images. Herein, the angle differences are calculated between neighboring landmarks, while the distance features consider combinations of all the available landmarks. Finally, a solution building on deep face representations has been described in the recently published work [33].

3. Detection Framework

The analyzed geometry-based detectors operate in the presence of the eMRTD and the probe live image depicting the physical subject. As explained in Section 1, the detection is intended to be applied after the FV outcome if an identity match is detected.

In fact, advanced FV algorithms for ABC are designed and calibrated to robustly link faces belonging to the same subject, which are generally in frontal position with close-to-neutral expression but also contain common disturbance factors (such as differences in pose, illumination, and subject's age/haircut). On the other hand, morphing attacks specifically challenge the FV's ability to differentiate very similar yet strategically altered face geometries and thus to reject image pairs containing this kind of inconsistency. For this reason, the geometry-based detectors act as specialized modules based on facial geometry for the detection of potential morphing attacks among image pairs where an identity match results from the FV system, as depicted in Figure 3. Thus, the following classes of image pairs are used for training and testing:

- *Bona fide pairs:* the eMRTD contains a genuine face image of the physical subject.
- *Attacked pairs:* the eMRTD contains a morphed face image of which physical subject is a donor.

The geometry-based detector is a machine learning model that classifies the pair as either bona fide or attacked, based on the facial landmark information extracted from the two images. In Section 3.1, we describe the workflow adopted for the extraction and processing of the landmarks. Moreover, the extracted landmark vector $\mathbf{L}$ can be further combined and transformed through a function Φ to obtain derived feature representations $\Phi(\mathbf{L})$. This can be done in order to reduce the feature dimensionality (and thus to facilitate training also in the case of scarce training data) or to provide more interpretable outcomes, which is typically an advantage of handcrafted features. Thus, in addition to the full set of landmarks, we define different transformations of **L** inspired by studies in craniofacial anthropometry [34], the discipline that analyzes measurements and proportions of human faces.

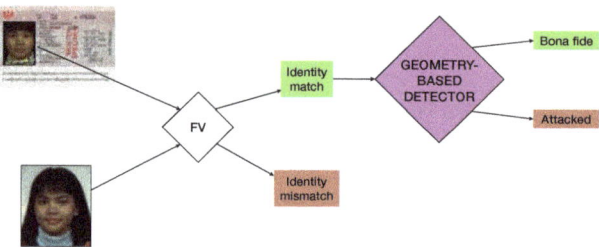

Figure 3. Detection framework.

3.1. Landmark Extraction

Facial landmarks are biologically meaningful keypoints of human faces, widely used for many tasks in computer vision. Several algorithms have been proposed for the automatic detection and localization of these keypoints, and in our work, we use the `dlib` library, which outputs the coordinates of 68 landmarks as depicted in Figure 4. The eye centers are computed starting from the 6 landmarks of each eye, and the landmark coordinates are rotated so that the eye centers lie on the same horizontal line. After being mapped into the interval $[0, 1]$ through a min-max normalization, they are scaled in such a way that the two eye centers of each face are aligned.

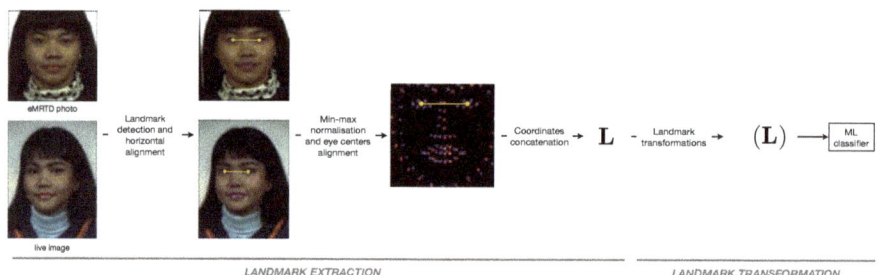

Figure 4. Landmark extraction and transformation.

The resulting vectors containing the bidimensional coordinates of the face in the passport photo and in the live image, respectively, are then concatenated together into a $68 \times 2 \times 2 = 272$-dimensional vector **L**.

3.2. Landmark Transformations

In order to better encode in the feature vectors geometric characteristics of the two compared faces, handcrafted feature transformations can be applied to **L**. Here, we introduce for comparative testing (see Section 4) two different transformations inspired by anthropometric studies Φ_R and Φ_A (and their union), and we recall previously proposed landmark-based feature representations.

3.2.1. Anthropometry-Based Features

Anthropometric craniofacial proportions [34] are characteristic ratios of distances between specific cranial and facial keypoints. They have been widely studied by anthropologists and used in different domains (ranging from art to medicine and from computer graphics to forensic sciences), and they have also been explored for 2D and 3D face recognition purposes [35,36]. We define the following transformations, yielding different features vectors:

- **Ratios (Φ_R):** for each face, we consider 47 pairs of landmarks and compute the distance between them, as depicted in (Figure 5, left). Those landmarks are selected as highly involved in the morphing process and less sensitive to slight expression variations. Then, those distances are divided individually by the two benchmark distances depicted in red in (Figure 5, middle) and chosen so that they are reliably detected and relatively stable through the morphing process, according to the approach proposed in [36]. Those 94 ratio values from each face are then concatenated, resulting in a feature vector $\Phi_R(\mathbf{L})$ of size 188.
- **Angles (Φ_A):** we take the 47 distances and the 2 benchmark distances used for Φ_R transformation. The angle between each of these distances and the horizontal line are then computed for the two faces (see Figure 5, right) and stored in a vector, resulting into a feature vector $\Phi_A(\mathbf{L})$ of size $49 \times 2 = 98$.
- **Ratios+Angles ($\Phi_R + \Phi_A$):** in this case, $\Phi_R(\mathbf{L})$ and $\Phi_A(\mathbf{L})$ are simply concatenated, the size of the feature vector being $188 + 98 = 286$.

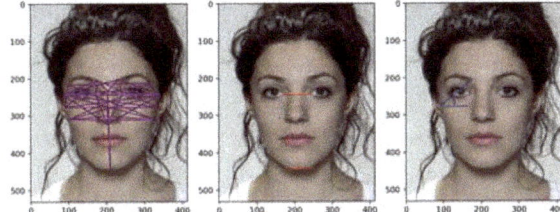

Figure 5. (**Left**) Forty-seven distances used in Φ_R. (**Middle**) Two benchmark distances used in Φ_R. (**Right**) Angle calculation as in Φ_A.

3.2.2. Previously Proposed Landmark-Based Features

As mentioned in Section 2.3, previous approaches in morphing detection have utilized facial landmarks which consist of transformations of the vector $\mathbf{L}$:

- **Directed Distances (Φ_{DD}):** proposed in [13], the transformation yields a 136-dimensional vector containing shifting patterns between corresponding landmarks in the two faces.
- **All Distances and Neighbour Angles (Φ_{AD}, Φ_{NA}):** the approach in [14] leads to two transformations: Φ_{AD} calculates a 2278-dimensional feature vector based on distances between all extracted landmarks of a face image; Φ_{NA} only considers angle differences between neighbouring landmarks and yields a 68-dimensional feature vector.

A common trait of these two landmark transformations is that they perform a one-to-one comparison of differente landmarks among the two faces, thus heavily relying on an accurate alignment of the two landmark sets. Instead, Φ_A and Φ_R process the landmark vectors separately for each face (ratios and angles are always computed within the same face) and then concatenate the two feature vectors of every pair. This mitigates potential inaccuracies of the alignment process, for instance, caused by slight pose variations.

4. Experimental Results

We now report the results of our experimental campaign, where the effectiveness of landmark-based geometric detectors is assessed. In Section 4.1, we describe the experimental setup adopted for our tests, including the datasets used, the machine learning classifier, and the evaluation metrics. Section 4.2 reports the results of our approach when the feature vector **L** containing all landmark locations is used for discrimination in different training and testing scenarios. An ablation study on different face areas is performed in Section 4.3, while in Section 4.4, we compare the different landmark transformation approaches described in Section 3.2. Finally, the robustness of the developed detectors in the presence of unknown processing in the testing phase is assessed in Section 4.5.

4.1. Experimental Setup

We used different datasets to create bona fide and attacked image pairs. Since most of the datasets were created for different tasks, in each case, we have selected images with frontal facing subjects exhibiting neutral expressions, according to the structure of each dataset. For the sake of clarity, in the following, we define multiple pair sets.

- Bona-fide pairs:

  - **AR**: 472 pairs formed starting from images in the AR dataset [37]. For every subject, pictures taken in two different acquisitions and distinct poses are available. We selected the 2 available frontal facing images where the face shows neutral expressions from both sessions and paired them with each other.
  - **REPLAY**: 140 pairs formed from frames extracted from the Replay dataset [38], which was originally proposed to benchmark detectors of face spoofing attacks.
  - **MISC**: a collection of 1000 pairs extracted from different datasets, including the Radboud Faces Dataset [39], the CVL Face Database [40], PUT Face Database [41], the FEI Face Database [42], and the Chicago Face Database [43].

- Attacked pairs:

  - **AMSL**: a total of 8700 pairs built from the publicly available AMSL Face Morph Image Dataset [44] used in [11]. A subset **AMSL**$_{1000}$ is also determined by randomly selecting 1000 pairs from **AMSL**.
  - **FERET**: 4306 pairs composed from a dataset of morphed images released by Biometix [5]. The morphs have been created starting from images of the Feret database [45], which includes multiple acquisitions of the same subject.

Those sets will be differently combined for creating the training set $\mathcal{TR}$ (i.e., the union of bona fide and attacked training pair sets $\mathcal{TR}_{BF}$ and $\mathcal{TR}_A$) and the testing set $\mathcal{TS}$ (i.e., the union of bona fide and attacked testing pair sets $\mathcal{TS}_{BF}$ and $\mathcal{TS}_A$) for supervised machine learning models, as described in the following subsections. The operator $|\cdot|$ will indicate the number of pairs contained in each set.

In each test, an SVM classifier with radial basis function (RBF) kernel has been used for classification. The parameters *gamma* and *C* of the SVM have been selected via grid-search over a logarithmic grid ranging from 10^{-4} to 10^1 for each dataset composition. Note that we have focused on the RBF kernel as it always outperformed linear and polynomial kernels in our tests. All the experiments have been performed in Python 3 and the `scikit-learn`, `OpenCV`, and `dlib` packages.

Consistently with other works in this domain, we adopt the metrics defined for the detection of presentation attacks in biometrics to measure the performance of the classification (i.e., thresholding the SVM score at 0):

- *APCER* (Attack Presentation Classification Error Rate): ratio of attacked pairs erroneously classified as bona fide pairs;
- *BPCER* (Bona fide Presentation Classification Error Rate): ratio of bona fide pairs erroneously classified as attacked pairs;
- *ACC* (Accuracy): fraction of image pairs that are correctly classified (either as bona-fide or attacked)

In addition, for selected cases, we show the Detection Error Tradeoff (DET) curve plotting *APCER* vs. *BPCER* obtained by varying the decision threshold on the output score of the SVM, and we will report the *EER* (Equal Error Rate), i.e., the error rate at the operating point where *APCER* = *BPCER*.

4.2. Full Landmark Set

We first test the effectiveness of the feature representation given by the full set of facial landmarks extracted from both images, i.e., the vector **L**.

We consider different experimental scenarios, always arranging the pairs in such a way that no subject appearing in the testing set is part of any pair used in the training set, not even as a donor of one morphed face. This is in fact the case for real-world applications where we cannot expect the identities in the testing phase to be present in the training set. To this purpose, we define a splitting procedure to form training and testing groups, where we select a part of the subjects appearing in a certain pair set and isolate all the pairs that contain those subjects. Note that the attack pairs consist of a morph and a probe image of one of its donors which was preferably not used during the morphing process. Thus, each morph yields at least 2 attack pairs with 2 images of its different donors. Given $p \in [0,1]$ and a set **SET**, the following steps are performed:

1. a fraction p of the subjects appearing in **SET** are randomly chosen;
2. all the pairs in **SET** which depict any of these subjects in one or both images or as donors of a morphed fac, are stored in **SET**(p)
3. the remaining pairs in **SET** are stored in $\overline{\textbf{SET}(p)}$

This procedure has been used to create $\mathcal{TR}$ and $\mathcal{TS}$ by varying p. In particular, we consider three scenarios differing for the composition of $\mathcal{TS}$, as described in Table 1. The bona fide pairs are the same for each row, and the share of **AR** between training and testing varies with p. In the first two scenarios, the attacked pairs in $\mathcal{TR}_A$ and $\mathcal{TS}_A$ are drawn from the same pair set. In the third more challenging scenario, $\mathcal{TS}_A$ is composed by 1000 **AMSL** pairs plus a number of **FERET** pairs (depending on p), while only **FERET** pairs are tested; thus, only a fraction of training samples are from the same set as the testing samples. By doing so, we can observe how performance are affected by the numerosity and composition of $\mathcal{TR}$ and $\mathcal{TS}$.

Table 1. Training/testing scenarios adopted in Section 4.2.

	$\mathcal{TR}_{BF}$	$\mathcal{TR}_A$	$\mathcal{TS}_{BF}$	$\mathcal{TS}_A$
AMSL-*only*		**AMSL**(p)		$\overline{\textbf{AMSL}(p)}$
FERET-*only*	**MISC** $\cup$ **AR**(p)	**FERET**(p)	$\overline{\textbf{AR}(p)} \cup$ **REPLAY**	$\overline{\textbf{FERET}(p)}$
Mixed		**AMSL**$_{1000}$ $\cup$ **FERET**(p)		$\overline{\textbf{FERET}(p)}$

Results for the **AMSL**-*only*, **FERET**-*only*, and *Mixed* scenarios are reported in Figures 6–8, respectively. In Figures 6a–8a, we plot the metrics *ACC*, *APCER*, and *BPCER* for different values of p. Since step 1 of the splitting procedure involves a random choice of a fraction p of subjects (for which the images are then included in $\mathcal{TR}$), the metrics are averaged over 5 different splitting instances for validation. Figures 6b–8b report the cardinality of the resulting training and testing groups for each class on a single splitting instance, for which we report in Figures 6c–8c the DET curve and the performance metrics at $p = 0.1$.

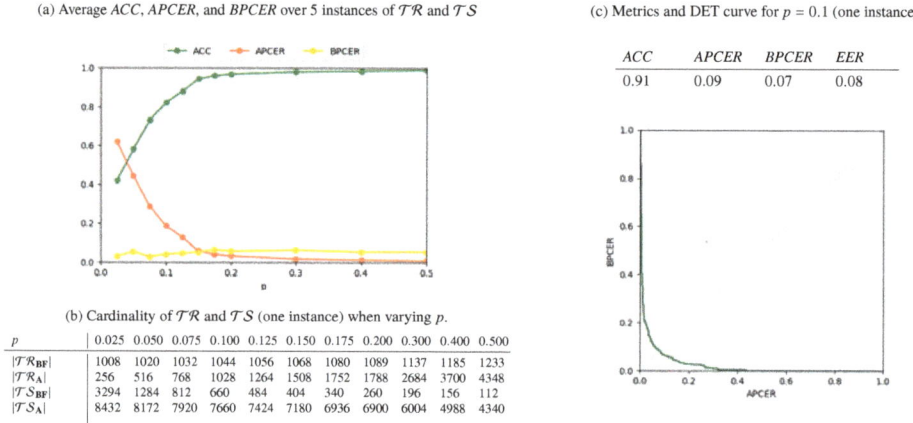

Figure 6. Results for the **AMSL**-*only* scenario.

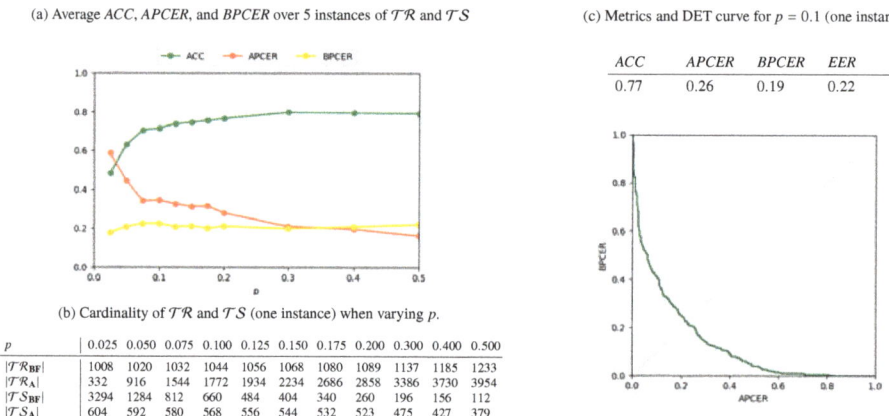

Figure 7. Results for the **FERET**-*only* scenario.

As expected, the performance increases with p, i.e., when more numerous and representative training samples are available. Overall, the best results are obtained in the **AMSL**-*only* scenario, with a global accuracy approaching 1 for $p > 0.2$. The **FERET**-*only* scenario instead shows a lower accuracy, which stabilizes at around 0.77 even when p increases. This is explained by the higher variability of acquisition conditions of the probe images in the **FERET** pairs, which makes it harder to discriminate face geometry anomalies due to variabilities in the probe images or due to morphing operations, thus causing increased *APCER*, *BPCER*, and *EER*.

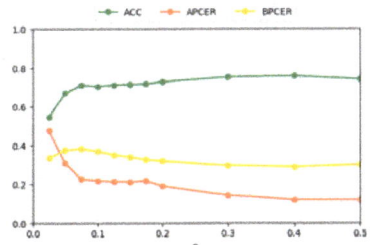

(a) Average *ACC*, *APCER*, and *BPCER* over 5 instances of $\mathcal{TR}$ and $\mathcal{TS}$

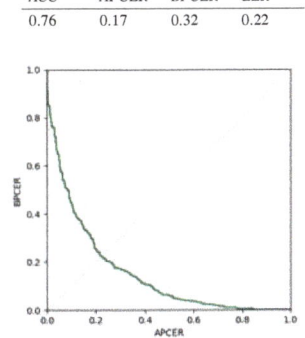

(c) Metrics and DET curve for $p = 0.1$ (one instance).

ACC	APCER	BPCER	EER
0.76	0.17	0.32	0.22

(b) Cardinality of $\mathcal{TR}$ and $\mathcal{TS}$ (one instance) when varying p.

p	0.025	0.050	0.075	0.100	0.125	0.150	0.175	0.200	0.300	0.400	0.500
$|\mathcal{TR}_{BF}|$	1008	1020	1032	1044	1056	1068	1080	1089	1137	1185	1233
$|\mathcal{TR}_A|$	1332	1916	2544	2772	2934	3234	3686	3858	4386	4730	4954
$|\mathcal{TS}_{BF}|$	3294	1284	812	660	484	404	340	260	196	156	112
$|\mathcal{TS}_A|$	604	592	580	568	556	544	532	523	475	427	379

Figure 8. Results for the *Mixed* scenario.

Finally, the *Mixed* scenario results show that, when trained mostly on the 1000 **AMSL** pairs, the detector struggles in recognizing **FERET** attacked pairs and performs well when samples in $\mathcal{TR}_A$ are roughly equally splitted in **AMSL** and **FERET** pairs. This suggests that different datasets carry peculiar characteristics and, as it typically happens for supervised machine learning solutions, there exists a risk of overfitting on specific sources.

For the sake of completeness, we have also investigated the use of a 1D convolutional neural network (CNN) classifier to better process the information contained in the landmark vector. We considered an architecture with 4 1-dimensional convolutional layers with a kernel size of 3 and $[64, 128, 256, 256]$ filters each. Succeeding the second convolution, we apply instance normalisation after every feature extraction layer. Before the classification, we apply a dense layer with 128 neurones.

In Table 2, we provide a comparison between the RBF SVM and the 1D CNN classifier for the *Mixed* scenario and $p = 0.1$ (one instance) both in terms of performance and training/testing time. In fact, we report the average training time over different values of p and the average prediction time for the two classifiers; for the SVM, tests have been conducted on a 2.3 GHz 8-core Intel Core i9, while the CNN was trained and tested on an NVIDIA GTX 1080Ti GPU.

As it can be observed, the gain in performance with respect to the RBF SVM is rather marginal, in front of a much higher computational effort. We therefore employ the RBF SVM for the following analyses. Moreover, for the sake of brevity, we will stick to the *Mixed* scenario and the case $p = 0.1$.

Table 2. Performance metrics of different classifiers: the average training time is computed as the mean of training times over distinct values of p. We define the average prediction time as the mean of the time (measured over 100 examples) that it takes for our models to classify one image pair.

Model	ACC	APCER	BPCER	Average Training Time per p	Average Prediction Time per Pair
RBF SVM	0.76	0.17	0.32	0.69 min	0.0031 s
1D CNN	0.77	0.19	0.29	36.08 min	0.1768 s

4.3. Ablation Study

In order to determine the importance of different landmarks, we group them into distinct semantic groups, as shown in Figure 9, and observe their detection results. These groups correspond to facial attributes and are inspired by the semantic landmark groupings in [46].

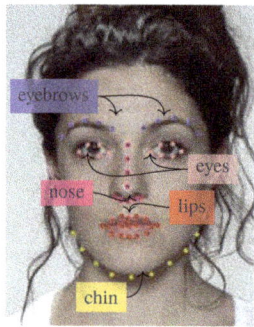 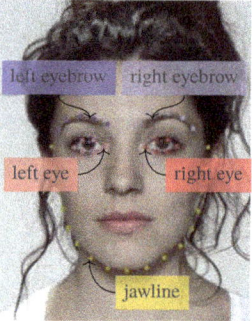 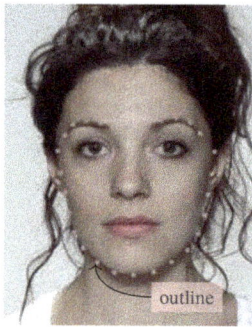

Figure 9. Landmark groups for our ablation study.

We separately test landmarks corresponding to different semantic groups for each image pair and concatenate them to obtain a feature vector $\mathbf{sL}_g$, where g indicates a single semantic group or a combination of them. We then feed $\mathbf{sL}_g$ to a RBF SVM, just like we did for **L**.

The results are reported in Table 3. It can be observed that **L** is generally better performing. However, $\mathbf{sL}_{outline}$ achieves comparable results, thus suggesting that most of the relevant geometric information resides in the relative position of the face line and the eyes.

Moreover, it is worth noticing that the accuracy drop of different variants of $\mathbf{sL}_g$ is mostly due an increase in *BPCER* while the *APCER* remains rather low. This bias towards false alarms might be due to the selected features being less distinctive and the training set not containing enough information for characterizing non-attacked samples, so that bona fide pairs likely exhibit unseen patterns at testing time and are classified as attacked.

Table 3. Results for the ablation tests.

Feature Representation	ACC	APCER	BPCER	EER
L	0.67	0.17	0.32	0.22
$\mathbf{sL}_{eyes}$	0.37	0.07	0.77	0.39
$\mathbf{sL}_{left\ eye}$	0.11	0.06	0.93	0.40
$\mathbf{sL}_{right\ eye}$	0.25	0.05	0.85	0.42
$\mathbf{sL}_{eyebrows}$	0.51	0.07	0.73	0.38
$\mathbf{sL}_{left\ eyebrow}$	0.32	0.01	0.89	0.35
$\mathbf{sL}_{right\ eyebrow}$	0.36	0.02	0.85	0.41
$\mathbf{sL}_{eyebrows\ +\ eyes}$	0.52	0.16	0.57	0.34
$\mathbf{sL}_{left\ eyebrow\ +\ eye}$	0.37	0.08	0.77	0.36
$\mathbf{sL}_{right\ eyebrow\ +\ eye}$	0.46	0.09	0.75	0.39
$\mathbf{sL}_{nose}$	0.21	0.11	0.83	0.43
$\mathbf{sL}_{lips}$	0.44	0.15	0.48	0.30
$\mathbf{sL}_{chin}$	0.20	0.05	0.79	0.39
$\mathbf{sL}_{jawline}$	0.41	0.06	0.69	0.34
$\mathbf{sL}_{outline}$	0.64	0.09	0.38	0.23

4.4. Comparison of Landmark Transformations

We now compare the performance of the different feature representations derived from the landmark location vector **L** introduced in Section 3.2, comparing them with other transformations proposed in the literature.

We report the results for the case of $p = 0.1$ in Figure 10. On the left, the DET curves for the different transformations are reported, and for each of them, the performance metrics are reported on the right. Higher *ACC* and *EER* are obtained by the anthropometry-based transformations $\Phi_R + \Phi_A$ and Φ_A. In general, the angle-based features in $\Phi_A(\mathbf{L})$ are more informative than the ratio-based ones in $\Phi_R(\mathbf{L})$, although their dimensionality is lower than all the other considered transformations. Φ_{DD} also has competitive performance, but its *APCER* and *BPCER* are strongly unbalanced. Φ_{AD}, Φ_{NA}, and their combinations yield less accurate classifications.

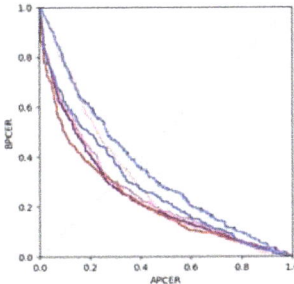

Color	Feature representation	ACC	APCER	BPCER	EER
	$\Phi_R(\mathbf{L})$	0.64	0.21	0.54	0.35
	$\Phi_A(\mathbf{L})$	0.70	0.27	0.33	0.30
	$\Phi_R(\mathbf{L}) + \Phi_A(\mathbf{L})$	**0.72**	0.26	0.31	**0.29**
	$\Phi_{DD}(\mathbf{L})$ [9]	0.68	0.06	0.62	0.30
	$\Phi_{AD}(\mathbf{L})$ [42]	0.63	0.06	0.72	0.34
	$\Phi_{NA}(\mathbf{L})$ [42]	0.59	0.11	0.75	0.38
	$\Phi_{AD}(\mathbf{L}) + \Phi_{NA}(\mathbf{L})$ [42]	0.59	0.11	0.75	0.38

Figure 10. Results for different feature representations.

However, note that all feature representations underperform with respect to **L**. This suggests that, in the considered experimental scenario, the SVM model is powerful enough to learn effective classification boundaries directly in the feature space of **L**, and further, handcrafted transformations are not beneficial in terms of global accuracy.

4.5. Robustness to Processing Operations

We assess the robustness of our detector in the case of diverse processing operations applied to the eMRTD photo. This is in fact known to be a typical issue of for previous detectors, especially single-image ones, as passport pictures can undergo several operations in its digital history (e.g., printing/scanning and compression). To this purpose, we run our models also on different variants of the testing set, where selected postprocessing operations are applied to the passport photos as listed and described in Table 4.

Examples of the different processing operations are reported in Figure 11, where a portion of the image is magnified.

In each case, we measure the performance loss with respect to the baseline case, where neither training nor testing underwent any processing. If *ACC* is the accuracy in the baseline case and ACC_P is the accuracy when a certain processing *P* is applied to the testing set, we calculate the accuracy loss as

$$ACC_{\text{Loss}} = ACC - ACC_P. \tag{1}$$

Figure 12 reports ACC_{Loss} for each processing operation and for the feature representations $\mathbf{L}$, $\Phi_R(\mathbf{L})$, $\Phi_A(\mathbf{L})$, and $\Phi_R(\mathbf{L}) + \Phi_A(\mathbf{L})$.

Table 4. Manipulations applied for the robustness test.

Name	Description
Noise	Additive Gaussian noise with $\sigma = 0.5$
Blur	Blurring with normalized box filter
Scaling V	Downscaling the vertical dimension by 1–2%
Scaling H	Downscaling the horizontal dimension by 1–2%
Affine 1	Applying small offsets to three selected landmarks and the corresponding affine transform to the whole image
Affine 2	Applying a small offset to one selected landmark and the corresponding affine transform to the whole image
Rotation	Rotating the image by $\pm 3\%$ degrees
Speckle	Multiplicative noise
Salt and pepper	Punctual noise on 4% of pixels

We can see that the accuracy loss is always below 5% and involves mostly angle-based feature representations. The loss for the full landmark feature vector $\mathbf{L}$ is however very small (always below 2%) and essentially oscillates around 0. We can then conclude that the trained models generally preserve their effectiveness also in the presence of these unseen processing operations appearing in the testing set.

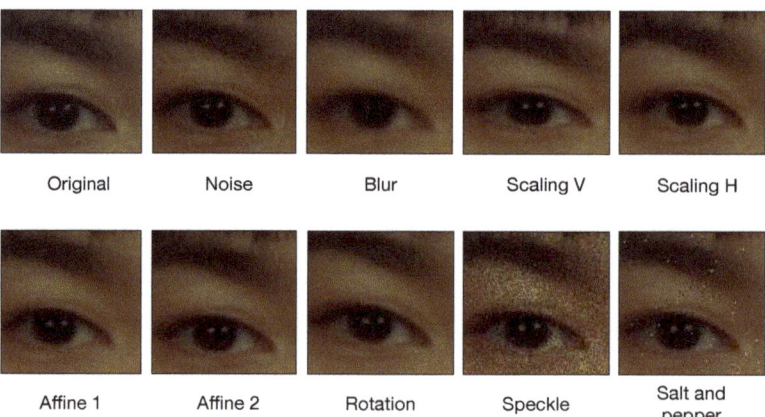

Figure 11. Example of processed electronic Machine Readable Travel Documents (eMRTD) pictures with different manipulations.

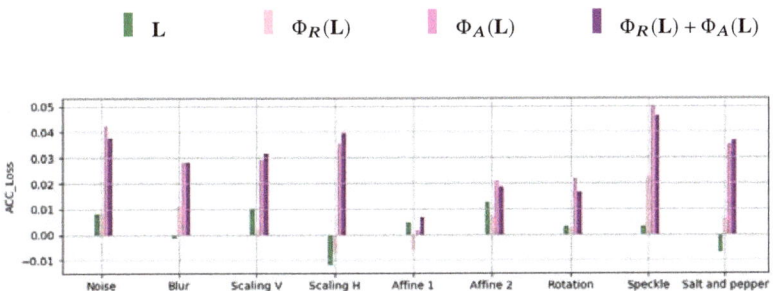

Figure 12. Values of ACC_P for different processing operations and feature representation.

5. Conclusions

We have addressed the problem of detecting morphed faces in electronic passports at border control in a differential scenario, i.e., by jointly analyzing the photo contained in the electronic passport and the live probe image acquired on site. In doing so, we have performed a comparative analysis of geometric face features by developing detectors based on the facial landmarks and by exploring their effectiveness in different directions.

In different scenarios, best results are obtained by operating directly in the feature space of the 2D coordinates of the 68 facial landmarks extracted from the two face images of the pair under investigation. The performance remains essentially stable even when the testing samples are modified via processing operations that are unseen in the training phase. This confirms the advantage of relying on geometric cues like landmarks, for which extraction is generally reliable even after visual alterations that are not too impactful.

Moreover, ablation tests suggests that a non-processed full set of landmark coordinates provides more discriminative information in every case. Among the compared handcrafted features, the ones based on facial anthropometry concepts are generally more effective with respect to approaches previously proposed in the literature.

The obtained results confirm the potential of a geometric differential analysis leveraging also the probe image for detecting morphing attacks. The extracted features are indeed limited in dimensionality (thus are lighter to process with respect to more computationally expensive techniques [32]), while offering fair detection performance and high interpretability of the detector's outcome. This is an advantage with respect to other differential detection approaches based on deep networks [33], which do not explicitly look for geometric distortions that are inherent to morphing attacks but rather rely on the distribution of deep features used for general face-recognition problems. However, our study also exposes typical issues affecting supervised machine learning techniques, namely the risk of overfitting training data and reduced generalization abilities when different data sources are tested. Multi-clue detectors would in fact be recommended for improved performance in realistic scenarios. In fact, a promising direction for future work would be to analyze geometric cues in conjuction with richer representations like the ones based on deep networks [33], which has brought a significant performance boost in many related tasks.

Author Contributions: Conceptualization, C.P. and S.A.; methodology, C.P.; software, S.A.; validation, S.A.; data curation, S.A.; writing–original draft preparation, S.A.; writing–review and editing, C.P. All authors have read and agreed to the published version of the manuscript.

Funding: The second author was partially supported by the project PREMIER (PREserving Media trustworthiness in the artificial Intelligence ERa), funded by the Italian Ministry of Education, University, and Research (MIUR) within the PRIN 2017 program.

Conflicts of Interest: The authors declare no conflict of interest.

References

1. Parkhi, O.M.; Vedaldi, A.; Zisserman, A. Deep Face Recognition. In Proceedings of the British Machine Vision Conference (BMVC), Swansea, UK, 7–10 September 2015; BMVA Press: Durham, UK, 2015; pp. 41.1–41.12.
2. Balaban, S. Deep learning and face recognition: The state of the art. In *Proceedings Volume 9457 Biometric and Surveillance Technology for Human and Activity Identification XII*; SPIE: Bellingham, WA, USA, 2015. [CrossRef]
3. Neubert, T.; Kraetzer, C.; Dittmann, J. A Face Morphing Detection Concept with a Frequency and a Spatial Domain Feature Space for Images on eMRTD. In Proceedings of the ACM Workshop on Information Hiding and Multimedia Security, Paris, France, 3–5 July 2019; pp. 95–100.
4. Ferrara, M.; Franco, A.; Maltoni, D. The magic passport. In Proceedings of the IEEE International Joint Conference on Biometrics, 2014, Clearwater, FL, USA, 29 September–2 October 2014; pp. 1–7. [CrossRef]
5. Biometix Pty Ltd. New Face Morphing Dataset (for Vulnerability Research). 2018. Available online: http://www.biometix.com/2017/09/18/new-face-morphing-dataset-for-vulnerability-research/ (accessed on 1 December 2019.)
6. Makrushin, A.; Neubert, T.; Dittmann, J. Automatic Generation and Detection of Visually Faultless Facial Morphs. In Proceedings of the Internation Joint Conference on Computer Vision, Imaging and Computer Graphics Theory and Applications, Porto, Portugal, 27 February–1 March 2017; pp. 39–50. [CrossRef]
7. Scherhag, U.; Rathgeb, C.; Busch, C. Performance variation of morphed face image detection algorithms across different datasets. In Proceedings of the 2018 International Workshop on Biometrics and Forensics (IWBF), Sassari, Italy, 7–8 June 2018; pp. 1–6. [CrossRef]
8. Pasquini, C.; Schöttle, P.; Böhme, R.; Boato, G.; Pèrez-Gonzàlez, F. Forensics of High Quality and Nearly Identical JPEG Image Recompression. In Proceedings of the ACM Information Hiding and Multimedia Security Workshop, Vigo, Spain, 20–22 June 2016; pp. 11–21.
9. Shang, S.; Kong, X. Printer and Scanner Forensics. In *Handbook of Digital Forensics of Multimedia Data and Devices*; John Wiley & Sons, Ltd.: Hoboken, NJ, USA, 2015; Chapter 10; pp. 375–410.
10. Pasquini, C.; Böhme, R. Information-Theoretic Bounds for the Forensic Detection of Downscaled Signals. *IEEE Trans. Inf. Forensics Secur.* **2019**, *14*, 1928–1943. [CrossRef]
11. Neubert, T.; Makrushin, A.; Hildebrandt, M.; Krätzer, C.; Dittmann, J. Extended StirTrace benchmarking of biometric and forensic qualities of morphed face images. *IET Biom.* **2018**, *7*, 325–332. [CrossRef]
12. Scherhag, U.; Rathgeb, C.; Busch, C. Morph Detection from Single Face Image: A Multi-Algorithm Fusion Approach. In *Proceedings of the 2018 2Nd International Conference on Biometric Engineering and Applications*; ICBEA '18; ACM: New York, NY, USA, 2018; pp. 6–12. [CrossRef]
13. Damer, N.; Boller, V.; Wainakh, Y.; Boutros, F.; Terhörst, P.; Braun, A.; Kuijper, A. Detecting Face Morphing Attacks by Analyzing the Directed Distances of Facial Landmarks Shifts. In *Pattern Recognition*; Brox, T., Bruhn, A., Fritz, M., Eds.; Springer International Publishing: Berlin, Germany, 2019; pp. 518–534.
14. Scherhag, U.; Budhrani, D.; Gomez-Barrero, M.; Busch, C. Detecting Morphed Face Images Using Facial Landmarks. In *Image and Signal Processing*; Springer International Publishing: Cham, Switzerland, 2018; pp. 444–452. [CrossRef]
15. Scherhag, U.; Rathgeb, C.; Merkle, J.; Breithaupt, R.; Busch, C. Face Recognition Systems Under Morphing Attacks: A Survey. *IEEE Access* **2019**, *7*, 23012–23026. [CrossRef]
16. FaceMorpher. Available online: https://github.com/stheakanath/facemorpher (accessed on 27 July 2020).
17. FaceMorpher Luxand. Available online: https://www.luxand.com/facemorpher/ (accessed on 27 July 2020).
18. Damer, N.; Saladié, A.M.; Braun, A.; Kuijper, A. MorGAN: Recognition Vulnerability and Attack Detectability of Face Morphing Attacks Created by Generative Adversarial Network. In Proceedings of the 2018 IEEE 9th International Conference on Biometrics Theory, Applications and Systems (BTAS), Los Angeles, CA, USA, 22–25 October 2018; pp. 1–10. [CrossRef]

19. Venkatesh, S.; Zhang, H.; Ramachandra, R.; Raja, K.B.; Damer, N.; Busch, C. Can GAN Generated Morphs Threaten Face Recognition Systems Equally as Landmark Based Morphs?-Vulnerability and Detection. In Proceedings of the IEEE International Workshop on Biometrics and Forensics (IWBF), Porto, Portugal, 29–30 April 2020; pp. 1–6.
20. Scherhag, U.; Rathgeb, C.; Busch, C. Towards Detection of Morphed Face Images in Electronic Travel Documents. In Proceedings of the 2018 13th IAPR International Workshop on Document Analysis Systems (DAS), Vienna, Austria, 24–27 April 2018; pp. 187–192. [CrossRef]
21. Wandzik, L.; Kaeding, G.; Garcia, R.V. Morphing Detection Using a General- Purpose Face Recognition System. In Proceedings of the 2018 26th European Signal Processing Conference (EUSIPCO), Rome, Italy, 3–7 September 2018; pp. 1012–1016.
22. Jassim, S.; Asaad, A. Automatic Detection of Image Morphing by Topology-based Analysis. In Proceedings of the 2018 26th European Signal Processing Conference (EUSIPCO), Rome, Italy, 3–7 September 2018; pp. 1007–1011.
23. Rashid, R.D.; Asaad, A.; Jassim, S. Topological data analysis as image steganalysis technique. In Proceedings of the Mobile Multimedia/Image Processing, Security, and Applications, Bellingham, WA, USA, 16–17 April 2018; Volume 10668, pp. 103–111.
24. Kraetzer, C.; Makrushin, A.; Neubert, T.; Hildebrandt, M.; Dittmann, J. Modeling Attacks on Photo-ID Documents and Applying Media Forensics for the Detection of Facial Morphing. In Proceedings of the 5th ACM Workshop on Information Hiding and Multimedia Security, Philadelphia, PA, USA, 20–21 June 2017; IH&MMSec '17; ACM: New York, NY, USA, 2017; pp. 21–32. [CrossRef]
25. Debiasi, L.; Rathgeb, C.; Scherhag, U.; Uhl, A.; Busch, C. PRNU Variance Analysis for Morphed Face Image Detection. In Proceedings of the 2018 IEEE 9th International Conference on Biometrics Theory, Applications and Systems (BTAS), Los Angeles, CA, USA, 22–25 October 2018; pp. 1–9. [CrossRef]
26. Scherhag, U.; Debiasi, L.; Rathgeb, C.; Busch, C.; Uhl, A. Detection of Face Morphing Attacks Based on PRNU Analysis. *IEEE Trans. Biom. Behav. Identity Sci.* **2019**, *1*, 302–317. [CrossRef]
27. Makrushin, A.; Kraetzer, C.; Neubert, T.; Dittmann, J. Generalized Benford's Law for Blind Detection of Morphed Face Images. In Proceedings of the ACM Workshop on Information Hiding and Multimedia Security, Innsbruck, Austria, 20–22 June 2018; pp. 49–54. [CrossRef]
28. Seibold, C.; Hilsmann, A.; Eisert, P. Reflection Analysis for Face Morphing Attack Detection. In Proceedings of the 2018 26th European Signal Processing Conference (EUSIPCO), Rome, Italy, 3–7 September 2018; pp. 1022–1026.
29. Seibold, C.; Samek, W.; Hilsmann, A.; Eisert, P. Detection of Face Morphing Attacks by Deep Learning. In *Digital Forensics and Watermarking*; Kraetzer, C., Shi, Y.Q., Dittmann, J., Kim, H.J., Eds.; Springer International Publishing: Berlin, Germany, 2017; pp. 107–120.
30. Raghavendra, R.; Raja, K.B.; Venkatesh, S.; Busch, C. Transferable Deep-CNN Features for Detecting Digital and Print-Scanned Morphed Face Images. In Proceedings of the 2017 IEEE Conference on Computer Vision and Pattern Recognition Workshops (CVPRW), Honolulu, HI, USA, 21–26 July 2017; pp. 1822–1830. [CrossRef]
31. Ferrara, M.; Franco, A.; Maltoni, D. Face Demorphing. *IEEE Trans. Inf. Forensics Secur.* **2018**, *13*, 1008–1017. [CrossRef]
32. Peng, F.; Zhang, L.; Long, M. FD-GAN: Face-demorphing generative adversarial network for restoring accomplice's facial image. *IEEE Access* **2019**, *7*, 75122–75131. [CrossRef]
33. Scherhag, U.; Rathgeb, C.; Merkle, J.; Busch, C. Deep Face Representations for Differential Morphing Attack Detection. *IEEE Trans. Inf. Forensics Secur.* **2020**, *15*, 3625–3639. [CrossRef]
34. Farkas, L.G.; Munro, I.R. Anthropometric facial proportions in medicine. *Am. J. Orthod. Dentofac. Orthop.* **1987**, *92*, 522.
35. Gupta, S.; Markey, M.; Bovik, A.C. Anthropometric 3D Face Recognition. *Int. J. Comput. Vis.* **2010**, *90*, 331–349. [CrossRef]
36. Shi, J.; Samal, A.; Marx, D. How Effective Are Landmarks and Their Geometry for Face Recognition? *Comput. Vis. Image Underst.* **2006**, *102*, 117–133. [CrossRef]
37. Martinez, A.; Benavente, R. The AR Face Database. Tech. Rep. CVC Tech. Rep. 1998 Available online: http://www2.ece.ohio-state.edu/~aleix/ARdatabase.html (accessed on 1 March 2020)

38. Chingovska, I.; Anjos, A.; Marcel, S. On the Effectiveness of Local Binary Patterns in Face Anti-spoofing. In Proceedings of the International Conference of Biometrics Special Interest Group (BIOSIG), Darmstadt, Germany, 6–7 September 2012.
39. Langner, O.; Dotsch, R.; Bijlstra, G.; Wigboldus, D.; Hawk, S.; Knippenberg, A. Presentation and validation of the Radboud Face Database. *Cogn. Emot. Cogn. Emot.* **2010**, *24*, 1377–1388. [CrossRef]
40. Peer, P. CVL Face Database. 2010. Available online: http://lrv.fri.uni-lj.si/facedb.html (accessed on 1 March 2020).
41. Kasiński, A.; Florek, A.; Schmidt, A. The PUT face database. *Image Process. Commun.* **2008**, *13*, 59–64.
42. Thomaz, C.; Giraldi, G. A new ranking method for Principal Components Analysis and its application to face image analysis. *Image Vis. Comput.* **2010**, *28*, 902–913. [CrossRef]
43. Ma, D.; Correll, J.; Wittenbrink, B. The Chicago face database: A free stimulus set of faces and norming data. *Behav. Res. Methods* **2015**, *47*. [CrossRef] [PubMed]
44. AMSL Face Morph Image Data Set. 2018. Available online: https://omen.cs.uni-magdeburg.de/disclaimer/index.php (accessed on 1 December 2019).
45. Phillips, P.J.; Hyeonjoon Moon.; Rizvi, S.A.; Rauss, P.J. The FERET evaluation methodology for face-recognition algorithms. *IEEE Trans. Pattern Anal. Mach. Intell.* **2000**, *22*, 1090–1104. [CrossRef]
46. Dabouei, A.; Soleymani, S.; Dawson, J.M.; Nasrabadi, N.M. Fast Geometrically-Perturbed Adversarial Faces. In Proceedings of the IEEE Winter Conference on Applications of Computer Vision, Waikoloa Village, HI, USA, 7–11 January 2019. [CrossRef]

Publisher's Note: MDPI stays neutral with regard to jurisdictional claims in published maps and institutional affiliations.

© 2020 by the authors. Licensee MDPI, Basel, Switzerland. This article is an open access article distributed under the terms and conditions of the Creative Commons Attribution (CC BY) license (http://creativecommons.org/licenses/by/4.0/).

Article

Media Forensics Considerations on DeepFake Detection with Hand-Crafted Features

Dennis Siegel *, Christian Kraetzer *, Stefan Seidlitz and Jana Dittmann

Department of Computer Science, Otto-von-Guericke University, 39106 Magdeburg, Germany; stefan.seidlitz@ovgu.de (S.S.); jana.dittmann@ovgu.de (J.D.)
* Correspondence: dennis.siegel@ovgu.de (D.S.); christian.kraetzer@ovgu.de (C.K.)

Abstract: DeepFake detection is a novel task for media forensics and is currently receiving a lot of research attention due to the threat these targeted video manipulations propose to the trust placed in video footage. The current trend in DeepFake detection is the application of neural networks to learn feature spaces that allow them to be distinguished from unmanipulated videos. In this paper, we discuss, with features hand-crafted by domain experts, an alternative to this trend. The main advantage that hand-crafted features have over learned features is their interpretability and the consequences this might have for plausibility validation for decisions made. Here, we discuss three sets of hand-crafted features and three different fusion strategies to implement DeepFake detection. Our tests on three pre-existing reference databases show detection performances that are under comparable test conditions (peak AUC > 0.95) to those of state-of-the-art methods using learned features. Furthermore, our approach shows a similar, if not better, generalization behavior than neural network-based methods in tests performed with different training and test sets. In addition to these pattern recognition considerations, first steps of a projection onto a data-centric examination approach for forensics process modeling are taken to increase the maturity of the present investigation.

Keywords: DeepFake detection; hand-crafted features; forensic process model; plausibility of decisions

1. Introduction

DeepFakes (a neologism combining the terms "deep learning" and "fake") are synthetic videos (or images) in which a person's face (and optionally also voice) is replaced with someone else's likeness using deep learning technologies. Having emerged in late 2017, DeepFakes nowadays pose a serious threat to the trust placed in video footage. Papers such as [1,2] elaborate on the effect of DeepFakes on current politics, disinformation and trust.

Like countering any other form of image, audio or video manipulation, detecting DeepFakes is an important task for media forensics and is currently receiving a lot of research attention due to the significance of the threat.

According to a well established definition given in [3], information technology (IT) forensics is: *"The use of scientifically derived and proven methods toward the preservation, collection, validation, identification, analysis, interpretation, documentation and presentation of digital evidence derived from digital sources for the purpose of facilitating or furthering the reconstruction of events found to be criminal, [...]"*.

This paper focuses on DeepFake detection as a novel challenge in the IT forensics subdiscipline of media forensics. In contrast to many other forensic subdisciplines, such as, e.g., the field of fingerprint analysis, this field is an especially young and immature research field, currently being far away from achieving the ultimate goal of courtroom readiness.

Regarding the basic methodology applied in the state-of-the-art work in DeepFake detection, it can be stated that most of the current research work is based on pattern recognition approaches using feature spaces learned with the help of neural networks. While this method achieves promising detection rates for small scale empirical evaluations with selected DeepFake datasets, it has the inherent drawback that it is extremely hard to validate the plausibility of decisions made by a neuronal network since the semantics of the features learned cannot easily be interpreted by humans. For other, more established, pattern recognition disciplines such as template matching or statistical pattern recognition, the issue of plausibility testing also exists, because the results generated by the application of machine learning strategies lack the intuitive verification that usually accompanies human decision-making processes. Nevertheless, for these disciplines, validation methods have been developed over the decades to establish whether the results of the learning and decision processes are reasonable. In practice, this means to establish that the patterns trained and detected are really the patterns that the user wants to distinguish between and that side-effects as well as external influence factors are known for the pattern recognition process. Such methods, which include, amongst others, feature selection strategies, as well as model analysis methods aimed at establishing the exact decision (or detection) performance and error behavior of an analysis method. The reason to do this is that this knowledge determines the plausibility of the result of the application of pattern recognition mechanisms in a forensic application scenario and should therefore be directly linked to the trust we place in their decisions.

In addition to the problems in estimating the plausibility of decisions of current (mostly neural network-driven) DeepFake detection methods, a second shortcoming in the current state of the art in this field has to be mentioned here: Apart from the considerations of efficiency (i.e., detection performance and plausibility), all forensic methods should aim at fulfilling some form of forensic conformity. Criteria for such conformity should address the admissibility of methods as a basis for expert witnesses' testimony as evidence in legal proceedings. For the United States of America (by far the most active legal system worldwide), those criteria are codified, amongst other regulations, by the so called Daubert standard (see e.g., [4] or [5] for a detailed discussion of this US case-law standard) in combination with the US Federal Rules of Evidence (FRE) [6]. In addition to those admission criteria for expert witnesses' testimony questions of evidence handling (i.e., chain of custody) also have to be looked into.

To address aspects of these two identified shortcomings (i.e., the explainability issues of feature spaces learned using a neural network on one hand and the lack of adherence to forensic process models on the other hand), this paper provides the following two main contributions :

- Using hand-crafted features for DeepFake detection and comparison with the performance of state-of-the-art deep learning-driven approaches, we discuss three sets of hand-crafted features and three different fusion strategies to implement DeepFake detection. Those features analyze the blinking behavior, the texture of the mouth region as well as the degree of texture found in the image foreground. Our tests on three pre-existing reference databases show detection performances that are under comparable test conditions to those of state-of-the-art methods using learned features (in our case obtaining a maximum AUC of 0.960 in comparison to a maximum AUC of 0.998 for a recent approach using convolutional neural networks). Furthermore, our approach shows a similar, if not better, generalization behavior (i.e., AUC drops from values larger than 0.9 to smaller than 0.7) than neural network based methods in tests performed with different training and test sets .

  In addition to those detection performance issues, we discuss at length that the main advantage which hand-crafted features have over learned features is their interpretability and the consequences this might have for plausibility validation for decisions made.
- Projection onto a forensic process model: With the aim to improve the maturity of pattern recognition-driven media forensics, we perform first steps of the projection of our work onto an established forensic process model. For this, a derivative of the forensic process model for IT forensics published in 2011 by the German Federal Office for Information Security (BSI) is used here. This derivative, or more precisely extension,

is called the Data-Centric Examination Approach (DCEA) and has seen its latest major overhaul in 2020 in [7]. While it is not yet perfectly capable of fitting the needs of media forensics analyses, our work shows first benefits of this modeling as well as points where DCEA would need to undergo further extension to fit those purposes.

The paper is structured as follows: In Section 2, the background and state of the art in DeepFake detection (Section 2.1), feature space design alternatives (Section 2.2) and the forensic process model chosen for this paper (Section 2.3) are discussed. Section 3 discusses the chosen solution concept for implementing DeepFake detection with hand-crafted features, while Section 4 focuses on implementation details.

Section 5 presents and discusses our evaluation results, structured into results for individual detectors (Section 5.1) and for fusion operators (Section 5.2). In Section 6, we provide a summary of the results and a comparison with other approaches from the state of the art (in Section 6.1) as well as our conclusion on the comparison between hand-crafted and learned features for DeepFake detection (in Section 6.2). Section 7 closes the paper with some indication for potential future work.

2. Background and State of the Art

By arguing that "Multimedia Forensics is not Computer Forensics", the authors of [8] point out that *"multimedia forensics and computer forensics belong to the class of digital forensics, but they differ notably in the underlying observer model that defines the forensic investigator's view on (parts of) reality, [...] while perfect concealment of traces is possible for computer forensics, this level of certainty cannot be expected for manipulations of sensor data"*. Even though this statement dates back to 2009, before the rise of neural network-driven data generation methods, such as generative adversarial networks (GANs), it still holds true; additionally, modern-day targeted media manipulations such as DeepFake generation, either leave telltale traces of the manipulation (here, the synthesis and insertion of a face into a video) or violate the source characteristics (e.g., violating the noise pattern of the camera). Recent papers on DeepFake detection, such as [9], provide strong indication that, if applied correctly, targeted detection using pattern recognition methods might be a viable media forensics approach to counter DeepFakes.

In Section 2.1 of this chapter, the state of the art regarding recent DeepFake detection methods is briefly summarized. Following this survey, which points out that nearly all recent methods found in the literature are looking at learned feature spaces as a means of tackling this pattern recognition problem, Section 2.2 discusses the existing alternatives for feature space design and reflects upon their suitability in sensitive decision processes, such as e.g., medical image processing or (media) forensics. Additionally, in Section 2.3, a discussion on the needs for integration of pattern recognition-driven methods into a forensic process model is summarized.

2.1. DeepFake Detection

Usually, the detection of DeepFakes happens with various combined Convolutional Neural Network (CNN) architectures such as autoencoders (AEs). The reasons behind this are obvious: First, most DeepFakes are produced with AEs because internet platforms such as YouTube provide many video sources with different human faces which are usable for the training of DeepFake generators based on neural networks. FakeApp [10] is one example of an autoencoder–decoder structure which is able to swap the latent features of two different faces [11]. These architectures introduce several artifacts to the video while creating a DeepFake that are, in most cases, not visible for the human eye but are potential artifacts that could be utilized for DeepFake detection using image or video analysis methods. It stands to reason that neural networks are also useful for the detection of DeepFake videos, assuming that there is a sufficiently large set of representative data to train features, allowing for the localization of the aforementioned artifacts. Second, which is also a consequence of the first reason, several large and publicly available DeepFake databases (such as FaceForensic++ [12] or Celeb-DF [13]) already exist and provide huge datasets, which can easily be used for the training of CNN-based DeepFake detectors.

The survey paper from Nguyen et al. [11] summarizes different DeepFake detection approaches into the two main categories of *temporal features across video streams* (i.e., inter-frame analysis) and *visual artifacts within video frames* (i.e., intra-frame analysis). For example, the approach of Sabir et al. [14] extracts temporal features of video streams for the detection of DeepFake videos: The authors analyze a potential DeepFake video frame-by-frame for low level artifacts which are only present in single frames to class a video as a DeepFake. Then, they use a Recurrent Convolutional Network (RCN) model to detect and track the temporal artifacts across frames [11,14]. In Li et al.'s work [15], another CNN-based inter-frame analysis approach addresses the eye blinking of a person in a video under the assumption that many DeepFake generated videos are not able to reproduce a natural blinking behavior. The authors first extract the eye areas based on six eye landmarks from a segmented face region. After that, they use the extracted eye area of all video frames in a long-term recurrent convolutional network (LRCN) to detect temporal discrepancies in the blinking behavior [11,15]. An approach which should also be considered for these temporal features across video streams category is described in [16]. Here, the authors analyze (amongst other detection strategies) the lip movements with a combined neural network structure of Mel-Frequency Cepstral Coefficients (MFCCs), Principal Coefficients (PCAs) and an RNN-based (recurrent neural network) Long Short-Term Memory (LSTM) and check whether the lip movement is synchronized to the audio signal [16,17].

The second category for DeepFake detectors, defined by Nguyen et al. [11] (i.e., the intra-frame analyses), is divided into the subcategories of deep and shallow classifiers: During the DeepFake creation process, it is necessary to warp the face area by scaling, rotation and shearing. Deep classifiers address resolution inconsistencies between the warped face area and the surrounding context. These inconsistencies are represented in artifacts which are detectable by CNNs (see, e.g., [11,18]). In contrast, the so called shallow classifiers refer to different visual feature artifacts in head pose, eyes, teeth or in facial contours. In particular, the last three features are addressed in Matern et al.'s work [19]. They solve the DeepFake detection by analyzing the eye and teeth areas for missing reflections or details as well as the texture features from the facial region [11,19].

Other survey papers in this rapidly growing research field, such as the work of, e.g., Yu et al. [20], use the main structure of the DeepFake detection method to classify these methods into several detector categories. Similar to Nguyen et al., they distinguish broadly between inter- and intra-frame analyses. In their scheme, the first (i.e., temporal) features are covered by temporal consistency-based methods using mainly network structures such as recurrent CNNs which are able to detect temporal features frame-by-frame. The latter category is addressed by general network-based methods, which are divided into transfer learning methods and specially designed networks. The methods of transfer learning re-train detectors originally trained for a different recognition problem, while specially designed networks construct and train entirely novel architectures and detectors dedicated entirely to the task of detecting DeepFake videos.

In summary of the (survey) papers discussed above, it can be stated that most DeepFake detection approaches are based on (convolutional) neural networks to learn the feature space to be used. This approach usually requires big databases of real and DeepFake videos to generate detectors that usually perform with very high detection rates on test material that is similar to the used training material in terms of its characteristics.

Hand-crafted feature methods, as an alternative to features learned with neural networks, have the benefit that they (at least theoretically) could work without training. In addition to this and other potential benefits (see Section 2.2), hand-crafted feature spaces for the detection of DeepFake videos are much less common in the literature than neural network-based approaches. Most of the existing research papers relying on hand-crafted approaches (such as [21–23]) use Support Vector Machines (SVMs) for a fast and efficient detection of DeepFake videos.

For the DeepFake detection of persons of interest (POIs) such a Barack Obama, Hillary Clinton or Donald Trump, Gu et al. [23] analyzed speech in combination with face and head movements. They followed the assumption that a person has individual facial expressions and head movements while they are speaking. Their detection pipeline starts with a single video were they tracked facial and head movements first. These facial expressions are defined by 2D and 3D facial landmark positions and several facial action units which are then used for further evaluation steps. For the DeepFake detection, they trained and tested one-class SVMs only with extracted features from authentic videos of specific POIs.

Jung et al. [24] present a hand-crafted DeepFake detector called DeepVision [24], which evaluates eye blinking behavior. In their first step, they extract the face region from a potential DeepFake video. In the following, they use an eye tracker to detect the eye area of a person. After this step they check the eye area of each frame for closed or open eyes and calculate the eye blink elapsed times and eye blink periods.

Unfortunately, the authors of some survey papers, such as [25,26], refer to learned features using specially designed networks (such as those proposed in [15,18]) and also as being "hand-crafted". This is not our perspective of hand-crafted features because they only design the neural network architectures and not the actual features and their semantics. In the following section, we will provide working definitions for the terms hand-crafted and learned features to be used in this paper.

2.2. Feature Space Design Alternatives

In pattern recognition, feature extraction starts from an initial set of input data and builds derived values (features) intended to be informative and non-redundant, facilitating the subsequent learning and generalization steps. It is generally seen to be one form of dimensionality reduction projecting the input into an easier to process and (optimally) less noisy representation. In applied pattern recognition, there generally exist two distinct approaches for feature design:

(a) Features are especially designed (so-called hand-crafted) by domain experts for an application scenario in a process, which, despite the fact that it is sometimes also called intuition-based feature design, usually requires strong domain knowledge. Here, the domain expert uses his/her own experience to construct the features to encode his/her own knowledge about the semantics (and internal as well as external influence factors) inherent to the different pattern classes in the problem at hand. As a result, usually rather low-dimensional feature spaces are designed, which require only small sets of training data (or none at all) for the training (i.e., adaptation/calibration) to a specific application scenario. The semantic characteristics intrinsic to these feature spaces can easily be exploited to validate decisions made using such a feature space.

Such features can also be the result of the transfer of features from other, related or similar pattern processing problems.

(b) Feature spaces are g by methods such as neural networks, where a structure (or architecture) for the feature space is designed (or chosen from a set of known goods) and then labelled training specimens are used to train the network from scratch or re-train an already existing network in transfer learning. The inherent characteristic of this process is that it requires very large sets of labelled, representative data for the training of the network (a little less so in case of transfer learning). The resulting feature spaces and trained models usually lack the encoding of easily interpretable semantics.

While neural network-based methods have seen a growing popularity in the field of media forensics in the last few years, they are still burdened by the problem that the plausibility of a decision made on the basis of such features is extremely hard to verify. One of the main reasons for this is the fact that the learned features as such hardly ever encode semantics that could be interpreted by a human expert. Instead, with the help of decision validation approaches such as the expert interpretation of heatmaps using methods such as

Layer-wise Relevance Propagation (LRP; [27]), it can be shown that these methods assign meaning to regions in the input (see e.g. [28]).

For this reason, i.e., problems with the interpretability of the feature space and corresponding decisions, many application fields with sensitive tasks are hesitant to rely on learned features. A good example of a very thorough discussion of the pros and cons of hand-crafted features in contrast to those learned using convolutional neural networks can be found in Lin et al.'s work [29]. In this paper, the authors discuss this issue for specific medical data analysis problems, which, similar to forensics, is another very sensitive research field applying pattern recognition. In their work, they highlight and demonstrate with their datasets three main drawbacks of neural network-based feature space learning:

1. In the case of only small amounts of training data being available (which seems to be a problem encountered often in medical data analysis problems, including clinical studies where *"the recruitment of a large number of patients or collection of large number of images is often impeded by patient privacy, limited number of disease cases, restricted resources, funding constraints or number of participating institutions"* [29]), the classification performance of hand-crafted features (which usually show persistent detection performances with small training datasets) outperformed their feature spaces learned by neural networks. This is hardly astonishing since it is well known that CNNs require a large amount of training data for reliable imaging classification. This situation changes with increasing training dataset sizes.

2. Another advantage of hand-crafted features is interpretability. Lin et al. summarize this issue as follows: *"Therefore, interpretability of* [hand-crafted] *features reveal why liver* [magnetic resonance] *images are classified as suboptimal or adequate"* [29], i.e., these features allow for expert reasoning on errors, loss or uncertainty in decision making.

3. Feature selection strategies help learning about significance and contextual relationship for hand-crafted features, while they fail to produce interpretable results for learned features.

For the more traditional feature space designs (i.e., using hand-crafted features), the question of plausibility verification is usually easier to address. A multitude of methods for feature space analysis have been discussed in the past, including feature space-driven plausibility validation as well as model-driven validation.

Initially, there existed two main approaches for feature selection: wrapper methods, in which the features are selected using the classifier, and filter methods, in which the selection of features is independent of the classifier used. Around 2001, both main approaches were joined into a so-called hybrid method (see, e.g., [30,31]), which are usually used nowadays to analyze hand-crafted feature spaces.

2.3. A Data-Centric Examination Approach for Incident Response and Forensic Process Modeling

Forensic process models are an important cornerstone in science and more importantly the practice of forensics. They guide investigations and make them comparable, reproducible as well as certifiable. Usually, the adherence to strict guidelines (i.e., process models) is regulated within any legal system (e.g., in the US by the fourth Daubert criterion (*"the existence and maintenance of standards and controls"* [4])). For mature forensic sciences, such as, for example, dactyloscopy, internationally accepted standards (such as the ACE-V process model for dactyloscopy) have been established over recent decades.

Due to the fact that IT forensics is a rather young discipline in this field (with media forensics being an even younger subdiscipline), it is hardly astonishing that here the forensic process models have not yet achieved the same degree of maturity as in other fields. Nevertheless, they would still be important to achieve universal court acceptability of methods. One well established forensic process model for IT forensics is the one proposed by the German Federal Office for Information Security (BSI). When it was originally published in 2011, its sole focus was on computer and network forensics, but since then it has evolved to also include suite and also some extend the needs of other subdisciplines such as digitized forensics. The latest major revision of this process model, which is used within this paper, can be found in [7] and is called the Data-Centric Examination Approach (DCEA). The core of the DCEA consists of three main aspects: a model of the *phases* of a phase-driven forensic process, a classification scheme for *forensically relevant data types* and *forensic method classes*.

The DCEA phases are briefly summarized in Table 1.

Table 1. Sets of examination steps for digital forensics, as defined in [7] (updated from [32]).

Sets of Examination Steps	Description (According to [7])
Strategic preparation (SP)	Includes measures taken by the operator of an IT system and by the forensic examiners in order to support a forensic investigation prior to an incident
Operational preparation (OP)	Includes measures of preparation for a forensic investigation after the detection of a suspected incident
Data gathering (DG)	Includes measures to acquire and secure digital evidence
Data investigation (DI)	Includes measures to evaluate and extract data for further investigation
Data analysis (DA)	Includes measures for detailed analysis and correlation between digital evidence from various sources
Documentation (DO)	Includes measures for the detailed documentation of the proceedings, also for the transformation into a different form of description for the report of the incident

One important reason for this paper to use the DCEA to model our own work is the separation of preparation steps in an investigation into two distinct phases (the strategic preparation (SP) on one hand an the operational preparation (OP) on the other). In [7], the SP is generally defined as: *"The strategic preparation [...] includes all preparation procedures taken ahead of the actual occurrence of a specific incident"*. Exemplary measures for SP in the context of digital forensics are given by [7] as: *"Documentation and extension of knowledge of IT systems specifics, tool testing for forensic data types and sets of methods determination for error loss and uncertainty estimation, setup of logging capabilities, performance of system landscape analysis, data protection considerations, [...]"*. In contrast, the OP is specified to *"[...] include all preparation procedures taken after of the actual occurrence of a specific incident. Those procedures by definition do not alter any data on the targeted system"*. These preparation phases are then followed by the actual application of forensic procedures, separated in DCEA into the triplet of data gathering (DG), data investigation (DI) and data analysis (DA). The whole process is, in every phase (including SP and OP), supported by accompanying documentation, which is in the last phase (documentation (DO)) used as basis for the generation of the official documents regarding the investigation (e.g. the evidence to be interpreted in expert testimony in a court case).

The second core aspect of DCEA is the classification scheme for forensically relevant data types, as summarized in Table 2. The categories in this scheme are not classes in a mathematical sense, since all other later data types are interpreted out of raw data. More recent publications, such as [33], have shown that this scheme needs to be extended accordingly if new investigation domains are considered.

Table 2. Forensic data types defined in [7] (updated from [34]).

Forensic Data Type	Description (According to [7])
Raw data	A sequence of bits or data streams of system components not (yet) classified
Hardware data	Data not or only in a limited way influenced by the OS and application
Details about data	Meta data describing other data
Configuration data	Modify the behavior of the system and applications
Communication protocol data	Modify the communication behavior of the system
Process data	Data about a running process
Session data	Data collected by a system during a session
User data	Content created, edited or consumed by the user

This original set of data types, which was designed with digital (IT) forensics in mind, needs to be adapted to every investigation domain. In [7,32], such an adaptation for the field of digitized forensics has been discussed for the field of dactyloscopy (forensic fingerprint analysis and comparison). This adaptation is summarized in Table 3 below because it is much closer to the requirements we face within this paper than the original data types summarized in Table 2.

Table 3. Forensic data types defined in [7] for an exemplary selected process in digitized forensics (here, digital dactyloscopy) (updated from [32]).

Forensic Data Type	Description (According to [7])
Raw sensor data (DD1)	Digital input data from the digitalization process (e.g., scans of test samples)
Processed signal data (DD2)	Results of transformations to raw sensor data (e.g., visibility enhanced fingerprint pattern)
Contextual data (DD3)	Contain environmental data (e.g., spatial information, spatial relation between traces, temperature, humidity)
Parameter data (DD4)	Contain settings and other parameters used for acquisition, investigation and analysis
Trace characteristic feature data (DD5)	Describe trace specific investigation results (e.g., level 1/2/3 fingerprint features)
Substrate characteristic feature data (DD6)	Describe trace carrier specific investigation results (e.g., surface type, individual surface characteristics)
Model data (DD7)	Describe trained model data (e.g., surface specific scanner settings, reference data)
Classification result data (DD8)	Describes classification results gained by applying machine learning and comparable approaches
Chain of custody data (DD9)	Describe data used to ensure integrity and authenticity and process accompanying documentation (e.g., cryptographic hash sums, certificates, device identification, time stamps)
Report data (DD10)	Describe data for the process accompanying documentation and for the final report

The third core aspect of DCEA is the definition of forensic method classes as presented in Table 4. For a detailed discussion on these method classes, including considerations on the estimation of availability in certain investigation contexts, practicalities of the forensic process, etc., we refer to [7].

Table 4. Grouping of sets of methods for the forensic process in digital forensics defined in [7] (updated from [32]).

Sets of Methods for the Forensic Process in Digital Forensics	Description (According to [7])
Operating system (OS)	Methods that provide forensically relevant data as well as serving their main purpose of distributing computing resources
File system (FS)	Methods that provide forensically relevant data as well as serving their main purpose of maintaining the file system
IT application (ITA)	Methods provided by IT applications that provide forensically relevant data as well as serving their main purpose
Explicit means of intrusion detection (EMID)	Methods that are executed autonomous on a routine basis and without a suspicion of an incident
Scaling of methods for evidence gathering (SMG)	Methods that are unsuited for routine usage in a production environment (e.g., due to false positives or high computation power requirements)
Data processing and evaluation (DPE)	Dedicated methods of the forensic process that display, process or document information

The DCEA is relevant for the work presented in this paper for two different reasons: On one hand, we will use it in Section 3 to provide a comparative description of the solution concept to address the issue of DeepFake detection in this paper. On the other hand, we will elaborate on the question related to how well this process model fits the needs of media forensics investigations and which changes or extensions would be required in DCEA to provide better support for this very young subdiscipline in IT forensics.

3. Solution Concept for DeepFake Detection with Hand-Crafted Features

The main findings considering the background and state of the art in Section 2 can be summarized as follows: DeepFake detection is a very active research field trying to address a significant recent threat. While many detection approaches have been published in the last few years (some reporting astonishing detection performances), only a small number of publications have been tackling the questions of interpretability and plausibility of results. We attribute this lack of studies mainly to the type of features used in the majority of the research published so far, which rely on neural networks to learn feature spaces used, a method that has inherent difficulties with interpretability (see Section 2.2). Additionally, this question of creating the feature spaces required for a pattern recognition-driven media forensics method such as DeepFake detection, a close integration of forensic procedures and *"the existence and maintenance of standards and controls"* [4] is an open issue. This can contribute to the comparative novelty of many media forensics methods, including DeepFake detection.

To address both of these apparent gaps (interpretability of feature spaces and projection into forensic procedures), our work in this paper focuses on the usage of hand-crafted features for this pattern recognition problem as well as discussions on the applicability of the Data-Centric Examination Approach (DCEA, see Section 2.3) to map out our work. Regarding the pattern recognition aspects, the concept in this paper focuses on four items:

- The design, implementation and empirical evaluation of features for DeepFake detection: Here, two feature spaces hand-crafted especially for DeepFake detection and a hand-crafted feature space derived from a different but similar pattern recognition problem domain (face morph detection) are implemented and evaluated. For the empirical evaluation, pre-existing reference databases containing DeepFake as well as

benign ("original") face video sequences are used together with a pre-existing out of the box classification algorithm implementation. To facilitate the interpretation of results and the comparability with other detector performances reported in the state of the art, different well established metrics are used: detection accuracy, Cohen's kappa as well as (ROC) AUC (Area Under the Curve (of the Receiver Operating Characteristic)).
- The discussion of different information fusion techniques and the empirical comparison with detection performances of individual classifiers: Here, with feature-level fusion and decision-level fusion, two different concepts are applied. For the latter, with the majority voting and weighted linear combination, two popular choices are used and compared with single classifiers in terms of the classification performance achieved.
- The comparison of the detection performance of our hand-crafted features with performances of learned feature spaces from the state of the art in this field: Here, the results obtained by single classifiers as well as fusion approaches are compared in terms of detection accuracy with different approaches from the state of the art, relying on learned features.
- Attempts at validating the detectors' decisions on basis of the features and trained models: Some classifiers, such as the decision tree algorithm used in this paper, train models that can be read, interpreted and compared by humans. Here, we analyze the decision trees trained on different training sets to identify the most relevant features and see how much these trees have in common and where they differ.

In addition to these pattern recognition aspects, we project the different operational aspects in training, validating and applying the DeepFake detectors into the established process model DCEA to show how such media forensics methods would have to be integrated into forensic procedures. In this projection, the first question to be asked concerns where the detector is supposed to be used. There exist two potential operation points in the phases described by the DCEA: either as a method of explicit means of intrusion detection (EMID) as part of incident detection mechanisms, which would place the whole DeepFake detection with the training of the method and its application into the phase of strategic preparation (SP), or in scaling of methods for evidence gathering (SMG), which would place DeepFake detection after an incident is detected or suspected and place the corresponding components in the operational preparation (OP), data gathering (DG), data investigation (DI) and data analysis (DA) phases. These two distinct operation points as a live detector or as means of post-mortem (or a posteriori) analysis in data investigation have, amongst other effects, significant impact on the training scenario that can be assumed: In the case of application as an live detector (EMID), in SP, only pre-trained models can be applied. In the case of a post-mortem (SMG) detector, in the OP the material to be investigated can be analyzed to design targeted training datasets perfectly matching the characteristics encountered. Using those sets (and own DeepFake algorithms to also generate a specimen for this class) optimal models could be trained for each case. In this paper, the conceptual choice made is that of a live detector, reserving considerations on targeted training for future work.

The concept of training brings us to a second issue where the principles of the DCEA can help structuring of the description of media forensics methods such as DeepFake detectors: The accompanying documentation in the DCEA is meant to allow for interpretability and plausibility validation steps while compiling the case documentation in DO. For our work, this implies not only documenting all details of the pattern recognition process at hand but also using these data to reason about the plausibility of decisions (e.g., by comparing the characteristics of training and test sets to determine questions of generalization power).

One important realization when trying to apply the DCEA data types for digital or digitized forensics, as summarized in Tables 2 and 3, is that they do not perfectly match the media forensics task at hand. Using the original model for digital forensics, only four of the data types would be covered (raw data differentiated into different user data media streams (video, audio, network stream) and possibly hardware data (derived from the camera/microphone used) as well as details about data). If the model for digitized dactyloscopy is used, which slightly better matches with the characteristics of our application scenario, then eight of the ten data types would be directly relevant (processed signal data (DD2), contextual data (DD3), parameter data (DD4), trace characteristic feature data (DD5), model data (DD7), classification result data (DD8), chain of custody data (DD9) and report data (DD10)), while one other would very likely also to be of significance (raw sensor data (DD1), which might be used to calibrate specific cameras or camera models, etc.).

It is apparent that an adapted data type model for media forensics would be required to be able to make use of the full potential of the DCEA in this context. Nevertheless, it is outside the scope of this paper to propose such an adapted data type model.

4. Implementation of the Individual Detectors and the Fusion Operators

For our DeepFake detection methods, the input video is evaluated frame-wise with the intention to analyze inter-frame patterns (e.g., the time between two blinks of one eye). In a pre-processing step, the presence of a face in a frame is determined, the face region is segmented and annotated frame-wise with a semantic model localizing 68 facial landmarks. This semantic model [35] is provided by the dlib library [36]. The output of this pre-processing is shown in Figure 1.

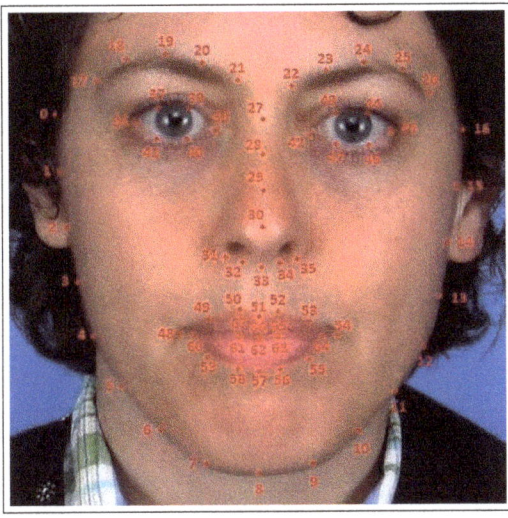

Figure 1. Visual representation of the 68 facial landmark model [35]. Image originates from Utrecht ECVP [37] with application of keypoints generation by dlib [36] followed by cropping.

In case no face can be localized in a frame, this event is logged, if a face is found, and the segmented face pixel matrix and the positions of these 68 facial landmarks are then forwarded to the feature extraction component of each individual detector as well as the concatenation operator for the feature-level fusion. This process is repeated frame-wise until the end of the video is reached, which initializes the detection operations performed. The entire processing sequence is shown in Figure 2. Due to the specific recording conditions of the datasets used in this paper (which all represent a single person in an ideal interview-like recording setting with perfectly illuminated faces and none of the facial key regions, such as eye and mouth, occluded), the pre-processing could be kept that simple. In case more realistic/averse videos have to be analyzed, this pre-processing would necessarily have to be extended.

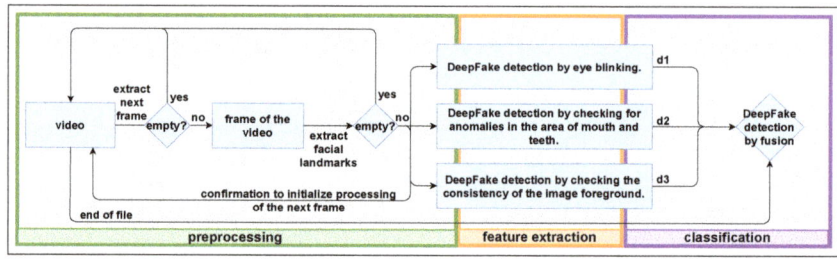

Figure 2. Concept pipeline considered in this paper.

The domain knowledge used here in hand-crafting features for DeepFake detection is based on the fact that DeepFake generators (similar to face morphing algorithms) rely on blending operations in the face region, which is a well established fact in the state-of-the-art research in this field [13]. Blending itself describes the process of a weighted combination of two or more faces to create a new identity [38]. This often goes hand in hand with a loss of local details in the face regions, while the background of a video or image is usually not affected, which is a fact also used in similar media forensics detectors such as, e.g., morphing attack detectors [39].

This knowledge is translated in Section 4.1 into three distinct hand-crafted feature spaces aiming at solving the following pattern recognition tasks to distinguish between DeepFake and genuine videos: (a) anomaly detection for eye blinking (Section 4.1.1), (b) anomaly detection in mouth and teeth region level of detail (Section 4.1.3), and (c) DeepFake detection based on image foreground texture (Section 4.1.3). In terms of the DCEA data type model, these features would make up the Trace characteristic feature data (DD5) from the data model discussed in [7] for digitized forensics. While the broad category actually fits, the extensive discussion on feature space design alternatives for DeepFake detection presented in Section 2.2 indicates that more detailed modeling would be required to sufficiently address this aspect.

To implement the actual classification, we decided not to design or implement our own but instead rely on a proven classification algorithm detection which does facilitate feature space as well as model-driven plausibility considerations. The actual algorithm that we use here is the WEKAs [40] J48 decision tree, which is an open source implementation of Ross Quinlans C4.5 decision tree algorithm [41]. The classifier is used here in its default parameterization, i.e., without parameter optimization being applied.

To further increase the performance and robustness of DeepFake detection, different fusion operators for feature-level fusion and decision-level fusion are implemented, as shown in Section 4.2.

In terms of datasets (i.e., processed signal data (DD2)), the pre-existing, publicly available and widely accepted reference datasets TIMIT-DF [16,42], FaceForensics++ [12,43,44] and Celeb-DF [13] are used in our evaluations. VidTIMIT [42], which was used to create TIMIT-DF [16], is a long-established reference database for various video processing tasks. It represents recording criteria that are ideal for face recognition and similar tasks: uniform lighting, the presence of exactly one person in each video, a frontal position to the camera, an average duration of 3 to 5 s and the speaking of ten different, pre-defined sentences. A total of 430 videos are included in the set, recorded using 43 volunteers. The resulting DeepFake videos were generated for TIMIT-DF by face swapping in two different resolutions with the autoencoder resolutions 64 × 64 and 128 × 128, respectively. Through prior selection, 16 suitable pairs of faces were selected for the generation, resulting in 32 DeepFake entities. This yields a total of 640 DeepFakes, which were taken into account in the TIMIT-DF dataset [16].

The second dataset considered is called DeepFakeDetection (DFD) [44], which originates from the FaceForensics++ [12] dataset. It contains a total of 363 source videos based on 28 actors (*DFD-source*). DeepFake synthesis was performed with an autoencoder resolution of 256 × 256 pixels and a total of 3068 DeepFake videos (*DFD-DF*) were generated. All videos considered were compressed with H.264 at CRF 23. Due to time constraints, only a subset of the DFD dataset, containing 55 DFD-source and 55 DFD-DF videos, were used. Video selection was carried out manually, selecting videos in which only a single person can be found speaking towards the camera. In the DFD dataset, this was carried out by searching for the keyword *talking* in conjunction with *against wall* or *outside*.

The third dataset is Celeb-DF [13], which includes videos (harvested from YouTube) of celebrities being interviewed. These source videos were divided in [13] into the two datasets *Celeb-YouTube* and *Celeb-real*, whereby only *Celeb-real* was considered for the DeepFake synthesis. The synthesis method is more advanced than the one from TIMIT-DF in terms of quality, using an autoencoder resolution of 256 × 256. Due to an average video duration of about 13 to 15 s, only a subset of this dataset is used in our own paper. For our evaluations, 120 source and 120 DeepFake videos were chosen. For simplification, the entire dataset is subsequently also referred to as *Celeb-DF*.

Those three datasets, summarized in Table 5 were used to design different training and testing scenarios to be able to establish facts about the generalization power of the detectors trained, which is an important aspect of the quality assessment for every method. Such evaluations would have to be performed as part of quality assurance in the strategic preparation (SP) phase of each forensic process.

Table 5. Collection of datasets used for this paper.

Dataset	Number of Videos	Reference
VidTIMIT	430 *	[42]
TIMIT-DF	640	[16,42]
DFD-source	55 *	[12,44]
DFD-DF	55 *	[12,44]
Celeb-YouTube	60 *	[13]
Celeb-real	60 *	[13]
Celeb-DF (v2)	120 *	[13]

*: Numbers do not reflect the total but rather the number of videos used in the context of this work.

4.1. Individual Detectors Using Hand-Crafted Features

In general, the 68 facial landmark model [35] used in this paper (see Section 4) can be structured into different facial areas, as shown in Figure 1. Here, the following segmentation alternatives are used to derive the features for our individual detectors: The first set of keypoints, numbers 0 to 26, describes the edges of the face along the chin and eyebrows. These keypoints are used to segment the image foreground, as explained in Section 4.1.3. Keypoints 27 to 35 describe the nose, which is neglected in this work. The eyes are described with the help of keypoints 36 to 47 and form the basis for the detection of blinking behavior considered in Section 4.1.1. The final keypoints, 48 to 67, are used to model the mouth, which is examined in more detail in Section 4.1.2.

In the following subsections, our three distinct detectors relying on different hand-crafted features spaces are described. A summarizing overview over all features extracted is presented in Table A1 at the end of the document in Appendix A.

4.1.1. DeepFake Detection Based on Eye Blinking

The first implemented detector is based on the biometric modality eye and acts on the behavior of eye blinking. Using the 68 facial landmark model [35], each eye is described by six keypoints (keypoints 36 to 41 and 42 to 47, respectively). The process of blinking itself occurs subconsciously about 10 to 15 times per minute. On average one blink takes 0.3 to 0.4 s between closing and reopening the eyes. It should be noted that blinking behavior is also influenced by gender, age, time of day and how tired the person is [24]. In some publications, the minimum duration of human blinking is noted as 0.1 s [45]. To enable the detection of blinking, the eyes are modeled to two possible states—*open* and *closed*. To distinguish between these two states, the degree of aperture for each eye is determined individually by the formula:

$$AspectRatio = \frac{y_{Max} - y_{Min}}{x_{Max} - x_{Min}}$$

The parameters of this bounding box are determined from the six keypoints of the 68 facial landmark model, which describe the respective eye. The main idea of the feature design here is strong likeliness of DeepFake synthesis artifacts leading to lower average AspectRatio values, due to the inherent impact of the blending operation. Considering diversity in eye shapes and the inclusion of emotions, as shown in Figure 3, results on the use of a dynamic threshold (determined empirically on the training data used) were used to distinguish the eye states.

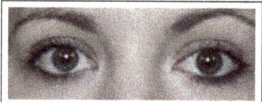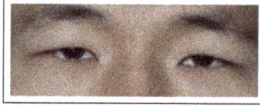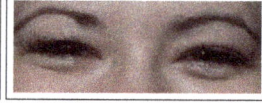

Figure 3. Illustration of the challenges of correctly detecting the aperture of eye opening as widely open (**left**), based on ethnicity (**center**) and inclusion of emotions (**right**). Images originate from LondonDB [46] dataset with application of cropping.

The eye state classification is carried out as binary decision, under the assumption that the aspect ratio always represents exactly one of two values, representing the two eye states (open and closed). The threshold under consideration was implemented as a bimodal distance function. Here, both states are described by a value which corresponds to the most frequent value of the upper and lower thirds of values found in the training data. The *closed* state is described by the most frequent value of the lower third of the value range. Conversely, *open* is described by the most frequent value, which is found in the upper third of the value range. Subsequently, the state for each eye and frame is determined via smaller distance to one of the two values representing the states.

For DeepFake classification based on eye blinking, a feature vector of fixed size of 13 dimensions was designed. Seven out of these 13 features are directly based on the AspectRatio, one is based on the difference between the two eyes and the other six are based on eyelid movements. This eyelid movement is detected as a rate of change on a frame-by-frame basis. Features 8 to 13 are based on the given eye state modeling. One feature introduces a new metric of anomaly, hereinafter referred to as *noise*. This noise is described as a frequent change in eye states below the expected frequency. In detail, this timespan is set to 0.05 s and thus corresponds to half the duration of a blink to detect anomalies only. Another feature describes the percentage of time in the video that the person has their eyes open. The last four features considered refer to the extreme values given the duration in each eye state.

In the summarizing overview of all features in this paper, given in Table A1 at the end of the document in Appendix A, these eye blinking features are the first 13 feature vector elements.

4.1.2. DeepFake Detection Based on Mouth Region

The second implemented detector is based on the biometric modality lip-movement. The focus of this approach is on analyzing the highly detailed teeth region. Under the assumption of blending as part of DeepFake creation, a blurred, less detailed image of the teeth is expected. The 68 facial landmark model is also used to localize the mouth region by using keypoints 48 to 67. These keypoints allow the mouth to be displayed as two separate images, one of which represents the entire mouth described by keypoints 48 to 59. This representation is henceforth called the OuterBoundRegion (OBR). The other keypoints (60 to 67) can be used show another representation considered in this work. This, in the following, is called the InnerBoundRegion (IBR) and represents the mouth area with the exception of the lips. The IBR is used to determine whether the mouth is open, since a closed mouth can be represented by a non-existent IBR. The third and last representation considered to describe the mouth region is the so-called TeethRegion (TR). The TR is created by segmenting the OBR to preserve potential teeth found in the image. An example of the representations can be found in Figure 4. In addition, the degree of aperture of the mouth is determined as an additional parameter based on the OBR. Here, the x and y dimensions are considered separately in order to act independently of the spoken phoneme. The respective values are determined by the bounding box of the OBR using $Aperture_x = x_{Max} - x_{Min}$ and $Aperture_y = y_{Max} - y_{Min}$ for each frame.

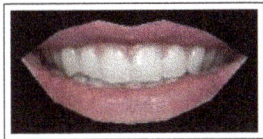
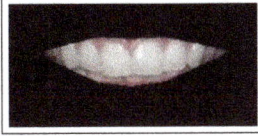
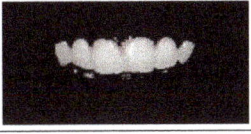

Figure 4. Illustration of the proposed representations for the mouth region OBR (**left**), IBR (**center**) and TR (**right**). Mouth image originates from LondonDB [46] dataset with application of keypoint generation by dlib [36], segmentation and cropping.

Based on these representations, a total of three states are conceived to describe the mouth. These states are: *closed mouth*, *open mouth without detectable teeth* and *open mouth with detectable teeth*. The subdivision of the states is made by two binary decisions. The first decision is based on the IBR and describes whether the mouth is open. The metric used for the decision is the number of pixels found in the IBR. Here, a conscious decision is made against cropping and scaling of the representations in order to prevent distortion of the image when viewing different visemes [47]. As a consequence, the number of pixels of the OBR is taken as a reference. Thus, the decision threshold is determined empirically on training data as: $\frac{PixelCount_{IBR}}{PixelCount_{OBR}} > 0.211137$, for criteria for an open mouth. The second decision, if the mouth is classified as open, is made with the help of the number of pixels in the TR, once again using the OBR as a reference. The threshold considered (after empirical determination from training data) is $\frac{PixelCount_{TR}}{PixelCount_{OBR}} > 0.11455$ for detectable teeth. An example of each state considered can be found in Figure 5.

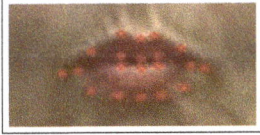
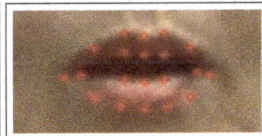
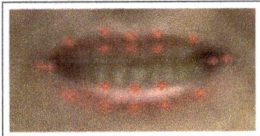

Figure 5. Illustration of the proposed mouth states: closed (**left**), open without detectable teeth (**center**) and open with detectable teeth (**right**). Image originates from VidTIMIT [42] dataset with application of keypoint generation by dlib [36] and cropping.

For the detection of DeepFakes based on mouth region, a feature vector of dimensionality 16 is designed. Six of these features are based on mouth movements. This mouth movement is recognized image-wise as the rate of change, which corresponds to the extreme values for the x- and y-dimensions, respectively. The other 10 features are based on the detected mouth states, leaving out the *closed mouth* state. Thus, the focus of this review is based on the description of the level of detail in the mouth region. For this purpose, FAST and SIFT keypoint detectors as well as Sobel edge detection and the number of closed regions are considered. All of them are implemented by OpenCV [48] and used with default parameters. For the *open without teeth* state, the maximum of each feature, and for state *open with teeth*, the minimum of each feature are determined over all frames. Lastly, the percentage of time in both states is considered. The expectation for this approach is a low level of detail in the *open with teeth* state for DeepFakes or even a wrong assignment to the *open without teeth* state, although teeth are recognisable, due to blending of artifacts.

In the summarizing overview over all features in this paper, given in Table A1 at the end of the document in Appendix A, these mouth movement features are elements 14 to 29 of the feature vector.

4.1.3. DeepFake Detection Based on Image Foreground

The third and last proposed detector is based on domain transfer of hand-crafted features from a similar media forensics task. As shown by Kraetzer et al. [39], such a domain transfer seems plausible to detect blending anomalies in face morph attack detection. This requires an image foreground, which is characterized by a uniform distance towards the camera. Image foreground $Img_{Foreground}$ is designed as an extension of the facial region Img_{Face}, which is determined based on the 68 facial landmark model—more precisely, keypoints 0 to 26. The extension of the facial region is carried out by widening along the vertical axis to include the upper body, which is potentially shown in the image. A third representation, called Img_{ROI}, is conceived as the differential image of the previous two, formally described as $Img_{ROI} = Img_{Foreground} - Img_{Face}$. A visual example of each representation can be found in Figure 6.

Figure 6. Illustration of the proposed representations for anomaly detection based on image foreground Img_{Face} (**right**). Image originates from VidTIMIT [42] dataset with application of keypoint generation by dlib [36] and segmentation.

For the detection of DeepFakes based on the image foreground, a feature vector of fixed size of eight elements was designed. The first subset of features is based on face detection itself, counting the number of frames and sequences where no face can be found. Here, it is assumed that a failure is due to anomalies of the DeepFake synthesis. The second set of features is based on the level of detail in Img_{Face} relative to Img_{ROI}. For each frame and representation, the characteristics of FAST and SIFT keypoints as well as the Sobel edge image are determined. The implementation of these metrics is carried out using the default parameters given by OpenCV [48] and the scoring for each frame corresponds to $\frac{Img_{Face}}{Img_{ROI}}$. Lower values for DeepFakes are expected here. Lastly, the respective extreme values of all frames are extracted as features.

In the summarizing overview of all the features in this paper, given in Table A1 at the end of the document in Appendix A, these features are elements 30 to 37 of the feature vector.

4.2. Fusion Operators

To further increase the performance as well as robustness of the detection, different methods of fusion were implemented for our evaluation. The fusion itself is considered here both at *feature level* and *decision level* [49]. At the feature level, the feature spaces of the individual detectors are concatenated, without additional pre-processing such as weighting or filtering. At the decision level, a total of four operators are applied: The first operator makes an unbiased decision using *simple majority voting* [50]. In contrast, the other three operators implement weighted linear combinations and derive the weights for each individual detector based on its classification performance on the training set. Considering the different training scenarios, there are two sets of weights, each based on the training using dataset TIMIT-DF [16,42], DFD ([12,44]) or Celeb-DF [13]. The explicit weights determined this way can be found in Section 5.2. In summary, the following five fusion operators are considered:

1. Feature-level fusion: concatenation of all features;
2. Decision-level fusion: simple majority voting;
3. Decision-level fusion: weighted, based on accuracy using TIMIT-DF for training;
4. Decision-level fusion: weighted, based on accuracy using DFD for training;
5. Decision-level fusion: weighted, based on accuracy using Celeb-DF for training.

5. Evaluation Results

The evaluation of the created approaches (i.e., our three feature spaces used in training and testing with the used J48 classifier) for DeepFake detection is looking into aspects of *performance*, *generalizability* and *plausibility* of the decisions made (i.e., the kind of information summarized in the DCEA data type model for digitized forensics as Classification result data (DD8)). To address *performance* and *generalizability*, the three datasets used for training and testing are presented as different scenarios (as shown in Table 6). Scenarios S1, S5 and S9, which represent evaluations in a simplistic (i.e., very naive) setup, split one dataset in disjointed training and test subsets. These three scenarios are used to validate the *performance* of detectors under optimal conditions.

In contrast, for evaluations on the *generalizability*, separate training and testing datasets are used in scenarios S2, S3, S4, S6, S7 and S8. Since the individual detectors classify binary according to {DeepFake, OK}, the evaluation is carried out using the metrics' true positive rate (TPR; a true positive (TP) in our case being a DeepFake detected as a *DeepFake*), true negative rate (TNR; a true negative (TN) being an unmodified video classified as *OK*), accuracy and Cohen's kappa (κ).

Table 6. Representation of the considered training and testing scenarios, given by differentiation of the training and testing datasets used.

↓ Training/Testing →	TIMIT-DF	DFD	Celeb-DF
TIMIT-DF	scenario 1 (S1)	scenario 2 (S2)	scenario 3 (S3)
DFD	scenario 4 (S4)	scenario 5 (S5)	scenario 6 (S6)
Celeb-DF	scenario 7 (S7)	scenario 8 (S8)	scenario 9 (S9)

In addition, the hand-crafted features are evaluated in terms of *interpretability* and *relevance*. This is carried out by manually evaluating the trained decision trees in model-driven decision validation, looking at the individual features used to make the decision, the threshold used, and their distance from the root node. To support this analysis, the complete list of all features and experts' assumptions about their content behavior can be found in Table A1 at the end of the document in Appendix A. To extend the initial model-driven decision validation, a comparison of the three decision trees trained on the different datasets, TIMIT-DF, DFD and Celeb-DF, is made.

5.1. Results for Individual Detectors

The detection approach based on *blink behavior* has a generally higher TPR than TNR, regardless of the scenario considered. For S1, it has a TNR of 70.47% and a TPR of 90.94%, resulting in an accuracy of 82.15% and κ of 0.6306. In comparison, S9 shows a TNR of 63.33% and TPR of 75.00%, resulting in an accuracy of 69.17% and κ of 0.3833. It is assumed that the Celeb-DF dataset also represents an improvement of the DeepFake synthesis over the older TIMIT-DF by incorporating more realistic blinking behavior. Considering the generalizability, a drastic decrease in detection rates can be seen in S7, S8 and S9, with a tendency to label all videos as DeepFake. In numbers, S3 indicates a TNR of 33.33% and TPR of 75.00%, with an accuracy of 54.17% and κ of 0.0833. In comparison, S7 shows a TNR of 6.05% and TPR of 99.53%, resulting in an accuracy of 61.96% and κ of 0.0659. By performing feature selection on the 13 features considered, only the eyelid movement-based features ($ID2_{blink}$ to $ID7_{blink}$) seem suitable. In addition, looking at the two eyes separately shows added value. As a result of the model-driven comparison of both trained decision trees, a DeepFake can be described by a higher difference between opening and closing speeds, relative to a non-manipulated video. However, the ranges of the values found as well as the associated thresholds are different for the TIMIT-DF and Celeb-DF datasets, explaining the drastic performance decrease for S3 and S7. Training on the DFD dataset shows only the use of features $ID9_{blink}$ and $ID10_{blink}$ for decision making.

The second detection approach considered, based on the *mouth region*, has the highest individual classification performances. For S1, a TNR of 88.84%, TPR of 97.81%, accuracy of 94.21% and κ of 0.8779 was achieved. In contrast, S9 resulted in a TNR of 91.67%, TPR of 97.50%, accuracy of 94.58% and κ of 0.8917, thus showing better results in direct comparison. Based on this result, it is suspected that newer DeepFake generators, such as the one used to create Celeb-DF, also exhibit said blending artifacts. Once again, there are clear losses in generalizability for S3 and S7: For S3, a TNR of 40.83%, TPR of 72.50%, accuracy of 56.67% and κ of 0.1333 were observed. S7 shows slightly better results with a TNR of 63.02%, TPR of 71.09%, accuracy of 67.85% and κ of 0.3378, which are justified by more general inclusion conditions of the Celeb-DF data and more general classification model. Based on the 16 features considered in feature selection, the set of features describing the grade of detail, excluding the ones using Sobel operator, are used to classify a DeepFake. This clearly shows that blending results in a loss of detail in the facial region, which can be found for both states *open without teeth* and *open with teeth*. Additionally, the assumption that the state *open with teeth* is found less frequently for DeepFakes is correct. However, it should be noted here that the approach only works if an open mouth can be found—for example, if a person is speaking.

The trend of high TPR at the expense of TNR is also emerging for the *detector based on the image foreground*. For S1, a TNR of 52.33%, TPR of 87.50%, accuracy of 73.36% and κ of 0.4182 were observed. For S9, the results look similar, with a TNR of 56.67%, TPR of 85.00%, accuracy of 70.83% and κ of 0.4167. This approach also shows poor generalizability, with a TNR of 43.33%, TPR of 70.00%, accuracy of 56.67% and κ of 0.1333 for S3. Lastly, S7 shows a TNR of 32.79%, TPR of 79.38%, accuracy of 60.83% and κ of 0.1297. For the decision making itself, the features based on the level of detail except for the Sobel operator, as well as the number of frames without a found face, are used. However, the $ID1_{foreground}$ shows a different classification strategy depending on the dataset considered, when at least one frame without a face is found. While for TIMIT-DF and DFD it is interpreted as a DeepFake, for Celeb-DF it serves the classification OK. It is suspected that for TIMIT-DF and DFD, the synthesis may result in artifacts, making the face undetectable. On the other hand, less strict recording conditions in Celeb-DF do not exclude side shots that cannot be detected by the facial landmark model. The use of features $ID3_{foreground}$ to $ID6_{foreground}$ corresponds to the assumptions about blending, whereby lower levels of detail are taken as an indication of a DeepFake.

In conclusion, regardless of the detection approach considered, in all cases, a value for Cohen's kappa > 0 was obtained, implying for all cases a detector performance better than chance agreement (i.e., better than guessing). Nevertheless, it has to be admitted that the differences between the more naive setups (S1 and S9 with $\kappa > 0.35$) and the more realistic setups (S3 and S7 with $\kappa < 0.15$ for all but one case) indicate a very limited generalization power of the trained detectors.

Analyzing the trained models in more detail, it has to be highlighted that the decision tree trained on Celeb-DF is shown to be smaller and more compact. This is justified by a lower number of suitable features for the detection of higher quality DeepFakes. In addition, S3 generalizes better than S7, which goes hand in hand with the preceding statement. Here, Celeb-DF represents a more general dataset, with fewer indicators of DeepFakes, where the trained model applies better to TIMIT-DF than vice versa.

5.2. Results for Fusion Operators

For all fusion operators considered, the metrics TPR, TNR, accuracy and Cohen's kappa are used to allow comparability between fusion and individual detectors. In addition, the *receiver operating characteristic* (ROC) for all scenarios considered, based on the different approaches of fusion at the decision level, are determined. The resulting graphs can be found in Figure 7. Based on the ROC, the *area under curve* (AUC) is determined in order to realize a better comparison with research results in the state of the art in the literature.

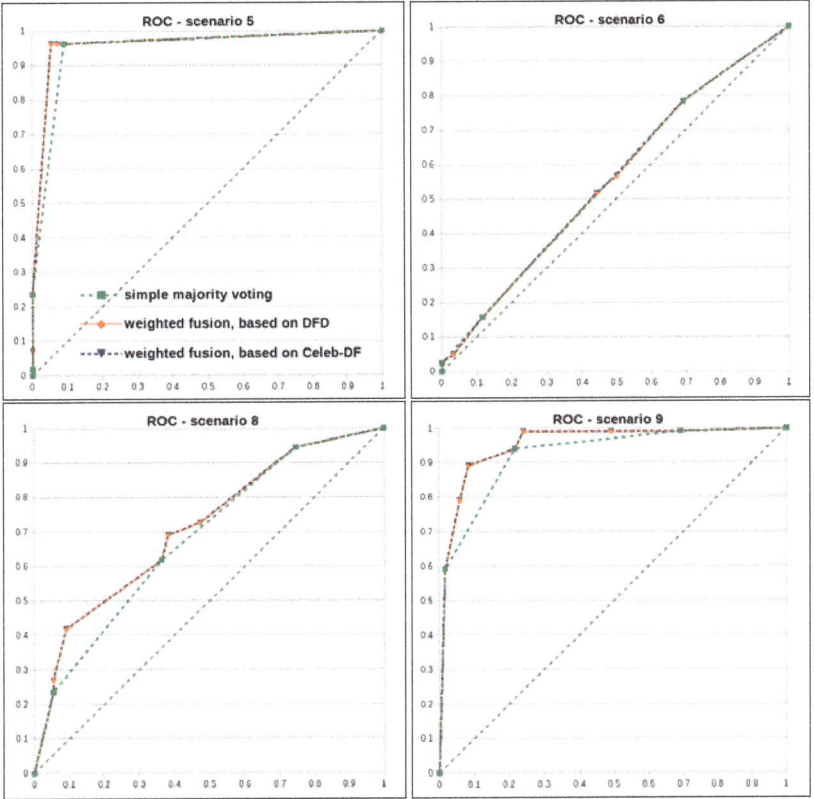

Figure 7. Receiver operation curves (ROCs) for the decision-level fusion methods simple majority voting and weighted fusion, based on DFD and Celeb-DF. Scenarios S5, S6, S8 and S9, which consider both the DFD and Celeb-DF datasets, are presented here. The false alarm rate (false positive rate) is plotted on the x-axis. The sensitivity (true positive rate) is plotted on the y-axis.

The first fusion approach considered is carried out at the *feature level* by concatenating all features without prior adjustments or filtering. A descriptor of this vector can be found in Table A1. For S1, a TNR of 96.74%, TPR of 98.13%, accuracy of 97.57% and κ of 0.9494 and for S9 a TNR of 92.50%, TPR of 95.83%, accuracy of 94.17% and κ of 0.8833 are achieved. This outperforms the best individual detector from Section 5.1. However, this performance is accompanied by even more significant losses for generalizability seen for S3 and S7: A TNR of 70.83%, TPR of 38.33%, accuracy of 54.58% and κ of 0.0917 are achieved for S3 and a TNR of 63.02%, TPR of 64.22%, accuracy of 63.74% and κ of 0.2653 are achieved for S7.

The model-driven feature selection shows that mainly features of the mouth region are used here. From the other two feature spaces, only ID2$_{blink}$ and ID6$_{foreground}$ are considered (the latter is found in the root of the respective decision trees). This again implies that the individual features based on blinking and image foreground appear more unsuitable than the features based on the mouth region. In addition, the differences between the performances on the datasets and corresponding differences in threshold determination described at the end of Section 5.1 are again apparent.

The second approach of the fusion operators takes place at *decision-level* in the form of *simple majority voting*. Here, detection rates of TNR of 79.53%, TPR of 98.75%, accuracy of 91.03% and κ of 0.8075 for S1 and TNR of 78.33%, TPR of 94.17%, accuracy of 86.25% and κ of 0.7250 for S9 are determined. Furthermore, simple majority voting shows the best generalizability of all approaches for S3, with a TNR of 53.33%, TPR of 64.17%, accuracy of 58.75% and κ of 0.1750. A TNR of 26.74%, TPR of 91.41%, accuracy of 65.42% and κ of 0.2015 are determined for S7.

For the considered weighted *decision-level* fusion approaches, the weight combinations $w_{blink} = 0.328967$, $w_{mouth} = 0.377246$ and $w_{foreground} = 0.293787$ based on the use of TIMIT-DF for training, $w_{blink} = 0.257934$, $w_{mouth} = 0.420621$ and $w_{foreground} = 0.321445$ based on the use of DFD as well as $w_{blink} = 0.294849$, $w_{mouth} = 0.403197$ and $w_{foreground} = 0.301954$ based on the use of Celeb-DF for training are derived based on the determined detection performances in training. In addition, the optimal threshold value for the classification is determined manually. For both cases, the ideal threshold can be described as:

$$w_{blink} + w_{foreground} < \text{threshold} < w_{mouth} + w_{blink\,|\,foreground}$$

It is therefore necessary that both the detector based on the mouth region and another one arrive at the classification result *DeepFake* so that the fusion also arrives at that conclusion. In the following, a threshold value of 0.65 is used. Considering the results, these resemble the detector based on the mouth region and show S1 with a TNR of 91.40%, TPR of 97.03%, accuracy of 94.77% and κ of 0.8904, as well as a TNR of 91.67%, TPR of 94.17%, accuracy of 90.42% and κ of 0.8083 for S9. In the context of generalizability, this fusion approach for S3 shows a TNR of 59.17%, TPR of 55.83%, accuracy of 57.50% and κ of 0.1500. Scenario S7 has a TNR of 63.72%, TPR of 70.94%, accuracy of 68.04% and κ of 0.3427 are determined, representing the best results of all considered implementations for S7. A marginal improvement of the weights based on the Celeb-DF can be found in consideration of the ROC AUC, as shown in Figure 7.

In conclusion, previous trends are confirmed showing that S7 has a higher performance than S3 and thus more refined DeepFakes and less limiting factors of acquisition are necessary for a more accurate classifier.

Table 7 summarizes and compares the performances of the individual and fusion detectors. While the best performances are very similar, the fusion-based approaches show a much smaller range in their results, which implies that the strongest of the three single detectors (using the mouth region features) has a dominating impact out of all three fusion operators tested. By switching from single classifiers to fusion approaches, here no gain could be made in terms of increasing generalization power. The reason has to be sought in the different thresholds that were derived for both training sets (see the corresponding discussion at the end Section 5.1).

Table 7. Classification results based on accuracy in percent, followed by Cohen's kappa in parenthesis, for the different methods proposed in this paper. Best result for each combination of training and test data is highlighted bold.

Training Dataset →	TIMIT-DF [16,42]			DFD [12,44]			Celeb-DF [13]		
↓ proposed method test dataset →	TIMIT-DF	DFD	Celeb-DF	TIMIT-DF	DFD	Celeb-DF	TIMIT-DF	DFD	Celeb-DF
DeepFake detection based on eye blinking	82.15% (0.63)	50.00% (0.00)	**57.50%** (0.15)	58.32% (0.15)	59.09% (0.18)	52.92% (0.06)	62.06% (0.07)	58.18% (0.16)	69.17% (0.38)
DeepFake detection based on mouth region	94.21% (0.88)	**76.36%** (0.53)	56.67% (0.13)	64.95% (0.29)	**96.36%** (0.93)	53.75% (0.08)	67.85% (0.34)	69.09% (0.38)	**94.58%** (0.89)
DeepFake detection based on image foreground	73.36% (0.42)	53.64% (0.07)	56.67% (0.13)	58.33% (0.17)	73.64% (0.47)	**54.02%** (0.11)	60.83% (0.13)	54.55% (0.09)	70.83% (0.42)
Feature-level fusion	**97.57%** (0.95)	66.36% (0.33)	54.58% (0.09)	65.05% (0.30)	**97.27%** (0.95)	56.25% (0.13)	63.74% (0.27)	60.00% (0.20)	94.17% (0.88)
Decision-level fusion: simple majority voting	91.03% (0.81)	69.09% (0.38)	**58.75%** (0.18)	59.72% (0.24)	61.18% (0.24)	52.08% (0.04)	65.42% (0.20)	62.73% (0.25)	86.25% (0.73)
Decision-level fusion: weighted (threshold=0.65)	94.77% (0.89)	70.91% (0.42)	57.50% (0.15)	**67.00%** (0.33)	95.45% (0.91)	53.75% (0.08)	**68.04%** (0.34)	65.45% (0.31)	90.42% (0.81)

6. Summary and Conclusions

To allow for a direct comparison of hand-crafted and learned features, Section 6.1 discusses our obtained performances and the generalization behavior observed in direct comparison with a state-of-the-art paper using deep learning under comparable evaluation conditions. Furthermore, we compare our feature concept implementations for *eye blinking*, *mouth region* and *foreground texture analysis* with other hand-crafted and learned features considering the same facial regions.

In Section 6.2, we summarize our conclusions on the comparison of hand-crafted and learned features for DeepFake detection.

6.1. Summary of the Results and Comparison with other Approaches from the State of the Art

In the sections below, we provide a comparison of the results obtained in our experiments with selected work from the state of the art in this fast growing research field. Section 2.1 shows that there exists a wide range of different approaches to distinguish DeepFake from real videos, with a strong tendency towards relying on features learned by using neural networks. In subsection 6.1.1, we compare our results with selected detection performances and generalization behaviors observed in the state of the art. In Section 6.1.2, we compare our concepts for feature designs (looking at hand-crafted features, especially for eye blinking, mouth region and image foreground) with similar approaches by other authors.

6.1.1. Performances and Generalization Power

Table 8 consists of two parts, the upper half represents our results on fusion-based detectors trained on the DFD and Celeb-DF dataset and tested on TIMIT-DF, DFD and Celeb-DF. The values given above are the results taken from Table 7 translated into area under curve (AUC).

The second half are the results resented by Bondi et al. in [9], where the authors performed very similar experiments like us only with a feature space learned with a convolutional neural network (CNN). In their paper, they also used a total of four sets to design training and test setups as we did with our S1 to S9. Two of the sets are Celeb-DF and DFD, which are also used by us. Comparing our work and the AUC results from Bondi et al. on the sets that are used in both papers, we can state that our approach with hand-crafted features performs only slightly worse (maximum AUC = 0.960) than their method relying on learned features (maximum AUC = 0.998). Furthermore, we can point out that their experiments with training and testing on different sets of DeepFakes results in very similar, if not worse problems in terms of generalization power (i.e., AUC drops from values larger than 0.9 to smaller than 0.7).

Table 8. Comparison (in terms of AUC) of different state-of-the-art DeepFake detectors with the presented methods. Further separation based on differentiating training and test dataset.

Training Dataset →		DeepFakeDetection (DFD) [12,44]			Celeb-DF [13]		
↓ fusion method	test dataset →	TIMIT-DF	DFD	Celeb-DF	TIMIT-DF	DFD	Celeb-DF
Ours: simple majority		0.668	0.947	0.556	0.690	0.685	0.925
Ours: weighted based on accuracy using DFD for training		0.685	0.960	0.556	0.682	0.712	0.954
Ours: weighted based on accuracy using Celeb-DF for training		0.685	0.960	0.556	0.698	0.712	0.955
[9]: Baseline		-	0.987	0.754	-	0.708	0.998
[9]: Triplet Training		-	0.882	0.759	-	0.554	0.995
[9]: EfficientNetB4. Binary Cross Entropy with augmentation		-	0.990	0.842	-	0.795	0.998
[9]: EfficientNetB4. Triplet Loss with augmentation		-	0.982	0.809	-	0.604	0.995

6.1.2. Comparison of Feature Concepts

In the case of DeepFake detection, *eye blinking* is a feature which is used for hand-crafted as well as learned feature space approaches. Section 2.1 also recaps the main functionality of DeepVision by Jung et al. [24] where they describe a hand-crafted detection method of the eye blinking behavior of persons in potential DeepFake videos. This approach is similar to our proposed feature detector for the eye blinking behavior. After the face detection happens in both cases, the detection of both eyes frame-by-frame. In our work, for every detected eye the AspectRatio changes are tracked over time. Jung et al. [24] evaluate only the amount of blinking events in a video and also the blink elapsed time as well as the blinking period time, which would correspond to the features $ID8_{blink}$ to $ID13_{blink}$ of our work. Implementation differences are visible in handling the threshold for state (open vs. closed) determination.

Li et al. [15] used a CNN for the segmentation of the eyes after they located the face area in a video. For their inter-frame blinking analysis they use an RNN with LSTM cells. The output of each RNN neuron is connected to a fully connected network, which estimate the output of the LSTM cells if an eye is open or closed.

Unfortunately, a direct comparison with these other publications in terms of performances is not possible here, since entirely different datasets were used.

To our knowledge, there is currently in the literature no similar DeepFake detection approach analyzing only the visible *mouth region* in the video with hand-crafted features. Currently, our approach only analyzes the mouth region in the video stream but does not consider of the spoken speech in the audio stream combined with the lip movements. Extending it with methods for fake voice detection, as in [51], would be an interesting next step for this method.

Considering neural network-based approaches for analysing the mouth region, Agarwal et al. [47] present the hypothesis that DeepFake videos are not able to reproduce spoken phoneme such as "M", "B" or "P", where the mouth is normally completely closed for the pronunciation. Their detection pipeline starts with the extraction of all phoneme locations. The phoneme generation is managed by the transcribing API Speech-To-Text of Google and then manually reduced to six phoneme groups ({OY,UH,UW}, {AA}, {M,B,P}, {L}, {F,V}, {CH,JH,SH}). The video stream is then aligned to these phonemes. After that, they measure the visemes for several evaluation tests in three different ways (manual, profile, CNN) [47]. This approach corresponds to a simplified lip-sync approach for a DeepFake detection, which is realized in [16] (see Section 2.1).

To the best of our knowledge, in the current literature, no hand-crafted approach analyzing only the *image foreground* to detect DeepFakes using image foreground can be found.

Looking for neural network-based approaches implementing such a feature space, the papers of Zhang et al. [52,53] have to be mentioned here. In contrast to our approach, they developed an automatic approach using a CNN. The idea behind their approach is that the image compression ratio of the face and background is different between the DeepFake and original. The reason behind this issue is that the resolution all current DeepFake algorithms is very limited. In addition, the generated fake faces are modified by affine transformations such as scaling, rotating and shearing. Based on this hypothesis, Zhang et al. try to detect the resulting artifacts of these affine transformations. The detection of the compressing distortions happens in their case with the well known error level analysis (ELA) method [54]. It follows that the training of a CNN with these ELA images which extracts the counterfeit features of the ELA images. If the CNN is able to extract these counterfeit features, then the input image of the CNN is a DeepFake. Even though the detection in [52,53] uses only DeepFake images in its tests, it would be possible to upgrade this approach for a DeepFake detection of videos.

6.2. Comparison of Hand-Crafted and Learned Features for DeepFake Detection and Conclusions

Our proposed hand-crafted features as well as hand-crafted features from other sources such as [21–24] have shown that also such expert knowledge-driven approaches are able to distinguish real from DeepFake videos. The detection rates are usually high but in most cases slightly lower than the performance achieved with learned feature spaces. The main advantage that hand-crafted features have over learned features is their interpretability and the consequences this might have for plausibility validation for decisions made.

All current approaches for DeepFake detection in the literature show error rates which are far from perfect. In particular, when DeepFake detectors are evaluated in a realistic setting, i.e., with independent training and test sets, then current hand-crafted as well as learned feature space approaches suffer generalization problems if the characteristics of training and test data are different. This has been demonstrated in our results but also in papers performing similar tests with learned feature spaces, such as Bondi et al. in [9].

Obviously, the problems of individual detectors could be increased if the DeepFake generators would include active mechanisms (counter-forensics) into the generation process to enforce false results with known detectors. Various strategies could and should be applied to address these performance and reliability issues. In this paper, we performed fusion operations to improve detection performances of hand-crafted feature spaces. In their work, Lin et al. [29] propose to extend fusion even further by combining hand-crafted features and CNN features. By doing so, they imply that it would enable us to find a solution that combines the interpretability of hand-crafted features with the potentially higher classification accuracy of learned features. The main benefit of such fusion approaches is that they generate complexer decision constructs that could compensate the problems of individual detectors in the set and might be more resilient against counter-forensics. However, these benefits would be bought at the cost of throughput/runtime behavior and a much more difficult interpretability of decisions.

In most cases, hand-crafted approaches do not need much data for model training, which may also result in lower process costs for memory or calculation time. Additionally, approaches which are including neuronal networks and specially convolutional neuronal networks need much more memory (mostly graphic memory) and CPU or GPU power for the training of the detection networks. In particular, the analyzing process of whole videos and specially a recurrent network structure have a huge impact to the needed memory. These learned approaches are also expensive in purchase costs for (new) hardware architectures. However, when the networks are finally trained, the networks are able to detect DeepFake videos in a very short time, similar to models created/trained with hand-crafted features. Therefore, neither choice would limit the application in incident response procedures (EMID), where fast (close to real time) detector responses would be required for live detectors.

7. Future Work

Our proposed hand-crafted features reach acceptable detection rates for DeepFake videos. However, not every video was classified correctly. Some DeepFake videos were detected as real video and vice versa. It is necessary to detect, analyze and find the reasons for a misclassification to improve our proposed approaches for DeepFake detection. A further improvement can be achieved by investigating different feature selection methods to strengthen the suitability of the proposed features. Possible improvements would also affect approaches from other sources, as it is extremely unlikely that any detection method can correctly classify every video, especially considering potential counter-forensics methods included in the DeepFake generation. Different detection approaches should be analyzed and the benefits of these approaches should be finally combined into a single detection method with a better detection rate and higher robustness against counter-forensics. This also concerns the fusion of hand-crafted and learned features whereat also the integration of hand-crafted methods into learned approaches are meant. In this context, the evaluation of our approaches should expand to other DeepFake databases to create a wider base for training or construct more evaluation scenarios to validate the generalizability of the approach.

A DeepFake video usually consists of two media types: the visible video and the underlying audio. These different media types should be analyzed in combination at the same time. For example, our handcrafted detector for the mouth region should be expanded to include a lip synchronization detector. It is also possible to extract the current emotion of a person in a video. Here, it is imaginable to analyze the emotion of one area (e.g., the left eye) and compare it to another (e.g., the right eye and/or the mouth). Possible aspects to determine emotions are facial expression (e.g., gesture of mouth and eyes), as well as the way of speaking.

In this paper, we started with trying to project the media forensics method of DeepFake detection onto a forensic process model (here, the data-centric examination approach (DCEA) introduced in Section 2.3). In future work, more effort is required to extend this projection, including a required extension of the DCEA data type model to make it suitable for the media data characteristics encountered here. As discussed in Section 3, the most significant change would be the design of a new, domain specific data type model for this media forensics task. While many components (such as the Processed signal data (DD2), Contextual data (DD3), Classification result data (DD8), Chain of custody data (DD9) and Report data (DD10)) could be re-used with only minor modifications, others (esp. Parameter data (DD4), Trace characteristic feature data (DD5) as well as Model data (DD7)) would need a major overhaul. The updated data modeling would also have to reflect that, in this media forensics task, different correlated (media) data streams such as video, audio, network, meta and synchronization data would have to be analyzed in parallel to substantiate the findings.

In addition to the data-driven nature of DCEA, a second reason for its choice as a forensic process model here is that it explicitly requests of modeling the error, (information) loss and (decision) uncertainty of forensic methods [7]. These considerations have to by extended for media forensics from closed set tests (where the ground truth class label in a pattern recognition problem is known) to field applicability (where only the detector response is available and the true class of a specimen encountered will remain unknown).

Author Contributions: Conceptualization, D.S., C.K. and J.D.; data curation, D.S.; funding acquisition, C.K. and J.D.; investigation, D.S. and S.S.; methodology, C.K. and J.D.; project administration,

C.K.; software, D.S.; supervision, C.K. and J.D.; validation, C.K. and S.S.; visualization, D.S.; writing—original draft, D.S.; writing—review and editing, C.K., S.S. and J.D. All authors have read and agreed to the published version of the manuscript.

Funding: The work in this paper is funded in part by the German Federal Ministry of Education and Research (BMBF) under grant number FKZ: 13N15736.

Institutional Review Board Statement: Not applicable.

Informed Consent Statement: Not applicable.

Data Availability Statement: In this work, the following the pre-existing reference databases have been used for our evaluations: TIMIT-DF ([16,42]), Celeb-DF ([13]) and FaceForensics++ ([12,43,44]). They are publicly available at: https://www.idiap.ch/en/dataset/deepfaketimit (last accessed: 30 June 2021); https://github.com/yuezunli/celeb-deepfakeforensics (last accessed: 30 June 2021); https://github.com/ondyari/FaceForensics (last accessed: 30 June 2021).

Conflicts of Interest: The funders had no role in the design of the study; in the collection, analyses, or interpretation of data; in the writing of the manuscript, or in the decision to publish the results.

Appendix A. Collection of Features Proposed in this Paper

Table A1. Collection of all features and their expected behaviors proposed in this paper.

ID	Feature	Description
$ID1_{fusion}$ $ID1_{blink}$	Maximum AspectRatio difference between both eyes.	The expected difference is close to 0, whereby a larger distance is suspected as an indication of a DeepFake. Additionally, the absence of winking is required for this feature.
$ID2_{fusion}$ $ID2_{blink}$	Absolute maximum AspectRatio rate of change for the left eye.	Based on several studies the eyelid movement varies based on different aspects, e.g., age and gender [24,45]. Nevertheless, the maximum speeds, as well as the relation of opening and closing speeds, could be an indication for DeepFake detection. This rate of change for each frame is determined by the difference between previous and following frame. Normalization is carried out by multiplying the rate of change by the frame rate of the video. This results in the AspectRatio change every 3 seconds, described as $\frac{\Delta AspectRatio}{3s}$. The suitability of these features is based on the disregard of blink behavior in DeepFake synthesis.
$ID3_{fusion}$ $ID3_{blink}$	Maximum AspectRatio rate of change for the left eye. Maximum opening speed of the left eye.	
$ID4_{fusion}$ $ID4_{blink}$	Minimum AspectRatio rate of change for the left eye. Maximum closing speed of the left eye.	
$ID5_{fusion}$ $ID5_{blink}$	Absolute maximum AspectRatio rate of change for the right eye.	
$ID6_{fusion}$ $ID6_{blink}$	Maximum AspectRatio rate of change for the right eye. Maximum opening speed of the right eye.	
$ID7_{fusion}$ $ID7_{blink}$	Minimum AspectRatio rate of change for the right eye. Maximum closing speed of the right eye.	
$ID8_{fusion}$ $ID8_{blink}$	Noise count in the eye state signal.	*Noise* is defined as a rapid change of eye state, where one state lasts for a maximum of 0.08 seconds. A higher number of these noises is expected for DeepFakes.
$ID9_{fusion}$ $ID9_{blink}$	Percentage of video time at which the state *open* is classified.	Another feature that can be justified by studies about human blinking behavior [24,45]. Assuming a healthy person in a non-manipulated video, on average a value of about 0.9 should be expected.
$ID10_{fusion}$ $ID10_{blink}$	Minimum duration detected for the eye state *open* in seconds.	Features based on the durations of the states are again based on the knowledge of human blinking behavior. It is assumed that the eyes are open longer than they are closed. As a conclusion $ID12_{blink} < ID10_{blink}$ and $ID13_{blink} < ID11_{blink}$ are expected.
$ID11_{fusion}$ $ID11_{blink}$	Maximum duration detected for the eye state *open* in seconds.	
$ID12_{fusion}$ $ID12_{blink}$	Minimum duration detected for the eye state *closed* in seconds.	
$ID13_{fusion}$ $ID13_{blink}$	Maximum duration detected for the eye state *closed* in seconds.	

Table A1. Cont.

ID	Feature	Description
ID14$_{fusion}$ ID1$_{mouth}$	Absolute maximum rate of change in y-dimension.	This rate of change for each frame is determined by the difference between previous and following frame. Normalization is carried out by multiplying the rate of change by the frame rate of the video. This results in the AspectRatio change every 3 s, described as $\frac{\Delta AspectRatio}{3s}$. For these features, a maximum speed is assumed, which is determined by training the model. Exceeding this maximum speed is assumed to be an indication for the classification DeepFake. Limitation: only works with videos where the person moves their lips during the video, e.g., when speaking.
ID15$_{fusion}$ ID2$_{mouth}$	Maximum rate of change in y-dimension. Lip opening movement in y-dimension.	
ID16$_{fusion}$ ID3$_{mouth}$	Minimum rate of change in y-dimension. Lip closing movement in y-dimension.	
ID17$_{fusion}$ ID4$_{mouth}$	Absolute maximum rate of change in x-dimension.	
ID18$_{fusion}$ ID5$_{mouth}$	Maximum rate of change in x-dimension. Lip opening movement in x-dimension.	
ID19$_{fusion}$ ID6$_{mouth}$	Minimum rate of change in x-dimension. Lip closing movement in x-dimension.	
ID20$_{fusion}$ ID7$_{mouth}$	Percentage of video time at which the state *open without teeth* is classified.	The assumption for feature ID7$_{mouth}$ is that DeepFakes are more often classified in this state compared to non-manipulated videos. The cause is the blending subprocess in the creation of DeepFakes, which leads to a loss of information and detail in the mouth region due to smoothing. As a consequence, DeepFakes are assumed to have both a comparatively low level of detail due to said blending and a comparatively high level of detail due to possible misclassification of *open with teeth* as *open without teeth*. Normalization takes place relative to the number of pixels in the TR (see Figure 4). Default value is set to -1 to be outside the considered range.
ID21$_{fusion}$ ID8$_{mouth}$	Maximum number of regions based on all frames of the video for state *open without teeth*.	
ID22$_{fusion}$ ID9$_{mouth}$	Maximum number of FAST keypoints based on all frames of the video for state *open without teeth*.	
ID23$_{fusion}$ ID10$_{mouth}$	Maximum number of SIFT keypoints based on all frames of the video for state *open without teeth*.	
ID24$_{fusion}$ ID11$_{mouth}$	Maximum number of Sobel edge pixels based on all frames of the video for state *open without teeth*.	
ID25$_{fusion}$ ID12$_{mouth}$	Percentage of video time at which the state *open with teeth* is classified.	The assumption for feature ID12$_{mouth}$ is that non-manipulated videos are more often classified in this state compared to DeepFakes. The cause is the blending subprocess in the creation of DeepFakes, which leads to a loss of information and detail in the mouth region due to smoothing. As a consequence, DeepFakes are assumed to have a comparatively low level of detail due to said blending. Normalization takes place relative to the number of pixels in the TR (see Figure 4). Default value is set to -1 to be outside the considered range.
ID26$_{fusion}$ ID13$_{mouth}$	Minimum number of regions based on all frames of the video for state *open with teeth*.	
ID27$_{fusion}$ ID14$_{mouth}$	Minimum number of FAST keypoints based on all frames of the video for state *open with teeth*.	
ID28$_{fusion}$ ID15$_{mouth}$	Minimum number of SIFT keypoints based on all frames of the video for state *open with teeth*.	
ID29$_{fusion}$ ID16$_{mouth}$	Minimum number of Sobel edge pixels based on all frames of the video for state *open with teeth*.	
ID30$_{fusion}$ ID1$_{foreground}$	Total number of frames in the video without a detectable face.	The consideration of these features is made under the assumption that DeepFake synthesis could result in artifacts, causing the face detection to fail. Normalization is relative to the number of frames of the video to ensure comparability regardless of the video length.
ID31$_{fusion}$ ID2$_{foreground}$	Total number of segments in the video without a detectable face.	

Table A1. *Cont.*

ID	Feature	Description
ID32$_{fusion}$ ID3$_{foreground}$	Maximum number of FAST keypoints based on all frames of the video for the image foreground.	
ID33$_{fusion}$ ID4$_{foreground}$	Minimum number of FAST keypoints based on all frames of the video for the image foreground.	The assumption for this set of features is that an almost constant value can be found throughout the course of the video. As a result, no significant differences between minimum and maximum of each feature are expected. Greater distances are seen as an indication of DeepFakes. Normalization is carried out on the basis of the two representations *Face* and *ROI* (see Figure 6 for reference) based on the level of detail as well as the number of pixels. Formally, this takes the form of $\frac{Feature_{Face}}{Feature_{ROI}}$, where $Feature_{Face\,|\,ROI} = \frac{FeatureCount_{Face\,|\,ROI}}{Pixelcount_{Face\,|\,ROI}}$. In order to prevent division by 0, the default value is set to -1 to be outside the considered range.
ID34$_{fusion}$ ID5$_{foreground}$	Maximum number of SIFT keypoints based on all frames of the video for the image foreground.	
ID35$_{fusion}$ ID6$_{foreground}$	Minimum number of SIFT keypoints based on all frames of the video for the image foreground.	
ID36$_{fusion}$ ID7$_{foreground}$	Maximum number of Sobel edge pixel based on all frames of the video for the image foreground.	
ID37$_{fusion}$ ID8$_{foreground}$	Minimum number of Sobel edge pixel based on all frames of the video for the image foreground.	

References

1. Chesney, R.; Citron, D. Deepfakes and the new disinformation war: The coming age of post-truth geopolitics. *Foreign Aff.* **2019**, *98*, 147.
2. Vaccari, C.; Chadwick, A. Deepfakes and disinformation: Exploring the impact of synthetic political video on deception, uncertainty, and trust in news. *Soc. Media Soc.* **2020**, *6*. [CrossRef]
3. Palmer, G.L. *A Road Map for Digital Forensics Research—Report from the First Digital Forensics Research Workshop (DFRWS) (Technical Report DTR-T001-01 Final)*; Technical Report; Air Force Research Laboratory, Rome Research Site: Utica, NY, USA, 2001.
4. Champod, C.; Vuille, J. Scientific Evidence in Europe—Admissibility, Evaluation and Equality of Arms. *Int. Comment. Evid.* **2011**, *9*. [CrossRef]
5. Krätzer, C. Statistical Pattern Recognition for Audio-forensics—Empirical Investigations on the Application Scenarios Audio Steganalysis and Microphone Forensics. Ph.D. Thesis, Otto-von-Guericke-University, Magdeburg, Germany, 2013.
6. U.S. Congress. *Federal Rules of Evidence*; Amended by the United States Supreme Court in 2021; Supreme Court of the United States: Washington, DC, USA, 2021.
7. Kiltz, S. Data-Centric Examination Approach (DCEA) for a Qualitative Determination of Error, Loss and Uncertainty in Digital and Digitised Forensics. Ph.D. Thesis, Otto-von-Guericke-University, Magdeburg, Germany, 2020.
8. Böhme, R.; Freiling, F.C.; Gloe, T.; Kirchner, M. Multimedia forensics is not computer forensics. In *Computational Forensics*; Geradts, Z.J.M.H., Franke, K.Y., Veenman, C.J., Eds.; Springer: Berlin/Heidelberg, Germany, 2009; pp. 90–103.
9. Bondi, L.; Cannas, E.D.; Bestagini, P.; Tubaro, S. Training Strategies and Data Augmentations in CNN-based DeepFake Video Detection. *arXiv* **2020**, arXiv:2011.07792.
10. FakeApp 2.2.0. Available online: https://www.malavida.com/en/soft/fakeapp (accessed on 30 June 2021).
11. Nguyen, T.T.; Nguyen, C.M.; Nguyen, D.T.; Nguyen, D.T.; Nahavandi, S. Deep Learning for Deepfakes Creation and Detection. *arXiv* **2021**, arXiv:1909.11573.
12. Rössler, A.; Cozzolino, D.; Verdoliva, L.; Riess, C.; Thies, J.; Nießner, M. FaceForensics++: Learning to Detect Manipulated Facial Images. In Proceedings of the IEEE/CVF International Conference on Computer Vision, Seoul, Korea, 27 October–2 November 2019.
13. Li, Y.; Yang, X.; Sun, P.; Qi, H.; Lyu, S. Celeb-DF: A Large-Scale Challenging Dataset for DeepFake Forensics. In Proceedings of the 2020 IEEE/CVF Conference on Computer Vision and Pattern Recognition (CVPR), Virtual, Seattle, WA, USA, 14–19 June 2020; pp. 3204–3213.
14. Sabir, E.; Cheng, J.; Jaiswal, A.; AbdAlmageed, W.; Masi, I.; Natarajan, P. Recurrent Convolutional Strategies for Face Manipulation Detection in Videos. *arXiv* **2019**, arXiv:1905.00582.
15. Li, Y.; Chang, M.; Lyu, S. In Ictu Oculi: Exposing AI Generated Fake Face Videos by Detecting Eye Blinking. *arXiv* **2018**, arXiv:1806.02877.
16. Korshunov, P.; Marcel, S. DeepFakes: A New Threat to Face Recognition? Assessment and Detection. *arXiv* **2018**, arXiv:1812.08685.
17. Tolosana, R.; Vera-Rodríguez, R.; Fiérrez, J.; Morales, A.; Ortega-Garcia, J. DeepFakes and Beyond: A Survey of Face Manipulation and Fake Detection. *arXiv* **2020**, arXiv:2001.00179.

18. Li, Y.; Lyu, S. Exposing DeepFake Videos By Detecting Face Warping Artifacts. *arXiv* **2018**, arXiv:1811.00656.
19. Matern, F.; Riess, C.; Stamminger, M. Exploiting Visual Artifacts to Expose Deepfakes and Face Manipulations. In Proceedings of the 2019 IEEE Winter Applications of Computer Vision Workshops (WACVW), Waikoloa Village, HI, USA, 7–11 January 2019; pp. 83–92. [CrossRef]
20. Yu, P.; Xia, Z.; Fei, J.; Lu, Y. A Survey on Deepfake Video Detection. *IET Biom.* **2021**. [CrossRef]
21. Yang, X.; Li, Y.; Lyu, S. Exposing Deep Fakes Using Inconsistent Head Poses. *arXiv* **2018**, arXiv:1811.00661.
22. McCloskey, S.; Albright, M. Detecting GAN-generated Imagery using Color Cues. *arXiv* **2018**, arXiv:1812.08247.
23. Agarwal, S.; Farid, H.; Gu, Y.; He, M.; Nagano, K.; Li, H. Protecting World Leaders Against Deep Fakes. In Proceedings of the IEEE/CVF Conference on Computer Vision and Pattern Recognition (CVPR) Workshops, Long Beach, CA, USA, 16–20 June 2019.
24. Jung, T.; Kim, S.; Kim, K. DeepVision: Deepfakes Detection Using Human Eye Blinking Pattern. *IEEE Access* **2020**, *8*, 83144–83154. [CrossRef]
25. Ciftci, U.A.; Demir, I. FakeCatcher: Detection of Synthetic Portrait Videos using Biological Signals. *arXiv* **2019**, arXiv:1901.02212.
26. Verdoliva, L. Media Forensics and DeepFakes: An overview. *arXiv* **2020**, arXiv:2001.06564.
27. Bach, S.; Binder, A.; Montavon, G.; Klauschen, F.; Müller, K.R.; Samek, W. On Pixel-Wise Explanations for Non-Linear Classifier Decisions by Layer-Wise Relevance Propagation. *PLoS ONE* **2015**, *10*, e0130140. [CrossRef]
28. Samek, W.; Binder, A.; Montavon, G.; Lapuschkin, S.; Müller, K.R. Evaluating the Visualization of What a Deep Neural Network Has Learned. *IEEE Trans. Neural Netw. Learn. Syst.* **2017**, *28*, 2660–2673. [CrossRef]
29. Lin, W.; Hasenstab, K.; Cunha, G.M.; Schwartzman, A. Comparison of handcrafted features and convolutional neural networks for liver MR image adequacy assessment. *Sci. Rep.* **2020**, *10*, 20336. [CrossRef] [PubMed]
30. Sánchez-Maroño, N.; Alonso-Betanzos, A.; Tombilla-Sanromán, M. Filter Methods for Feature Selection—A Comparative Study. In *Intelligent Data Engineering and Automated Learning—IDEAL 2007*; Yin, H., Tino, P., Corchado, E., Byrne, W., Yao, X., Eds.; Springer: Berlin/Heidelberg, Germany, 2007; pp. 178–187.
31. Law, M.; Figueiredo, M.; Jain, A. Simultaneous feature selection and clustering using mixture models. *IEEE Trans. Pattern Anal. Mach. Intell.* **2004**, *26*, 1154–1166. [CrossRef] [PubMed]
32. Kiltz, S.; Dittmann, J.; Vielhauer, C. Supporting Forensic Design—A Course Profile to Teach Forensics. In Proceedings of the 2015 Ninth International Conference on IT Security Incident Management and IT Forensics, Magdeburg, Germany, 18–20 May 2015; pp. 85–95.
33. Altschaffel, R. Computer Forensics in Cyber-Physical Systems: Applying Existing Forensic Knowledge and Procedures from Classical IT to Automation and Automotive. Ph.D. Thesis, Otto-von-Guericke-University, Magdeburg, Germany, 2020.
34. Kiltz, S.; Hoppe, T.; Dittmann, J. A New Forensic Model and Its Application to the Collection, Extraction and Long Term Storage of Screen Content off a Memory Dump. In Proceedings of the 16th International Conference on Digital Signal Processing, DSP'09, Santorini, Greece, 5–7 July 2009; IEEE Press: New York, NY, USA , 2009; pp. 1135–1140.
35. Sagonas, C.; Antonakos, E.; Tzimiropoulos, G.; Zafeiriou, S.; Pantic, M. 300 Faces In-The-Wild Challenge. *Image Vis. Comput.* **2016**, *47*, 3–18. [CrossRef]
36. King, D.E. Dlib-ml: A Machine Learning Toolkit. *J. Mach. Learn. Res.* **2009**, *10*, 1755–1758.
37. 2d Face Sets—Utrecht ECVP. Available online: http://pics.stir.ac.uk/2D_face_sets.htm (accessed on 19 May 2021).
38. Makrushin., A.; Neubert., T.; Dittmann., J. Automatic generation and detection of visually faultless facial morphs. In Proceedings of the 12th International Joint Conference on Computer Vision, Imaging and Computer Graphics Theory and Applications—Volume 6: VISAPP, (VISIGRAPP 2017), INSTICC, Porto, Portugal, 27 February–1 March 2017; SciTePress: Setubal, Portugal, 2017; pp. 39–50. [CrossRef]
39. Kraetzer, C.; Makrushin, A.; Neubert, T.; Hildebrandt, M.; Dittmann, J. Modeling Attacks on Photo-ID Documents and Applying Media Forensics for the Detection of Facial Morphing. In Proceedings of the 5th ACM Workshop on Information Hiding and Multimedia Security, IH&MMSec '17, Philadelphia, PA, USA, 20–22 June 2017; Association for Computing Machinery: New York, NY, USA, 2017; pp. 21–32. [CrossRef]
40. Hall, M.; Frank, E.; Holmes, G.; Pfahringer, B.; Reutemann, P.; Witten, I.H. The WEKA data mining software: An update. *SIGKDD Explor.* **2009**, *11*, 10–18. [CrossRef]
41. Quinlan, J.R. *C4.5: Programs for Machine Learning*; Morgan Kaufmann Publishers Inc.: San Francisco, CA, USA, 1993.
42. Sanderson, C.; Lovell, B. Multi-Region Probabilistic Histograms for Robust and Scalable Identity Inference. *LNCS* **2009**, *5558*, 199–208. [CrossRef]
43. Rössler, A.; Cozzolino, D.; Verdoliva, L.; Riess, C.; Thies, J.; Nießner, M. FaceForensics: A Large-scale Video Dataset for Forgery Detection in Human Faces. *arXiv* **2018**, arXiv:1803.09179.
44. Dufour, N.; Gully, A.; Karlsson, P.; Vorbyov, A.V.; Leung, T.; Childs, J.; Bregler, C. DeepFakes Detection Dataset by Google & JigSaw. Available online: https://ai.googleblog.com/2019/09/contributing-data-to-deepfake-detection.html (accessed on 19 May 2021).
45. Wubet, W.M. The Deepfake Challenges and Deepfake Video Detection. *Int. J. Innov. Technol. Explor. Eng.* **2020**, *9*. [CrossRef]
46. DeBruine, L.; Jones, B. Face Research Lab London Set. Available online: https://figshare.com/articles/dataset/Face_Research_Lab_London_Set/5047666/1 (accessed on 19 May 2021).
47. Agarwal, S.; Farid, H.; Fried, O.; Agrawala, M. Detecting Deep-Fake Videos From Phoneme-Viseme Mismatches. In Proceedings of the IEEE/CVF Conference on Computer Vision and Pattern Recognition (CVPR) Workshops, Seattle, WA, USA, 14–19 June 2020.

48. Bradski, G. The OpenCV Library. *Dobb J. Softw. Tools*, **2000**, *120*, 122–125.
49. Ross, A.A.; Nandakumar, K.; Jain, A.K., Levels of Fusion in Biometrics. In *Handbook of Multibiometrics*; Springer: Boston, MA, USA, 2006; pp. 59–90. [CrossRef]
50. Kuncheva, L.I. *Combining Pattern Classifiers: Methods and Algorithms*; Wiley: Hoboken, NJ, USA, 2004. [CrossRef]
51. Rana, S.; Ridwanul, M. DeepFake Audio Detection. *GitHub Repos.* Available online: https://github.com/dessa-oss/fake-voice-detection (accessed on 30 May 2021).
52. Zhang, W.; Zhao, C.; Li, Y. A Novel Counterfeit Feature Extraction Technique for Exposing Face-Swap Images Based on Deep Learning and Error Level Analysis. *Entropy* **2020**, *22*, 249. [CrossRef] [PubMed]
53. Zhang, W.; Zhao, C. Exposing Face-Swap Images Based on Deep Learning and ELA Detection. *Proceedings* **2020**, *46*. [CrossRef]
54. Krawetz, N. A Picture's Worth... Digital Image Analysis and Forensics. In Proceedings of the Black Hat Briefings 2007, Las Vegas, NV, USA, 28 July–2 August 2007; pp. 1–31.

Article

Fighting Deepfakes by Detecting GAN DCT Anomalies

Oliver Giudice [1,*], Luca Guarnera [1,2] and Sebastiano Battiato [1,2]

[1] Department of Mathematics and Computer Science, University of Catania, 95125 Catania, Italy; luca.guarnera@unict.it (L.G.); battiato@dmi.unict.it (S.B.)
[2] iCTLab s.r.l., Spinoff of University of Catania, 95125 Catania, Italy
* Correspondence: giudice@dmi.unict.it

Abstract: To properly contrast the Deepfake phenomenon the need to design new Deepfake detection algorithms arises; the misuse of this formidable A.I. technology brings serious consequences in the private life of every involved person. State-of-the-art proliferates with solutions using deep neural networks to detect a fake multimedia content but unfortunately these algorithms appear to be neither generalizable nor explainable. However, traces left by Generative Adversarial Network (GAN) engines during the creation of the Deepfakes can be detected by analyzing ad-hoc frequencies. For this reason, in this paper we propose a new pipeline able to detect the so-called GAN Specific Frequencies (GSF) representing a unique fingerprint of the different generative architectures. By employing Discrete Cosine Transform (DCT), anomalous frequencies were detected. The β statistics inferred by the AC coefficients distribution have been the key to recognize GAN-engine generated data. Robustness tests were also carried out in order to demonstrate the effectiveness of the technique using different attacks on images such as JPEG Compression, mirroring, rotation, scaling, addition of random sized rectangles. Experiments demonstrated that the method is innovative, exceeds the state of the art and also give many insights in terms of explainability.

Keywords: deepfake detection; Generative Adversarial Networks; multimedia forensics; image forensics

1. Introduction

Artificial Intelligence (AI) techniques to generate synthetic media and their circulation on the network led to the birth, in 2017, of the Deepfake phenomenon: altered (or created) multimedia content by ad-hoc machine learning generative models, e.g., the Generative Adversarial Network (GAN) [1]. Images and videos of famous people, available on different media like TV and Web, could appear authentic at first glance, but they may be the result of an AI process which delivers very realistic results. In this context the 96% of these media are porn (deep porn) [2]. If we think that anyone could be the subject of this alteration we can understand how a fast and reliable solution is needed to contrast the Deepfake phenomenon. Most of the techniques already proposed in literature act as a "black box" by tuning ad-hoc deep architectures to distinguish "real" from "fake" images generated by specific GAN machines. It seems not easy to find a robust detection method capable of working in the wild; even current solutions need a considerable amount of computing power. Let's assume that any generative process based on GAN, presents an automated operating principle, resulting from a learning process. In [3], it has been already demonstrated that it is possible to attack and retrieve the signature on the network's deconvolutional layers; in this paper a method to identify any anomaly of the generated "fake" signal, only partially highlighted in some preliminary studies [4,5] is presented. The Fourier domain demonstrated to be prone and robust into understanding semantic at superordinate level [6]. Spatial domain has been recently further investigated by [7–9] to gain robustness and exploit related biasness [10]. To improve the efficiency, the 8 × 8 DCT has been exploited, by employing similar data analysis made in [11,12] and extracting simple statistics of the underlying distribution [13]. The final classification engine based on gradient boosting, properly manages and isolates the GAN Specific Frequencies (*GSF*), of each specific architecture, a sort of fingerprint/pattern, outperforming state-of- the-art methods. In this paper a new "white box" method of Deepfake detection called CTF-DCT (Capture the Fake by DCT Fingerprint Extraction) is proposed, based on the analysis of the Discrete Cosine Transform (DCT) coefficients. Experiments on Deepfake images of human faces proved that a proper signature of the generative process is embedded on the given spatial frequencies. In particular we stress the evidence, that such kind of images, have in common global shape and main structural elements allowing to isolate artefacts that are not only unperceivable but also capable to discriminate between the different GANs. Finally, the robust classifier is able to demonstrate its generalizing ability in the wild even on Deepfakes not generated by GAN-engines demonstrating the ability to catch artefacts related to reenactment forgeries.

The main contributions of this research are the following:

- A new high-performance Deepfake face detection method based on the analysis of the AC coefficients calculated through the Discrete Cosine Transform, which delivered not only great generalization results but also impressive classification results with respect to previous published works. The method does not require computation via GPU and "hours" of training to perform Real Vs Deepfake classifications;
- The detection method is "explainable" (white-box method). Through a simple estimation of the characterizing parameters of the Laplacian distribution, we are able to detect those anomalous frequencies generated by various Deepfake architectures;
- Finally, the detection strategy was attacked to simulated situations in the wild. Mirroring, scaling, rotation, addition of random size rectangles, position and color were applied to the images, also demonstrating the robustness of the proposed method and the ability to perform well even on video dataset never taken into account during training.

The paper is organized as follows: Section 2 presents the state-of-the-art of Deepfake generation and detection methods. The proposed approach is described in Section 3. Section 5, a discussion of GSF is reported. Experimental results, robustness test and comparison with competing methods are reported in Section 6. Section 7 concludes the paper with suggestions for future works.

2. Related Works

AI-synthetic media are generally created by techniques based on GANs, firstly introduced by Goodfellow et al. [1]. GANs train two models simultaneously: a generative model *G*, that captures the data distribution, and a discriminative model *D*, able to estimate the probability that a sample comes from the training data rather than from *G*. The training procedure for *G* is to maximize the probability of *D* making a mistake thus resulting to a min-max two-player game.

An overview on Media forensics with particular focus on Deepfakes has been recently proposed in [14,15].

Five of the most famous and effective architectures in state-of-the-art for Deepfakes facial images synthesis were taken into account (StarGAN [16], StyleGAN [17], Style-GAN2 [18], ATTGAN [19] GDWCT [20]) used in our experiments as detailed below.

2.1. Deepfake Generation Techniques of Faces

StarGAN [16], proposed by Choi et al., is a method capable of performing image-to-image translations on multiple domains (such as change hair color, change gender, etc.) using a single model. Trained on two different types of face datasets—CELEBA [21] containing 40 labels related to facial attributes such as hair color, gender and age, and RaFD dataset [22] containing 8 labels corresponding to different types of facial expressions ("happy", "sad", etc.)—this architecture, given a random label as input (such as hair color, facial expression, etc.), is able to perform an image-to-image translation operation with impressive visual result.

An interesting study was proposed by He et al. [19] with a framework called AttGAN in which an attribute classification constraint is applied in the latent representation to the generated image, in order to guarantee only the correct modifications of the desired attributes.

Another style transfer approach is the work of Cho et al. [20], proposing a group-wise deep whitening-and coloring method (GDWCT) for a better styling capacity. They used CELEBA, Artworks [23], cat2dog [24], Ink pen and watercolor classes from Behance Artistic Media (BAM) [25], and Yosemite datasets [23] as datasets improving not only computational efficiency but also quality of generated images.

Finally, one of the most recent and powerful methods regarding the entire-face synthesis is the Style Generative Adversarial Network architecture or commonly called StyleGAN [17], where, by means of mapping points in latent space to an intermediate latent space, the framework controls the style output at each point of the generation process. Thus, StyleGAN is capable not only of generating impressively photorealistic and high-quality photos of faces, but also offers control parameters in terms of the overall style of the generated image at different levels of detail. While being able to create realistic pseudo-portraits, small details might reveal the fakeness of generated images. To correct those imperfections, Karras et al. made some improvements to the generator (including re-designed normalization, multi-resolution, and regularization methods) proposing StyleGAN2 [18] obtaining extremely realistic faces. Figure 1 shows an example of facial images created by five different generative architectures.

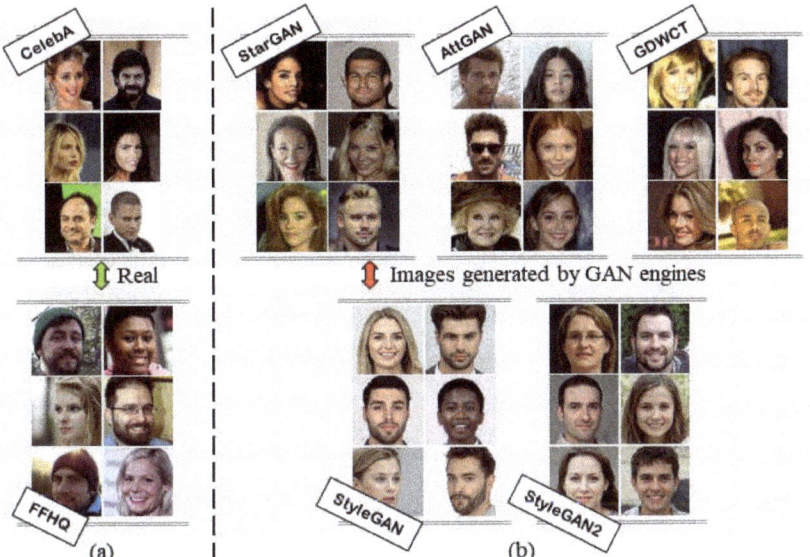

Figure 1. Example of real (**a**) and deepfake datasets (**b**) used in our experiments. The CelebA dataset was used to generate human face images with the StarGAN, AttGAN and GDWCT architectures. The FFHQ dataset was used to generate human face images with the StyleGAN and StyleGAN2 architectures.

2.2. Deepfake Detection Techniques

Almost all currently available strategies and methods for Deepfake detection are focused on anomalies detection trying to find artefact and traces of the underlying generative process. The Deepfake images could contain a pattern pointed out by the analysis of anomalous peaks appearing in the spectrum in the Fourier domain. Zhang et al. [5] analyze the artefacts induced by the up-sampler of GAN pipelines in the frequency domain. The authors proposed to emulate the synthesises of GAN artefacts. Results obtained by the spectrum-based classifier greatly improves the generalization ability, achieving very good performances in terms of binary classification between authentic and fake images. Also Durall et al. [26] presented a method for Deepfakes detection based on the analysis in the frequency domain. The authors combined high-resolution authentic face images from different public datasets (CELEBA-HQ data set [27], Flickr-Faces-HQ data set [17]) with fakes (100K Faces project (https://generated.photos/, accessed on 14 February 2021), this person does not exist (https://thispersondoesnotexist.com/, accessed on 14 February 2021)), creating a new dataset called Faces-HQ. By means of naive classifiers they obtained effective results in terms of overall accuracy of detection.

Wang et al. [28] proposed FakeSpotter, a new method based on monitoring single neuron behaviors to detect faces generate by Deepfake technologies. The authors used in the experiments CELEBA [21] and FFHQ (https://github.com/NVlabs/ffhq-dataset, accessed on 14 February 2021) images (real datasets of faces) and compared Fakespotter with Zhang et al. [5] obtaining an average detection accuracy of more than 90% on the four types of fake faces: Entire Synthesis [18,27], Attribute Editing [16,29], Expression Manipulation [17,29], DeepFake [30,31].

The work proposed by Jain et al. [32] consists of a framework called DAD-HCNN which is able to distinguish unaltered images from those that have been retouched or generated through different GANs by applying a hierarchical approach formed by three distinct levels. The last level is able to identify the specific GAN model (STARGAN [16], SRGAN [33], DCGAN [34], as well as the Context Encoder [35]). Liu et al. [36] proposed an architecture called Gram-Net, where, through the analysis of a global image texture representations, they managed to create a robust fake image detection. The results of the experiments, done both with Deepfake (DCGAN, StarGAN, PGGAN, StyleGAN) and real images (CelebA, CelebA-HQ, FFHQ), demonstrate that this new type of detector delivers effective results.

Recently, a study conducted by Hulzebosch [37] describes that the CNN solutions presented till today for Deepfake detection are limited to lack of robustness, generalization capability and explainability, because they are extremely specific to the context in which they were trained and, being very deep, tend to extract the underlying semantics from images. For this reason, in literature new algorithms capable to find the Deepfake content without the use of deep architectures were proposed. As described by Guarnera et al. [3,38], the current GAN architectures leaves a pattern (through convolution layers) that characterizes that specific neural architecture. In order to capture this forensic trace, the authors used the Expectation-Maximization Algorithm [39] obtaining features able to distinguish real images from Deepfake ones. Without the use of deep neural networks, the authors exceeded state-of-the-art in terms of accuracy in the real Vs Deepfake classification test, using not only Deepfake images generated by common GAN architectures, but also testing images generated by modern FaceApp mobile application.

Differently from the described approaches, in this paper, the possibility to capture the underlying pattern of a possible Deepfake is investigated extracting the discriminative features through the DCT transform.

3. The CTF Approach

In [37], Dutch law enforcement experts were tasked with discriminating between images from the FFHQ dataset and StyleGAN images, which were created starting from FFHQ. The results reached only the 63% of accuracy while state-of the-art methods [28,38] are able to deliver a better outcome. Algorithms were used for extracting black-box features that likely are not related to the visible domain but are somehow encoding anomalies strictly dependent on the way Deepfakes are generated. In particular, a refined evaluation of the StyleGAN images, shows that some abnormal patterns are visible in the most structured part of the images (e.g., skin, hair, etc.). Given such a repetitive pattern, which would have to be subsisting on the middle bands of the Deepfake image frequency spectrum, a frequency-based approach might be able to detect it and describe it. To this end, the CTF approach will take place by leveraging more than a decade of JPEG compression pipeline studies employing DCT block-based processing, which is effectively used for many computer vision and image forensics tasks not strictly related to compression itself [11,12,40–42].

The CTF approach transform and analyse images on the DCT domain in order to detect the most discriminant information related to the pattern shown in Figure 2 which is typical of the employed Generative Model (e.g., GAN).

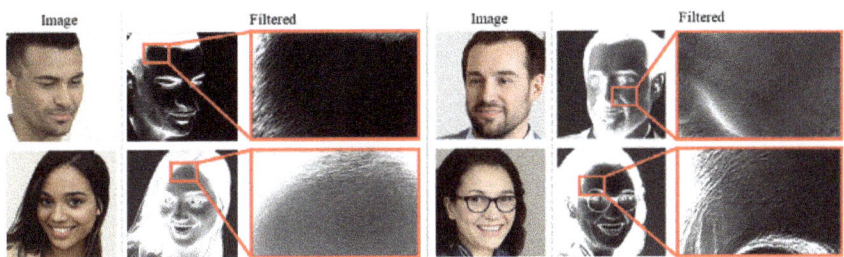

Figure 2. Example of image generated by StyleGAN properly filtered to highlight patterns resulting from the generative process.

Let I be a digital image. Following the JPEG pipeline, I is divided into non-overlapping blocks of size 8×8. The Discrete Cosine Transform (DCT) is then applied to each block, formally:

$$F[u,v] = \frac{1}{4}C(u)C(v)\left[\sum_{x=0}^{7}\sum_{y=0}^{7} I[x,y]\cos(a)\cos(b)\right] \quad (1)$$

where $a = \frac{(2x+1)u\pi}{16}$, $b = \frac{(2y+1)v\pi}{16}$, $C(u) = \begin{cases} \frac{1}{\sqrt{2}} & u=0 \\ 1 & u>0 \end{cases}$ and $C(v) = \begin{cases} \frac{1}{\sqrt{2}} & v=0 \\ 1 & v>0 \end{cases}$.

For each 8×8 block, the 64 elements $F[u,v]$ form the DCT coefficients. They are sorted into a zig-zag order starting from the top-left element to the bottom right (Figure 3). The DCT coefficient at position 0 is called DC and represents the average value of pixels in the block. All others coefficients namely AC, corresponds to specific bands of frequencies.

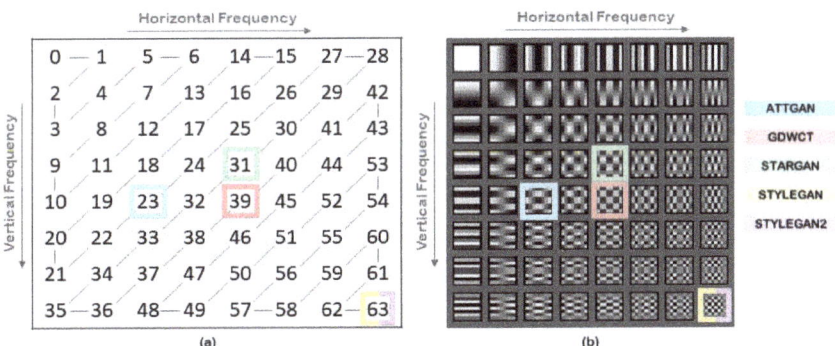

Figure 3. GSF that identify the generative architectures. (**a**) Zig-zag order after DCT transform. (**b**) DCT 8×8 frequencies.

Given all the DCT transformed 8×8 blocks of I, it is possible to assess some statistics for each DCT coefficient. By applying evidence reported in [13], the DC coefficient can be modelled with a Gaussian distribution while the AC coefficients were demonstrated to follow a zero-centred Laplacian distribution described by:

$$P(x) = \frac{1}{2\beta} exp\left(\frac{-|x-\mu|}{\beta}\right) \qquad (2)$$

with $\mu = 0$ and $\beta = \sigma/\sqrt{2}$ is the scale parameter where σ corresponds to the standard deviation of the AC coefficient distributions. The proposed approach is partially inspired by [11] where a GMM (Gaussian Mixture Model) over different β values has been properly adopted for scene classification at superordinate level.

An accurate estimation of such β values for each coefficient and involved GAN-engine, is crucial for the purpose achievement. Figure 4 graphically summarizes the statistical trend of the β-values of each involved datasets showing empirically the intrinsic discriminative power devoted to distinguish almost univocally images generated by GAN-engines or picked-up from real datasets. Let $\vec{\beta}_I = \{\beta_{I_1}, \beta_{I_2}, \ldots, \beta_{I_N}\}$ with $N = 63$ (DC coefficient is excluded) the corresponding feature vector of the image I. We exploited related statistics on different image-datasets DT_g with g = {StarGAN, AttGAN, GDWCT, StyleGAN, StyleGAN2, CelebA, FFHQ}.

For the sake of comparisons in our scenario we evaluated pristine images generated by StarGAN [16], AttGAN [19], GDWCT [20], StyleGAN [17], StyleGAN2 [18], and genuine images extracted by CelebA [21] and FFHQ. E.g., $DT_{StyleGAN}$ represents all the available images generated by StyleGAN engine. For each image-set DT_g let's consider the following representation:

$$\beta_{DT_g} = \begin{pmatrix} \vec{\beta}_1 \\ \vec{\beta}_2 \\ \vdots \\ \vec{\beta}_{|DT_g|} \end{pmatrix} = \begin{pmatrix} \beta_{1,1} & \beta_{1,2} & \cdots & \beta_{1,63} \\ \beta_{2,1} & \beta_{2,2} & \cdots & \beta_{2,63} \\ \vdots & \vdots & \ddots & \vdots \\ \beta_{|DT_g|,1} & \beta_{|DT_g|,2} & \cdots & \beta_{|DT_g|,63} \end{pmatrix} \qquad (3)$$

where $|.|$ is the number of images in DT_g. For sake of simplicity, in the forthcoming notation all dataset DT_g have been selected to have the same size $|DT_g| = K$. Note that β_{DT_g} have been normalised w.r.t. each column. To extract GSF we first computed the distance among the involved AC distributions modelled by β_{DT_g} for each dataset. We computed a χ^2 distance as follows:

$$\chi^2(\beta_{DT_i}, \beta_{DT_j}) = \sum_{r=1}^{K} \frac{(\beta_{DT_i}[r,c] - \beta_{DT_j}[r,c])^2}{\beta_{DT_j}[r,c]} \quad \text{with} \quad c = 1,\ldots,63 \qquad (4)$$

where $i, j \in g, i \neq j$, c is the column which corresponds to the AC coefficient and r are the rows in (3) that represents all $\vec{\beta}_I$ features. The distance $\chi^2(\beta_{DT_i}, \beta_{DT_j})$ is a vector with size of 63. Finally, it is possible to define the GAN Specific Frequency (GSF) as follows:

$$GSF_{DT_i, DT_j} = \underset{c}{\mathrm{argmax}} \sum_{r=1}^{K} \frac{\left(\beta_{DT_i}[r,c] - \beta_{DT_j}[r,c]\right)^2}{\beta_{DT_j}[r,c]} \qquad (5)$$

where, $i, j \in g, i \neq j$. GSF allow to realize a one-to-one evaluation between image sets.

Practically, the most discriminative DCT frequency is selected among two datasets in a greedy fashion and, as proven by experiments, there is no need to add further computational steps (e.g., frequency ranking/sorting, etc.). In Figure 5c, GSF computed for a set of pair of image-sets, are highlighted just to provide a first toy example where 200 images ($K = 200$) for each set have been employed. Specifically AttGAN, StarGAN and GDWCT were compared with the originating real image-set (CelebA) and for the same reason StyleGAN and StyleGAN2 were compared with FFHQ.

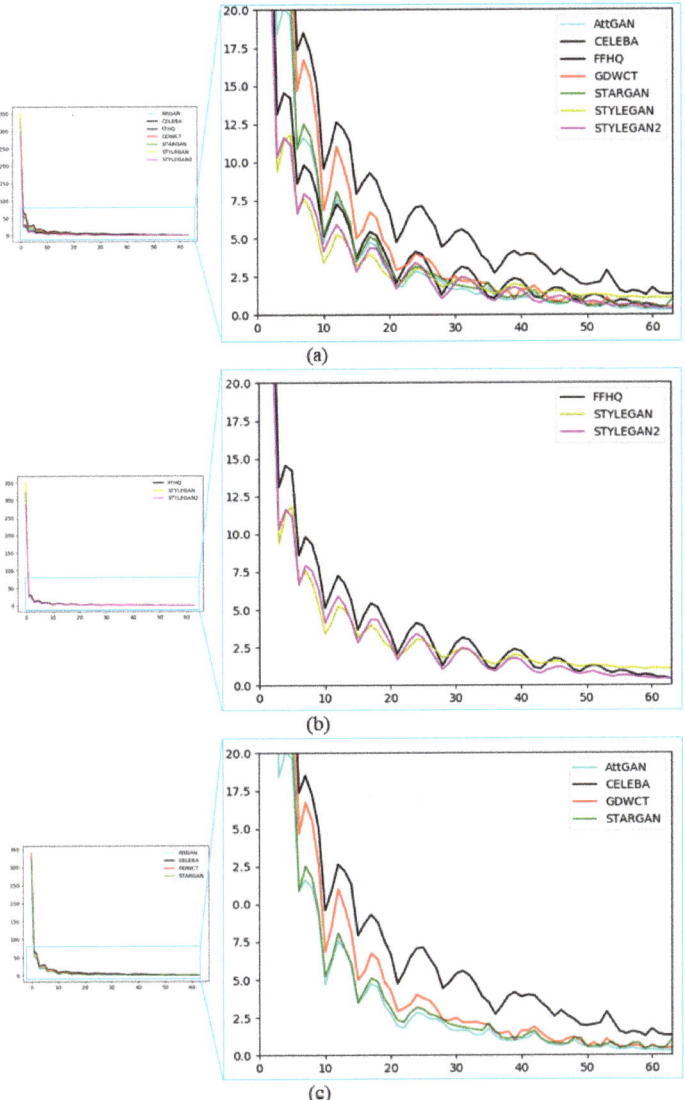

Figure 4. Plot of β statistics of each involved dataset. The average β value for each i-th coefficient is reported. (**a**) Shows the average β trend of all datasets (real and deepfake); (**b**) Shows the average β trend of StyleGAN and StyleGAN2 compared to the real image dataset used for their creation (FFHQ); (**c**) Shows the average β trend of StarGAN, AttGAN and GDWCT compared to the real image dataset used for their creation (CelebA). For each plot, the abscissa axis represents the 64 coefficients of the 8×8 block, while the ordinate axis are the respective inferred β values (in our case the average of the β values computed for all images of the respective datasets).

The β values as described in the experiments, are very discriminative when it comes to deepfake detection. Figure 4 shows the average trend of β of all images from the respective Real and Deepfake datasets. It is interesting to analyze the trend of β of the Deepfake images compared to the statistics of the Real dataset used for the generation task. Figure 4c shows StarGAN, AttGAN, and GDWCT Vs CelebA. All DCT coefficients are sorted in terms of JPEG zigzag order as shown in Figure 3a. It is worth noting that if we consider even only one of the β values we can roughly establish if an image is a deepfake simply by properly thresholding specific frequencies according to the definition of GSF (Equation (5)). Please note that the discriminative power of the GSFs, even if in some sense they bring energies due to the involved DCT frequencies as demonstrated by the detection results, are not fully dependent by the involved resolution.

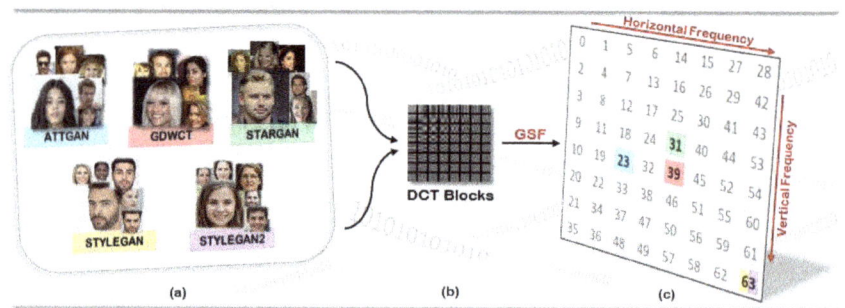

Figure 5. CTF-DCT approach: (**a**) Dataset used for our experiments; (**b**) Discrete Cosine Transform (DCT) of a given image at each 8 × 8 blocks; (**c**) GAN Specific Frequencies (GSF) that identify involved GAN architectures.

4. Datasets Details

Two datasets of real face images were used for the employed experimental phase: CelebA and FFHQ. Different Deepfake images were generated considering StarGAN, GDWCT, AttGAN, StyleGAN and StyleGAN2 architectures. In particular, CelebA images were manipulated using pre-trained models available on Github, taking into account StarGAN, GDWCT and AttGAN. Images of StyleGAN and StyleGAN2 created through FFHQ were downloaded ad detaled in the following:

- CelebA (CelebFaces Attributes Dataset): a large-scale face attributes dataset with more than 200 K celebrity images, containing 40 labels related to facial attributes such as hair color, gender and age. The images in this dataset cover large pose variations and background clutter. The dataset is composed by 178 × 218 JPEG images.
- FFHQ (Flickr-Faces-HQ): is a high-quality image dataset of human faces with variations in terms of age, ethnicity and image background. The images were crawled from Flickr and automatically aligned and cropped using dlib [43]. The dataset is composed by high-quality 1024 × 1024 PNG images.
- StarGAN is able to perform Image-to-image translations on multiple domains using a single model. Using CelebA as real images dataset, every image was manipulated by means of a pre-trained model (https://github.com/yunjey/stargan, accessed on 14 February 2021) obtaining a final resolution equal to 256 × 256.
- GDWCT is able to improve the styling capability. Using CelebA as real images dataset, every image was manipulated by means of a pre-trained model (https://github.com/WonwoongCho/GDWCT, accessed on 14 February 2021) obtaining a final resolution equal to 216 × 216.
- AttGAN is able to transfers facial attributes with constraints. Using CelebA as real images dataset, every image was manipulated by means of a pre-trained model (https://github.com/LynnHo/AttGAN-Tensorflow, accessed on 14 February 2021) obtaining a final resolution equal to 256 × 256.
- StyleGAN is able to transfers semantic content from a source domain to a target domain characterized by a different style. Images have been generated considering FFHQ as dataset in input with 1024 × 1024 resolution (https://drive.google.com/drive/folders/1uka3a1noXHAydRPRbknqwKVGODvnmUBX, accessed on 14 February 2021).
- StyleGAN2 improves STYLEGAN quality with the same task. Images have been generated considering FFHQ as dataset in input with 1024 × 1024 resolution (https:

//drive.google.com/drive/folders/1QHc-yF5C3DChRwSdZKcx1w6K8JvSxQi7, accessed on 14 February 2021).

For all the carried out experiments, 3000 Deepfake images for each GAN architecture and 3000 from CelebA and FFHQ were collected and divided into training and test set as will be reported in experimental dedicated Sections. Figure 1 shows some examples of the employed real and Deepfake images.

5. Discussion on GSF

Although differentiating between a Deepfake and a real image could be easy, given the high accuracy values demonstrated by state-of-the-art methods [44], it becomes difficult when the test is carried out on fake images obtained from a specific set of real images: for instance differentiating between FFHQ images and StyleGAN ones, which are generated from FFHQ images, is more difficult than differentiating StyleGAN vs. CelebA images. As a matter of fact, state-of-the-art methods like Fakespotter [28] employs for training, mixed sets of Deepfake and real images. Results are then unbalanced by the extremely-easy-to-spot-difference like CelebA vs. StyleGAN. This can be demonstrated by means of *GSF* analysis.

Through *GSF* it is possible to perform a one-to-one test between sets of images. This was carried out specifically for the harder case as described before: taking 200 images for each set, *GSF* was calculated for each pair of image sets, whose values obtained are shown in Figure 3b. In particular, AttGAN, StarGAN and GDWCT were compared with the starting real images (CelebA) and for the same reason StyleGAN and StyleGAN2 were compared with FFHQ.

Torralba et al. [45] demonstrated that scenes semantic-visual components are captured precisely with analogous statistics on spectral domain used also to build fast classifiers of scenes [11]. In this sense, the comparison between images that represent close-ups of faces showing the some overall visual structure raising extremely similar statistical characteristics of AC coefficients and their β values. This allows the *GSF* analysis to focus on the unnatural anomalies introduced by the convolutional generative process typical of Deepfakes. To demonstrate the discriminative power of the *GSF* a simple binary classifier (logistic regression) was trained using the β (e.g., that corresponds the set of values of a given column/coefficient in Equation (3)) of the corresponding *GSF* as unique feature.

For all the experiments carried out, the number of collected images has been equally set considering $K = 3000$. In particular the classifier was trained using only the 10% of the entire dataset, while the remaining part was used as test set. For each binary classification test, the simple classification solution obtained the results shown in Figure 6. Results demonstrated that Deepfakes are easily detectable by just looking at the β value of the *GSF* for that specific binary test. This is empirically found to be discriminative (wider range of values) than expected on natural images, given the semantic context of facial images. This finding is what state-of-the-art is exploiting with much more complex and computational intensive solutions. For instance, Fakespotter [28], at a first step compares real against fake images and finds these unnatural frequencies with an ad-hoc trained CNN. As a matter of fact, frequencies found are different for forgeries made with Photoshop which certainly do not bear traces of convolution and for this reason they are easily discriminated from the Deepfake images.

As already stated, the combination of different resolution and frequency bands image-sets is the major problem encountered in the state of the art methods, while the most problematic issue is differentiating the original images from the transformed Deepfake. Let's take into account FFHQ vs. STYLEGAN: a task in which even the human being had difficulties [37]. Applying GSF analysis among all involved proper datasets, we obtain impressive generalization results as reported in Figure 7. Further demonstration of the importance of the *GSF* will be visual. In addition to the anomalies visually identified in Figure 8, in Guarnera et al. [4] the authors already identified some strange components in the Fourier spectrum. Given an image from a specific image-set, after having computed the

GSF (Figure 5), it is possible for sake of explainability, to apply the following amplification process: to multiply in the DCT domain each DCT coefficient different from the *GSF* by a value k_1 (with $0 < k_1 \leq 1$) while the coefficient corresponding to the *GSF* by a value k_2 (with $k_2 > 1$). Figure 8 shows an example of such amplification procedure with $k_1 = 0.1$ and $k_2 = 100$. This operation will create an image where the *GSF* is amplified. Figure 8 shows that the original Fourier Spectrum and the amplified one share the same abnormal frequency appearance. Thus, *GSF* becomes an explanation of those anomalies with a clear boost of forensics analysis.

	StarGAN		AttGAN		GDWCT		StyleGAN		StyleGAN2	
	GSF	Acc(%)	GSF	Acc(%)	GSF	Acc(%)	GSF	Acc(%)	GSF	Acc(%)
CelebA	31	94%	23	89%	39	91%				
FFHQ							63	99%	63	99%

Figure 6. Average Accuracy results (%) obtained for the binary classification task employing only the *GSF*. 700 images were employed for testing, 200 images for training, 5-fold cross validated, classes are balanced.

	StarGAN		AttGAN		GDWCT		StyleGAN		StyleGAN2	
	GSF	Acc(%)	GSF	Acc(%)	GSF	Acc(%)	GSF	Acc(%)	GSF	Acc(%)
CelebA	31	94%	23	89%	39	91%	2	100%	2	100%
FFHQ	63	96%	2	95%	2	94%	63	99%	63	99%
StarGAN			63	100%	63	95%	50	100%	63	100%
AttGAN					7	72%	62	99%	2	95%
GDWCT							2	98%	2	99%
StyleGAN									54	99%

Figure 7. GSF and classification accuracy results (%) obtained for each binary classification task.

It has to be noted that the *GSF* approach described in this section is a great instrument to white-box GAN-generated image processing. A *GSF* is able to identify a set of GAN-generated images. On the other hand, it is not enough to properly being employed in the wild or against fakes not generated by neural approaches. For this reason, in the following section, we "finalize" the approach by presenting a more robust and complete feature vector but, on the other hand, we will lose explainability.

Finalizing the CTF Approach

Given the ability of the *GSF* to make one-to-one comparisons even between image-sets of GANs it is possible to use it to resolve further discrimination issues. Figure 5 shows that the two StyleGANs actually have the same $GSF_{StyleGAN,FFHQ} = GSF_{StyleGAN2,FFHQ} = 63$, while $GSF_{StyleGAN,StyleGAN2} = 54$ was obtained (Figure 7). Also upon this *GSF* it is possible to train a classifier that quickly obtains an accuracy value in the binary test between StyleGAN and StyleGAN2 close to 99%.

The *GSF* analysis can be exploited to give explainability to unusual artifacts and behaviors that appear in the Fourier domain of Deepfakes. Obviously, using only the corresponding β to *GSF* can be reductive for a scenario in the wild and this is the reason why the CTF approach will be completed by means of a robust classifier which will be outlined in the next section. Instead of using only the corresponding β to the *GSF*, it will employ a feature vector with all 63 β, consequently used as input to a Gradient Boosting classifier [46] and tested in a noisy context that includes a number of plausible attacks on the images under analysis. Gradient Boosting was selected as the best classifier for data and the following hyper-parameters were selected by means of a 10% of the dataset employed as validation set. We selected the following hyper parameters: *number-of-estimators* = 100, *learning-rate* = 0.6, $max_{depth} = 2$.

The robust classifier thus created, fairly identify the most probable GAN from which the image has been generated, providing hints for "visual explainability". By considering the growing availability of Deepfakes to attack people reputation such aspects become fundamental to assess and validate forensics evidence. All the employed data and code will be publicly available after the review process at a public link.

 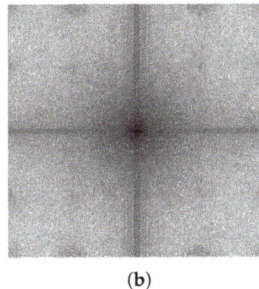 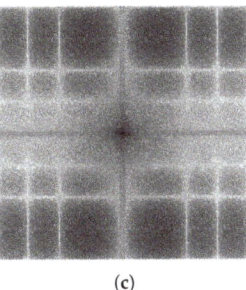

(a) (b) (c)

Figure 8. Abnormal frequencies inspection. (**a**) Image example from the StarGAN dataset; (**b**) Fourier Spectra of the input image (**a**); (**c**) Abnormal frequency shown by means of *GSF* amplification.

6. Experimental Results

In this section experimental results are presented. Primarily, to finalize the CTF approach, a robust classifier was trained and tested by means of several attacks on images and consequently tested in a different scenario, namely the FaceForensics++ dataset of Deepfake videos [30]. The above-mentioned deepfake dataset is used only during the testing phase to classify real Vs deepfake. 3000 real and fake images were collected to train the "robust classifier" for the validation, employing only the 10% of the entire dataset while the remaining part was used as test set. Multiple attack types augmented the dataset; Figure 9 provides examples of images after each attack. Cross-validation was carried out.

6.1. Testing with Noise

All the images collected in the corresponding *DT* have been put through different kinds of attacks as addition of a random size rectangle, position and color, Gaussian blur, rotation and mirroring, scaling and various JPEG Quality Factor compression (QF), in order to demonstrate the robustness of the CTF approach.

As shown in Table 1 this type of attacks do not destroy the *GSF* obtaining high accuracy values.

Gaussian Blur applied with different kernel sizes (3×3, 9×9, 15×15) could destroy different main frequencies in the images. This filtering preserves low frequencies by almost totally deleting the high frequencies, as the kernel size increases. It is possible to see in Table 1, that the accuracy decreases at increasing of the kernel size. This phenomenon, is particularly visible for images generated by AttGAN, GDWCT and StarGAN which have the lowest resolution.

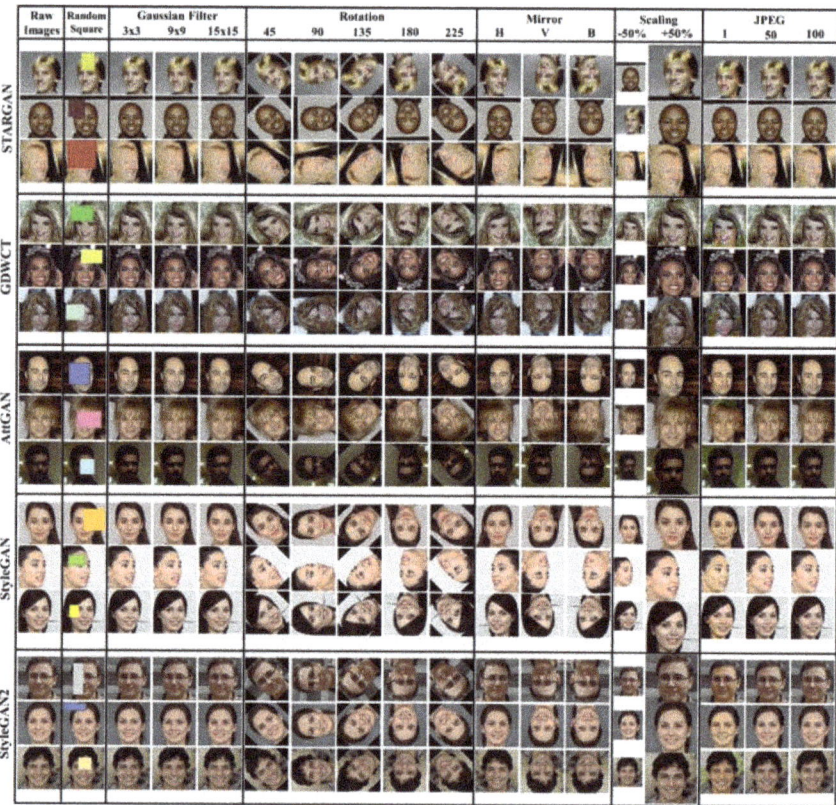

Figure 9. Examples of ATTGAN, GDWCT, STARGAN, STYLEGAN, STYLEGAN2 images in which we applied different attacks: Random Square, Gaussian Blur, Rotation, Mirror, Scaling and JPEG Compression. They were also applied in the real dataset (CelebA and FFHQ).

Several degrees of rotation (45, 90, 135, 180, 255) were considered since they can modify the frequency components of the images. Rotations with angles of 90, 180, and 270 do not alter the frequencies because the [x,y] pixels are simply moved to the new [x',y'] coordinates without performing any interpolation function, obtaining high values of detection accuracy. On the other hand, when considering different degrees of rotation, it is necessary to interpolate the neighboring pixels to get the missing ones. In this latter case, new information is added to the image that can affect the frequency information. In fact, considering rotations of 45, 135, 225 degree, the classification accuracy values decrease; except for the two StyleGANs for the same reason described for the Gaussian filter (i.e., high resolution).

The mirror attack reflects the image pixels along one axis (horizontal, vertical and both). This does not alter image frequencies, obtaining extremely high accuracy detection values.

The resizing attacks equal to −50% of resolution causes a loss of information, hence, already small images tend to totally lose high-frequency components presenting a behavior similar to low-pass filtering; in this case accuracy values are inclined to be low. Vice versa, a resizing of +50% doesn't destroy the main frequencies obtaining a high classification accuracy values.

Table 1. Percentage of Precision, Recall, F1-score and accuracy obtained in the robustness test. "Raw Images" shows the results without the attack process. For the "Real" column the CelebA and FFHQ datasets were considered. Different attacks were carried out in the datasets: Random square; Gaussian filter with different kernel size (3 × 3, 9 × 9, 15 × 15); Rotations with *degree* = {45, 90, 135, 180, 225}; Mirror with Horizontal (H), Vertical (V) and Both (B) ways; Scaling (+50%, −50%); JPEG Compression with different Quality Factor (QF = {1, 50, 100}).

		Real			AttGAN			GDWCT			StarGAN			StyleGAN			StyleGAN2			Overall
		Prec	Rec	F1	Prec	Rec	F1	Prec	Rec	F1	Prec	Rec	F1	Prec	Rec	F1	Prec	Rec	F1	Accuracy
Raw Images		99	97	98	99	100	99	98	98	98	99	100	100	99	98	99	98	100	99	99
Random Square		98	94	96	90	96	93	92	89	91	100	98	99	98	99	98	99	99	99	96
Gaussian Filter	3 × 3	98	95	96	83	88	86	89	92	91	92	86	89	97	98	98	99	99	99	93
	9 × 9	98	99	98	62	59	60	70	79	74	59	53	56	99	98	99	98	99	98	81
	15 × 15	100	97	98	58	64	61	72	64	68	55	53	54	98	99	98	95	100	97	80
Rotation	45°	97	93	95	85	82	83	92	98	95	84	84	84	97	99	98	99	98	98	92
	90°	98	99	98	95	99	97	98	93	95	100	99	99	99	98	98	99	99	99	98
	135°	95	96	96	85	83	84	97	94	96	83	86	85	96	95	96	96	97	97	92
	180°	98	94	96	95	100	97	97	95	96	99	100	99	98	99	99	100	99	99	98
	225°	96	95	95	88	85	87	96	96	96	86	89	88	96	97	97	97	97	97	93
Mirror	H	99	96	98	99	100	99	98	99	98	99	100	99	99	99	99	100	100	100	99
	V	99	96	98	99	100	99	97	99	98	99	100	100	99	99	99	100	100	100	99
	B	99	94	97	98	100	99	97	99	98	99	100	100	99	99	99	100	100	100	99
Scaling	+50%	99	98	99	94	95	95	95	93	94	98	99	99	99	99	99	99	100	99	97
	−50%	74	95	84	77	66	71	74	72	73	81	77	79	82	85	84	90	81	85	80
JPEG	1	78	69	73	63	65	64	59	67	63	59	57	58	78	83	80	84	80	82	70
	50	93	95	94	98	99	98	87	80	83	84	89	86	88	88	88	90	89	89	90
	100	99	99	99	100	99	99	98	98	98	99	100	99	99	99	99	99	99	99	99

Finally, different JPEG compression quality factors were applied ($QF = 1, 50, 100$). As expected in Table 1, a compression with $QF = 100$ does not affect the results. The overall accuracy begins to be affected as the QF decreases, among other things, destroying the DCT coefficients. However, at $QF = 50$ the mid-level frequencies are still preserved and the results maintain a high level of accuracy. This is extremely important given that this level of QF is employed by the most common social platforms such as Whatsapp or Facebook, thus demonstrating that the CTF approach is extremely efficient in real-world scenarios.

6.2. Comparison and Generalization Tests

The CTF approach is extremely simple, fast, and demonstrates a high level of accuracy even in real-world scenarios. In order to better understand the effectiveness of the technique, a comparison with state-of-the-art methods was performed and reported in this section. The trained robust classifier was compared to the most recent work in the literature and in particular Zhang et al. [5] (AutoGAN), Wang et al. [28] (FakeSpotter) and Guarnera et al. [38] (Expectation-Maximization) were considered for the use of a few GAN architectures in common with the analysis performed in this paper: StyleGAN, StyleGAN2, StarGAN. Table 2 shows that the CTF approach achieves the best results with an unbeatable accuracy of 99.9%.

Table 2. Comparison with state-of-the-art methods [5,28,38]. Classification of Real images (CelebA and FFHQ) vs. Deepfake images. Accuracy values (%) of each classification task are reported.

	StarGAN	StyleGAN	StyleGAN2
AutoGAN [5]	65.6	79.5	72.5
FakeSpotter [28]	88	99.1	91.9
EM [38]	90.55	99.48	99.64
CTF (our)	99.9	100	100

Another comparison was made on the detection of StyleGAN and StarGAN with respect to [38,44]. The obtained results are shown in the Table 3 in which the average classification values of each classification task are reported.

A specific discussion is needed for testing the FaceForensics++ dataset [30] which is a challenging dataset of fake videos of people speaking and acting in several contexts. The fake videos were created by means of four different techniques (Face2Face [47] among them) on videos taken from YouTube. By means of OpenCV's face detectors, cropped images of faces were taken from fake videos of FF++ (with samples from all four categories, at different compression levels) and a dataset of 3000 images with different resolutions ($min_{resolution} = 162 \times 162$ px, $max_{resolution} = 895 \times 895$ px). The CTF approach was employed to construct the β feature vector computed on the DCT coefficients and the robust classifier (trained in the Section 6.1), was used for binary classification in order to perform this "in the wild" test. We emphasize that the latter datasets were only used in the testing phase with the robust classifier. Since the classifier detected FaceForensics++ images as well as StyleGAN images, we also tried to calculate the *GSF* by comparing FaceForensics++ images with FFHQ obtaining a value of 61 which is extremely close to the *GSF* of StyleGANs. This leads to the explanation that the *GSF*s are also dependent not only on the generative process but also to the reenactment phase done on images. The reenactment is done analytically in Face2Face and trained in StyleGANs as a part of the model (similarly to Face2face but as a cost function).

The results obtained on FaceForensics++ are reported in Table 3 showing how the CTF approach is an extremely simple and fast method capable of beating the state-of-the-art even on datasets on which it has not been trained and being able to catch not only convolutional artefacts but also those created by reenactment phase which is an important part for the most advanced Deepfake techniques.

Table 3. Comparison with state-of-the-art methods [38,44]. Classification of Real images (CelebA and FFHQ) vs. Deepfake images. The CTF approach was tested and compared also considering the dataset of Deepfake video's FaceForensics++ (FF++). Average Precision values (%) of each classification task are reported.

	StyleGAN	StarGAN	FF++
Wang [44]	96.3	100	98.2
EM [38]	99	93	98.8
CTF (our)	99.9	99.9	99.9

7. Conclusions

In this paper, the CTF approach was presented as a detection method for Deepfake images. The approach is extremely fast, explainable, and does not need intense computational power for training. By exploiting and analyzing the overall statistics of the DCT coefficients it is possible to discriminate among all known GAN's by means of the GAN Specific Frequency band (GSF). The GSF has many interesting properties demonstrated through empirical and visual analysis; among others it is possible to give some explainability to the underlying generation process, especially for forensics purposes. In order to achieve higher accuracy values, all frequency bands must be taken into account and the CTF approach is finalized by means of a G-boost classifier which demonstrated to be robust to attacks and able to generalize even in a dataset of Deepfake videos (FaceForensics++) not used during training. Further investigation could be carried out on GSF frequencies in order to detect not only GAN artefacts but also information coming from the reenactment phase. Finally, the CTF approach could give useful suggestions for the GSF analysis (explainability, etc.) in new scenarios with more challenging modalities (attribute manipulation, expression swap, etc.) and media (audio,video).

Author Contributions: Conceptualization, O.G. and L.G.; Data curation, O.G. and L.G.; Formal analysis, O.G. and L.G.; Investigation, O.G. and L.G.; Methodology, O.G. and L.G.; Resources, O.G. and L.G.; Software, L.G.; Supervision, S.B.; Validation, L.G. and S.B.; Writing—original draft, O.G. and L.G.; Writing—review and editing, O.G., L.G. and S.B. All authors have read and agreed to the published version of the manuscript.

Funding: This research received no external funding.

Institutional Review Board Statement: Not applicable.

Informed Consent Statement: Not applicable.

Data Availability Statement: https://iplab.dmi.unict.it/mfs/Deepfakes/PaperGANDCT-2021/, accessed on 14 February 2021.

Conflicts of Interest: The authors declare no conflict of interest.

References

1. Goodfellow, I.; Pouget-Abadie, J.; Mirza, M.; Xu, B.; Warde-Farley, D.; Ozair, S.; Courville, A.; Bengio, Y. Generative adversarial nets. In Proceedings of the Advances in Neural Information Processing Systems, Montreal, QC, Canada, 8–13 December 2014; pp. 2672–2680.
2. Vaccari, C.; Chadwick, A. Deepfakes and disinformation: Exploring the impact of synthetic political video on deception, uncertainty, and trust in news. *Soc. Media+ Soc.* **2020**, *6*, 2056305120903408. [CrossRef]
3. Guarnera, L.; Giudice, O.; Battiato, S. DeepFake Detection by Analyzing Convolutional Traces. In Proceedings of the IEEE/CVF Conference on Computer Vision and Pattern Recognition Workshops, Seattle, WA, USA, 14–19 June 2020; pp. 666–667.
4. Guarnera, L.; Giudice, O.; Nastasi, C.; Battiato, S. Preliminary Forensics Analysis of DeepFake Images. In Proceedings of the 2020 AEIT International Annual Conference (AEIT), Catania, Italy, 23–25 September 2020; pp. 1–6. [CrossRef]
5. Zhang, X.; Karaman, S.; Chang, S.F. Detecting and simulating artifacts in gan fake images. In Proceedings of the 2019 IEEE International Workshop on Information Forensics and Security (WIFS), Delft, The Netherlands, 9–12 December 2019; pp. 1–6.
6. Oliva, A.; Torralba, A. Modeling the shape of the scene: A holistic representation of the spatial envelope. *Int. J. Comput. Vis.* **2001**, *42*, 145–175. [CrossRef]

7. Xu, K.; Qin, M.; Sun, F.; Wang, Y.; Chen, Y.K.; Ren, F. Learning in the frequency domain. In Proceedings of the IEEE/CVF Conference on Computer Vision and Pattern Recognition, Seattle, WA, USA, 14–19 June 2020; pp. 1740–1749.
8. Xu, Z.Q.J.; Zhang, Y.; Xiao, Y. Training behavior of deep neural network in frequency domain. In *International Conference on Neural Information Processing*; Springer: Berlin/Heidelberg, Germany, 2019; pp. 264–274.
9. Yin, D.; Gontijo Lopes, R.; Shlens, J.; Cubuk, E.D.; Gilmer, J. A Fourier Perspective on Model Robustness in Computer Vision. In Proceedings of the Advances in Neural Information Processing Systems, Vancouver, BC, Canada, 8–14 December 2019; Volume 32, pp. 13276–13286.
10. Rahaman, N.; Baratin, A.; Arpit, D.; Draxler, F.; Lin, M.; Hamprecht, F.; Bengio, Y.; Courville, A. On the spectral bias of neural networks. In Proceedings of the International Conference on Machine Learning, Long Beach, CA, USA, 9–15 June 2019; pp. 5301–5310.
11. Farinella, G.M.; Ravì, D.; Tomaselli, V.; Guarnera, M.; Battiato, S. Representing scenes for real-time context classification on mobile devices. *Pattern Recognit.* **2015**, *48*, 1086–1100. [CrossRef]
12. Ravì, D.; Bober, M.; Farinella, G.M.; Guarnera, M.; Battiato, S. Semantic segmentation of images exploiting DCT based features and random forest. *Pattern Recognit.* **2016**, *52*, 260–273. [CrossRef]
13. Lam, E.Y.; Goodman, J.W. A mathematical analysis of the DCT coefficient distributions for images. *IEEE Trans. Image Process.* **2000**, *9*, 1661–1666. [CrossRef] [PubMed]
14. Tolosana, R.; Vera-Rodriguez, R.; Fierrez, J.; Morales, A.; Ortega-Garcia, J. Deepfakes and beyond: A survey of face manipulation and fake detection. *arXiv* **2020**, arXiv:2001.00179.
15. Verdoliva, L. Media Forensics and DeepFakes: An overview. *IEEE J. Sel. Top. Signal Process.* **2020**, *14*, 910–932. [CrossRef]
16. Choi, Y.; Choi, M.; Kim, M.; Ha, J.W.; Kim, S.; Choo, J. Stargan: Unified generative adversarial networks for multi-domain image-to-image translation. In Proceedings of the IEEE Conference on Computer Vision and Pattern Recognition, Salt Lake City, UT, USA, 18–22 June 2018; pp. 8789–8797.
17. Karras, T.; Laine, S.; Aila, T. A style-based generator architecture for generative adversarial networks. In Proceedings of the IEEE Conference on Computer Vision and Pattern Recognition, Long Beach, CA, USA, 16–20 June 2019; pp. 4401–4410.
18. Karras, T.; Laine, S.; Aittala, M.; Hellsten, J.; Lehtinen, J.; Aila, T. Analyzing and improving the image quality of stylegan. In Proceedings of the IEEE/CVF Conference on Computer Vision and Pattern Recognition, Seattle, WA, USA, 14–19 June 2020; pp. 8110–8119.
19. He, Z.; Zuo, W.; Kan, M.; Shan, S.; Chen, X. Attgan: Facial attribute editing by only changing what you want. *IEEE Trans. Image Process.* **2019**, *28*, 5464–5478. [CrossRef] [PubMed]
20. Cho, W.; Choi, S.; Park, D.K.; Shin, I.; Choo, J. Image-to-image translation via group-wise deep whitening-and-coloring transformation. In Proceedings of the IEEE Conference on Computer Vision and Pattern Recognition, Long Beach, CA, USA, 16–20 June 2019; pp. 10639–10647.
21. Liu, Z.; Luo, P.; Wang, X.; Tang, X. Deep learning face attributes in the wild. In Proceedings of the IEEE International Conference on Computer Vision, Santiago, Chile, 7–13 December 2015; pp. 3730–3738.
22. Langner, O.; Dotsch, R.; Bijlstra, G.; Wigboldus, D.H.; Hawk, S.T.; Van Knippenberg, A. Presentation and validation of the Radboud Faces Database. *Cogn. Emot.* **2010**, *24*, 1377–1388. [CrossRef]
23. Zhu, J.Y.; Park, T.; Isola, P.; Efros, A.A. Unpaired image-to-image translation using cycle-consistent adversarial networks. In Proceedings of the IEEE International Conference on Computer Vision, Venice, Italy, 22–29 October 2017; pp. 2223–2232.
24. Lee, H.Y.; Tseng, H.Y.; Huang, J.B.; Singh, M.; Yang, M.H. Diverse image-to-image translation via disentangled representations. In Proceedings of the European Conference on Computer Vision (ECCV), Munich, Germany, 8–14 September 2018; pp. 35–51.
25. Wilber, M.J.; Fang, C.; Jin, H.; Hertzmann, A.; Collomosse, J.; Belongie, S. Bam! the behance artistic media dataset for recognition beyond photography. In Proceedings of the IEEE International Conference on Computer Vision, Venice, Italy, 22–29 October 2017; pp. 1202–1211.
26. Durall, R.; Keuper, M.; Pfreundt, F.J.; Keuper, J. Unmasking deepfakes with simple features. *arXiv* **2019**, arXiv:1911.00686.
27. Karras, T.; Aila, T.; Laine, S.; Lehtinen, J. Progressive growing of gans for improved quality, stability, and variation. *arXiv* **2017**, arXiv:1710.10196.
28. Wang, R.; Ma, L.; Juefei-Xu, F.; Xie, X.; Wang, J.; Liu, Y. Fakespotter: A simple baseline for spotting AI-synthesized fake faces. *arXiv* **2019**, arXiv:1909.06122.
29. Liu, M.; Ding, Y.; Xia, M.; Liu, X.; Ding, E.; Zuo, W.; Wen, S. Stgan: A unified selective transfer network for arbitrary image attribute editing. In Proceedings of the IEEE Conference on Computer Vision and Pattern Recognition, Long Beach, CA, USA, 16–20 June 2019; pp. 3673–3682.
30. Rossler, A.; Cozzolino, D.; Verdoliva, L.; Riess, C.; Thies, J.; Nießner, M. Faceforensics++: Learning to detect manipulated facial images. In Proceedings of the IEEE International Conference on Computer Vision, Seoul, Korea, 27–28 October 2019; pp. 1–11.
31. Li, Y.; Yang, X.; Sun, P.; Qi, H.; Lyu, S. Celeb-DF: A Large-scale Challenging Dataset for DeepFake Forensics. In Proceedings of the IEEE/CVF Conference on Computer Vision and Pattern Recognition, Seattle, WA, USA, 14–19 June 2020; pp. 3207–3216.
32. Jain, A.; Majumdar, P.; Singh, R.; Vatsa, M. Detecting GANs and Retouching based Digital Alterations via DAD-HCNN. In Proceedings of the IEEE/CVF Conference on Computer Vision and Pattern Recognition Workshops, Seattle, WA, USA, 14–19 June 2020; pp. 672–673.

33. Ledig, C.; Theis, L.; Huszár, F.; Caballero, J.; Cunningham, A.; Acosta, A.; Aitken, A.; Tejani, A.; Totz, J.; Wang, Z.; et al. Photo-realistic single image super-resolution using a generative adversarial network. In Proceedings of the IEEE Conference on Computer Vision and Pattern Recognition, Honolulu, HI, USA, 21–26 July 2017; pp. 4681–4690.
34. Radford, A.; Metz, L.; Chintala, S. Unsupervised representation learning with deep convolutional generative adversarial networks. *arXiv* **2015**, arXiv:1511.06434.
35. Pathak, D.; Krahenbuhl, P.; Donahue, J.; Darrell, T.; Efros, A.A. Context encoders: Feature learning by inpainting. In Proceedings of the IEEE Conference on Computer Vision and Pattern Recognition, Las Vegas, NV, USA, 27–30 June 2016; pp. 2536–2544.
36. Liu, Z.; Qi, X.; Torr, P.H. Global texture enhancement for fake face detection in the wild. In Proceedings of the IEEE/CVF Conference on Computer Vision and Pattern Recognition, Seattle, WA, USA, 14–19 June 2020; pp. 8060–8069.
37. Hulzebosch, N.; Ibrahimi, S.; Worring, M. Detecting CNN-Generated Facial Images in Real-World Scenarios. In Proceedings of the IEEE/CVF Conference on Computer Vision and Pattern Recognition Workshops, Seattle, WA, USA, 14–19 June 2020; pp. 642–643.
38. Guarnera, L.; Giudice, O.; Battiato, S. Fighting Deepfake by Exposing the Convolutional Traces on Images. *IEEE Access* **2020**, *8*, 165085–165098. [CrossRef]
39. Moon, T.K. The expectation-maximization algorithm. *IEEE Signal Process. Mag.* **1996**, *13*, 47–60. [CrossRef]
40. Jing, X.Y.; Zhang, D. A face and palmprint recognition approach based on discriminant DCT feature extraction. *IEEE Trans. Syst. Man Cybern. Part B (Cybern.)* **2004**, *34*, 2405–2415. [CrossRef] [PubMed]
41. Thai, T.H.; Retraint, F.; Cogranne, R. Camera model identification based on DCT coefficient statistics. *Digit. Signal Process.* **2015**, *40*, 88–100. [CrossRef]
42. Lam, E.Y. Analysis of the DCT coefficient distributions for document coding. *IEEE Signal Process. Lett.* **2004**, *11*, 97–100. [CrossRef]
43. King, D.E. Dlib-ml: A Machine Learning Toolkit. *J. Mach. Learn. Res.* **2009**, *10*, 1755–1758.
44. Wang, S.Y.; Wang, O.; Zhang, R.; Owens, A.; Efros, A.A. CNN-generated images are surprisingly easy to spot... for now. In Proceedings of the IEEE Conference on Computer Vision and Pattern Recognition, Seattle, WA, USA, 14–19 June 2020; Volume 7.
45. Zhou, B.; Zhao, H.; Puig, X.; Fidler, S.; Barriuso, A.; Torralba, A. Scene parsing through ade20k dataset. In Proceedings of the IEEE Conference on Computer Vision and Pattern Recognition, Honolulu, HI, USA, 21–26 July 2017; pp. 633–641.
46. Bishop, C.M. *Pattern Recognition and Machine Learning*; Springer: Berlin/Heidelberg, Germany, 2006.
47. Thies, J.; Zollhofer, M.; Stamminger, M.; Theobalt, C.; Nießner, M. Face2face: Real-time face capture and reenactment of rgb videos. In Proceedings of the IEEE Conference on Computer Vision and Pattern Recognition, Las Vegas, NV, USA, 27–30 June 2016; pp. 2387–2395.

Article

Detection of Manipulated Face Videos over Social Networks: A Large-Scale Study

Federico Marcon, Cecilia Pasquini * and Giulia Boato

Department of Information Engineering and Computer Science, Via Sommarive 9, 38123 Trento, Italy; federico.marcon@alumni.unitn.it (F.M.); giulia.boato@unitn.it (G.B.)
* Correspondence: cecilia.pasquini@unitn.it

Abstract: The detection of manipulated videos represents a highly relevant problem in multimedia forensics, which has been widely investigated in the last years. However, a common trait of published studies is the fact that the forensic analysis is typically applied on data prior to their potential dissemination over the web. This work addresses the challenging scenario where manipulated videos are first shared through social media platforms and then are subject to the forensic analysis. In this context, a large scale performance evaluation has been carried out involving general purpose deep networks and state-of-the-art manipulated data, and studying different effects. Results confirm that a performance drop is observed in every case when unseen shared data are tested by networks trained on non-shared data; however, fine-tuning operations can mitigate this problem. Also, we show that the output of differently trained networks can carry useful forensic information for the identification of the specific technique used for visual manipulation, both for shared and non-shared data.

Keywords: deepfakes; video forensics; facial manipulations; social networks; deep learning

Citation: Marcon, F.; Pasquini, C.; Boato, G. Detection of Manipulated Face Videos over Social Networks: A Large-Scale Study. *J. Imaging* **2021**, *7*, 193. https://doi.org/10.3390/jimaging7100193

Academic Editors: Irene Amerini and Siwei Lyu

Received: 2 August 2021
Accepted: 17 September 2021
Published: 28 September 2021

Publisher's Note: MDPI stays neutral with regard to jurisdictional claims in published maps and institutional affiliations.

Copyright: © 2021 by the authors. Licensee MDPI, Basel, Switzerland. This article is an open access article distributed under the terms and conditions of the Creative Commons Attribution (CC BY) license (https://creativecommons.org/licenses/by/4.0/).

1. Introduction

Latest advancements in artificial photo-realistic generation enabled new outstanding possibilities for media data manipulations. So-called *deepfakes*, i.e., credible digital media depicting untruthful content, can be obtained either through the manipulation of pristine material or generated from scratch thanks to automated algorithms based on Artificial Intelligence (AI). The web abounds with tutorials and applications for the creation of simple deepfakes products that can easily run on a commercial smartphone or PCs (such as FakeApp, Impressions, Reface App, MyVoiceyourface, Snapchat Cameos, FaceSwap), and more sophisticated creation techniques are developed at a fast pace.

These technologies poses significant threats to the reliability of visual information, and can represent harmful tools to undermine the digital identity and reputation of individuals. The many cases of abuses reported in the last months involving public figures in politics and cconomics, confirm these concerns, and we can only expect this phenomenon to increase in the upcoming years. As a response, the detection of the employment of new efficient techniques for synthetic media generation has drawn many research efforts in the last years [1]. An ever increasing number of tools and approaches have been proposed in the last years, together with the development of benchmark datasets (e.g., FaceForensics++ [2]) and world-wide open challenges (e.g., Facebook Deepfake Detection Challenge).

While earlier approaches were focused on the detection of imperfections, artifacts, distortions in the outcomes, the recent success of deep learning for visual analysis brought researchers to employ also purely data-driven detection methodologies. Indeed, general purpose neural networks have shown encouraging results in detecting video frames that have been manipulated [2,3].

While several methodologies and datasets have been published during the last years, one rather unexplored aspect is the generalization capability of those deep descriptors in situations where data are shared through social platforms [3,4]. This is a known and ever emerging problem in multimedia forensics [5], given the pervasive role of popular social media platforms in the dissemination and exchange of visual content on a daily basis.

In this regard, this work presents the results of an extensive detection analysis which goes beyond controlled laboratory conditions, typically adopted in previous works [1], and deals with a scenario where data are not only analyzed as direct outputs of manipulation algorithms but also after upload/download operations through a popular sharing service. As it has been observed in previous studies [6,7], the uploading/downloading steps involved in the sharing process typically operate heavily on the data under investigation, for instance through resizing and recompression to save memory and bandwidth. Thus, while non-shared data better exhibit the inter-pixel statistics at the center of feature-based extraction and analysis, such sharing operations impacts pixel distribution and potentially compromise the detection capabilities of forensics detectors.

While the addressed scenario is of high practical relevance due to the massive daily use of social media platforms for content dissemination, extensive experimental studies in this context are hindered by the high workload required in the data collection phase. In fact, the upload/download operations through different platforms can rarely be automated efficiently and are typically performed in a semi-manual fashion.

We can then summarize the contributions of this work as follows:

- we created an enlarged data collection of shared manipulated videos that is available to the scientific community (Data can be downloaded at: https://tinyurl.com/puusfcke, accessed on 17 September 2021);
- we provide empirical evidences of generalization and transfer learning capabilities of CNN-based detectors;
- we devise and evaluate a simple ensemble strategy to trace the specific manipulation algorithm of data that are detected as fake.

The remainder of the paper is structured as follows: in Section 2, we provide an overview of previous works addressing the discrimination between synthetic and real faces, focusing in particular on manipulated video sequences. In Section 3, we presents our experimental design and setting with the involved deep architectures, data and sharing platforms. In Section 4, we describe the results emerging from our experimental campaign on pre-social and post-social videos, also with respect to the ability of identifying the manipulation technique and performing a video-based decision. Finally, in Section 5 we draw some conclusive remarks.

2. Related Work

In this section, we recall the main approaches employed in the literature for the detection of manipulated facial data. Due to the abundance of techniques proposed in the recent years, we outline here a general categorization and group the different approaches according to their main rationale, while referring the interested reader to [1] for a detailed review.

2.1. Methods Based on Physical Inconsistencies

The first generation of deepfakes contents used to exhibit visible visual inconsistencies in generating human faces and expressions. For this reason, the research was initially directed at detecting, for instance, miss-matching eye blinking [8], as the manipulation algorithms, being trained on images showing people with open eye, were unable to realistically reproduce this phenomena. However, creation technologies have been constantly improving and reducing those artefacts, as it is shown in [9].

The work proposed in [10] exploits the limitations of AI in producing faces at fixed size, and adapted through affine transformation to different target poses, by training a CNN on "good" and "bad" fake examples to recover the warping artifacts.

Similarly, the strategy proposed in [11] is focused on alignment errors of synthesized faces in non-frontal head poses or critical situations such as rapid changes in illumination or distance from camera. Moreover, detection approaches operate on the basis of color disparities [12] since fake media, being usually generated using only on RGB images, exhibit substantial differences in other color spaces with respect to real contents that, through acquisition process, are subjected to specific relation in their color components.

2.2. Methods Based on Handcrafted Descriptors

Earlier studies perform classification between real and manipulated content focusing on statistical features related to specific traces of real data during acquisition process [13], such as color filter array interpolation [14] and lens chromatic aberration [15].

A detection based on handcrafted feature starting from noise residual [16] from videos in FaceForensics++ are used to train a SVM classifier with good performance, but only without compression present. The process of residual-based forgery detection is also implemented through CNN architecture in [17]. In this context, other approaches include the analysis of the spatio-temporal texture [18–20] and of distributions of coefficients in wavelet domain [21,22]. Moreover, differently from common approaches where the analysis is usually performed in the image domain, [23] examined GAN-generated images in the frequency domain demonstrating how artifacts can be recovered with this representation.

2.3. Methods Based on Biological Signals Extraction

Along with the idea to develop fake detection on the natural characteristics or behaviors of human beings, several works have been presented [24]. DeepRhythm [25] classifies real or computer generated faces exploiting heart rate (HR) manifestations in the periodic color skin variations caused by the flowing of blood. FakeCatcher [26] has been designed building on photoplethysmography, the optical technique used to detect volume variation of blood flowing, thanks to its robustness against dynamic changing of the scene. The aim of DeepPhyON [27] is to adapt the features learned for HR estimation with DeepPhys [28], a model designed to isolate the information of color changes caused by fluctuations of oxygen level in blood from the one related to other factor like illumination and noise conditions.

In this context, another promising stream of research analyzes the facial spatio-temporal dynamics by tracking face landmarks over time and building soft biometrics models of individuals [29,30].

2.4. Methods Based on Deep Descriptors

In light of the success of deep learning in many close fields, researchers have extensively applied Convolutional Neural Networks (CNN) as manipulation detectors [31], due to their ability to automatically learn the more relevant descriptors.

In [32], a CNN-based analysis is performed for the distinction between real and computer-generated images by combining the contribution of small patches under the same image. Inspired by the Inception architecture [33], mesoscopic features are employed in [34]. In general, the work in [2] shows that deeper general-purpose networks like Xception largely outperform shallow ones such as [32,34,35], as well as re-adapted feature-based methods originating from steganalysis [16]. One of the most recent studies [36] addresses the problem of identifying and locating fake faces when more than one are present in the same scene. After creating a new large scale dataset, the authors implemented the detection based on CNNs to obtain an algorithm that could be more robust when varying the number of targets in a video and that could automatically learn where the manipulation occured.

The majority of proposed studies are based on benchmark datasets, but rarely consider the scenario where data undergo further post-processing after the manipulation process. In particular, the impact of sharing operations on social networks, routinely performed to acquired data, is largely unexplored and, to the best of our knowledge, the only contribution in this regard can be found in [4]. However, such work operates on data where the upload/download operation is only simulated through hard-coded compression and no actual sharing through existing and active platforms is performed.

3. Experimental Design and Settings

We now outline the design of our empirical analysis and describe the experimental settings considered. The overall framework is depicted in Figure 1, where the *pre-social* and *post-social* scenario are represented.

In the first case, data are analyzed as direct outputs of the manipulation operations, followed only by a high-quality compression. In the second case, data are uploaded and downloaded through social networks.

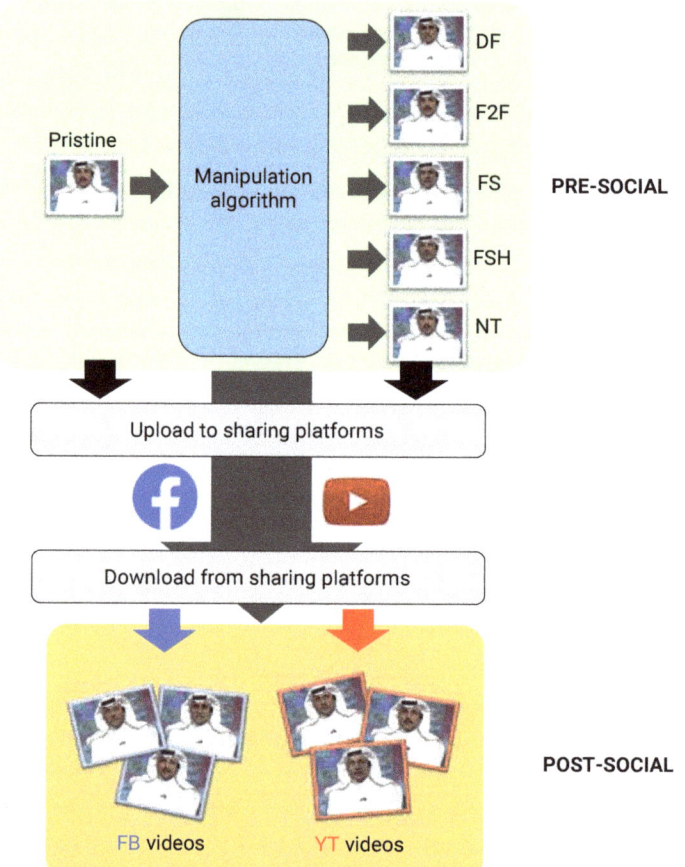

Figure 1. Experimental design of our comparative evaluation.

3.1. Initial Data Corpus

In order to carry out our quantitative experiments, we build on the state-of-the-art dataset FaceForensics++ [2], created under the necessity of providing the community with a large-scale video dataset for face manipulation analysis.

FaceForensics++ consists of 1000 original videos, each of them manipulated through 5 different manipulation techniques Deepfake (DF), Face2Face ($F2F$), FaceSwap (FS), NeuralTextures (NT) and FaceShifter (FSH) techniques. All the videos depict one person, typically in a central position within the frame. In terms of manipulation type, Face2Face and NeuralTextures perform video re-enactment, thus the facial dynamics of a source video is transferred into a target video. The Deepfake, FaceShifter and FaceSwap technique instead implement face substitution, thus superimposing the face taken from a source video into the facial dynamics of a target video.

Also, different techniques present diversity in terms of tools they employ: Deepfakes, NeuralTextures, FaceShifter are based on pre-trained learning-based schemes, while FaceSwap and Face2Face rely on computer graphics rule-based methodologies. FaceForensics++ offers three different quality versions: raw (unprocessed video frames), high-quality (HQ) with 23 factor compression and low-quality (LQ) 40-compressed. While raw video frames are unlikely to be encountered, LQ videos are strongly degraded; thus, we focus our analysis on HQ compressed videos as a tradeoff between visual quality and practical relevance.

The dataset comes with a predefined partition of the 1000 videos into training, validation and testing set (composed by 720, 140 and 140 videos, respectively), which we also employed in our experiments.

3.2. Deep Architectures for Detection

For comparison purposes, we consider three different general purpose CNNs that proved to be effective in the classification of real and manipulated contents:

- *Xception (XC)* [37] was born as "extreme" version of Inception architecture and it is proved in [36,38,39] as proficient backbone architecture for forensic detectors (in [2] it is reported as the most successful architecture on the FaceForensics++ dataset).
- *InceptionV3 (INC)* [40] is the result of improvements to the original Inception structure [33] and based on multiple filters of different sizes in the same module to enhance scalability of descriptors. It has been used in image forensics for copy-move forgery detection [41] and GAN-generated image detection [3].
- *Densenet (DEN)* [42] is designed on dense connections ensuring large diversity of features with few parameters. It has found applications in image classification [43], steganalysis [44], and the identification of GAN-generated images shared on social networks [3].

All of them operate in a frame-wise fashion, thus the analysis is performed on single frames without considering the temporal relation between them. In each training phase, we reproduce the procedure adopted in [2]: starting from models pretrained on Imagenet, the classification layer is separately pretrained for 3 epochs, and then the full network is trained for 15 epochs and the model with best validation accuracy is chosen. Regarding training hyperparameters, samples are grouped in batches of 32 and Adam optimizer is applied with its default values and learning rate equal to 0.0002.

3.3. Data Creation

Both pristine and manipulated videos have been uploaded to and downloaded from two popular platforms, YouTube (YT) and Facebook (FB). Such operations have been performed in a semi-manual fashion for each video in the validation and testing set and for each manipulated version, leading to a total number of shared videos equal to $(140+140) \times 6 \times 2 = 3360$.

In particular, on YouTube the procedure is managed through the YouTube Studio interface where video playlists can be created with a maximum of 15 videos uploaded per day. Successively, each sequence is downloaded individually from the playlist. For the case of Facebook, since no constraints on the number of videos are in place, videos have been published as private albums; the downloading operation is applied in batch through the "Download album" functionality.

The degradation of the videos, once shared, is confirmed when observing the downscaling in resolution and the decrease in size of files. In terms of resolution, pre-social videos undergo a reduction of an average factor of 0.8 on Facebook and 0.64 on YouTube. Similarly, the file dimension is respectively impacted of 0.5 and 0.7 after the downloading.

4. Experimental Analysis

We now report the main results of our evaluation campaign.

In our analysis, the three architectures are always trained individually to distinguish real from manipulated frames for each single technique of FaceForensics++. In order to conduct extensive comparative tests, a set of *baseline* binary detectors have been trained by employing the 3 different architectures and the 5 different manipulation techniques. This leads to 15 baseline models indicated as XC_m, INC_m and DEN_m, where $m \in \{DF, F2F, FS, FSH, NT\}$.

By following the same settings as in [2], the binary video classification is always performed at frame level (unless otherwise stated) by extracting 10 frames from each video. In doing so, a face detector is applied to identify the face area, which is then cropped and fitted to the input size of the networks. Thus, according to the data splits provided, for every detector we have 7200 training frames, 1400 validation frames and 1400 testing frames for each class.

The remainder of the section is structured as follows:

- *Detection Performance in the Pre-Social Scenario (Section 4.1)*
  videos are first analyzed in their pre-social version, showing consistent results with what reported in [2];
- *Generalization Performance in the Post-Social Scenario (Section 4.2)*
  the analysis is extended to shared data and the performance of deep networks is evaluated in a standard and transfer learning mode;
- *Identification of the Manipulation Technique (Section 4.3)*
  we evaluate the possibility of identifying the manipulation technique that has been used to create the video by exploiting the different network outputs;
- *Accuracy of Video-based Aggregated Decisions (Section 4.4)*
  the analysis of individual frame is combined to obtain a decision on the full video.

4.1. Detection Performance in the Pre-Social Scenario

The chart in Figure 2 reports the accuracy results for all the deep networks when distinguishing pristine and manipulated video frames extracted from videos in the pre-social scenario. Results are reported separately for each manipulation technique and show in general good discrimination capabilities.

Among the considered nets, Xception (XC) always provides superior performance against every manipulation, in line with what obtained in [2] when comparing Xception to other forensic detectors. However, InceptionV3 (INC) and Densenet (DEN) also exhibit rather high accuracy, with a maximum decrease with respect to Xception equal to 1.0% and 2.54%, respectively.

When observing the results across different manipulations, we can moreover observe that the detection accuracy on data manipulated through NT is significantly lower (no higher than 92.0%), while for all the other four techniques we achieve an accuracy above 96% in all cases.

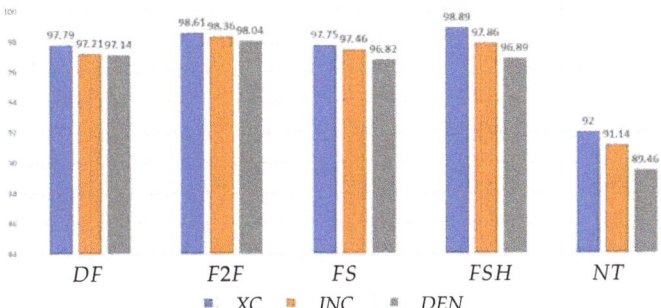

Figure 2. Accuracy of different networks in the pre-social scenario.

4.2. Generalization Performance in the Post-Social Scenario

We now report the results of the post-social analysis, which include measuring different effects, as described below.

First, we directly test the baseline models already trained in Section 4.1 on video frames extracted from shared videos. This first allows us to measure what we indicate as the *misalignment loss*, defined as the decrease in accuracy observed for the baseline models when moving from tests on pre-social data to tests on post-social data.

Then, we evaluate the effectiveness of a simple transfer learning strategy via finetuning. In particular, pretrained baseline models are further trained on a number of frames extracted from shared videos. For this purpose, we used the videos in the validation set (140 for each binary class). We applied this procedure for every baseline model and both sharing platforms, leading to 30 so-called *specialized* models. Thus, each of them is first trained on real and manipulated frames created to a specific manipulation and then fine-tuned with real and manipulated frames of videos shared from a given platform. We indicate as subscript the platform on which detectors are specialized, so that, for instance, XC_m^{YT} is the specialized model obtained by fine-tuning XC_m with validation data shared through YouTube.

By doing so, we can then evaluate two other effects, namely:

- the *fine-tuning gain*, defined as the increase in accuracy observed on post-social data when specialized models are employed in place of baseline models;
- the *forgetting loss*, the decrease in accuracy observed on pre-social data when specialized models are employed in place of baseline models. (The terms "loss" and "gain" are used by definition to indicate a decrease and an increase in accuracy, respectively, due to direction of the expected effect. They might however assume negative values, thus indicating a reversed effect (e.g., a negative loss indicates an increase in accuracy)).

In fact, in addition to measuring the advantages of using specialized detectors on the newly seen post-social data, it is also important to evaluate to which extent they remain accurate on pre-social data, for which they had been originally trained.

In order to effectively visualize those observed effects, we report the results of the different tests in a condensed format by adopting in the plots the following convention:

△ → accuracy of baseline models on pre-social data
○ → accuracy of baseline models on post-social data
● → accuracy of specialized models on post-social data
▲ → accuracy of specialized models on pre-social data

By doing so, in each case we can represent the results as depicted in Figure 3:

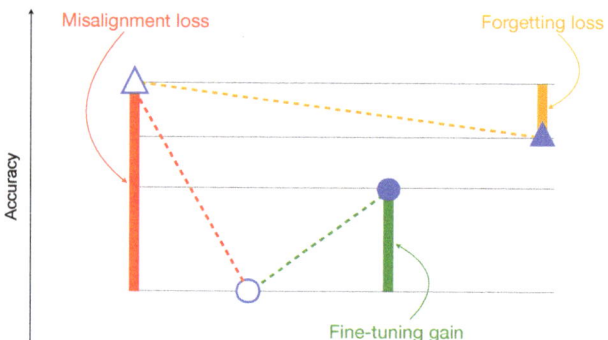

Figure 3. Example of result visualization.

Figures 4 and 5 report the results of such analysis for the different networks, manipulation techniques and sharing platforms.

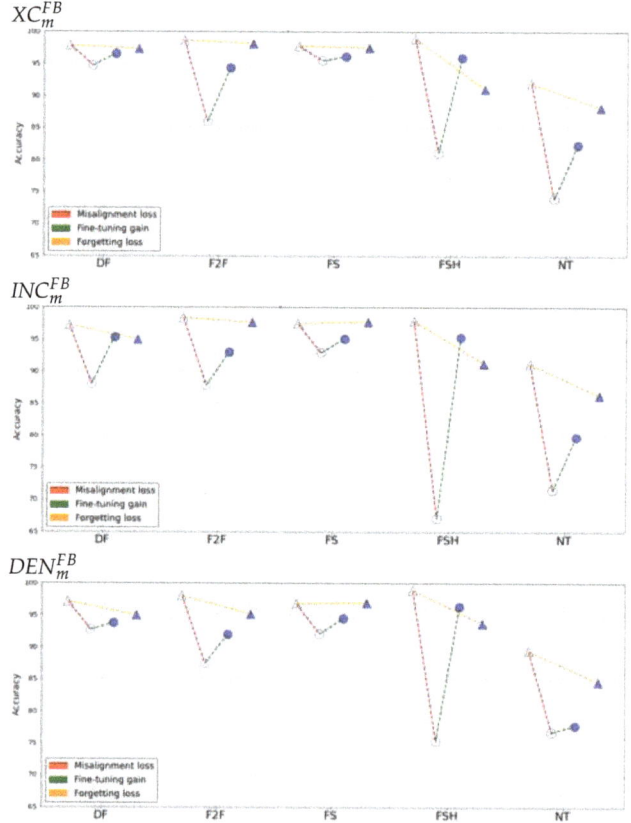

Figure 4. Accuracy results in the post-social scenario on FB.

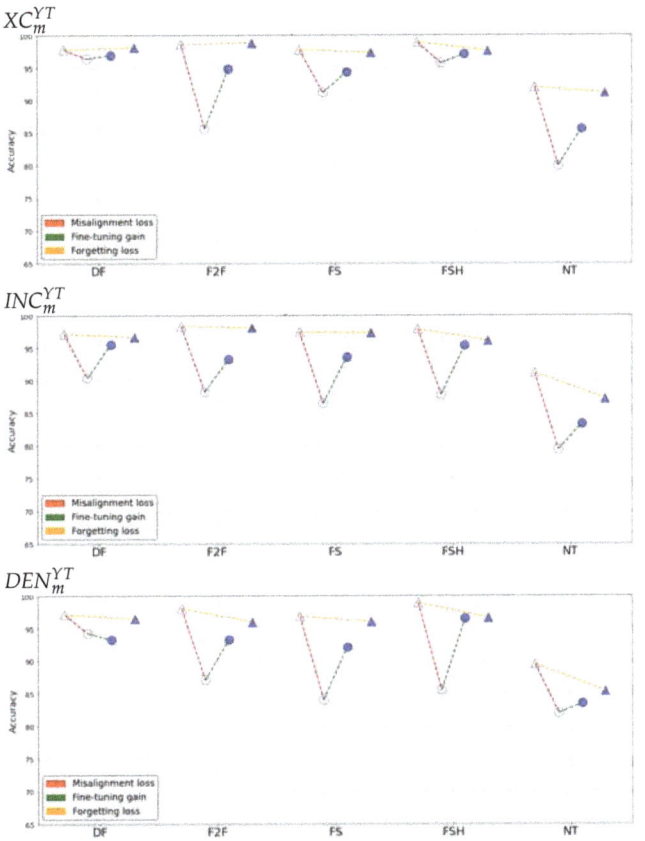

Figure 5. Accuracy results in the post-social results on YT.

We can then observe the different effects separately:

Misalignment loss

The extent of the loss varies across the manipulations considered, the employed architecture and the sharing platform. In general, we can deduce that XC is on average the most robust in detecting manipulated content in presence of strong degradation of information, while Densenet seems to be relatively less susceptible against NT. By looking at different manipulation techniques, the two platforms seem to have different impact: for FB, FSH and NT are the ones resulting more challenging to detect, while for YT higher misalignment losses are observed also on $F2F$ and FS. In general, the loss is particularly small for DF data.

Fine-tuning gain

When fine-tuning is applied to post-social data, the gain is always positive and sometimes reaches 20%. Accuracy is brought above 90% in every case, except for NT data for which the detection capabilities are strongly compromised in the post-social scenario. The only exception is given by the DEN_{DF}^{YT} model, which slightly decreases the performance of DEN_{DF} on post-social data. This confirms the peculiar behaviour of the DF manipulated data with respect to the other techniques.

For the sake of completeness, we report in Tables 1 and 2 the full accuracy results obtained through specialized models.

Table 1. Accuracy of networks fine tuned on Facebook videos.

	DF	F2F	FS	FSH	NT
XC	96.54	94.39	96.11	95.39	82.29
INC	95.36	93.00	95.11	95.29	79.82
DEN	93.79	92.04	94.50	95.36	77.82

Table 2. Accuracy of networks fine tuned on YouTube videos.

	DF	F2F	FS	FSH	NT
XC	96.96	94.86	94.36	97.07	85.57
INC	95.57	93.32	93.64	95.39	83.36
DEN	93.38	93.12	92.07	96.50	83.46

Forgetting loss

By looking at the forgetting loss, we can notice that its behaviour varies considerably among different manipulation techniques, showing essentially small performance fluctuations on not-shared content when adopting baseline and specialized detectors for the DF, $F2F$ and FS techniques. For FSH and NT, the forgetting loss increases, mostly in correspondence to higher values of the misalignment loss.

4.3. Identification of the Manipulation Technique

Although less investigated with respect to the distinction between real and manipulated content, one interesting aspect in this experimental framework would be the ability to blindly identify the manipulation technique used for altering the video. In fact, in a video verification scenario, determining which algorithmic pipeline has been employed on data that have been reported as manipulated could aid the process of tracing users or services which provided the untruthful visual content [5].

Therefore, we address this problem and explore the possibility of exploiting for this purpose the outputs of our different binary networks. In fact, predictions on single frames made by the considered deep networks come in the form of a value in $[0, 1]$ (the softmax layer output), which is interpreted as the probability of the sample to belong to the manipulated class and successively binarized. Thus, if is $\mathbf{x}$ a generic frame and F as a generic model, we can indicate as $F(\mathbf{x}) \in [0, 1]$ the model output; when $F(\mathbf{x}) > 0.5$, the $\mathbf{x}$ is classified as manipulated.

In each configuration, both our baseline and specialized models are exposed during training to manipulated data created with only a certain technique; we can then expect that the network predictions will be higher when manipulated frames produced through this specific technique are tested, with respect to other kinds of frames.

For a generic testing frame $\mathbf{x}$ and the tree architectures considered, we then define the sets

$$\mathbf{XC}(\mathbf{x}) = \{XC_{DF}(\mathbf{x}), XC_{F2F}(\mathbf{x}), XC_{FS}(\mathbf{x}), XC_{FSH}(\mathbf{x}), XC_{NT}(\mathbf{x})\} \quad (1)$$
$$\mathbf{INC}(\mathbf{x}) = \{INC_{DF}(\mathbf{x}), INC_{F2F}(\mathbf{x}), INC_{FS}(\mathbf{x}), INC_{FSH}(\mathbf{x}), INC_{NT}(\mathbf{x})\} \quad (2)$$
$$\mathbf{DEN}(\mathbf{x}) = \{DEN_{DF}(\mathbf{x}), DEN_{F2F}(\mathbf{x}), DEN_{FS}(\mathbf{x}), DEN_{FSH}(\mathbf{x}), DEN_{NT}(\mathbf{x})\}. \quad (3)$$

Analogous sets can be defined in the same way when specialized models are used by simply adding the corresponding superscript.

Building on this rationale, one can conjecture that the maximum response observed among the five different available deep detectors can act as an indicator of the manipulation technique on a generic frame. Then, we blindly analyze each testing frame $\mathbf{x}$ and provide three estimates of the manipulation technique as the ones corresponding to $\max \mathbf{XC}(\mathbf{x})$, $\max \mathbf{INC}(\mathbf{x})$ and $\max \mathbf{DEN}(\mathbf{x})$.

We report in Figures 6–8 the confusion matrices obtained with such methodology for the different architectures. In each case, we tested both the pre-social and the post-social scenarios, the latter being addressed with specialized models.

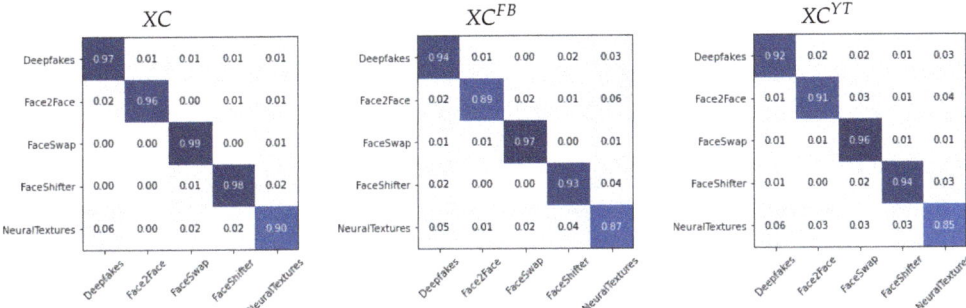

Figure 6. Confusion matrices obtained from **XC**(**x**) in the pre-social and post-social scenarios.

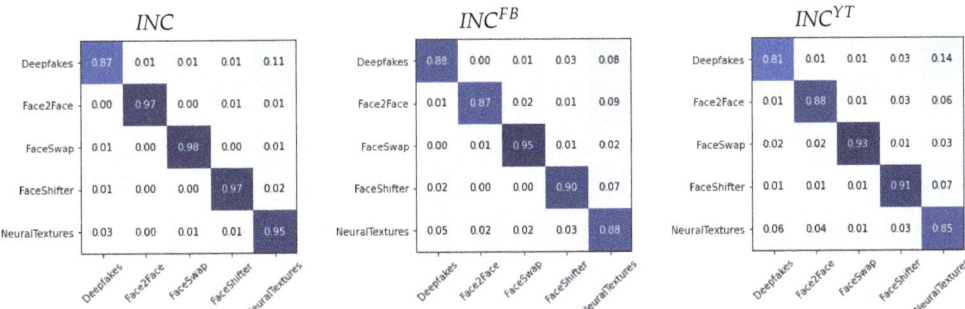

Figure 7. Confusion matrices obtained from **INC**(**x**) in the pre-social and post-social scenarios.

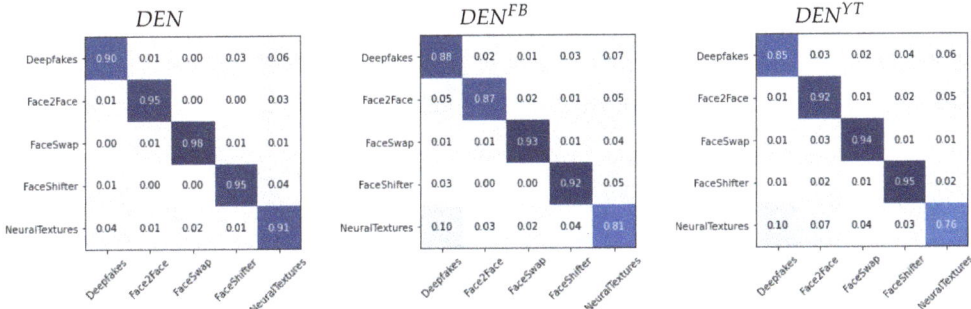

Figure 8. Confusion matrices obtained from **DEN**(**x**) in the pre-social and post-social scenarios.

We observe a clear diagonal in each case, with comparable performance when comparing the pre- and post-social scenarios, thus demonstrating that the network outputs indeed carry useful forensic information for this task. When observing the behaviour of specific manipulation techniques, we notice that Deepfakes (*DF*) and NeuralTextures (*NT*) consistently present a higher error.

4.4. Accuracy of Video-Based Aggregated Decisions

While the analyzed models perform a forensic analysis on individual frames (by extracting 10 frames per video), in practical situations those predictions are typically combined in order to take a decision on the entire multimedia object, i.e., the full video.

Thus, we here evaluate the ability of frame-wise decisions (based on deep network predictions) to support a video-wise decision. In particular, instead of selecting a limited number of frames per video, we now analyze all of them through the nets.

For each full video, we compute all the binary responses of individual frames and the ratio of frames that are classified as manipulated.

Such ratio value can be thresholded in order to take a decision on each video, so that a Receiver Operating Curve can be produced for a varying threshold $t \in [0, 1]$. When $t = 0.5$, the decision rule corresponds to a majority voting criterion over multiple frames. False and true positive rate are here computed on the total number of test videos.

For the sake of brevity, we limit this analysis to FSH and NT analyzed through specialized models in the post-social scenario. The resulting ROCs are reported in Figures 9 and 10. We can notice that Area Under the Curve (AUC) values are rather high in all cases, thus showing that lower accuracy values on individual frames can indeed be mitigated by the aggregation of multiple ones.

In general, the discrimination capability seems however to decrease when videos are shared through YT. This holds for both the selected manipulations.

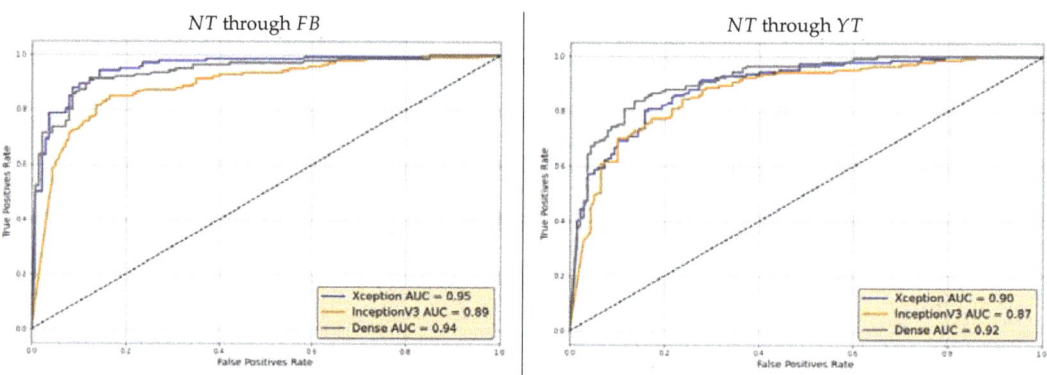

Figure 9. ROC curves of the video-based decision through specialized models on NT videos shared on Facebook (**left**) and YouTube (**right**).

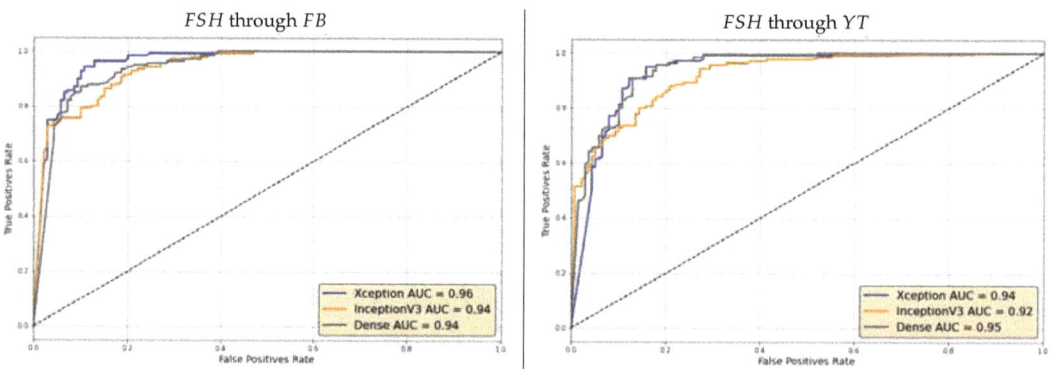

Figure 10. ROC curves of the video-based decision through specialized models on FSH videos shared on Facebook (**left**) and YouTube (**right**).

5. Conclusions

In this work we have addressed the challenging scenario where forensics analysis is applied to manipulated videos shared through social media platforms.

Indeed, we have presented an extensive evaluation going beyond controlled laboratory conditions and analyzing detection performance both in what we have called pre-social and post-social scenarios, involving several general purpose deep networks, state-of-the-art manipulated data and two popular sharing platforms (Facebook and YouTube).

We have shown generalization and transfer learning capabilities of CNN-based detectors measuring misalignment loss, fine-tuning gain and forgetting loss for all different types of data and architecture. Moreover, we have presented an ensemble strategy to identify the specific manipulation algorithm of data that are detected as fake. Finally we have analyzed detection performance when moving from single frame prediction to full video sequence decision, where predictions on every frame are aggregated and the decision between real and fake is given by the percentage of fake frames identified.

All such results show promising directions for an effective forensic analysis in real-world scenarios where deceptive media are shared after manipulation. In particular, simple transfer learning via fine-tuning seems a viable strategy for re-gaining accuracy when the testing data deviates from the training one due to the sharing operation. In this regard, alternative and possibly more efficient data augmentation techniques could be explored that simulate the various resizing and recompression pipelines of social networks, which are however not fully known. In this framework, issues can be however foreseen due to the purely data-driven nature of this methodology. In fact, in our tests a limited number of platforms were selected and analyzed separately, always assuming some kind of knowledge on this regard. Dealing with a higher number of platforms in the training phase, as well as in blind scenarios where unseen platforms are involved in the testing phase represent open problems for future investigations. Related to this, provenance studies could also be performed with the goal of identifying the sharing pipeline of the analyzed content and thus facilitate the forensic analysis. Moreover, a possible way to overcome the need for extensive training data in the data-driven techniques would be to employ methods based on physiological cues or physical inconsistencies, whose robustness to sharing processes should be assessed. Finally, one open point which would deserve further investigation is the relation between the specific manipulation technique with respect to the detector performance.

Author Contributions: Conceptualization, G.B. and C.P.; methodology, C.P. and G.B.; software, F.M.; validation, F.M.; formal analysis, C.P.; investigation, F.M., C.P. and G.B.; resources, F.M.; data curation, F.M.; writing—original draft preparation, F.M. and C.P.; writing—review and editing, G.B.; visualization, C.P.; supervision, G.B.; project administration, G.B.; funding acquisition, G.B. All authors have read and agreed to the published version of the manuscript.

Funding: This research was funded by the project PREMIER (PREserving Media trustworthiness in the artificial Intelligence ERa), funded by the Italian Ministry of Education, University, and Research (MIUR) within the PRIN 2017 program.

Data Availability Statement: The initial data corpus (FaceForensics++ data) is available at https://github.com/ondyari/FaceForensics, accessed on 17 September 2021.

Conflicts of Interest: The authors declare no conflict of interest.

References

1. Verdoliva, L. Media Forensics and DeepFakes: An Overview. *IEEE J. Sel. Top. Signal Process.* **2020**, *14*, 910–932. [CrossRef]
2. Rössler, A.; Cozzolino, D.; Verdoliva, L.; Riess, C.; Thies, J.; Nießner, M. FaceForensics++: Learning to Detect Manipulated Facial Images. In Proceedings of the International Conference on Computer Vision (ICCV), Seoul, Korea, 27 October–2 November 2019.
3. Marra, F.; Gragnaniello, D.; Cozzolino, D.; Verdoliva, L. Detection of GAN-Generated Fake Images over Social Networks. In Proceedings of the IEEE Conference on Multimedia Information Processing and Retrieval (MIPR), Miami, FL, USA, 10–12 April 2018; pp. 384–389.

4. Hu, J.; Liao, X.; Wang, W.; Qin, Z. Detecting Compressed Deepfake Videos in Social Networks Using Frame-Temporality Two-Stream Convolutional Network. *IEEE Trans. Circuits Syst. Video Technol.* **2021**, 2021. [CrossRef]
5. Pasquini, C.; Amerini, I.; Boato, G. Media forensics on social media platforms: A survey. *EURASIP J. Inf. Secur.* **2021**, *2021*, 1–19.
6. Moltisanti, M.; Paratore, A.; Battiato, S.; Saravo, L. Image manipulation on facebook for forensics evidence. In Proceedings of the International Conference on Image Analysis and Processing, Genoa, Italy, 7–11 September 2015; pp. 506–517.
7. Phan, Q.; Pasquini, C.; Boato, G.; De Natale, F.G.B. Identifying Image Provenance: An Analysis of Mobile Instant Messaging Apps. In Proceedings of the IEEE International Workshop on Multimedia Signal Processing (MMSP), Vancouver, BC, Canada, 29–31 August 2018; pp. 1–6.
8. Li, Y.; Chang, M.C.; Lyu, S. In Ictu Oculi: Exposing AI Created Fake Videos by Detecting Eye Blinking. In Proceedings of the 2018 IEEE International Workshop on Information Forensics and Security (WIFS), Hong Kong, China, 11–13 December 2018; pp. 1–7. [CrossRef]
9. Fox, G.; Liu, W.; Kim, H.; Seidel, H.P.; Elgharib, M.; Theobalt, C. Videoforensicshq: Detecting high-quality manipulated face videos. In Proceedings of the 2021 IEEE International Conference on Multimedia and Expo (ICME), Shenzhen, China, 5–9 July 2021; pp. 1–6.
10. Li, Y.; Lyu, S. Exposing DeepFake Videos By Detecting Face Warping Artifacts. *arXiv* **2018**, arXiv:1811.00656.
11. Yang, X.; Li, Y.; Lyu, S. Exposing deep fakes using inconsistent head poses. In Proceedings of the ICASSP 2019—2019 IEEE International Conference on Acoustics, Speech and Signal Processing (ICASSP), Brighton, UK, 12–17 May 2019; pp. 8261–8265.
12. Li, H.; Li, B.; Tan, S.; Huang, J. Identification of deep network generated images using disparities in color components. *Signal Process.* **2020**, *174*, 107616. [CrossRef]
13. Ng, T.T.; Chang, S.F.; Hsu, J.; Xie, L.; Tsui, M.P. Physics-motivated features for distinguishing photographic images and computer graphics. In Proceedings of the 13th annual ACM international conference on Multimedia, Singapore, 6–11 November 2005; pp. 239–248.
14. Gallagher, A.C.; Chen, T. Image authentication by detecting traces of demosaicing. In Proceedings of the IEEE Computer Vision and Pattern Recognition Workshops (CVPRW), Anchorage, AK, USA, 23–28 June 2008.
15. Dirik, A.E.; Sencar, H.T.; Memon, N. Source Camera Identification Based on Sensor Dust Characteristics. In Proceedings of the IEEE Workshop on Signal Processing Applications for Public Security and Forensics, Washington, DC, USA, 11–13 April 2007; pp. 1–6.
16. Fridrich, J.; Kodovsky, J. Rich models for steganalysis of digital images. *IEEE Trans. Inf. Forensics Secur.* **2012**, *7*, 868–882. [CrossRef]
17. Cozzolino, D.; Poggi, G.; Verdoliva, L. Recasting residual-based local descriptors as convolutional neural networks: An application to image forgery detection. In Proceedings of the 5th ACM Workshop on Information Hiding and Multimedia Security, Philadelphia, PA, USA, 20–22 June 2017; pp. 159–164.
18. Pan, F.; Chen, J.; Huang, J. Discriminating between photorealistic computer graphics and natural images using fractal geometry. *Sci. China Ser. Inf. Sci.* **2009**, *52*, 329–337. [CrossRef]
19. Ke, Y.; Min, W.; Du, X.; Chen, Z. Detecting the composite of photographic image and computer generated image combining with color, texture and shape feature. *J. Theor. Appl. Inf. Technol.* **2013**, *49*, pp. 844–851.
20. Bonomi, M.; Pasquini, C.; Boato, G. Dynamic texture analysis for detecting fake faces in video sequences. *J. Vis. Commun. Image Represent.* **2021**, *79*, 103239. [CrossRef]
21. Lyu, S.; Farid, H. How realistic is photorealistic? *IEEE Trans. Signal Process.* **2005**, *53*, pp. 845–850. [CrossRef]
22. Chen, D.; Li, J.; Wang, S.; Li, S. Identifying computer generated and digital camera images using fractional lower order moments. In Proceedings of the 2009 4th IEEE Conference on Industrial Electronics and Applications, Xian, China, 25–27 May 2009; pp. 230–235.
23. Frank, J.; Eisenhofer, T.; Schönherr, L.; Fischer, A.; Kolossa, D.; Holz, T. Leveraging frequency analysis for deep fake image recognition. In Proceedings of the International Conference on Machine Learning, Virtual, 13–18 July 2020; pp. 3247–3258.
24. Bonomi, M.; Boato, G. Digital human face detection in video sequences via a physiological signal analysis. *J. Electron. Imaging* **2020**, *29*, 1–10. [CrossRef]
25. Qi, H.; Guo, Q.; Juefei-Xu, F.; Xie, X.; Ma, L.; Feng, W.; Liu, Y.; Zhao, J. DeepRhythm: Exposing deepfakes with attentional visual heartbeat rhythms. In Proceedings of the 28th ACM International Conference on Multimedia, Seattle WA USA, 12–16 October 2020; pp. 4318–4327.
26. Ciftci, U.A.; Demir, I.; Yin, L. Fakecatcher: Detection of synthetic portrait videos using biological signals. *IEEE Trans. Pattern Anal. Mach. Intell.* **2020**. [CrossRef] [PubMed]
27. Hernandez-Ortega, J.; Tolosana, R.; Fierrez, J.; Morales, A. Deepfakeson-phys: Deepfakes detection based on heart rate estimation. *arXiv* **2020**, arXiv:2010.00400.
28. Chen, W.; McDuff, D. Deepphys: Video-based physiological measurement using convolutional attention networks. In Proceedings of the European Conference on Computer Vision (ECCV), Munich, Germany, 8–14 September 2018; pp. 349–365.
29. Agarwal, S.; Farid, H.; Gu, Y.; He, M.; Nagano, K.; Li, H. Protecting World Leaders Against Deep Fakes. In Proceedings of the IEEE/CVF Conference on Computer Vision and Pattern Recognition (CVPR) Workshops, Long Beach, CA, USA, 16–20 June 2019.
30. Cozzolino, D.; Rössler, A.; Thies, J.; Nießner, M.; Verdoliva, L. ID-Reveal: Identity-aware DeepFake Video Detection. *arXiv* **2021**, arXiv: 2012.02512.

31. Bayar, B.; Stamm, M.C. A deep learning approach to universal image manipulation detection using a new convolutional layer. In Proceedings of the 4th ACM workshop on information hiding and Multimedia Security, Vigo Galicia, Spain, 20–22 June 2016; pp. 5–10.
32. Rahmouni, N.; Nozick, V.; Yamagishi, J.; Echizen, I. Distinguishing computer graphics from natural images using convolution neural networks. In Proceedings of the IEEE Workshop on Information Forensics and Security (WIFS), Rennes, France, 4–7 December 2017; pp. 1–6.
33. Szegedy, C.; Liu, W.; Jia, Y.; Sermanet, P.; Reed, S.; Anguelov, D.; Erhan, D.; Vanhoucke, V.; Rabinovich, A. Going deeper with convolutions. In Proceedings of the IEEE Conference on Computer Vision and Pattern Recognition, Boston, MA, USA, 7–12 June 2015; pp. 1–9.
34. Afchar, D.; Nozick, V.; Yamagishi, J.; Echizen, I. MesoNet: A Compact Facial Video Forgery Detection Network. In Proceedings of the IEEE International Workshop on Information Forensics and Security, Hong Kong, China, 11–13 December 2018; pp. 1–7.
35. Bayar, B.; Stamm, M.C. Constrained Convolutional Neural Networks: A New Approach Towards General Purpose Image Manipulation Detection. *IEEE Trans. Inf. Forensics Secur.* **2018**, *13*, 2691–2706. [CrossRef]
36. Zhu, X.; Wang, H.; Fei, H.; Lei, Z.; Li, S.Z. Face Forgery Detection by 3D Decomposition. In Proceedings of the IEEE/CVF Conference on Computer Vision and Pattern Recognition, Virtual, 19–25 June 2021; pp. 2929–2939.
37. Chollet, F. Xception: Deep learning with depthwise separable convolutions. In Proceedings of the IEEE Conference on Computer Vision and Pattern Recognition, Honolulu, HI, USA, 21–26 July 2017; pp. 1251–1258.
38. Kumar, A.; Bhavsar, A.; Verma, R. Detecting deepfakes with metric learning. In Proceedings of the 2020 8th International Workshop on Biometrics and Forensics (IWBF), Porto, Portugal, 29–30 April 2020; pp. 1–6.
39. Jiang, L.; Li, R.; Wu, W.; Qian, C.; Loy, C.C. Deeperforensics-1.0: A large-scale dataset for real-world face forgery detection. In Proceedings of the IEEE/CVF Conference on Computer Vision and Pattern Recognition, Virtual, 14–19 June 2020; pp. 2889–2898.
40. Szegedy, C.; Vanhoucke, V.; Ioffe, S.; Shlens, J.; Wojna, Z. Rethinking the inception architecture for computer vision. In Proceedings of the IEEE Conference on Computer Vision and Pattern Recognition, Las Vegas, NV, USA, 26 June–1 July 2016; pp. 2818–2826.
41. Zhong, J.L.; Pun, C.M. An end-to-end dense-inceptionnet for image copy-move forgery detection. *IEEE Trans. Inf. Forensics Secur.* **2019**, *15*, 2134–2146. [CrossRef]
42. Huang, G.; Liu, Z.; Van Der Maaten, L.; Weinberger, K.Q. Densely connected convolutional networks. In Proceedings of the IEEE Conference on Computer Vision and Pattern Recognition, Honolulu, HI, USA, 21–26 July 2017; pp. 4700–4708.
43. Zhang, K.; Guo, Y.; Wang, X.; Yuan, J.; Ding, Q. Multiple feature reweight DenseNet for image classification. *IEEE Access* **2019**, *7*, 9872–9880. [CrossRef]
44. Yang, J.; Shi, Y.Q.; Wong, E.K.; Kang, X. JPEG steganalysis based on densenet. *arXiv* **2017**, arXiv: 1711.09335.

Article

Factors that Influence PRNU-Based Camera-Identification via Videos

Lars de Roos [1,2,*] and Zeno Geradts [2,3]

1. Faculty of Technology, Amsterdam University of Applied Sciences, 1097 DZ Amsterdam, The Netherlands
2. Department of Digital and Biometric Traces, Netherlands Forensic Institute, 2467 GB The Hague, The Netherlands; geradts@uva.nl
3. Faculty of Science, University of Amsterdam, 1098 XH Amsterdam, The Netherlands
* Correspondence: larssamderoos@gmail.com

Abstract: The Photo Response Non-Uniformity pattern (PRNU-pattern) can be used to identify the source of images or to indicate whether images have been made with the same camera. This pattern is also recognized as the "fingerprint" of a camera since it is a highly characteristic feature. However, this pattern, identically to a real fingerprint, is sensitive to many different influences, e.g., the influence of camera settings. In this study, several previously investigated factors were noted, after which three were selected for further investigation. The computation and comparison methods are evaluated under variation of the following factors: resolution, length of the video and compression. For all three studies, images were taken with a single iPhone 6. It was found that a higher resolution ensures a more reliable comparison, and that the length of a (reference) video should always be as high as possible to gain a better PRNU-pattern. It also became clear that compression (i.e., in this study the compression that Snapchat uses) has a negative effect on the correlation value. Therefore, it was found that many different factors play a part when comparing videos. Due to the large amount of controllable and non-controllable factors that influence the PRNU-pattern, it is of great importance that further research is carried out to gain clarity on the individual influences that factors exert.

Keywords: PRNU; photo response non-uniformity; source camera identification; videos; compression; snapchat; resolution

1. Introduction

Each camera creates a highly characteristic pattern: The Photo Response Non-Uniformity pattern (PRNU-pattern). The PRNU-pattern is caused by differences in material properties and due to proximity effects during the production process of the image sensor. This pattern can be compared with various software in order to answer the following questions: 'which camera is the source of a specific photo or video' and 'are certain photos or videos taken with the same camera'. After this comparison, a correlation value is linked to it, which describes the degree of similarity. In some cases, inexplicable low correlation values were measured when comparing videos. Several initiatives have already been taken by the Netherlands Forensic Institute (NFI) to determine the causes of these low correlation values. This was done by conducting small studies and proficiency tests in which international organizations participated. Since the size of these studies was limited, in most cases this matter has not been published. This study therefore made an overview of the factors already investigated. Based on this list of more than 50 different factors, three factors were chosen that could contribute to the broadening of knowledge regarding the factors that influence the PRNU-pattern. These factors include the following: compression, resolution and the length of the video. It is expected that these factors will negatively influence the PRNU-pattern, resulting in a low correlation value when a comparison is made. In previous studies [1–3] it was found that compression had a

negative influence on the PRNU-pattern. Since Snapchats compression had not yet been investigated, this factor was chosen. Currently not much is possible in terms of getting information from the Snapchat application. A method to determine whether an image comes from the Snapchat application of a phone is therefore a welcome addition. These "Snapchat image comparisons" can also be very important to increase the burden of proof when normal reference images are missing or when large quantities of social media images have to be compared with each other. In this report the investigation regarding Snapchat serves as a starting point for further investigations. In addition to this partial study, the influence of resolution on the PRNU-pattern is being investigated. Some research has been conducted into video resolutions higher than 720p, but not enough to draw more general conclusions [3]. This partial study attempts to contribute to the formation of these more general conclusions. The last factor, the influence of the length of the video, was chosen on the basis of a recommendation that was given in a study into the influence of movement and stabilization of drones on the PRNU-pattern [4]. In this last study it was described that this factor may contribute to the deterioration of the PRNU-pattern. This paper therefore looks at three different factors that can influence the PRNU-pattern and with that the correlation value that comes from the comparison of these PRNU-patterns. The factors that have already been investigated by the NFI are also included. The aim of this research is therefore to determine which factors may provide low correlation values when comparing videos. It evaluates the computation and comparison methods used, under variation of these certain factors.

Now that an introduction has been given, the rest of this paper consists of the following: The chapter state of the art describes the basics of PRNU-investigation. The materials and methods chapter gives information regarding the choices made. The results are presented and later discussed in the chapters results and discussion. Subsequently, a conclusion has been formulated. All chapters are written by Lars de Roos, under the supervision of Zeno Geradts.

2. State of the Art

2.1. Photo Response Non-Uniformity

Photo Response Non-Uniformity is a way in which errors in the output of the image sensor are expressed [5,6]. PRNU describes the difference between the actual response of the image sensor and a uniform response [7]. During the production process PRNU occurs due to the impurity of the raw material or by the variation in size of the photodiode due to proximity effects. Since PRNU is caused by these physical properties, the characteristic differences cannot be eliminated [7]. Furthermore, the amount of noise depends on the light: if there is a lot of light, or if settings are used that let much light enter the camera, this will lead to a lot of noise. The differences and variations that arise create a noise pattern (also called a PRNU-pattern). This pattern is present in every photograph that the image sensor produces. The pattern is often seen as the "fingerprint" of the image sensor, and therefore also of a camera [8,9]. The production of the fingerprint of the camera has grown over the years to be the golden standard when comparing digital images.

The PRNU-pattern can be made visible with advanced software, such as PRNUCompare [10]. With this software the source of an image can be retrieved. This is done with the same steps as described by Meij and Geradts [2]. In this study, steps 4 and 5 whereby the zero mean and Wiener filter are used to remove noise and artifacts created due to compression, were skipped in order to investigate the influence of compression. Reference cameras are needed to make reference images, also called flatfield images. These are images of a gray surface where the light is distributed as evenly as possible over the pixels of the image sensor. The PRNU-patterns that come from the reference images can then be compared to the images whose source has to be retrieved. In the software, such a comparison can be performed. A correlation value is calculated for this comparison which describes the degree of similarity between the PRNU-patterns.

2.2. Related Work

Multiple studies have been conducted over the past few years regarding the analysis of camera images. In the early stages these were mainly focused on the possibilities that Fixed Pattern Noise (FPN)—which includes Photo Response Non-Uniformities—had to offer [5,6]. Furthermore, it was also discovered that it was possible to identify a camera on the basis of pixel defects [11]. Ultimately, the method of Photo Response Non-Uniformities was further developed. For example, more complex filters and algorithms were introduced [12–14]. Due to further developments within this subject, even images of poorer quality could be analyzed. [15–17]. The goals were also adjusted. In addition to identifying the camera, it became possible to identify fake images [18–21]. Even before the turn of the century it was possible to identify a video camera on the basis of videos. However, this did not concern current digital videos but video tapes [22]. The identification of current digital videos started around 2007, when it was found possible to identify a camcorder using PRNU [23]. From that moment on, developments have progressed, and it became possible to prevent the copying and illegal downloading of movies [24]. The emergence of drones, smartphones and social media has led to yet another change in the playing field of digital images. To keep up with this, several studies have been conducted in recent years concerning smartphones, WhatsApp, YouTube and drones [2,4,25,26]. For example, it is now possible to identify the brand and model of a smartphone via video analysis [27]. In most literature that has been discussed so far, there is no explicit mention in the results, or in the interpretation and discussion of those results, that there were problems with, for instance, factors influencing the (PRNU-)patterns. Unfortunately, despite all the rapid advances, these problems can still occur. These problems are also referred to as (unexpected) artifacts or defects [28,29]. Observations made in the "Dresden Image Database" study revealed several of those artifacts [30]. In many other studies the defects are seen as beneficial since this increases the characteristic value of the noise pattern [29]. In order to identify more factors that influence the PRNU-pattern, a large number of studies have been done by the NFI. To provide insight into this, a table is made in which all the factors, and their influences on the PRNU-pattern, have been presented. In Table A1 the distinction is made between six different groups: type of camera, resolution, compression, digital processing, physical adaptation and other factors. Examples of previously investigated factors are the influence of the framerate [31], the influence of compression and resolution of YouTube videos [3,32,33] and the influence of stabilization and movement of drones [4].

3. Materials and Methods

The most important information about the PRNU-pattern, including a brief overview of studies that have been conducted in recent years into (factors influencing) the PRNU-pattern, has just been discussed. This knowledge is applied in this chapter to determine the research method. In this way an attempt has been made to exclude most unwanted influences and to create the opportunity to examine only the chosen factors. This chapter successively describes the camera, software and images used.

3.1. Camera

An iPhone 6 was used for this study. This iPhone was chosen because it had the ability to adjust the resolution, so videos could be made in 720p and 1080p, both with 30 fps (30 frames per second). No updates were made at the time of the investigation. The Snapchat application was also downloaded on this iPhone.

3.2. PRNUCompare

Software program "PRNUCompare" was developed by the Netherlands Forensic Institute (NFI) in order to answer the following questions: 1: Which camera is the source of a specific photo or video? And 2: Are photos or videos taken with the same camera? PRNUCompare can analyze individual or multiple photos and/or videos, including YouTube clips. It is equipped with a large selection of advanced algorithms which, when they are combined, have the ability to analyze multiple images simultaneously. Different filters can be chosen to obtain the PRNU-pattern: 2nd order extraction filter (FSTV), 4th order extraction filter and wavelet denoising/filter [2,10]. The 2nd order extraction filter (FSTV) works best for videos relative to the other filters [2,3]. The differences between the filters are mainly based on the relationship between speed and quality. In PRNUCompare it is also possible to use "frame averaging". During the examination of all factors, the 2nd order extraction filter was used and 1 in 10 frames was extracted each time (frame averaging). When interpreting the results, the NFI uses a minimum correlation value in order to make a reliable statement about finding the source of an image. This correlation value, which can be between 0 and 1, has to be at least 0.15. In this study, this value was also used to draw conclusions about the reliability of the correlation values of the factors studied. The correlation value is a result of the equation below, which is carried out using PRNUCompare. NCC stands for the normalized cross-correlation. This is a matrix of the values between X and Y (in short, the coordinates of an image) [34]. In the rest of the article, PRNUCompare is referred to as 'algorithm'.

$$NCC[i,j] = \frac{\sum_{k=1}^{m}\sum_{l=1}^{n}\left(X[k,l]-\overline{X}\right)\left(Y[k+i,l+j]-\overline{Y}\right)}{\|X-\overline{X}\|\,\|Y-\overline{Y}\|} \tag{1}$$

3.3. Images

Different amounts of videos were used for the examined factors, an overview of the images per factor examined can be found in Table 1. This table also explains the type of videos (flatfield or natural) that have been used. All videos were made with the rear camera of the iPhone 6, without filters and other custom settings. All videos taken with the iPhone were stationary flatfield images, which means that the videos all consisted of a still shot of a grey background. This also insured that the light distribution was as favorable as possible and that influence on the pixels was minimal. The standard video format for Apple devices (.mov) was used, which may not be representative of non-iOS devices such as Samsung or Huawei. The videos used for the investigation of the compression of Snapchat and the resolution were all between 10 and 11 s long. Before the start of the investigation into the compression of Snapchat, it was first investigated whether there was actually a compression. This was done with images made with the Snapchat application on the iPhone 6. There were two sets, or rather parts, of Snapchat videos made: part 1 consisted of 7 flatfield videos and part 2 consisted of 15 flatfield videos. The two sets of videos were made on two different days.

Table 1. Overview of the amount of videos per factor examined.

Factor	Amount of Videos
Resolution	23 videos (720p) and 23 videos (1080p)
Snapchat	22 Snapchat videos (720 × 1080)
Video length	10 videos same length and 10 videos different length

When researching the length of the videos, the first set consisted of 10 videos with different lengths (10, 14, 15 and 16 s) and the second set consisted of 10 videos with a length of 10 s. QuickTime Player was used to shorten the videos with different lengths to a length of 10 s.

During the production of all videos, it was taken into account that the factors, from Table A1, might still have an influence on the results of the examined factors. For instance, camera settings and the amount of light. To limit these random and systematic errors as much as possible work was carried out in the same lab, in this lab use was made of controlled light, air and temperature conditions. The same device (the iPhone 6) was used and this device was in the lab at all times. Camera settings have remained unchanged, except for the change in resolution. The settings were adjusted, through the settings of the iPhone 6, from the standard 1080p with 30 fps to 720p with 30 fps and later back to 1080p with 30 fps for the other examined factors.

3.4. Snapchat: Extraction and Comparison of Snapchat Images

Snapchat, together with Instagram, Facebook and Twitter, is one of the most used social media in the world. In Snapchat it is possible to take photos and videos, with or without the large amount of filters and augmented reality (AR) techniques that Snapchat offers.

Both the images and the videos were created in the same way in Snapchat and stored on the iPhone 6. Since Snapchat offers no option to save photos directly on a smartphone, the following method was chosen: first the image or the video was made, it was saved in "memories" and then exported to the photo application of the iPhone 6. The images were then taken from the iPhone to investigate on a desktop which had the PRNUCompare software. Here the images were compared to each other and to images and videos from the iPhone 6.

3.5. From Images to Results

It is important to zoom in a little further on what happens between the production of the images and obtaining the results of the comparisons in the form correlation values. After the images are structured in a way that is easy to load into the algorithm, the images are converted as batches to PRNU-patterns. As discussed above, certain settings and factors are taken into account and the method of Meij and Geradts is used [2]. After the images have been converted to PRNU-patterns, it is possible to perform comparisons. The patterns are compared one by one on the basis of similarities between the noise pattern, using the aforementioned equation [34]. It is possible to compare a single pattern with a single other pattern, but it is also possible to perform an entire set of comparisons directly. In the latter case, a certain number of other patterns are compared per single pattern (for example 1 vs. 20). This creates a kind of "ranking" of the best matches per pattern based on the correlation value. As mentioned, a correlation value is generated for each performed comparison, which is displayed in a table and in a graph. These tables can be exported in Excel, after which a visual presentation can easily be made, as can be found in the results of this paper.

4. Results

For interpreting the figures that can be found in the results this information may be relevant: the highest and lowest correlation values are indicated in each figure, these are the values of mutual comparisons of images from the same telephone. The negative (red) result therefore relates to the lowest correlation value that came from a mutual comparison between two images of the same telephone. This result is considered negative since it would be "normal" if there was no or very little difference between mutual comparison of images from the same phone (with the same settings).

4.1. Resolution

First, we investigated whether the resolution of the videos could have an influence on the correlation value, and therefore would influence the comparison of visual material. Since previous studies only looked at a maximum resolution of 720p, we chose devices that had the ability to make videos with resolutions higher than 720p. Therefore, we decided to use an iPhone 6 video with resolutions of 720p and 1080p, both with 30 fps. Table 2 and Figures 1 and 2 show the correlation values of the different video comparisons made using the algorithm. One video comparison means that different videos with a same resolution from the same device, the iPhone 6, are compared (with a one-to-one video comparison). This resulted in a highest, lowest, and average correlation value per comparison. Since the algorithm always takes the same picture into the equation, a maximum correlation value of 1.00 is always achieved. This value was omitted here as it had to be investigated how well the other images of the same device could be matched.

Table 2. Overview of the highest, average and lowest correlation values for both resolutions.

	Figure 1 (720p)	Figure 2 (1080p)
Highest correlation value	between 0.13 and 0.23	between 0.27 and 0.67
Average correlation value	between 0.08 and 0.15	between 0.25 and 0.58
Lowest correlation value	between 0.06 and 0.12	between 0.22 and 0.44

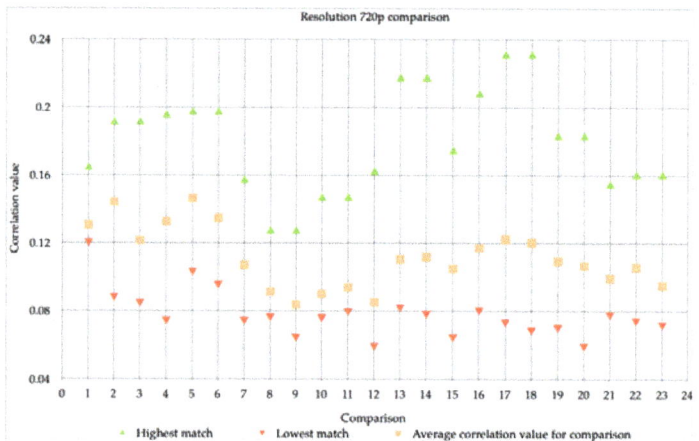

Figure 1. 23 comparisons, done with images made with an iPhone 6, all with a resolution of 720p.

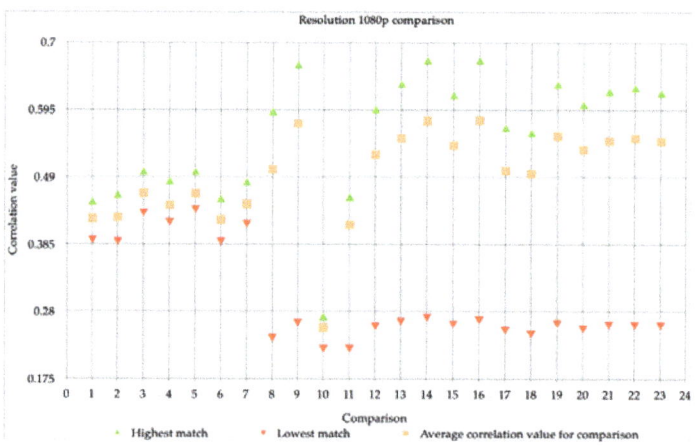

Figure 2. 23 comparisons, done with images made with an iPhone 6, all with a resolution of 1080p.

In Figure 1 all 23 comparisons have a comparable lowest correlation value and the average correlation value varies a little. The highest correlation values per comparison vary more. In Figure 1 comparison 1 has a little spread, compared to the other comparisons. In Figure 2 the first seven comparisons are very close together, the rest of the 23 comparisons are more scattered. The highest and lowest value are much further apart. Comparison 10 is noticeable; it only has a highest correlation value of 0.27.

When looking at the average correlation values in Figures 1 and 2. It shows that these average correlation values of the resolutions are very different. The images with a resolution of 1080p have a much higher correlation value for all comparisons than the images with a resolution of 720p. Furthermore, the videos with a resolution of 720p cannot be reliably matched several times, they do not meet the requirement of a minimum correlation value of 0.15 used by the NFI. The difference with the videos with a resolution of 1080p is big, since a valid match can always be made with this resolution. The stability of the correlation values also differs. For example, the highest and lowest correlation values of the images with a resolution of 720p fluctuate more, this may have to do with the influence that stabilization and/or movements had during the making of the videos. Videos with a lower resolution seem to be more sensitive to this, as a result of which the correlation values differ. At higher resolutions, in this case at a resolution of 1080p, this mutual difference is much less (almost minimal). What can be concluded of this is the following: as the resolution improves, it becomes increasingly possible to obtain a PRNU-pattern (that is more resistant to influence by other factors) from a video. This makes it possible to carry out a reliable comparison with the algorithm.

4.2. Snapchat Compression

Subsequently, research was done into the compression of Snapchat. In order to determine whether Snapchat made any adjustments at all, a small investigation was conducted into the differences between normal iPhone 6 images and Snapchat images (which were also made with an iPhone 6). It turned out that when Snapchat was used, the resolution was adjusted to 720×1280. This could be caused by a different utilization of the image sensor within the iPhone 6. The resolution of the normal iPhone 6 images was 3264×2448 (pixel height: 3264 and pixel width: 2448). For this reason, no direct comparison could be made.

The Snapchat images could be compared to each other, but it was noticeable that the correlation values were all far below the limit of a possible match. This made it clear that Snapchat makes very big adjustments to images. The algorithm could not recognize that the images were all made by the same phone with the same Snapchat application. After that it was investigated whether Snapchat makes a compression on videos.

In Figure 3 the 22 video comparisons of the Snapchat videos are shown. In this case, one single video comparison means that several videos of Snapchat from the same device, the iPhone 6, are compared. The highest correlation value is displayed with green; this value varies between 0.17 and 0.28. Orange shows the average correlation value for the comparison performed this value also varies. Correlation values between 0.10 and 0.21 have been measured here. Red indicates the lowest correlation value; these values vary between 0.08 and 0.18. In Figure 3 it is striking that there is a difference between the first 7 comparisons (part 1) and the last 15 comparisons (part 2). The lowest correlation value here is much lower than that of comparisons 8 to 22. Additionally, in comparison 6 and 7 the highest correlation value is lower than in the other 20 comparisons. There is no direct explanation for these results. Because very many factors have been taken into account, the conditions have been kept as equal as possible, see the materials and methods section. Yet it seems that making images on two different days can still cause a slight difference, even if the circumstances have remained the same.

To determine whether a match could be found on the basis of regular images of the iPhone 6, the videos that were used in researching the resolution in this study were used to perform various comparisons. Thus, the videos of the resolution study all served as reference images.

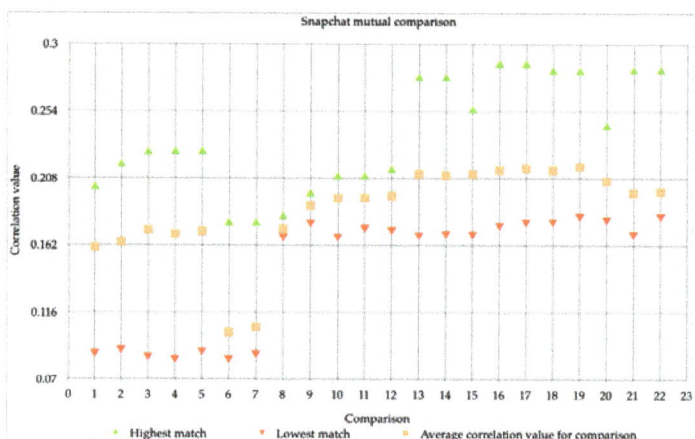

Figure 3. 22 comparisons, done with Snapchat images made with an iPhone 6, all with a resolution of 720 × 1280.

The previous figures (see Figures 1–3) showed the individual comparisons, with the highest, lowest and average values. The results that can be found in these figures can be seen as check whether the images can be matched (and thus meet the requirements set in the method). Because the correlation values, with some exceptions, were sufficient to perform mutual comparisons, the images were then compared with each other: the iPhone 6 videos with a resolution of 720p, as well as videos with a resolution of 1080p were compared to Snapchat videos. The result of these comparisons can be found in Figure 4.

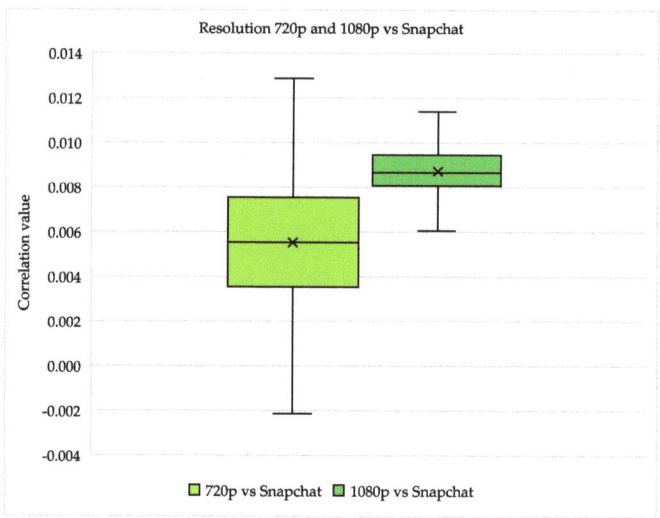

Figure 4. Boxplot of two times 506 individual comparisons between Snapchat images, all with a resolution of 720 × 1280, made with an iPhone 6 and images, all with a resolution of either 720p or 1080p, made with an iPhone 6.

The spread of the comparison between images with a resolution of 720p and Snapchat is larger than that of images with a resolution of 1080p and Snapchat. This is not comparable to the difference already seen between Figures 1 and 2, in which it became clear that images with a resolution of 1080p achieve higher correlation values, but also fluctuate on a larger scale, namely between 0.22 and 0.67 (see Figure 2). In Figure 4 this spread, when comparing 1080p videos to Snapchat videos, is between 0.006 and 0.012. Which immediately shows the decrease in the correlation values and thus the decrease in the reliability of the comparisons performed. The same drop can be observed when comparing the 720p videos to Snapchat videos, the correlation value there is between −0.002 and 0.013 instead of 0.06 and 0.23 (see Figure 1). In all cases, the highest correlation value is below the limit used by the NFI when it comes to a reliable comparison with the algorithm.

With regard to the comparison between 1080p videos and Snapchat, it is striking that not only the spread is smaller, but also the average is higher. The 1080p vs. Snapchat comparison average is around 0.008, while it is 0.005 for the 720p vs. Snapchat comparison. This was unexpected since it was expected that this comparison would not be possible due to the difference in resolution between the Snapchat videos (720p) and regular iPhone 6 videos with a resolution of 1080p. However, slightly higher correlation values were measured in the 720p vs. Snapchat comparison. Apart from the outlier, all values in the 1080p vs. Snapchat comparison are below 0.012. In Table 3 the above mentioned highest, lowest and average correlation values of both comparisons are shown. Here it becomes clear again that no reliable comparison could be made. None of the values came close to the limit of 0.15 used by the NFI.

Table 3. Overview of the highest, average and lowest correlation values for both resolutions compared to Snapchat.

	720p vs. Snapchat	1080p vs. Snapchat
Highest correlation value	0.013	0.012
Average correlation value	0.005	0.008
Lowest correlation value	−0.002	0.006

Thus, it was found that Snapchat was making a major adjustment, not only on photos, but also on videos. It also became clear that, partly due to this adaptation, the comparisons with regular iPhone 6 videos of both 720p and 1080p could not contribute to the reliable matching of the Snapchat videos. For this reason, it was investigated in which way it could be determined whether the camera of the iPhone 6 had made the Snapchat images. A comparison has been made between both sets of the Snapchat videos: part 1 vs. part 2. In Figure 5 this comparison between the first and second set is shown. The following results were found: The highest correlation value (correlation value) varies between 0.12 and 0.19. The average correlation values, between 0.11 and 0.18, for the comparisons are close to the highest values. The lowest correlation value varies between 0.10 and 0.17.

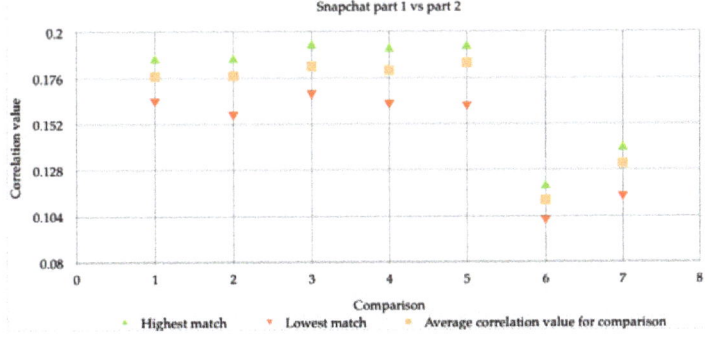

Figure 5. Mutual comparisons of Snapchat video's (part 1) and Snapchat video's (part 2).

Aside from comparisons 6 and 7, this means that the comparison between Snapchat exceeds 0.15 and can therefore be seen as "reliable". The difference in the mean correlation value with the comparisons with the two resolutions (720p and 1080p) is at least 0.17.

4.3. Length of the Video

The last factor consisted of the influence of the length of a video. As mentioned earlier, only flatfield images were used here. The results of the comparisons made can be observed in Table 4. Here it becomes clear that with shorter videos (with a length of 10 s) a lower correlation value arises. The correlation values of the videos with a length of 14, 15 and 16 s are relatively close to each other. These results correspond to the following expectation: if a video is longer, it contains more frames (single images). So, if the video is longer and the algorithm extracts a pattern every 10 frames (three per second in this study, since the framerate is 30 fps), more patterns can be extracted from one video. This creates a more reliable PRNU-pattern since the average pattern over all frames of that single video is more stable.

Table 4. Results of the mutual comparisons of both videos with different lengths and videos with the same length (10 s).

Name of Video	Length in Seconds	Lowest Correlation	Highest Correlation	Name of Cut Video	New Length in Seconds	Lowest Correlation	Highest Correlation
1a	15	0.669	0.711	1b	10	0.526	0.537
2a	15	0.710	0.808	2b	10	0.534	0.759
3a	15	0.709	0.819	3b	10	0.536	0.725
4a	14	0.702	0.819	4b	10	0.533	0.738
5a	14	0.703	0.814	5b	10	0.533	0.749
6a	10	0.675	0.778	6b	10	0.537	0.744
7a	10	0.669	0.773	7b	10	0.534	0.743
8a	16	0.711	0.836	8b	10	0.526	0.731
9a	16	0.710	0.836	9b	10	0.535	0.757
10a	16	0.709	0.832	10b	10	0.531	0.759

To investigate whether the length of the videos caused a direct difference in the correlation values during the comparison, the same videos of the iPhone 6 were investigated. These videos were cut to a length of 10 s with QuickTime Player. Table 4 shows the results of the mutual comparison of the cut videos. Here you can see the correction values of the comparison of the iPhone images when they were cut to a length of 10 s. This table clearly shows the difference between the videos that are cut and those that are not. The highest correlation values of the videos of 10 s are almost all about 0.05 (or more) lower than the videos of different lengths. The same applies to the lowest correlation values for the cut videos, which are even >0.10 lower than the videos with different lengths. What is also striking is that the measurements of the videos of 10 s are all very close to each other compared to the videos with different lengths. This is possible because a longer video provides more information about the PRNU-pattern, so that more differences can be detected. Even the video that was already 10 s long was cut to exactly 10 s. As a result, a small difference has arisen. In the Table 4, for both the comparison of the images with a different length and the images with a length of 10 s, the maximum correlation value that the algorithm always calculates is omitted. This was done because this value was unimportant in this study, as it was investigated how well the images of the same device could be matched.

Finally, it was investigated whether a cut video could be matched with the accompanying full video. This has not been processed in a report in this way before and is therefore interesting. The results of this study are shown in Table 5. The comparison performed is the following: videos of different lengths (1a to 10a) vs. videos of 10 s (1b to 10b). Table 5 shows whether the match was successful and which correlation values could be linked to these comparisons. In these results it can be seen that in some cases even a 0.99 correlation value has been achieved, which is exceptionally high. However, this has the following reason: these two videos (video 6 and 7) were already 10 s, only a few milliseconds were cut out, so only a very small adjustment was made. This has led to the exceptionally high correlation value of almost 1.00. The other correlation values also offer a positive result: it is more than clear that the algorithm is able to match cut videos to the original images.

Table 5. The correlation values of the comparison of videos of different lengths (1a to 10a) with videos of 10 s (1b to 10b).

	1b	2b	3b	4b	5b	6b	7b	8b	9b	10b
1a	0.882	0.674	0.675	0.676	0.677	0.674	0.664	0.678	0.677	0.678
2a	0.563	0.946	0.761	0.765	0.760	0.759	0.744	0.766	0.771	0.769
3a	0.559	0.756	0.947	0.778	0.771	0.768	0.752	0.775	0.781	0.779
4a	0.554	0.751	0.767	0.960	0.772	0.769	0.751	0.777	0.782	0.779
5a	0.558	0.746	0.760	0.772	0.959	0.764	0.748	0.771	0.776	0.775
6a	0.537	0.716	0.728	0.738	0.733	0.996	0.718	0.739	0.743	0.742
7a	0.532	0.709	0.719	0.728	0.724	0.725	0.991	0.733	0.738	0.734
8a	0.561	0.759	0.773	0.785	0.779	0.778	0.763	0.948	0.797	0.795
9a	0.558	0.761	0.775	0.786	0.781	0.779	0.767	0.794	0.948	0.797
10a	0.559	0.756	0.771	0.780	0.777	0.775	0.760	0.787	0.792	0.950

5. Discussion

In the investigation into the differences between resolutions and their influence on the PRNU-pattern, two comparisons stand out: Comparison 1 of the video comparison with resolution 720p has a striking little spread, the smallest of all 23 comparisons. This could be due to other factors such as light (settings), which may have caused the video to be clearer than the other videos. Comparison 10 of the video comparison with resolution 1080p is noticeable, since it only has a highest correlation value of 0.27. This is lower than the correlation values of the remaining 22 comparisons. Most likely motion or light caused an unclear video, which meant that a less good PRNU-pattern could be extracted. Correlation values differ between the two resolutions, in most cases this difference is above 0.30. This is a very big difference, as this can indicate whether a match is considered reliable or not.

It was already known that lower resolutions (i.e., resolutions below 720p) resulted in reduced correlation values [3,4,32]. The same conclusion could be drawn from the experiment that was carried out. It also appeared that a lower resolution is less stable than videos of 1080p that were compared. As mentioned earlier, this may be due to the influence of stabilization and movement. In the literature nothing is known about this, but it is quite possible to imagine: at a lower resolution, fewer pixels are available to register (major) changes, so that details are missed.

It is recommended to carry out further research into even higher resolutions and to involve the framerate. As mentioned, it is possible to change the resolution settings on many smartphones, it is also possible to adjust the framerate: this increases the number of frames per second, which may result in an even more stable PRNU-pattern. Further research on multiple devices might help to increase the reliability of this experiment.

In the experiment on the influence of the compression performed by Snapchat, it quickly became apparent that a major adjustment was being made. This adjustment was visible on both images and videos that were created with the Snapchat application. This was not inconceivable as already known from previous studies that social media applications almost always make adjustments to visual material [1–3,25]. It was striking that Snapchat lowers the resolution to 720p with videos. The comparisons with the videos of 720p gave a slightly higher correlation value than the comparisons with the videos of 1080p. This can be explained by the fact that the resolution of the Snapchat videos (standard 720p) corresponds to the videos with a resolution of 720p, so that a more equal performance can be seen. What emerges from these two comparisons is that the algorithm cannot make a reliable comparison between videos that were made with Snapchat, and those that were not. So, if there is a Snapchat video that needs to be investigated whether it comes from a certain device, it is recommended not to include reference pictures of the device itself in the comparison. However, it is recommended to create Snapchat reference images with a reference device on which the application Snapchat is installed. This allows the creation of Snapchat reference images that can be compared with the algorithm. Again, it might be interesting to investigate whether the same correlation values occur with other devices. Possibly also because there is a difference between the Snapchat that is available for iOS (the operating system of Apple) and Android (the operating system of almost all other smartphones). On Android smartphones, a "screengrab" (screenshot of what the camera receives) is made instead of making an image or video with the camera of the smartphone. Capturing with the camera is what happens on an iPhone. This leads to the higher quality of the images and videos that come from an iPhone compared to an android smartphone.

In the research into the influence of the length of a video, one video of 15 s stands out, which had a lower correlation value than the other videos of 15 s. It is unclear how this difference could have arisen in this single video. It was investigated whether there was a direct influence by shortening the length of the video and it was also checked whether the videos could still be matched to the complete videos after cutting. The videos from the iPhone 6 have been duplicated and cut to a length of 10 s, using QuickTime Player. Important here is that cutting images is actually destructive research, therefore it is not recommended to cut images to an equal length during a case study. The best solution is to make reference images of the same length as the images to be examined. Incidentally, QuickTime Player, as mentioned earlier, can still have influence on the final correlation values. Unfortunately, nothing is known about the influence of this program on the PRNU-pattern.

Some recommendations have been drawn up on the basis of the research into the factors discussed above. It summarizes what can be taken into account or where the method could be adjusted in relation to the current state of affairs. These recommendations can be found in Table 6.

Table 6. Overview of recommendations for implementation per factor investigated.

Factor	Recommendation
Compression (Snapchat)	With images: virtually no comparison possible due to large differences in compression. It is recommended to compare as many regular images as possible and omit Snapchat photos. With videos: comparison of Snapchat videos with regular videos of the device is not possible. It might be an option to make reference videos with the Snapchat application located on the reference device. However, further research is required to confirm this finding.
Resolution	It is recommended to compare only equal resolutions (was already known). Higher resolutions give higher correlation values but take into account the fact that comparisons of lower resolutions are still reliable.
Length of the video	When creating reference images, it is recommended to make videos of the same length as the suspicious images. The reference images may also be longer, in this way more information is extracted from the video, which improves the comparison. Videos that have been cut can still be compared, the same applies as above: it is best to use videos of the same length, or longer than the suspicious images, as a reference.

6. Conclusions

From the table (Table A1) that was made, several factors were known that could be responsible for low correlation values when comparing videos. In addition to this overview, three factors were examined in this study, which lead to the following conclusions:

Compression has a negative effect on the comparison since it leads to a decrease in the correlation value. This was already known for many programs, but not specifically for Snapchat. In this research we found that through Snapchat the images (photos and videos) can be negatively influenced, in most cases so bad that a match with a normal reference is not possible. Further research is needed to confirm whether it is actually possible that a reliable comparison can be made with reference images of Snapchat.

The better (higher) the resolution, the better (higher) the reliability of the comparison of videos will be. This was already known with resolutions up to and including 720p. This research shows that it gets even better with resolutions of 1080p.

The longer the video is, the more reliable the PRNU-pattern that can be extracted from the video. Vice versa: the shorter the video is, the worse a PRNU-pattern can be made (however, a reliable match is still possible). It is also possible, as it turns out, to match cut videos to the original videos. Often even with a very high correlation value.

Thus, it appears from the experiments that many different factors play a part in comparing videos. Due to the large amount of controllable and non-controllable factors that influence a PRNU-pattern, it is of great importance that further research is done to gain clarity on the individual influences that factors exert.

Author Contributions: Conceptualization, L.d.R. and Z.G.; methodology, L.d.R. and Z.G.; software, L.d.R. and Z.G.; validation, L.d.R. and Z.G.; formal analysis, L.d.R.; investigation, L.d.R.; resources, Z.G.; data curation, L.d.R.; writing—original draft preparation, L.d.R.; writing—review and editing, L.d.R.; visualization, L.d.R.; supervision, Z.G.; project administration, L.d.R. and Z.G.; funding acquisition, Z.G. All authors have read and agreed to the published version of the manuscript.

Funding: This research received no external funding.

Institutional Review Board Statement: Not applicable.

Informed Consent Statement: Not applicable.

Data Availability Statement: Data available in a publicly accessible repository that does not issue DOIs. This data can be found here: https://drive.google.com/drive/folders/1w_vkluq1oy-lMNTXmtuTIvxSjjhqtXhH?usp=sharing.

Conflicts of Interest: The authors declare no conflict of interest.

Appendix A

Table A1. Overview of possible factors that influence a decrease of the (PRNU) correlation value in videos (or images in general).

	Factor	Influence
Type of camera	Exposure	Variation large, small differences
	Focal length	Zoom = drop (no identification possible)
	Camera setting (general)	This has influence
	Aperture (with shutter speed)	Little difference
	Focus	Possible factor
	Focus (middle or angle)	Middle = standard Angle(s) = more noise, so actually better
	Framerate	Higher rate = higher correlation (when comparing same rate video to video) Different rate impossible to compare
	Frames	More = better (video/video-comparison) Video/photo-comparison not (yet) possible
	I- and P-frames	Whole video or single frames highest correlation, not I- and/or P-frames
	ISO (CCD)	ISO 100 or 200 best for comparing
	ISO (CMOS)	Everything possible, if comparison with reference is made with equal (and otherwise middle) ISO value
	ISO (foveon x3)	Variation large
	Quality (camera)	Possible factor
	Shutter speed	Variation large, shorter shutter speed = lower correlation
	Temperature (decrease/increase)	This has no influence
	White balance	Variation large

Table A1. Cont.

	Factor	Influence
Resolution	480p	No identification possible
	720p	Depending on the camera possible or not possible
	Resolution (photo)	Low = Decrease High = Increase
	Resolution (mutual difference)	No identification possible
	Resolution (video)	Low = Decrease High = Increase
	Photos with Video (resolution)	Comparison not (yet) possible
Compression	Compression	Possible factor
	Compression (online)	Compression increase = reliability decrease
	Compression (online) 2.0	So much loss, no comparison possible
	Compression (comparison)	Using the same type of compression, otherwise the correlation value decreases
	Compression/Cropped (256 × 256)	No loss and faster, lower than this value leads to degradation
	Photos with Video (compression)	Comparison not (yet) possible
	JPEG fine vs. JPEG standard	No identification possible
Digital processing	Cropped areas	No identification possible
	Grayscale (photos)	Best way to make reference images for comparison
	Increasing image	Bad and another research says good (640 × 480 to 1920 × 1080)
	Enlarge/reduce (PC)	VGA/9M = Best way
	Enlarge/reduce (camera)	Superfine = Best way
	Reducing image	This has a positive influence on the comparison
Physical adaptation	Gimbal (drone)	In combination with lower quality camera, it leads to a decrease
	Switch camera module	This has no influence
Other factors	2nd Order filter	Best result, match will be higher
	Distance to camera	Possible factor
	Motion of image	Identification possible if reference is also in motion
	Contrasts	Bad results (Usage of homogeneous substrates recommended)
	Dark/light	Darker = Decrease Lighter = Decrease Middle = Works the best
	Halogen light	Leads to lower correlation values
	Color of reference image	Green and gray show high correlation values, red and blue show lower correlation values
	Length of video	Mutual difference = Decrease
	Light (inside/outside)	Different per case
	Light (intensity)	Possible factor
	Fluorescent light	This has no direct influence
	Aging	This has no influence

References

1. Khanna, N.; Mikkilineni, A.; Delp, E. Forensic Camera Classification: Verification of Sensor Pattern Noise Approach. *Forensic Sci. Commun.* **2009**, *11*, 1.
2. Meij, C.; Geradts, Z. Source camera identification using Photo Response Non-Uniformity on WhatsApp. *Digit. Investig.* **2018**, *24*, 142–154. [CrossRef]
3. Brouwers, M.; Mousa, R. Automatic Comparison of Photo Response Non Uniformity (PRNU) on Youtube. Master's Thesis, University of Amsterdam, Amsterdam, The Netherlands, 2017.
4. Bramer, S. *The Influence of Motion Stability on the PRNU-Pattern of the Camera of a Drone*; Netherlands Forensic Institute: The Hague, The Netherlands, 2018.

5. Lukas, J.; Fridrich, J.J.; Goljan, M. Determining digital image origin using sensor imperfections. *Proc. SPIE* **2005**, *5685*, 249–261. [CrossRef]
6. Lukas, J.; Fridrich, J.; Goljan, M. Digital Camera Identification from Sensor Pattern Noise. *IEEE Trans. Inf. Forensics Secur.* **2006**, *1*, 205–214. [CrossRef]
7. van Houten, W. Understanding Image Sensors Noise, Non-Uniformities and Obtaining a Likelihood Ratio in the Process of Device Identification. Master's Thesis, University of Amsterdam, Amsterdam, The Netherlands, 2008.
8. Bayram, S.; Sencar, H.T.; Memon, N. Efficient sensor fingerprint matching through fingerprint binarization. *IEEE Trans. Inf. Forensics Secur.* **2012**, *7*, 1404–1413. [CrossRef]
9. Satta, R.; Beslay, L. *Camera Fingerprinting Based on Sensor Pattern Noise as a Tool for Combatting Child Abuse Online. Project AVICAO, JRC Technical Reports*; European Commission: Brussels, Belgium, 2014.
10. van der Mark, M.; van Houten, W.; Geradts, Z. *PRNUCompare*; Netherlands Forensic Institute: The Hague, The Netherlands, 2010.
11. Dirik, A.E.; Sencar, H.; Memon, N. Digital Single Lens Reflex Camera Identification from Traces of Sensor Dust. *IEEE Trans. Inf. Forensics Secur.* **2008**, *3*, 539–552. [CrossRef]
12. Matsushita, K.; Kitazawa, H. An Improved Camera Identification Method Based on the Texture Complexity and the Image Restoration. In Proceedings of the 2009 International Conference on Hybrid Information Technology, Daejeon, Korea, 27–29 August 2009; pp. 171–175.
13. Cooper, A.J. Improved photo response non-uniformity (PRNU) based source camera identification. *Forensic Sci. Int.* **2013**, *226*, 132–141. [CrossRef] [PubMed]
14. Gisolf, F.; Malgoezar, A.; Baar, T.; Geradts, Z. Improving source camera identification using a simplified total variation based noise removal algorithm. *Digit. Investig.* **2013**, *10*, 207–214. [CrossRef]
15. Alles, E.J.; Geradts, Z.; Veenman, C.J. Source Camera Identification for Low Resolution Heavily Compressed Images. In Proceedings of the International Conference on Computational Sciences and Its Applications, Perugia, Italia, 30 June–31 July 2008; pp. 557–567.
16. Goljan, M.; Fridrich, J. Camera Identification from Cropped and Scaled Images—Art. No. 68190E. In Proceedings of the SPIE, Media Forensics and Security Conference, San Jose, CA, USA, 26–31 January 2008; pp. 1–13.
17. Goljan, M.; Fridrich, J. Sensor Fingerprint Digests for Fast Camera Identification from Geometrically Distorted Images. In Proceedings of the IS&T/SPIE Electronic Imaging Conference, Burlingame, CA, USA, 3–7 January 2013; p. 86650B.
18. Zhang, C.; Zhang, H. Exposing Digital Image Forgeries by Using Canonical Correlation Analysis. In Proceedings of the 2010 20th International Conference on Pattern Recognition, Istanbul, Turkey, 23–26 August 2010; pp. 838–841.
19. Lukás, J.; Fridrich, J.; Goljan, M. Detecting Digital Image Forgeries Using Sensor Pattern Noise—Art. No. 60720Y. *Int. Soc. Opt. Eng.* **2006**, *6072*, 362–372.
20. Chierchia, G.; Parrilli, S.; Poggi, G.; Sansone, C.; Verdoliva, L. On the Influence of Denoising in PRNU based Forgery Detection. In Proceedings of the 2nd ACM Workshop on Multimedia in Forensics, Security and Intelligence, Firenze, Italy, 25–29 October 2010.
21. Chierchia, G.; Parrilli, S.; Poggi, G.; Verdoliva, L.; Sansone, C. PRNU-Based Detection of Small-Size Image Forgeries. In Proceedings of the 2011 17th International Conference on Digital Signal Processing (DSP), Corfu, Greece, 13–15 June 2011; pp. 1–6.
22. Kurosawa, K.; Kuroki, K.; Saitoh, N. CCD Fingerprint Method-Identification of a Video Camera from Videotaped Images. In Proceedings of the 1999 International Conference on Image Processing (Cat. 99CH36348), Kobe, Japan, 24–28 October 2003; pp. 537–540.
23. Chen, M.; Fridrich, J.; Goljan, M.; Lukás, J. Source digital camcorder identification using sensor photo response non-uniformity—Art. No. 65051G. *SPIE* **2007**, *6505*. [CrossRef]
24. Bayram, S.; Sencar, T.; Memon, N. Video Copy Detection Based on Source Device Characteristics: A Complementary Approach to Content-Based Methods. In Proceedings of the 1st ACM SIGMM International Conference on Multimedia Information Retrieval, MIR 2008, Vancouver, BC, Canada, 30–31 October 2008; pp. 435–442.
25. Caldelli, R.; Becarelli, R.; Amerini, I. Image Origin Classification Based on Social Network Provenance. *IEEE Trans. Inf. Forensics Secur.* **2017**, *12*, 1299–1308. [CrossRef]
26. Villalba, L.J.G.; Orozco, A.L.S.; Corripio, J.R.; Hernandez-Castro, J. A PRNU-based counter-forensic method to manipulate smartphone image source identification techniques. *Futur. Gener. Comput. Syst.* **2017**, *76*, 418–427. [CrossRef]
27. Villalba, L.J.G.; Orozco, A.L.S.; López, R.R.; Castro, J.H. Identification of smartphone brand and model via forensic video analysis. *Expert Syst. Appl.* **2016**, *55*, 59–69. [CrossRef]
28. Gloe, T.; Pfennig, S.; Kirchner, M. Unexpected Artefacts in PRNU-Based Camera Identification: A 'Dresden Image Database' Case-Study. MM and Sec'12. In Proceedings of the 14th ACM Multimedia and Security Workshop, Coventry, UK, 6–7 September 2012; pp. 109–114.
29. Fridrich, J. *Sensor Defects in Digital Image Forensic. Digital Image Forensics: There is More to a Picture than Meets the Eye*; Springer: New York, NY, USA, 2013; pp. 179–218.
30. Gloe, T.; Böhme, R. The Dresden Image Database for Benchmarking Digital Image Forensics. *J. Digit. Forensic Pract.* **2010**, *3*, 150–159. [CrossRef]
31. Opmeer, S. *Finding the Difference between Digital Photos and Digital Videos with PRNU-Patterns*; Netherlands Forensic Institute: The Hague, The Netherlands, 2015.

32. Scheelen, Y.; van der Lelie, J.; Geradts, Z.; Worring, M. Camera Identification on YouTube. *Chin. J. Forensic Sci.* **2012**, *64*, 19–39.
33. Kiegaing, E.; Emir Dirik, A. PRNU-based source device attribution for YouTube videos. *Digit. Investig.* **2019**, *29*, 91–100.
34. Goljan, M.; Fridrich, J. Camera Identification from Cropped and Scaled Images. In *Security, Forensics, Steganography, and Watermarking of Multimedia Contents*; SPIE: Bellingham, WA, USA, 2008.

Article

Performance Evaluation of Source Camera Attribution by Using Likelihood Ratio Methods

Pasquale Ferrara *,†, Rudolf Haraksim † and Laurent Beslay †

Joint Research Centre, European Commission, 21027 Ispra, Italy; rudolf.haraksim@ec.europa.eu (R.H.); laurent.beslay@ec.europa.eu (L.B.)
* Correspondence: pasquale.ferrara@ec.europa.eu
† These authors contributed equally to this work.

Abstract: Performance evaluation of source camera attribution methods typically stop at the level of analysis of hard to interpret similarity scores. Standard analytic tools include Detection Error Trade-off or Receiver Operating Characteristic curves, or other scalar performance metrics, such as Equal Error Rate or error rates at a specific decision threshold. However, the main drawback of similarity scores is their lack of probabilistic interpretation and thereby their lack of usability in forensic investigation, when assisting the trier of fact to make more sound and more informed decisions. The main objective of this work is to demonstrate a transition from the similarity scores to likelihood ratios in the scope of digital evidence evaluation, which not only have probabilistic meaning, but can be immediately incorporated into the forensic casework and combined with the rest of the case-related forensic. Likelihood ratios are calculated from the Photo Response Non-Uniformity source attribution similarity scores. The experiments conducted aim to compare different strategies applied to both digital images and videos, by considering their respective peculiarities. The results are presented in a format compatible with the guideline for validation of forensic likelihood ratio methods.

Keywords: forensic evidence evaluation; video source attribution; likelihood ratio; performance

Citation: Ferrara, P.; Haraksim, R.; Beslay, L. Performance Evaluation of Source Camera Attribution by Using Likelihood Ratio Methods. *J. Imaging* **2021**, *7*, 116. https://doi.org/10.3390/jimaging7070116

Academic Editors: Irene Amerini, Gianmarco Baldini and Francesco Leotta

Received: 31 May 2021
Accepted: 10 July 2021
Published: 15 July 2021

Publisher's Note: MDPI stays neutral with regard to jurisdictional claims in published maps and institutional affiliations.

Copyright: © 2021 by the authors. Licensee MDPI, Basel, Switzerland. This article is an open access article distributed under the terms and conditions of the Creative Commons Attribution (CC BY) license (https://creativecommons.org/licenses/by/4.0/).

1. Introduction

Evaluation of forensic evidence relies on the concept of likelihood ratios (LRs), derived from the Bayes theorem. In fact, reporting LRs is the preferred way of presenting findings from criminal investigations across the spectrum of forensic disciplines [1]. This is reflected by a number of best-practice manuals [2,3] published by the European Network of Forensic Science Institutes (ENFSI)—covering disciplines of handwriting, fingerprints, document examination and others.

In the vast majority of cases, the result of a comparison between a questioned sample and the reference database leads to a similarity score, which is often dimensionless, lacking any kind of probabilistic interpretation and is therefore very difficult to incorporate into the forensic work-flow, unlike the LRs. It is the case of source camera attribution based on the Sensor Pattern Noise (SPN) or Photo Response Non-Uniformity (PRNU) [4,5], where most of the time the Peak to Correlation Energies (PCEs) [6] are compared to camera-related noise patterns.

Calculation of LRs from similarity scores is described in the literature [7–15], including a LR framework for camera source attribution using SPN and PRNU of still images [16]. Vast majority of these approaches use the plug-in scoring methods, which rely on post-processing of similarity scores using statistical modeling for computation of LRs. Direct methods, which output LR values instead of similarity scores have likewise been described in the literature [17]. These are much more complex to implement mainly due to the necessity to integrate-out the uncertainties when the feature vectors are compared under either of the propositions. The direct methods, as the title suggests, produce probabilistically sound LRs. Due to the continuous similarity score output of PRNU based methods, we use the plug-in score-based approach in order to facilitate a "fair" evaluation and inter-model comparison.

The main contribution of this article is the assignment of probabilistic interpretation to the set of similarity scores obtained from PRNU comparisons in the context of source camera attribution. This aim is reached by converting similarity scores into LRs within a Bayesian interpretation framework [18]. The performance of the resulting LR values, and by extension their usefulness for forensic investigation, is measured following the methodology developed in [19–23]. The objective is to reinforce the reliability of innovative tools such as source camera attribution, allowing them to be used not only as simple new investigation leads but also to contribute in a more determinant way to the investigation of digital forensic evidence. As underlined in the recently adopted EU strategy [24] to tackle Organized Crime 2021–2025, law enforcement and judiciary authorities need to fit for the digital age. The consolidation of their tactics and techniques for digital investigation with new approaches such as the one presented here, will reinforce the acceptability of those digital evidence submitted to the court.

The article is structured in the following way: in the next section we introduce the fundamentals of PRNU analysis. Section 3 presents the score-based plug-in Bayesian evidence evaluation methods for calculation of LRs and tools used for evaluation of performance of these methods. In Section 4, we describe the experimental protocol, the similarity scores and their mapping into LR values. Results obtained from a comparison of different methodologies are presented in Section 5. The contributions and future works are summarized in the conclusions in Section 6.

2. Prnu-Based Source Camera Attribution

PRNU is a unique noise pattern that every camera sensor implants like a passive watermark into every digital image [4,5] and video [25,26]. Due to its uniqueness, the extraction of PRNU signal allows to link a media content to its source device like a digital "fingerprint". More in depth, PRNU is a 2D multiplicative noise pattern and can be modelled as a zero-mean white Gaussian noise [27], as a first approximation. Formally, a generic image can be described as

$$I = I_{(0)} + I_{(0)} \cdot K_I + \Theta \quad (1)$$

where $I_{(0)}$ is an ideal noiseless image, K_I is the PRNU and Θ is a noise term which considers other noisy contributions (i.e., dark current, quantization noise, etc.).

Several techniques were proposed to extract PRNU from an image but in this paper we refer to the one described in [28]. At image level, sensor noise is extracted by means of 2D discrete wavelet decomposition; then, saturated pixels are attenuated, and the noise pattern is normalized to erase liner patterns. Finally, 'blockiness' artifacts due to JPEG compression are removed by means of Wiener filtering.

As best practice, the PRNU associated to a given sensor is estimated by replicating the previous processing for a large enough set of flat-field images, in order to reduce the impact of the images content. The PRNU is then estimated according to the Maximum Likelihood criterion [28] as:

$$\hat{K}(x,y) = \frac{\sum_l I_l(x,y) \cdot K_l(x,y)}{\sum_l I_l^2(x,y)} \quad (2)$$

where $I_l(x,y)$ and $K_l(x,y)$ are, respectively, the images and their associated PRNU estimate.

2.1. Peak-to-Correlation Energy

A similarity measure is needed in order to compare two PRNUs and classify whether they come from the same camera or not. Goljan et al. [6] proposed Peak-to-Correlation Energy (PCE) instead of correlation. PCE consists of measuring the ratio between the correlation peak energy and the energy of correlations evaluated for shifts outside from a neighborhood around the peak value. In order to calculate the PCE, the correlation matrix $\varrho(u,v)$ between two noise pattern of size $r \times c$ needs to be computed in the following way:

$$PCE = \frac{\varrho(u_0, v_0)^2}{\frac{1}{rc-|\mathcal{N}|} \sum_{(u,v) \notin \Omega} \varrho(u,v)^2} \qquad (3)$$

where $\mathcal{N}$ is a neighborhood of $|\mathcal{N}|$ pixels surrounding the correlation peak in position (u_0, v_0).

2.2. Extension to Videos

A straightforward solution for extracting a unique PRNU from a video is to consider video frames as images, and then to apply (2). This approach implicitly assumes geometric alignment of all noise patterns. Unfortunately, such an assumption does not hold for the most recent imaging devices which feature Digital Motion Stabilization (DMS). The DMS aims to generate high quality videos by minimizing any visual impact of vibrations and shaky hands which are often present when using hand-held devices, as illustrated in Figure 1. It performs a geometric alignment of each video frame according to the frame content. This processing alters the geometrical frame-by-frame alignment of the PRNU, so that the assumption of geometrical alignment between PRNUs of the frames is not true any more, consequently leading to worse PRNU estimates if (2) is applied.

In order to address DMS challenge, several matching strategies have been proposed in the literature [29–33]. Although authors propose different approaches, all are based on PCE as similarity measures.

Figure 1. Digital motion video stabilization on subsequent frames. Undesired camera shakes are compensated for in order to have stable contents.

2.3. Reference PRNU Creation

The objective of the analysis is to attribute or dissociate a questioned image or video to a specific device. As a first step, the reference PRNU needs to be extracted for the camera. In the case of the images, the process is quite straightforward: a set of flat-field images is acquired, from which the PRNU is extracted according to (2). In the case of the videos, the process is a bit more elaborated. There are at least two options proposed in the literature:

1. Using flat-field video recording to extract key-frame sensor noise and compute PRNU camera digital fingerprint according to (2). Still videos are used to limit the effect of motion stabilization. For the sake of simplicity, we name it RT1.
2. Employing both flat-field images and flat-field videos [34] in order to lessen the impact of motion stabilization as well as the impact of video compression, which is typically stronger for video frames compared to images. We name this second type RT2.

In order to use both, video recordings and images, we briefly recall how a camera generates a video frame. The process involves three steps: acquisition of a full-frame image, cropping of an internal region with a different aspect ratio (e.g., 16:9 for High Definition videos) and scaling to the final resolution. By assuming that the crop is symmetric with respect to the optical centre and posing the reference system at the centre of the frame, the relation between image and video PRNUs, namely K_I and K_V, can be modeled by the scaling factor $s \in \mathbb{R}$. Once the scaling factor is estimated [30,31,35], the PRNU extracted from images K_I is resized accordingly, as shown in Figure 2.

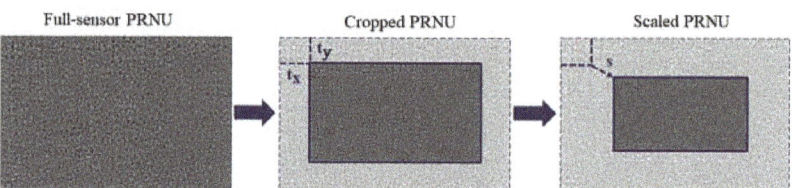

Figure 2. In-camera processing involved in video creation.

2.4. Similarity Scores

As we explained in Section 2.1, similarity scores between two PRNU patterns are based on the computation of PCE. However, its computation does not follow a standard procedure, it is adapted from time to time to the particular use-case. For instance, if a certain robustness against image cropping is needed [6], the analyst can adopt an extended version of PCE where the position of the correlation peak is calculated as:

$$(u_0, v_0) = \arg\max_{u,v \in U}\{\varrho(u,v)\} \quad (4)$$

where U is an arbitrary neighbourhood in which the correlation peak is searched. The operation of maximization clearly impacts on the distribution of the similarity scores. Similar considerations can be made in the case of the video recordings, for those approaches that try to minimize the impact of DMS by adopting (4).

In order to simplify our analysis, we assume that no operation aiming to maliciously modify the PRNU is applied to the data. In this setting, the similarity scores for images are computed according to (3). In the case of the video recordings, we compared three different PRNU comparison strategies:

(a) Baseline: PRNU is obtained by cumulating the noise patterns extracted frame-by-frame according to (2), and the PCE is computed.
(b) Highest Frame Score (HFS): PRNU is extracted and compared frame-by-frame against the reference PRNU, and the maximum PCE is taken [30].
(c) Cumulated Sorted Frames Score (CSFS): PRNUs, extracted from each frame and compared with the reference signal, are first sorted in a descending order according to their individual PCE values; then, they are progressively cumulated, according to (2); finally, the maximum of PCE values obtained at each cumulation step is taken [31].

All the above-mentioned methods compute the PCE as described in (4).

Finally, it is worth noting that, according to the Equation (3), PCE can assume values in the range $[0, +\infty)$. Because in practice the PCE covers a very large range about 0 to $\sim 10^6$, we consider a $\log_{10}$ scale.

3. Performance Evaluation

Couple of key components are necessary in order to compute LRs from the similarity scores: the ground truth regarding the source of origin of the image/video (same source or different source), a set of forensic propositions (hypotheses set for the defence and for the prosecution), and similarity scores, which are produced by different methods described in the previous section. Unlike the traditional performance assessment, which is usually limited to the analysis of the Detection Error Trade-off (DET) and Receiver Operating Characteristic (ROC) curves, we add the probabilistic meaning and interpretation to the similarity scores by transforming them into LRs. In order to do this, we set the hypotheses at the source level:

- H_P (Prosecution): the Questioned Data (QD) comes from the camera C (mated trial).
- H_D (Defense): the QD does not come from the camera C (non-mated trial).

It should be noted here that it is possible, and encouraged, to set the propositions at other than the source level [36]. Once the hypotheses are set, we proceed with the evaluation of forensic evidence under the Bayesian LR framework.

3.1. Bayesian Interpretation Framework

Different ways have been described in the forensic literature to calculate the LRs from continuous similarity scores [19,22]. Once the hypotheses are set, the strength of forensic evidence E is calculated in the following way:

$$LR = \frac{P(E|H_P, I)}{P(E|H_D, I)} \quad (5)$$

where in the numerator of the LR we have the probability of observing $E(QD)$ under the prosecution hypothesis (and additional related case information) and in the denominator of the LR we have the probability of observing the same evidence $E(QD)$ under the defence hypothesis (and additional case-related information). We use a leave-one out cross-validation strategy [20], in which the role of evidence is taken by the left-out similarity score and the LRs are calculated in the following way:

$$LR = \frac{f(S|H_P)}{f(S|H_D)} \quad (6)$$

where the $f(\cdot)$ represents the probability density function of the remaining scores and the S represents the left-out observation.

3.2. Performance Evaluation Tools

Performance assessment of the LR values under either of the propositions follows the methodology proposed in [19,21,22]. In their work on validation of LR values for forensic casework the authors propose measurement of two sets of performance characteristics—primary and secondary.

Given the limited amount of data we focus on evaluation of performance using the primary characteristics and leave the concept of validation of the LRs for forensic casework for future research. Although the full scope of the proposed "validation" framework cannot be applied, the basic concepts presented are valid and provide supplementary information, complementing the typically reported ROC/DET representations and accuracy measures at a fixed operating point.

The following performance characteristics and corresponding graphical representations are presented in the results section:

- *accuracy*, as sum of discriminating power and calibration, represented by the Empirical Cross Entropy (ECE) plot and measured by the log LR cost (CLLR) [37];
- *discriminating power* represented by the DET and ECE^{min} plots and measured by the Equal Error Rate (EER) and $CLLR^{min}$ [38];
- *calibration* represented by the Tippet and the ECE plots and measured by $CLLR^{cal}$ [37].

4. Experimental Protocol

In this section, we first describe the data set we used in the experiments. Afterwards, the experimental protocol follows a logical separation, based on the type of data, namely images and video recordings. For videos, we separate the analysis in function of the type of PRNU reference and the presence or the absence of DMS, in order to perform the four basic experiments mentioned in Section 5. All the experiments produce a set of similarity scores calculated in the course of comparison between the questioned and reference samples.

4.1. Data Corpus

We used the Vision Dataset [39] (except for device D13, according to the names convention) to create a benchmark dataset for pictures and videos. Among the devices, 16 produce motion stabilized videos, whereas the other 18 produce only non-stabilized videos. For each device, we have at our disposal:

- A set of 30 randomly selected flat-field images, from which we extracted the image PRNU K_I.
- A set of flat-field static (labelled as still) and moving (labeled as panrot and move) videos. These videos are used to create reference PRNU K_V per device.
- A set of images with natural content that we used as query data. The set is composed of at least 200 pictures per devices.
- A set of non-flat query videos including still, pan-rotating and moving videos.

In summary, we used 34 different devices, 34 × 30 = 1020 flat-field images, 218 flat-field video recordings, 7393 natural images, 223 non-stabilized and 190 stabilized questioned videos. The number of mated and non-mated scores is summarized in Table 1.

Table 1. Number of similarity scores per experiment.

	# Mated Scores	# Non-Mated Scores
Images	7393	243,969
Non-stabilized videos	223	3791
Stabilized videos	190	2850

4.2. Preliminary Analysis of the Similarity Scores

The two types of experiments (images and videos) present slightly different challenges. For example, let us consider the scores distributions obtained from images analysis and shown in Figure 3. The empirical distributions of $P(E|H_P, I)$ and $P(E|H_D, I)$ are overlapping to some extent. At the same time, if we look closer at the distribution for each device, we observe that for some devices, see Figure 3b, the two distributions are perfectly separated. On the other hand, for some other devices, the score distributions show a non-negligible proportion of mated similarity scores attaining the non-mated similarity score magnitudes, effectively heavily contributing to the False Rejection rates Figure 3c. In other words, the PRNU obtained from these devices compromises the overall performance of the methods under evaluation.

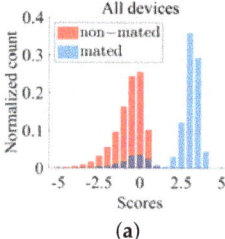
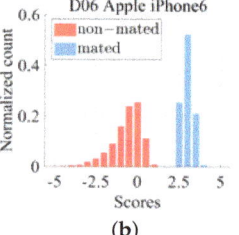
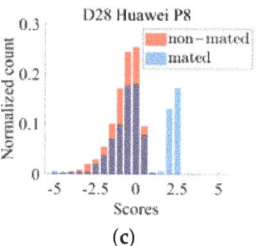

(a) (b) (c)

Figure 3. Histograms of empirical score distributions obtained from images. (**a**): empirical distributions by considering all the devices within the benchmark dataset. (**b**): scores obtained from query images coming from an Apple iPhone 6. (**c**): scores distributions for images acquired through a Huawei P8.

In some cases, for example non-stabilized video recordings against RT1 result in "perfect separation" of the mated and non-mated score distributions (see Figure 4a). While the perfect separation is highly desirable, in the case when number of comparisons is relatively small (as in our case), it usually points in the direction of one of the following problems (or a combination of any of these): plain lack of data, over-fitting (sub-optimal separation of the dataset into training and testing subsets), or a feature space being much greater than the actual dataset.

For some cases however, such as PRNUs obtained from the images, a significant proportion of the mated scores attains the magnitudes of the non-mated scores, thus contributing heavily to the False Rejection error rates. Again, PRNU obtained from these devices compromises the overall performance of the methods under evaluation.

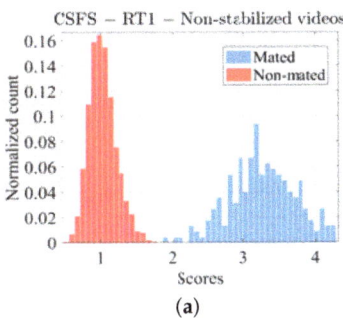
(a)

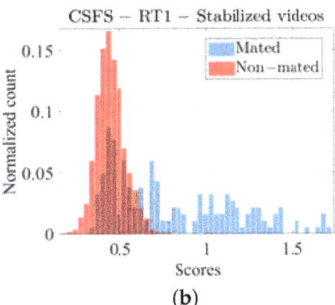
(b)

Figure 4. Histograms of empirical score distributions obtained from non-stabilized (**a**) and stabilized video recordings (**b**). The scores are obtained by using the reference Photo Response Non-Uniformity (PRNU) of type RT1 and by applying the Cumulated Sorted Frame Score (CSFS) method.

4.3. Score to LR Calibration Transformation

4.3.1. Images

Our analysis into the distribution of similarity scores produced by the image test and reference samples showed that the mated samples (H_P) were distributed following the inverted chi squared probability distribution function (PDF) with 1 degree of freedom and shape parameter equal to zero [28]. The non-mated similarity scores (H_D) followed a similar PDF with 1 degree of freedom and a non-zero shape parameter.

Although the inverted chi-squared PDF's provided a reasonably good estimate, they did not generalize well to the previously unseen data when subjected to cross-validation. The generalization issue, or in our case inability to generalize well to the previously unseen data, can be explained by large inter and intra variability among the sensors embedded within different devices, even when coming from the same manufacturer.

Since we do not have at our disposal a fully exhaustive database of mobile devices/cameras from different manufacturers, we opted for a simpler solution and transformed the similarity scores into LRs using regularized logistic regression with a uniform prior regularization [40]. The process of calibration using linear logistic regression can be described in the following way:

- Iterative use of leave-one-out cross validation for both mated and non-mated scores, where each of the left-out scores "plays" the role of the evidence;
- One-to-one mapping from probability to log-odds domain is performed using a logit function [37];
- Calibrated LRs are calculated iteratively for each evidence score.

More detailed description of the use of LR calibration is beyond the scope of this article, but the reader might refer to [23] for more details.

4.3.2. Video Recordings

In the case of the video recordings, we note that while the similarity scores under the hypothesis H_P for the non-stabilized videos follows a Gaussian-like distribution in the logarithmic scale (see Figure 4a), the analogous similarity scores for stabilized videos do not (see Figure 4b). We therefore adopt a different calibration strategy for both cases.

Score distributions under hypothesis H_D follow in both cases a Gaussian-like distribution in the logarithmic domain. This result is in agreement with the outcome of [31], where authors demonstrated that scores under hypothesis H_D are distributed according to a Generalized Extreme Value [41] distribution on the linear scale.

The fact that both mated and non-mated distributions are positive indicates the need of calibration. In the subsequent step we perform a leave-one-out cross-validation calibration and calculate the LR values at the same time.

Knowing the ground truth regarding the origin of the pair of videos and the reference sample (RT1 or RT2), we proceed iteratively through the set of similarity scores, exclude one similarity score (mated or non-mated) to "play" the role of observed evidence. We use remaining similarity scores to model score distributions under either of the propositions.

The Gaussian calibration with optimal risk smoothing is used for the non-stabilized videos as both, the mated (H_P) and non-mated (H_D) scores resemble a "well-behaved" normal distribution (Figure 4a).

The calibration for the case of non-stabilized video sequences can be summarized in the following steps:

- Iterative use of leave-one-out cross-validation for mated and non-mated scores, where each of the left-out scores "plays" the role of the evidence;
- A normal distribution is fitted to the rest of the mated and non-mated scores;
- Calculation of the numerator and denominator of the LR for each left-out score;
- Calibrated LRs are calculated according to (6).

More detailed description of the calculation of LR values from normally distributed similarity scores is beyond the scope of this article, but the interested reader is kindly referred to [20] for more details.

Similarity scores, in particular the mated scores (H_P) produced in the course of comparison between the stabilized videos and reference PRNU do not follow any obvious distribution pattern (Figure 4b). In fact, it is very difficult to fit any particular distribution, given the fact that the mated comparison counts drop to zero on multiple occasions. One could argue that a kernel density function could serve the purpose with which we in principle agree, however given the relatively small number of comparisons we opted for a linear logistic regression calibration in a process identical to that described above in Section 4.3.

5. Performance Evaluation Results

In this section, we provide the experimental results of the PRNU source attribution presented in the likelihood ratios framework. Alike the experimental protocol Section 4, results section follows the same comparative analysis between images, stabilized and non-stabilized videos.

5.1. Images

By assuming that the images are exactly like the ones that the device produces, the most significant parameter that affects the PRNU is the image resolution, which varies from one camera model to another. For this reason, we repeated our analysis for three different resolutions: 1024×1024, 512×512 and 256×256, in order to see the effects of the resolution on the performance of the PRNU.

The DET plots present the discriminating capabilities of the different methods. They (Figure 5) show the probability of false acceptance versus the probability of false rejection of the non-stabilized video on a Gaussian-warped scale. The main advantage of this representation over ROC curves is that the DET curves get close to linear when the LR values follow Gaussian distribution. At the intersection of each DET curve with the main diagonal we find the EER which is a measure of discrimination [37]. The best discriminating capabilities were observed for the highest tested resolution (1024×1024) with the ERR 6%. Reducing the image resolution to one fourth (512×512 pixels) significantly reduce the discriminating capabilities of the PRNU and nearly doubles the EER = 11.8%. Additional reduction of the image size to 256 × 256 pixels lower the discriminating capabilities and rises the EER to 12.8%.

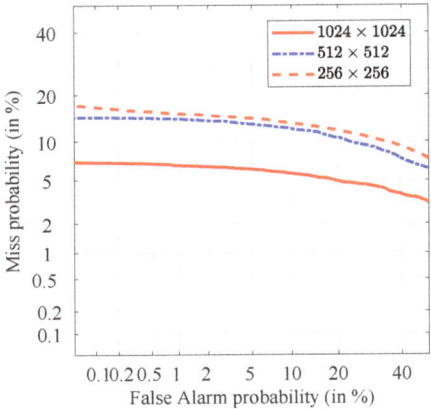

Figure 5. Detection Error Trade-off (DET) plots for picture at different resolutions: 1024 × 1024, 512 × 512 and 256 × 256.

Figure 6 shows the Empirical Cross-Entropy plots, which have information-theoretical interpretation [42]. They provide summary of accuracy, discriminating capabilities and a calibration of a given method, conveniently all in one plot. The black dotted line represents a neutral system (effectively equivalent to making decisions based on a coin-toss using a fair coin). The red line shows the measure of accuracy (CLLR) at the prior-$\log_{10}$-odds = 0, blue dashed line shows the measure of discriminating capabilities of a method (CLLR^{MIN}) at the prior-$\log_{10}$-odds = 0. The difference between the CLLR and CLLR^{MIN} is a measure of calibration (CLLR^{CAL}). When the LRs support the correct hypotheses, the CLLR values tend to be lower (e.g., the lower the CLLR the better the accuracy, the lower the CLLR^{MIN} the better the discriminating capabilities and the lower the CLLR^{CAL} the better he calibration of a given method).

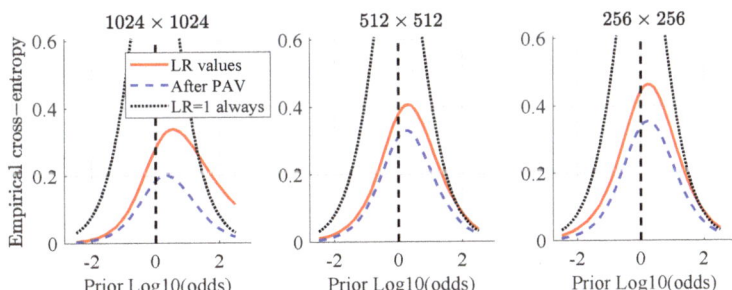

Figure 6. Empirical Cross Entropy (ECE) plots for pictures at different resolutions: 1024 × 1024, 512 × 512 and 256 × 256.

As already introduced in the DET plots, the best discriminating capability of the PRNU is observed for 1024 × 1024 images, confirmed in the ECE plots, achieving CLLR^{MIN} of 0.18. It also shows the highest overall accuracy out of the three image resolutions considered with CLLR = 0.28. Although showing the best discriminating capabilities and accuracy, this method presents the second worst calibration with the calibration loss equal to one third of the overall accuracy (CLLR^{CAL} = 0.096). ECE curves, unlike the DET plots, reveal a weak spot. At prior-log-odds = 1.8 the CLLR (red curve of the 1024 × 1024 images) crosses the line of the reference system (black dotted line), effectively making decisions at the prior-log-odds > 1.8 worse than a coin toss using a fair coin.

Tippett plots as additional measure of calibration presented in Figure 7 show cumulative distribution functions of LRs [38]. Individual curves represent the proportion of comparisons supporting either of the two propositions. The rates of misleading evidence are observed at the intersection of the Tippett plots with the $\log_{10}(LR) = 0$. The symmetry between the two curves (supporting either of the propositions) is likewise used as an indicator of calibration.

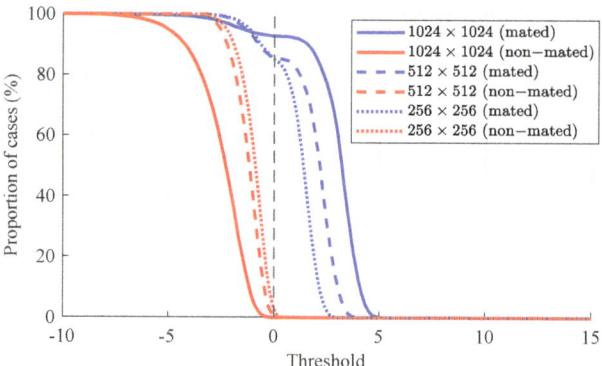

Figure 7. Tippet plots for pictures at different resolutions: 1024 × 1024, 512 × 512 and 256 × 256. Cumulated distributions of mated (blue) and non-mated (red) scores are presented.

The the lowest probabilities of misleading evidence are observed for 1024 × 1024 resolution images ($PME_{HP} = 7.074\%$ and $PME_{HD} = 0.02\%$), and complement the calibration results indicated by the ECE plots above. The probabilities of misleading evidence for the 512 × 512 and 256 × 256 resolution images are show in Table 2.

Table 2. Performance metrics observed for different resolutions of the images. The best performance is highlighted in bold.

	Image Resolution		
	1024 × 1024	**512 × 512**	**256 × 256**
(%) EER	5.984	11.83	12.83
CLLR	**0.2798**	0.3802	0.4428
$CLLR^{MIN}$	**0.1836**	0.3127	0.3377
$CLLR^{CAL}$	0.09614	**0.06744**	0.1051
(%)PME_{HP}	**7.074**	14.12	14.27
(%)PME_{HD}	**0.2049**	1.347	5.24

5.2. Non-Stabilized Video Recordings

DET curves in the case of non-stabilized videos are shown in Figure 8. As an element of comparison, it should be noted here that the discriminating capabilities of well-established biometric systems produce EER typically below 5%, which is also true for some of the methods presented in the non-stabilized subsection. The relatively high EER values achieved with the stabilized video recordings, in contrast with the non-stabilized videos point out potential for additional improvement.

The baseline method shows the best discriminating capabilities in terms of EER in case of comparison of non-stabilized videos against the reference for both types of reference PRNU. The proposed method offers identical or comparable performance (in the worst case, 1% of loss). Due to the near-perfect separation of the mated and non-mated scores, the baseline method and the CSFS method are not visible in the DET plot as their EERs are close to zero.

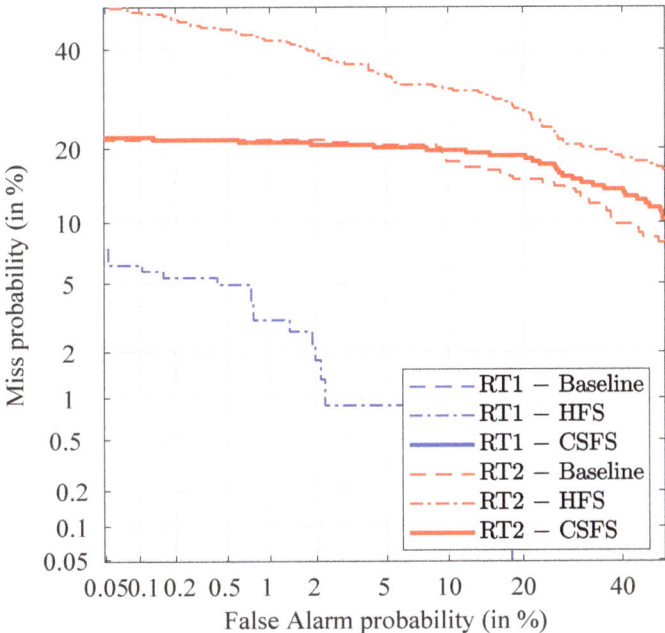

Figure 8. DET plots for non-stabilized videos.

Among the methods compared by means of ECE plots (Figure 9), the baseline method shows the best performance in terms of discriminating capabilities and accuracy for the comparisons of non-stabilized videos versus RT2. The best accuracy and discriminating capabilities in the case of comparisons against reference RT1 is nearly identical for the CSFS and the baseline method, while the baseline method shows slightly better calibration. It is worth adding that the differences observed between these two methods are negligible. Accuracy of LR values produced by the CSFS and the baseline method show sub-optimal performance for the prior-$\log_{10}$-odds ≥ 1, where the red line crosses the black dotted line. LRs of both of these methods in this region are unreliable [20] and the fact-finder trusting these will be effectively making worse decisions than using a coin-toss. Further tests using different calibration methods are necessary to eradicate the source of this behaviour.

By looking at the Tippett plots (Figure 10), the lowest probabilities of misleading evidence in the case of non-stabilized videos in the scope of RT2 experiments is observed for the CSFS method. On the other hand, lowest probability of misleading evidence in the case of non-stabilized videos in the scope of RT1 experiments supporting the H_P is observed for the CSFS method and supporting the H_D for the baseline method. It should likewise be noted that on average, lower rates of misleading evidence have been observed in the context of RT1 experiments, which means that LR in this case provide stronger support to the correct propositions. The results for the non-stabilized videos are summarized below in Table 3 (the best performance is highlighted in bold).

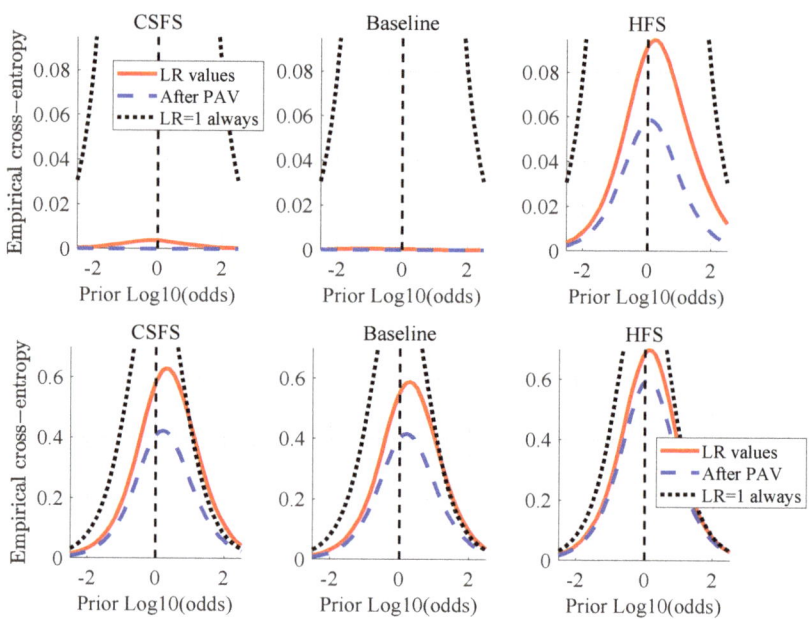

Figure 9. ECE plots: non-stabilized videos vs. RT1 (first row) and RT2 (second row).

Table 3. Summary of the results for accuracy, discriminating power and calibration for the non-stabilized videos. The best performance is highlighted in bold.

	RT1			RT2		
	CSFS	**Baseline**	**HFS**	**CSFS**	**Baseline**	**HFS**
(%) EER	**0.08**	**0.08**	1.98	17.43	**16.48**	23.85
CLLR	0.004	0.003	0.092	0.58	**0.55**	0.69
CLLR^{MIN}	**0.003**	**0.003**	0.062	0.41	**0.4**	0.59
CLLR^{CAL}	0.001	0	0.03	0.17	**0.15**	0.1
(%) PME$_{HP}$	0	0	1.34	21.07	21.5	36.77
(%) PME$_{HD}$	0.13	0	2.24	**1.5**	1.66	3.66

LRs produced in the course of non-stabilized videos show "perfect" accuracy and calibration when compared in the scope of RT1 experiments for proposed and baseline methods. Given the relatively small dataset, these results should be further analysed and followed up by a series of experiments to show the robustness of methods to the previously unseen data and potential overfitting. Slightly better accuracy and calibration was observed for the baseline method when comparing RT2 video recordings however, lower rates of misleading evidence were observed for the proposed method. In general, the performance of baseline and proposed methods can be considered equivalent. Decisions based on the LR values observed for prior log10odds greater than 1.0 for the questioned videos in the scope of RT2 experiments should not be trusted due to the fact that the ECE curve crosses the reference line and these decisions are effectively worse than decisions based on a coin toss.

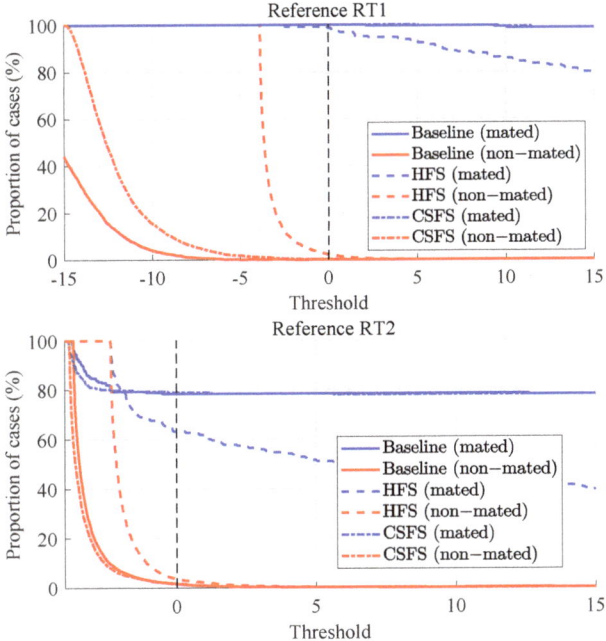

Figure 10. Tippett plots: non-stabilized videos vs. RT1 (upper) and RT2 (lower).

5.3. Stabilized Videos

Before discussing the results, we provide an analysis of the resulting LR values for the stabilized videos by means of normalized-count histograms, which perfectly suit the purpose. As shown in Figure 11, a significant proportion of the LRs supporting the H_P proposition (blue histogram) is overlapping with the LRs supporting the H_D proposition (red histogram). As a result, all of these LRs provide support to the wrong hypothesis (H_D). From the two groups of the stabilized videos (compared against the reference RT1 or RT2) we conclude that the method showing the best discriminating capabilities is in both cases the CSFS method (see Figure 12). The CSFS method shows the best performance in terms of EER for comparisons of stabilized images against the reference set of both types of reference PRNU.

Figure 13 shows the ECE plots in the case of stabilized videos. Amongst the methods compared, the CSFS method shows the best performance in terms of discriminating capabilities and accuracy, while the HFS method shows the best calibration (all be it the difference in calibration between the method proposed and the HFS method is negligible and both of these methods can be described as rather well calibrated).

High rates of misleading evidence of the LR's supporting the H_P on average are the result of small similarity scores (which resulted in low LR values) observed for mated comparisons as discussed above (see Figure 14).

The results for the stabilized video recordings compared against reference RT1 and RT2 are summarized in Table 4 (the best performance is indicated in bold). LRs produced during stabilized videos experiments show better performance in terms of accuracy and discriminating power for the CSFS method over the remaining two methods. In the case of videos compared against RT1 reference the best calibration was observed for the HFS method. It should be noted that the calibration losses observed in the course of this set of experiments were minimal and decisions regarding which method to favour should not be based on the calibration measure alone.

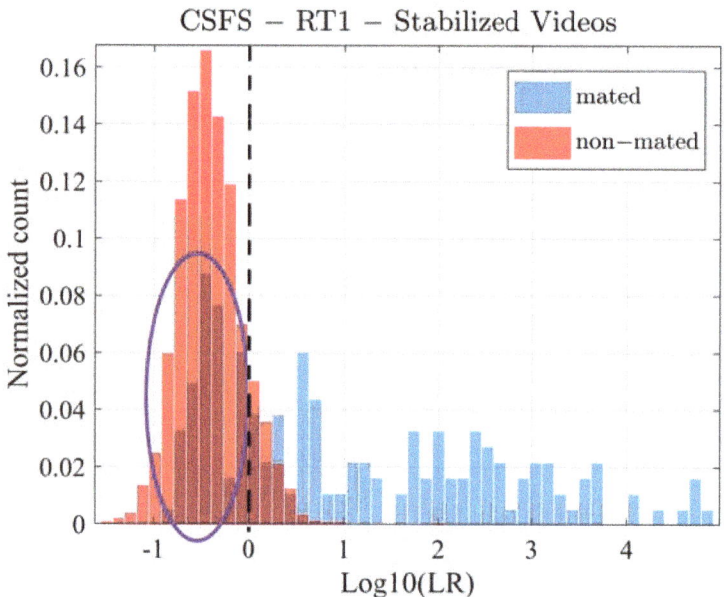

Figure 11. Likelihood ratio distribution after the linear logistic regression calibration. Magenta ellipse indicates the issue with the mated scores, black line shows $log_{10}(LR) = 0$.

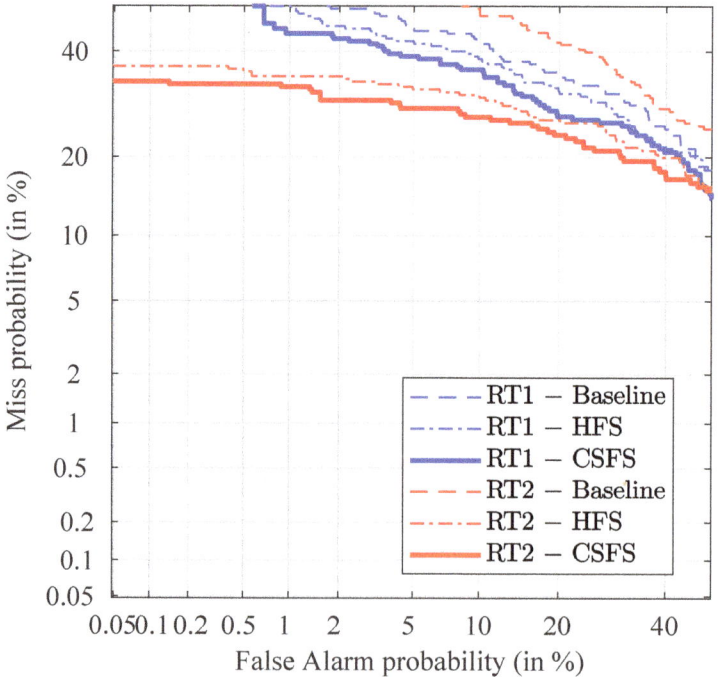

Figure 12. DET plots for stabilized videos.

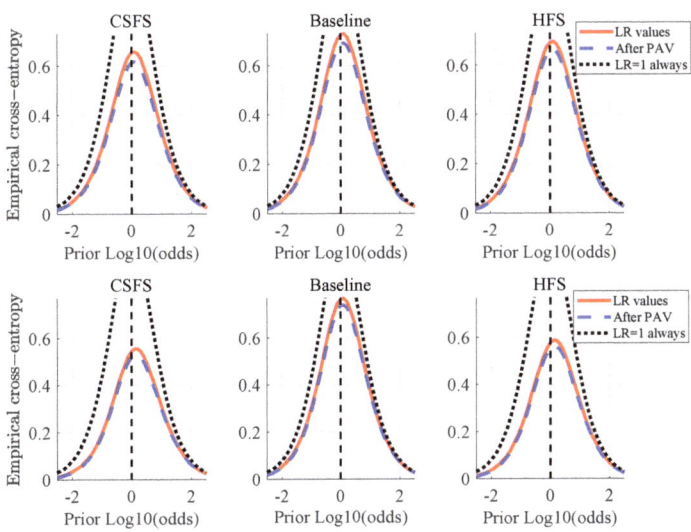

Figure 13. ECE plots: stabilized videos vs. RT1 (first row) and RT2 (second row).

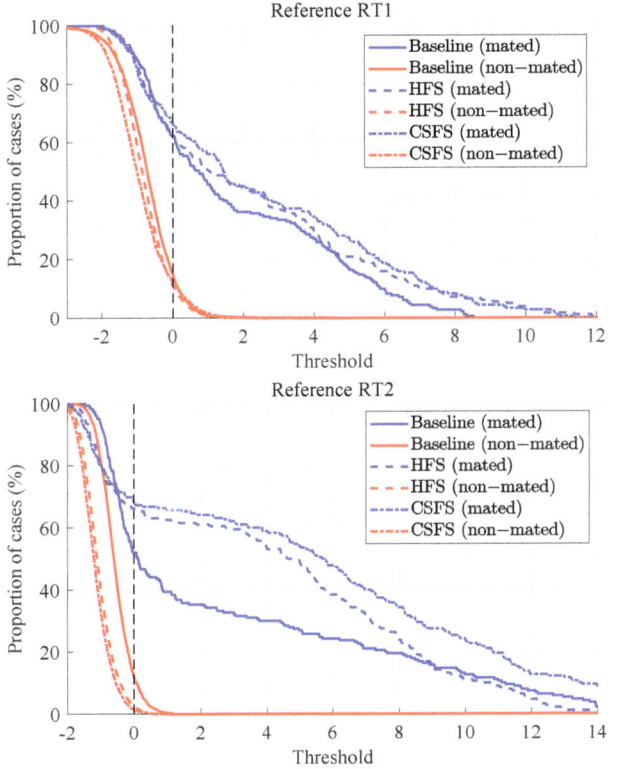

Figure 14. Tippett plots: stabilized videos vs. RT1 (upper) and RT2 (lower).

Table 4. Summary of the results for accuracy, discriminating power and calibration for the stabilized videos. The best performance is highlighted in bold.

	RT1			RT2		
	CSFS	Baseline	HFS	CSFS	Baseline	HFS
(%) EER	**26.46**	30.85	28.64	**22.7**	33.5	25.86
CLLR	**0.66**	0.73	0.69	**0.55**	0.77	0.58
$CLLR^{MIN}$	**0.62**	0.69	0.66	**0.52**	0.74	0.56
$CLLR^{CAL}$	0.04	0.04	**0.03**	**0.03**	0.03	0.04
(%)PME_{HP}	**33.52**	37.91	37.36	**31.58**	47.89	33.68
(%)PME_{HD}	12.37	15.07	**10.9**	**1.47**	12.35	2.49

6. Conclusions

In this article we addressed to our best knowledge for the first time the challenge of source camera attribution for video recordings from a perspective of a forensic evidence evaluation using likelihood ratios, and complemented previous research [16] on source camera attribution for still images. We have taken multiple continuous sets of similarity scores (mated and non-mated), converted them into LRs using the probability density function and measured their performance. In essence, we gave the difficult-to-interpret set of similarity scores a probabilistic meaning and interpretation.

Reflecting on the analysis of the results of different methods and settings, particularly ECE plots prove useful as they point out regions where produced LRs provide unreliable support to forensic evidence for both still images as well as video recordings. Considering the fact that there is a lot more information present in the video recordings (sequence of images) than in a single still image, it is not surprising that the best performance in terms of accuracy, calibration and discriminating capabilities was observed for the non-stabilized video recordings. However, performance dramatically drops if digital motion stabilization is adopted. A particular attention should be paid to the analysis of images, for which apart from the image resolution the device model should be considered as a deciding parameter. The latter might affect in a positive or negative manner the overall performance of the system.

Additional validation experiments accompanied by further analysis of the similarity scores will be performed in the near future. Particular attention will be given to the "perfectly separated" similarity scores and regions of high correlation, with the aim to demonstrate robustness to the lack of data, generalization and coherence [23]—which present the secondary performance characteristics necessary for the validation of the methods presented for forensic casework. Likewise, different probability distribution functions will be used to convert the hard-to-interpret similarity scores into reliable likelihood ratios.

Author Contributions: Conceptualization, L.B.; methodology, R.H. and P.F.; software, R.H. and P.F.; validation, P.F. and R.H.; formal analysis, R.H.; investigation, P.F. and R.H.; resources, P.F.; data curation, P.F.; writing—original draft preparation, P.F. and R.H.; writing—review and editing, L.B.; visualization, P.F. and R.H.; supervision, L.B.; project administration, L.B. All authors have read and agreed to the published version of the manuscript.

Funding: This research received no external funding.

Institutional Review Board Statement: Not applicable.

Informed Consent Statement: Not applicable.

Data Availability Statement: Publicly available datasets were analyzed in this study. This data can be found here: https://lesc.dinfo.unifi.it/VISION/ (last accessed: 23 September 2020).

Conflicts of Interest: The authors declare no conflict of interest.

Abbreviations

The following abbreviations are used in this manuscript:

PRNU	Photo Response Non-Uniformity
DMS	Digital Motion Stabilization
LR	Likelihood Ratio
ENFSI	European Network of Forensic Science Institutes
SPN	Sensor Pattern Noise
PCE	Peak-to-Correlation Energy
RT1	Reference Type 1
RT2	Reference Type 2
HFS	Highest Frame Score
CSFS	Cumulated Sorted Frame Score
QD	Questioned Data
ROC	Receiver Operating Characteristic
DET	Detection Error Trade-off
ECE	Empirical Cross Entropy
CLLR	Curves and Log LR (cost)
EER	Equal Error Rate

References

1. Casey, E. Standardization of forming and expressing preliminary evaluative opinions on digital evidence. *Forensic Sci. Int. Digit. Investig.* **2020**, *32*, 200888. [CrossRef]
2. European Network of Forensic Science Institutes. Best Practice Manuals. Available online: http://enfsi.eu/documents/best-practice-manuals/ (accessed on 15 February 2021).
3. European Network of Forensic Science Institutes—Forensic Information Technology Working Group. Best Practice Manual for the Forensic Examination of Digital Technology. Available online: https://enfsi.eu/wp-content/uploads/2016/09/1._forensic_examination_of_digital_technology_0.pdf (accessed on 15 February 2021).
4. Lukas, J.; Fridrich, J.; Goljan, M. Digital camera identification from sensor pattern noise. *IEEE Trans. Inf. Forensics Secur.* **2006**, *1*, 205–214. [CrossRef]
5. Li, C.T. Source camera identification using enhanced sensor pattern noise. *IEEE Trans. Inf. Forensics Secur.* **2010**, *5*, 280–287.
6. Goljan, M.; Fridrich, J. Camera identification from cropped and scaled images. In *Security, Forensics, Steganography, and Watermarking of Multimedia Contents X*; SPIE: San Jose, CA, USA, 2008; Volume 6819, p. 68190E.
7. Gonzalez-Rodriguez, J.; Fierrez-Aguilar, J.; Ramos-Castro, D.; Ortega-Garcia, J. Bayesian analysis of fingerprint, face and signature evidences with automatic biometric systems. *Forensic Sci. Int.* **2005**, *155*, 126–140. [CrossRef] [PubMed]
8. Egli, N.; Champod, C.; Margot, P. Evidence evaluation in fingerprint comparison and automated fingerprint identification systems–modelling within finger variability. *Forensic Sci. Int.* **2007**, *167*, 189–195. [CrossRef]
9. Hepler, A.B.; Saunders, C.P.; Davis, L.J.; Buscaglia, J. Score-based likelihood ratios for handwriting evidence. *Forensic Sci. Int.* **2012**, *219*, 129–140. [CrossRef]
10. Champod, C.; Evett, I.; Kuchler, B. Earmarks as evidence: A critical review. *J. Forensic Sci.* **2001**, *46*, 1275–1284. [CrossRef]
11. Meuwly, D. Forensic individualization from biometric data. *Sci. Justice* **2006**, *46*, 205–213. [CrossRef]
12. Zadora, G.; Martyna, A.; Ramos, D.; Aitken, C. *Statistical Analysis in Forensic Science: Evidential Values of Multivariate Physicochemical Data*; John Wiley and Sons: Hoboken, NJ, USA, 2014.
13. Perlin, M.; Legler, M.; Spencer, C.; Smith, J.; Allan, W.; Belrose, J.; Duceman, B. Validating true allele DNA mixture interpretation. *J. Forensic Sci.* **2011**, *56*, 1430–1447. [CrossRef]
14. Hoffman, K. Statistical evaluation of the evidential value of human hairs possibly coming from multiple sources. *J. Forensic Sci.* **1991**, *36*, 1053–1058. [CrossRef]
15. Champod, C.; Baldwin, D.; Taroni, F.; Buckleton, S.J. Firearms and tool marks identification: The Bayesian approach. *AFTE J.* **2003**, *35*, 307–316.
16. van Houten, W.; Alberink, I.; Geradts, Z. Implementation of the likelihood ratio framework for camera identification based on sensor noise patterns. *Law Probab. Risk* **2011**, *10*, 149–159. [CrossRef]
17. Ramos, D. Forensic Evaluation of the Evidence Using Automatic Speaker Recognition Systems. Ph.D. Thesis, Escuela Politecnica Superior, Universidad Autonoma de Madrid, Madrid, Spain, 2007.
18. Champod, C.; Taroni, F. *Interpretation of Evidence: The Bayesian Approach*; Taylor and Francis: London, UK, 1999; pp. 379–398.
19. Haraksim, R. Validation of Likelihood Ratio Methods Used for Forensic Evidence Evaluation: Application in Forensic Fingerprints. Ph.D. Thesis, University of Twente, Enschede, The Netherlands, 2014.
20. Haraksim, R.; Ramos, D.; Meuwly, D. Validation of likelihood ratio methods for forensic evidence evaluation handling multimodal score distributions. *IET Biom.* **2016**, *6*, 61–69. [CrossRef]

21. Meuwly, D.; Ramos, D.; Haraksim, R. A guideline for the validation of likelihood ratio methods used for forensic evidence evaluation. *Forensic Sci. Int.* **2017**, *276*, 142–153. [CrossRef]
22. Ramos, D.; Haraksim, R.; Meuwly, D. Likelihood ratio data to report the validation of a forensic fingerprint evaluation method. *Data Brief* **2017**, *10*, 75–92. [CrossRef] [PubMed]
23. Ramos, D.; Meuwly, D.; Haraksim, R.; Berger, C. Validation of Forensic Automatic Likelihood Ratio Methods. In *Handbook of Forensic Statistics*; Chapman & Hall/CRC Handbooks of Modern Statistical Methods; Banks, D., Kafadar, K., Kaye, D., Eds.; Chapman & Hall/CRC: Boca Raton, FL, USA, in press.
24. European Commission. EU Security Union Strategy: Connecting the Dots in a New Security Ecosystem. Available online: https://ec.europa.eu/commission/presscorner/detail/en/ip_20_1379 (accessed on 15 September 2020).
25. Chen, M.; Fridrich, J.; Goljan, M.; Lukáš, J. Source digital camcorder identification using sensor photo response non-uniformity. In Proceedings of the SPIE 6505, Security, Steganography, and Watermarking of Multimedia Contents IX, San Jose, CA, USA, 29 January–1 February 2007.
26. van Houten, W.; Geradts, Z. Using sensor noise to identify low resolution compressed videos from YouTube. In *Computational Forensics*; Springer: Berlin/Heidelberg, Germany, 2009; pp. 104–115.
27. Chen, M.; Fridrich, J.; Goljan, M.; Lukáš, J. Determining image origin and integrity using sensor noise. *IEEE Trans. Inf. Forensics Secur.* **2008**, *3*, 74–90. [CrossRef]
28. Goljan, M.; Fridrich, J.; Filler, T. Large scale test of sensor fingerprint camera identification. In *Media Forensics and Security*; SPIE: San Jose, CA, USA, 2009; Volume 7254, p. 72540I.
29. Taspinar, S.; Mohanty, M.; Memon, N. Source camera attribution using stabilized video. In Proceedings of the IEEE International Workshop on Information Forensics and Security, Abu Dhabi, United Arab Emirates, 4–7 December 2016; pp. 1–6.
30. Mandelli, S.; Bestagini, P.; Verdoliva, L.; Tubaro, S. Facing device attribution problem for stabilized video sequences. *IEEE Trans. Inf. Forensics Secur.* **2020**, *15*, 14–27. [CrossRef]
31. Ferrara, P.; Beslay, L. Robust video source recognition in presence of motion stabilization. In Proceedings of the 8th IEEE International Workshop on Biometrics and Forensics, Porto, Portugal, 29–30 April 2020; pp. 1–6.
32. Mandelli, S.; Argenti, F.; Bestagini, P.; Iuliani, M.; Piva, A.; Tubaro, S. A Modified Fourier-Mellin Approach For Source Device Identification On Stabilized Videos. In Proceedings of the 2020 IEEE International Conference on Image Processing (ICIP), Abu Dhabi, United Arab Emirates, 25–28 October 2020; pp. 1266–1270.
33. Altinisik, E.; Sencar, H.T. Source Camera Verification for Strongly Stabilized Videos. *IEEE Trans. Inf. Forensics Secur.* **2021**, *16*, 643–657. [CrossRef]
34. Iuliani, M.; Fontani, M.; Shullani, D.; Piva, A. Hybrid reference-based Video Source Identification. *Sensors* **2019**, *19*, 649. [CrossRef]
35. Bellavia, F.; Iuliani, M.; Fanfani, M.; Colombo, C.; Piva, A. PRNU pattern alignment for images and videos based on scene content. In Proceedings of the IEEE International Conference on Image Processing, Taipei, Taiwan, 22–25 September 2019; pp. 91–95.
36. Ommen, D.M.; Saunders, C.P. Building a unified statistical framework for the forensic identification of source problems. *Law Probab. Risk* **2018**, *17*, 179–197. [CrossRef]
37. Brümmer, N.; du Preez, J. Application-independent evaluation of speaker detection. *Comput. Speech Lang.* **2006**, *20*, 230–275. [CrossRef]
38. Meuwly, D. Reconnaissance de Locuteurs en Sciences Forensiques: L'apport d'une Approche Automatique. Ph.D. Thesis, Université de Lausanne, Lausanne, Switzerland, 2000.
39. Shullani, D.; Fontani, M.; Iuliani, M.; Shaya, O.A.; Piva, A. VISION: A video and image dataset for source identification. *EURASIP J. Inf. Secur.* **2017**, *2017*, 15. [CrossRef]
40. Morrison, G.; Poh, N. Avoiding overstating the strength of forensic evidence: Shrunk likelihood ratios/Bayes factors. *Sci. Justice J. Forensic Sci. Soc.* **2018**, *58*, 200–218. [CrossRef]
41. Leadbetter, M.R.; Lindgren, G.; Rootzen, H. *Extremes and Related Properties of Random Sequences and Processes*; Springer Science & Business Media: Berlin/Heidelberg, Germany, 2012.
42. Ramos, D.; Gonzalez-Rodriguez, J. Reliable support: Measuring calibration of likelihood ratios. *Forensic Sci. Int.* **2013**, *230*, 156–169. [CrossRef] [PubMed]

Journal of Imaging

Article

CNN-Based Multi-Modal Camera Model Identification on Video Sequences

Davide Dal Cortivo, Sara Mandelli *, Paolo Bestagini and Stefano Tubaro

Dipartimento di Elettronica, Informazione e Bioingegneria, Politecnico di Milano, 20133 Milan, Italy; davide.dalcortivo@mail.polimi.it (D.D.C.); paolo.bestagini@polimi.it (P.B.); stefano.tubaro@polimi.it (S.T.)
* Correspondence: sara.mandelli@polimi.it

Citation: Dal Cortivo, D.; Mandelli, S.; Bestagini, P.; Tubaro, S. CNN-Based Multi-Modal Camera Model Identification on Video Sequences. *J. Imaging* **2021**, *7*, 135. https://doi.org/10.3390/jimaging7080135

Academic Editors: Irene Amerini, Gianmarco Baldini and Francesco Leotta

Received: 25 June 2021
Accepted: 2 August 2021
Published: 5 August 2021

Publisher's Note: MDPI stays neutral with regard to jurisdictional claims in published maps and institutional affiliations.

Copyright: © 2021 by the authors. Licensee MDPI, Basel, Switzerland. This article is an open access article distributed under the terms and conditions of the Creative Commons Attribution (CC BY) license (https:// creativecommons.org/licenses/by/ 4.0/).

Abstract: Identifying the source camera of images and videos has gained significant importance in multimedia forensics. It allows tracing back data to their creator, thus enabling to solve copyright infringement cases and expose the authors of hideous crimes. In this paper, we focus on the problem of camera model identification for video sequences, that is, given a video under analysis, detecting the camera model used for its acquisition. To this purpose, we develop two different CNN-based camera model identification methods, working in a novel multi-modal scenario. Differently from mono-modal methods, which use only the visual or audio information from the investigated video to tackle the identification task, the proposed multi-modal methods jointly exploit audio and visual information. We test our proposed methodologies on the well-known Vision dataset, which collects almost 2000 video sequences belonging to different devices. Experiments are performed, considering native videos directly acquired by their acquisition devices and videos uploaded on social media platforms, such as YouTube and WhatsApp. The achieved results show that the proposed multi-modal approaches significantly outperform their mono-modal counterparts, representing a valuable strategy for the tackled problem and opening future research to even more challenging scenarios.

Keywords: camera model identification; video forensics; audio forensics; convolutional neural networks

1. Introduction

Camera model identification has gained significant importance in multimedia forensic investigations as digital multimedia contents (i.e., digital images, videos and audio sequences) are increasingly widespread and will continue to spread in the future with the advance of technological progress. This phenomenon is mainly attributable to the advent of the internet and social media, which have allowed a very rapid diffusion of digital contents and, consequently, made it extremely difficult to trace their origin.

For instance, in forensic investigations, tracing the origin of digital contents can be essential to identify the perpetrators of such crimes as rape, drug trafficking or acts of terrorism. There is also the possibility that certain private content become viral through the internet, as has sadly happened in recent times with revenge porn. Being able to retrieve the source of multimedia content, therefore, assumes a fundamental role.

This paper aims at determining the smartphone model used to acquire digital video sequences by jointly exploiting visual and audio information from the videos themselves. We mainly focus on video source identification because little work has been done specifically for digital video sequences in the forensic literature [1]. On the contrary, the analysis of digital images is widely addressed [2]. We can identify the camera model used to acquire an image, thanks to the various peculiar traces left on the photograph at the time of shooting. In this vein, the two main families of approaches related to image camera model identification are defined as model-based and data-driven.

Model-based approaches specifically rely on exploiting the traces released by the digital image acquisition process in order to identify the camera model. Several works in the literature exploit specific features associated with the Color Filter Array (CFA)

configuration (i.e., the specific arrangement of color filters in the sensor plane) [3,4] and the CFA interpolation algorithm [5–9] to retrieve information about the source camera model. Undesired optical aberration effects generated by the lens are exploited as well in [10–14]. Moreover, other processing operations and defects (typical of the image acquisition pipeline), such as dust particles left on the sensor [15] and noise patterns [16], have been demonstrated to carry information about the used camera model.

In the last few years, the availability of digital data and computational resources has lead to the growth of data-driven approaches, which have greatly outperformed many model-based solutions proposed in the past. Instead of focusing on a specific trace left by the image acquisition process, as is typically done in model-based methodologies, data-driven approaches are able to capture model traces, due to various components' interplay [2]. The most recent and best-performing data-driven methodologies are those based on learned features, that is, methods directly feeding digital images to a deep-learning paradigm in order to learn model-related features and to associate images with their original source. In this field, Convolutional Neural Networks (CNNs) are now the most widespread solution [17–22].

To our knowledge, the only work that investigates the problem of camera model identification on video sequences is proposed in [1]. The authors exploit a CNN to produce camera model identification scores for small patches extracted from video frames, and then fuse the achieved scores to produce a single accurate classification result per video.

In this paper, we rely on advanced deep-learning approaches to develop effective methods for camera model identification on video sequences. Specifically, our proposed method involves the use of CNNs capable of classifying videos by jointly extracting suitable features from their visual and audio content. We define the proposed strategy as multi-modal since we exploit both visual and audio information coming from the query video to solve the identification task. Given a video, as visual content, we use patches cropped from the frames; as audio content, we use patches cropped from the Log-Mel Spectrogram (LMS) of its audio track. In this vein, the approach suggested by [1] falls into the mono-modal category, as the authors only exploit the visual content to classify a query video.

We propose two distinct multi-modal camera model identification approaches. In both proposed approaches, we make use of CNNs and feed them with pairs of visual and audio patches. In the first approach, we compare and fuse the scores individually obtained from two CNNs, trained following a mono-modal strategy, i.e., one CNN only deals with visual information and the other one only with audio. In the second approach, we train a single multi-input CNN, which deals with both visual and audio patches. Moreover, for each proposed approach, we investigate three different network configurations and data pre-processings, exploiting effective CNN architectures that are well known in the state of the art [23,24].

We evaluate results on the Vision dataset, which contains approximately 650 native video sequences with their related social media versions, collecting almost 2000 videos recorded by 35 modern smartphones. The videos on which we conduct experiments are not only the original native ones; we also use those compressed by the WhatsApp and YouTube algorithms so as to explore the effects of data recompression and to investigate challenging scenarios in which the training and testing datasets do not share common characteristics.

To provide a baseline strategy for comparing the achieved results, we investigate the mono-modal attribution problems as well. Indeed, the vast majority of state-of-the-art works in multimedia forensics always deal with video sequences by only exploiting their visual or audio content in a separate way [25–29]. Only a few works have been proposed that employ both visual and audio cues for multimedia forensics purposes, but they do not tackle the camera model identification task [30–33]. We evaluate the mono-modal results achieved by exploiting only visual or audio patches to classify the query video sequence. The performed experimental campaign highlights the effectiveness of the proposed multi-modal methodology with respect to mono-modal strategies. In general, the pursued multi-modal approaches demonstrate to be significantly more effective than standard mono-modal solutions. As expected, we verify that data that undergo stronger compression (e.g., videos uploaded to the WhatsApp application) are more challenging to classify. Nonetheless, the proposed multi-modal methods outperform the mono-modal strategies also in this complicated scenario.

Our work is organized as follows. In Section 2, we introduce some general concepts in order to better understand the tackled problem and the proposed methodology. In Section 3, we report the formulation of the problems of mono-modal and multi-modal camera model attribution. In Section 4, we report a detailed explanation of the resolution method proposed. In Section 5, we analyze the achieved results. Finally, Section 6 draws some conclusions.

2. Background

Identifying the camera model used to acquire an image or a video frame is possible, thanks to the many peculiar traces left on them at the shooting time. To better understand the traces that we are referring to, in this section, we provide the reader with some background on the generic acquisition pipeline of digital images. Then, since we investigate also the audio content of video sequences, we introduce the definition of the Mel scale and Log-Mel Spectrogram (LMS) of digital audio signals. In particular, the LMS is a very powerful tool for analyzing the spectral and temporal evolution of an audio track.

2.1. Digital Image Acquisition Pipeline

Whenever we take a photograph with a digital camera or smartphone, we trigger an elaborate process consisting of several operations. This process, which lasts a few fractions of a second, starts when we press the shutter button and ends when we can visualize the shot taken. In general, the acquisition pipeline of a digital image is not unique. There can be differences among the vendors, the device models and the on-board technologies that are available. Nonetheless, we can reasonably model the image acquisition pipeline as a series of common steps [34], as depicted in Figure 1.

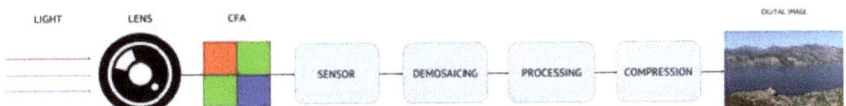

Figure 1. Typical steps of a common digital image acquisition pipeline.

Light rays hit a lens that focuses them on the sensor [35]. The surface of a sensor is covered by a grid of microscopic pits called photosites, which represent the pixels of a digital image and return a different voltage depending on the intensity of the light that hits them. To capture colors, most sensors use color filters. The most common one is the Color Filter Array (CFA) (or Bayer filter), which covers each photosite with a colored filter (red, green or blue), specializing it in capturing that particular color. The shape of the CFA determines the color captured by each pixel, and this is a vendor choice. Beyond the CFA grid, we end up with three partially sampled color layers, where only one color (i.e., red, blue or green) is impressed at each pixel location. To retrieve the missing color information (e.g., blue and red for pixels that only acquired green light), an interpolation is made between the color captured by the photosite itself and the colors captured by the neighboring photosites. This procedure, namely the demosaicing, debayering or CFA interpolation process, allows to obtain a raw version of color images and can be implemented using proprietary interpolation techniques.

After that, we have a processing phase consisting of additional operations. For instance, as lenses may introduce various kinds of optical aberrations (e.g., radial lens distortion, chromatic aberration, and vignetting), camera vendors typically apply some digital correction; this may introduce forensic traces. Furthermore, other common operations that are vendor-specific are the white balancing and the color correction. Eventually, a step of image compression is typically applied. In this regard, JPEG compression is the most widespread operation and again introduces implementation-specific and quality degrees of freedom.

2.2. Mel Scale and Log-Mel Spectrogram

The Mel scale is a perceptual scale of pitches proposed in 1940 by [36]. In particular, the Mel scale aims at mimicking the non-linear human ear perception of sound by being more discriminative at lower frequencies and less discriminative at higher frequencies. The relation between pitch (in Mel scale) and frequency (in Hz) is as follows:

$$p = \text{Mel}(f) = 2595 \cdot \log\left(1 + \frac{f}{700}\right), \quad (1)$$

where $p = \text{Mel}(f)$ indicates the perceived pitch $p[\text{Mel}]$ of a sound at frequency $f[\text{Hz}]$. Conversely, we can define as $f = \text{Mel}^{-1}(p)$ the inverse relationship, by means of which we can compute the frequency (Hz) starting from the pitch (Mel).

The human ear's behavior can be simulated with the so-called Mel filterbank, a set of K triangular filters, where each filter has a maximum response at the center frequency and decreases linearly toward 0 until it reaches the center frequency of the two adjacent ones. Specifically, the filter centered around the pitch p in Mel scale can be modeled as follows:

$$H_p(f) = \begin{cases} \frac{f - \text{Mel}^{-1}(p-1)}{\text{Mel}^{-1}(p) - \text{Mel}^{-1}(p-1)}, & \text{Mel}^{-1}(p-1) \leq f < \text{Mel}^{-1}(p) \\ \frac{\text{Mel}^{-1}(p+1) - f}{\text{Mel}^{-1}(p+1) - \text{Mel}^{-1}(p)}, & \text{Mel}^{-1}(p) \leq f \leq \text{Mel}^{-1}(p+1) \\ 0, & \text{otherwise} \end{cases} \quad (2)$$

The entire Mel filterbank can be modeled as a two-dimensional matrix $\mathbf{H}$ with size $F \times K$, where columns contain the coefficients associated with the different filters $H_p(f)$ (related to K distinct pitches), and rows are associated with frequencies.

By applying the Mel filterbank $\mathbf{H}$ to the spectrogram of an audio signal, we can compute the Log-Mel Spectrogram (LMS), which is an important tool widely used for speech and audio processing [24,37,38]. Considering a signal evaluated over T temporal samples and F frequency bins, LMS can be represented as a 2D matrix $\mathbf{L}$ with size $T \times K$, computed as follows:

$$\mathbf{L} = \ln(\mathbf{S} \cdot \mathbf{H} + \epsilon). \quad (3)$$

where $\mathbf{S}$ is a 2D matrix with size $T \times F$ containing the spectrogram of the audio signal (i.e., the magnitude of the Short-Time Fourier Transform (STFT), with frequency information along columns and time information along rows), $\cdot$ computes the matrix multiplication, $\ln(\cdot)$ computes the natural logarithm, and ϵ is a small constant used to avoid feeding zeros to the logarithm. The resulting LMS brings information about the spectral content of the audio signal (in Mel scale) as a function of the temporal evolution: along columns, we find pitches in Mel scale; along rows, the temporal evolution.

3. Problem Formulation

The problem we address in this paper is that of camera model identification on video sequences. We mainly focus on identifying the source camera model of digital video sequences, as the analysis of digital images has been widely addressed in the forensic literature, with excellent results [2,18,21,22]. In particular, we work with video sequences recorded from different smartphone models and propose an innovative approach that combines visual and audio information of the considered videos. In the following sections, we first introduce the standard mono-modal problem, which aims at identifying the source camera model of a video sequence, exploiting only its visual or audio information. Then, we introduce the actual multi-modal problem tackled in this paper, which employs both visual and audio cues to identify the source camera model from videos.

3.1. Mono-Modal Camera Model Identification

The problem of mono-modal camera model identification consists of detecting the device model used to acquire a specific kind of media at a single modality, for instance, given a photograph, understanding the model of the camera used to take it, or, alternatively, given an audio recording, detecting the used recorder model. Given a video, which is the case of our interest, the mono-modal model attribution consists of identifying the device model that shot it, using only the visual or audio information of the video itself.

3.2. Multi-Modal Camera Model Identification

Given a video sequence, the problem of multi-modal camera model identification converts to identifying the device model that shot it, using both the visual and audio information of the video itself. In our case, we consider a closed-set identification, which consists of detecting the camera model used to shoot a video sequence within a set of known devices. In this scenario, the investigator assumes that the video being analyzed is taken with a device belonging to a family of devices that she/he knows. If the video does not come from any of those devices, the investigator will wrongly attribute the video to one of those.

4. Methodology

In this paper, we propose to solve the problem of closed-set multi-modal camera model identification on video sequences. Figure 2 represents the general scheme of the proposed methodology. Starting from the video under analysis, we jointly exploit its visual and audio content to retrieve the smartphone model used to shoot it. In particular, we extract both visual and audio cues of query video sequences and feed these data into one or multiple CNNs that can discriminate among different source camera models. In a nutshell, the proposed method includes two main steps:

1. Content extraction and pre-processing: extraction of visual and audio content from the video sequence under analysis and manipulation of data prior to feeding them to CNNs;
2. CNN processing: feature extraction and classification block composed of one or multiple CNNs.

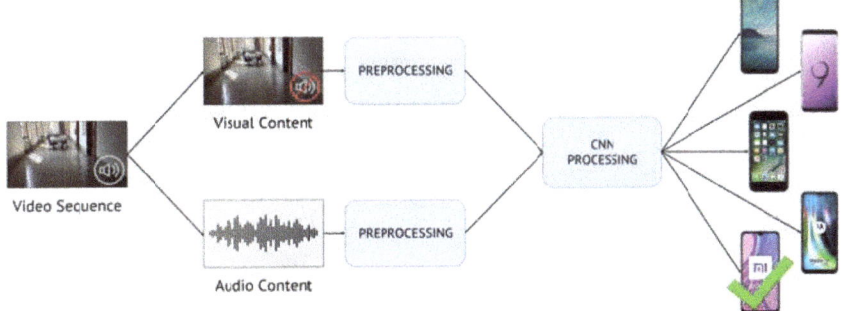

Figure 2. Pipeline of the proposed method to solve multi-modal camera model identification on video sequences. Given a query video sequence, we extract and pre-process its visual and audio content, then feed these data to CNNs in order to identify the actual source camera model.

In the following lines, we enter more in detail for each step of the proposed pipeline.

4.1. Content Extraction and Pre-Processing

The extraction and pre-processing phase consists of visual and audio content manipulation and data normalization.

Considering the extraction and pre-processing of visual content from the video under analysis, this phase consists of three steps (see Figure 3):

1. Extraction of N_v color frames equally distant in time and distributed over its entire duration. The video frames have size $H_v \times W_v$, which depends on the resolution of the video under analysis;
2. Random extraction of N_{P_v} color patches of size $H_{P_v} \times W_{P_v}$;
3. Patch normalization in order to have zero mean and unitary variance as is commonly done prior to feeding data to CNNs.

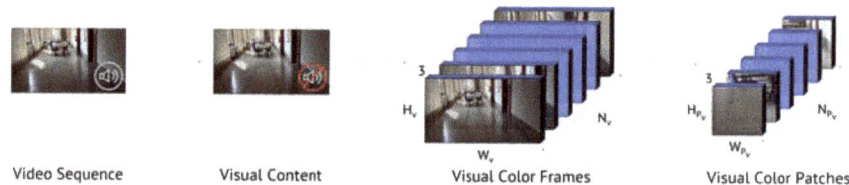

Figure 3. Extraction of visual patches from a video sequence. We extract N_v color frames, with size H_v and W_v. From these frames, we randomly extract N_{P_v} visual patches with size $H_{P_v} \times W_{P_v}$.

Regarding the audio content of the video under analysis, the extraction and pre-processing phase consists of three steps as well (see Figure 4):

1. Extraction of the LMS **L** of the audio content related to the video sequence. Indeed, the LMS represents a very informative tool for audio data and was used several times as a valuable feature for audio and speech classification and processing [24,37–41]. During some preliminary experiments, we compared different audio features extracted from the magnitude and phase of the signal STFT, and we verified that the LMS (based on the STFT magnitude) was the most informative one. Phase-based strategies reported accuracy of lower than 80%, achieved by LMS. The LMS **L** has size $H_a \times W_a$, where rows refer to the temporal information (varying with the video length) and columns to the frequency content in Mel scale;
2. Random extraction of N_{P_a} patches of size $H_{P_a} \times W_{P_a}$ from **L**;
3. Patch normalization in order to have zero mean and unitary variance, as previously described for visual patches.

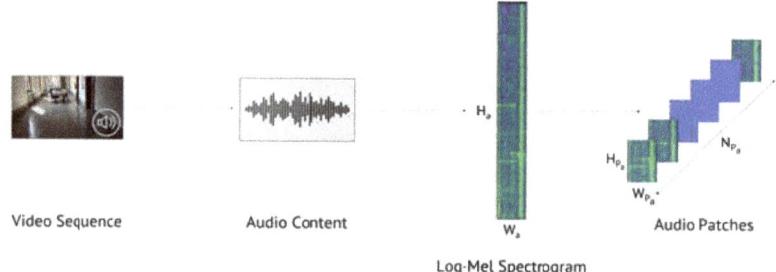

Figure 4. Extraction of audio patches from a video sequence. Once we select the audio content, we compute the LMS, which has size $H_a \times W_a$. Then, we randomly extract N_{P_a} audio patches with size $H_{P_a} \times W_{P_a}$.

4.2. CNN Processing

In the CNN processing step, the extracted pre-processed content is fed to one or multiple CNNs to extract distinguishable features among the different source camera models and classify the original one.

The mono-modal camera identification problem can be solved by feeding the visual or audio information extracted as shown in Section 4.1 to a CNN. In principle, any CNN architecture performing classification could be used at this point; in the next section, we comment our choice in detail. The final layer of the classification network is a fully-connected layer with a number of nodes equal to the total number of models, M, where each node is associated with a particular camera model. The output value is an M-element vector defined as $\mathbf{y}$, where each element y_m represents the probability that input data have been acquired by the model associated with that node. To extract the predicted model $\hat{m}$ in the classification process, we can select the node associated with the maximum score obtained:

$$\hat{m} = \underset{m}{\mathrm{argmax}}\, y_m. \tag{4}$$

Considering multi-modal camera model identification, which is our actual task, we propose two distinct methods to solve the problem:

1. Late Fusion methodology: compare the classification scores of visual and audio patches, separately obtained from two single-input CNNs;
2. Early Fusion methodology: build one multi-input CNN, feed this with both visual and audio content and exploit it to produce a single classification score.

In both proposed methods, we always provide pairs of patches as input to the network(s), composed of one visual patch and one audio patch extracted from the same video sequence under analysis.

4.2.1. Late Fusion Methodology

In the first method, defined as Late Fusion methodology, we follow three steps to determine the predicted model $\hat{m}$ for a visual/audio patch pair coming from the same query video sequence:

1. Separately feed a CNN with a visual patch and a CNN with an audio patch;
2. Extract the classification scores associated with the two patches. In particular, we define $\mathbf{y}_v$ as the classification scores related to the visual patch and $\mathbf{y}_a$ as those related to the audio patch;
3. Select the classification score vector (choosing between $\mathbf{y}_v$ and $\mathbf{y}_a$) that contains the highest score; the estimated source model $\hat{m}$ by the Late Fusion methodology is related to the position in which that score is found:

$$\hat{m} = \underset{m}{\mathrm{argmax}}\, y_{\mathrm{LF}_m}, \tag{5}$$

where y_{LF_m} is the m-th element of the score vector $\mathbf{y}_{\mathrm{LF}}$, defined as follows:

$$\mathbf{y}_{\mathrm{LF}} = \begin{cases} \mathbf{y}_v & \text{if } \max_m y_{v_m} \geq \max_m y_{a_m} \\ \mathbf{y}_a & \text{if } \max_m y_{v_m} < \max_m y_{a_m} \end{cases}. \tag{6}$$

To summarize, Figure 5 depicts the pipeline of the proposed Late Fusion method.

The training phase of Late Fusion method consists of training the two networks (one dealing with visual patches and the other one with audio patches) separately. More specifically, the network working with visual patches updates its weights by optimizing the classification problem on the scores returned by $\mathbf{y}_v$; the network working with audio patches is optimized basing on the scores returned by $\mathbf{y}_a$. The two networks are separately trained following the very same mono-modal methodology seen at the beginning of Section 4.2. In the evaluation phase, the results obtained from the two CNN branches are compared and fused.

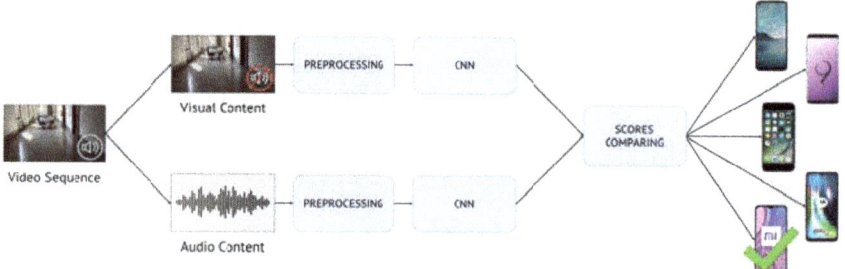

Figure 5. Late Fusion method pipeline. Given a query video, we extract and pre-process its visual and audio content. Then, we separately feed two distinct CNNs: one only with visual information and the other one only with audio information. Eventually, we compare and fuse the classification scores to identify the actual source camera model.

4.2.2. Early Fusion Methodology

In the second method, defined as Early Fusion, we build a multi-input CNN by joining together two CNNs. The union is made by concatenating the final fully-connected layers of the two networks and by adding three fully-connected layers up to the prediction of the camera model (see Figure 6 for details about the layers dimensionality). For each visual/audio patch pair, Early Fusion predicts the estimated camera model based on the scores obtained at the output of the last fully-connected layer, namely $\mathbf{y}_{EF}$:

$$\hat{m} = \operatorname*{argmax}_{m} y_{EF_m}. \tag{7}$$

In the training phase, we train the whole network in its entirety using visual and audio patch pairs. Unlike Late Fusion, there is no separate training between the visual and audio branches. Both training and testing phases are analogous to those of the mono-modal methodology, but this time, we provide the whole network with visual/audio patch pairs, not single patches only (e.g., limited to visual or audio content). Figure 6 draws the pipeline of the Early Fusion method. The dimensions of input and output features to the fully-connected layers are reported as well. Notice that the output feature at the last network layer has size equal to M, i.e., the number of investigated camera models.

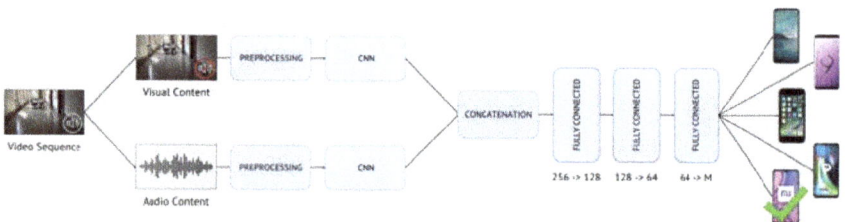

Figure 6. Early Fusion method pipeline. Given a query video, we extract and pre-process its visual and audio content. Then, we feed these data to one multi-input CNN, composed of two CNNs whose last fully-connected layers are concatenated. Three additional fully-connected layers follow to identify the actual source camera model.

4.3. CNN Architectures

The CNNs we use to solve the problem are the EfficientNetB0 [23] and the VGGish [24].

The EfficientNetB0 belongs to the recently proposed EfficientNet family of CNN models [23], which has achieved very good results in multimedia forensics tasks [21]. It is the simplest EfficientNet model; we selected this in order to have faster training phases and, consequently, much more time to experiment with different evaluation setups. Moreover, as shown in [21] and verified by means of preliminary tests, there is no significant difference between the performance of EfficientNetB0 with respect to computationally heavier network models requiring more parameters. The VGGish [24] is a CNN widely used for audio classification [42], and it is inspired by the famous VGG networks [43] used for image classification.

We use EfficientNetB0 for processing visual patches; audio patches can be processed by means of both EfficientNetB0 and VGGish. To solve the proposed multi-modal camera model identification problem, we make some modifications to the network architectures in order to match the input audio data. In particular, to correctly process audio patches, we add an extra convolutional layer at the beginning of EfficientNetB0. We need this additional layer because EfficientNetB0 accepts three-channel patches as input (i.e., color patches). The extra layer applies a 2D convolution using $3 \times 3 \times 3$ kernels, resulting in a transformed color patch suitable for EfficientNetB0.

5. Results

In this section, we first present the dataset we work with, and the experimental setup (i.e., the network training parameters and the configurations we use in the experiments). Then, we report the evaluation metrics and comment on the achieved results.

5.1. Dataset

We select video sequences from the Vision dataset [44], a recent image and video dataset, purposely designed for multimedia forensics investigations. The Vision dataset collects approximately 650 native video sequences captured by 35 modern smartphones/tablets, including also their related social media versions. Overall, the dataset comprises almost 2000 video sequences, clearly indicating the source device used to acquire them. To perform our experiments, we select non-flat videos (i.e., videos depicting natural scenes containing objects): both the original native ones (i.e., videos acquired by the smartphone camera without any post-processing) and those compressed by WhatsApp and YouTube algorithms. Since our analysis is aimed at the granularity model-level, we group videos from different devices that belong to the same model. Videos from devices D04, D12, D17 and D22 (considering the Vision dataset nomenclature provided in [44]) are excluded because they give problems in the extraction of the frames or the audio track. We also exclude the original videos that do not feature a WhatsApp or YouTube compressed version. Notice that we do not limit our investigations to high resolution videos: even though the majority of native videos presents resolutions higher than or equal to 720p, we also explore native sequences limited to 640×480. In doing so, we end up with 1110 videos of about 1 min, belonging to 25 different camera models. For each video sequence, we exploit the provided information about its source camera model as the ground truth to evaluate the classification performance of our proposed method.

For what concerns the visual content of videos, we extract 50 frames per video sequence, equally distant in time and distributed over its entire duration. Then, we extract 10 patches per frame (taken in random positions), for a total of $N_{P_v} = 500$ color patches per video. We select a patch-size equal to 256×256 pixels as suggested in [1].

As for the audio, we extract the LMS based on the default parameters purposely designed for the VGGish network [24]. The investigated frequency range spans from 125 Hz to 7500 Hz; we exploit a sampling rate of 16,000 Hz and a window length of 0.025 s with hop length of 0.010 s. We end up with an LMS consisting of H_a temporal samples and 64 Mel bins. Notice that the number of rows of LMS depends on the temporal length of the audio content, while the 64 Mel bins belong to the default parameters required by VGGish. Furthermore, after some preliminary experiments on how the exploited frequency range influences the classification performance, we propose to expand the investigated frequency range from 125 Hz to 20,000 Hz, changing the sampling rate to 44,100 Hz. Being that the investigated spectrum is enlarged by almost three times, we consider also three times as much the amount of Mel bins for computing the LMS. Therefore, we end up with an LMS with 192 Mel bins. In both the two situations, we randomly extract $N_{P_a} = 500$ patches per LMS. As regards H_{P_a} (i.e., the temporal dimension associated with the audio patches), we exploit the default parameter required by VGGish, i.e., 96 temporal bins. Thus, in the former scenario, the audio patch size is 96 × 64; in the latter one, the audio patch size is 96 × 192.

5.2. Network Setup and Training

As reported in Section 4.3, we always employ the EfficientNetB0 architecture for processing visual patches. On the contrary, we can use both VGGish and EfficientNetB0 architectures for processing the audio patches. Furthermore, the LMS can be calculated either on a reduced frequency range purposely designed for being processed by VGGish, or on an expanded range. In light of these considerations, we can work with three different network configurations per multi-modal method:

- Configuration EV, which uses EfficientNetB0 for processing visual patches and VGGish for audio patches, considering the default audio frequency range required by VGGish (i.e., 64 Mel bins);
- Configuration EE_{64}, which uses EfficientNetB0 for both visual and audio patches, considering the same audio frequency range required by VGGish (i.e., 64 Mel bins);
- Configuration EE_{192}, which uses EfficientNetB0 for both visual and audio patches, considering an expanded audio frequency range (i.e., 192 Mel bins).

Following a common procedure applied in CNN training, we initialize the EfficientNetB0 weights, using those trained on ImageNet database [45], while we initialize the VGGish ones using those trained on the AudioSet database [46]. We initialize in the same way also the weights of the EfficientNetB0 and of the VGGish networks that are part of the multi-input CNNs in the Early Fusion methodology. All CNNs are trained using the Cross-Entropy Loss and Adam optimizer with default parameters. The learning rate is initialized to 0.001 and is decreased by a factor of 10 whenever the validation loss does not improve for 10 epochs. We train the networks for at most 50 epochs, and training is stopped if the validation loss does not decrease for more than 20 epochs. The model providing the best validation loss is selected.

Concerning the dataset split policy, we always keep 80% of the video sequences of each device for the training phase (further divided in 85–15% for training set and validation set, respectively), leaving the remaining 20% to the evaluation set. All tests were run on a workstation equipped with one Intel® Xeon E5-2687W v4 (48 Cores @3 GHz), RAM 252 GB, one TITAN V (5120 CUDA Cores @1455 MHz), 12 GB, running Ubuntu 20.04.2. We resort to Pytorch [47] as the Deep Learning framework.

5.3. Evaluation Metrics

To evaluate the goodness of the system in classifying video sequences we use confusion matrices, where rows and columns are associated with the smartphone models under analysis. The value at position (i, j) represents the probability that a patch of a video recorded by the i-th model is classified as a patch of a video recorded by the j-th model. The more effective the method, the more the confusion matrix tends to be diagonal. In particular, we evaluate results by means of the achieved balanced classification accuracy. These metrics can be computed as the average of the values lying on the confusion matrix diagonal.

5.4. Mono-Modal Results

In order to provide a baseline comparison with our proposed multi-modal attribution, we start showing the results achieved in the case of standard mono-modal attribution on the same dataset. Specifically, for both visual-based and audio-based attributions, we select the networks' configuration achieving the average highest accuracy. In doing so, we select the EfficientNetB0 network for evaluating visual patches and the VGGish architecture for the audio ones, i.e., the networks' configuration defined as EV.

We report in Figures 7 and 8 the confusion matrices obtained in the mono-modal scenarios, considering only visual patches or audio patches of native video sequences, respectively. As previously specified in Section 5.1, we group devices of the same camera model, such as D05, D14 and D18 (using the Vision dataset nomenclature), which are different instances of the Apple iPhone 5c model. It is worth noticing that there is some uncertainty in classification, especially in the second scenario. Nonetheless, as regards the visual mono-modal approach (see Figure 7), mismatches in classification only appear between very similar camera models, e.g., Apple iPhone 6 Plus (D19) is sometimes confused with Apple iPhone 6 (D06-D15). For what concerns the audio counterpart (see Figure 8), the classification errors are more distributed and may also occur between models of different vendors, e.g., OnePlus A3003 (D32) can be confused with Huawei P8 GRA-L09 (D28), and Asus Zenfone 2 Laser (D23) can be confused with Apple iPhone 5c (D05-D14-D18).

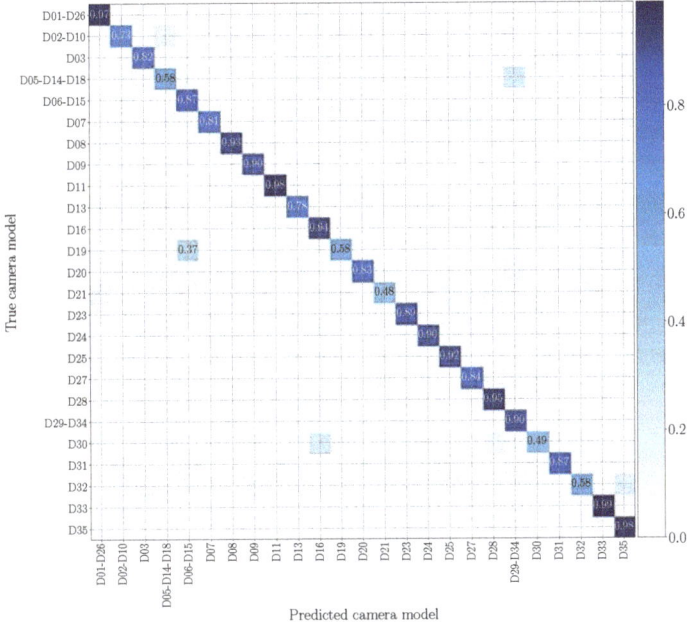

Figure 7. Confusion matrix achieved by mono-modal camera model identification exploiting visual patches only. We report results by training and testing on the native video set, and we only show the numbers which exceed 0.3. Device nomenclature is that of [44].

Having available the compressed versions of the videos with WhatsApp and YouTube algorithms, we investigate further by evaluating the cross test results, i.e., scenarios in which the data being tested have different characteristics than the training ones. For instance, we evaluate the achieved accuracy in testing WhatsApp video sequences by exploiting a network trained on native or YouTube compressed data. Table 1 shows the accuracy of cross tests and non-cross tests in both visual and audio modalities. We achieve the highest accuracy on the visual patches (82%) in the non-cross test configuration by working with native video sequences. Both the two mono-modal methods report similar performance on the WhatsApp and YouTube data in non-cross tests. Overall, we can leverage the visual content to achieve a better or comparable non-cross test performance.

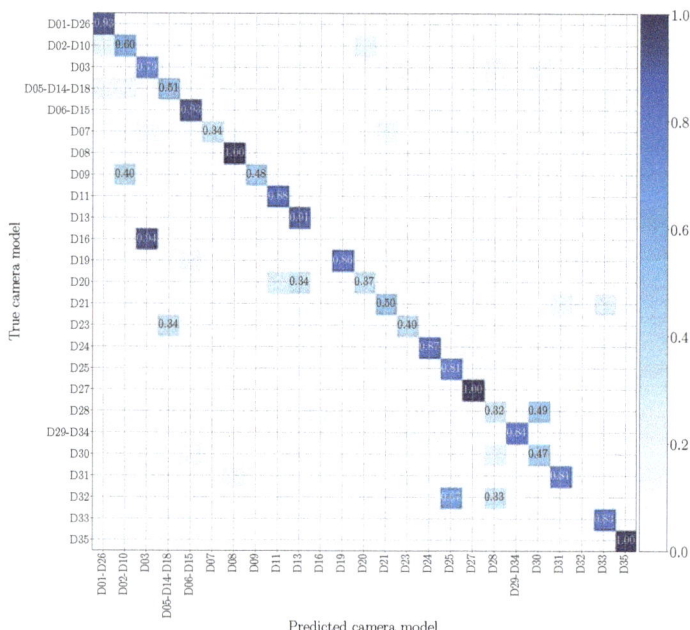

Figure 8. Confusion matrix achieved by mono-modal camera model identification exploiting audio patches only. We report results by training and testing on the native video set, and we only show the numbers which exceed 0.3. Device nomenclature is that of [44].

Not surprisingly, the cross test results are worse than the non-cross test results, especially those including data from WhatsApp. In particular, we focus on the setup in which we train on native sequences and test on videos passed through WhatsApp and YouTube (see the first row of Table 1). Indeed, this represents a realistic scenario in which the forensics analyst has only available original data, but must investigate videos coming from social networks. The audio-based method is actually the best performing solution, outperforming its visual counterpart by almost 20% accuracy points. We think this superior performance may be due to a lighter compression applied by social media to the audio content with respect to the visual content. Since the audio content requires considerably less storage space than video frames, the audio track might undergo reduced compression operations, thus reporting weaker compression artifacts than those occurring in video frames. Therefore, the network trained on native audios can be better representative of WhatsApp and YouTube audio with respect to the network trained only on native visual content and tested on social network visual patches.

Table 1. Classification accuracy of mono-modal methods as a function of training/testing sets. In bold is the highest achieved classification accuracy.

	Visual—EfficientNetB0			Audio—VGGish		
Testing Set → Training Set ↓	Native	WhatsApp	YouTube	Native	WhatsApp	YouTube
Native	**0.8202**	0.3579	0.4869	0.6578	0.5304	0.6654
WhatsApp	0.5599	0.6739	0.5158	0.5028	0.6757	0.5245
YouTube	0.7271	0.5531	0.7404	0.6954	0.5924	0.7010

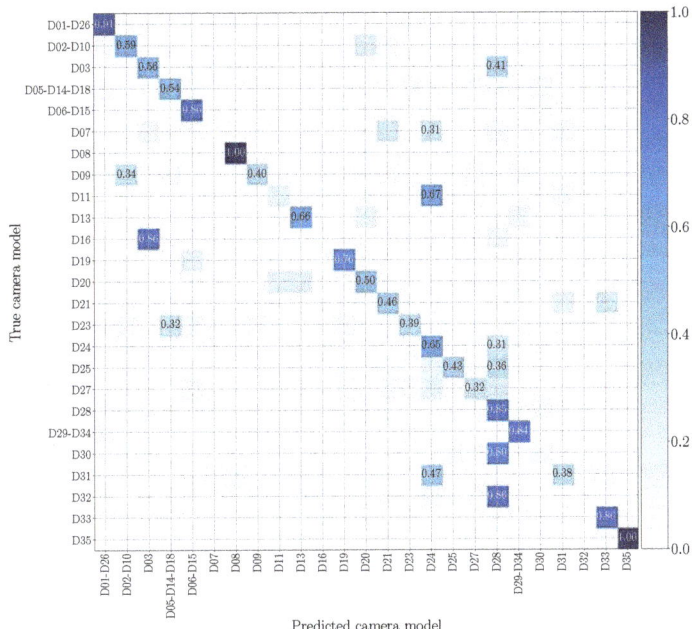

Figure 9. Confusion matrix achieved by mono-modal camera model identification, exploiting audio patches only. We report results by training on the native video set and testing on the WhatsApp set, and we only show the numbers that exceed 0.3. The device nomenclature is that of [44].

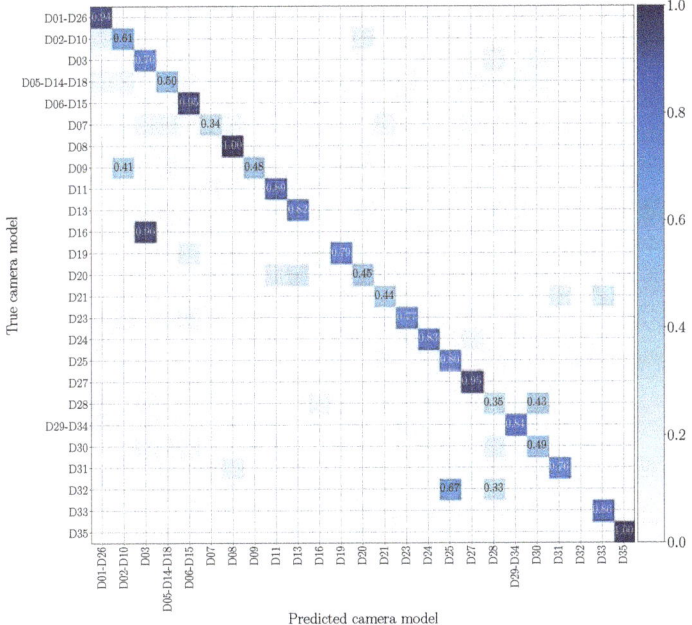

Figure 10. Confusion matrix achieved by mono-modal camera model identification, exploiting audio patches only. We report results by training on the native video set and testing on the YouTube set, and we only show the numbers which exceed 0.3. The device nomenclature is that of [44].

Figures 9 and 10 draw the confusion matrices achieved in cross test scenarios by training on original audio patches and testing on WhatsApp and YouTube audio patches, respectively. WhatsApp data (see Figure 9) are the most challenging to model, and many camera models are confused with others of different vendors. This may be due to the compression operations performed by WhatsApp, which are more significant than those of YouTube, making classification more difficult. On the contrary, on YouTube data (see Figure 10), misclassifications mostly occur on models from the same brand, e.g., Huawei P9 Lite VNS-L31 (D16) is confused with Huawei P9 EVA-L09 (D03), and OnePlus A3003 (D32) is sometimes confused with OnePlus A3000 (D25).

5.5. Multi-Modal Results

As seen in Section 5.2, we can work with three different network configurations per multi-modal method: configuration EV (i.e., EfficientNetB0 for visual patches and VGGish for audio patches), configuration EE_{64} (i.e., EfficientNetB0 for both visual and audio patches, considering an audio frequency range composed by 64 Mel bins as required by VGGish), and configuration EE_{192} (i.e., EfficientNetB0 for both visual and audio patches, considering an expanded audio frequency range).

In Figures 11 and 12, we show the confusion matrices related to multi-modal camera model identification in a non-cross test scenario on the native video sequences. Specifically, Figure 11 refers to Early Fusion EV and Figure 12 to Late Fusion EV. In both cases, we consider the network's configuration EV and the native video set to make a direct comparison with the mono-modal results previously reported in Figures 7 and 8. The confusion matrix of Early Fusion has a similar behavior to the visual mono-modal results reported in Figure 7; the matrix approaches a diagonal style, but classification is not yet very effective. On the contrary, Late Fusion reports better performance; some misclassifications still occur (especially among models of the same vendor) but it shows a reduced error percentage.

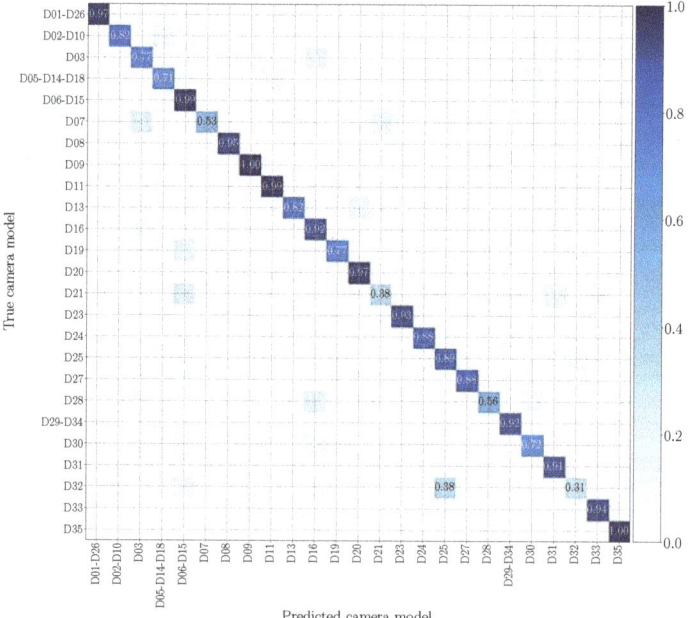

Figure 11. Confusion matrix achieved by multi-modal camera model identification exploiting Early Fusion EV. We report results by training and testing on the native video set, and we only show the numbers which exceed 0.3. Device nomenclature is that of [44].

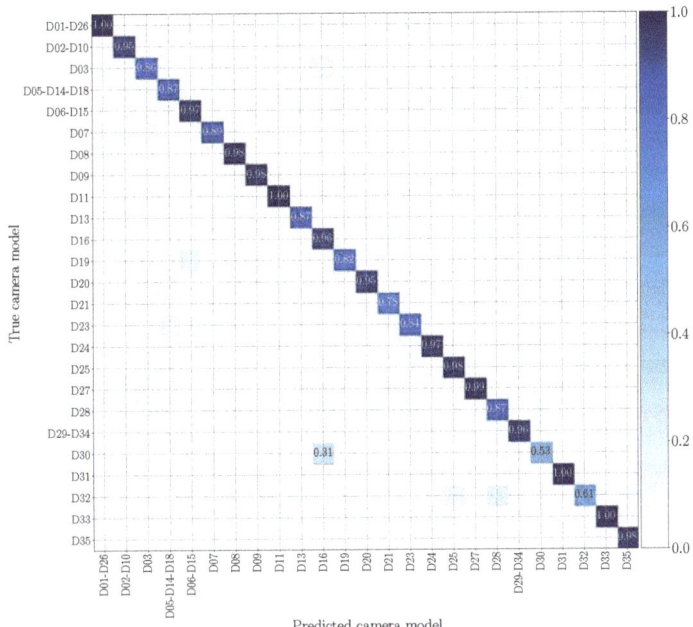

Figure 12. Confusion matrix achieved by multi-modal camera model identification exploiting Late Fusion EV. We report results by training and testing on the native video set, and we only show the numbers which exceed 0.3. Device nomenclature is that of [44].

Tables 2 and 3 report the classification accuracy of Early Fusion and Late Fusion multi-modal methods, respectively. In particular, we investigate both non-cross and cross test scenarios, considering all the network configurations. As regards the non-cross tests on the native video set, the results obtained with multi-modal methods are always greater or comparable to those obtained with mono-modal methods. For instance, configuration EE_{192} achieves extremely high accuracy (up to 99%). In general, we obtain substantially better results also in the other non-cross tests, including YouTube and WhatsApp. For example, configuration EE_{192} always exceeds 91% accuracy on WhatsApp and 95% on YouTube.

Cross tests, including native and YouTube video sequences, follow this trend as well. On the other hand, cross tests on WhatsApp do not always significantly outperform the results achieved by mono-modal methods, being often comparable or superior.

In particular, as was previously done for the mono-modal problem, we investigate the challenging scenario in which the training set consists of native video sequences, and testing data are picked from social media platforms (see the first row of Tables 2 and 3). In this scenario, for WhatsApp, the proposed multi-modal methodologies achieve the best results with the Early Fusion EV configuration, outperforming the highest mono-modal accuracy by more than 15%. Interestingly, it is worth noticing that Early Fusion EV is the configuration that achieves the lowest non-cross test accuracy if compared to the remaining options. We think that a reduced overfitting on the training native set enables better results' generalization also on testing data, which show quite different characteristics than training ones, WhatsApp videos being an example. Figure 13 depicts the confusion matrix corresponding to Early Fusion EV in the analyzed cross-test scenario. Contrarily to Figure 9 (which shows the confusion matrix for the same cross test scenario in the mono-modal setup), few misclassifications mainly occur among same-brand models.

Table 2. Classification accuracy of Early Fusion as a function of training/testing sets. In bold is the highest achieved accuracy in non-cross test scenarios.

	Early Fusion EV			Early Fusion EE_{64}			Early Fusion EE_{192}		
Testing Set → Training Set ↓	Native	WhatsApp	YouTube	Native	WhatsApp	YouTube	Native	WhatsApp	YouTube
Native	0.8210	0.6879	0.7784	0.8396	0.6120	0.7956	**0.9598**	0.1795	0.7968
WhatsApp	0.5810	0.7519	0.5766	0.5930	0.8076	0.5873	0.5091	**0.9120**	0.4954
YouTube	0.7548	0.6212	0.7590	0.8071	0.6903	0.8090	0.8731	0.4146	**0.9513**

Table 3. Classification accuracy of Late Fusion as a function of training/testing sets. In bold, the highest achieved accuracy in non-cross test scenarios.

	Late Fusion EV			Late Fusion EE_{64}			Late Fusion EE_{192}		
Testing Set → Training Set ↓	Native	WhatsApp	YouTube	Native	WhatsApp	YouTube	Native	WhatsApp	YouTube
Native	0.9039	0.5960	0.7069	0.8945	0.6020	0.8039	**0.9900**	0.4544	0.8389
WhatsApp	0.6413	0.7610	0.6368	0.6262	0.8198	0.6208	0.5703	**0.9163**	0.5602
YouTube	0.8163	0.6595	0.8274	0.8321	0.6976	0.8390	0.9172	0.4957	**0.9519**

Cross-test performance, by training on the native set and testing on YouTube, always exceeds that achieved by mono-modal methods. More specifically, Late Fusion EE_{192} outperforms the best mono-modal accuracy by 17%. In general, YouTube data are less prone to classification errors than WhatsApp. We are convinced that this is due to the weaker compression operations applied by YouTube, compared to WhatsApp, which render YouTube data more similar to the native ones. To provide an example, Figure 14 depicts the confusion matrix of Late Fusion EE_{192} in the analyzed cross-test scenario. Notice the diagonal behavior of the matrix; however, misclassifications sometimes occur among models of different vendors.

Comparing the two proposed multi-modal methods, Late Fusion always outperforms Early Fusion in non-cross tests scenarios. Nonetheless, the cross-test results show comparable accuracy between the two methods, and, on average, both the proposed methodologies report valid performance. Based on the scenario of our interest, we can prefer one proposed method over the other.

As for the comparison between the three networks' configurations, EE_{192} obtains the best results in all non-cross-test scenarios for both the two proposed fusion methodologies. This consideration is valid for cross tests as well, considering data from the native and YouTube sets. However, when evaluating the cross test results with highly compressed data, such as those of WhatsApp, this is the configuration that works worst.

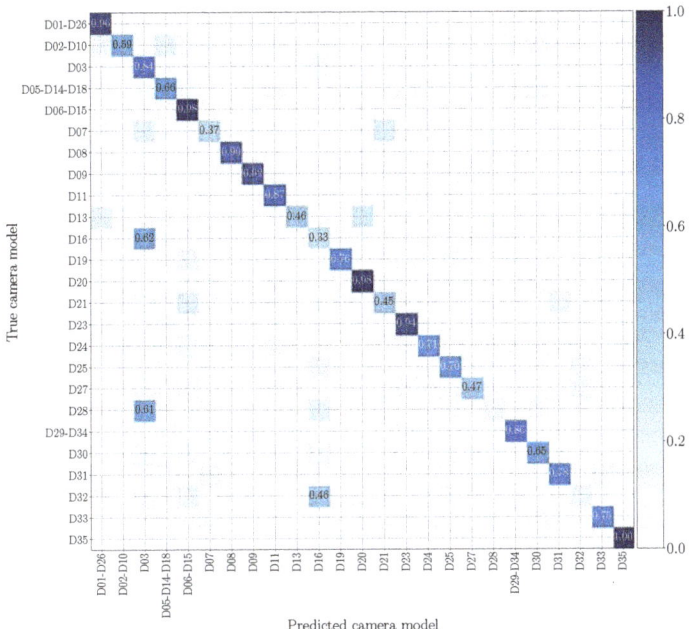

Figure 13. Confusion matrix achieved by multi-modal camera model identification exploiting Early Fusion EV. We report results by training on the native video set and testing on WhatsApp videos, and we only show the numbers that exceed 0.3. Device nomenclature is that of [44].

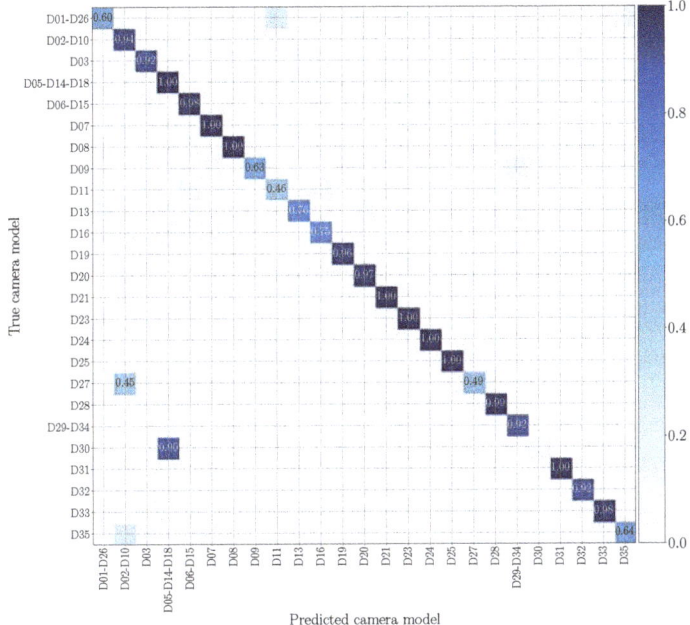

Figure 14. Confusion matrix achieved by multi-modal camera model identification exploiting Late Fusion EE_{192}. We report results by training on the native video set and testing on YouTube videos, and we only show the numbers which exceed 0.3. Device nomenclature is that of [44].

In general, we believe that the Late Fusion methodology associated with the EE_{192} configuration can be chosen as the best-preferred strategy among all the others. Indeed, it always reports the highest accuracy in both non-cross and cross test scenarios when dealing with native and YouTube video sequences. Cross-test results, including WhatsApp data, are comparable to the other two configurations, even if slightly worse. This lower performance can be attributable to the fact that, in this configuration, the trained CNNs adapt very well to the data seen in the training phase (i.e., visual and audio patches selected from native or YouTube video sequences), thus resulting in being less general and being more sensitive to significant data compression, such as that applied by WhatsApp.

6. Conclusions and Future Works

This paper proposes a novel multi-modal methodology for closed set camera model identification related to digital video sequences. In a nutshell, we propose to determine the smartphone model used to acquire a query video by exploiting both visual and audio information from the video itself. The devised methodology is based on CNNs capable of classifying videos by extracting suitable features from their visual and audio content. Given a video, as visual content, we use patches cropped from its video frames, while as audio content, we use patches cropped from the Log-Mel Spectrogram of its audio track.

We propose two multi-modal camera model identification approaches: in the Late Fusion method, we combine the scores individually obtained from two mono-modal networks (one working with visual patches and the other with audio patches) to classify the query video; in the Early Fusion method, we build one multi-input network and feed it with visual/audio patch pairs extracted from the query video. For each methodology, we compare three different networks' configurations, exploiting distinct architectures and data pre-processing.

We evaluate our experimental campaign over video sequences selected from the Vision dataset. The videos on which we experiment are not only the original native ones, i.e., those directly acquired by the smartphone camera. We also use videos compressed by the WhatsApp and YouTube algorithms so as to explore many different training and testing configurations as well as to simulate realistic scenarios in which we have to classify data compressed through internet services (e.g., social media, and upload sites). Moreover, we compare our proposed multi-modal methodologies with a mono-modal attribution strategy selected as the baseline.

The achieved results show that the proposed multi-modal methods are significantly more effective than standard mono-modal methods; on average, the Late Fusion approach reports the best results. In general, we can correctly identify native and YouTube video sequences with accuracy of up to 99%. WhatsApp videos are yet the most challenging to model, probably due to the massive data compression applied. This opens the door to future challenges and improvements focused on identifying the source camera model on video sequences shared (or re-shared multiple times) on social media. Furthermore, it is worth noticing that the proposed multi-modal strategies could be straightforwardly extended to potential situations, including more data modalities (i.e., more than two). The Late Fusion methodology would only require separately training one CNN per modality, while the Early Fusion methodology would require training one multi-input CNN with a number of inputs equal to the available modalities.

Author Contributions: Conceptualization, D.D.C., S.M. and P.B.; Methodology, D.D.C., S.M. and P.B.; Software, D.D.C.; Validation, D.D.C., S.M. and P.B.; Formal Analysis, D.D.C.; Investigation, D.D.C.; Resources, S.M. and P.B.; Data Curation, D.D.C.; Writing—Original Draft Preparation, D.D.C. and S.M.; Writing—Review and Editing, S.M. and P.B.; Visualization, D.D.C. and S.M.; Supervision, P.B. and S.T.; Project Administration, P.B. and S.T.; Funding acquisition, P.B. and S.T. All authors have read and agreed to the published version of the manuscript.

Funding: This material is based on research sponsored by the Defense Advanced Research Projects Agency (DARPA) and the Air Force Research Laboratory (AFRL) under agreement number FA8750-20-2-1004. The U.S. Government is authorized to reproduce and distribute reprints for governmental purposes notwithstanding any copyright notation therein. The views and conclusions contained herein are those of the authors and should not be interpreted as necessarily representing the official policies or endorsements, either expressed or implied, of DARPA and AFRL or the U.S. Government. This work was supported by the PREMIER project, funded by the Italian Ministry of Education, University, and Research within the PRIN 2017 program.

Conflicts of Interest: The authors declare no conflict of interest.

References

1. Hosler, B.C.; Mayer, O.; Bayar, B.; Zhao, X.; Chen, C.; Shackleford, J.A.; Stamm, M.C. A Video Camera Model Identification System Using Deep Learning and Fusion. In Proceedings of the IEEE International Conference on Acoustics, Speech and Signal Processing, ICASSP 2019, Brighton, UK, 12–17 May 2019; pp. 8271–8275. [CrossRef]
2. Kirchner, M.; Gloe, T. Forensic camera model identification. In *Handbook of Digital Forensics of Multimedia Data and Devices*; Wiley-IEEE Press: Piscataway, NJ, USA, 2015; pp. 329–374.
3. Takamatsu, J.; Matsushita, Y.; Ogasawara, T.; Ikeuchi, K. Estimating demosaicing algorithms using image noise variance. In Proceedings of the Twenty-Third IEEE Conference on Computer Vision and Pattern Recognition, CVPR 2010, San Francisco, CA, USA, 13–18 June 2010; pp. 279–286. [CrossRef]
4. Kirchner, M. Efficient estimation of CFA pattern configuration in digital camera images. In Proceedings of the Media Forensics and Security II, IS&T-SPIE Electronic Imaging Symposium, San Jose, CA, USA, 18–20 January 2010; Volume 7541, p. 754111. [CrossRef]
5. Popescu, A.C.; Farid, H. Exposing digital forgeries in color filter array interpolated images. *IEEE Trans. Signal Process.* **2005**, *53*, 3948–3959. [CrossRef]
6. Bayram, S.; Sencar, H.T.; Memon, N.; Avcibas, I. Improvements on source camera-model identification based on CFA interpolation. In Proceedings of the WG 2006, Kobe, Japan, 11–14 October 2006; Volume 11.
7. Swaminathan, A.; Wu, M.; Liu, K.J.R. Nonintrusive Component Forensics of Visual Sensors Using Output Images. *IEEE Trans. Inf. Forensics Secur.* **2007**, *2*, 91–106. [CrossRef]
8. Cao, H.; Kot, A.C. Accurate detection of demosaicing regularity for digital image forensics. *IEEE Trans. Inf. Forensics Secur.* **2009**, *4*, 899–910.
9. Chen, C.; Stamm, M.C. Camera model identification framework using an ensemble of demosaicing features. In Proceedings of the 2015 IEEE International Workshop on Information Forensics and Security, WIFS 2015, Roma, Italy, 16–19 November 2015; pp. 1–6, doi:10.1109/WIFS.2015.7368573. [CrossRef]
10. San Choi, K.; Lam, E.Y.; Wong, K.K. Automatic source camera identification using the intrinsic lens radial distortion. *Opt. Express* **2006**, *14*, 11551–11565. [CrossRef] [PubMed]
11. Lanh, T.V.; Emmanuel, S.; Kankanhalli, M.S. Identifying Source Cell Phone using Chromatic Aberration. In Proceedings of the 2007 IEEE International Conference on Multimedia and Expo, ICME 2007, Beijing, China, 2–5 July 2007; pp. 883–886. [CrossRef]
12. Gloe, T.; Borowka, K.; Winkler, A. Efficient estimation and large-scale evaluation of lateral chromatic aberration for digital image forensics. In Proceedings of the Media Forensics and Security II, IS&T-SPIE Electronic Imaging Symposium, San Jose, CA, USA, 18–20 January 2010; Volume 7541, p. 754107. [CrossRef]
13. Yu, J.; Craver, S.; Li, E. Toward the identification of DSLR lenses by chromatic aberration. In Proceedings of the Media Forensics and Security III, San Francisco, CA, USA, 24–26 January 2011; Volume 7880, p. 788010. [CrossRef]
14. Lyu, S. Estimating vignetting function from a single image for image authentication. In Proceedings of the Multimedia and Security Workshop, MM&Sec 2010, Roma, Italy, 9–10 September 2010; Campisi, P., Dittmann, J., Craver, S., Eds.; ACM: New York, NY, USA, 2010; pp. 3–12. [CrossRef]
15. Dirik, A.E.; Sencar, H.T.; Memon, N.D. Digital Single Lens Reflex Camera Identification From Traces of Sensor Dust. *IEEE Trans. Inf. Forensics Secur.* **2008**, *3*, 539–552. [CrossRef]
16. Thai, T.H.; Retraint, F.; Cogranne, R. Camera model identification based on the generalized noise model in natural images. *Digit. Signal Process.* **2016**, *48*, 285–297. [CrossRef]
17. Tuama, A.; Comby, F.; Chaumont, M. Camera model identification with the use of deep convolutional neural networks. In Proceedings of the IEEE International Workshop on Information Forensics and Security, WIFS 2016, Abu Dhabi, United Arab Emirates, 4–7 December 2016; pp. 1–6. [CrossRef]
18. Bondi, L.; Baroffio, L.; Guera, D.; Bestagini, P.; Delp, E.J.; Tubaro, S. First Steps Toward Camera Model Identification With Convolutional Neural Networks. *IEEE Signal Process. Lett.* **2017**, *24*, 259–263. [CrossRef]
19. Stamm, M.C.; Bestagini, P.; Marcenaro, L.; Campisi, P. Forensic Camera Model Identification: Highlights from the IEEE Signal Processing Cup 2018 Student Competition [SP Competitions]. *IEEE Signal Process. Mag.* **2018**, *35*, 168–174. [CrossRef]
20. Rafi, A.M.; Kamal, U.; Hoque, R.; Abrar, A.; Das, S.; Laganière, R.; Hasan, M.K. Application of DenseNet in Camera Model Identification and Post-processing Detection. In Proceedings of the IEEE Conference on Computer Vision and Pattern Recognition Workshops, CVPR Workshops 2019, Long Beach, CA, USA, 16–20 June 2019; pp. 19–28.
21. Mandelli, S.; Bonettini, N.; Bestagini, P.; Tubaro, S. Training CNNs in Presence of JPEG Compression: Multimedia Forensics vs Computer Vision. In Proceedings of the 12th IEEE International Workshop on Information Forensics and Security, WIFS 2020, New York, NY, USA, 6–11 December 2020; pp. 1–6. [CrossRef]

22. Rafi, A.M.; Tonmoy, T.I.; Kamal, U.; Wu, Q.M.J.; Hasan, M.K. RemNet: Remnant convolutional neural network for camera model identification. *Neural Comput. Appl.* **2021**, *33*, 3655–3670. [CrossRef]
23. Tan, M.; Le, Q.V. EfficientNet: Rethinking Model Scaling for Convolutional Neural Networks. In Proceedings of the 36th International Conference on Machine Learning, ICML 2019, PMLR, Long Beach, CA, USA, 9–15 June 2019; Volume 97, pp. 6105–6114.
24. Hershey, S.; Chaudhuri, S.; Ellis, D.P.W.; Gemmeke, J.F.; Jansen, A.; Moore, C.; Plakal, M.; Platt, D.; Saurous, R.A.; Seybold, B.; et al. CNN Architectures for Large-Scale Audio Classification. In Proceedings of the International Conference on Acoustics, Speech and Signal Processing (ICASSP), New Orleans, LA, USA, 5–9 March 2017.
25. Seferbekov, S.; Lee, E. DeepFake Detection (DFDC) Solution by @selimsef. 2020. Available online: https://github.com/selimsef/dfdc_deepfake_challenge (accessed on 27 July 2021).
26. Verdoliva, D.C.G.P.L. Extracting camera-based fingerprints for video forensics. In Proceedings of the CVPRW, Long Beach, CA, USA, 16–20 June 2019.
27. Mandelli, S.; Bestagini, P.; Verdoliva, L.; Tubaro, S. Facing device attribution problem for stabilized video sequences. *IEEE Trans. Inf. Forensics Secur.* **2019**, *15*, 14–27. [CrossRef]
28. Mayer, O.; Hosler, B.; Stamm, M.C. Open set video camera model verification. In Proceedings of the ICASSP 2020–2020 IEEE International Conference on Acoustics, Speech and Signal Processing (ICASSP), Barcelona, Spain, 4–8 May 2020; pp. 2962–2966.
29. Verdoliva, L. Media forensics and deepfakes: An overview. *IEEE J. Sel. Top. Signal Process.* **2020**, *14*, 910–932. [CrossRef]
30. Hosler, B.; Salvi, D.; Murray, A.; Antonacci, F.; Bestagini, P.; Tubaro, S.; Stamm, M.C. Do Deepfakes Feel Emotions? A Semantic Approach to Detecting Deepfakes via Emotional Inconsistencies. In Proceedings of the IEEE/CVF Conference on Computer Vision and Pattern Recognition (CVPR) Workshops, Online, 19–25 June 2021; pp. 1013–1022.
31. Mittal, T.; Bhattacharya, U.; Chandra, R.; Bera, A.; Manocha, D. Emotions Don't Lie: An Audio-Visual Deepfake Detection Method Using Affective Cues. In Proceedings of the 28th ACM International Conference on Multimedia, MM '20, Seattle, WA, USA, 12–16 October 2020; Association for Computing Machinery: New York, NY, USA, 2020; pp. 2823–2832. [CrossRef]
32. Agarwal, S.; Farid, H.; Fried, O.; Agrawala, M. Detecting Deep-Fake Videos from Phoneme-Viseme Mismatches. In Proceedings of the 2020 IEEE/CVF Conference on Computer Vision and Pattern Recognition Workshops (CVPRW), Seattle, WA, USA, 14–19 June 2020; pp. 2814–2822. [CrossRef]
33. Agarwal, S.; Farid, H. Detecting Deep-Fake Videos From Aural and Oral Dynamics. In Proceedings of the IEEE/CVF Conference on Computer Vision and Pattern Recognition (CVPR) Workshops, Online, 15–19 June 2021; pp. 981–989.
34. Ramanath, R.; Snyder, W.E.; Yoo, Y.; Drew, M.S. Color image processing pipeline. *IEEE Signal Process. Mag.* **2005**, *22*, 34–43. [CrossRef]
35. Tabora, V. Photo Sensors In Digital Cameras. 2019. Available online: https://medium.com/hd-pro/photo-sensors-in-digital-cameras-94fb26203da1 (accessed on 7 April 2021).
36. Stevens, S.S.; Volkmann, J. The relation of pitch to frequency: A revised scale. *Am. J. Psychol.* **1940**, *53*, 329–353. [CrossRef]
37. Shen, J.; Pang, R.; Weiss, R.J.; Schuster, M.; Jaitly, N.; Yang, Z.; Chen, Z.; Zhang, Y.; Wang, Y.; Skerrv-Ryan, R.; et al. Natural TTS synthesis by conditioning Wavenet on mel spectrogram predictions. In Proceedings of the IEEE International Conference on Acoustics, Speech and Signal Processing (ICASSP), Calgary, AB, Canada, 15–20 April 2018.
38. Meng, H.; Yan, T.; Yuan, F.; Wei, H. Speech emotion recognition from 3D log-mel spectrograms with deep learning network. *IEEE Access* **2019**, *7*, 125868–125881. [CrossRef]
39. Mascia, M.; Canclini, A.; Antonacci, F.; Tagliasacchi, M.; Sarti, A.; Tubaro, S. Forensic and anti-forensic analysis of indoor/outdoor classifiers based on acoustic clues. In Proceedings of the European Signal Processing Conference (EUSIPCO), Nice, France, 31 August–4 September 2015.
40. Liang, B.; Fazekas, G.; Sandler, M. Piano Sustain-pedal Detection Using Convolutional Neural Networks. In Proceedings of the IEEE International Conference on Acoustics, Speech and Signal Processing (ICASSP), Brighton, UK, 12–17 May 2019. [CrossRef]
41. Comanducci, L.; Bestagini, P.; Tagliasacchi, M.; Sarti, A.; Tubaro, S. Reconstructing Speech from CNN Embeddings. *IEEE Signal Process. Lett.* **2021**. [CrossRef]
42. Shi, L.; Du, K.; Zhang, C.; Ma, H.; Yan, W. Lung Sound Recognition Algorithm based on VGGish-BiGRU. *IEEE Access* **2019**, *7*, 139438–139449. [CrossRef]
43. Simonyan, K.; Zisserman, A. Very Deep Convolutional Networks for Large-Scale Image Recognition. *arXiv* **2014**, arXiv:1409.1556.
44. Shullani, D.; Fontani, M.; Iuliani, M.; Shaya, O.A.; Piva, A. VISION: a video and image dataset for source identification. *EURASIP J. Inf. Secur.* **2017**, *2017*, 15. [CrossRef]
45. Deng, J.; Dong, W.; Socher, R.; Li, L.; Li, K.; Li, F. ImageNet: A large-scale hierarchical image database. In Proceedings of the 2009 IEEE Computer Society Conference on Computer Vision and Pattern Recognition (CVPR 2009), Miami, FL, USA, 20–25 June 2009; pp. 248–255. [CrossRef]
46. Gemmeke, J.F.; Ellis, D.P.W.; Freedman, D.; Jansen, A.; Lawrence, W.; Moore, R.C.; Plakal, M.; Ritter, M. Audio Set: An ontology and human-labeled dataset for audio events. In Proceedings of the 2017 IEEE International Conference on Acoustics, Speech and Signal Processing (ICASSP), New Orleans, LA, USA, 5–9 March 2017.
47. Paszke, A.; Gross, S.; Massa, F.; Lerer, A.; Bradbury, J.; Chanan, G.; Killeen, T.; Lin, Z.; Gimelshein, N.; Antiga, L.; et al. PyTorch: An Imperative Style, High-Performance Deep Learning Library. In Proceedings of the Advances in Neural Information Processing Systems 32: Annual Conference on Neural Information Processing Systems 2019, NeurIPS 2019, Vancouver, BC, Canada, 8–14 December 2019; pp. 8024–8035.

Journal of
Imaging

Article

VIPPrint: Validating Synthetic Image Detection and Source Linking Methods on a Large Scale Dataset of Printed Documents

Anselmo Ferreira *,†, Ehsan Nowroozi † and Mauro Barni †

Department of Information Engineering and Mathematics, University of Siena, 53100 Siena, SI, Italy; ehsan.nowroozi65@gmail.com (E.N.); barni@dii.unisi.it (M.B.)
* Correspondence: anselmo.castelo@unisi.it
† These authors contributed equally to this work.

Abstract: The possibility of carrying out a meaningful forensic analysis on printed and scanned images plays a major role in many applications. First of all, printed documents are often associated with criminal activities, such as terrorist plans, child pornography, and even fake packages. Additionally, printing and scanning can be used to hide the traces of image manipulation or the synthetic nature of images, since the artifacts commonly found in manipulated and synthetic images are gone after the images are printed and scanned. A problem hindering research in this area is the lack of large scale reference datasets to be used for algorithm development and benchmarking. Motivated by this issue, we present a new dataset composed of a large number of synthetic and natural printed face images. To highlight the difficulties associated with the analysis of the images of the dataset, we carried out an extensive set of experiments comparing several printer attribution methods. We also verified that state-of-the-art methods to distinguish natural and synthetic face images fail when applied to print and scanned images. We envision that the availability of the new dataset and the preliminary experiments we carried out will motivate and facilitate further research in this area.

Keywords: digital image forensics; source identification; GAN-generated image detection

Citation: Ferreira, A.; Nowroozi, E.; Barni, M. VIPPrint: Validating Synthetic Images Detection and Source Linking Methods on a Large Scale Dataset of Printed Documents. *J. Imaging* **2021**, *7*, 50. https://doi.org/10.3390/jimaging7030050

Academic Editor: Mohamed Daoudi

Received: 1 February 2021
Accepted: 25 February 2021
Published: 8 March 2021

Publisher's Note: MDPI stays neutral with regard to jurisdictional claims in published maps and institutional affiliations.

Copyright: © 2021 by the authors. Licensee MDPI, Basel, Switzerland. This article is an open access article distributed under the terms and conditions of the Creative Commons Attribution (CC BY) license (https://creativecommons.org/licenses/by/4.0/).

1. Introduction

The abundant availability of new technologies for generating physical documents such as printers and scanners has raised many concerns about their misuse, examples of which include generating illegal documents, misguiding investigations through the generation of fake evidence, or even hiding relevant evidence in criminal investigations. For instance, child pornography can be printed and distributed between pedophiles in order to avoid virtual monitoring from the police, and illegal amendments can be incorporated in printed contracts without previous notice. Furthermore, professional printers can be used to print fake currency and packages of fake products, causing several negative effects on the economy. Finally, printing and scanning can be used to hide the traces of image manipulation or the synthetic nature of the images, since the artifacts commonly found in manipulated, and synthetic images are not present or detectable after the images have been printed and scanned.

As a countermeasure to the diffusion of counterfeited printed documents, most of the major manufacturers of color laser printers have signed a secret agreement with governments to let the printers include secret (invisible) yellow dots onto printed documents [1]. Such dots, also called machine identification codes (MIC) or simply printer steganography, are used to identify the source of printed documents, as unique yellow-dots patterns are used to identify different printers. However, such a feature is not enabled in all laser printers, and as shown in [2], the yellow-dot patterns can be easily anonymized, leaving the authentication of printed documents problem unsolved.

The challenges posed by printed document forensics have pushed the multimedia forensics research community to look for viable solutions based on the analysis of the artifacts left by the printers on the printed documents. In general, printed document forensics can be split into three main research areas: (i) source linking (also known as printer attribution); (ii) detection of printed manipulated images; and (iii) detection of printed and scanned synthetic images. Solutions for printer attribution are mostly based on the analysis of the extrinsic artifacts contained in printed documents, with the most popular ones for laser printers being banding, jitter, and skewed jitters. The presence of these artifacts has been exploited by several works to identify the sources of printed texts [3–22], color images [23–33], or both [34–36]. Manipulation detection in printed documents has received some attention only recently [37] and mainly refers to unveiling post-processing operations that could alter the semantic meanings of the images. It usually exploits texture descriptors and deep neural networks to identify the visual artifacts introduced by such manipulations. Finally, as far as we know, despite the intense research devoted to the detection of images generated by generative adversarial networks (GANs) [38–40], scarce attention has been paid to the detection of such images in printed documents.

The research carried out so far notwithstanding, progresses in this area is hindered by the lack of large reference datasets. The few existing datasets, in fact, present at least one of the following issues: (i) they contain ad hoc data prepared for specific research only; (ii) the printed patterns are often simple ones, such as icons, text, and halftone patterns; (iii) most of them consider old and non-professional printers; (iv) they do not consider copies of the same printer brand and model; and (v) to the best of our knowledge, no dataset with complex fake printed images exists. This last issue is particularly important and challenging, as most of the artifacts used to detect image manipulations, such as the correlation between RGB channels, discrete cosine transform irregularities, and even illumination inconsistencies, are gone after the images are printed and scanned. This problem is worsened by the observation that printing and scanning back a manipulated image is one of the most powerful and simplest attacks an adversary can conceive of to fool manipulation detectors. The availability of a large reference dataset overcoming the above problems may be of great help to foster new advances in printed document investigations, concerning both the detection of manipulated and synthetic documents and the attribution of printed documents to the device that generated them.

In this paper, we aim at filling said gaps by presenting a large scale dataset that can be used for both applications: source attribution and synthetic image detection. Due to their relevance in image forensics applications, the dataset focuses on face images. In particular, the initial version of the dataset (we are planning to update it continuously in the next years) is composed of images printed by several printers and scanned back with a high-quality scanner. The images in the dataset are divided into (i) pristine images, to be used for the source attribution problem; and (ii) synthetic face images generated by three different generative adversarial networks (GANs). The dataset is further split into several subsets, containing regions of interest with different sizes for the investigation of localized artifacts. To evaluate the difficulties associated with the forensic analysis of the images contained in the dataset, we carried out an extensive comparative study including several source attribution and synthetic image detection baseline methods.

In summary, the contributions of this paper are:

1. We present a large scale dataset of color-printed face images for digital image forensics purposes, such as source attribution and synthetic images detection (deep fake images).
2. We increased the diversity of the images in our dataset to make it suitable for approaches working on images of different sizes. Full scanned images and regions of interest with different sizes are available.
3. To the best of our knowledge, our dataset is the first large scale dataset with printed and scanned artificial images created with GANs such as StyleGAN2 [41], ProgressiveGAN [42], and StarGAN [43].

4. We present the results of an in-depth comparative study conducted on the new dataset regarding several baseline approaches, including both data-driven methods and methods based on handcrafted features. The comparison regards both source attribution and synthetic image detection.

The rest of this paper is organized as follows: in Section 2 we report some related work and discuss the limitations of datasets used in the literature. In Section 3, we present our dataset and several configurations considered to generate data. In Section 4, we discuss the experimental setup considered to assess the difficulty of such a dataset. Finally, Section 5 reports the achieved results and, in Section 6, we conclude this paper and discuss the future work that we are aiming to do in such a dataset.

2. Related Work

Several works have investigated the exploitation of the artifacts left by the printers into the printed documents to identify their source. Here we focus our works aiming at source linking after document scanning, as they are usually cheaper, non-destructive, and fast.

Common surveys in the literature [44–47] divide source linking methods according to the kind of documents they focus on, namely: printed text documents, printed color image documents, or both. Moreover, we can distinguish between methods aimed at identifying the technology used to print the documents—inkjet, laser, etc.—and those trying to link the printed document to the single device that was used to print it [48–52]. In this section, we briefly review the second class of methods, since research in that area is more advanced.

Generally speaking, there are two kinds of clues in printed documents that could guide a forensic investigation aimed at identifying the specific source of the document: intrinsic and extrinsic signatures. Intrinsic signatures are introduced by the printing process itself, whereas extrinsic signatures are intentionally inserted into the printed material. Three of the most investigated intrinsic signatures in laser printers are banding, jitter, and skewed jitters. Eid et al. [24] characterized banding as a textural pattern composed of horizontal, low frequency, and periodic artifacts caused by the laser printer components variation, vibration, and speed regulation that can uniquely identify different printers. Similarly, the jitter consists of horizontal artifacts, but with a different frequency range and duration, and is caused by oscillatory disturbances of the printer's drum and the developer roller. Finally, skewed jitter is also a periodic artifact like the others, but it differs from the previous ones as it is formed by vertical lines. With regard to extrinsic signatures, some relevant works include embedding code sequences in electrophotographic halftone images [53] and also machine identification codes [54]. Approaches based on extrinsic signatures require expensive modifications in the printing device, and also some of these extrinsic signatures can even be erased from the printed material [2].

With regard to the attribution of printed texts (i.e., black and white dots only), most of the techniques based on intrinsic signatures treat such a problem as a texture identification problem, as artifacts such as banding are not easy to be obtained from text [26]. For this set of techniques, the same patterns are extracted from the documents and subtle differences among them can be discriminated when printed by different printers [34]. One of the pioneers works in this regard comes from Ali et al. in 2004 [3]. The authors consider the pixel values of letters "I" as features in a multi-class classification problem. After the letters are classified, the source of a document can be found by verifying the most voted class among all the individual letters "I" classification. Several other techniques used a similar pipeline with few modifications, such as considering the statistics of gray-level co-occurrence matrices [4–6,11], Distance Transform [8], Discrete Cosine Transform [10], statistics of gray-level co-occurrence matrices together with residual noise and sub-bands of wavelet transform [12–14,17], deep neural networks [18,20], ad hoc texture descriptors [19,22] among others [7,9,15,16,21].

A second set of techniques to identify the source of any printed document focuses on the intrinsic signatures of documents containing colored pictures. In this case, banding artifacts are more evident as more patterns are printed (including the background). In this regard, one of the pioneer works is the one from Ali et al. [23], where the authors proposed to capture banding artifacts by applying the Fourier transform in image patches to get different banding frequencies. Eid et al. [24] applied a similar strategy to jitter artifacts by using Gabor filtering and discrete Fourier transform.

Another set of research on colored documents source linking treated intrinsic artifacts as noise. Choi et al. [26] discriminated printers by calculating 39 noise features from the diagonal (HH) sub-band of the discrete wavelet transform in pairwise and individual RGB and CMYK channels. In a subsequent work by the same authors [27], noise was estimated after Wiener filtering and gray level co-occurrence matrix statistics. Tsai et al. [29] calculated 45 statistics in HH, LH and HL sub-bands of a discrete wavelet transform with further feature selection. Choi et al. [30] extended their previous work in [26] by estimating noise with Wiener filtering and a 2D discrete wavelet transform, and characterizing it with 384 statistical filters on gray level co-occurrence matrices that described single channels of residual images and pair-wise channels. Other important techniques for color documents source attribution involve describing geometric distortions [25,32] and halftone texture descriptors [28,31,33].

Finally, a number of techniques aim at identifying the sources of printed documents regardless of their content. Ferreira et al. [34] proposed an extension of the gray level co-occurrence matrix descriptor considering more directions and scale and also a new descriptor, called convolutional texture gradient filter, that builds histograms of filtered textures with specific gradients intervals. The authors validated these approaches not only on the letter "E" of printed text, but also on regions of interest called frames, which are rectangular areas with sufficient printed material—images, text, or both. Bibi et al. [36] used a similar strategy using chunks of printed materials, but their solution involves convolutional neural networks. Finally, Tsai et al. [35] apply nine different filters, fusing several previous strategies such as extracting features from gray-level co-occurrence matrices, discrete wavelet transform, spatial filters, Gabor filter, Wiener filter, gray level co-occurrence matrices features, and fractal features.

The abundant development of source linking approaches for printed documents notwithstanding, the identification of image forgeries and synthetic images from a printed and scanned version of a digital image has received considerably less attention. One of the few works in this area has been published in [37], where simple print and scan attacks of manipulated printed documents with recompression, filtering, noise addition, and other simple image operations are detected by a specialized CNN architecture.

Therefore, although printed document forensics (especially printer source attribution) has received much attention in the last few years, there are still several issues to be tackled before solutions applicable to real-world scenarios are developed. Among them, the following two issues are relevant for the present paper:

1. There is a need for a publicly available dataset that grows through time to include modern printers with different technologies and manufacturing procedures. We expect that different printers manufactured at different times generate different artifacts in printed documents that cannot be detected by previous works.
2. There is a need for multimedia forensic techniques able to detect deepfake printed images. This is a very challenging problem, since several artifacts, such as the correlation between RGB channels, discrete cosine transform irregularities, and even illumination inconsistencies in the digital image versions are usually removed by the print and scan process. In this way, although several adversarial attacks have been discussed in the literature [55], the print and scan procedure is the easiest yet most powerful attack an adversary could perform against deepfake digital image detectors.

Therefore, the present work aims at moving a first step towards the solution of the above problems. This is done by presenting a long term dataset addressing both tasks: real-world source attribution with modern printers, and deepfake detection in printed and scanned documents. The details of the dataset we have constructed are described in the following sections.

3. The VIPPrint Dataset

In this work, we present a new dataset trying to minimize some of the issues of existing datasets. The new dataset, which we call VIPPrint (the dataset is named after the VIPP group), consists of two sections. The first one focuses on printer source attribution and solves some common limitations in previous works, such as (i) lack of diversity and (ii) lack of redundancy. Concerning the lack of diversity, the dataset contains printers of different models and printing resolutions. This is an important issue when considering source attribution in real-world applications such as anti-counterfeiting detection, where the printing resolution used for printing a counterfeited document or package is unknown. The inclusion in the dataset of diverse printers marks a significant difference concerning existing datasets, which usually look at artifacts associated with specific printing technologies at fixed resolutions. As to lack of redundancy, very few works have analyzed the effect of the presence of two or more printers of the same model and brand in the dataset, thus neglecting the overlapping effect associated with the presence of two identical printers. The second section of the dataset considers an important, yet understudied, problem in digital image forensics: the detection of synthetic fake images such as those created by Generative Adversarial Networks after print and scan.

The importance of the new dataset for digital image forensics is twofold: (i) it can foster the development of novel solutions for digital image forensics capable of withstanding a print and scan procedure, and (ii) it can inspire new techniques for source attribution of fake colored documents printed by modern printers, thereby linking the fake content to the owner, or user, of the printer.

Concerning the content of the images composing the dataset, we decided to consider face images. The first reason for such a choice is that face images are particularly relevant in many applications related to biometric recognition, criminal investigations, and misinformation. A second reason is the availability of large scale datasets of face images that can be used as a starting point for the construction of the printed and scanned dataset. Giving researchers the possibility to work both with the digital images and their printed and scanned versions can represent an added value in many applications. Finally, AI-based techniques to generate synthetic images are particularly advanced in the case of face images, whose quality has reached unprecedented levels with no or very few semantic artifacts the forensic analysis can rely on [41].

The details of the two sections the VIPPrint dataset consists of are discussed in the following.

3.1. VIPPrint Dataset for Source Attribution

To select the images to print in the first dataset, we choose images from a dataset that has particular importance in the digital image forensics literature. These images come from the original subset of human faces from the Flickr-Faces-HQ (FFHQ) dataset [41]. We use these images for two reasons: (i) they have enough samples to generate a large dataset of printed images, which can be used by data-hungry techniques such as those based on deep learning; and (ii) they can be used to develop methods focusing on applications (e.g., child pornography) for which printing patterns usually found in other datasets (e.g., barcodes and text) are not useful. Some examples of the images included in the first section of the dataset are shown in Figure 1.

Figure 1. Some digital images considered from the work of Karras et al. [41] to build our dataset of printed images.

We choose to print the images in the dataset with printers that are diverse enough to make the source attribution problem challenging enough for state-of-the-art techniques. The initial version (As we said, we are planning to continuously update the dataset with new images, printed with other printers.) of such sub-dataset for source attribution contains 1600 printings from the printers listed in Table 1. We would like to highlight the difficulties associated with such a dataset as it contains modern printers, with some of them being professional laser printers that were commercialized in the last five years. The dataset also contains printers with different printing resolutions: for example, printers #1 and #8 have native resolutions different from the others (600 × 600 dpi).

Table 1. A list of eight laser printers that compose the first version of the VIPPrint dataset.

VIPPrint Dataset- Printer Source Linking					
ID	Brand	Model	Resolution	Type	#Images
#1	Epson	WorkForce WF-7715	4800 × 2400 dpi	Laser	200
#2	Kyocera	Color Laser	600 × 600 dpi	Laser	200
#3	Kyocera	TaskAlfa 3551	600 × 600 dpi	Laser	200
#4	Kyocera	TaskAlfa 3551	600 × 600 dpi	Laser	200
#5	Samsung	Multiexpress X3280NR	600 × 600 dpi	Laser	200
#6	HP	Color LaserJet Pro rfp-r479fdw	600 × 600 dpi	Laser	200
#7	HP	Color LaserJet rfp-r377dw	600 × 600 dpi	Laser	200
#8	OKI	C612 LaserColor	1200 × 600 dpi	Laser	200

The printers used were available in normal conditions (that means they were not exclusively used to print our dataset). Most of the printers were realtively new (they were from weeks to years old), and some of them needed toner replacements while printing. As for the scanner, we used the scanner from the Kyocera TaskAlfa3551ci multifunctional printer (printer #3 in Table 1), with 600 × 600 dpi scanning resolution. Moreover, we used the default sharpness for scanning and images are saved in a lossless compression configuration. As shown in Table 1, we printed 200 images per printer. For that, we used 50 A4 sheets of paper, printing four images per sheet using the landscape orientation, and then extracting individual patches.

To illustrate the difficulties associated with source-linking of the images in the dataset, in Figure 2 we show the same image printed by different printers and its HH DWT subbands, which were used by Choi et al. [26] to perform source attribution of colored documents. Very subtle differences can be seen in HH subbands of different printers from the same brand but different models (Printers #6 and #7 in Figure 2), but no clear differences in the HH subband when using the same brand and model (Printers #3 and #4 in Figure 2).

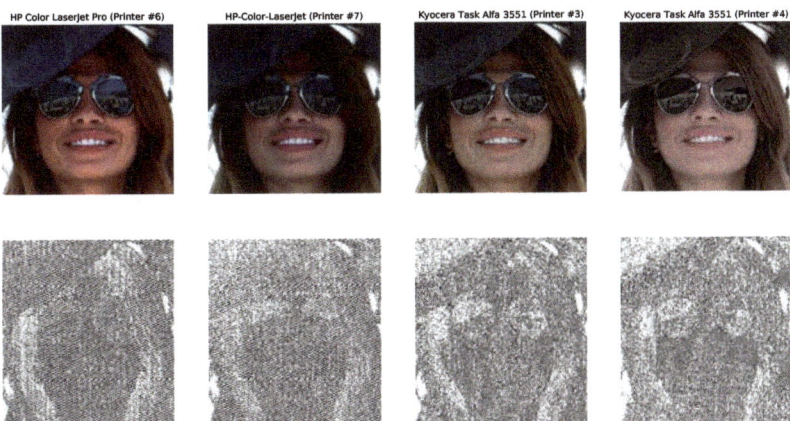

Figure 2. The same image (193.jpg) printed by four different printers and their corresponding HH discrete wavelet transform subbands (luminance component).

As we were aware that 200 images per printer may not be enough for data-hungry techniques such as those based on deep learning, we produced a second set of images containing Regions of Interest (ROI) extracted from the full images set. The importance of the ROI sub-dataset for classification algorithms is three-fold: (i) it may filter only areas that are useful for recognition (e.g, areas containing edges); (ii) such areas can be input to techniques that require lots of data such as data-driven approaches; and (iii) they allow the classification of documents through the fusion of their ROIs classification, providing the most accurate results. Such a strategy was validated several times before in the digital forensics domain, such as in works for camera source attribution [56,57], anti-spoofing solutions [58] and other works in laser printer source attribution [34,36].

To extract the ROI patches, we used an approach inspired by the one adopted in [58] to tackle rebroadcast attacks in a data-driven classification scenario. In particular, we extract image patches by firstly applying Canny filter to the whole input image, and then dividing the resulting binary edge image into squared blocks of varying sizes. Then, we calculate the energy E of the image patches using the horizontal (H), vertical(V), and diagonal (D) sub-bands of the discrete wavelet transform as follows:

$$E = \frac{\sum_{i=1}^{N}\sum_{j=1}^{N} H(i,j)^2 + \sum_{i=1}^{N}\sum_{j=1}^{N} V(i,j)^2 + \sum_{i=1}^{N}\sum_{j=1}^{N} D(i,j)^2}{M^2}, \quad (1)$$

where N is the number of values in the sub-bands of DWT and M is the fixed size of the squared patches. Afterwards, we ranked the image patches according to their E and selected the top 10 energy patches per image. The patches selected in this way compose the RoI subdataset. We chose to calculate the Energy after the binary image is created as we are looking for areas with more edges, instead of those with the highest edge strength. This approach is quite useful when printer noise is hidden in the background or flat areas. . For this second set of images, we choose patch sizes of 28×28, 32×32, 64×64, 128×128, 224×224, 227×227, 256×256 and 299×299 in agreement with the most common input formats accepted by the deep learning approaches available today. The RoI subdataset contains, therefore, 128,000 high energy patches. Figure 3 shows some example of high energy patches selected according to the proposed criterion.

Figure 3. Image 139.jpg of the dataset (first column) and the top 10 energy blocks of size 128 × 128 for different versions of the image printed by various printers (remaining columns).

3.2. VIPPrint Dataset for Synthetic GAN Images Detection

Detecting if an image is a deepfake, i.e., if it has been artificially generated by a GAN, is an increasingly trendy topic in multimedia forensics. In the context of a criminal investigation, for instance, assessing that an image has been taken by a digital camera rather than having been generated artificially can be of fundamental importance to assess the trustfulness of a proof. As another example, in a social media scenario, detecting synthetic images may be useful to understand that a misinformation campaign supported by fake media is ongoing.

So far, research in this area has focused on digital documents, as they are intrinsically linked to fake news in social media. Several strategies have been proposed to deal with such a problem, including analysing the co-occurrence behavior of pixels in RGB channels [39], cross-spectral co-occurrence between pairs of RGB channels [40], discrepancies in color spaces [59], contrastive loss between original and fake images [60] and also other variations of deep learning approaches [38,61]. On the contrary, very few works have considered the detection of deepfake printed images. To date and to the best of our knowledge, the only approach available to deal with the detection of printed manipulated images focuses on the identification of simple manipulations such as Gaussian blurring, Median filtering, resizing and JPEG compression [37]. Yet, printing and scanning back deepfake images is one of the easiest and most effective ways to fool media forensic techniques thought to work in the digital domain.

To promote further research on this topic, we built a second section of the VIPPrint dataset, containing a very large number of natural and GAN-generated face images. Specifically, we printed and scanned a total of 40,000 face images using a Kyocera TaskAlfa3551ci (Printer #3 in Table 1) in the following configurations:

- 16,000 pristine and 16,000 fake images generated by StyleGAN2 [41].
- 3500 pristine and 3500 fake images generated by ProgressiveGAN [42].
- 500 pristine and 500 fake images generated by StarGAN [43].

The first difficulty with these images is the heavy distortion introduced in pixels after printing and scanning. Figure 4 shows how a GAN image is degraded after printing and scanning. The calculated Structural Similarity Index [62] of such images is 0.41 and the Peak Noise to Signal Ratio is 17.65 dB, which corresponds to intense image degradation. The noisy texture of the degradation is visible in the zoomed regions of the digital and printed images highlighted in Figure 5. It is pretty clear from the analysis of this picture that distinguishing between printed pristine and GAN images by looking at textural artifacts only is an extremely difficult task. To further substantiate this hypothesis, in Figure 6 we show the co-occurrence matrices of the RGB bands before and after scanning and printing. The change between the matrices is dramatic, as the image is basically rebroadcasted by another image generation device (i.e., a scanner), possibly erasing the artifacts used to distinguish between natural and GAN images.

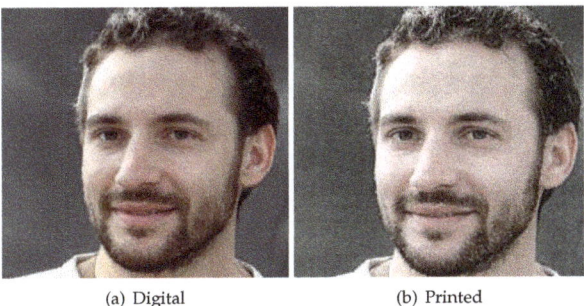

Figure 4. A StyleGAN2 generated image in its original and printed–scanned versions.

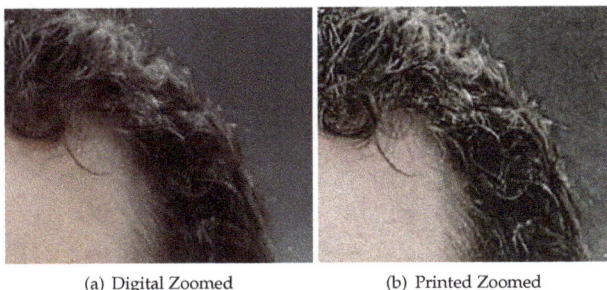

Figure 5. Zoomed regions of the same pictures in Figure 4.

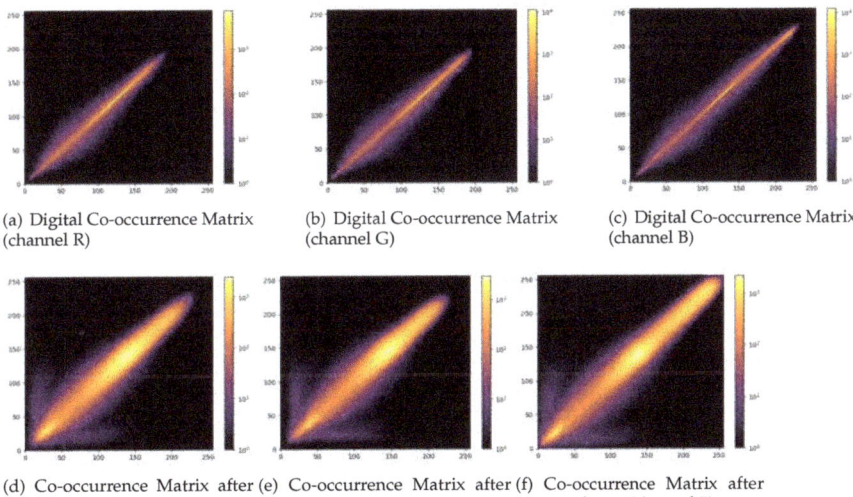

Figure 6. Co-occurrence matrices proposed in [39] to discriminate GAN-generated images from natural ones and their behavior in digital and printed and scanned images: (**top**) GAN image co-occurrence matrices in the digital format (**bottom**); GAN image co-occurrence matrices after printing and scanning.

As for the source attribution dataset, we also built a ROI dataset by applying high energy patch extraction and ranking. However, for this specific problem, the top 100 energy patches were selected (depending on the size of the patches, the selection may correspond to selecting all the patches with non-zero energy). This new subset contained, for the StyleGAN2 case 1109.822 patches for the size 299 × 299, and 2392.469 patches for the 224 × 224 size. Patches for other dimensions and GANs can also be extracted by following the same approach. In the rest of the paper, we will focus on StyleGAN2 images, since they are by far the most difficult to discriminate. Figure 7 shows an example of some GAN images of our dataset along with the selected patches.

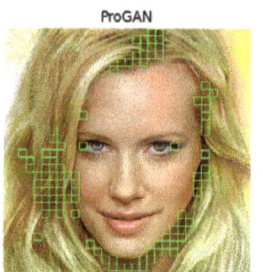

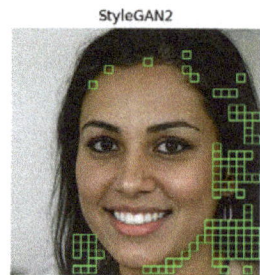

Figure 7. Sample printed pictures from each of the GANs in our dataset with their 64 × 64 top 100 energy blocks.

4. Experimental Setup

In this section, we discuss the experimental setup we used to assess the difficulties associated with source attribution (a multiclass classification problem) and GAN image detection (a binary classification problem) on the images of the VIPPrint dataset. Specifically, we present the metrics used for the experiments, the experimental methodology, the statistical tests we adopted (when applicable), and the baseline approaches we tested together with their implementation details.

4.1. Metrics

Even if authentication and source linking are different classification problems (i.e., a binary and a multi-class problem respectively), the performance achieved by different methods on such tasks can be measured with similar metrics, by paying attention to interpret them properly according to the considered task. The set of metrics we have used is described in the following.

4.1.1. Recall

For binary classification problems, the recall, also known as true positive rate, indicates the percentage of correctly classified positive samples and is calculated as

$$Recall = \frac{TP}{TP + FN}, \qquad (2)$$

where TP (True Positives) represents the number of samples correctly classified as positives, and FN (False Negatives) is the number of positive samples wrongly labeled as negative. In our binary classification problem, the Recall metric measures how many GAN images in the testing set were correctly detected as such.

For the multiclass problem of source attribution, a similar metric can be used, with the difference of considering the recall for each class and calculating the weighted mean for all classes as a final metric.

4.1.2. Precision

As a metric complementary to the Recall, we are interested in the classification precision, which is the fraction of correctly classified positives out of all the instances classified as such in a binary classification problem (in our case, GAN images detection). That is

$$Precision = \frac{TP}{TP + FP}. \tag{3}$$

For the case of source attribution (a multiclass problem), we considered the precision in a way similar to what we did for the recall. That means, we calculate the precision for each class and then consider the final precision as being the weighted mean of precisions from all classes.

4.1.3. F-Measure

The most important metric for both problems is f-measure (F). It measures the harmonic mean of precision and recall and is calculated as follows for the binary classification case:

$$F = 2 \times \frac{P \times R}{P + R}. \tag{4}$$

For the multi-class source attribution problem, we calculate the f-measure individually for each class by using per-class precisions and recalls and weighting them over all classes, exactly as done for the precision and the recall.

4.1.4. Accuracy

As a final metric, we considered the accuracy. In a binary classification problem, it is defined as the total number of samples correctly classified (in both classes) divided by the number of samples under investigation:

$$Accuracy = \frac{TP + TN}{TP + TN + FP + FN}. \tag{5}$$

In the multiclass problem, we repeated the steps done for other multiclass metrics: we calculated the accuracy per printer and then the weighted average of all the accuracies for all classes was calculated.

4.2. Experimental Methodology

To validate the experiments carried out on the VIPPrint dataset, we followed two different approaches, depending on which application we were considering. In the source attribution scenario, we chose the 5 × 2 cross-validation protocol, as it is considered an optimal benchmarking protocol for machine learning algorithms [63] and was also used in other works on printer attribution [18,34]. According to such a protocol, five iterations of twofold cross-validation were carried out. In other words, the data were firstly randomized, and 50% of data was selected as the training set with the other 50% being used for testing. Then the process was inverted. As stated before, this process was repeated five times (five rounds), resulting in ten experiments of training and testing the machine learning classifiers. Additionally, when using deep learning approaches, we also needed validation data in order to help training. Therefore, we further split the 50% of training data into training data and validation data, with a ratio equal to 70:30.

It is important to notice that, in contrast to camera source attribution validation approaches commonly used in the literature [56,57] that use totally random images generated by different cameras, for source attribution of printed documents, the same document can be printed by different printers [18,34]. In this paper, we consider the source attribution problem as a closed set multiclass problem, where we classify documents printed by known printers in our dataset.

For the GAN-image detection task, we took a set of detectors and trained them on the original digital images, as done in the original papers, and assessed their performance on printed and scanned images. We focus on the detection of the StyleGAN2 images in the VIPPrint dataset, as they are by far the best quality GAN images in the dataset. The procedure we followed to evaluate the performances of the detectors was a simple one: we used 24,000 digital images for training and 6000 digital images for validation, and then we used 2000 printed and scanned images from our dataset for testing the detectors. All the sets were independent and stratified (i.e., images in one set were not present in the others and there was an equal number of images per class).

4.3. Statistical Tests

To verify that the source attribution results were statistically significant, we performed a series of two tests in the 5×2 cross-validation procedure. The first one, which we call a pre-test, was used to confirm that all the techniques considered in the experiment are statistically different. If they passed this test, then we did a post test that compared the results in a pairwise manner. The pre-test was done in the distributions of f-measures calculated after ten runs of the 5×2 cross-validation experiments for each technique. The test was applied to an input matrix of n rows (where n is the number of tested approaches) and ten columns, which were the ten f-measures resulting from the 10 runs. The test aimed at verifying whether the distributions of all the sets of f-measures changed significantly. We used the Friedmann test [64] for this first step, with a confidence level of 95%. In other words, if the calculated p-value was below 0.05, then the null hypothesis, which said that there is no statistically significant difference between the f-measures' distributions, was rejected and we could move on to the next test.

For the post test, which tested the statistical relevance of each pair of approaches, we considered the Student's t-test [65]. This test can determine if there is a significant difference between the means of f-measures distributions taken pairwise. To apply this test to our scenario, we also considered the same set of 5×2 f-measure results, but now for each possible pair of approaches. In this test, we set the confidence level to 95%: if the calculated p-value was below 0.05, then the null hypothesis, which stated that there is no statistical significance between the performance of the pair of approaches, was rejected.

4.4. Baseline Methods

In this section, we briefly describe the baseline methods considered in our tests.

Source Attribution

For this problem, we selected 12 approaches divided into three sets. In the first set, which we call image texture descriptors, we used a set of common descriptors that are mainly used for image characterization. For a source attribution task, such descriptors can be useful to differentiate printers' banding artifacts efficiently if the analyzed patterns do not change much, and therefore, they normally exhibit good performance in some printer source attribution tasks [18,20,22,34]. We considered four approaches in this set as follows.

- The gray histogram [66] (hereafter referred to as GH) divides the grayscale version of the analyzed image into a fixed number of blocks. Then, a histogram of gray intensities is calculated for each block and all the histograms together are used to generate a description vector.
- The histogram of oriented gradients [67] (hereafter referred to as HOG) extracts the edges in the image by means of the Sobel kernel gradients; then it computes the gradients for all the orientations. Finally, a histogram of such orientations is fed into the input of a machine learning classifier.
- The edge histogram [66] (hereafter referred to as EH) is similar to HOG. However, it calculates, for each block, the dominant edge orientation instead of all of them, and the descriptor is a histogram of these orientations.
- The local binary patterns [68] divide the image into blocks and compare each pixel in a block to all its neighbors. If the pixel in the center of the block is greater than a neighbor's value, then a 0 digit is written (1 otherwise). Considering eight neighbors in

each block, 8-digit binary numbers are generated for each pixel in a block. Such digits are converted to decimals and histograms for each block are calculated, normalized, and concatenated to describe the image.

The second class of approaches has already been introduced in Section 2, and they are referred to as feature based source printer source attribution baseline techniques. These approaches were already validated in the printer source attribution problem by previous works in the literature, and they are:

- The multidirectional version of the gray level co-occurrence matrix (GLCM-MD) from Ferreira et al. [34].
- The multidirectional and multiscale version of the same approach proposed in [34] (GLCM-MD-MS).
- The convolutional texture gradient filter in a 3 × 3 window [34] (CTGF-3X3).
- The 39 statistical features from the diagonal discrete wavelet transform sub-band from Choi et al. [26] (DWT-STATS).

Finally, the third set of approaches belong to the class of data-driven baselines and rely on the training of deep neural networks. For this set, we considered several convolutional neural network approaches analyzed in [36] for printer source attribution. These are:

- The 16 and 19 layer versions of the VGG convolutional neural network [69] (VGG−16 and VGG−19).
- The 50 and 101 layer versions of the RESNET convolutional neural networks [70] (RESNET-50 and RESNET−101).

Printed and Scanned GAN Image Detection

For the deepfake detection task, we chose a set of deep learning classifiers proposed in the literature for digital images. The first three approaches were based on ImageNet dataset pre-trained models and their use for GAN images detection was validated in the work of Marra et al. [38]. They are:

- The Densely connected networks [71] (DENSENET)
- The third version of InceptionNet [72] (INCEPTION-V3);
- The InceptionNet evolution considering fully separable filters [73] (XCEPTION)

The other set of deep neural networks were ad hoc networks designed for the GAN detection problem. These networks act on pre-processed data, namely, the co-occurency matrices of image channels, and they are:

- A CNN that acts on three co-occurence intra-channel matrices [39] (CONET);
- A CNN that acts on six co-occurence matrices considering both intra- and inter-channel co-occurrences [40] (CROSSCONET).

All these five CNNs have been retrained on StyleGAN2 and pristine digital images as described in Section 4.2. In conclusion, we considered 12 baseline methods for the source attribution tasks and 5 for the GAN-image detection task.

4.5. Implementation Details

To ensure the reproducibility of our results, we provide all the implementation details we used to achieve our results. We start with the source attribution approaches that we had to re-train from scratch. We had to do that because the eight printers used to build the VIPPrint dataset had never been used before in a source attribution problem. Then, we report the implementation details of the pre-trained baseline models on digital we used to distinguish printed and scanned GAN and pristine images.

We start with the feature engineering approaches. For GH, LBP, EH, HOG, and DWT we used Python implementations, whereas for GLCM-MD, GLCM-MD-MS and CTGF-3X3 we used MATLAB implementations available at the authors' source code website [74]. Although the implementations used different programming languages, we used them only to extract the features, using a Linear SVM from Python's sci-kit-learn library (http://scikit-learn.

org, accessed on 11 February 2021) for the final classification stage. We chose a linear kernel support vector machines classifier, as it is well suitable to deal efficiently with high-dimensional features. We performed a grid-search approach to find the best parameters to train the classifiers for each of the 10 experiments. This was done by applying a five-fold cross-validation procedure to the training data only. The classifiers' parameter C was varied in the set $C = \{0.1, 1, 10, 100, 1000\}$, and the best value was used to train the classifier.

In contrast to the previous approaches, those based on convolutional neural networks were applied patch-wise, with patches of size 224×224 for VGG−16, VGG−19, RESNET-50, RESNET−101, INCEPTION_NET-V3, and DENSENET; and 299×299 for XCEPTION_NET. The final classification result for an image was set to be the mode of the classifications obtained on single patches. This approach is commonly known as majority voting and was also validated in printed document forensics research [18–20,22,34]. To choose the patches, we applied the highest-energy procedure already described in Section 3. The only exceptions to this rule were the CONET and CROSS-CONET networks for GAN image detection, which acted on 256×256 co-occurence matrices computed on the entire images. We implemented these techniques by using Python's Tensorflow (https://www.tensorflow.org/, accessed on 11 February 2021), and Keras (https://keras.io/, accessed on 11 February 2021) libraries.

For a fair comparison of the data-driven approaches, we used the following common procedure to train the neural networks:

1. We fine-tuned the neural networks pre-trained on ImageNet with the input training data (e.g., high energized patches), by initializing the weights with Imagenet pre-trained weights. We tried other procedures, such as fine-tuning, only the tops of the networks (i.e., the fully connected layers) and freezing the other layers, but the results were not worthwhile.
2. In the fine-tuning procedure, we cut off the tops of these networks, replacing them with a layer of 512 fully connected neurons, followed by a 50% dropout layer and a final layer with eight or two neurons, depending on the task.
3. The networks were trained with the steepest gradient descent optimizer [75], with an initial learning rate of 0.01. The learning rate was reduced by a factor of $\sqrt{0.1}$ once the validation loss stagnated after five epochs. We fixed the learning rate lower bound to 0.5×10^{-6}. We trained the networks on minibatches of size 32 for source attribution and 16 for GAN detection.
4. We set the maximum number of epochs for source attribution to 300 epochs. However, after 20 epochs we implemented an early stopping procedure if the validation loss did not improve. For deepfake detection, we chose 10 epochs and the early stopping condition was implemented after five epochs, as we were using much more data.
5. We used data augmentation for the source attribution task by using the following image processing operations: rotation, zoom, width shifts, height shifts, shears, and horizontal flips. For GAN detection, since much more training data are available (more than 300,000 images), we did not use any data augmentation.

Finally, all the data presented in this paper, including the two datasets, the scripts for generating the high-energy blocks, 5×2 cross-validation data, and some of the source code used are all available at https://tinyurl.com/vipprint, accessed on 11 February 2021.

5. Experimental Results

In this section, we discuss the results of our comparative study for both source attribution and GAN-image detection.

5.1. Source Attribution

An overall view of the average results we got for the 12 baseline source attribution techniques we have tested is reported in Table 2.

Table 2. Average performance for the source attribution problem. The approaches are divided by category, and boldfaced entries denote the solutions specifically designed for the source printer attribution problem. The best results for each metric are highlighted in yellow.

Type	Method	5 × 2 Cross Validation Results–Close Set Printer Attribution			
		Input Size	F	Precision	Recall
TEXTURE DESCRIPTORS	GH [66]	Image	0.52 ± 0.01	0.53 ± 0.01	0.52 ± 0.01
	HOG [67]	Image	0.68 ± 0.01	0.69 ± 0.01	0.68 ± 0.01
	EH [66]	Image	0.69 ± 0.01	0.69 ± 0.01	0.69 ± 0.01
	LBP [68]	Image	0.75 ± 0.01	0.75 ± 0.01	0.75 ± 0.01
FEATURE-BASED BASELINES	**DWT-STATS** [26]	Image	0.76 ± 0.01	0.76 ± 0.01	0.76 ± 0.01
	GLCM-MD [34]	Image	0.78 ± 0.01	0.79 ± 0.01	0.78 ± 0.01
	GLCM-MD-MS [34]	Image	0.84 ± 0.01	0.84 ± 0.01	0.84 ± 0.01
	CTGF-3x3 [34]	Image	0.79 ± 0.01	0.79 ± 0.01	0.79 ± 0.01
DATA-DRIVEN BASELINES	**RESNET-50** [36,70]	224×224 patches	**0.91 ± 0.01**	**0.92 ± 0.00**	**0.91 ± 0.00**
	RESNET-101 [36,70]	224×224 patches	0.90 ± 0.01	**0.92 ± 0.00**	**0.91 ± 0.00**
	VGG-16 [36,69]	224×224 patches	0.46 ± 0.45	0.45 ± 0.46	0.51 ± 0.40
	VGG-19 [36,69]	224×224 patches	0.37 ± 0.44	0.37 ± 0.44	0.42 ± 0.39

The first aspect to be noticed in the results shown in Table 2 is the bad performance obtained by methods based on general-purpose texture descriptors. The GH descriptor, for example, tries to discriminate printers by assuming that different printers print the same images using different colors, which is supposed to be seen in different histograms plotted in the n-dimensional space and clustered by hyperplanes such as those from the SVM classifiers. That assumption failsm as the resulting f-measure (0.53) is pretty similar to a random guess. The approaches relying more on the effects of gradients and edges (EH and HOG), where the banding and other printing artifacts are more evident [34], achieve slightly better but still poor performance. The best f-measure in this class of techniques was obtained by the LBP descriptor ($F = 0.75$). A possible explanation for the better performance of LBP compared to other texture descriptors is that it explores gradient information by encoding, in several regions, the neighborhood relationships. This can better identify the behavior of printer patterns compared to other texture descriptors.

The second set of techniques included approaches based on handcrafted features specifically tailored for the source attribution problem. To start with, we found that the performance of DWT-STATS ($F = 0.76$) dropped with respect to the performance reported in the original paper [26], highlighting that different datasets with modern printers may confuse such characterization. Additionally, from the discussion done in Section 3, we found that considering statistics from a specific wavelet channel allows identifying different brands, but does not work well when identical devices are included in the set. Other descriptors from [34] show better, but still unsatisfactory results. CTGF-3X3 filters convolutional generated features, building their histogram in a gradient interval. Said approach yielded an average $F = 0.79$, which is considered a good result when compared with the common texture descriptors we considered and discussed in the previous paragraph. We can also see from Table 2 that better performances were also obtained by GLCM-MD ($F = 0.78$) and GLCM-MD-MS ($F = 0.84$). These approaches consider more directions in the neighborhood of pixels and more statistics in the co-occurrence matrices. Additionally, for GLCM-MD-MS, more scales were used in order to achieve invariance with respect to the size of the printed pattern. Such features can be considered ad hoc texture features specific for laser printer attribution, thereby achieving better performance than general texture descriptors.

Finally, the last set of techniques are based on CNNs [36]. Let us consider first the shallower networks, namely, VGG−16 and VGG−19. They provide the two worst results for all metrics, while also showing a very high standard deviation, indicating very unstable training. Two possible reasons for such bad performance are the shallowness of the networks and their very simple architecture, including only convolutional and pooling layers. Those explanations were confirmed by the results gotten by deeper and more complex networks, RESNET-50 and RESNET−101 CNNs. These networks exhibited (by far) the top two results of our tests, with $F = 0.91$ for RESNET-50 and $F = 0.90$ for RESNET−101.

To better investigate the differences between these networks, we start to discuss where they fail and succeed in the printer attribution task. Tables 3 and 4 show the confusion matrix of these approaches. It can be seen that both approaches have strong difficulties to discriminate two printers from Kyocera: the Color-Laser and a specific Taskalfa model (printers #2 and #3 of our dataset). This result is somewhat surprising because these printers are quite different physically (Taskalfa is a multifunctional printer and Color-Laser is an ordinary laser printer). One possible explanation is that the two printers could have shared some components in their manufacturing process. RESNET-50 showed slightly better performance, as it is less affected by said problem and also because it classified 4 out of 10 printers perfectly, instead of 3 out of 10.

Table 3. Confusion matrix of RESNET-50 for the source attribution problem.

Printer	Epson-WorkForce WF-7715	Kyocera ColorLaser	Kyocera TaskAlfa3551ci	Kyocera TaskAlfa3551ci-2	Samsung Multiexpress X3280NR	HP Color-LaserJet Pro rfp-r479fdw	HP Color-LaserJet rfp-r377dw	OKI-C612 LaserColor
Epson-WorkForce WF-7715	100.00%							
Kyocera ColorLaser		56.00%	41.00%	3.00%				
Kyocera TaskAlfa3551ci		5.00%	92.00%	3.00%				
KyoceraTaskAlfa 3551ci-2		1.00%		99.00%				
Samsung Multiexpress-X3280NR					100.00%			
HP Color-LaserJet Pro rfp-r479fdw						98.00%	2.00%	
HP-Color-LaserJet rfp-r377dw							100.00%	
OKI-C612 LaserColor								100.00%

Table 4. Confusion matrix of RESNET−101 for the source attribution problem.

Printer	Epson-WorkForce WF-7715	Kyocera ColorLaser	Kyocera TaskAlfa3551ci	Kyocera TaskAlfa3551ci-2	Samsung Multiexpress X3280NR	HP Color-LaserJet Pro rfp-r479fdw	HP Color-LaserJet rfp-r377dw	OKI-C612 LaserColor
Epson-WorkForce WF-7715	100.00%							
Kyocera ColorLaser		35.00%	60.00%	5.00%				
Kyocera TaskAlfa3551ci		5.00%	93.00%	2.00%				
KyoceraTaskAlfa 3551ci-2			1.00%	99.00%				
Samsung Multiexpress-X3280NR					100.00%			
HP Color-LaserJet Pro rfp-r479fdw						98.00%	2.00%	
HP-Color-LaserJet rfp-r377dw						1.00%	99.00%	
OKI-C612 LaserColor								100.00%

As a final step of the printer attribution experiments, we analyzed the statistical significance of the results. By applying the Friedmann test to 12 vectors (one for each approach) with the 10 f-measures, we got a p-value lower than 0.01, thereby proving that the differences in the f-measures between all the approaches are statistically significant. As a second step, the results of the pairwise statistical tests (Student's t-test) are shown in Table 5.

The first noticeable behavior in Table 5 is that the large standard deviation of VGG−16 does not allow one to draw statistically significant conclusions for some of the comparisons, namely, those with GH, HOG, EH, and LBP. Other cases where no statistically significant conclusions can be drawn are the comparisons of DWT-STATS and LBP, and HOG with EH.

Finally, we notice that the superior performances of RESNET-50 and RESNET−101 were confirmed by the results of the Student's t-tests with all the other methods. At the same time, the difference between the performances of these two networks was not statistically significant. Based on these observations, we can conclude that RESNET-50 and RESNET−101 represent the better solutions for the source attribution problem, even though their best performance, with an f-measure equal to 0.91, along with the difficulties in distinguishing some Kyocera printers, leave room for further improvement.

Table 5. Pairwise statistical comparison between different source attribution techniques.

Method	GH [66]	HOG [67]	EH [66]	LBP [68]	DWT-STATS [26]	GLCM-MD [34]	GLCM-MD-MS [34]	CTGF-3x3 [34]	RESNET-50 [36,70]	RESNET-101 [36,70]	VGG-16 [36,69]	VGG-19 [36,69]	TOTAL
GH [66]	0	-1	-1	-1	-1	-1	-1	-1	-1	-1	0	0	-9
HOG [67]	1	0	0	-1	-1	-1	-1	-1	-1	-1	0	1	-5
EH [66]	1	0	0	-1	-1	-1	-1	-1	-1	-1	0	1	-5
LBP [68]	1	1	1	0	0	-1	-1	-1	-1	-1	0	1	-1
DWT-STATS [26]	1	1	1	0	0	-1	-1	-1	-1	-1	1	1	0
GLCM-MD [34]	1	1	1	1	1	0	-1	0	-1	-1	1	1	4
GLCM-MD-MS [34]	1	1	1	1	1	1	0	1	-1	-1	1	1	7
CTGF-3x3 [34]	1	1	1	1	1	0	-1	0	-1	-1	1	1	4
RESNET-50 [36,70]	1	1	1	1	1	1	1	1	0	0	1	1	10
RESNET-101 [36,70]	1	1	1	1	1	1	1	1	0	0	1	1	10
VGG-16 [36,69]	0	0	0	0	-1	-1	-1	-1	-1	-1	0	0	-6
VGG-19 [36,69]	0	-1	-1	-1	-1	-1	-1	-1	-1	-1	0	0	-9

1 = Line method is better than column method
0 = Line method is equivalent to column method
−1 = Line method is worse than column method

5.2. Detection of GAN Images

We now discuss the results of GAN image detection on printed and scanned documents. For that, we considered a set of CNNs trained on different patch sizes (i.e., 224 × 224 and 299 × 299) with majority voting and also 256 × 256 co-occurrence matrices without majority voting. We first show, in Figure 8, the training and validation behavior of these networks considered for this experiment when trained on digital images.

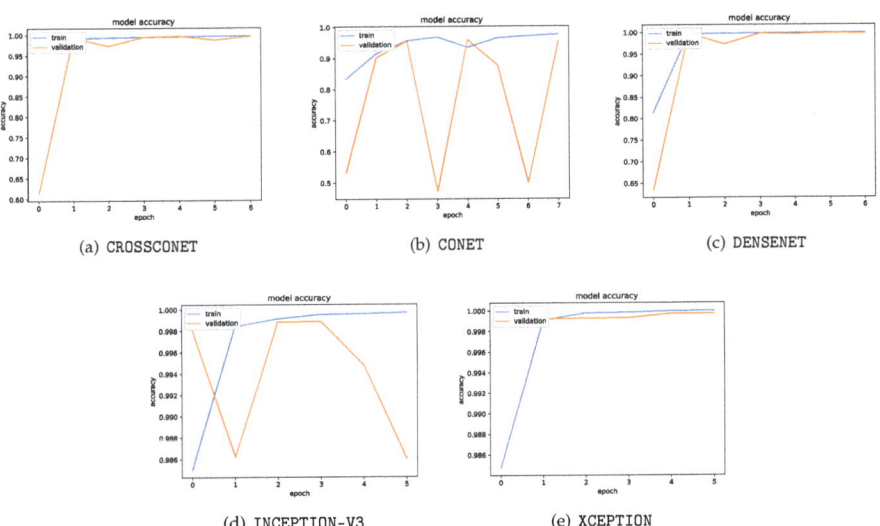

(a) CROSSCONET   (b) CONET   (c) DENSENET

(d) INCEPTION-V3   (e) XCEPTION

Figure 8. Models of training and validation curves when applied to digital images.

Figure 8 shows the training and validation curves' behavior for INCEPTION-V3 and CONET CNNs. The different patterns visible in the figure can be explained by the different complexity of the architectures we used, the number of layers, and the diversity of training data: INCEPTION-V3 has a very simple architecture with some inception modules in 48 layers, whereas CONET was trained on RGB co-occurrence matrices with seven layers only and with 10 times less data. Those issues notwithstanding, it is expected that, without the early stopping criterion on such a low number of epochs as we used for our CNNs' training, the curves' behavior would stabilize after some iterations. However, even with these irregular training curves, the early stopping criterion required less than 10 epochs to be fulfilled, and all models' training and validation accuracies selected for further testing were higher than 95% when classifying digital images.

As anticipated in Section 3.2, the print and scan process eliminated most of artifacts commonly found on digital images, being the simplest but most efficient attack against such approaches. In Table 6, we show the classification results considering both digital and printed and scanned test images. For the digital case, all the approaches achieved an accuracy higher than 95%, with the worst approach being CONET with 96% accuracy. The CROSSCONET [40] showed better performance than CONET for digital images, as it also looks for artifacts in cross-band co-occurrence matrices. The best approaches in the digital scenario were DENSENET, INCEPTION-V3, and XCEPTION, with virtually perfect results. The power of ROIs majority voting is exemplified by the confusion matrix of the XCEPTION CNN in Table 7. It can be seen from that table that the approach misclassifies only seven $299 \times 299 \times 3$ high-energy testing patches, explaining the perfect classification after majority voting.

Table 6. Results of GAN image detection tests for digital (left) and printed and scanned images (right). Best results are highlighted in yellow

Method	Training/Validation Data	Input Size	Digital Images Testing Results				Printed and Scanned Testing Images Results			
			Acc	F	Precision	Recall	Acc	F	Precision	Recall
DENSENET [38,71]	Images Patches	$224 \times 224 \times 3$	1.00	1.00	1.00	1.00	0.50	0.00	0.00	0.00
INCEPTION-V3 [38,72]	Images Patches	$224 \times 224 \times 3$	1.00	1.00	1.00	1.00	0.50	0.00	0.00	0.00
XCEPTION [38,73]	Images Patches	$299 \times 299 \times 3$	1.00	1.00	1.00	1.00	0.50	0.00	0.00	0.00
CONET [39]	Co-occurency Matrices	$256 \times 256 \times 3$	0.96	0.96	0.95	0.98	0.50	0.00	0.00	0.00
CROSSCONET [40]	Co-occurency Matrices	$256 \times 256 \times 6$	0.99	0.99	0.98	1.00	0.50	0.29	0.50	0.21

Table 7. Confusion matrix of XCEPTION $299 \times 299 \times 3$ patches classified for digital GAN-image detection.

| | Confusion Matrix | |
| | Xception | |
	Digital Test Patches	
Class	Real	Fake
Real	8914	5
Fake	2	8983

When faced with printed and scanned images, though, all methods failed, as can be seen on the rightmost part of Table 6. These results confirm that most of the artifacts used by the detectors to distinguish between GAN and real images, such as warping, blur, noise, correlation, and image statistics, are gone when images are printed and recaptured. In fact, all the approaches provided accuracy equal to 0.5 with zero precision and recall, meaning that all the images were classified as natural ones. The only minor exception is represented by CROSSCONET, which correctly classified 21% of StyleGAN2 images as fake images, as can be seen from the confusion matrix shown in Table 8.

Table 8. Confusion matrix of CROSSCONET for printed and scanned GAN-image detection.

| | Confusion Matrix | |
| | CrossCoNet | |
	PrintScan Test Images	
Class	Real	Fake
Real	796	204
Fake	788	212

The poor results obtained when GAN-image detectors were trained on digital images and applied to printed and scanned images call for new research on this topic, in order to face the fact that counterfeiters could print and scan fake images in order to avoid being revealed as such. We are, therefore, confident that the availability of the VIPPrint dataset will help researchers to solve this challenging task.

6. Conclusions

The accessibility and constant upgrading of devices capable of generating high-quality physical documents have raised the necessity for forensic methods to attest to the reliability of printed documents and possibly link illegal or criminal documents to their creators. Authentication and source linking of printed documents may also have huge economic impacts, since it may help to tackle the diffusion of counterfeited products. Although several works in the scientific literature have addressed said issue, all of them failed in two aspects: (i) they did not consider a dataset that grows with time, including more recent and professional printing devices; and (ii) they did not consider the authentication of printed artificial images.

In this paper, we showed the extent of such limitations by validating existing authentication and source linking methodologies on a novel dataset specifically made for printed document forensics. The new dataset, the VIPPrint dataset, presents the first version of an ongoing effort to build a challenging environment for printed image forensics. To the best of our knowledge, the dataset contains the richest publicly available corpus of printed natural and artificial images, with 40,000 images addressing deepfake face-image detection, and 1600 images focusing on source attribution in a closed set of eight printer sources. The experiments we have run showed that this dataset results in an error probability of at least 9% for the best baseline source attribution methods. The dataset raises even more challenging problems in the case of GAN-image detection, given that StyleGAN2 images look like the original ones for all the tested methods after they are printed and scanned.

The experiments we ran have guided us toward a lot of further work. First of all, we will continue updating the dataset to include new printers, more scanners, other GANs, and acquisition devices such as digital single lens reflex (DSLR) cameras. Second, we aim at investigating novel ways of selecting regions of interest in the digitized images and also considering other color spaces in addition to RGB. Finally, we are also headed toward investigating and applying adversarial attacks in the printed domain; we will add relevant features to our dataset in order to evaluate the effectiveness of printed document forensic methods.

Author Contributions: Conceptualization, A.F. and M.B.; methodology, A.F.; software, A.F. and E.N.; validation, A.F. and E.N.; formal analysis, A.F., E.N. and M.B.; investigation, A.F., E.N., and M.B.; resources, M.B.; data curation, A.F., E.N., and M.B.; writing—original draft preparation, A.F. and M.B.; writing—review and editing, A.F. and M.B.; visualization, A.F. and M.B.; supervision, M.B.; project administration, A.F. and M.B.; funding acquisition, A.F. and M.B. All authors have read and agreed to the published version of the manuscript.

Funding: This research was funded by the European Union Marie Sklodowska-Curie project PrintOut (grant number 892757).

Acknowledgments: The authors would like to thank Davide Rossi for his outstanding help with building the dataset presented in this paper.

Institutional Review Board Statement: Not applicable.

Informed Consent Statement: Not applicable.

Data Availability Statement: Our data is available on a public repository. The address is informed in the paper (http://tinyurl.com/vipprint, accessed on 11 February 2021). The DOI for our dataset is http://doi.org/10.5281/zenodo.4454971 , accessed on 11 February 2021.

Conflicts of Interest: The authors declare no conflict of interest. The funders had no role in the design of the study; in the collection, analyses, or interpretation of data; in the writing of the manuscript, or in the decision to publish the results.

References

1. Electronic Frontier Foundation. List of Printers Which Do or Do Not Display Tracking Dots. Available online: https://www.eff.org/pages/list-printers-which-do-or-do-not-display-tracking-dots (accessed on 5 October 2020).
2. Richter, T.; Escher, S.; Schönfeld, D.; Strufe, T. Forensic Analysis and Anonymisation of Printed Documents. In *ACM Workshop on Information Hiding and Multimedia Security*; Association for Computing Machinery: New York, NY, USA, 2018; pp. 127–138.
3. Ali, G.; Mikkilineni, A.; Delp, E.; Allebach, J.; Chiang, P.J.; Chiu, G. Application of principal components analysis and Gaussian Mixture Models to printer identification. In *NIP & Digital Fabrication Conference*; Society for Imaging Science and Technology: Springfield, VA, USA, 2004; pp. 301–305.
4. Mikkilineni, A.; Chiang, P.; Ali, G.; Chiu, G.; Allebach, J.; Delp, E. Printer identification based on texture features. In *NIP & Digital Fabrication Conference*; Society for Imaging Science and Technology: Springfield, VA, USA, 2004;pp. 306–311.
5. Mikkilineni, A.K.; Chiang, P.J.; Ali, G.N.; Chiu, G.T.C.; Allebach, J.P.; Delp, E.J., III. Printer identification based on graylevel co-occurrence features for security and forensic applications. In *Security, Steganography, and Watermarking of Multimedia Contents VII*; Delp, E.J., III., Wong, P.W., Eds.; International Society for Optics and Photonics: Bellingham, WA, USA, 2005; Volume 5681, pp. 430–440. [CrossRef]
6. Mikkilineni, A.; Arslan, O.; Chiang, P.J.; Kumontoy, R.; Allebach, J.; Chiu, G.; Delp, E. Printer Forensics using SVM Techniques. In *NIP & Digital Fabrication Conference*; Society for Imaging Science and Technology: Springfield, VA, USA, 2005; pp. 223–226.
7. Kee, E.; Farid, H. Printer Profiling for Forensics and Ballistics. In Proceedings of the ACM Workshop on Multimedia and Security, Oxford, UK, 22–23 September 2008; Association for Computing Machinery: New York, NY, USA, 2008; pp. 3–10. [CrossRef]
8. Deng, W.; Chen, Q.; Yuan, F.; Yan, Y. Printer Identification Based on Distance Transform. In Proceedings of the International Conference on Intelligent Networks and Intelligent Systems, Wuhan, China, 1–3 November 2008; pp. 565–568.
9. Wu, Y.; Kong, X.; Guo, Y. Printer forensics based on page document's geometric distortion. In Proceedings of the IEEE International Conference on Image Processing (ICIP), Cairo, Egypt, 7–10 November 2009; pp. 2909–2912.
10. Jiang, W.; Ho, A.T.S.; Treharne, H.; Shi, Y.Q. A Novel Multi-size Block Benford's Law Scheme for Printer Identification. In *Pacific-Rim Conference on Multimedia*; Qiu, G.; Lam, K.M.; Kiya, H.; Xue, X.Y.; Kuo, C.C.J.; Lew, M.S., Eds.; Springer: Berlin/Heidelberg, Germany, 2010; pp. 643–652.
11. Mikkilineni, A.K.; Khanna, N.; Delp, E.J. Forensic printer detection using intrinsic signatures. In *Media Watermarking, Security, and Forensics III*; Memon, N.D., Dittmann, J., Alattar, A.M., Delp, E.J., III, Eds.; International Society for Optics and Photonics: Bellingham, WA, USA, 2011; Volume 7880, pp. 278–288. [CrossRef]
12. Tsai, M.; Liu, J. Digital forensics for printed source identification. In Proceedings of the IEEE International Symposium on Circuits and Systems (ISCAS), Beijing, China, 19–23 May 2013; pp. 2347–2350.
13. Elkasrawi, S.; Shafait, F. Printer Identification Using Supervised Learning for Document Forgery Detection. In Proceedings of the International Workshop on Document Analysis Systems, Tours, France, 7–10 April 2014; pp. 146–150.
14. Tsai, M.J.; Yin, J.S.; Yuadi, I.; Liu, J. Digital Forensics of Printed Source Identification for Chinese Characters. *Multimed. Tools Appl.* **2014**, *73*, 2129–2155. [CrossRef]
15. Hao, J.; Kong, X.; Shang, S. Printer identification using page geometric distortion on text lines. In Proceedings of the IEEE China Summit and International Conference on Signal and Information Processing (ChinaSIP), Chengdu, China, 12–15 July 2015; pp. 856–860.
16. Shang, S.; Kong, X.; You, X. Document forgery detection using distortion mutation of geometric parameters in characters. *J. Electron. Imaging* **2015**, *24*, 1–10. [CrossRef]
17. Tsai, M.; Hsu, C.; Yin, J.; Yuadi, I. Japanese character based printed source identification. In Proceedings of the Proceedings of the IEEE International Symposium on Circuits and Systems (ISCAS), Lisbon, Portugal, 24–27 May 2015; pp. 2800–2803.
18. Ferreira, A.; Bondi, L.; Baroffio, L.; Bestagini, P.; Huang, J.; dos Santos, J.A.; Tubaro, S.; Rocha, A. Data-Driven Feature Characterization Techniques for Laser Printer Attribution. *IEEE Trans. Inf. Forensics Secur.* **2017**, *12*, 1860–1873. [CrossRef]
19. Joshi, S.; Khanna, N. Single Classifier-Based Passive System for Source Printer Classification Using Local Texture Features. *IEEE Trans. Inf. Forensics Secur.* **2018**, *13*, 1603–1614. [CrossRef]
20. Joshi, S.; Lomba, M.; Goyal, V.; Khanna, N. Augmented Data and Improved Noise Residual-Based CNN for Printer Source Identification. In Proceedings of the IEEE International Conference on Acoustics, Speech and Signal Processing (ICASSP), Calgary, AB, Canada, 15–20 April 2018; pp. 2002–2006.
21. Jain, H.; Gupta, G.; Joshi, S.; Khanna, N. Passive classification of source printer using text-line-level geometric distortion signatures from scanned images of printed documents. *Multimed. Tools Appl.* **2019**, *79*, 7377–7400. [CrossRef]
22. Joshi, S.; Khanna, N. Source Printer Classification Using Printer Specific Local Texture Descriptor. *IEEE Trans. Inf. Forensics Secur.* **2020**, *15*, 160–171. [CrossRef]
23. Ali, G.; Mikkilineni, A.; Chiang, P.J.; Allebach, J.; Chiu, G.; Delp, E. Intrinsic and Extrinsic Signatures for Information Hiding and Secure Printing with Electrophotographic Devices. In Proceedings of the International Conference on Digital Printing Technologies, New Orleans, MS, USA, 28 September–3 October 2003.

24. Eid, A.H.; Ahmed, M.N.; Rippetoe, E.E. EP printer jitter characterization using 2D Gabor filter and spectral analysis. In Proceedings of the IEEE International Conference on Image Processing, San Diego, CA, USA, 12–15 October 2008; pp. 1860–1863.
25. Bulan, O.; Mao, J.; Sharma, G. Geometric distortion signatures for printer identification. In Proceedings of the IEEE International Conference on Acoustics, Speech and Signal Processing (ICAASP), Taipei, Taiwan, 19–24 April 2009; pp. 1401–1404.
26. Choi, J.H.; Im, D.H.; Lee, H.Y.; Oh, J.T.; Ryu, J.H.; Lee, H.K. Color laser printer identification by analyzing statistical features on discrete wavelet transform. In Proceedings of the IEEE International Conference on Image Processing (ICIP), Cairo, Egypt, 7–10 November 2009; pp. 1505–1508.
27. Choi, J.H.; Lee, H.K.; Lee, H.Y.; Suh, Y.H. Color Laser Printer Forensics with Noise Texture Analysis. In Proceedings of the ACM Workshop on Multimedia and Security, Cairo, Egypt, 7–10 November 2009; Association for Computing Machinery: New York, NY, USA, 2010; p. 19–24.
28. Ryu, S.; Lee, H.; Im, D.; Choi, J.; Lee, H. Electrophotographic printer identification by halftone texture analysis. In Proceedings of the IEEE International Conference on Acoustics, Speech and Signal Processing (ICAASP), Dallas, TX, USA, 14–19 March 2010; pp. 1846–1849.
29. Tsai, M.; Liu, J.; Wang, C.; Chuang, C. Source color laser printer identification using discrete wavelet transform and feature selection algorithms. In Proceedings of the IEEE International Symposium of Circuits and Systems (ISCAS), Rio de Janeiro, Brazil, 15–18 May 2011; pp. 2633–2636.
30. Choi, J.H.; Lee, H.Y.; Lee, H.K. Color laser printer forensic based on noisy feature and support vector machine classifier. *Multimed. Tools Appl.* **2013**, *67*, 363–382. [CrossRef]
31. Kim, D.; Lee, H. Color laser printer identification using photographed halftone images. In Proceedings of the European Signal Processing Conference (EUSIPCO), Lisbon, Portugal, 1–5 September 2014; pp. 795–799.
32. Wu, H.; Kong, X.; Shang, S. A printer forensics method using halftone dot arrangement model. In Proceedings of the IEEE China Summit and International Conference on Signal and Information Processing (ChinaSIP), Chengdu, China, 12–15 July 2015; pp. 861–865.
33. Kim, D.; Lee, H. Colour laser printer identification using halftone texture fingerprint. *Electron. Lett.* **2015**, *51*, 981–983. [CrossRef]
34. Ferreira, A.; Navarro, L.C.; Pinheiro, G.; dos Santos, J.A.; Rocha, A. Laser printer attribution: Exploring new features and beyond. *Forensics Sci. Int.* **2015**, *247*, 105–125. [CrossRef] [PubMed]
35. Tsai, M.; Yuadi, M.; Tao, Y.; Yin, J. Source Identification for Printed Documents. In Proceedings of the International Conference on Collaboration and Internet Computing (CIC), San Jose, CA, USA, 15–17 October 2017; pp. 54–58.
36. Bibi, M.; Hamid, A.; Moetesum, M.; Siddiqi, I. Document Forgery Detection using Printer Source Identification—A Text-Independent Approach. In Proceedings of the International Conference on Document Analysis and Recognition Workshops, Sydney, Australia, 22–25 September 2019; Volume 8, pp. 7–12.
37. James, H.; Gupta, O.; Raviv, D. Printing and Scanning Attack for Image Counter Forensics. *arXiv* **2020**, arXiv:2005.02160.
38. Marra, F.; Gragnaniello, D.; Cozzolino, D.; Verdoliva, L. Detection of GAN-Generated Fake Images over Social Networks. In Proceedings of the IEEE Conference on Multimedia Information Processing and Retrieval (MIPR), Miami, FL, USA, 10–12 April 2018; pp. 384–389.
39. Nataraj, L.; Mohammed, T.M.; Manjunath, B.; Chandrasekaran, S.; Flenner, A.; Bappy, M.J.; Roy-Chowdhury, A. Detecting GAN generated Fake Images using Co-occurrence Matrices. *Electron. Imaging* **2019**, *2019*, 532–1–532–1.–1173.2019.5.MWSF-532. [CrossRef]
40. Barni, M.; Kallas, K.; Nowroozi, E.; Tondi, B. CNN Detection of GAN-Generated Face Images based on Cross-Band Co-occurrences Analysis. In Proceedings of the IEEE Workshop on Information Forensics and Security (WIFS), Delft, The Netherlands, 9–12 December 2020; pp. 1–6.
41. Karras, T.; Laine, S.; Aila, T. A Style-Based Generator Architecture for Generative Adversarial Networks. In Proceedings of the IEEE/CVF Conference on Computer Vision and Pattern Recognition (CVPR), Long Beach, CA, USA, 15–20 June 2019; pp. 4396–4405.
42. Karras, T.; Aila, T.; Laine, S.; Lehtinen, J. Progressive Growing of GANs for Improved Quality, Stability, and Variation. *arXiv* **2017**, arXiv:1710.10196.
43. Choi, Y.; Choi, M.; Kim, M.; Ha, J.W.; Kim, S.; Choo, J. StarGAN: Unified Generative Adversarial Networks for Multi-Domain Image-to-Image Translation. *arXiv* **2017**, arXiv:1711.09020.
44. Khanna, N.; Mikkilineni, A.K.; Martone, A.F.; Ali, G.N.; Chiu, G.T.C.; Allebach, J.P.; Delp, E.J. A survey of forensic characterization methods for physical devices. *Digit. Investig.* **2006**, *3*, 17–28. [CrossRef]
45. Khanna, N.; Mikkilineni, A.K.; Chiu, G.T.C.; Allebach, J.P.; Delp, E.J. Survey of Scanner and Printer Forensics at Purdue University. In *International Workshop on Computational Forensics*; Srihari, S.N.; Franke, K., Eds.; Springer: Berlin/Heidelberg, Germany, 2008; pp. 22–34.
46. Chiang, P.J.; Khanna, N.; Mikkilineni, A.; Segovia, M.; Suh, S.; Allebach, J.; Chiu, G.; Delp, E. Printer and Scanner Forensics. *IEEE Signal Process. Mag.* **2009**, *26*, 72–83. [CrossRef]
47. Devi, M.U.; Rao, C.R.; Agarwal, A. A Survey of Image Processing Techniques for Identification of Printing Technology in Document Forensic Perspective. *Int. J. Comput. Appl.* **2010**, *1*, 9–15.
48. Oliver, J.; Chen, J. Use of signature analysis to discriminate digital printing technologies. In *Proceedings of the NIP & Digital Fabrication Conference*; Society for Imaging Science and Technology: Springfield, VA, USA, 2002; pp. 218–222.

49. Lampert, C.H.; Mei, L.; Breuel, T.M. Printing Technique Classification for Document Counterfeit Detection. In Proceedings of the International Conference on Computational Intelligence and Security, Guangzhou, China, 3–6 November 2006; Volume 1, pp. 639–644.
50. Schulze, C.; Schreyer, M.; Stahl, A.; Breuel, T. Using DCT Features for Printing Technique and Copy Detection. In *Advances in Digital Forensics V*; Peterson, G.; Shenoi, S., Eds.; Springer: Berlin/Heidelberg, Germany, 2009; pp. 95–106.
51. Schreyer, M.; Schulze, C.; Stahl, A.; Effelsberg, W. Intelligent Printing Technique Recognition and Photocopy Detection for Forensic Document Examination. In *Informatiktage: Fachwissenschaftlicher Informatik-Kongress*; Informatiktage: Bonn, Germany, 2009; pp. 39–42.
52. Roy, A.; Halder, B.; Garain, U. Authentication of Currency Notes through Printing Technique Verification. In Proceedings of the Indian Conference on Computer Vision, Graphics and Image Processing (ICVGIP), Chennai, India, 12–15 December 2010; Association for Computing Machinery: New York, NY, USA, 2010; pp. 383–390.
53. Chiang, P.; Allebach, J.P.; Chiu, G.T. Extrinsic Signature Embedding and Detection in Electrophotographic Halftoned Images Through Exposure Modulation. *IEEE Trans. Inf. Forensics Secur.* **2011**, *6*, 946–959. [CrossRef]
54. Beusekom, J.V.; Shafait, F.; Breuel, T. Automatic authentication of color laser print-outs using machine identification codes. *Pattern Anal. Appl.* **2012**, *16*, 663–678. [CrossRef]
55. Nowroozi, E.; Dehghantanha, A.; Parizi, R.M.; Choo, K.K.R. A survey of machine learning techniques in adversarial image forensics. *Comput. Secur.* **2021**, *100*, 102092. [CrossRef]
56. Bondi, L.; Baroffio, L.; Güera, D.; Bestagini, P.; Delp, E.J.; Tubaro, S. First Steps Toward Camera Model Identification With Convolutional Neural Networks. *IEEE Signal Process. Lett.* **2017**, *24*, 259–263. [CrossRef]
57. Ferreira, A.; Chen, H.; Li, B.; Huang, J. An Inception-Based Data-Driven Ensemble Approach to Camera Model Identification. In Proceedings of the IEEE International Workshop on Information Forensics and Security (WIFS), Hong Kong, China, 11–13 December 2018; pp. 1–7.
58. Agarwal, S.; Fan, W.; Farid, H. A Diverse Large-Scale Dataset for Evaluating Rebroadcast Attacks. In Proceedings of the International Conference on Acoustics, Speech and Signal Processing (ICASSP), Calgary, AB, Canada, 15–20 April 2018; pp. 1997–2001.
59. Li, H.; Li, B.; Tan, S.; Huang, J. Identification of deep network generated images using disparities in color components. *Signal Process.* **2020**, *174*, 107616. [CrossRef]
60. Hsu, C.; Lee, C.; Zhuang, Y. Learning to Detect Fake Face Images in the Wild. In Proceedings of the International Symposium on Computer, Consumer and Control (IS3C), Taichung, Taiwan, 6–8 December 2018; pp. 388–391.
61. Bonettini, N.; Cannas, E.D.; Mandelli, S.; Bondi, L.; Bestagini, P.; Tubaro, S. Video Face Manipulation Detection Through Ensemble of CNNs. *arXiv* **2020**, arXiv:2004.07676.
62. Wang, Z.; Bovik, A.C.; Sheikh, H.R.; Simoncelli, E.P. Image quality assessment: From error visibility to structural similarity. *IEEE Trans. Image Process.* **2004**, *13*, 600–612. [CrossRef] [PubMed]
63. Dietterich, T.G. Approximate Statistical Test For Comparing Supervised Classification Learning Algorithms. *Neural Comput.* **1998**, *10*, 1895–1923. [CrossRef] [PubMed]
64. Friedman, M. The Use of Ranks to Avoid the Assumption of Normality Implicit in the Analysis of Variance. *J. Am. Stat. Assoc.* **1937**, *32*, 675–701. [CrossRef]
65. Gosset, W.S. The Probable Error of a Mean. *Biometrika* **1908**, *6*, 1–25.
66. Jain, A.K.; Vailaya, A. Image retrieval using color and shape. *Pattern Recognit.* **1996**, *29*, 1233–1244. [CrossRef]
67. Dalal, N.; Triggs, B. Histograms of oriented gradients for human detection. In Proceedings of the IEEE Computer Society Conference on Computer Vision and Pattern Recognition (CVPR), San Diego, CA, USA, 20–26 June 2005; Volume 1, pp. 886–893.
68. Ojala, T.; Pietikäinen, M.; Harwood, D. A comparative study of texture measures with classification based on featured distributions. *Pattern Recognit.* **1996**, *29*, 51–59. [CrossRef]
69. Simonyan, K.; Zisserman, A. Very Deep Convolutional Networks for Large-Scale Image Recognition. In Proceedings of the International Conference on Learning Representations, San Diego, CA, USA, 7–9 May 2015.
70. He, K.; Zhang, X.; Ren, S.; Sun, J. Deep Residual Learning for Image Recognition. In Proceedings of the IEEE Conference on Computer Vision and Pattern Recognition (CVPR), Las Vegas, NV, USA, 27–30 June 2016; pp. 770–778.
71. Huang, G.; Liu, Z.; Van Der Maaten, L.; Weinberger, K.Q. Densely Connected Convolutional Networks. In Proceedings of the IEEE Conference on Computer Vision and Pattern Recognition (CVPR), Honolulu, HI, USA, 21–26 July 2017; pp. 2261–2269.
72. Szegedy, C.; Vanhoucke, V.; Ioffe, S.; Shlens, J.; Wojna, Z. Rethinking the Inception Architecture for Computer Vision. In Proceedings of the IEEE Conference on Computer Vision and Pattern Recognition (CVPR), Las Vegas, NV, USA, 27–30 June 2016; pp. 2818–2826.
73. Chollet, F. Xception: Deep Learning with Depthwise Separable Convolutions. In Proceedings of the IEEE Conference on Computer Vision and Pattern Recognition (CVPR), Honolulu, HI, USA, 21–26 July 2017; pp. 1800–1807.

74. Ferreira, A. Printer Forensics Source Code. 2014. Available online: https://github.com/anselmoferreira/printer_forensics_source_code (accessed on 5 October 2020).
75. Wardi, Y. A stochastic steepest-descent algorithm. *J. Optim. Theory Appl.* **1988**, *59*, 307–323. [CrossRef]

Journal of Imaging

Article

Identification of Social-Media Platform of Videos through the Use of Shared Features

Luca Maiano [1,2,*], Irene Amerini [1], Lorenzo Ricciardi Celsi [2] and Aris Anagnostopoulos [1]

[1] Department of Computer, Control and Management Engineering, Sapienza University of Rome, via Ariosto, 25, 00185 Rome, Italy; amerini@diag.uniroma1.it (I.A.); aris@diag.uniroma1.it (A.A.)
[2] Elis Innovation Hub, via Sandro Sandri 81, 00159 Rome, Italy; l.ricciardicelsi@ELIS.ORG
* Correspondence: maiano@diag.uniroma1.it

Abstract: Videos have become a powerful tool for spreading illegal content such as military propaganda, revenge porn, or bullying through social networks. To counter these illegal activities, it has become essential to try new methods to verify the origin of videos from these platforms. However, collecting datasets large enough to train neural networks for this task has become difficult because of the privacy regulations that have been enacted in recent years. To mitigate this limitation, in this work we propose two different solutions based on transfer learning and multitask learning to determine whether a video has been uploaded from or downloaded to a specific social platform through the use of shared features with images trained on the same task. By transferring features from the shallowest to the deepest levels of the network from the image task to videos, we measure the amount of information shared between these two tasks. Then, we introduce a model based on multitask learning, which learns from both tasks simultaneously. The promising experimental results show, in particular, the effectiveness of the multitask approach. According to our knowledge, this is the first work that addresses the problem of social media platform identification of videos through the use of shared features.

Keywords: media forensics; social media platform identification; video forensics

1. Introduction

Researchers have been studying multimedia forensics for more than two decades in different experimental settings; however, the practical application of these techniques has been limited because of the high variability of real cases, which is difficult to reproduce in experiments. Today, the assessment of the authenticity and the source of multimedia content has become an essential element for building trust in images and videos shared across online platforms. When videos of military propaganda, revenge porn, cyberbullying, or other illegal content are shared on social media, they can easily go viral. While it is important to immediately identify and delete this content from social platforms, another problem to be addressed is to identify the authors of the video to proceed with any legal action. In many other cases, law enforcement may locate a device containing illegal content and to identify its source, it may be necessary to understand whether the video was recorded with the hijacked device or whether it was downloaded via messaging apps or social networks. In fact, in all these cases videos and images could be used as evidence in court and knowing how to identify videos shared on social platforms could help identify criminal networks operating online. However, for this to be possible, it is necessary to be able to prove the origin of such content. In particular, two problems must be solved: (1) Knowing how to reconstruct the source of acquisition (camera model or device) and (2) understanding whether some media content found on an offending device comes from social media. Being able to respond to the latter would allow the sharing network to be reconstructed and possible online criminal groups to be identified. Figure 1 summarizes these two problems.

Figure 1. An application example of the proposed solution. An attacker records a video with illegal content and shares it on social networks or messaging apps. Subsequently, the police seize a device with this video and want to trace the source.

Deep learning has pushed the design of new methods that can learn forensic fingerprints automatically from data [1–3], helping us to take a new step towards applying these techniques to real problems. Despite the promising results of artificial neural networks, some limitations still remain. Single-task learning has been very successful in computer vision applications, with many models performing as well or even exceeding human performance for a large number of tasks; however, they are extremely data dependent and poorly adaptable to new contexts. Recently, collecting data from social networks has become increasingly difficult because of data protection regulations and the most stringent policies introduced by the platforms (https://www.facebook.com/apps/site_scraping_tos_terms.php, https://twitter.com/en/tos—accessed on 4 August 2021). Indeed, it is mandatory to obtain end user consent or the platform's written permission before acquiring data via the API or web scraping of the most common social networks like Facebook, Instagram or Twitter. Moreover, new data protection regulations, such as GDPR (https://europa.eu/youreurope/citizens/consumers/internet-telecoms/data-protection-online-privacy/index_en.htm—accessed on 4 August 2021), CCPA (https://oag.ca.gov/privacy/ccpa—accessed on 4 August 2021), or the Australian privacy act are contributing to the introduction of new limitations in some countries around the world. All these limitations make difficult to collect enough data to train a deep-learning model. Moreover, the human ability to learn from experience and reuse what has been learned in new contexts is still difficult to reproduce in machine learning as well as in multimedia forensics. All these reasons, along with the unavailability of large training datasets containing both video and image content, have led researchers to treat the problems of social-media–platform identification of images [4–7] and videos [8] separately. Recently, Iuliani et al. [9] showed that it is possible to identify the source of a digital video by exploiting a reference sensor pattern noise generated by still images taken by the same device, suggesting that images and videos share some forensic traces. Based on this intuition, we build a model that classifies videos from different social-media platforms or messaging apps by taking advantage of the shared features between images and videos. More specifically, to overcome the aforementioned limitations, we try to answer the following question: *Is it possible to decide whether a video has been downloaded from a specific social-media platform? If so, do images and videos have any common forensic trace that can be used to solve video social-media platform identification using both media?* To answer these questions, we propose two methods: A method based on transfer learning and a one based on multitask learning. Both methods offer the possibility of reusing the features learned from one media into another using fewer training data, a feature that is very useful in this domain given the difficulty of finding datasets large enough to train neural networks.

In *transfer learning*, we first train the base model on the image task, and then reuse the learned features, or *transfer* them, to videos. This process tends to work if the features are general, that is, suitable to both tasks [10]. The forensics community has adopted widely transfer learning because, as new manipulation methods are continually introduced, there is a need of detection techniques that are able to detect fakes with little to no training data [11,12]. In *multitask learning*, a model shares weights across multiple tasks and makes multiple inferences in a forward pass. This method has proved to be more scalable and robust compared to single-task models, allowing for successful applications in several scenarios outside the forensic community [13]. Some applications of multitask learning have been even applied to multimedia forensics problems as well, for example, to solve camera model and manipulation detection tasks [14], as well as brand, model, and device-level identification, using original and manipulated images [15].

We apply both learning approaches in this work to accelerate the training of a deep-learning method for deciding whether a video has been downloaded from a social media platform. Because the collection of large datasets for this task is usually very difficult, if not impossible, in practical applications because of privacy reasons, it is worth investigating the effectiveness and the limits of transfer learning and multitasking learning on the task of social media platform identification of videos.

In this paper, we show how well low-level features generalize between images and videos, demonstrating that common platform-dependent features can be learned when the training data are not large enough to train a deep learning model from scratch to estimate the traces left by social media platforms during the upload phase on videos. The sharing process can combine multiple operations that leave different traces in the video signal. These alterations can be exposed in various ways. For example, as first observed in [16], compression and resizing are usually applied by Facebook to reduce the size of uploaded images and this may happen differently on different platforms based on the resolution and size of the input data before loading. As is widely known in multimedia forensics, such operations can be detected and characterized by analyzing the video signal where distinctive patterns can be exhibited. Indeed, these operations typically distort the original video signal with some artifacts that can be detected. When the signal is used as a source of information for the provenance analysis, different choices can be made to preprocess the signal and extract an effective feature representation. After the feature representation is extracted, different kinds of machine-learning or deep-learning classifiers can then be trained to perform platform identification (see Section 3.1). To detect videos shared through social media platforms, we propose two methods that can learn to detect the traces left by different social-media platforms without any preprocessing operation on the input frames. To our knowledge, this is the first work that analyzes the similarity of the traces left by social media platforms on images and videos used in combination. Next, we show that the features learned in the task of social-media identification of images can be successfully applied on social-media identification of videos, but not vice versa, thus suggesting a *task asymmetry*, which could possibly be explained by looking at social-media identification of videos as a special case of the image task. Indeed, as discussed in Section 3.1, shared videos may have both static and temporal artifacts, whereas shared images have static features only. These findings are particularly valuable in investigative scenarios where law-enforcement agencies have to trace the origin of multimedia content without being able to refer to other sources such as metadata. This scenario is depicted in Figure 1.

The rest of this paper is organized as follows: First, in Section 2 we present some related work. In Section 3 we describe our methods and provide a detailed explanation of methods based on transfer learning and multitask learning. In Section 4 we show the experimental results on the VISION dataset [17]. Finally, in Section 6 we draw the conclusions of our work.

2. Related Work

When shared on social media platforms and messaging apps, multimedia content is typically subjected to a series of processing and recompression operations to speed up the loading and optimize the display of images and videos on the platform. Videos are typically compressed as sequence of *groups of pictures* (GOP), each of which is made by an alternation of three different kinds of frames: *I-frames*, which are not derived from any other frame and are independently encoded using a process similar to JPEG compression, and *P-frames* and *B-frames*, which are predictively encoded using motion estimation and compensation. While the algorithms used by social platforms are not known, all of these operations leave traces that can be detected [4,6,7,18,19] and, since they typically differ between different platforms [19–21], they can be used to distinguish between distinct social networks. According to the survey by Pasquini et al. [21], we can identify two main possible steps in the digital life of a media object shared online, namely the acquisition and the upload. Initially, a real scene is captured through an acquisition device, then, a number of post-processing operations such as resizing, filtering, compressions, cropping, semantic manipulations may be applied. Finally, through the upload phase, the object is shared through social media.

Following these two steps, in the remainder of this section, we describe the state-of-the-art methods that can be used to analyze the acquisition source or integrity of a video (Section 2.1) and to reconstruct information on the sharing history of a video (see Section 2.2).

2.1. Forensic Analysis

The main problems in traditional media forensics are the identification of the source of images and videos and the verification of their integrity.

Source-camera identification is the problem of tracing back the origin of a video by identifying the device or model that captured a particular media file. This problem has been very often treated in a *closed-set* setting, meaning that all the devices that we want to be associated with a source video are known in advance. These methods typically rely on Photo Response Non-Uniformity (PRNU) [22]. Houten and Geradts [23] propose video camera source identification of YouTube videos showing the limitations to reach a correct identification on the shared video because of the numerous variations that affect PRNU (e.g., compression, codec, video resolution, and changes in the aspect ratio). Similarly, another work [24] performs an analysis on stabilized and non-stabilized videos proposing to use the spatial domain averaged frames for fingerprint extraction. A different method for PRNU fingerprint estimation [25] takes into account the effects of video compression on the PRNU noise selecting blocks of frames having at least one non-null discrete cosine transform (DCT) coefficient. Other works use PRNU to link social media profiles containing images and videos captured by the same sensor [9,26]. Similar approaches have been introduced for camera model identification [27,28]. Recently, some works have begun to deal with the problem of identifying the source of a video with *limited knowledge* or even an *open-set* of devices. Cozzolino et al. [29] introduce a siamese method based on [2] to estimate camera-based fingerprints (called *Noiseprints*) for video with no need of prior knowledge on the specific manipulation or any form of fine-tuning. Another work [30] from the same research group combines the PRNU and Noiseprint to boost the performance of PRNU-based analyses based on only a few images. In some works [8,31,32] video file containers have been considered for the source identification of videos without a prior training phase. To do this, López et al. [32] introduces a hierarchical clustering method whereas [8] proposes a likelihood-ratio framework. Mayer et al. [33] propose a similarity network based on [1] to extract features from video patches, and to fuse multiple comparisons to produce a video-level verification decision.

Even though most of the techniques described so far are based on deep learning, which has proved successful for camera model identification problems [34], there are other works using different techniques. Marra et al. [35] study a class of blind features based on the analysis of the image residuals of all color bands, where no hypothesis is made on the origin of camera-specific marks, and the identification task is regarded simply as a texture classification problem. Chen and Stamm [36] introduce a model of a camera's de-mosaicing algorithm by grouping together a set of submodels. Each submodel is a nonparametric model designed to capture partial information of the de-mosaicing algorithm. the diversity among these submodels, leads to the composition of a comprehensive representation of a camera's de-mosaicing algorithm. Finally, an ensemble classifier is trained on the information gathered by each sub model to identify the model of an image's source camera.

The application of forgery detection methods on shared videos has been very limited to date. Iuliani et al. [8] show that the dissimilarity between a query video and a reference file container can be estimated to detect video forgery. Mayer and Stamm [1,37] propose a graph-based representation of an image, named Forensic Similarity Graph, to detect manipulated digital images. A forgery can be detected as a separate cluster of patches with respect to the pristine-patches cluster in the graph. Even if the same idea has been applied [33] for video source identification, the robustness of this method has not been tested on forged videos as well.

The next section presents the methods that can be used for the second phase of the pipeline, which is the association of the platform of origin of a video.

2.2. Platform Provenance Analysis

Social-media–platform identification has been broadly explored for images. Amerini et al. [7] propose a CNN architecture that analyzes the histograms of image DCT coefficients to reconstruct the origin of images shared across Facebook, Flickr, Google+, Instagram, Telegram and Twitter. Another work [4] introduced a CNN-based model that was used to fuse the information extracted from the histograms of image DCT coefficients with a noise residual extracted from the image content through high-pass filtering. Moreover, by combining DCT features with metadata, Phan et al. [6] showed that is possible to track multiple sharing on social networks by extracting the traces left by each social network within the image file. Finally, PRNU)can be applied as suggested by Caldelli et al. [18] to train a CNN to detect the social network of origin of an image.

The proposal of social-media–platform identification techniques has been instead quite limited for videos. Amerini et al. [38] introduce a preliminary work in which they evaluate different methods to build a fingerprint to detect video shared in social networks and also introduce a method that generates a composite fingerprint by resorting to the use of PRNU noise. Two recent works [8,31] introduced simple yet effective container-based methods to identify video manipulation fingerprints and reconstruct the operating system of the source device, proving the robustness of the method on manipulation introduced by social media platforms. Amerini et al. [39] propose a two-stream neural network that analyze I-frames and P-frames in parallel. All frames are preprocessed converting them from RGB to YUV, and the Y-channel of each frame is used as input for the network. For P-frames, the authors subtract the Gaussian filtered version of the frame from the Y-channel to reduce the noise in these type of frames.

Nevertheless, because these preprocessing operations can change over time, it may be necessary to periodically learn new forensic traces for smaller training datasets. For this reason, in the next section, we propose two learning techniques to train models on little data, possibly taking advantage of what is learned on similar tasks to improve performance and speed up the learning.

3. Proposed Method

In this section, we propose a theoretical analysis of what could be the traces that can be left on videos by social media and we propose a framework for platform identification.

3.1. The Rationale

As discussed earlier, when we upload a video to a social-media platform, it usually goes through a series of operations, which most commonly may include recompression to reduce the bandwidth requirement for using the video on the platform, a resize, and in some cases the removal of some frames of the video to make it fit the maximum duration of the videos imposed by some platforms. While, as mentioned, these operations may vary depending on the platform, in this section we want to formalize as much as possible how these operations can leave information in the video. As shown in [40,41], these operations can leave both static and temporal artifacts in the video signal when a video sequence is subjected to double MPEG compression. Statically, the I-frames of an MPEG sequence are subjected to double JPEG compression. Temporally, frames that move from one GOP to another, as a result of frame deletion, give rise to a relatively larger motion estimation errors. Figure 2 shows an example of a short eleven-frame MPEG sequence. In this example, during the upload phase, the video is subjected to the removal of three frames and subsequent recompression. The second row shows the reordered frames, and the third line shows the re-encoded frames after recompressing the video as an MPEG video.

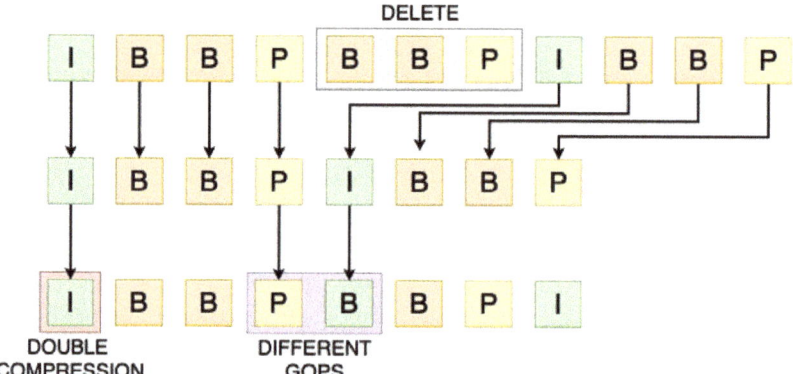

Figure 2. The top line shows an original MPEG encoded sequence. The next lines show the effect of deleting the three frames in the shaded area. The second line shows the reordered frames and the third line the recoded frames. The I-frame before erasing is subjected to double compression. Some of the frames following the deletion move from one GOP sequence to another. This double MPEG compression gives rise to specific statistical and temporal models that can be used to identify the platform of origin.

Statically, when an I-frame gets recompressed with different bit rates (i.e., quantization amounts), the DCT coefficients are subject to two quantization levels, leaving behind a specific statistical signature in the distribution of DCT coefficients [40,42]. Quantization is a pointwise operation, which can be calculated as:

$$Q_k(s_1) = \left\lfloor \frac{k}{s_1} \right\rfloor,$$

where s_1 indicates the quantization step and k denotes a value in the range of the input frame. Similarly, double quantization is also a pointwise operation given by:

$$Q_{s_1 s_2}(k) = \left\lfloor \left\lfloor \frac{k}{s_1} \right\rfloor \frac{s_1}{s_2} \right\rfloor,$$

where s_1 and s_2 are the quantization steps. From the equation above, double quantization can be described as a sequence of three operations: A quantization with step s_1, a de-quantization with step s_1, and a quantization with step s_2. As Wang and Farid show [41], the re-quantization introduces periodicity of the artifacts into the histograms of quantized frames. As these artifacts will differ depending on the quantization step used by every platform, they can be used to distinguish differences between social media platforms.

Temporarily, deleting a few frames of the video to fit the maximum length set by some platforms can in turn leave information. For example, consider deleting three frames in Figure 2. Within the first GOP of this sequence, the I-frame and the first P-frame come from the first GOP of the original sequence. The third B-frame, however, is the I-frame of the second GOP of the original sequence, and the second I-frame is the first P-frame of the second GOP of the original video. When this new sequence gets re-encoded, we will observe a larger motion error between the first and second P-frames, as they originated from different GOPs. Furthermore, this increase in motion error will be periodic, occurring in each of the GOPs after the frame gets deleted. Formally, consider a six-frame sequence that is encoded as $I_1, P_2, P_3, P_4, P_5, I_6$. Because of JPEG compression and motion error, each frame can be modeled by an additive noise, that is:

$$I_i = F_i + N_i \qquad P_j = F_j + N_j$$

with $i \neq j$, where each N_i, N_j is the additional noise and F_i, F_j are the original frames. Notice that the noise for I_1 through P_5 will be correlated to each other because they belong to the same GOP, but not to that of I_6. If we denote the motion compensation as $M(\cdot)$, we can derive the motion error for a frame $i, (i > 1)$ as:

$$\begin{aligned} e_i &= P_i - M(I_{i-1}) \\ &= F_i + N_i - M(F_{i-1} + N_{i-1}) \\ &= (F_i - M(F_{i-1})) + (N_i - M(N_{i-1})). \end{aligned}$$

Suppose now that we delete frame P_4, bringing frames P_5 and I_6 to the fourth and fifth positions, respectively. I_6 will now be encoded as the new P_5'. The motion error for this new frame will be:

$$e_5' = (F_6 - M(F_5)) + (N_6 - M(N_5)).$$

Notice that for frames belonging to the same GOP, the components of the additive noise term $N_i - M(N_{i-1})$ are correlated, thus, we can expect some noise cancellation. After the deletion of frame P_4, however, the two components of the additive noise term $(N_6 - M(N_5))$ are not correlated, leading to a relatively larger motion error compared to the others. This pattern can be learned by a deep neural network with sufficient training data samples.

3.2. Social Media Platform Identification Framework

In this section, we propose two learning methods to detect and classify different static and temporal recompression fingerprints left by social media platforms on shared videos exploiting a unified set of features. Through these learning methods, the goal is to evaluate the transferability of features between the image and video tasks and to show the hierarchical relation of these two tasks. In all the following sections, we construct our methods starting from the MISL network introduced by Bayar and Stamm [43] to train it with two different learning approaches. This network has proven successful in several multimedia forensics applications [1,14], so we decided to keep its architecture and optimize it for our setting. Because the MISL network was originally designed to work on greyscale images, we modified the initial constrained layer to work on RGB inputs, therefore, we doubled the number of kernels in the first convolutional layer from 3 to 6, to increase the expressive power of the network and match the more complex input the model is fed with. The network has 5 convolutional layers (called *constrained*, *conv1*, *conv2*, *conv3*, *conv4*) and three fully connected layers (called *fc1*, *fc2*, *fc3*). The *fc3* layer has a number of neurons corresponding to the number of output classes. The network is trained on RGB image patches for the image social media identification platform task, and on RGB I-frame and P-frame patches extracted from videos for the video source platform identification task. Differently from state-of-the-art methods reported in Section 2, we decided to use the constrained convolutional layer to automatically learn the best input transformation instead of feeding the network with DCT histograms or reference sensor pattern noise. Therefore, we train the network with RGB input patches extracted from video frames.

In the following sections, we use $\mathcal{I}$ and $\mathcal{V}$ to refer to the image task and video task respectively. Moreover, we use $X_{\mathcal{I}}$ and $X_{\mathcal{V}}$ to refer to the input image or video patches of the network and $Y_{\mathcal{I}}$ and $Y_{\mathcal{V}}$ to refer to the corresponding output classes.

3.2.1. Method Based on Transfer Learning

In this section we propose transfer learning to transfer the static features learned by a base model on images to the video domain, so as to increase the performance of the same model on this new target task. Because we want the model to learn a certain fingerprint in both image and video sharing tasks, we adopt this technique to measure how features learned on one of the two tasks generalize to the other and study the hierarchical structure of features extracted at different layers of the network.

In this setting, we initially train the model with image RGB inputs $X_\mathcal{I}$ to predict the platform of provenance $Y_\mathcal{I}$ of these images. The network is initialized with a Xavier initializer [44] and trained on 256 × 256 input patches to predict the output classes with a cross-entropy loss function. As shown in Figure 3, we train this network on native single-compressed images (i.e., images that have not been shared on any platform) and images shared across social networks. Next, we perform feature transfer by freezing a number of layers from the image task and we retrain the remaining network layers on RGB patches $X_\mathcal{V}$ extracted from video frames. We iterate this process starting from the lower *constrained* layer up to the higher *fc2* layer of the network. At each iteration, we freeze all the middle layers in between the constrained layer and the upper layer that we want to transfer. Figure 3 shows an example of this iterative feature-transfer approach. We initially train the model on the image task in a single-task learning fashion to predict the corresponding platforms of provenance. Then, we freeze all the convolutional layers from the *constrained* layer up to the *conv3* layer and retrain the remaining fully connected layers on the video task to predict the actual new social media platforms. In Section 4.3, we show that, according to the generic transfer learning behavior, low-level features generalize well across the two tasks, whereas deeper levels tend to learn more task-related representations. This information will be useful to understand how much the two tasks share with each other.

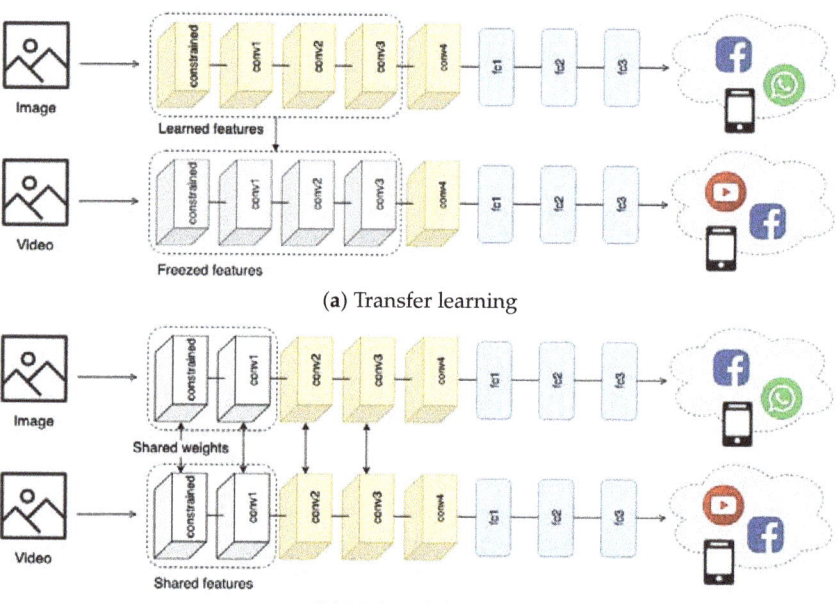

Figure 3. Learning approaches proposed in this paper: (**a**) Method based on transfer learning; (**b**) Method based on multitask learning. In the transfer-learning approach we initially train the model on the image task. Then we reuse the feature representations learned on images to train the model on the video source platform identification task. In multitask learning we share the weights of the *constrained* and *conv1* layers of two siamese networks while learning them on images and videos in parallel.

3.2.2. Method Based on Multitask Learning

In multitask learning, we constrain some layers of two models to learn a unique set of parameters for different tasks. In this way, we encourage the shared layers of the network to learn a generalized representation that should help to produce more robust and flexible classifiers with respect to both static and temporal features. As we mentioned previously, the collection large datasets of shared multimedia contents is very hard because of several limitations (mostly related to privacy policies and API restrictions); this approach instead helps to train the network on smaller training datasets. Therefore, in this setting, we force the two networks to share a number of layers to learn more adaptable feature representations.

Figure 3 shows the multitask learning-based network used in this paper. In the figure, the two proposed networks share the weights from the *constrained* layer up to the *conv1* layer to learn a common feature extractor given input images $X_\mathcal{I}$ and videos $X_\mathcal{V}$. Next, the two networks independently learn to predict the correct output classes $Y_\mathcal{I}$ and $Y_\mathcal{V}$. Clearly, as suggested by the hierarchical dependencies of features maps extracted by different layers of the network highlighted by transfer learning, for these tasks it is not helpful to share all the layers from the *constrained* layer up to the *fc2* layer (see Section 4.4). Thus, to choose which layers to share, we use what we have learned with transfer learning by selecting the layers that extract the more general representations useful for both images and videos, that is, the constrained layer and *conv1* layer.

Because detecting forensics traces left by social media on videos is harder than learning such fingerprints on images [38], we train the multitask learner by taking this information into consideration and slow down the learning process on images. More precisely, we train the model measuring the cross entropy loss on each task and weighing the overall loss according to the following equation:

$$L = \frac{1}{N}(w_\mathcal{I} L_\mathcal{I} + w_\mathcal{V} L_\mathcal{V}) \quad (1)$$

where $L_\mathcal{I}$ and $L_\mathcal{V}$ are the cross-entropy losses on images and videos respectively, N is the number of tasks (2 in our setting), and $w_\mathcal{I}$ and $w_\mathcal{V}$ are the weights assigned to each task. The weights can be experimentally adjusted on each task depending on the availability of training data and task complexity. In all our experiments, we fix $w_\mathcal{I} = 0.25$ and $w_\mathcal{V} = 1$ such as to reduce the loss on the image task and accelerate the improvements on videos. As for the method based on transfer learning, at each training iteration the weights and biases of the model are updated according to gradient descent $w^{(\ell)} = w^{(\ell)} - \alpha \frac{\partial L_t}{\partial w^{(\ell)}}$, where L_t indicates the loss measured on task $t \in \{\mathcal{I}, \mathcal{V}\}$ and $w^{(\ell)}$ represents the weights matrix at layer ℓ.

4. Experimental Evaluation

In this section, we experimentally evaluate the effectiveness of transfer learning and multitask learning with respect to a baseline single-task learning model fully trained on the target task. Specifically, (1) we measure the performance of two baseline single-task models trained on images and videos; (2) we evaluate the importance of hierarchical features with respect to images and videos, measuring the amount of information that the two tasks share at each level of depth through transfer learning; (3) we compare the results of the multitask-learning approach with those relative to transfer learning and single-task learning.

4.1. Dataset and Experimental Setting

We run our experiments on the VISION dataset [17]. The dataset includes 34,427 images and 1914 videos, both in the native format (original) and in their social media version (i.e., Facebook and WhatsApp for images, YouTube and WhatsApp for videos), captured by 35 portable devices of 11 major brands in many different settings. In our experiment, we split the dataset for training and validation with a proportion of 80% and 10%, respectively.

Moreover, we use the remaining 10% of the dataset for testing purposes. All the results reported in this section refer to this set. This ensures the robustness of the model with respect to completely unseen data. Finally, we use the *ffprobe* (https://ffmpeg.org/ffprobe.html—accessed on 4 August 2021) analyzer to extract the I-frames and P-frames from all videos in the dataset and crop each frame and image into non-overlapping patches of size $H \times W$, where $H = W = 256$.

All experiments were carried on a Google Cloud Platform n1-standard-8 instance with 8 vCPUs, 30 GB of memory, and an NVIDIA Tesla K80 GPU. The models have been implemented using Pytorch (https://pytorch.org/—accessed on 4 August 2021) v.1.6. For the first two sets of experiments, we trained all the networks with the learning rate set to 1×10^{-4}, a learning rate decay of 0.95 fixed at every epoch, weight decay set to 5×10^{-3}, and AdamW optimizer. In our experiments, we trained the networks for 100 epochs with batches of size 64 and early stopping set to 10. Finally, to train the multitask model, we set a learning rate to 1×10^{-3}, a learning rate decay of 0.99, and weight decay set to 1×10^{-2}. The model was trained for 250 epochs with a batch size of 64. All models were initialized with a Xavier initializer [44].

4.2. Evaluation of Single-Task Learning

To measure the effect of transfer learning and multitask learning, we introduce a baseline model trained on each task. We trained the network on images and videos, measuring the model effectiveness on both tasks. In single task, we achieved an accuracy of 97.84% for RGB image patches and 86.85% for RGB video patches extracted from frames (see Figure 4). Interestingly, we did not observe substantial differences when training the model with both I-frame and P-frame video versus I-frame alone. However, we decided to keep both types of frames to help generalize the model by exposing it to as different cases as possible. Finally, to validate our choice to train the model on RGB patches without any preprocessing on the input, we compared the performance of our method with the Y-channel of the input after converting RGB to YUV, and we observed a decrease in accuracy of 1.41% for images and 4.2% for videos.

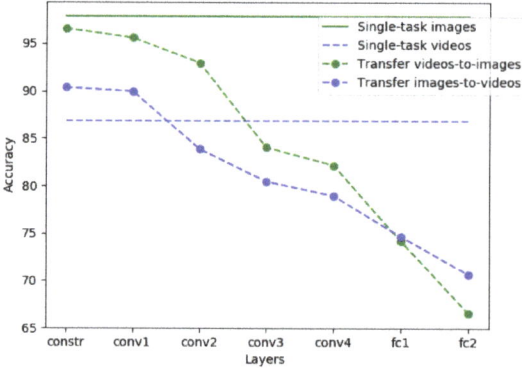

Figure 4. Comparison of baseline single-task learning, transfer-learning–based, and multitask-learning–based models accuracy on image (in green) and video (in blue) patches.

Tables 1 and 2 report the confusion matrices of the single-task detectors on both tasks. Even though we do not apply any preprocessing operation to the input patches, the model achieves state-of-the-art performance comparable to the much more complex FusionNET [4] for the image task. Indeed, the FusionNET has 99.97%, 98.65%, and 99.81% patch-level accuracy on Facebook, WhatsApp, and native images, respectively, with an average difference of +1.89% with respect respect to our single-task model. For videos, our method suffers a drop in accuracy compared to the image task, but it still achieves results around 86.85%. Finally, we tested the overall accuracy of the model at image level and video level applying *majority voting* (i.e., the class that is voted by the majority of input patches is selected as the predicted class of the entire image or video), reaching 98.52% and 85.48%, respectively.

Table 1. Confusion matrix of the baseline single-task model on patches extracted from images. FBH and FBL represent high-quality and low-quality patches from Facebook. WA and NAT represent WhatsApp and native image patches respectively.

	FB	WA	NAT
FB	**98.78%**	0.05%	1.17%
WA	0.23%	**98.37%**	1.40%
NAT	1.56%	1.31%	**97.13%**

Table 2. Confusion matrix of the baseline single-task model on patches extracted from video frames. YT, WA and NAT represent YouTube, WhatsApp and native video patches respectively.

	YT	WA	NAT
YT	**85.28%**	8.36%	6.45%
WA	11.56%	**72.35%**	16.09%
NAT	2.85%	11.15%	**86.00%**

4.3. Evaluation of Transfer Learning

We performed a set of experiments to measure the robustness of methods based on transfer learning to images and videos. To perform the experiments, we froze some layers of the network with the learned parameters in one task and we retrained the remaining layers in the other task. To track the hierarchical dependencies of each task and measure the similarity of the two, we repeated this process for each level in the network from the *constrained* layer up to the *fc2* layer. As shown in Figure 4, the two tasks share low-level features, whereas deeper representations are mostly related to the target task with the accuracy varying from 66.56% to 96.60% for images and from 70.69% to 90.39% for videos at the patch level. On images (in green), the accuracy deteriorates as more layers are shared from the pretrained *constrained* layer up to the *fc2* layer. When knowledge is transferred from the image domain to the video domain (in blue), the network achieves 90.39% accuracy, gaining 3.54% accuracy with respect to the single-task model. This result confirms the intuition that lower-level features are shared between the two tasks, and that the *hierarchical* dependence between the two tasks can be used to train a deep-learning model on a small set of images or videos originating from social networks. In fact, the features extracted from the deeper levels turn out to be specific to the task being solved and therefore less generalizable, whereas the features extracted from the first levels of the network are more generic and, therefore, can be shared between the two tasks. The accuracy increases when measuring the performance at the image and at the video level. Specifically, the accuracy on images varies from 80.15% to 97.87%, with maximum accuracy up to 98.37% obtained by transferring video features up to the *conv2* layer. Finally, when transferring from images to video, we can observe an increase in accuracy from 85.48% to 92.61% on the video classifier, but the same does not happen for the transfer from video to images. This result can probably be explained by considering the videos as a more specific case and then thinking of this task as a subset of the corresponding task on images, thus suggesting an *asymmetry* between the two tasks.

4.4. Evaluation of Multitask Learning

With this last experiment, we measured the performance of the proposed multitask learner. Specifically, we chose to train two networks on both tasks, by forcing them to share weights between the first two convolutional layers, namely the *constrained* and *conv1* layers. Because of the different complexity of the two tasks highlighted by transfer learning, it is not useful to share all the layers between the two networks and it becomes necessary to balance the learning speed on images with compared to the videos. Therefore, we initially run several experiments with variable weighted loss according to Equation (1). To speed up the training, in this exploratory phase we chose to train the networks on images and I-frames only for the videos. We report the results of this experiment in Figure 5. We have varied the images weight $w_\mathcal{I}$ from 0.5 down to 0.1. Then, we chose $w_\mathcal{I} = 0.25$ so as to maximize the accuracy of the multitask learner on the video task and we retrained the multitask-learning-based model sharing the *constrained* and *conv1* layers between the two tasks. In this configuration, the multitask-learning-based model achieved 85.91% accuracy on images and 81.70% accuracy on videos. Finally, we tested the overall accuracy of the model at the image and the video level, reaching 92.08% and 91.55% accuracy on the images and the videos respectively. In this setting the model reaches an accuracy comparable to the single-task learner for the video task.

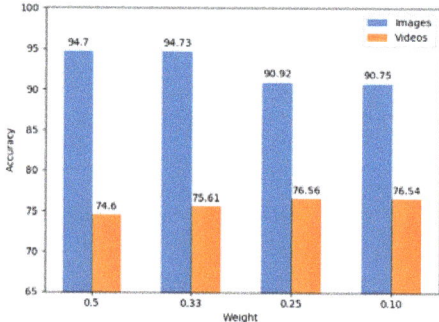

Figure 5. Test accuracy of the multitask learner on images and video I-frames obtained by fixing $w_\mathcal{V} = 1$ and varying the images weight $w_\mathcal{I}$ according to Equation (1).

To evaluate the performance of our method, we compared it with the state-of-the-art two-stream network introduced by Amerini et al. [39]. To compare the performance of the transfer-learning and multitask-learning–based methods with that of Amerini et al. [39], we retrained the model of that work in this new setting. Table 3 shows the results of this comparison. Splitting the dataset at video level instead of frame level, the method from Amerini et al. [39] records a drop in accuracy of 15.47% compared to the configuration used in the original paper.

Table 3. Comparison of video patch classification accuracy of our transfer-learning and multitask-learning methods with the one of Amerini et al. [39] on the VISION dataset.

Method	Accuracy
[39]	80.04%
TL (ours)	**90.39%**
MT (ours)	81.70%

5. Discussion

While the method based on transfer learning achieves a higher overall accuracy than the one based on multitask learning, we investigated the different performance of these two approaches. To analyze and compare the results of the two methods, we kept the best configuration of the multitask learning-based model and examined the results of the transfer learning-based model when transferring features from the *constrained* and *conv1* layers as for the multitask network. Table 4 shows the confusion matrices of these two methods on videos.

First, the transfer-learning model is able to achieve better results than the baseline model on YouTube and native videos (see Tables 2 and 4a). However, the WhatsApp class gets more easily confused with the other classes. Second, the multitask learner (Table 4b) tends to learn features representations that are more equally separated, with accuracy on all classes that oscillates between 79.25% and 83.68%, making the multitask learner less biased and more robust across all the classes. Moreover, thanks to this property, the multitask approach introduces an improvement in classification performance on WhatsApp compared to transfer learning (+10.74%, see Table 4) and the baseline model (+7.89%, see Tables 2 and 4b). Because WhatsApp is the only class shared by the image and video sets, it might suggest that training a model in a multitask setting on images and videos from the same social media platform could be even more beneficial. To evaluate this intuition we tested the model on WhatsApp with native images and videos, achieving encouraging results. The multitask-learning model achieves higher accuracy than transfer learning and single-task learning, again obtaining more stable accuracy across all classes. Most likely, images and videos shared through the same platform use very similar compression algorithms, favoring the learning of the alterations introduced when the content is recompressed when uploaded to the platform. Table 5b,c show the results of this experiment. However, because of the lack of publicly available datasets containing both images and videos we are not able to verify whether this is the case with more classes and leave this issue open for future research.

Table 4. Confusion matrices on video patches of the transfer-learning (a) and multitask learning (b) models sharing the *constrained* and *conv1* layers.

	(a) Transfer Learning		
	YT	WA	NAT
YT	**91.24%**	1.08%	7.66%
WA	13.33%	**69.50%**	17.15%
NAT	6.05%	1.49%	**92.45%**
	(b) Multitask Learning		
	YT	WA	NAT
YT	**83.68%**	6.19%	10.04%
WA	10.04%	**80.24%**	9.72%
NAT	10.58%	10.17%	**79.25%**

Table 5. Confusion matrices on video patches of the transfer-learning (a) and multitask learning (b) models sharing the *constrained* and *conv1* layers.

	(a) Single-Task Learning	
	WA	NAT
WA	**60.12%**	39.88%
NAT	28.07%	**71.93%**
	(b) Transfer Learning	
	WA	NAT
WA	**63.08%**	36.92%
NAT	23.69%	**76.30%**
	(c) Multitask Learning	
	WA	NAT
WA	**71.48%**	28.52%
NAT	26.16%	**73.84%**

6. Conclusions

In this paper, we propose two methods to identify the platform of origin of videos shared on different social networks through the use of joint features from images. Moreover, we show that images and videos share common forensic traces and a mixed approach may be beneficial in some cases where data are not enough to train a single-task model. By applying a transfer-learning–based method on both tasks, we experimentally showed that: (1) As expected, low-level features generalize well across images and videos, whereas deeper-feature mappings are more related to the target task, therefore suggesting that a common feature hierarchy exists between the two tasks; (2) image features can be successfully used to identify the social media platform in which videos have been uploaded, helping to improve performance over single task learning. Finally, we showed the promising effectiveness of a multitask-learning approach compared to single-task learning. In this way, the model can learn from images and videos simultaneously, learning more generic and robust features across all classes. These findings suggest that learning from multiple media could help to overcome the hurdle of training low-data models, by taking advantage of the similarity of different forensic tasks, usually treated separately.

Future work could be aimed at gathering a larger training dataset for social-media–platform identification of multimedia content and at studying the case of multiple sharing considering both images and videos. Moreover, a limitation of our method is that it appears susceptible to false positive classifications, leaving room for improvement.

Author Contributions: Conceptualization, L.M., I.A. and A.A.; methodology, L.M. and I.A.; software, L.M.; investigation, L.M., I.A., L.R.C. and A.A.; data curation, L.M.; writing and editing: L.M., I.A., L.R.C. and A.A.; supervision, A.A. All authors have read and agreed to the published version of the manuscript.

Funding: Partially supported by Supported by the ERC Advanced Grant 788893 AMDROMA and the EC H2020 RIA project "SoBigData++" (871042).

Data Availability Statement: No new data were created in this study.

Conflicts of Interest: The authors declare no conflicts of interest.

References

1. Mayer, O.; Stamm, M.C. Forensic Similarity for Digital Images. *IEEE Trans. Inf. Forensics Secur.* **2020**, *15*, 1331–1346. [CrossRef]
2. Cozzolino, D.; Verdoliva, L. Noiseprint: A CNN-Based Camera Model Fingerprint. *IEEE Trans. Inf. Forensics Secur.* **2020**, *15*, 144–159. [CrossRef]
3. Huh, M.; Liu, A.; Owens, A.; Efros, A.A. Fighting Fake News: Image Splice Detection via Learned Self-Consistency. *arXiv* **2018**, arXiv:cs.CV/1805.04096.
4. Amerini, I.; Li, C.; Caldelli, R. Social Network Identification Through Image Classification With CNN. *IEEE Access* **2019**, *7*, 35264–35273. [CrossRef]
5. Siddiqui, N.; Anjum, A.; Saleem, M.; Islam, S. Social Media Origin Based Image Tracing Using Deep CNN. In Proceedings of the 2019 Fifth International Conference on Image Information Processing (ICIIP), Waknaghat, India, 15–17 November 2019; pp. 97–101. [CrossRef]
6. Phan, Q.; Boato, G.; Caldelli, R.; Amerini, I. Tracking Multiple Image Sharing on Social Networks. In Proceedings of the ICASSP 2019—2019 IEEE International Conference on Acoustics, Speech and Signal Processing (ICASSP), Brighton, UK, 12–17 May 2019; pp. 8266–8270. [CrossRef]
7. Amerini, I.; Uricchio, T.; Caldelli, R. Tracing images back to their social network of origin: A CNN-based approach. In Proceedings of the 2017 IEEE Workshop on Information Forensics and Security (WIFS), Rennes, France, 4–7 December 2017; pp. 1–6. [CrossRef]
8. Iuliani, M.; Shullani, D.; Fontani, M.; Meucci, S.; Piva, A. A Video Forensic Framework for the Unsupervised Analysis of MP4-Like File Container. *IEEE Trans. Inf. Forensics Secur.* **2019**, *14*, 635–645. [CrossRef]
9. Iuliani, M.; Fontani, M.; Shullani, D.; Piva, A. Hybrid reference-based Video Source Identification. *Sensors* **2019**, *19*, 649. [CrossRef] [PubMed]
10. Yosinski, J.; Clune, J.; Bengio, Y.; Lipson, H. How transferable are features in deep neural networks? *arXiv* **2014**, arXiv:cs.LG/1411.1792.
11. Zhan, Y.; Chen, Y.; Zhang, Q.; Kang, X. Image Forensics Based on Transfer Learning and Convolutional Neural Network. In Proceedings of the 5th ACM Workshop on Information Hiding and Multimedia Security, Philadelphia, PA, USA, 20–22 June 2017; Association for Computing Machinery: New York, NY, USA, 2017; pp. 165–170. [CrossRef]

12. Cozzolino, D.; Thies, J.; Rössler, A.; Riess, C.; Nießner, M.; Verdoliva, L. ForensicTransfer: Weakly-supervised Domain Adaptation for Forgery Detection. *arXiv* 2019, arXiv:cs.CV/1812.02510.
13. Zhang, Y.; Yang, Q. A Survey on Multi-Task Learning. *arXiv* 2018, arXiv:cs.LG/1707.08114.
14. Mayer, O.; Bayar, B.; Stamm, M.C. Learning Unified Deep-Features for Multiple Forensic Tasks. In Proceedings of the 6th ACM Workshop on Information Hiding and Multimedia Security, Innsbruck, Austria, 20–22 June 2018; Association for Computing Machinery: New York, NY, USA, 2018; pp. 79–84. [CrossRef]
15. Ding, X.; Chen, Y.; Tang, Z.; Huang, Y. Camera Identification Based on Domain Knowledge-Driven Deep Multi-Task Learning. *IEEE Access* 2019, *7*, 25878–25890. [CrossRef]
16. Moltisanti, M.; Paratore, A.; Battiato, S.; Saravo, L. Image Manipulation on Facebook for Forensics Evidence. In *Image Analysis and Processing—ICIAP 2015*; Murino, V., Puppo, E., Eds.; Springer International Publishing: Cham, Switzerland, 2015; pp. 506–517.
17. Shullani, D.; Fontani, M.; Iuliani, M.; Alshaya, O.; Piva, A. VISION: A video and image dataset for source identification. *EURASIP J. Inf. Secur.* 2017, *2017*, 15. [CrossRef]
18. Caldelli, R.; Amerini, I.; Li, C.T. PRNU-based Image Classification of Origin Social Network with CNN. In Proceedings of the 2018 26th European Signal Processing Conference (EUSIPCO), Rome, Italy, 3–7 September 2018; pp. 1357–1361. [CrossRef]
19. Amerini, I.; Anagnostopoulos, A.; Maiano, L.; Celsi, L.R. Deep Learning for Multimedia Forensics. *Found. Trends Comput. Graph. Vis.* 2021, to appear.
20. Mullan, P.; Riess, C.; Freiling, F. Forensic source identification using JPEG image headers: The case of smartphones. *Digit. Investig.* 2019, *28*, S68–S76. [CrossRef]
21. Pasquini, C.; Amerini, I.; Boato, G. Media forensics on social media platforms: A survey. *EURASIP J. Inf. Secur.* 2021, *2021*, 4. [CrossRef]
22. Lukas, J.; Fridrich, J.; Goljan, M. Digital camera identification from sensor pattern noise. *IEEE Trans. Inf. Forensics Secur.* 2006, *1*, 205–214. [CrossRef]
23. Van Houten, W.; Geradts, Z. Source Video Camera Identification for Multiply Compressed Videos Originating from YouTube. *Digit. Investig.* 2009, *6*, 48–60. [CrossRef]
24. Taspinar, S.; Mohanty, M.; Memon, N. Camera Fingerprint Extraction via Spatial Domain Averaged Frames. *IEEE Trans. Inf. Forensics Secur.* 2020, *15*, 3270–3282. [CrossRef]
25. Kouokam, E.K.; Dirik, A.E. PRNU-based source device attribution for YouTube videos. *Digit. Investig.* 2019, *29*, 91–100. [CrossRef]
26. Bertini, F.; Sharma, R.; Iannì, A.; Montesi, D. Profile Resolution across Multilayer Networks through Smartphone Camera Fingerprint. In Proceedings of the 19th International Database Engineering and Applications Symposium, Yokohama, Japan, 13–15 July 2015; Association for Computing Machinery: New York, NY, USA, 2015; pp. 23–32. [CrossRef]
27. Rafi, A.M.; Kamal, U.; Hoque, R.; Abrar, A.; Das, S.; Laganière, R.; Hasan, M.K. Application of DenseNet in Camera Model Identification and Post-processing Detection. *arXiv* 2019, arXiv:eess.IV/1809.00576.
28. Kuzin, A.; Fattakhov, A.; Kibardin, I.; Iglovikov, V.; Dautov, R. Camera Model Identification Using Convolutional Neural Networks. *arXiv* 2018, arXiv:cs.CV/1810.02981.
29. Giovanni, C.; Luisa, P.; Verdoliva, D. Extracting camera-based fingerprints for video forensics. In Proceedings of the IEEE/CVF Conference on Computer Vision and Pattern Recognition (CVPR) Workshops, Long Beach, CA, USA, 16–20 June 2019.
30. Cozzolino, D.; Marra, F.; Gragnaniello, D.; Poggi, G.; Verdoliva, L. Combining PRNU and noiseprint for robust and efficient device source identification. *EURASIP J. Inf. Secur.* 2020, *2020*, 1–12. [CrossRef]
31. Yang, P.; Baracchi, D.; Iuliani, M.; Shullani, D.; Ni, R.; Zhao, Y.; Piva, A. Efficient Video Integrity Analysis Through Container Characterization. *IEEE J. Sel. Top. Signal Process.* 2020, *14*, 947–954. [CrossRef]
32. Ramos López, R.; Almaraz Luengo, E.; Sandoval Orozco, A.L.; Villalba, L.J.G. Digital Video Source Identification Based on Container's Structure Analysis. *IEEE Access* 2020, *8*, 36363–36375. [CrossRef]
33. Mayer, O.; Hosler, B.; Stamm, M.C. Open Set Video Camera Model Verification. In Proceedings of the ICASSP 2020—2020 IEEE International Conference on Acoustics, Speech and Signal Processing (ICASSP), Barcelona, Spain, 4–9 May 2020; pp. 2962–2966. [CrossRef]
34. Bondi, L.; Baroffio, L.; Güera, D.; Bestagini, P.; Delp, E.J.; Tubaro, S. First Steps Toward Camera Model Identification with Convolutional Neural Networks. *IEEE Signal Process. Lett.* 2017, *24*, 259–263. [CrossRef]
35. Marra, F.; Poggi, G.; Sansone, C.; Verdoliva, L. A study of co-occurrence based local features for camera model identification. *Multimed. Tools Appl.* 2016, *76*, 4765–4781. [CrossRef]
36. Chen, C.; Stamm, M.C. Camera model identification framework using an ensemble of demosaicing features. In Proceedings of the 2015 IEEE International Workshop on Information Forensics and Security (WIFS), Rome, Italy, 16–19 November 2015; pp. 1–6. [CrossRef]
37. Mayer, O.; Stamm, M.C. Exposing Fake Images with Forensic Similarity Graphs. *arXiv* 2020, arXiv:eess.IV/1912.02861.
38. Amerini, I.; Caldelli, R.; Mastio, A.D.; Fuccia, A.D.; Molinari, C.; Rizzo, A.P. Dealing with video source identification in social networks. *Signal Process. Image Commun.* 2017, *57*, 1–7. [CrossRef]
39. Amerini, I.; Anagnostopoulos, A.; Maiano, L.; Celsi, L.R. Learning Double-Compression Video Fingerprints Left From Social-Media Platforms. In Proceedings of the ICASSP 2021—2021 IEEE International Conference on Acoustics, Speech and Signal Processing (ICASSP), Toronto, ON, Canada, 6–12 June 2021; pp. 2530–2534. [CrossRef]

40. Popescu, A.C.; Farid, H. Statistical Tools for Digital Forensics. In *Information Hiding*; Fridrich, J., Ed.; Springer: Berlin/Heidelberg, Germany, 2005; pp. 128–147.
41. Wang, W.; Farid, H. Exposing Digital Forgeries in Video by Detecting Double MPEG Compression. In Proceedings of the 8th Workshop on Multimedia and Security, Geneva, Switzerland, 26–27 September 2006; Association for Computing Machinery: New York, NY, USA, 2006; pp. 37–47. [CrossRef]
42. Mahdian, B.; Saic, S.; Nedbal, R. JPEG Quantization Tables Forensics: A Statistical Approach. In *Computational Forensics*; Sako, H., Franke, K.Y., Saitoh, S., Eds.; Springer: Berlin/Heidelberg, Germany, 2011; pp. 150–159.
43. Bayar, B.; Stamm, M.C. Constrained Convolutional Neural Networks: A New Approach Towards General Purpose Image Manipulation Detection. *IEEE Trans. Inf. Forensics Secur.* **2018**, *13*, 2691–2706. [CrossRef]
44. Glorot, X.; Bengio, Y. Understanding the difficulty of training deep feedforward neural networks. In Proceedings of the Thirteenth International Conference on Artificial Intelligence and Statistics, Sardinia, Italy, 13–15 May 2010; pp. 249–256.

Article

No Matter What Images You Share, You Can Probably Be Fingerprinted Anyway

Rahimeh Rouhi [1,*], Flavio Bertini [2,*] and Danilo Montesi [2,*]

1 Université de Lorraine, CNRS, LORIA, F-54000 Nancy, France
2 Department of Computer Science and Engineering, University of Bologna, 40126 Bologna, Italy
* Correspondence: rahimeh.rouhi@loria.fr (R.R.); flavio.bertini2@unibo.it (F.B.); danilo.montesi@unibo.it (D.M.)

Abstract: The popularity of social networks (SNs), amplified by the ever-increasing use of smartphones, has intensified online cybercrimes. This trend has accelerated digital forensics through SNs. One of the areas that has received lots of attention is camera fingerprinting, through which each smartphone is uniquely characterized. Hence, in this paper, we compare classification-based methods to achieve *smartphone identification* (SI) and *user profile linking* (UPL) within the same or across different SNs, which can provide investigators with significant clues. We validate the proposed methods by two datasets, our dataset and the VISION dataset, both including original and shared images on the SN platforms such as *Google Currents, Facebook, WhatsApp,* and *Telegram*. The obtained results show that k-medoids achieves the best results compared with k-means, hierarchical approaches, and different models of convolutional neural network (CNN) in the classification of the images. The results show that k-medoids provides the values of F1-measure up to 0.91% for SI and UPL tasks. Moreover, the results prove the effectiveness of the methods which tackle the loss of image details through the compression process on the SNs, even for the images from the same model of smartphones. An important outcome of our work is presenting the *inter-layer UPL* task, which is more desirable in digital investigations as it can link user profiles on different SNs.

Keywords: camera fingerprint; smartphone identification; user profile linking; digital investigations; social network; classification

Citation: Rouhi, R.; Bertini, F.; Montesi, D. No Matter What Images You Share, You Can Probably Be Fingerprinted Anyway. *J. Imaging* **2021**, *7*, 33. https://doi.org/10.3390/jimaging7020033

Academic Editor: Irene Amerini
Received: 20 December 2020
Accepted: 8 February 2021
Published: 11 February 2021

Publisher's Note: MDPI stays neutral with regard to jurisdictional claims in published maps and institutional affiliations.

Copyright: © 2021 by the authors. Licensee MDPI, Basel, Switzerland. This article is an open access article distributed under the terms and conditions of the Creative Commons Attribution (CC BY) license (https://creativecommons.org/licenses/by/4.0/).

1. Introduction

In recent years, different social networks (SNs) have revolutionized the web by providing users with specific types of interaction, for instance by sending texts and sharing images and videos. Different SNs meet different needs of users. This means that users are usually active across multiple SNs. It has been reported that on average an Internet user used 8 different SNs at the same time in 2017 [1]. Moreover, many SNs have provided their own dedicated applications for major mobile devices (e.g., smartphones), which has introduced changes in user habits with respect to multimedia content on SNs [2]. In particular, it has led users to take more and more digital images and share them across various SNs [3], making it a challenging task to control the production and propagation of the images and to use the images as digital evidence. From the forensics point of view, the images shared by users on SN platforms could be considered as complementary clues to detect the evidence referenced in a digital crime [4]. In a real scenario, once a digital crime is reported on an SN platform, the police may identify a number of suspects (e.g., friends, relatives and most active users) and collect the electronic devices and the respective profile information on the SNs. With a set of "original images" coming directly from a specific number of the collected devices and the "shared images" taken from suspects' profiles, *smartphone identification* (SI) and *user profile linking* (UPL) could be achieved. These tasks represent an orthogonal work compared with the work presented in [5] and can provide the police with significant findings and the opportunity to update their dataset to apply to future investigations by creating new fingerprints of the criminals' smartphones.

More specifically, SI is the task used to identify the source camera generating a given set of images, while UPL is the task used to find the links among the suspects' profiles. It is worth mentioning that a user would be linked to other profiles even if there is not a direct friendship between the profiles on the same or different SN platforms. In recent years, methods based on camera sensor imperfections have been known as a robust approach for smartphone fingerprinting applied to digital investigations due to their stability against environmental conditions [6–8]. The photo-response non-uniformity (PRNU) approach is most suitable for defining the pattern noise (PN) of camera sensor imperfections [9,10]. The PN can be approximated as the average of residual noises (RNs) present in each image captured by the camera. The RN is estimated as the difference between the image content and its denoised version obtained through a denoising filter [10]. Due to the effectiveness of PRNU, in this paper, we take advantage of PRNU in the classification of both "original" (or native) and "shared images" within a set of investigated profiles on SNs to achieve SI and UPL.

1.1. Problem Statement

Given a set of images, "original" or "shared images", taken by a given number of smartphones, and a set of user profiles, as shown in Figure 1a, we aim to perform SI and UPL tasks based on classification of smartphones' camera fingerprints. In particular, a visual example of the proposed methods for two smartphones and two SNs, *Facebook* and *WhatsApp*, is provided in Figure 1b,c. For SI, we consider the following cases:

1.1 *Original-by-original SI* is the task used to detect the source cameras from which a set of "original images" directly coming from smartphones have been taken, see the arrow labeled "Classification (1)" in Figure 1b.

1.2 *Social-by-original SI* represents the task used to identify the source cameras of a given set of "shared images", see the arrow labeled "Classification (3)" in Figure 1c. In this case, the "original images" are input data and allow one to define the smartphone camera fingerprints.

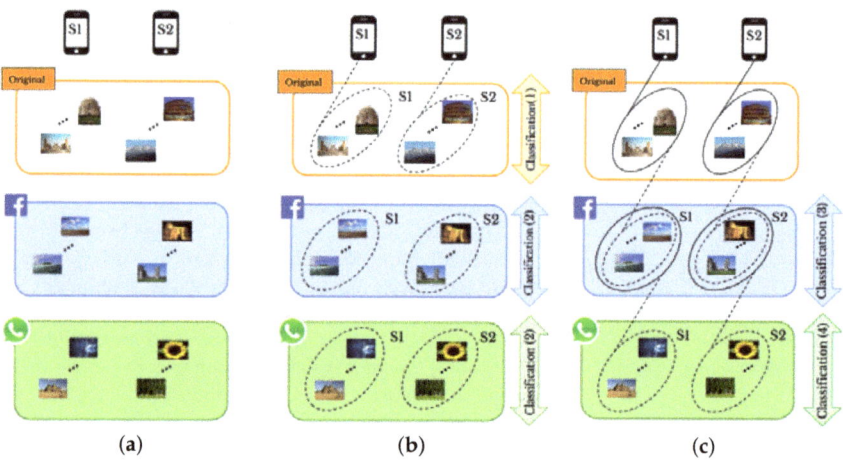

Figure 1. A visual example of the proposed methods: (**a**) domain of the problem, (**b,c**) classification-based approaches for smartphone identification (SI) and user profile linking (UPL) by "original" and "shared images", respectively. The labels (1) to (4) refer to Figure 2 presenting all the combinations of "original" and "shared images".

Moreover, the UPL task is categorized into two cases: within the same SN and across different SNs, resulting in the following:

2.1 *Intra-layer UPL* is the task used to link a given set of user profiles within the same SN using "shared images", see the arrows labeled "Classification (2)" on *Facebook* and *WhatsApp* in Figure 1b. Through this task, the profiles that share images from the same source are linked within the same SNs.

2.2 *Inter-layer UPL* represents the task used to link a set of user profiles across different SNs by using "shared images", see the arrow labeled "Classification (4)" in Figure 1c. Through this task, the profiles from different SNs that share images from the same source are linked.

1.2. Contribution

In this paper, we apply both "original" and "shared images" to fingerprint smartphones. We assume that the number of smartphones is known. Figure 2 shows all the combinations of both types of images. Labels (1)–(4) make a connection with Figure 1b,c, presenting the same meaning. We investigate different approaches, such as pre-trained CNN and clustering methods, for *original-by-original SI* and *intra-layer UPL* tasks, and we apply a neural network model for the *social-by-original SI* and *inter-layer UPL* tasks. According to the comparison results (see Sections 4.1 and 4.2 for more details), k-medoids technique [11] effectively classifies "original" and "shared images" and achieves *original-by-original SI* and *intra-layer UPL* (i.e., the green and magenta rounded arrows in Figure 2). In addition, a classification approach based on artificial neural networks (ANNs) effectively achieves *social-by-original SI* and *inter-layer UPL* (i.e., the blue and red straight arrows in Figure 2). In particular, we classify the "shared images" by exploiting the fingerprints derived from the obtained classes, refer to Section 3.4 for more details.

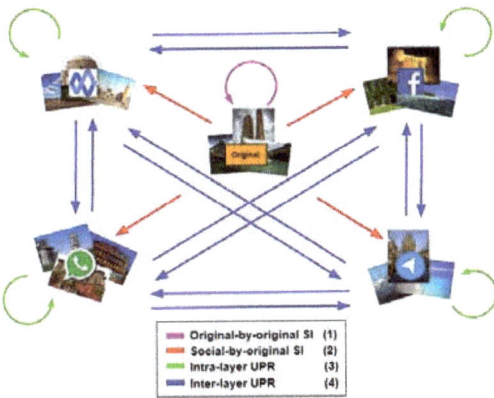

Figure 2. All the possible combinations of "original" and "shared images" in the proposed methods. The green and magenta rounded arrows from A to A imply classifying images of A, while the blue and red straight arrows from A to B mean that we use the classified images of A to classify the images of B.

Analyzing a huge number of images on all SN platforms is an unfeasible task; for this reason, in a real-world scenario investigators identify a restricted number of suspects and collect the relative devices and user profile information. Accordingly, to evaluate the proposed methods, we use our real dataset that consists of 4500 images captured by 18 different smartphones. The dataset was uploaded and downloaded on 4 of the most popular SNs, namely *Google Currents* (Google+ was discontinued in April 2019 and enterprise accounts were transitioned to Google Currents), *Facebook*, *WhatsApp*, and *Telegram*. In addition, we validate our proposed methods by the VISION image dataset [12]. The obtained results show the effectiveness of the proposed methods, even for the images degraded through the compression process on the applied SNs. Moreover, the methods are device-independent and able to distinguish the same model of smartphones. An important result of our work is applying the *inter-layer UPL* task to link a given set of user profiles on different SN platforms. This is more desirable in digital investigations because on average, users are active on multiple SNs [1].

The rest of the paper is organized as follows. Section 2 provides a summary of the SI and UPL tasks proposed in the literature. In Section 3, we describe the proposed methods. Experiments and their results are discussed in Section 4. In Section 5, limitation and significance of the proposed methods are presented. Some concluding remarks are made in Section 6.

2. Related Works

Smartphones have several built-in sensors that measure motion, orientation, and various environmental conditions. All of these components present hardware imperfections created during the manufacturing process that uniquely characterize each smartphone. The smartphone fingerprint formed by these imperfections has been known as a reliable characteristic making a smartphone trackable [7–9].

A lot of attempts have been made to get smartphone fingerprints using a variety of sensors such as accelerometers [13], gyroscopes [14], magnetometers [15,16], cameras [17], and paired microphones and speakers [18]. The camera could be considered a built-in sensor that is less invasive and more suitable for source camera identification [6]. A pioneering work [9] introduced the PRNU technique to obtain camera sensor noise. A significant advantage of the PRNU is that it remains stable under different environments. In addition, it is considered a reliable fingerprint that efficiently characterizes the digital device that generated the image [19,20].

Most of the works proposed for SI and smartphone image classification were implemented on the "original images", e.g., [20–23]. However, identification by "shared images" is challenging because of the images' compression. Only a few works, e.g., [12,24,25], applied shared images or videos from, for example, *Facebook*, *YouTube*, and *Twitter*. All the mentioned works used "shared images" for only SI not UPL.

Different approaches have been proposed for the UPL task. For example, [26] exploited user activities on SNs. They collected logs filed within the device through a manual investigation and used them to match user profiles. Their experiments showed that the method failed for BlackBerry devices. Similarly, reference [2] monitored user activities and collected a variety of artifacts, such as usernames, passwords, login information, personal information, uploaded posts, and exchanged messages. All of this information was gathered for the digital investigations. The authors of [27] used the Jaro–Winkler distance algorithm [28], to compare the account information of users, such as username, friends, and interests, from accounts on different SNs for profile matching. Iofciu et al. [29] introduced a method based on the combination of user IDs and tags to recognize users through the social tagging system.

The works of [30,31] presented a framework for UPL across SNs considering profile attributes. The framework assigns a different similarity measure to each attribute. The authors of [32] introduced a method that was not dependent on login credentials. The behavioral traits of users were applied to link users. Zafarani et al. [33] applied behavioral patterns to establish a mapping among identities of individuals across social media sites. The authors of [34] used datasets such as call records and matched the obtained histograms of users' data representing their fingerprints to identify users. In [35], user activities on SNs were analyzed to find trust interactions between the users. However, there are still some problems with these approaches. The information of users' identities could be diverse on different SNs [36]. The users may select different nicknames and E-mail addresses, resulting in incorrect matching between the real person and the accounts [33].

Hence, in this paper, we use a different approach based on supervised and unsupervised classification techniques, extending our previous works [37–39]. What makes our work innovative is using images from one SN to identify smartphones applied on another SN, which provides user profile linking across different SN platforms. In addition, we apply our proposed methods to larger datasets covering images from different or even identical models of smartphones.

3. Methodology

We first provide a brief background on RN extraction and PN computation, namely smartphone camera fingerprinting. Then, we describe the pre-processing phase that enables definition of several parameters, such as the orientation, size, and channel of the images. Finally, we explain SI and UPL across SNs based on classification techniques. To evaluate our methods, we gathered a dataset including 4500 images from 18 different smartphones. Through the paper, we call our dataset "Lab Dataset", i.e., $\mathcal{D}_L$. Based on our previous work [40], the minimum number of images per samrtphone to get a reliable fingerprint is 50. Hence, for each smartphone, we collected 250 images. Then, we kept a subset of 50 "original images" (O) and uploaded and downloaded 50 images on each of the four selected SNs: *Google Currents* (G), *WhatsApp* (W), *Facebook High Resolution* (FH), and *Telegram* (T). Correspondingly, we have the datasets $\mathcal{D}_L^O$, $\mathcal{D}_L^G$, $\mathcal{D}_L^W$, $\mathcal{D}_L^{FH}$, and $\mathcal{D}_L^T$. The characteristics of the applied smartphones in $\mathcal{D}_L$ are shown in Table 1. We use also the VISON image dataset including a different number of images taken by 35 smartphones. The images are divided into *flat*, which is a set of images of walls and skies, and *generic*, which is a set of images without limitations on orientation or scenario. The images were shared through WhatsApp and Facebook (in both high and low resolutions). We use only generic images in our experiments. We call the datasets $\mathcal{D}_V^O$, $\mathcal{D}_V^W$, $\mathcal{D}_V^{FH}$, and $\mathcal{D}_V^{FL}$ corresponding to the O, W, FH, and *Facebook Low Resolution* (FL) images. The lowest and the highest resolutions of images for each SN in the datasets $\mathcal{D}_L$ and $\mathcal{D}_V$ are presented in Table 2.

Table 1. Characteristics of smartphones in $\mathcal{D}_L$.

Phone ID	Brand	Model	Resolution
S1	LG	Nexus 4	3264×2448
S2	Samsung	Galaxy S2	3264×2448
S3	Apple	iPhone 6+	3264×2448
S4	LG	Nexus 5	3264×2448
S5	Huawei	Y550	2592×1944
S6	Apple	iPhone 5	3264×2448
S7	Motorola	Moto G	2592×1456
S8	Samsung	Galaxy S4	4128×3096
S9	LG	G3	4160×3120
S10	LG	Nexus 5	3264×2448
S11	Sony	Xperia Z3	5248×3936
S12	Samsung	Samsung S3	3264×2448
S13	HTC	One S	3264×2448
S14	LG	Nexus 5	3264×2448
S15	Apple	iPhone 6	3264×2448
S16	Samsung	Galaxy S2	3264×2448
S17	Nokia	Lumia 625	2592×1456
S18	Apple	iPhone 5S	3264×2448

Table 2. The lowest and highest image resolution in different datasets.

Dataset	Lowest Resolution	Highest Resolution
$\mathcal{D}_L^O$	960 × 544	5248 × 3936
$\mathcal{D}_L^G$	960 × 544	5248 × 3936
$\mathcal{D}_L^W$	960 × 544	1600 × 1200
$\mathcal{D}_L^{FH}$	960 × 544	2048 × 1536
$\mathcal{D}_L^T$	960 × 544	1280 × 960
$\mathcal{D}_V^O$	960 × 720	5248 × 3936
$\mathcal{D}_V^W$	960 × 720	1280 × 960
$\mathcal{D}_V^{FH}$	960 × 720	2048 × 1536
$\mathcal{D}_V^{FL}$	1040 × 584	1312 × 984

3.1. Smartphone Fingerprinting

We use the PRNU approach, proposed by [41], to extract the RN left by sensor imperfections in each image. Let I and $d()$ be, respectively, an image and a denoising filter. The RN is computed as follows:

$$RN = I - d(I) \qquad (1)$$

Then, the PN (i.e., the smartphone camera fingerprint) is approximated by averaging the RNs of n images of camera k as follows:

$$PN_k = \frac{1}{n} \sum_{j=1}^{n} RN_j \qquad (2)$$

According to (1) and (2), n and $d()$ are the two main factors that affect the quality of the PN. In particular, the more images taken by a certain source are provided, the higher the quality of PN is acquired [42]. We use Block-matching and 3D filtering (BM3D) as the denoising filter $d()$. It has shown promising effectiveness regarding the *peak signal-to-noise ratio* and visual quality, even for high levels of noise and scaled images [7,43,44].

3.2. Pre-Processing

The collected images come from different smartphones with different characteristics, such as orientation and size. We do the pre-processing phase to make a coordination between images in terms of orientation, size and channel. The aim is to balance a trade-off between the computational cost and the effectiveness of the proposed methods.

The image orientation depends on the rotation of the acquisition smartphone, which could be either portrait or landscape. Smartphone fingerprinting based on camera sensors is dependent on the orientation of images. Accordingly, the orientation has to be normalized for all the applied images. Although for "original images", the metadata, which are available through Exchangeable Image File Format (EXIF) [45], could be a solution to obtain the right orientation, this is not applicable to "shared images". The reason is that the SN platforms usually remove the metadata, such as orientation, during the uploading and downloading of the images. Hence, for the "shared images", we only align the images to either portrait or landscape orientation based on the spatial resolution [12]. This may not entirely resolve the orientation problem and affects the classification, but it can be alleviated.

In our previous work [38], in fingerprinting smartphones, we tested different channels of images, i.e., R, G, and B in RGB color space, and Y in YCbCr color space, among which the Y channel led to the best results. Therefore, we use the Y channel (gray-scale version) of images in this paper.

Unlike most of the presented works in the literature, which mostly cropped the central block of the extracted RNs, we use resizing. Generally, resizing the images involves up-scaling or down-scaling the images to a specific resolution. After extracting the RNs from gray-scale images, the obtained RNs are resized to an optimal size based on bicubic interpolation [46]. We will present some experiments in Section 4 to show the impact of resizing compared with cropping RNs.

3.3. Original-By-Original Smartphone Identification and Intra-Layer User Profile Linking

We apply supervised and unsupervised classification to images (see Figure 1b). More specifically, we do supervised classification using different pre-trained convolutional neural networks (CNN) such as GoogleNet [47], SqueezeNet [48], Densenet201 [49], and Mobilenetv2 [50]. In particular, we have added a convolutional layer to adapt the size of the images to the network input, retaining the weights from the previous training on the ImageNet dataset. As an unsupervised classification, we use k-means, k-medoids, and hierarchical techniques, which are performed based on a similarity measure in such a way that the objects in the same class have more similarity compared with those in different classes [51]. In the hierarchical classification technique, the objects are typically organized into a dendrogram (tree structure), where leaf nodes represent the individual data and the root is the whole dataset. The middle nodes show merged groups of similar objects [52]. In partitional classification such as k-means [53], and k-medoids the objects are divided into some partitions, each of which is considered as a group. The partitional classification starts by initializing a set of k class centers. Then, each object is assigned to the class whose center is the nearest [11,54]. K-medoids is an expensive approach, but it is a more reliable technique in the presence of noise and outliers compared to the other unsupervised classification methods [55].

We compare the CNN, hierarchical, k-means, and k-medoids techniques to classify the "original images" and achieve *original-by-original SI* and select the best technique for classification of smartphone camera fingerprints. Then, in a similar way, we classify the "shared images" to achieve *intra-layer UPL*. Figure 3 shows the task of *original-by-original SI*. Through the proposed methods, the number of smartphones under investigation has to be provided. Let I be a set of the "original images", and $S = \{S_1, S_2, \ldots, S_m\}$ be a set of m camera sources. We aim to classify the images of I into the right sources of S, where each camera source S_i has its own set of images, that is $I_{\langle 1,i \rangle}, \ldots, I_{\langle j,i \rangle}, \ldots, I_{\langle n,i \rangle} \in S_i$. Thus, we have the full dataset $I = \bigcup I_{\langle i,j \rangle}$, $\forall\, i = 1, \ldots, n$ and $j = 1, \ldots, m$, where n is the number of the collected images for each of the m smartphones. Firstly, we extract the RNs of the "original images" such that $RN_{<i,j>}$ is the RN corresponding to ith image taken by jth smartphone. Then, we use correlation as the similarity measure because it is the optimal metric for multiplicative signals such as PRNU [41]. The correlation between $RN_{\langle a,b \rangle} = [x_1, \ldots, x_l]$ from $I_{\langle a,b \rangle}$ and $RN_{\langle c,d \rangle} = [y_1, \ldots, y_l]$ from $I_{\langle c,d \rangle}$, such that l is the total number of pixels forming images $I_{\langle a,b \rangle}, I_{\langle c,d \rangle}$ and the two related RN vectors, is defined as follows:

$$\rho = \frac{\sum_{i=1}^{l}(x_i - \overline{RN}_{\langle a,b \rangle})(y_i - \overline{RN}_{\langle c,d \rangle})}{\sqrt{\sum_{i=1}^{l}(x_i - \overline{RN}_{\langle a,b \rangle})^2 \sum_{i=1}^{l}(y_i - \overline{RN}_{\langle c,d \rangle})^2}} \quad (3)$$

where $\overline{RN}_{\langle a,b \rangle}$ and $\overline{RN}_{\langle c,d \rangle}$ represent the means of the two RN vectors. We create a matrix ζ containing correlations between each pair of the extracted RNs. As a result of the varying qualities of PNs of different cameras, the average correlation between the RNs from one camera may differ from that of other camera [20]. This problem makes the classification of PNs more challenging. To address this problem, an alternative similarity measure is calculated based on shared κ-nearest neighbors (SNN) proposed by [56]:

$$\mathcal{W}(d_i, d_j) = |\mathbb{N}(\rho_i) \cap \mathbb{N}(\rho_j)| \quad (4)$$

where ρ_i and ρ_j are two elements in the correlation matrix ζ, and $\mathbb{N}(\rho_i)$ and $\mathbb{N}(\rho_j)$ are the SNN of ρ_i and ρ_j, so $\mathcal{W}(\rho_i, \rho_j)$ results in the number of κ-nearest neighbours shared by ρ_i and ρ_j. Then, we apply classification to the resulted matrix $\mathcal{W}$ from SNN.

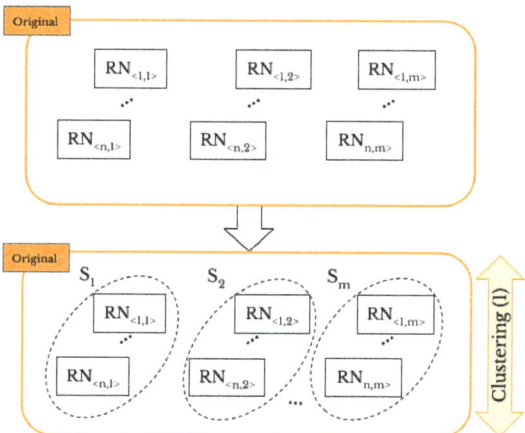

Figure 3. *Original-by-original SI*: the "original images" are classified according to the smartphone's source camera.

Smartphone identification deals with 1-to-m matching problem and determines which smartphone out of m took a given image. Therefore, the stopping criterion in hierarchical classification and the parameter k in k-means and k-medoids are set to the number of smartphones, i.e., $m = 18$ and $m = 35$ for $\mathcal{D}_L$ and $\mathcal{D}_V$, respectively. The number of smartphones represents the number of classes as the output of various networks used. All the classification approaches associate each RN with a label that represents the related source of the image. Similarly, we address the *intra-layer UPL* task, as shown in Figure 4.

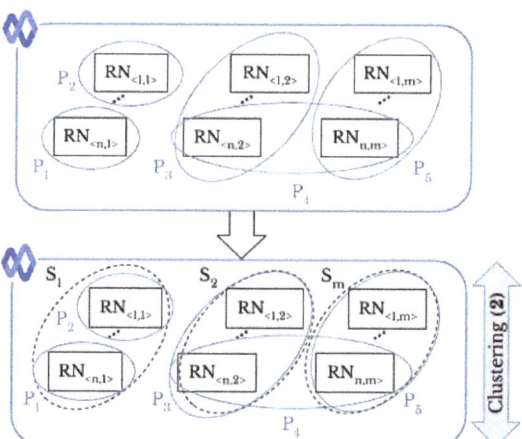

Figure 4. *Intra-layer UPL* task: profiles P_1 and P_2 are linked since they share images taken from the same smartphone S_1.

Let D^x be a set of images where $x \in \{G, W, FH, FL, T\}$. Each image in D^x has a specific profile tag P_i that represents the ith user's profile on the SN x the image comes from. Like *original-by-original SI*, we exploit the full pairwise correlation matrix of the extracted RNs to classify D^x images into the right sources of S. Then, by using the resulted classes and profile tags, we are able to link profiles. Moreover, we can determine whether a user uploaded images taken by one or more smartphones. In the first case, if within two different profiles there are images that are in the same class S_i, these profiles could be linked. For instance, in Figure 4, identification of smartphone S_1 leads to a matching between the profiles P_1 and P_2. In the second case, if the images belonging to the same profile are grouped in different classes, it means that the user uploaded the images from different smartphones. In Figure 4, the user of profile P_4 has shared images taken by two different smartphones, namely S_2 and S_m.

3.4. Social-By-Original Smartphone Identification and Inter-Layer User Profile Linking

Here, we exploit the obtained classes, from *original-by-original SI* and *intra-layer UPL* tasks, as ground truths of the fingerprinted smartphones to classify "original" or "shared images" into m classes. Generally, ANNs, inspired by the biological form of the human neural system, have proven their effectiveness in classification tasks [57]. They are very flexible in learning features and can solve non-linear problems. Compared with the other classifiers such as support vector machine, extreme learning machine, and random forest, ANNs are more fault tolerant [58]. As a mathematical model, an ANN consists of a set of attached neurons called processing units. Neurons are organized in layers. The output of a neuron is stated as $f(h)$, where $f()$ is the *activation function*, and h is computed as follows:

$$h = \sum_{i=1}^{s} w_i x_i + b \tag{5}$$

where x_i and w_i are the input data and weight of the neuron, respectively; b is the bias; and s is the total number of input connections of the neuron [59]. For a desirable classification, the weights of the ANN should be tuned. This process is called *training* or *learning* [60]. A *multi-layer perceptron* (MLP) is a kind of ANN composed of one or several hidden layers of neurons [61]. An MLP is trained by using a *back propagation* (BP) algorithm such that it minimizes the *mean squared error* (MSE), which is formulated by:

$$MSE = \frac{1}{N} \sum_{i=1}^{N} (T_i - O_i)^2 \tag{6}$$

where O and T are matrices representing the labels predicted by ANN and the class labels of the inputs, respectively, and N is the number of samples. We will use the classified images that are the outcome of the previous task and ANN to perform both *social-by-original SI* and *inter-layer UPL*. The *social-by-original SI* task is shown in Figure 5. We first define the fingerprint PN_i corresponding to the obtained classes from the set I, such that PN_i transitively identifies the smartphone S_i. Then, by (3), we calculate the correlation values between each pair of RNs extracted from the images in D^x, and the obtained PNs. For example, a correlation matrix of the size 900×18 is formed corresponding to 900 RNs in $\mathcal{D}_L^G$ to be classified according to 18 smartphones in $\mathcal{D}_L^O$ which have already been identified in the classification. The matrix is used for training and test the ANN through a 10-fold cross-validation model [62]. In particular, in every 10 iterations, the ANN is given 90% of the rows in the correlation matrix and corresponding class labels (smartphone labels by which the RNs in $\mathcal{D}_L^G$ were generated) as the ground truth. In the test, the trained ANN is provided by 10% of the rows in the correlation matrix to classify each image in $\mathcal{D}_L^G$, called *social-by-original SI*. By using the 10-fold approach, all the samples in the correlation matrix are tested as there is a swap between training and test in each iteration.

In *inter-layer UPL* task, as shown in Figure 6, the profile tag P_i, where i represents the ith profile on a given SN, allows one to link user profiles across different SNs. The PN_i is defined by using the classes obtained from *Google Currents*, and the ANN is trained to classify the *WhatsApp* images. After the classification, the profile P_1 on *WhatsApp* is linked to the profiles P_1, P_2, and P_3 on *Google Currents* because they share images taken from the same smartphones S_1 and S_2. Similarly, the profile P_5 on *WhatsApp* is linked to the profiles P_4 and P_5 on *Google Currents*.

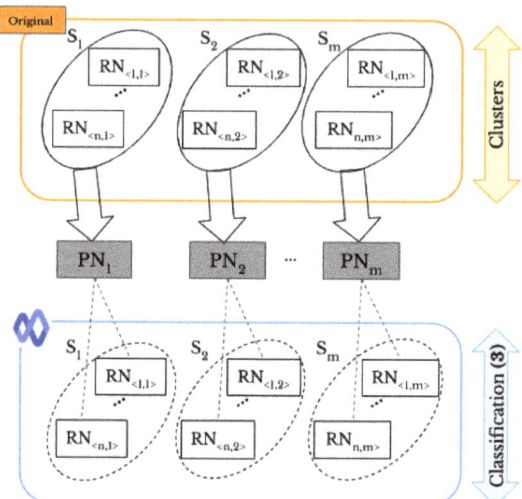

Figure 5. *Social-by-original SI* task based on classification approach: the classified "original images" are used to train the ANN and classify the "shared images".

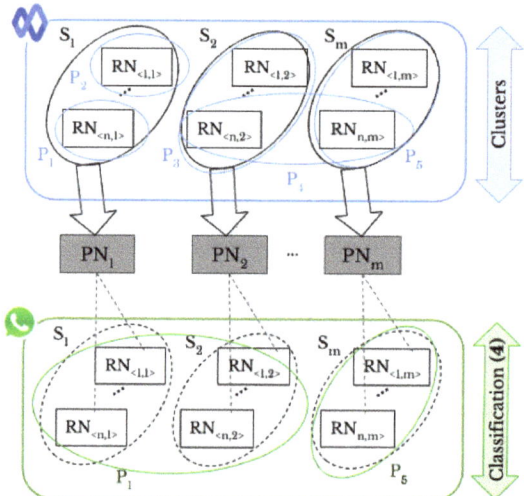

Figure 6. *Inter-layer UPL* task based on classification approach: to classify the "shared images" on a given social network (SN) (e.g., *WhatsApp*), the ANN is trained by using the obtained classes of "shared images" on a different SN (e.g., *Google Currents*).

We tested different topologies for the applied ANNs in terms of training method, activation function, and the number of hidden layers. As a result, an appropriate effectiveness of *social-by-original SI* and *inter-layer UPL* is achieved by the simple ANN's architecture shown in Table 3. In particular, we use *trainscg* as the training function that updates weight and bias values based on the *scaled conjugate gradient training* algorithm, and the *logistic sigmoid* as activation function that provides an appropriate convergence in the training. In particular, the applied activation function is defined as follows:

$$f(h) = \frac{1}{1 + e^{-h}} \tag{7}$$

where h is obtained by (5).

Table 3. ANN's architecture.

Type	Multi-Layer Perceptron (MLP)
Number of layers	2
Neurons in input layer	900 for $\mathcal{D}_L$ 7480 for $\mathcal{D}_V$
Neurons in hidden layer	50
Neurons in output layer	18 for $\mathcal{D}_L$ 35 for $\mathcal{D}_V$
Learning rule	Back Propagation (BP)
Training function	trainscg
Activation function	logsig
Error	Mean Squared Error (MSE)

4. Experimental Results

In this section, the results of SI and UPL are presented. In particular, the results of *original-by-original SI*, *social-by-original SI*, *intra-layer UPL*, and *inter-layer UPL* are provided, respectively. The proposed methods were implemented in MATLAB, version R2019a on a laptop with the following characteristics: Intel Core i7-6500U (2.93 GHz), 16 GB of RAM, and Windows 10 operating system. In each of these tests, to evaluate the classification processes, we calculate several measures. Let TP be a set of images to which the method has correctly assigned class labels, while that it has correctly not assigned is represented by TN. In addition, FP is the set of images to which the method has wrongly assigned class labels and FN is the set of images that the method has wrongly not assigned. Accordingly, Sensitivity ($\mathcal{SE}$), Specificity ($\mathcal{SP}$), Rand Index ($\mathcal{RI}$), Adjusted Rand Index ($\mathcal{ARI}$), F1-measure ($\mathcal{F}$), and Purity ($\mathcal{P}$) are defined as follows:

$$\mathcal{SE} = \frac{|TP|}{|TP| + |FN|} \tag{8}$$

$$\mathcal{SP} = \frac{|TN|}{|TN| + |FP|} \tag{9}$$

$$\mathcal{RI} = \frac{|TP| + |TN|}{|TP| + |FP| + |TN| + |FN|} \tag{10}$$

where $|.|$ denotes cardinality of the related set, i.e., True Positive (TP), True Negative (TN), False Positive (FP), or False Negative (FN). The value of $\mathcal{RI}$ varies between 0 and 1, respectively showing no agreement and full agreement between the classification results and the ground truth. For two random classes, the average of $\mathcal{RI}$, i.e., $\overline{\mathcal{RI}}$ is a non-zero value. To get rid of this bias, $\mathcal{ARI}$ was proposed by [63]:

$$\mathcal{ARI} = \frac{\mathcal{RI} - \overline{\mathcal{RI}}}{1 - \overline{\mathcal{RI}}} \tag{11}$$

$$\mathcal{F} = \frac{2.|TP|}{2.|TP| + |FP| + |FN|} \tag{12}$$

$$\mathcal{P} = \frac{\sum_{i=1}^{|C|} \frac{|\hat{c}_i|}{|c_i|}}{|C|} \tag{13}$$

where $C = \{c_1, c_2, \ldots, c_m\}$ is the set of the obtained classes corresponding to m smartphones in dataset, $\hat{c}_i$ denotes the number of RNs with the dominant class label in the class c_i, and $|c_i|$ is the total number of RNs in c_i.

As described before, we evaluate the effectiveness of the ANN in the training phase as well as its generalization capability by using 10-fold cross-validation. Firstly, a matrix including the correlations between the extracted RNs and the obtained PNs are calculated based on (3). The ith row of the matrix includes the similarities between the ith RN and all the resulted PNs from the classification. The rows related to the same smartphone are shuffled to have an order-independent evaluation. Then, they are divided into 10 folds so that each of them includes an equal number of samples for each smartphone. In each of 10 iterations of the cross-validation, nine folds and one independent fold are used respectively for "training set" and "test set". For example, in $\mathcal{D}_L^O$ we have 50 images for each smartphone, so we use 850 and 50 rows, respectively, in training and test at each iteration. The 10-fold cross-validation process is repeated 10 times, and finally, the average values obtained from the measures in (8)–(13) are considered as the ANN results.

4.1. Original-By-Original Smartphone Identification Results

In this experiment, we use "original images" to identify their acquisition smartphones, which is called the *original-by-original SI* task. As shown in Table 1, these images have a high resolution, so the results can be considered as a benchmark for the capability of the classification in the best case. Furthermore, we exploit this experiment to perform some pre-processing in terms of size for all the applied images in the datasets. In particular, in the pre-processing phase, we use the k-medoids method because it is a more reliable technique in the presence of noise and outliers.

Based on Table 4, to obtain the optimal resolution in resizing, we resize the extracted RNs form the images in $\mathcal{D}_L^O$ with different resolutions, i.e., 128 × 128, 256 × 256, 512 × 512, 960 × 544, 1024 × 1024, 1280 × 1024, and 1536 × 1536. Then, we do classification by k-medoids. We choose the size of 1024 × 1024 as it results in the highest values of all the measures, i.e., $\mathcal{SE}$, $\mathcal{SP}$, $\mathcal{RI}$, $\mathcal{ARI}$, $\mathcal{F}$, and $\mathcal{P}$ compared with the other resolutions. In addition, Figure 7 shows the impact of SNN on the pairwise correlation matrices of the datasets $\mathcal{D}_L^O$ and $\mathcal{D}_V^O$. Comparing the subfigures (c) and (d) with (a) and (b), it can be seen that the average of intra-camera correlations, i.e., the diagonal parts, has increased while the average of the inter-camera correlations has decreased. This improvement in the correlations between RNs produces better results for k-medoids. The value of κ in SNN for each dataset was experimentally determined. Different values were tested and $\kappa = 20$ and $\kappa = 70$ generated the best results in the classification for $\mathcal{D}_L^O$ and $\mathcal{D}_V^O$, respectively.

Table 4. Results (%) of resizing versus cropping the RNs in *original-by-original SI* on $\mathcal{D}_L^O$, by testing different image resolution.

	Resizing					Cropping *				
Size	$\mathcal{SE}$	$\mathcal{SP}$	$\mathcal{ARI}$	$\mathcal{F}$	$\mathcal{P}$	$\mathcal{SE}$	$\mathcal{SP}$	$\mathcal{ARI}$	$\mathcal{F}$	$\mathcal{P}$
1536 × 1536	0.91	0.99	0.88	0.88	0.95	—	—	—	—	—
1280 × 1024	0.89	0.99	0.85	0.86	0.94	—	—	—	—	—
1024 × 1024	0.91	0.99	0.90	0.91	0.96	—	—	—	—	—
960 × 544	0.90	0.99	0.87	0.88	0.95	0.91	0.99	0.89	0.90	0.95
512 × 512	0.90	0.99	0.87	0.88	0.94	0.85	0.98	0.81	0.82	0.89
256 × 256	0.58	0.97	0.55	0.57	0.75	0.76	0.98	0.74	0.75	0.87
128 × 128	0.18	0.94	0.12	0.17	0.37	0.43	0.96	0.39	0.42	0.66

* The highest resolution for cropping RNs is 960 × 544 px, based on Table 2.

The comparison results among CNN models, hierarchical clustering, k-means, and k-medoids techniques applied to $\mathcal{D}_V^O$ are shown in Figure 8. The results confirm that k-medoids is the best to classify RNs, even for RNs extracted from images from identical models of smartphones. According to Table 5, the results of k-medoids on both the datasets $\mathcal{D}_L^O$ and $\mathcal{D}_V^O$ show the effectiveness of the classification with the resolution 1024 × 1024.

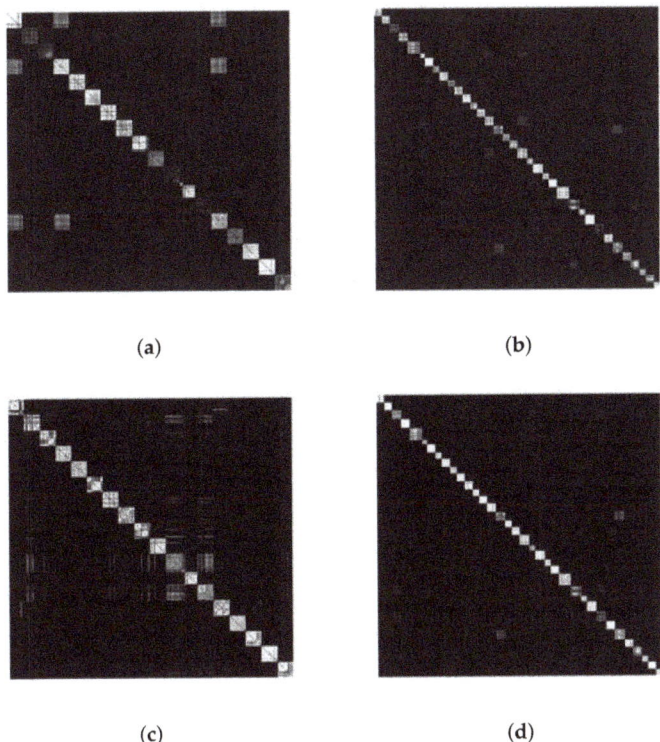

Figure 7. Pairwise similarities of residual noises (RNs): (**a**,**b**) without and (**c**,**d**) with using shared κ-nearest neighbor, respectively from left to right for $\mathcal{D}_L^O$, $\kappa = 20$, and $\mathcal{D}_V^O$, $\kappa = 70$.

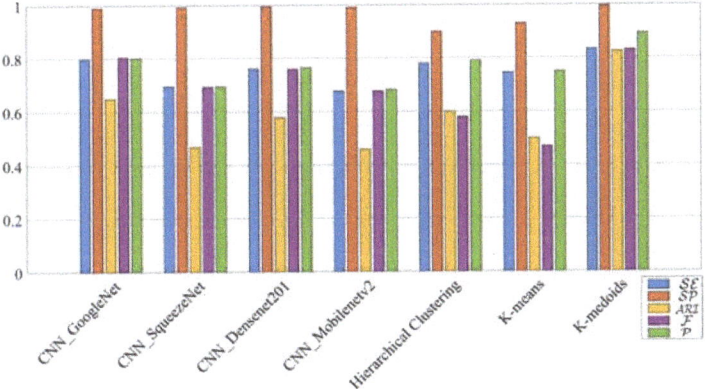

Figure 8. Results (%) of original-by-original SI by using different methods on $\mathcal{D}_V^O$ with the RN resolution 1024×1024.

Table 5. Results (%) of *original-by-original SI* on different datasets.

Dataset	$\mathcal{SE}$	$\mathcal{SP}$	$\mathcal{ARI}$	$\mathcal{F}$	$\mathcal{P}$
$\mathcal{D}_L^O$	0.91	0.99	0.90	0.91	0.96
$\mathcal{D}_V^O$	0.84	0.99	0.84	0.85	0.894

4.2. Social-By-Original Smartphone Identification Results

In this test, we use both "original" and "shared images" to present *social-by-original SI*. Firstly, we exploit *Google Currents* images in $\mathcal{D}_L$ to set up the architecture of the applied ANNs as *Google Currents* images provide the highest resolution. Accordingly, the test could also be considered as a benchmark for the ANNs used for the other SNs. In particular, to tune the number of neurons in the hidden layer, we consider the classes of the "original images" from the previous test and classify the *Google Currents* images.

Based on Figure 9, by systematically increasing the number of neurons, the classification results are improved in terms of $\mathcal{SE}, \mathcal{SP}, \mathcal{ARI}, \mathcal{F}$ and $\mathcal{P}$. Although the highest values are resulted in the cardinality of 35, up to the cardinality of 50, there are still some fluctuations in the values. For this reason, we set the number of the neurons to 50 in our experiments. The tuning phase of the ANNs can also be used as a benchmark for the capability of the classification in the best case because the "original images" and *Google Currents* images have the highest resolution in the dataset.

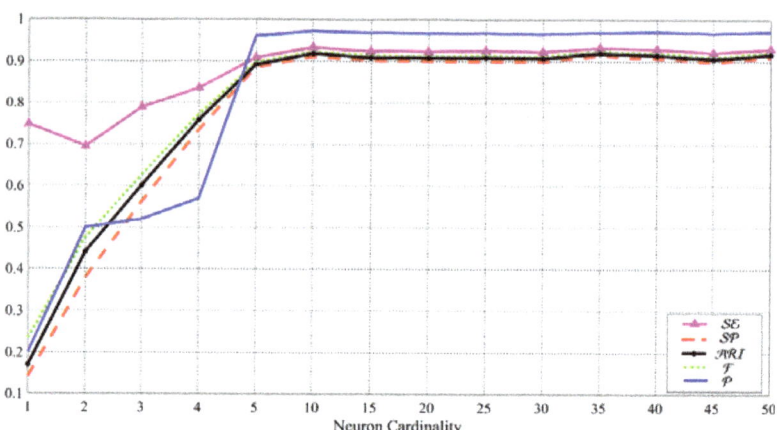

Figure 9. Results (%) of *social-by-original SI* for systematically increasing the number of neurons in the hidden layer of ANN. The images in $\mathcal{D}_L^G$ are classified by the obtained classes of images in $\mathcal{D}_L^O$ and the trained ANN.

The results of *social-by-original SI* for both datasets $\mathcal{D}_L$ and $\mathcal{D}_V$ are shown in Table 6. The *social-by-original SI* enables identification of smartphones in spite of the fact that the pictures get downgraded during the uploading and downloading process.

Table 6. Results (%) of *social-by-original SI* on different datasets.

Dataset	$\mathcal{SE}$	$\mathcal{SP}$	$\mathcal{ARI}$	$\mathcal{F}$	$\mathcal{P}$
$\mathcal{D}_L^G - \mathcal{D}_L^O$	0.92	0.99	0.91	0.91	0.97
$\mathcal{D}_L^W - \mathcal{D}_L^O$	0.85	0.99	0.82	0.83	0.92
$\mathcal{D}_L^{FH} - \mathcal{D}_L^O$	0.85	0.99	0.82	0.83	0.92
$\mathcal{D}_L^T - \mathcal{D}_L^O$	0.86	0.99	0.83	0.84	0.93
$\mathcal{D}_V^W - \mathcal{D}_V^O$	0.81	0.99	0.79	0.80	0.91
$\mathcal{D}_V^{FH} - \mathcal{D}_V^O$	0.80	0.99	0.77	0.77	0.90
$\mathcal{D}_V^{FL} - \mathcal{D}_V^O$	0.78	0.99	0.75	0.75	0.89

4.3. Intra-Layer User Profile Linking Results

In this section, we discuss the results of *intra-layer UPL*. In particular, this test exploits "shared images" to determine whether a given set of user profiles within the same SN are linked. Table 7 shows the results on the "shared images" in both $\mathcal{D}_L$ and $\mathcal{D}_V$. The best results are related to $\mathcal{D}_L^G$. The reason is that *Google Currents* images have the same resolution as the "original images" confirming that the compression algorithm on this SN results in less elimination of image details, (see Table 2). Although the other SNs compress the images more than *Google Currents*, the method has returned good results confirming the effectiveness of the method in the task of *intra-layer UPL*.

Table 7. Results (%) of *intra-layer UPL* on different datasets.

Dataset	$\mathcal{D}_L^G$	$\mathcal{D}_L^W$	$\mathcal{D}_L^{FH}$	$\mathcal{D}_L^T$	$\mathcal{D}_V^W$	$\mathcal{D}_V^{FH}$	$\mathcal{D}_V^{FL}$
$\mathcal{SE}$	0.91	0.87	0.88	0.87	0.75	0.73	0.43
$\mathcal{SP}$	0.99	0.98	0.99	0.99	0.99	0.99	0.98
$\mathcal{ARI}$	0.88	0.84	0.86	0.86	0.74	0.71	0.40
$\mathcal{F}$	0.89	0.86	0.85	0.85	0.75	0.71	0.42
$\mathcal{P}$	0.96	0.94	0.93	0.92	0.84	0.80	0.58

4.4. Inter-Layer User Profile Linking Results

This last test is the most challenging. We demonstrate that the proposed method is able to link a restricted set of user profiles across different SNs. In other words, we verify whether two sets of images from different user profiles on different SNs are linked, that is *inter-layer UPL*. The strengths of our method include the possibility to exploit images from different SNs, not only the "original images", but also the robustness in spite of the fact that some SNs degrade the resolution of the images more than others. We consider all the different combinations of the selected SNs for each dataset, as shown in Figure 2. The results for all the possible pairs of SNs are presented in Tables 8 and 9.

It is worth mentioning that the images in $\mathcal{D}_L$ used for experiments of *inter-layer UPL* on different SNs are not from the same scenes, making a more similar real-life situation. Among the results in Table 8, using *Google Currents* images to classify the images on the other SN datasets, i.e., $\mathcal{D}_L^W$, $\mathcal{D}_L^{FH}$, and $\mathcal{D}_L^T$ produce the highest values of $\mathcal{SE}$, $\mathcal{SP}$, $\mathcal{ARI}$, $\mathcal{F}$, and $\mathcal{P}$, as shown in the first rows of Table 8. For $\mathcal{D}_V$, using images in $\mathcal{D}_V^W$ to classify the images in the other datasets, i.e., $\mathcal{D}_L^{FH}$ and $\mathcal{D}_L^{FL}$ concluded the best results. It is interesting that the classification of the images in $\mathcal{D}_L^{FL}$ in inter-layer UPL compared with the classification of the images in intra-layer UPL generates better results. Given the results, it is proven that the proposed methods are reliable enough to match user profiles on the selected SNs.

Table 8. Results (%) of *inter-layer UPL* on $\mathcal{D}_L$.

Dataset	$\mathcal{SE}$	$\mathcal{SP}$	$\mathcal{ARI}$	$\mathcal{F}$	$\mathcal{P}$
$\mathcal{D}_L^W - \mathcal{D}_L^G$	0.90	0.99	0.87	0.88	0.96
$\mathcal{D}_L^{FH} - \mathcal{D}_L^G$	0.90	0.99	0.87	0.87	0.95
$\mathcal{D}_L^T - \mathcal{D}_L^G$	0.92	0.99	0.90	0.91	0.96
$\mathcal{D}_L^G - \mathcal{D}_L^W$	0.91	0.99	0.90	0.90	0.96
$\mathcal{D}_L^{FH} - \mathcal{D}_L^W$	0.86	0.99	0.83	0.83	0.94
$\mathcal{D}_L^T - \mathcal{D}_L^W$	0.90	0.99	0.88	0.87	0.95
$\mathcal{D}_L^G - \mathcal{D}_L^{FH}$	0.90	0.99	0.88	0.88	0.95
$\mathcal{D}_L^W - \mathcal{D}_L^{FH}$	0.86	0.98	0.82	0.83	0.94
$\mathcal{D}_L^T - \mathcal{D}_L^{FH}$	0.87	0.99	0.84	0.85	0.93
$\mathcal{D}_L^G - \mathcal{D}_L^T$	0.90	0.99	0.88	0.90	0.95
$\mathcal{D}_L^W - \mathcal{D}_L^T$	0.87	0.98	0.85	0.85	0.94
$\mathcal{D}_L^{FH} - \mathcal{D}_L^T$	0.87	0.98	0.85	0.86	0.94

Table 9. Results (%) of *inter-layer UPL* on $\mathcal{D}_V$.

Dataset	$\mathcal{SE}$	$\mathcal{SP}$	$\mathcal{ARI}$	$\mathcal{F}$	$\mathcal{P}$
$\mathcal{D}_V^{FH} - \mathcal{D}_V^W$	0.80	0.99	0.78	0.79	0.90
$\mathcal{D}_V^{FL} - \mathcal{D}_V^W$	0.80	0.99	0.78	0.78	0.88
$\mathcal{D}_V^W - \mathcal{D}_V^{FH}$	0.78	0.99	0.76	0.77	0.87
$\mathcal{D}_V^{FL} - \mathcal{D}_V^{FH}$	0.77	0.99	0.76	0.76	0.87
$\mathcal{D}_V^W - \mathcal{D}_V^{FL}$	0.61	0.99	0.58	0.59	0.72
$\mathcal{D}_V^{FH} - \mathcal{D}_V^{FL}$	0.61	0.99	0.59	0.60	0.73

5. Discussion

We have presented *smartphone identification* (SI) and *user profile linking* (UPL). Analyzing a huge number of images on all SN platforms is an unfeasible task. In addition, the digital investigation is operated on a restricted set of devices, suspects' profiles, and a given set of investigated images. Hence, we considered a scenario in which the number of smartphones has to be provided. Although in some applications it is not and clustering is used instead [5,23], applying classification is preferable which provides more accurate results compared with clustering.

Based on our work, it can be implied that despite the advances in deep learning techniques in classification with different CNN models, traditional techniques like k-medoids can still achieve high performing smartphone image classification tasks. K-medoids only needs one parameter to be set that is the number of smartphones in our application, while for CNN models lots of parameters have to be set which makes the classification more challenging and computationally expensive.

An important outcome of our work is presenting the *inter-layer UPL* task, which is more desirable in digital investigations as it links user profiles on different SNs. The proposed methods in the combination of the other types of information such as GPS, users' E-mail addresses, and login information can also help for user profile linking.

6. Conclusions

In this paper, we have compared different classification methods to achieve SI and UPL. The methods can help forensic investigators to find significant information from digital crimes when a set of images captured by a specific number of smartphones and shared on a set of investigated user profiles are provided. We have evaluated our methods on different datasets, i.e., our dataset and VISON dataset. The obtained results show that with an acceptable error margin, k-medoids achieves the best results compared with k-means, hierarchical approaches, and different models of convolutional neural network (CNN) in the classification of the images. In particular, the results indicate that even in the worst case k-medoids can provide the values of F1-measure 75% and 77%, for SI and UPL tasks, respectively. The results confirm the effectiveness of the methods, even with the same models of smartphones. The methods are applicable to images compressed on SNs, and there is no need to hack the user's smartphone for fingerprinting. An important outcome of our work is presenting the *inter-layer UPL* task, which is more desirable in digital investigations because it links user profiles on different SNs. The methods will become even more powerful when considering other types of information such as GPS, users' E-mail addresses, and login information, to name a few. Through the proposed methods, the number of smartphones under investigation has to be provided. However, in our future work, we plan to present an algorithm to classify all shared images on the suspect's profile, without prior knowledge of the source cameras. In addition, the relationship between the two parameters of the number of smartphones and the number of images needed per smartphone can be investigated to handle the uncertainty of these two parameters.

Author Contributions: Conceptualization, F.B. and R.R.; methodology, F.B. and R.R.; software, R.R.; validation, R.R., F.B. and D.M.; investigation, R.R.; data curation, F.B.; writing—original draft preparation, R.R.; writing—review and editing, R.R. and F.B.; supervision, D.M. All authors have read and agreed to the published version of the manuscript.

Funding: This research received no external funding.

Institutional Review Board Statement: Not applicable.

Informed Consent Statement: Not applicable.

Data Availability Statement: The dataset is available from: http://smartdata.cs.unibo.it/datasets#images, accessed on 10 February 2021.

Conflicts of Interest: The authors declare no conflict of interest.

References

1. Mander, J. *GWI Social Summary*; GlobalWebIndex: London, UK, 2017.
2. Norouzizadeh Dezfouli, F.; Dehghantanha, A.; Eterovic-Soric, B.; Choo, K.K.R. Investigating Social Networking applications on smartphones detecting Facebook, Twitter, LinkedIn and Google+ artefacts on Android and iOS platforms. *Aust. J. Forensic Sci.* **2016**, *48*, 469–488. [CrossRef]
3. Liu, Q.; Li, X.; Chen, L.; Cho, H.; Cooper, P.; Chen, Z.; Qiao, M.; Sung, A. Identification of smartphone-image source and manipulation. *Adv. Res. Appl. Artif. Intell.* **2012**, *7345*, 262–271.
4. Huang, N.; He, J.; Zhu, N.; Xuan, X.; Liu, G.; Chang, C. Identification of the source camera of images based on convolutional neural network. *Digit. Investig.* **2018**, *26*, 72–80. [CrossRef]
5. Rouhi, R.; Bertini, F.; Montesi, D.; Lin, X.; Quan, Y.; Li, C.T. Hybrid clustering of shared images on social networks for digital forensics. *IEEE Access* **2019**, *7*, 87288–87302. [CrossRef]
6. Van Lanh, T.; Chong, K.S.; Emmanuel, S.; Kankanhalli, M.S. A survey on digital camera image forensic methods. In Proceedings of the 2007 IEEE International Conference on Multimedia and Expo, Beijing, China, 2–5 July 2007; pp. 16–19.
7. Lin, X.; Li, C.T. Preprocessing reference sensor pattern noise via spectrum equalization. *IEEE Trans. Inf. Forensics Secur.* **2016**, *11*, 126–140. [CrossRef]
8. Taspinar, S.; Mohanty, M.; Memon, N. PRNU-Based Camera Attribution From Multiple Seam-Carved Images. *IEEE Trans. Inf. Forensics Secur.* **2017**, *12*, 3065–3080. [CrossRef]
9. Lukáš, J.; Fridrich, J.; Goljan, M. Digital camera identification from sensor pattern noise. *IEEE Trans. Inf. Forensics Secur.* **2006**, *1*, 205–214. [CrossRef]
10. Chen, Y.; Thing, V.L. A study on the photo response non-uniformity noise pattern based image forensics in real-world applications. In Proceedings of the International Conference on Image Processing, Computer Vision, and Pattern Recognition (IPCV). The Steering Committee of The World Congress in Computer Science, Computer Engineering and Applied Computing (WorldComp), Las Vegas, NV, USA, 16–19 July 2012; p. 1.
11. Park, H.S.; Jun, C.H. A simple and fast algorithm for K-medoids clustering. *Expert Syst. Appl.* **2009**, *36*, 3336–3341. [CrossRef]
12. Shullani, D.; Fontani, M.; Iuliani, M.; Al Shaya, O.; Piva, A. VISION: A video and image dataset for source identification. *EURASIP J. Inf. Secur.* **2017**, *2017*, 15. [CrossRef]
13. Dey, S.; Roy, N.; Xu, W.; Choudhury, R.R.; Nelakuditi, S. *AccelPrint: Imperfections of Accelerometers Make Smartphones Trackable*; NDSS: San Diego, CA, USA, 2014.
14. Willers, O.; Huth, C.; Guajardo, J.; Seidel, H. MEMS-based Gyroscopes as Physical Unclonable Functions. *IACR Cryptol. Eprint Arch.* **2016**, *2016*, 261.
15. Jin, R.; Shi, L.; Zeng, K.; Pande, A.; Mohapatra, P. Magpairing: Pairing smartphones in close proximity using magnetometers. *IEEE Trans. Inf. Forensics Secur.* **2016**, *11*, 1306–1320. [CrossRef]
16. Amerini, I.; Becarelli, R.; Caldelli, R.; Melani, A.; Niccolai, M. Smartphone Fingerprinting Combining Features of On-Board Sensors. *IEEE Trans. Inf. Forensics Secur.* **2017**, *12*, 2457–2466. [CrossRef]
17. Alles, E.J.; Geradts, Z.J.; Veenman, C.J. Source camera identification for low resolution heavily compressed images. In Proceedings of the 2008 ICCSA'08, International Conference on Computational Sciences and Its Applications, Perugia, Italy, 30 June–3 July 2008; pp. 557–567.
18. Das, A.; Borisov, N.; Caesar, M. Do you hear what i hear?: Fingerprinting smart devices through embedded acoustic components. In Proceedings of the 2014 ACM SIGSAC Conference on Computer and Communications Security, Scottsdale, AZ, USA, 3–7 November 2014; pp. 441–452.
19. Cortiana, A.; Conotter, V.; Boato, G.; De Natale, F.G. Performance comparison of denoising filters for source camera identification. In Proceedings of the Media Forensics and Security, San Francisco Airport, CA, USA, 24–26 January 2011; p. 788007.
20. Li, C.T.; Lin, X. A fast source-oriented image clustering method for digital forensics. *EURASIP J. Image Video Process.* **2017**, *2017*, 69. [CrossRef]

21. Caldelli, R.; Amerini, I.; Picchioni, F.; Innocenti, M. Fast image clustering of unknown source images. In Proceedings of the 2010 IEEE International Workshop on Information Forensics and Security, Seattle, WA, USA, 12–15 December 2010; pp. 1–5.
22. Villalba, L.J.G.; Orozco, A.L.S.; Corripio, J.R. Smartphone image clustering. *Expert Syst. Appl.* **2015**, *42*, 1927–1940. [CrossRef]
23. Lin, X.; Li, C.T. Large-scale image clustering based on camera fingerprints. *IEEE Trans. Inf. Forensics Secur.* **2017**, *12*, 793–808. [CrossRef]
24. Marra, F.; Poggi, G.; Sansone, C.; Verdoliva, L. Blind PRNU-based image clustering for source identification. *IEEE Trans. Inf. Forensics Secur.* **2017**, *12*, 2197–2211. [CrossRef]
25. Amerini, I.; Caldelli, R.; Del Mastio, A.; Di Fuccia, A.; Molinari, C.; Rizzo, A.P. Dealing with video source identification in social networks. *Signal Process. Image Commun.* **2017**, *57*, 1–7. [CrossRef]
26. Al Mutawa, N.; Baggili, I.; Marrington, A. Forensic analysis of social networking applications on mobile devices. *Digit. Investig.* **2012**, *9*, S24–S33. [CrossRef]
27. Jamjuntra, L.; Chartsuwan, P.; Wonglimsamut, P.; Porkaew, K.; Supasitthimethee, U. Social network user identification. In Proceedings of the 2017 9th International Conference on Knowledge and Smart Technology (KST), Chonburi, Thailand, 1–4 February 2017; pp. 132–137.
28. Winkler, W.E. *String Comparator Metrics and Enhanced Decision Rules in the Fellegi-Sunter Model of Record Linkage*; Education Resources Information Center-Institute of Education Sciences: Washington, DC, USA, 1990.
29. Iofciu, T.; Fankhauser, P.; Abel, F.; Bischoff, K. Identifying users across social tagging systems. In Proceedings of the Fifth International AAAI Conference on Weblogs and Social Media, Barcelona, Catalonia, Spain, 17–21 July 2011.
30. Bartunov, S.; Korshunov, A.; Park, S.T.; Ryu, W.; Lee, H. Joint link-attribute user identity resolution in online social networks. In Proceedings of the 6th International Conference on Knowledge Discovery and Data Mining, Workshop on Social Network Mining and Analysis, Beijing, China, 12–16 August 2012.
31. Raad, E.; Chbeir, R.; Dipanda, A. User profile matching in social networks. In Proceedings of the 2010 13th International Conference on Network-Based Information Systems, Takayama, Japan, 14–16 September 2010; pp. 297–304.
32. Gupta, S.; Rogers, M. *Using Computer Behavior Profiles to Differentiate between Users in a Digital Investigation*; Annual ADFSL Conference on Digital Forensics, Security and Law: Daytona Beach, FL, USA, 24–26 May 2016; pp. 37–46.
33. Zafarani, R.; Tang, L.; Liu, H. User identification across social media. *ACM Trans. Knowl. Discov. Data TKDD* **2015**, *10*, 16. [CrossRef]
34. Naini, F.M.; Unnikrishnan, J.; Thiran, P.; Vetterli, M. Where You Are Is Who You Are: User Identification by Matching Statistics. *IEEE Trans. Inf. Forensics Secur.* **2016**, *11*, 358–372. [CrossRef]
35. Agreste, S.; De Meo, P.; Ferrara, E.; Piccolo, S.; Provetti, A. Trust networks: Topology, dynamics, and measurements. *IEEE Internet Comput.* **2015**, *19*, 26–35. [CrossRef]
36. Shu, K.; Wang, S.; Tang, J.; Zafarani, R.; Liu, H. User identity linkage across online social networks: A review. *ACM Sigkdd Explor. Newsl.* **2017**, *18*, 5–17. [CrossRef]
37. Bertini, F.; Sharma, R.; Iannì, A.; Montesi, D. Smartphone Verification and User Profiles Linking Across Social Networks by Camera Fingerprinting. In Proceedings of the International Conference on Digital Forensics and Cyber Crime, Seoul, Republic of Korea, 6–8 October 2015; pp. 176–186.
38. Rouhi, R.; Bertini, F.; Montesi, D. A Cluster-based Approach of Smartphone Camera Fingerprint for User Profiles Resolution within Social Network. In Proceedings of the 22nd International Database Engineering & Applications Symposium, Villa San Giovanni, Italy, 18–20 June 2018; pp. 287–291.
39. Rouhi, R.; Bertini, F.; Montesi, D.; Li, C.T. Social Network Forensics through Smartphones and Shared Images. In Proceedings of the 2019 7th International Workshop on Biometrics and Forensics (IWBF), Cancun, Mexico, 2–3 May 2019; pp. 1–6.
40. Bertini, F.; Sharma, R.; Iannì, A.; Montesi, D. Profile resolution across multilayer networks through smartphone camera fingerprint. In Proceedings of the 19th International Database Engineering & Applications Symposium, Yokohama, Japan, 13–15 July 2015; pp. 23–32.
41. Lukáš, J.; Fridrich, J.; Goljan, M. Determining digital image origin using sensor imperfections. In Proceedings of the SPIE Electronic Imaging, Image and Video Communication and Processing, San Jose, CA, USA, 16–20 January 2005; Volume 5685, pp. 249–260.
42. Bloy, G.J. Blind camera fingerprinting and image clustering. *IEEE Trans. Pattern Anal. Mach. Intell.* **2008**, *30*, 532–534. [CrossRef]
43. Dabov, K.; Foi, A.; Katkovnik, V.; Egiazarian, K. Image denoising by sparse 3-D transform-domain collaborative filtering. *IEEE Trans. Image Process.* **2007**, *16*, 2080–2095. [CrossRef] [PubMed]
44. Chierchia, G.; Parrilli, S.; Poggi, G.; Sansone, C.; Verdoliva, L. On the influence of denoising in PRNU based forgery detection. In Proceedings of the 2nd ACM workshop on Multimedia in Forensics, Security and Intelligence, Firenze, Italy, 29 October 2010; pp. 117–122.
45. JEITA. Exchangeable Image File Format for Digital Still Cameras: Exif Version 2.2. 2002. Available online: http://www.exif.org/Exif2-2.PDF (accessed on 10 February 2021).
46. Carlson, R.E.; Fritsch, F.N. An algorithm for monotone piecewise bicubic interpolation. *SIAM J. Numer. Anal.* **1989**, *26*, 230–238. [CrossRef]

47. Szegedy, C.; Liu, W.; Jia, Y.; Sermanet, P.; Reed, S.; Anguelov, D.; Erhan, D.; Vanhoucke, V.; Rabinovich, A. Going deeper with convolutions. In Proceedings of the IEEE Conference on Computer Vision and Pattern Recognition, Boston, MA, USA, 7–12 June 2015; pp. 1–9.
48. Iandola, F.N.; Han, S.; Moskewicz, M.W.; Ashraf, K.; Dally, W.J.; Keutzer, K. SqueezeNet: AlexNet-level accuracy with $50\times$ fewer parameters and <0.5 MB model size. *arXiv* **2016**, arXiv:1602.07360.
49. Huang, G.; Liu, Z.; Van Der Maaten, L.; Weinberger, K.Q. Densely connected convolutional networks. In Proceedings of the IEEE Conference on Computer Vision and Pattern Recognition, Honolulu, HI, USA, 21–26 July 2017; pp. 4700–4708.
50. Sandler, M.; Howard, A.; Zhu, M.; Zhmoginov, A.; Chen, L.C. Mobilenetv2: Inverted residuals and linear bottlenecks. In Proceedings of the IEEE Conference on Computer Vision and Pattern Recognition, Salt Lake City, UT, USA, 18–22 June 2018; pp. 4510–4520.
51. Fahad, A.; Alshatri, N.; Tari, Z.; Alamri, A.; Khalil, I.; Zomaya, A.Y.; Foufou, S.; Bouras, A. A survey of clustering algorithms for big data: Taxonomy and empirical analysis. *IEEE Trans. Emerg. Top. Comput.* **2014**, *2*, 267–279. [CrossRef]
52. Shirkhorshidi, A.S.; Aghabozorgi, S.; Wah, T.Y.; Herawan, T. Big data clustering: A review. In Proceedings of the International Conference on Computational Science and Its Applications, Guimarães, Portugal, 30 June–3 July 2014; pp. 707–720.
53. Lloyd, S. Least squares quantization in PCM. *IEEE Trans. Inf. Theory* **1982**, *28*, 129–137. [CrossRef]
54. MacQueen, J. Some methods for classification and analysis of multivariate observations. In Proceedings of the fifth Berkeley symposium on mathematical statistics and probability, Oakland, CA, USA, 21 June–18 July 1967; Volume 1: Statistics, pp. 281–297.
55. Kaufman, L.; Rousseeuw, P.J. *Finding Groups in Data: An Introduction to Cluster Analysis*; John Wiley & Sons: Hoboken, NJ, USA, 2009; Volume 344.
56. Ertöz, L.; Steinbach, M.; Kumar, V. Finding clusters of different sizes, shapes, and densities in noisy, high dimensional data. In Proceedings of the 2003 SIAM International Conference on Data Mining, San Francisco, CA, USA, 1–3 May 2003; pp. 47–58.
57. Chauhan, S.; Dhingra, S. Pattern recognition system using MLP neural networks. *Pattern Recognit.* **2012**, *4*, 43–46. [CrossRef]
58. Abiodun, O.I.; Jantan, A.; Omolara, A.E.; Dada, K.V.; Mohamed, N.A.; Arshad, H. State-of-the-art in artificial neural network applications: A survey. *Heliyon* **2018**, *4*, e00938. [CrossRef]
59. Freeman, J.A.; Skapura, D.M. *Algorithms, Applications, and Programming Techniques*; Addison-Wesley Publishing Company: Boston, MA, USA, 1991.
60. Haykin, S. *Neural Networks: A Comprehensive Foundation*; Prentice Hall PTR: New York, NY, USA, 1994.
61. Yegnanarayana, B. *Artificial Neural Networks*; PHI Learning Pvt. Ltd.: Patparganj, India, 2009.
62. Refaeilzadeh, P.; Tang, L.; Liu, H. *Cross Validation, Encyclopedia of Database Systems (EDBS)*; Springer: New York, NY, USA, 2009; p. 6.
63. Hubert, L.; Arabie, P. Comparing partitions. *J. Classif.* **1985**, *2*, 193–218. [CrossRef]

Article

End-to-End Deep One-Class Learning for Anomaly Detection in UAV Video Stream

Slim Hamdi [1,2,*], Samir Bouindour [1], Hichem Snoussi [1], Tian Wang [3] and Mohamed Abid [2]

1. ICD-LM2S, CNRS, University of Technology of Troyes, 10000 Troyes, France; samir.bouindour@yahoo.fr (S.B.); hichem.snoussi@utt.fr (H.S.)
2. CES Laboratory, ENIS National Engineering School, University of Sfax, Sfax 3038, Tunisia; mohamed.abid_ces@yahoo.fr
3. School of Automation Science and Electrical Engineering, Beihang University, Beijing 100191, China; wangtian@buaa.edu.cn
* Correspondence: slim.hamdi@utt.fr

Abstract: In recent years, the use of drones for surveillance tasks has been on the rise worldwide. However, in the context of anomaly detection, only normal events are available for the learning process. Therefore, the implementation of a generative learning method in an unsupervised mode to solve this problem becomes fundamental. In this context, we propose a new end-to-end architecture capable of generating optical flow images from original UAV images and extracting compact spatio-temporal characteristics for anomaly detection purposes. It is designed with a custom loss function as a sum of three terms, the reconstruction loss (R_l), the generation loss (G_l) and the compactness loss (C_l) to ensure an efficient classification of the "deep-one" class. In addition, we propose to minimize the effect of UAV motion in video processing by applying background subtraction on optical flow images. We tested our method on very complex datasets called the mini-drone video dataset, and obtained results surpassing existing techniques' performances with an AUC of 85.3.

Keywords: anomaly detection; UAV videos; deep one-class

1. Introduction

The use of drones is booming around the world with a large variety of potential applications: wireless acoustic networking for amateur drone surveillance [1], updating of UAV networking using the software-defined radios (SDR) and software-defined networking (SDN) [2], the multi-agent reinforcement learning (MARL) framework [3] and malicious Wi-Fi hotspots detection [4]. In particular, the use of the UAV camera has become very important in the field of detecting abnormal behaviour in video footage. This importance stems from the fact that not only can a UAV monitor large and dangerous areas, but it is also cost-effective and can replace an entire installation of fixed cameras [5]. Moreover, processing video sequences from UAV for anomaly detection is a complex task compared to its counterpart with fixed cameras for two reasons: (a) Lack of video datasets from UAV in real conditions, and (b) dynamic, variable brightness and large-scale backgrounds. A video-drone protection system is a closed-circuit television CCTV system that describes a whole range of video surveillance technologies. Many factors can significantly reduce the effectiveness of CCTV systems, such as fatigue and lassitude caused by prolonged viewing of many surveillance videos. A possible solution to this problem would be the use of intelligent video surveillance systems. These systems must be capable of analysing and modelling the normal behaviour of a monitored scene and detecting any abnormal behaviour that could represent a security risk. In recent years, considerable technological advances in the fields of machine learning and computer vision have made it possible to process CCTV systems. Some of these are classics of machine learning: image classification [6], facial recognition [7], human pose estimation [8], natural language processing [9], automatic voice recognition [10], and even more atypical tasks; machine translation systems [11], lip reading [12] and automatic software code generation [13]. Moreover, Deep Learning (DL) is a sub-domain of Machine Learning (ML), it aims to learn high-level abstractions in data using multi-level architectures. These different levels are obtained by stacking several non-linear transformation modules. Each module transforms the data at a different level until a suitable representation is obtained to perform the target task. Deep learning has made it possible to go beyond the traditional model in certain application cases and to design efficient pattern recognition systems without in-depth expertise on the target elements. In fact, the most effective deep-learning methods are based on supervised learning, using large, labelled databases containing samples from different classes. To take advantage of these learning materials in an intelligent monitoring system, a large amount of training data representative of normal and abnormal events is required. Abnormal events are the rare events that does not appear redundantly at the scene. Thus, there are many barriers to the creation of such databases—for example, we can cite the following:

- The contextual aspect of the event. Indeed, an event is closely linked to its context, an abnormal event in one scene can be normal in another. This point makes it almost impossible to design common databases that can be used uniformly for different scenes.
- Risks and variability to reproduce some abnormal events make it impossible to identify and generate enough training samples.

Abnormal video events have been called by many names in the literature, such as abnormality, irregular behaviour, unusual behaviour, or abnormal behaviour. These different names will be used alternately without worrying about technical inconsistency. The detection of abnormal video events is also characterised by a variety of strategies for processing training data. The first approach is to carry out the training only on normal data and to consider any type of event outside the training phase as abnormal. Another approach, in contrast to the first, is to use only abnormal events for training [14]. This approach can be effective in identifying a certain type of abnormal events, but presents a high risk of missing abnormal events that are different from those that have been trained. Another approach is based on the use of data labelled in two different classes, normal and abnormal [15]. Other work uses more advanced classified and labelled data where each class represents a specific type of event [13]. Approaches that use abnormal events as learning data often have limitations. Some abnormal events are impossible to reproduce. The variability of abnormal events greatly complicates the learning task and can have a negative effect on modelling. Other approaches are based on clustering methods with the usage of unlabelled databases containing both normal and abnormal data [16]. It is assumed that normal events are those that occur frequently, and abnormal events are those that occur rarely. The advantage of this approach is that it does not require any labelling of training data, but its effectiveness is compromised by the assumption that all rare events are abnormal because, obviously, a rare event is not necessarily abnormal. Despite the different strategies for training data on the detection of abnormal events [15,17–19], the first approach of using only normal data during training has become the norm. In our work, we adopt this approach and we propose a new architecture capable of detecting abnormal event by training only with normal samples. The rest of the paper is organized as follows: Section 2 briefly reviews related literature of this research field. Section 3 introduces the proposed method. Experimental results are shown and discussed in Section 4. Section 5 concludes this paper and addresses some potential future studies.

2. Related Work

For many years, the development of a pattern recognition system based on the traditional model required expertise and in-depth knowledge to extract from the raw data appropriate representations that could be used to detect, identify or classify items among the input data. These methods require a priori knowledge to construct a feature extractor adapted to the targeted events and the scene being monitored. These constraints have led to the emergence of abnormal event detection methods based on learning representations and, more precisely, on deep learning. Representation learning or feature learning is a set of techniques allowing to automate the feature extraction step. These methods make it possible to define, by learning, the appropriate transformations to be applied to the input data in order to obtain representations to perform a targeted task, such as the recognition of an action, the classification of an image, the estimation of a human pose, semantic segmentation, and so forth [6,9,20,21].

2.1. Transfer Learning

The CNN is a type of artificial neural network inspired from the animal visual cortex. It consists of several layers that process data in a hierarchical pattern. It has been shown that a CNN trained to perform a target task can provide generic and robust functionality that can be used to perform another computer vision task different from the one for which it has been specifically trained. In [22], representations extracted with OverFeat, a CNN trained solely in object classification, are exploited by a linear SVM or Euclidean standard for different tasks (scene classification, detailed classification, attribute detection, visual instance retrieval). The results provide tangible evidence of the CNN's ability to provide generic and robust functionalities that can be used for different computer vision tasks. This principle has been applied in many works on abnormal event detection. In [23], a 2D CNN pre-formed from image classification databases is modified to extract representations of different regions from input images. An OC-SVM is then used to detect which of these regions have abnormal events. In [24], a pre-formed CNN is combined with a scattered self-coder that can be formed to provide a two-level feature extractor. At the output of the CNN, a first Gaussian classifier is used to classify regions of the image as normal, abnormal, or suspect. Representations of suspect regions are then transformed by the auto-coder to obtain more discriminating representations.

Methods based on transfer learning do not require a labelled database for feature extraction, and their results in terms of detection and localisation are very promising. However, the dependence of these methods on pre-trained models imposes a certain rigidity which considerably reduces their prospects for potential improvements. This drawback has originated the emergence of approaches based on generative and deep one-class models.

2.2. Generative Models

In recent years, the use of Generative Adversarial Networks (GANs) in machine learning has increased considerably. GAN is an unsupervised learning algorithm proposed for the first time by [25]. It consists of two sub-networks, a generator and a competing discriminator. During the learning phase, the generator tries to generate convincing data to deceive the discriminator which, in turn, tries to detect whether the generated samples are real (regular) or fakes (irregular). In [18], spatio-temporal adversary networks (STAN) was proposed to meet the challenge of video anomaly detection. It is composed of two sub-networks, a generator composed of convolution layers, ConvLSTM [26] and deconvolution layers and a discriminator composed of 3D convolution layers. The detection of abnormal events can be done directly by the discriminator or generator. However, the best results in [18] were obtained by combining the decisions of the two networks. The author of [27] also proposed the use of GANs for the detection of abnormal events. A thresholding of the generation error of the two GANs is used in order to identify the image regions containing the abnormal events. The first GAN is trained to generate optical flow representations from images, and the second GAN is trained to generate images from optical flow representations. However, the error between the generated images and the real images is not sufficient to obtain convincing results.

2.3. One-Class Models

Abnormal event detection approaches based on reconstructive, predictive or generative models are generally based on the assumption that a model formed on normal images will not be able to reconstruct, predict or generate abnormal images. Therefore, a threshold of reconstruction, prediction or degeneration error is often used to detect abnormal events. However, in the case of video events, the different elements of normal and abnormal situations are often similar and it is usually their interactions or the context that defines the normality or abnormality of a situation. In this respect, recent work aimed at developing one-class networks has been proposed. The ref. [28] proposes Deep One-Class (DOC), a convolutional neural network that can be trained end-to-end, using only one-class learning examples. The network is obtained by replacing the softmax usually used in CNNs with an OC-SVM. Moreover, The authors define an objective function that allows the formation of not only the OC-SVM layer, but also of all the layers of the network that can be formed. In this way, the network is optimised to extract compact representations and define the appropriate hyperplane to isolate data representations from the target class. On the other hand, many works based on one-class neural networks have been proposed for the detection of anomalies [29,30]. These works require very little adaptation to be used in the context of detection of abnormal video events. The ref. [31] proposes the use of transfer learning for adapting pre-trained networks to perform anomaly detection. The authors assume that two important aspects, compactness and description of the extracted features, must be imperatively considered. The description provides descriptive features. However, the compactness is used in order to ensure that images of the same class are described by similar representations, so they are positioned compactly in the feature space. These two aspects can significantly contribute to a decrease in the intra-class distance and an increase in the inter-class distance. To obtain these two aspects, the authors propose two networks. After the learning, the two identical networks are capable of providing both descriptive and compact representations. These networks can be applied with a One-Class classifier to dissociate the elements of a target class from the outliers. However, these methods proposed to use extra data sets or optical flow samples for analysing motion, which make these methods depend on handcrafted features and on the quality of extra datasets. In this work, we propose to build an architecture capable of analysing motion from raw images without using extra datasets.

2.4. Motivation and Contributions

In recent years, state-of-the-art methods have been based principally on generative or deep one-class models to treat the problem of anomaly detection efficiently. However, no single model has been proposed before being aimed at bringing together the benefits of both models. For that reason, the originality of our work is to propose a new architecture bringing together the advantages of both generative and deep one-class models for anomaly detection purposes in a UAV video footage. Our motivation is to design this new architecture in order to achieve high performance and a minimum Equal Error Rate (EER), compared to existing methods. Moreover, for many existing methods, optical flow features are computed by a pre-processing task before starting the inference. In this work, we propose an architecture capable of generating optical flow features at the testing phase, meeting the real-time constraint. The purpose of our work is to efficiently address the problem of anomaly detection by drone cameras. This purpose is ensured by creating a new deep one-class architecture capable of compacting the features of a given class into a half-hyper sphere. This classification method can be useful for many anomaly detection problems in other domains.

The contributions of our paper are summarized as follows:

- We propose a new end-to-end unsupervised generative learning architecture for deep one-class classification in order to guarantee not only the compactness of the different characteristics of normal events (optical flow and original images), but also the ability to automatically generate optical flow images from the UAV original video during

the test phase, which makes the processing chain faster for abnormal event detection. We have trained our architecture with a custom loss function as a sum of three terms, the reconstruction loss (R_l), the generation loss (G_l) and the compactness loss (C_l) to ensure an efficient classification of normal/abnormal events.
- In addition, we have applied background subtraction on the UAV optical flow to minimise the effect of camera movement, and we have tested our method on complex and hard-to-reach datasets in terms of variety of content and conditions, such as mini-video datasets.

3. Proposed Method

In this section, we propose a new end-to-end unsupervised architecture (Figure 1) for anomaly detection in UAV video footages. It is trained with only consecutive normal RGB and optical flow frames. Our architecture is capable of building new optical flow representations of a UAV video from consecutive original frames. It is based on a mix of convolution and deconvolution layers capable not only of automatically generating optical flow images, but also of extracting compact features from the original and optical flow images during the test phase. Classical computation of optical flow is then avoided and replaced by a fast and efficient convolution/deconvolution-based neural network. The proposed procedure can produce optical flow representations of abnormal samples with higher optical flow error (OFE) generation than normal samples, intuitively by decreasing the intra-class distance of the normal class during the training phase, as in the following equation:

$$OFE = \frac{1}{n}\sum_{1}^{n}(\phi(i) - \hat{\phi}(i))^2, \qquad (1)$$

where $\phi(i)$ is the original optical flow and $\hat{\phi}(i)$ is the generated optical flow. Thanks to this architecture, our model is able to correctly represent shapes and motion in videos. The neural network is composed of eight convolution layers: a concatenation layer, to combine the feature maps of each of the four convolution layers, and eight deconvolution layers to reconstruct the input composed of the consecutive original images and to generate the consecutive optical flow images. The concatenation layer is our bottleneck layer. We called our architecture a CNN optical flow generator because of its ability to generate optical flow samples from original images. The hyper-parameters of our architecture are provided in the following Table 1.

Table 1. Our architecture hyperparameters.

Layer	Filters	Kernel (h,w,d)	Stride (h,w,d)
Conv1	64	[11,11,1]	[2,2,1]
Conv2	128	[3,3,1]	[1,1,1]
Conv3	256	[3,3,3]	[2,2,1]
Conv4	512	[3,3,1]	[2,2,1]
Conv5	64	[11,11,1]	[2,2,1]
Conv6	128	[3,3,1]	[1,1,1]
Conv7	256	[3,3,3]	[2,2,1]
Conv8	512	[3,3,1]	[2,2,1]
Concat	1024	—	—
Deconv1	512	[3,3,1]	[2,2,1]
Deconv2	256	[3,3,3]	[2,2,1]
Deconv3	128	[3,3,1]	[1,1,1]
Deconv4	1	[11,11,1]	[2,2,1]
Deconv5	512	[3,3,1]	[2,2,1]
Deconv6	256	[3,3,3]	[2,2,1]
Deconv7	128	[3,3,1]	[1,1,1]
Deconv8	1	[11,11,1]	[2,2,1]

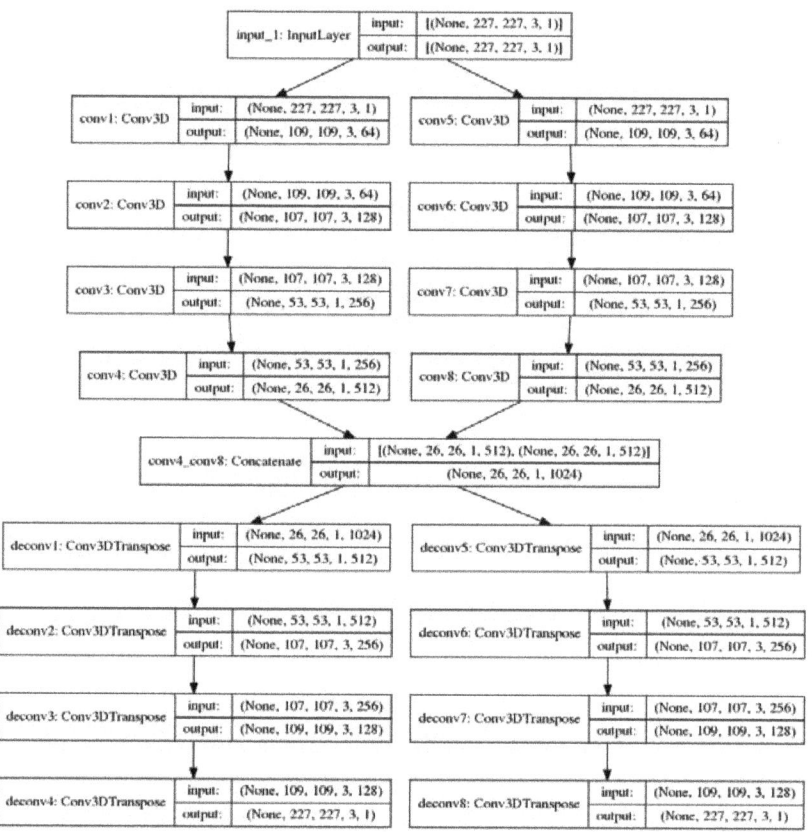

Figure 1. The proposed deep-learning architecture.

The Concat represents our concatenation layer; it does not need any filters or any strides as hyper-parameters, as it concatenates the outputs of the Conv4 and Conv8 layers. In the next section, we will discuss the proposed training strategy which is not limited to reconstruction error, but introduces a new concept of compactness. We will also detail the testing phase for our architecture during the inference.

3.1. Loss Function and Training Phase

We propose to train our architecture using only normal samples. We have used, as input volumes, three consecutive frames $F = \{F_t; F_{t-1}; F_{t-2}\}$ to describe not only the shapes, but also the motion encoded in these three frames. Only in the training, the frames and their corresponding optical flow representations are extracted from the raw videos and resized to 227 × 227. We scaled the pixels values in [1, −1]. In the testing phase, we used the same scaling values as in the training to ensure the condition of real-world applications. Our architecture was trained by the Adam optimizer with a learning rate equal to 0.00001. A hyperbolic tangent is used as the activation function of each convolution and deconvolution layer to ensure the symmetry of the reconstructed and the input video volume. The original aspect of our work is to design a custom loss function (L) as the sum of three terms, as given in Equation (2): a term related to compactness C_l, a term related to generation loss G_l and a term related to the reconstruction loss R_l. The aim of using those three loss components is to maximize the inter-class distance (between normal and abnormal samples) and to minimize the intra-class distance (between normal samples).

The objective of the C_l and G_l loss terms is to obtain features capable of generalization for normal samples and also of generating optical flow images with minimum OFE. Thus, those terms aim at maximizing the inter-class distance between normal and abnormal samples. The compactness loss allows to obtain compact features (both for shape and motion) of training data by minimizing their distance to a fixed point C_0. We have fixed the point C_0 at the maximum of our data range, which is a vector of ones. The overall loss L is then written as:

$$L = \frac{1}{n}(\sum_{i=1}^{n}(V - \hat{V})^2 + \sum_{i=1}^{n}(W - \hat{W})^2) + \alpha|M(x_i) - 1| \qquad (2)$$

$$L = R_l + G_l + \alpha C_l, \qquad (3)$$

where V represents the volume of the original image input, $\hat{V}$ is the corresponding shape-reconstructed volume, W is the optical flow volume, and $\hat{w}$ is its corresponding reconstructed volume. $M(X_i)$ is the mean value of features X_i at each patch in the Concat layer. α is a hyper-parameter between [0, 1] of our custom loss function, and it controls the influence of the compactness of our features. In practice, we fixed α to 0.1 to ensure the scale condition of other terms of L. It should be noted that when $\alpha = 0$, the model is trained without compactness loss and limited to reconstruction and generation loss. When $M(x_i)$ tends to 1, the features X_i tends to C_0. Then, we ensure that all normal features at the training are converging near the same point C_0 (see Figure 2).

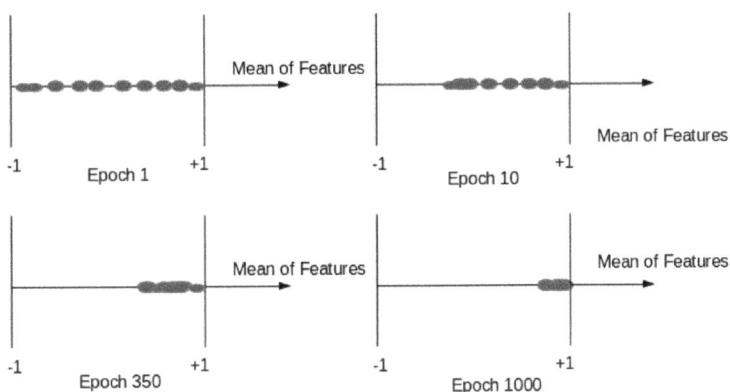

Figure 2. Average features during training.

3.2. Testing Phase

After training our architecture, we were able to obtain a model capable of extracting a robust spatio-temporal representation of each patch. Thanks to this architecture, each small region of the input video volume is represented by a 1024-vector of features capable of describing the shapes and motion contained in that region.

In the test phase, only the original images were used. Optical flow samples were generated by our architecture, which allows for fast implementation of the global detector. The compactness is used to constrain feature vectors inside a half-hypersphere (S) with centre C_0 and a small radius R, enhancing the performance of the classification procedure. For each new video volume, we extract the mean of the features $M'(x_i)$ at the Concat layers and compare its distance to C_0 to the radius R:

$$\begin{cases} \text{Normal if } (C_0 - M'(x_i)) \pm \varepsilon \leq R \\ \text{Abnormal if } (C_0 - M'(x_i)) \pm \varepsilon > R \end{cases} \qquad (4)$$

where ε defines the insensitivity zone.

4. Experimental Results

We have used different datasets to evaluate the proposed detection method. The model was trained with only normal events contained in datasets, and then it was tested within different abnormal events. The used datasets are listed as follows:

- Mini-Drone Video Dataset :
  Mini-Drone Video Dataset (MDVD) [32] is a dataset filmed by a drone of type Phantom 2 in a car park. It is mainly used for events identification. It is composed of 38 videos captured in high resolution, with a duration up to 24 s each. The videos in MDVD were divided into three categories: normal, suspicious, and abnormal, and they are defined by the actions of the persons involved in the videos. The normal case is defined by several events, such as people walking, getting in their cars, or parking correctly. The abnormal cases are represented by people fighting or stealing. Finally, for suspicious cases, nothing is wrong, but people do suspicious behavior which could distract the surveillance staff. In order to use the MDVD dataset in unsupervised mode for anomaly detection, we split this dataset into: 10 videos for the training containing only normal samples, and 10 videos for the test containing both abnormal and normal events.

- USCD Ped2 :
  UCSD Peds2 [33] is an anomaly detection dataset consisting of video footage of a crowded pedestrian walkway captured by a stationary camera. It contains both normal and abnormal events, like the walking movement of bikers, skaters, cyclists, and small carts. However, in the walkways, the motion of the pedestrian in an unexpected area is also considered as an anomalous event. It contains 16 training and 12 testing video samples, and provides frame-level ground truth, which helps us to evaluate the detection performance and to compare our method with other stat-of-the-art anomaly-detection methods.

- Brutal running dataset:
  We propose a new small dataset with 1000 samples (340 training samples and 660 samples for test) called the brutal running dataset captured by a Phantom 4 pro drone. The normal event consists of a girl walking outside, and the abnormal event occurs when she is running. This kind of anomaly is largely used in anomaly detection by fixed cameras.

4.1. Minimization of the Effect of UAV Motion on Optical Flow Images

Optical flow is the pattern of apparent motion of objects between two consecutive frames. It is a 2D vector field, where each vector is a displacement vector showing the movement of points from the first frame to the second. For training, we used the OpenCV Gunner Farneback algorithm to extract dense optical flows. We obtained a two-channel array with optical flow vectors (u,v). The Figure 3 shows same samples of optical flow calculated by Farneback's algorithm.

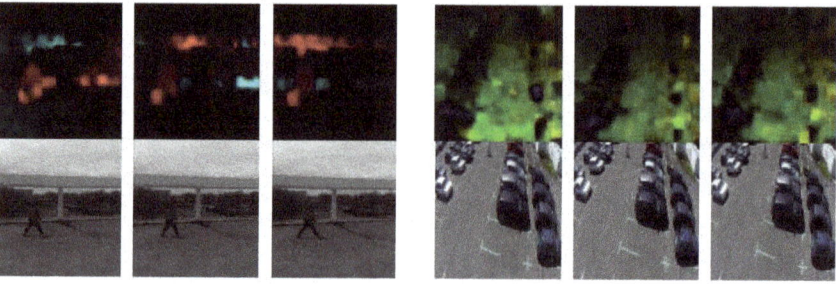

Figure 3. Optical flow samples of MDVD and other examples.

In order to denoise and minimize the effect of UAV motion on optical flow images, we propose to subtract the mean optical flow at the train and apply the same centering for the optical flow samples during testing.

Figures 4 and 5 show some examples of the optical flow of the Mini drone dataset and some other examples captured in a different scene. These figures prove that subtracted mean drone motion can minimize the drone motion effect on optical flow frames which become less noisy. We have used this version of optical flow to train our architecture.

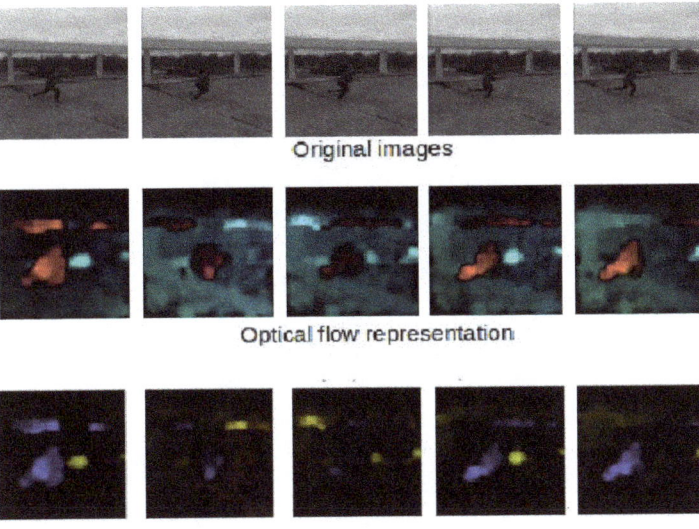

Figure 4. Subtraction of mean optical flow.

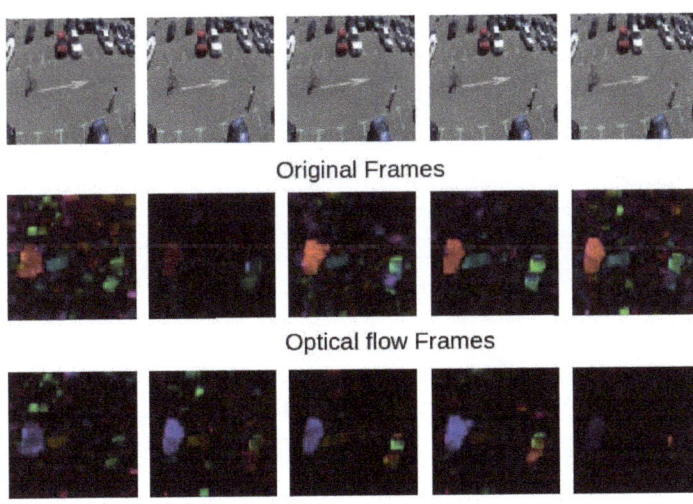

Figure 5. Subtraction of mean optical flow in the MDVD dataset.

4.1.1. Optical Flow Generating

Figure 6 shows the generated optical flow frames of both normal and abnormal samples of MDVD. It shows that our architecture can reproduce optical flow frames from original video frames. Then, at the testing phase (inference), it does not need a handcraft algorithm to extract optical flow. The proposed architecture is fed only with a raw video, directly ensuring the real-time implementation of the detection algorithm, even on constrained embedded processing units.

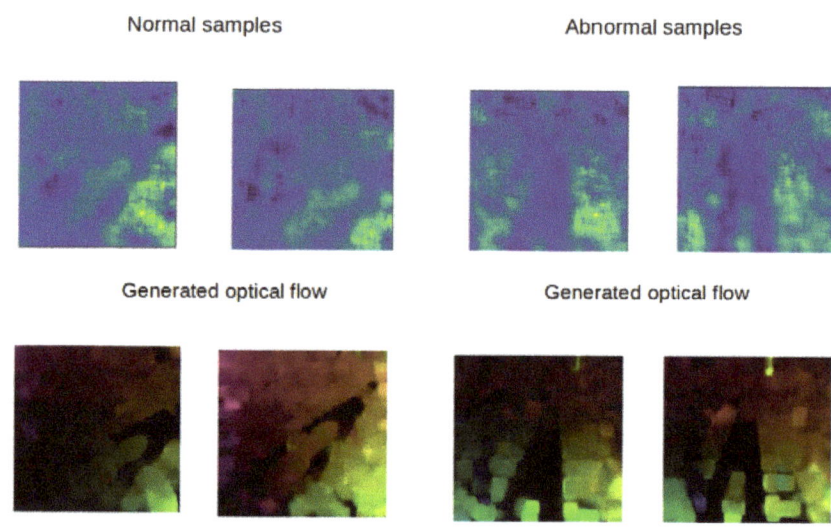

Figure 6. Samples of optical flow generated by our architecture.

4.1.2. Architecture Evaluation

We used Error Equal Rate (EER) and Area Under Curve ROC (AUC) as evaluation criteria. A smaller EER corresponds to better performance. As for the AUC, a bigger value corresponds to better performance. The Table 2 summarizes our results on MDVD, and a comparison was done with existing methods.

Table 2. EER and AUC for frame-level comparisons on MDVD.

Methods	EER	AUC
VGG+LSTM [5]	–	72.75
VGG [5]	–	50.12
Ours	19.85	85.3

Figure 7 illustrates algorithm results on MDVD, and proves that our method can localize anomalies: biker and fighting events. However, when the drone motion is fast, our system can give some localisation errors, but it still can dissociate between abnormal and normal events at frame level. Despite the difference between the movements and trajectories of the drone in the training phase and the testing phase, the results corroborate the effectiveness of the proposed architecture which works properly in detecting and localizing abnormal events.

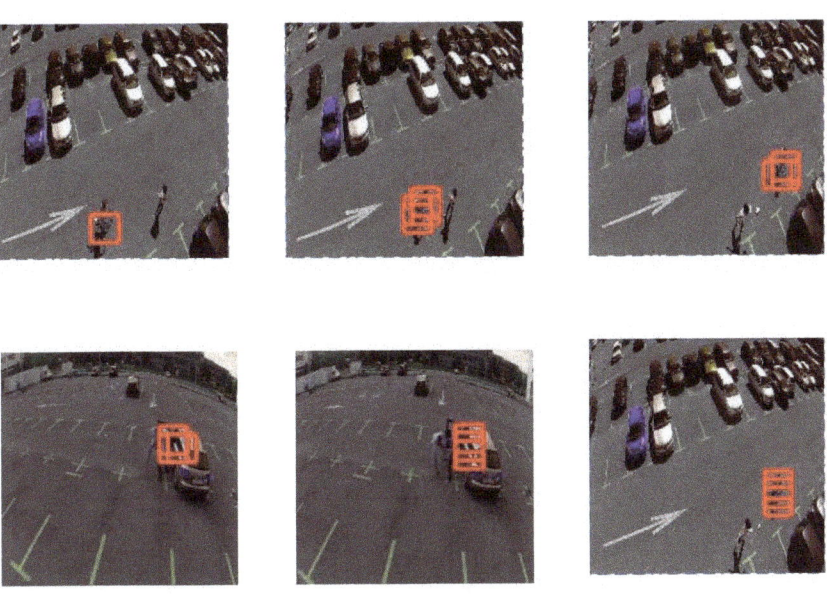

Figure 7. Our results on the MDVD dataset.

Figure 8 represents our results on the brutal running dataset. It shows that our method is capable of detecting abnormal brutal motion (running, in this case).

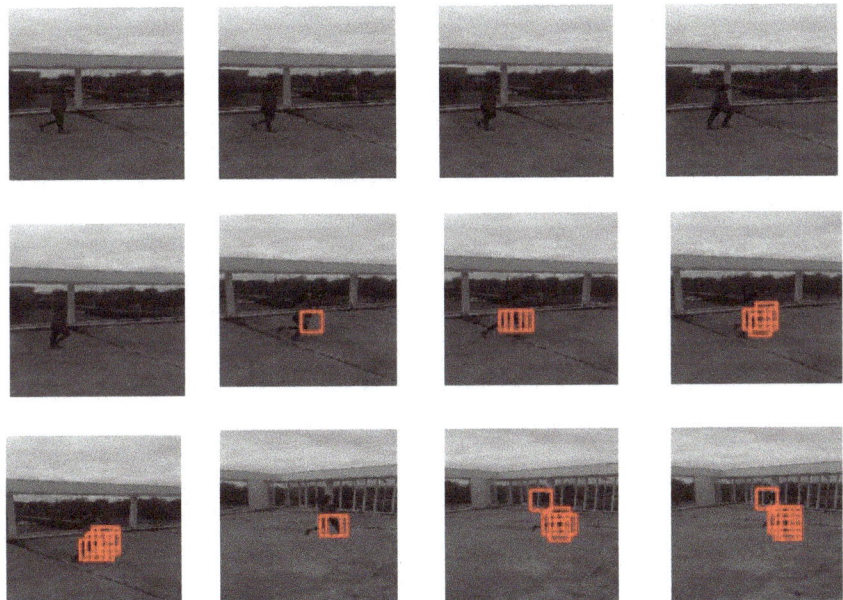

Figure 8. Our results on the brutal running dataset.

In order to further evaluate of the proposed method, we have tested on UCSD Ped2 datasets with fixed cameras and compared our results with state-of-the-art methods. Table 3 and Figure 9 report these comparative results, showing again the effectiveness of our method in video anomaly detection.

Table 3. EER and AUC for frame-level comparisons on the Ped2 dataset.

Methods	EER	AUC
Mehran. [34]	40	-
Kim. [35]	30.71	-
PCA [36]	29.20	73.98
CAE(FR) [37]	26.00	81.4
S. Hamdi [38]	14.50	-
Sabokrou [39]	8.2	-
ours	8.1	94.9

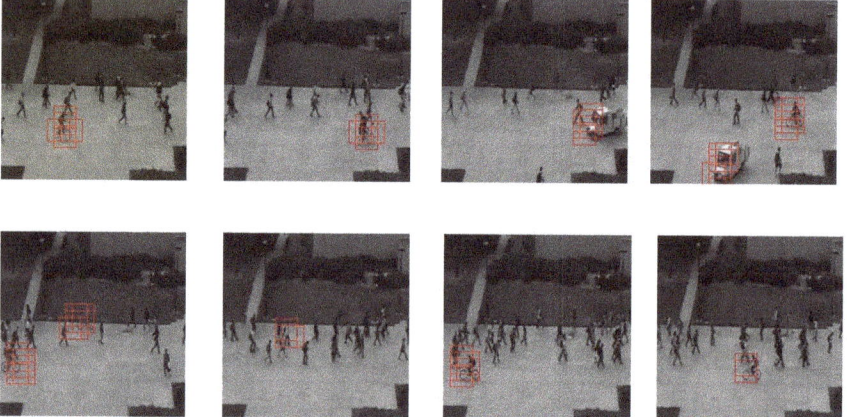

Figure 9. Ourresults on the Ped2 dataset.

4.1.3. Compactness Evaluation

In order to evaluate the advantages of compactness loss, we trained our model with and without this loss term. Table 4 shows the obtained results from MDVD using the Mahalanobis distance (Equation (5)):

$$D = (y_j - M) \times Q \times (y_j - M)' \quad \text{Mahalanobis distance} : \begin{cases} \text{Normal if} & D \leq \alpha \\ \text{Abnormal if} & D > \alpha \end{cases}, \quad (5)$$

where M is the mean and Q is the inverse of the covariance matrix of the training data X. If the distance exceeds a threshold α, the testing vector y_j is considered as an outlier, and the corresponding frame is labeled as abnormal. The results of Table 4 show that the compactness feature enhances the detection performances compared to the Mahalanobis classifier based on the extracted features from the Concat layer.

Figure 10 shows that the characteristics of the normal samples have an average very close to 1, but those of the abnormal samples are less close to 1. The confused samples are obtained when the anomalies start to appear. This illustrates the capacity of the algorithm to detect the abnormal events in a timely manner.

Table 4. Compactness loss importance.

	EER	AUC
our (without compactness)	23	78.2
our (with compactness)	19.85	85.3

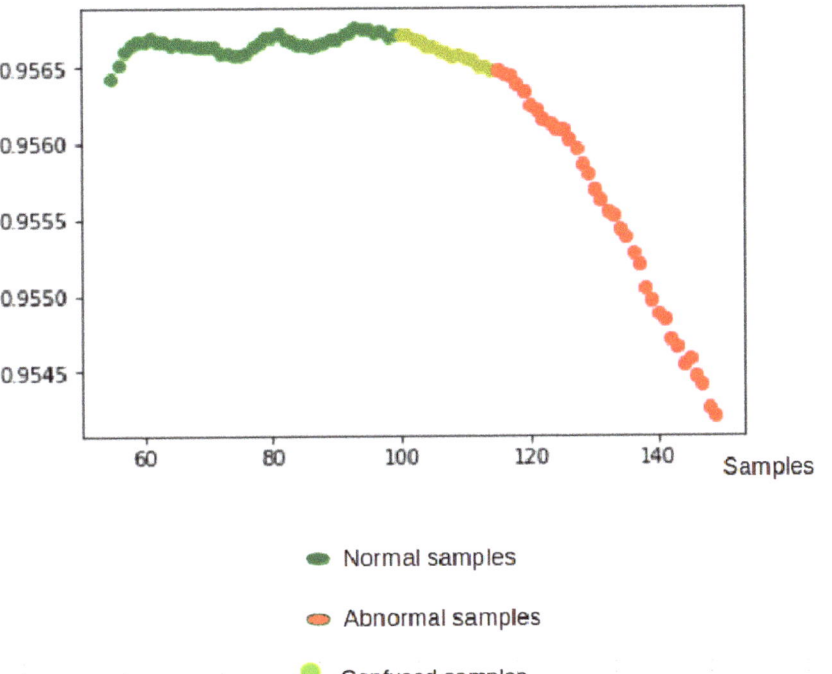

Figure 10. Mean of features at the testing phase.

From the presented results, we can see that our architecture is able to separate normal events from abnormal events. This is due to the specificity of our architecture, which is the ability to automatically extract deep features and contextual information from input frames that correctly express the difference between normal and abnormal events.

5. Conclusions

In this paper, we propose a new, unsupervised learning method based on deep end-to-end architecture for the detection of anomalies in UAV video streams. The main advantage of this method is its efficiency to jointly extract the optical flow features and to integrate a compactness regularization term during training. This method proves promising in terms of detection and localization of anomalies by UAV cameras and gives very high performance experimental results compared to state-of-the-art methods. Our future work is to study these results by setting up an on-board computer on the UAV for real-time anomaly detection application.

Author Contributions: S.H. and S.B. conceived of the presented idea. S.H. developed the theory and performed the computations. H.S. , T.W. and M.A. verified the analytical methods. H.S. encouraged S.H. to investigate and supervised the findings of this work. All authors discussed the results and contributed to the final manuscript. All authors have read and agreed to the published version of the manuscript.

Funding: This research received no external funding.

Institutional Review Board Statement: Not applicable.

Informed Consent Statement: Informed consent was obtained from all subjects involved in the study.

Data Availability Statement: The study did not report any data.

Conflicts of Interest: The funders had no role in the design of the study; in the collection, analyses, or interpretation of data; in the writing of the manuscript, or in the decision to publish the results.

References

1. Yue, X.; Liu, Y.; Wang, J.; Song, H.; Cao, H. software-defined radio and wireless acoustic networking for amateur drone surveillance. *IEEE Commun. Mag.* **2018**, *56*, 90–97. [CrossRef]
2. Wang, J.; Liu, Y.; Niu, S.; Song, H. Integration of software-defined Radios and software-defined Networking Towards Reinforcement Learning Enabled Unmanned Aerial Vehicle Networks. In Proceedings of the 2019 IEEE International Conference on Industrial Internet (ICII), Orlando, FL, USA, 11–12 November 2019; pp. 44–49.
3. Cui, J.; Liu, Y.; Nallanathan, A. Multi-agent reinforcement learning-based resource allocation for UAV networks. *IEEE Trans. Wirel. Commun.* **2019**, *19*, 729–743. [CrossRef]
4. Wang, J.; Juarez, N.; Kohm, E.; Liu, Y.; Yuan, J.; Song, H. Integration of SDR and UAS for malicious Wi-Fi hotspots detection. In Proceedings of the 2019 Integrated Communications, Navigation and Surveillance Conference (ICNS), Herndon, VA, USA, 9–11 April 2019; pp. 1–8.
5. Henrio, J.; Nakashima, T. Anomaly Detection in Videos Recorded by Drones in a Surveillance Context. In Proceedings of the 2018 IEEE International Conference on Systems, Man, and Cybernetics (SMC), Miyazaki, Japan, 7–10 October 2018; pp. 2503–2508.
6. He, K.; Zhang, X.; Ren, S.; Sun, J. Deep residual learning for image recognition. In Proceedings of the IEEE Conference on Computer Vision and Pattern Recognition, Las Vegas, NV, USA, 27–30 June 2016; pp. 770–778.
7. Taigman, Y.; Yang, M.; Ranzato, M.A.; Wolf, L. Deepface: Closing the gap to human-level performance in face verification. In Proceedings of the IEEE Conference on Computer Vision and Pattern Recognition, Columbus, OH, USA, 24–27 June 2014; pp. 1701–1708.
8. Toshev, A.; Szegedy, C. Deeppose: Human pose estimation via deep neural networks. In Proceedings of the IEEE Conference on Computer Vision and Pattern Recognition, Columbus, OH, USA, 24–27 June 2014; pp. 1653–1660.
9. Conneau, A.; Schwenk, H.; Barrault, L.; Lecun, Y. Very deep convolutional networks for natural language processing. *arXiv* **2016**, arXiv:1606.01781.
10. Amodei, D.; Ananthanarayanan, S.; Anubhai, R.; Bai, J.; Battenberg, E.; Case, C.; Chen, J. Deep speech 2: End-to-end speech recognition in english and mandarin. In Proceedings of the International Conference on Machine Learning, New York, NY, USA, 20–22 June 2016; pp. 173–182.
11. Wu, Y.; Schuster, M.; Chen, Z.; Le, Q.V.; Norouzi, M.; Macherey, W.; Krikun, M.; Cao, Y.; Gao, Q.; Macherey, K.; et al. Google's neural machine translation system: Bridging the gap between human and machine translation. *arXiv* **2016**, arXiv:1609.08144.
12. Chung, J.S.; Senior, A.; Vinyals, O.; Zisserman, A. Lip reading sentences in the wild. In Proceedings of the 2017 IEEE Conference on Computer Vision and Pattern Recognition (CVPR), Honolulu, HI, USA, 21–26 July 2017; pp. 3444–3453.
13. Lao, W.; Han, J.; De With, P.H. Automatic video-based human motion analyzer for consumer surveillance system. *IEEE Trans. Consum. Electron.* **2009**, *55*, 591–598. [CrossRef]
14. Zhang, C.; Chen, W.B.; Chen, X.; Yang, L.; Johnstone, J. A Multiple Instance Learning and Relevance Feedback Framework for Retrieving Abnormal Incidents in Surveillance Videos. *J. Multimed.* **2010**, *5*, 310–321 [CrossRef]
15. Zhou, S.; Shen, W.; Zeng, D.; Fang, M.; Wei, Y.; Zhang, Z. Spatial–temporal convolutional neural networks for anomaly detection and localization in crowded scenes. *Signal Process. Image Commun.* **2016**, *47*, 358–368. [CrossRef]
16. Javan Roshtkhari, M.; Levine, M.D. Online dominant and anomalous behavior detection in videos. In Proceedings of the IEEE Conference on Computer Vision and Pattern Recognition, Portland, OR, USA, 23–28 June 2013; pp. 2611–2618.
17. Hasan, M.; Choi, J.; Neumann, J.; Roy-Chowdhury, A.K.; Davis, L.S. Learning temporal regularity in video sequences. In Proceedings of the IEEE Conference on Computer Vision and Pattern Recognition, Las Vegas, NV, USA, 27–30 June 2016; pp. 733–742.
18. Lee, S.; Kim, H.G.; Ro, Y.M. STAN: Spatio-temporal adversarial networks for abnormal event detection. In Proceedings of the 2018 IEEE International Conference on Acoustics, Speech and Signal Processing (ICASSP), Calgary, AB, Canada, 15–20 April 2018; pp. 1323–1327.
19. Oza, P.; Patel, V.M. One-class convolutional neural network. *IEEE Signal Process. Lett.* **2018**, *26*, 277–281. [CrossRef]
20. Krizhevsky, A.; Sutskever, I.; Hinton, G.E. Imagenet classification with deep convolutional neural networks. *Commun. ACM* **2017**, *60*, 84–90. [CrossRef]
21. Szegedy, C.; Liu, W.; Jia, Y.; Sermanet, P.; Reed, S.; Anguelov, D.; Rabinovich, A. Going deeper with convolutions. In Proceedings of the IEEE Conference on Computer Vision and Pattern Recognition, Boston, MA, USA, 7–12 June 2015; pp. 1–9.
22. Sharif Razavian, A.; Azizpour, H.; Sullivan, J.; Carlsson, S. CNN features off-the-shelf: An astounding baseline for recognition. In Proceedings of the IEEE Conference on Computer Vision and Pattern Recognition Workshops, Columbus, OH, USA, 23–28 June 2014; pp. 806–813.
23. Bouindour, S.; Hittawe, M.M.; Mahfouz, S.; Snoussi, H. Abnormal event detection using convolutional neural networks and 1-class SVM classifier. In Proceedings of the 8th International Conference on Imaging for Crime Detection and Prevention (ICDP 2017), Madrid, Spain, 13–15 December 2017; pp. 1–6.
24. Sabokrou, M.; Fayyaz, M.; Fathy, M.; Klette, R. Fully Convolutional Neural Network for Fast Anomaly Detection in Crowded Scenes. *arXiv* **2016**, arXiv:1609.00866.

25. Goodfellow, I.; Pouget-Abadie, J.; Mirza, M.; Xu, B.; Warde-Farley, D.; Ozair, S.; Bengio, Y. Generative adversarial networks. *Commun. ACM* **2020**, *63*, 139–144. [CrossRef]
26. Shi, X.; Chen, Z.; Wang, H.; Yeung, D.Y.; Wong, W.K.; Woo, W.C. Convolutional LSTM network: A machine learning approach for precipitation nowcasting. *Adv. Neural Inf. Process. Syst.* **2015**, *28*, 802–810.
27. Ravanbakhsh, M.; Nabi, M.; Sangineto, E.; Marcenaro, L.; Regazzoni, C.; Sebe, N. Abnormal event detection in videos using generative adversarial nets. In Proceedings of the 2017 IEEE International Conference on Image Processing (ICIP), Beijing, China, 17–20 September 2017.
28. Furht, B. (Ed.) *Multimedia Tools and Applications*; Springer: Berlin, Germany, 2012; Volume 359.
29. Chalapathy, R.; Menon, A.K.; Chawla, S. Anomaly detection using one-class neural networks. *arXiv* **2018**, arXiv:1802.06360.
30. Ruff, L.; Vandermeulen, R.; Goernitz, N.; Deecke, L.; Siddiqui, S.A.; Binder, A.; Kloft, M. Deep one-class classification. In Proceedings of the International Conference on Machine Learning, Stockholm, Sweden, 10–15 July 2018; pp. 4393–4402.
31. Perera, P.; Patel, V.M. Learning deep features for one-class classification. *IEEE Trans. Image Process.* **2019**, *28*, 5450–5463. [CrossRef] [PubMed]
32. Bonetto, M.; Korshunov, P.; Ramponi, G.; Ebrahimi, T. Privacy in mini-drone based video surveillance. In Proceedings of the 2015 11th IEEE International Conference and Workshops on Automatic Face and Gesture Recognition (FG), Ljubljana, Slovenia, 4–8 May 2015; Volume 4, pp. 1–6.
33. Chong, Y.S.; Tay, Y.H. Abnormal event detection in videos using spatiotemporal autoencoder. In Proceedings of the International Symposium on Neural Networks, Shanghai, China, 6–9 June 2017; pp. 189–196.
34. Mehran, R.; Oyama, A.; Shah, M. Abnormal crowd behavior detection using social force model. In Proceedings of the IEEE Conference on Computer Vision and Pattern Recognition (CVPR 2009), Miami, FL, USA, 20–25 June 2009; pp. 935–942.
35. Kim, J.; Grauman, K. Observe locally, infer globally: A space-time mrf for detecting abnormal activities with incremental updates. In Proceedings of the IEEE Conference on Computer Vision and Pattern Recognition (CVPR 2009), Miami, FL, USA, 20–25 June 2009; pp. 2921–2928.
36. Pham, D.S.; Saha, B.; Phung, D.Q.; Venkatesh, S. Detection of cross-channel anomalies from multiple data channels. In Proceedings of the 2011 IEEE 11th International Conference on Data Mining, Vancouver, BC, Canada, 11–14 December 2011; pp. 527–536.
37. Ribeiro, M.; Lazzaretti, A.E.; Lopes, H.S. A study of deep convolutional auto-encoders for anomaly detection in videos. *Pattern Recognit. Lett.* **2018**, *105*, 13–22. [CrossRef]
38. Hamdi, S.; Bouindour, S.; Loukil, K.; Snoussi, H.; Abid, M. Hybrid deep learning and HOF for Anomaly Detection. In Proceedings of the 2019 6th International Conference on Control, Decision and Information Technologies (CoDIT), Paris, France, 23–26 April 2019; pp. 575–580.
39. Sabokrou, M.; Fayyaz, M.; Fathy, M.; Klette, R. Deep-cascade: Cascading 3d deep neural networks for fast anomaly detection and localization in crowded scenes. *IEEE Trans. Image Process.* **2017**, *26*, 1992–2004. [CrossRef] [PubMed]

Article

An Automated Approach for Electric Network Frequency Estimation in Static and Non-Static Digital Video Recordings

Georgios Karantaidis * and Constantine Kotropoulos

Department of Informatics, School of Sciences, Aristotle University of Thessaloniki, 54124 Thessaloniki, Greece; costas@csd.auth.gr
* Correspondence: gkarantai@csd.auth.gr

Abstract: Electric Network Frequency (ENF) is embedded in multimedia recordings if the recordings are captured with a device connected to power mains or placed near the power mains. It is exploited as a tool for multimedia authentication. ENF fluctuates stochastically around its nominal frequency at 50/60 Hz. In indoor environments, luminance variations captured by video recordings can also be exploited for ENF estimation. However, the various textures and different levels of shadow and luminance hinder ENF estimation in static and non-static video, making it a non-trivial problem. To address this problem, a novel automated approach is proposed for ENF estimation in static and non-static digital video recordings. The proposed approach is based on the exploitation of areas with similar characteristics in each video frame. These areas, called superpixels, have a mean intensity that exceeds a specific threshold. The performance of the proposed approach is tested on various videos of real-life scenarios that resemble surveillance from security cameras. These videos are of escalating difficulty and span recordings from static ones to recordings, which exhibit continuous motion. The maximum correlation coefficient is employed to measure the accuracy of ENF estimation against the ground truth signal. Experimental results show that the proposed approach improves ENF estimation against the state-of-the-art, yielding statistically significant accuracy improvements.

Keywords: estimation by rotational invariant techniques (ESPRIT); short-time Fourier transform (STFT); multiple signal classification (MUSIC); simple linear iterative clustering (SLIC); video forensics

Citation: Karantaidis, G.; Kotropoulo, C. An Automated Approach for Electric Network Frequency Estimation in Static and Non-Static Digital Video Recordings. *J. Imaging* **2021**, *7*, 202. https://doi.org/10.3390/jimaging7100202

Academic Editors: Irene Amerini, Gianmarco Baldini and Francesco Leotta

Received: 23 July 2021
Accepted: 29 September 2021
Published: 2 October 2021

Publisher's Note: MDPI stays neutral with regard to jurisdictional claims in published maps and institutional affiliations.

Copyright: © 2021 by the authors. Licensee MDPI, Basel, Switzerland. This article is an open access article distributed under the terms and conditions of the Creative Commons Attribution (CC BY) license (https://creativecommons.org/licenses/by/4.0/).

1. Introduction

The vast amount of information contained in multimedia content, i.e., audio, image, and video recordings, has prompted perpetrators to commit forgery attacks distorting the digital content. Digital forensics advancements have experienced an exponential growth in the last decades, as digital manipulation methods are constantly evolving and affecting various aspects of social and economic life. To this end, emphasis has been put on advancing emerging technologies in the field of digital forensics, which can efficiently verify the authenticity of multimedia content and cope with multimedia forgeries. A comprehensive survey of image forensics techniques can be found in [1].

In recent years, the Electric Network Frequency (ENF) has been employed as a tool in forensic applications. The ENF is a time-varying signal, which fluctuates around its nominal frequency, i.e., 50 Hz in Europe and 60 Hz in the United States. These fluctuations are due to the instantaneous load differences of the power network (i.e., the power grid). They exhibit an identical trend within the same interconnected network. The ENF is a non-periodic signal, which can act as a fingerprint for digital forensics applications [2]. It can be embedded in digital audio recorded by devices plugged into the power mains or by devices placed near the electric outlets and power cables. The ENF can be captured in video recorded in indoor environments due to fluorescent light. Illumination intensity variations resemble ENF variations in the power grid [3]. Thus, ENF estimation can be exploited for multimedia authentication, timestamp verification, and forgery detection in audio and video recordings. Until recently, the research has mainly been focused on audio recordings, where many advances have been achieved.

To begin with, let us briefly survey ENF estimation in audio recordings, because the same ENF estimation methods are also applied to a one-dimensional (1D) time-series extracted from video recordings. A comprehensive study addressing the ENF detection problem was presented in [4], where many practical detectors were introduced. The detectors were shown to have a reliable performance in relatively short recordings, enabling accurate ENF detection in real-world forensic applications. An alternative to the conventional Short-Time Fourier Transform (STFT) is advanced spectral estimation [5], offering high-resolution at the expense of increased computational complexity. For example, an iterative adaptive approach accompanied by a dynamic programming was applied to frequency tracking. An optimized maximum-likelihood estimator for ENF estimation was proposed by employing a multi-tone harmonic model [6]. Multiple harmonics were combined to provide a more accurate estimation of the ENF signal and the Cramer–Rao bound was used to bound the variance of the proposed estimator. Following the same reasoning, a spectral estimation approach was presented in [7], combining the ENF at multiple harmonics. Each harmonic was weighted depending on its signal-to-noise (SNR) ratio. A pre-processing approach was proposed in [8] that was based on robust principal component analysis to reduce noise interference and to enable accurate ENF estimation. There, a weighted linear prediction approach was also employed for ENF estimation. In [9], a lag window was designed to offer an optimal trade-off between smearing and leakage by maximizing the relative energy in the main lobe of the window. It was incorporated in the Blackman–Tukey method, offering accurate ENF estimation with low computational requirements. A Fourier-based algorithm for high-resolution frequency estimation was introduced in [10]. Specific spectral lines were taken into consideration instead of the entire frequency band. In [11], a comprehensive study of the parameters that affect ENF estimation accuracy was undertaken. In the pre-processing stage, signal filtering and temporal window choice were found to be critical in delivering accurate estimation results. A fast version of Capon spectral estimator based on Gohberg–Semencul factorization was presented in [12]. That method along with the use of a Parzen temporal window led to accurate ENF estimation. To address the problem of noise and interference, frequency demodulation was employed for ENF estimation [13]. Several high-resolution frequency estimation methods were discussed in [14]. That work aimed to achieve high performance and to maintain low computational complexity by using as few samples per frame as possible. An integrated and automated scheme for ENF estimation was developed in [15]. A framework for ENF estimation from real-world audio recordings was presented in [16]. First, signal enhancement was proposed, which was based on harmonic filtering. Second, graph-based harmonic selection was elaborated. In [17], a unified approach was proposed to detect multiple weak frequency components under low SNR conditions. Iterative dynamic programming and adaptive trace compensation were employed to identify the frequency components. A multi-tone model for ENF detection applied prior to ENF estimation was presented in [18].

The ENF can also be exploited to detect tampering in multimedia recordings. An edit detection approach taking advantage of the time-varying nature of ENF was proposed in [19]. Multimedia authentication was formulated as a problem of phase change analysis employing the Fourier Transform in [20]. An audio verification system for tamper detection and timestamp verification was proposed in [21]. The system employed absolute-error-maps. A tamper detection framework based on support vector machines was introduced in [22]. That framework exploited abnormal ENF variations caused by tampered regions.

In [23], it was demonstrated that the ENF can be exploited to determine the location of recordings even if they are captured within the same interconnected grid. A multi-class machine learning system was proposed to identify region-of-recordings in [24]. It took advantage of features related to ENF differences among power grids without the need for a reference ENF signal. A convolution neural network system was tested for identifying audio recordings that have been recaptured in [25]. The system worked properly for very short audio clips and was able to combine both the fundamental ENF and its harmonics. To cope with noise interference, a filtering algorithm was introduced in [26]. It employed a kernel function to create a time–frequency representation facilitating ENF estimation. The existence of reliable ENF reference databases is critical for multimedia authentication applications. A method to create ENF reference databases based on geographical information systems (GIS) was presented in [27]. Recently, ENF was explored as a tool for device identification [28]. The proposed method was based on the analysis of harmonic amplitude coefficients, which were employed to deliver an accurate identification of acquisition devices. The ENF is a stochastic signal and its values depend on various exogenous and endogenous factors. In [29], a study was carried out on the factors affecting the capture of ENF in audio recordings as well as on the impact of the audio characteristics.

Although significant attention has been paid to ENF estimation in audio recordings, it was found that the ENF can also be traced in video recordings. The ENF can be estimated in videos captured under the illumination of fluorescent bulbs in indoor environments [3]. ENF variations caused by power grid networks affect the illumination intensity, and each frame captures a time-snapshot of ENF. ENF video estimation approaches can be divided into two categories based on the recording sensor type. The first category consists of videos captured by charge-coupled device (CCD) sensors, which employ a global shutter mechanism. This type of sensor instantly captures all pixels of a frame. Thus, each frame depicts a specific time snapshot. When CCD sensors are used, the state-of-the-art approach for ENF estimation is based on averaging all pixels in each frame of static videos [3]. For non-static videos, state-of-the-art ENF estimation suggests averaging all steady pixels in each video frame. The second category consists of videos captured by complementary metal oxide semiconductor (CMOS) sensors. Such sensors employ a rolling shutter mechanism, which acquires a row at a time in each video frame [3,30]. A comprehensive analysis of the rolling shutter effect was conducted in [31]. An analytical model for videos captured using a rolling shutter mechanism was developed, demonstrating the relation between ENF variations and the idle period length. ENF-based video forensics are not trivial, especially for non-static video recordings. ENF presence detection based on superpixels (i.e., multiple pixels) was proposed in [32]. The proposed approach could be applied to static and non-static videos captured by both CCD and CMOS camera sensors. Recently, a method for ENF estimation in non-static videos was presented in [33]. This method could be accurately utilized in video recordings whose frame rate is unknown. The ENF was applied to video recordings for camera identification in [34]. Video synchronization can be efficiently achieved by employing the ENF. Video synchronization methods were developed in [35,36] that were based on ENF signal alignment. A forgery detection algorithm based on ENF signal was proposed in [37] without needing any ground truth signal. A technique to detect false frame injection attacks in video recordings using the ENF was discussed in [38]. ENF was employed to authenticate video feeds from surveillance cameras. ENF estimation and detection in single images captured by CMOS camera sensors constitutes a challenging task. Novel investigations taking into consideration the ENF strength were described in [39]. ENF estimation in videos with a rolling shutter mechanism was presented in [40]. Both parametric and non-parametric spectral estimation methods were combined for accurate ENF estimation.

In this paper, inspired by [32], an automated approach is proposed for ENF estimation from CCD video recordings based on Simple Linear Iterative Clustering (SLIC) [41]. Areas of common characteristics that include superpixels are generated using the SLIC algorithm. The proposed approach takes into consideration only the superpixels whose average intensity exceeds a predefined threshold. It is shown that within these areas, the embedded ENF is not hindered by any interference, resulting in more accurate estimation regardless of whether the video recording is static or not. The novelty of the proposed approach lies in (1) the creation of areas with similar characteristics and (2) the estimation of ENF exploiting only these areas in contrast to what has been achieved for ENF estimation in videos so far. The motivation for the development of the proposed approach is to mitigate the interference and noise caused by textures, shadows, and brightness that are present in real-life applications, such as surveillance videos. By doing so, we advance the related literature, where static videos are mostly used, such as the "white wall" recordings. From a practical point of view, the proposed approach enables automated ENF estimation regardless of whether the video recording is static or non-static. Thus, it can be applied to practical forensics applications, such as multimedia content authentication, indicating the place where a recording was captured, and revealing the time the recording was made. It is worth noting that the proposed approach is tested on real-world static and non-static videos of escalating difficulty in order to simulate real conditions. The maximum correlation coefficient (MCC) between the estimated ENF and the reference signal is employed to measure ENF estimation accuracy. Moreover, hypothesis testing is performed to assess the statistical significance of the improvements delivered by the proposed approach.

The remainder of the paper is organized as follows. Section 2 details ENF fundamentals, and Section 3 presents the proposed approach; Section 4 describes the dataset and discusses the derived results; conclusions, limitations, and future research are drawn in Section 5.

2. ENF Fundamentals

The ENF was initially introduced by C. Grigoras [2,42] to attest to the authenticity of digital recordings, to determine the time they were recorded, and to indicate the area they were captured. In particular, when it comes to video recordings, ENF estimation can determine whether the multimedia content has undergone major alterations. Moreover, ENF can reveal the area where the indoor video was recorded. When the estimated ENF is compared against a reference ground truth, the time the video was recorded is revealed. The proposed approach aims at improving ENF estimation, whose practical applications fall into forensic science. The importance of ENF is due to its unique properties, which makes it a powerful tool in forensic applications. Once the ENF signal has been estimated, a comparison against a reference ENF database should be made in order to assess estimation accuracy.

The most remarkable properties of the ENF signal are summarized as follows:

- The ENF is a non-periodic signal randomly fluctuating around the fundamental frequency.
- ENF fluctuations are identical within the same interconnected network.
- The ENF signal can also be found in higher harmonics [43].

Many approaches have been proposed to efficiently estimate ENF depending on the particularities of each recording.

2.1. ENF Estimation

The ENF is embedded in the electric light signal. Assuming stationarity within short-time segments of the signal, the ENF is modeled as

$$s(t) = A\sin(2\pi f t + \phi) \qquad (1)$$

where f is the fluctuating frequency representing the ENF component, A is the signal magnitude, and ϕ corresponds to signal phase. There are more complex ENF models, such as that proposed in [44].

It has been shown recently that ENF traces can be embedded in video recordings due to light intensity variations. Such recordings are captured in the presence of fluorescent light or the light emitted by incandescent bulbs [35]. The light intensity is directly connected to electric current and its nominal frequency is influenced by the ENF signal, fluctuating at twice the nominal frequency of ENF, i.e., 100 Hz in Europe, and 120 Hz in the United States. The lower temporal sampling rate of cameras capturing video recordings compared to frequency components in light flickering results in a significant aliasing of ENF signals. Thus, ENF is present at different frequencies than those appearing in audio recordings.

These frequencies can be derived by applying the sampling theorem [45]. In addition to the fundamental frequency of power mains, it is the frame rate of video camera that influences the aliased base frequency of ENF in video recordings [3]. The aliased frequency f_E emanated from fluorescent illumination is given as follows [46]:

$$f_E = |f_l - \gamma f_s| \leq \frac{f_s}{2} \qquad (2)$$

where f_s denotes the sampling frequency of camera, f_l denotes the frequency of light source illumination, and γ denotes an integer. Aliased frequencies of ENF based on different camera frame rates and power main frequencies are listed in Table 1.

Table 1. Aliased frequencies of ENF with respect to (w.r.t.) camera frame rate and fundamental ENF at power mains frequency [3].

Power Mains (Hz)	Camera Frame Rate f_s (fps)	Aliased Base Frequency (Hz)
50	29.97	10.09
50	30	10
60	29.97	0.12
60	30	0

The ENF estimation procedure in video recordings differs slightly from that employed in audio ones. The difference is in the pre-processing stage. Two cases are examined depending on whether the video recordings are static or non-static. Regarding static videos, the state-of-the-art [3] suggests computing the mean intensity of each frame, transforming the two-dimensional (2D) images into a 1D time-series. It is worth noting that the majority of experiments conducted so far employ static recordings of white wall videos. Here, we employ a variety of static recordings different than white wall videos, as detailed in Section 4.1. Regarding non-static videos, the current practice is to compute the mean intensity of relatively stationary areas of each frame. In both categories, a 1D time-series is formed and the estimation procedure follows that employed for audio recordings. This time-series is treated as a raw signal that is passed through a zero-phase bandpass filter around the frequencies where ENF appears. Specifically, the bandpass edges of the filter are set at 9.9 and 10.1 Hz when the nominal frame rate is 30 Hz despite the fact that the nominal frame rate was claimed to be 29.97 Hz in [33]. The bandpass edges employed herein accommodate also the aliased base frequency, which corresponds to a nominal frame rate of 29.97 Hz. The filtering procedure is of crucial importance in ENF estimation [11]. Subsequently, the signal is split into V overlapping segments of L samples size. Each segment is shifted by S s from its immediate predecessor and is multiplied by an L-size rectangular window. Any temporal window can be employed in the pre-processing procedure. Afterward, the prevalent frequency of each segment is estimated by spectral estimation. Frequently, a quadratic interpolation is used to overcome the interference that hinders the entire procedure and results in more precise ENF estimation [5,9]. Here, the estimated ENF signal f is calculated by employing shifts of 1 s (i.e., $S = 1$).

3. Proposed Method

Here, a video ENF estimation approach for static and non-static video recordings is proposed. It is based on the SLIC algorithm for image segmentation. The SLIC algorithm generates superpixels, which are regions of similar characteristics. The idea behind the proposed approach is that in regions having high luminance levels and not hindered by shadows or dark areas, light source variations can easily be detected, and thus, the ENF signal can be estimated more accurately. The first step of the proposed approach generates N regions with similar characteristics in the first frame of a video recording. Afterward, the mean intensity values $\zeta_n(1)$, $n = 1, 2, \ldots, N$ of all regions in the first frame are computed and only those exceeding a predefined threshold τ are retained. Let $\zeta(1)$ be the vector with elements $\zeta_n(1)$. If $\overline{N} = |\{n : \zeta_n(1) > \tau\}|$ denotes the size of region mean intensity values exceeding the threshold, then the mean intensity value for the first frame is given as follows:

$$x(1) = \frac{1}{\overline{N}} \sum_{n=1}^{N} \zeta_n(1) u(\zeta_n(1) - \tau) \qquad (3)$$

where $u(\zeta_n(1) - \tau)$ denotes the Heaviside function.

In the next step, the generated regions from the first frame are located in all Λ frames of the video recording. For a video recording with a duration of 12 min, $\Lambda = 21{,}600$ frames. Employing these regions, the mean intensity values of the regions are computed and, then, the mean intensity value in each frame is calculated, as in (3). In this way, each video frame is represented by an intensity value $x(t)$, $t = 1, 2, \ldots, \Lambda$.

A non-parametric, namely the STFT, and a parametric method, i.e., the Estimation by Rotational Invariant Techniques (ESPRIT), were employed for ENF estimation. Hereafter, the frames, indexed by t, will be referred to as samples.

The STFT is one of the most common methods in time-frequency analysis of signals. Assuming stationary within the short-time segments of the signal, the Discrete-Time Fourier transform is computed for each time segment [47]:

$$X_l(\omega) = \sum_{t=-\infty}^{\infty} x(t) w(t - lG) e^{-j\omega t} \qquad (4)$$

where $w(t)$ denotes a window function of length L, $X_l(\omega)$ is the discrete-time Fourier transform of the windowed data centered around lG, and $G = S f_s$ is the hop size in samples. The proper selection of window function constitutes a very important issue in STFT and, generally, in the majority of time–frequency analysis methods. This is because an optimal trade-off between time and frequency resolution is sought. Let $\hat{\phi}_l(\omega_\kappa) \propto |X_l(\omega_\kappa)|^2$ be the periodogram of the $L = D f_s$ samples long lth segment, where ω_κ, $\kappa = 0, 1, \ldots, Q-1$ are the frequency samples with $Q = 4L$. Specifically, the frequency sample ω_κ that corresponds to the maximum periodogram value is extracted as a first ENF estimate. Afterward, a quadratic interpolation is employed to obtain a refined ENF estimate.

ESPRIT is also employed to estimate the ENF signal. Let $\hat{R}$ be the sample covariance matrix

$$\hat{R} = \frac{1}{L} \sum_{t=m}^{L} \tilde{x}(t) \tilde{x}^\top(t) \qquad (5)$$

where $^\top$ stands for transposition and

$$\tilde{x}(t) \triangleq [x(t), x(t-1), \ldots, x(t-m+1)]^\top. \qquad (6)$$

Let $\hat{S}$ be the subspace spanned by the W principal eigenvectors of $\hat{R}$. Let $\hat{S}_1 = [I_{m-1}|0] \hat{S}$ and $\hat{S}_2 = [0|I_{m-1}] \hat{S}$, where I_{m-1} denotes the $(m-1) \times (m-1)$ identity matrix. ESPRIT estimates the angular frequencies $\{\omega_\kappa\}_{\kappa=1}^{W}$ as $-\arg(\hat{v}_\kappa)$, where $\{\hat{v}_\kappa\}_{\kappa=1}^{W}$ are the eigenvalues of the estimated matrix $\hat{\phi}$ [48]:

$$\hat{\phi} = (\hat{S}_1^\top \hat{S}_1)^{-1} \hat{S}_1^\top \hat{S}_2 \qquad (7)$$

The frequency $-\frac{1}{2\pi} \arg(\hat{v}_\kappa) f_s$ (in Hz), which is closest to the aliased base frequency is the ENF estimate. Here, $m = 10$ and $W = 3$.

The proposed approach combines the generation of the mean intensity time-series $x(t)$ with either the ESPRIT or the STFT method. An outlook of the proposed approach is depicted in Algorithm 1.

Algorithm 1 Proposed SLIC-based approach for ENF estimation in video recordings.

Inputs: Number of video frames Λ, number of superpixels N, threshold τ, cut-off frequencies, segment duration L, number of overlapping segments V, ESPRIT parameters m and W, and reference ground truth.
Output: Estimated ENF vector f.

1. Perform SLIC in the first frame of the video recording to generate N regions of similar characteristics and luminance, i.e., superpixels.
2. Compute mean intensity values $\zeta_n(1)$ of each generated region.
3. The mean intensity values of regions exceeding threshold τ in the computation of x_1.
4. Locate the generated regions in the $\Lambda - 1$ remaining frames and repeat steps 2-3 to compute $x(t)$, $t = 2, 3, \ldots, \Lambda$.
5. Having computed the 1-D time-series $x(t)$, $x(t)$ is bandpass filtered using the cut-off frequencies described in Section 2.1.
6. The filtered signal is split into V overlapping segments. Each segment is obtained by multiplying the filtered signal with an L-size rectangular window. Any segment is shifted from its immediate predecessor segment by S s.
7. In each segment, the prevalent frequency derived by the ESPRIT method is employed as the ENF estimate. In the case of STFT, the frequency that corresponds to the maximum periodogram value is extracted as the ENF estimate.
8. Compute the MCC between the estimated ENF and the reference ground truth.

Evaluation Metric

Having estimated ENF, a matching procedure is applied in order to objectively assess estimation accuracy. Having calculated the reference ENF captured by power mains, the MCC [49] is used to compare the estimated ENF from video recordings against the reference one. Let $f = [f_1, f_2, \ldots, f_K]^\top$ be the estimated ENF signal at each second. Let also $g = [g_1, g_2, \ldots, g_{\tilde{K}}]^\top$ for $\tilde{K} > K$ be the reference ground truth ENF, which is known, and $\tilde{g}(p) = [g_p, g_{p+1}, \ldots, g_{p+K-1}]^\top$ be a segment of g starting at p. The following index is determined:

$$p_{opt} = \underset{p}{\arg\max}\, c(p) \qquad (8)$$

where $p = 1, 2, \ldots, \tilde{K} - K + 1$ and $c(p)$ is the sample correlation coefficient between f and $\tilde{g}(p)$ defined as:

$$c(p) = \frac{f^\top \tilde{g}(p)}{\|f\|_2 \|\tilde{g}(p)\|_2}. \qquad (9)$$

In Section 4.9, Fisher's transformation was employed to assess whether the pairwise differences between the MCC delivered by the proposed approach and that of state-of-the-art one are statistically significant at a significance level of 5%.

4. Results

The estimation of the ENF signal is significantly affected by the nature of video recordings. In static videos, ENF presence is not affected and, thus, estimation accuracy is much higher than that in non-static videos. There, continuous motion hinders ENF estimation accuracy. Many approaches aim at overcoming this difficulty. For this reason, the state-of-the-art approach for ENF estimation in video [3], which employs intensity averaging with the Multiple Signal Classification (MUSIC) method, examines whether the video to be analyzed is a static or a non-static one. For brevity, from now on, the state-of-the-art [3] approach for both static and non-static videos will be referred to as MUSIC. The proposed approach employs either ESPRIT or STFT after SLIC. The novelty of the proposed approach lies in the fact that CCD sensors capture a time snapshot using a global shutter mechanism, which makes the distinction between static and non-static video obsolete. Thus, the proposed approach is applied regardless of whether the video recording is a static or a non-static one. It is tested on six video recordings of escalating difficulty from the publicly available dataset [50]. These recordings are either static and non-static ones. A reference ground truth signal is also available. The results are compared to those obtained by MUSIC [3]. The video recordings of the dataset employed in the paper are publicly available (https://zenodo.org/record/3549379#.YUIK7bgzaUl, accessed in 8 September 2021).

4.1. Dataset

Six different video recordings were recorded in Vigo, Spain, at a nominal ENF 50 Hz. Two different cameras were employed, namely, a GOPRO Hero 4 Black and an NK AC3061-4KN without an anti-flicker filter [50]. The video recordings are named as mov_i, $i = 1, 2, 3, 4, 5, 6$ and their types are listed in Table 2.

Table 2. Types of six video recordings employed for ENF estimation.

Video Name	Video Type
mov_1	static
mov_2	static
mov_3	non-static
mov_4	non-static
mov_5	non-static
mov_6	non-static

Recording mov_1 is closer to what is known as "white wall" video in the literature. Going a step further, it depicts a flat colored wall of low brightness. This kind of recording can be exploited to evaluate whether ENF variations can be embedded and, subsequently, estimated in such a static and seemingly noise-free environment. mov_2 is also a static video, which contains regions with different textures, brightness, and shadows. This video is more challenging than mov_1. mov_3 can be categorized as a non-static video. It starts showing a white wall and a wooden table. Then, an object is placed on the table and a human hand rapidly shakes white papers at regular intervals on the right region of the recording. mov_4 is a non-static video, where human movement appears. It is a complex recording and consists of several textures. It takes place within an office, where a human is constantly moving. Both the background wall and the floor are captured. mov_5 constitutes one of the most challenging recordings, which resembles a real-life scene captured by a security camera. It is recorded within the complex environment of a room. The scene contains several objects with different colors and textures. The most significant challenge of mov_5 is that the movement affects the majority of the frames and more than 50% of the pixels of each frame. mov_6 represents another challenging video recording, which contains a constant movement of a person inside a room. The movement takes place close to the camera, affecting most pixels in each frame. In all cases, the camera is fixed. Sample frames of the video recordings are depicted in Figure 1. The estimated ENF signal is compared against a reference ground truth obtained from power mains.

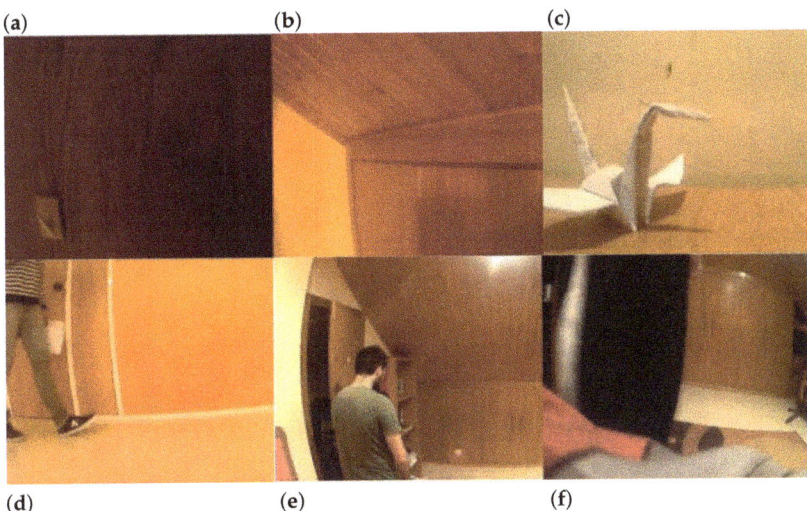

Figure 1. Sample frames of the six video recordings employed. (**a**) On the top left, there is a snapshot of a static video, recording a dark wall, while (**b**) on the top middle there is a snapshot of a static video, which captures the interior of a room. (**c**) On the top right, a table is depicted on which an object is placed. (**d**) On the bottom left, a person is constantly moving in an office. (**e**) On the bottom middle, there is a room with different textures and a person is moving covering a large part of the camera field many times. (**f**) On the bottom right, a person is moving in front of the camera lens inside a room.

4.2. Experimental Evaluation

The approach detailed in Section 2.1 was applied to the six video recordings and the estimated ENF was compared against the MUSIC [3] for static and non-static videos. Particularly, for static videos, the state-of-the-art approach [3] suggests averaging intensity values in each frame, while for non-static videos, intensity values are averaged within relatively static regions of each frame. In all comparisons, a rectangular temporal window was employed. The predefined threshold τ was set at $^{MV}/3$, where MV is the median of N average intensity values within the generated regions in each frame. All approaches were implemented in MATLAB 2016a. A 64-bit operating system with an Intel(R) Core(TM) i7 − 5930K CPU at 3.5 GHz was used in the experiments conducted.

4.3. ENF Estimation in Static Video mov_1

The ESPRIT method was tested for ENF estimation in mov_1. The static nature of mov_1 enables an accurate ENF estimation. The proposed approach, which employs the SLIC-based segmentation and intensity averaging resulted in an MCC of 0.9926, outperforming the MUSIC [3] where the MCC was measured to be 0.9658. When STFT was employed, the MCC was found to be 0.8662. Different segment durations in ENF estimation affect the results obtained. The MCC was computed for various segment durations D, as depicted in Figure 2. When a segment duration of 1 s was employed, the proposed approach using the ESPRIT worked satisfactorily, yielding an MCC of about 0.79, while the MCC was measured to be about 0.5, when the MUSIC [3] was used. The performance of ENF estimation depends also on the filter order ν of the bandpass filter. The MCC is plotted versus various filter orders in Figure 3. The top performance of the proposed approach, employing the ESPRIT, is achieved when $\nu = 111$. Despite mov_1 is a trivial recording, the proposed approach offers significant improvements in ENF estimation accuracy against the method in [3]. The computational time of the proposed approach employing SLIC+ESPRIT was about 506.8 s, while the MUSIC [3] required about 492.5 s.

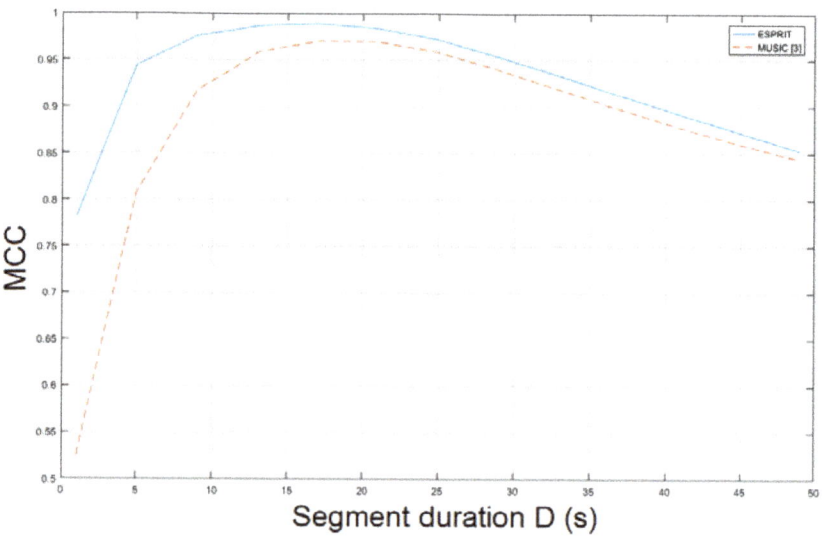

Figure 2. Maximum correlation coefficient of the proposed approach employing SLIC+ESPRIT for various segment durations against the MUSIC [3] (mov1).

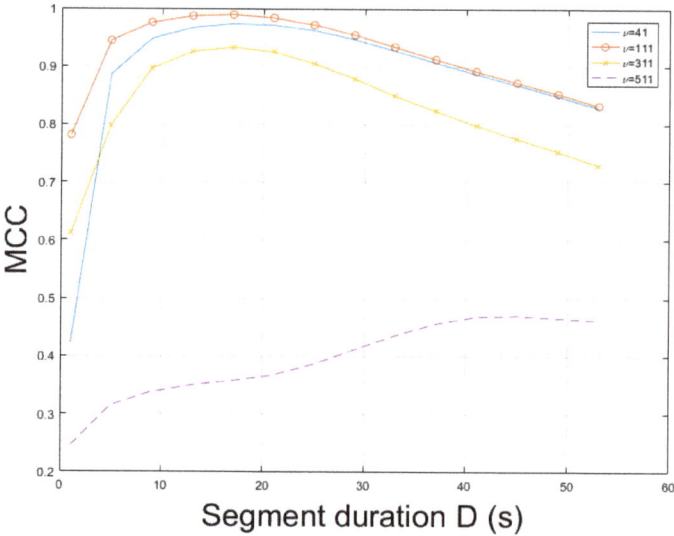

Figure 3. Maximum correlation coefficient of the proposed approach employing SLIC+ESPRIT for various filter orders and segment durations (mov1).

4.4. ENF Estimation in Static Video mov_2

The static recording mov_2 is more challenging than mov_1 due to different textures and various levels of luminance. The STFT was employed for ENF estimation yielding an MCC of 0.9704. The MUSIC [3] resulted in an MCC of 0.9466. The ESPRIT method achieved an MCC of 0.9526. In this case, there is a strong correlation between the proposed approach and the method in [3] w.r.t. segment duration. Smaller segment durations resulted in lower MCCs in both approaches. For longer segment durations, both approaches yielded a higher MCC, as shown in Figure 4. Similar behavior was noticed when different filter orders were employed. When the bandpass filter order $\nu = 81$ was used, the top performance was observed. The MCC of the proposed approach employing SLIC+STFT for various values of bandpass filter order and segment duration is plotted in Figure 5. The proposed approach employing SLIC+STFT required about 627.2 s. The computational time of the MUSIC [3] one was approximately 704.7 s.

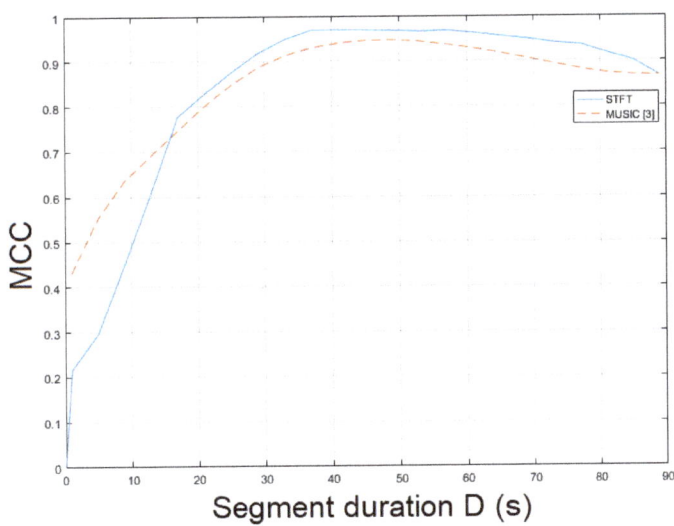

Figure 4. Maximum correlation coefficient of the proposed approach employing SLIC+STFT for various segment durations against the MUSIC [3] (mov2).

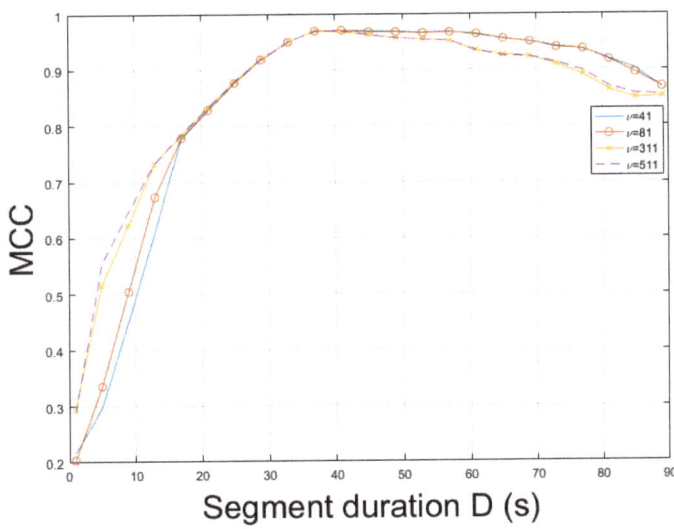

Figure 5. Maximum correlation coefficient of the proposed approach employing SLIC+STFT for various bandpass filter orders and segment durations (mov2).

4.5. ENF Estimation in Non-Static Video mov_3

The STFT method was employed for ENF estimation. mov_3 is a challenging video depicting movements and different textures. Thus, ENF estimation is a non-trivial task. The STFT achieved an MCC of 0.9877, outperforming the method in [3], which reached an MCC of 0.9191. The ESPRIT method resulted in an MCC of 0.7271. As can be seen in Figure 6, the longer the segment duration, the more accurate the ENF estimation. The top result w.r.t. the MCC was measured for bandpass filter order $\nu = 51$. In mov$_3$, improper values of filter order can lead to a significant reduction in MCC. Increasing the segment duration usually results in a more accurate ENF estimation w.r.t. the MCC. In this experiment, it has been noticed that when a large value of bandpass filter order is employed, increasing segment duration deteriorates estimation accuracy. The impact of filter order in MCC is demonstrated in Figure 7. The computational time of the proposed approach employing SLIC+STFT was about 468.5 s, while the MUSIC [3] required 531.4 s.

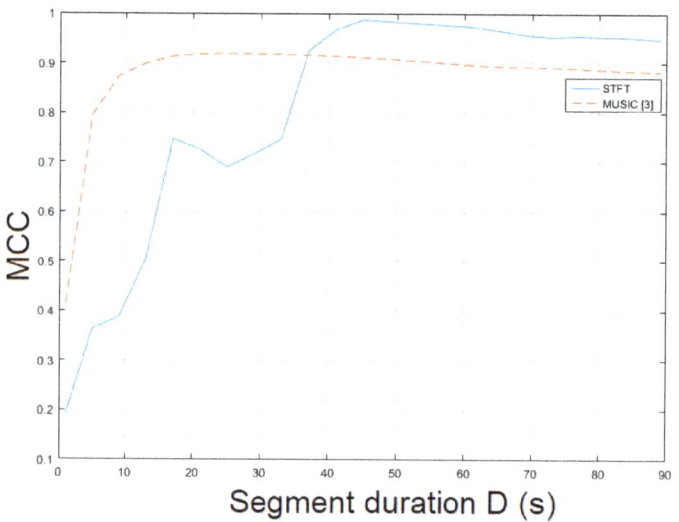

Figure 6. Maximum correlation coefficient of the proposed approach employing SLIC+STFT for various segment durations against the MUSIC [3] (mov3).

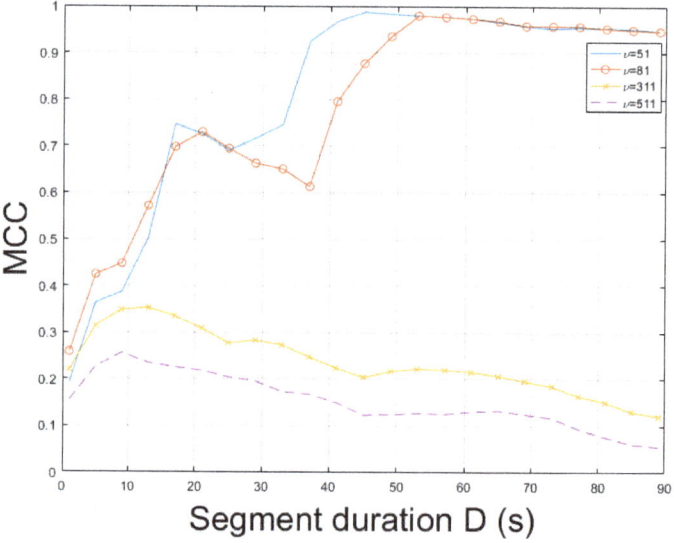

Figure 7. Maximum correlation coefficient of the proposed approach employing SLIC+STFT for various bandpass filter orders and segment durations (mov3).

4.6. ENF Estimation in Non-Static Video mov_4

The non-static video mov_4 captures a much more complex scene, where the human presence and movement is closer to real-life applications than the previous videos. Here, the STFT was employed for ENF estimation. The STFT yielded an MCC of 0.9837, which outperformed the MUSIC, which attained 0.8700 [3]. When the ESPRIT method was used, an MCC of 0.7605 was measured. The top performance was achieved for $\nu = 51$. The MCC of the proposed approach employing SLIC+STFT for various segment durations is shown in Figure 8. MCC values of different segment durations and various bandpass filter orders are plotted in Figure 9. The computational time required by the proposed method employing SLIC+STFT was about 423.3 s, while the execution of the MUSIC [3] required 487.2 s to conclude.

4.7. ENF Estimation in Non-Static Video mov_5

Video mov_5 is one of the most challenging recordings. It resembles a scene captured by a security camera. Here, the STFT was employed for ENF estimation. The STFT achieved an MCC of 0.9432, outperforming the MUSIC [3] whose MCC was measured to be 0.8441 [3]. When the ESPRIT was employed, the MCC reached 0.8959. The MCC of STFT is plotted for various segment durations against the MUSIC [3] in Figure 10. When different values of bandpass filter order were employed, a longer segment duration was found to yield an increase in MCC, as can be seen in Figure 11. On the contrary, for a segment duration longer than or equal to 40, a plateau is noticed. The top MCC was achieved for a bandpass filter order of $\nu = 511$. The execution of the proposed approach employing SLIC+STFT required 523.4 s to conclude, while the computational time of the MUSIC [3] was about 602.6 s.

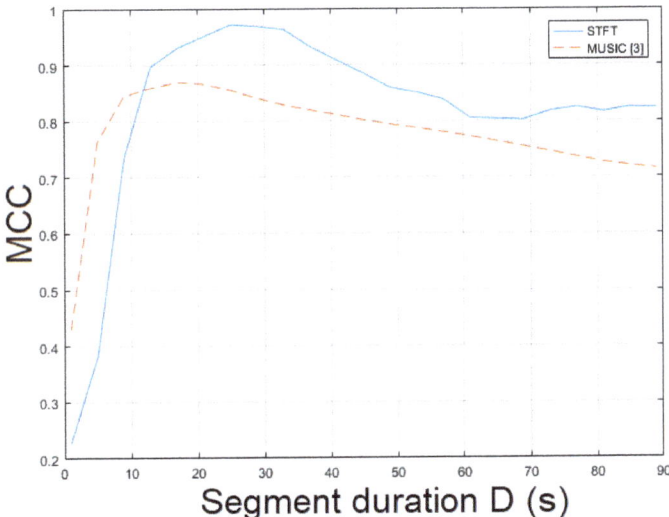

Figure 8. Maximum correlation coefficient of the proposed approach employing SLIC+STFT for various segment durations against the MUSIC [3] (mov4).

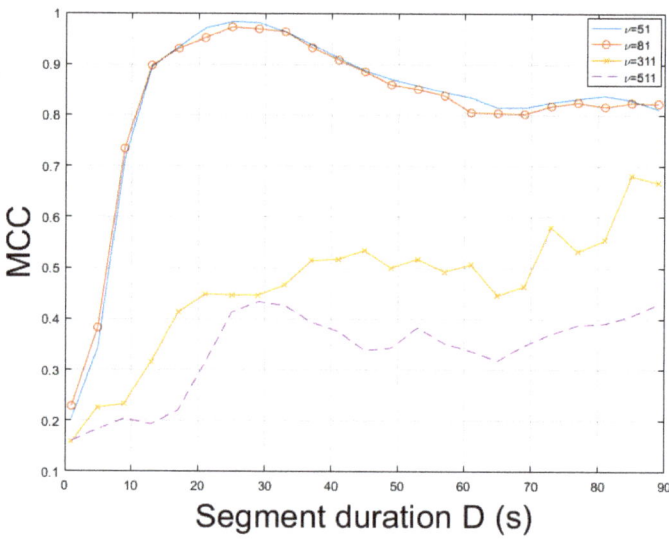

Figure 9. Maximum correlation coefficient of the proposed approach employing SLIC+STFT for various bandpass filter orders and segment durations (mov4).

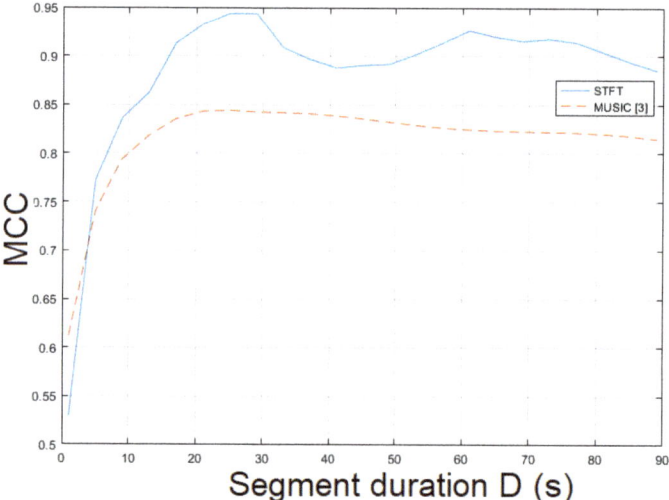

Figure 10. Maximum correlation coefficient of the proposed approach employing SLIC+STFT for various segment durations against the MUSIC [3] (mov5).

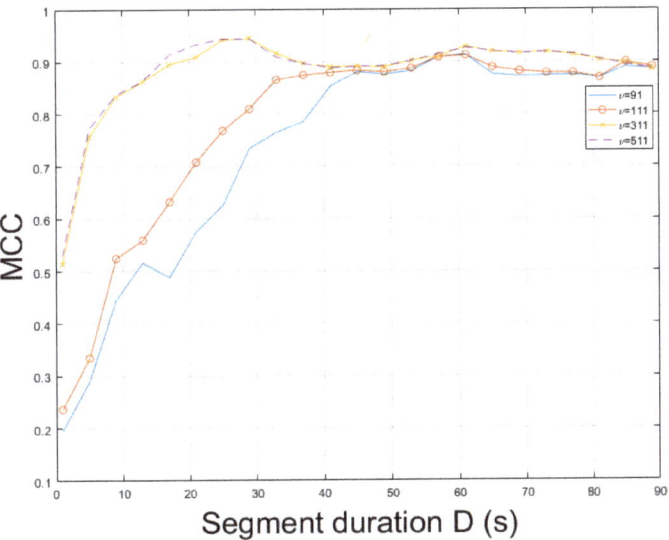

Figure 11. Maximum correlation coefficient of the proposed approach employing SLIC+STFT for various bandpass filter orders and segment durations (mov5).

4.8. ENF Estimation in Non-Static Video mov_6

Similarly to video mov_5, mov_6 constitutes a challenging real-world indoor recording. This recording resembles a scene captured by a hidden camera under special conditions, which could hinder ENF estimation accuracy. Nevertheless, the proposed approach employing STFT resulted in an MCC of 0.9309, outperforming the MUSIC [3] whose MCC was measured to be 0.9115. The MCC of SLIC+STFT is plotted for various segment durations against the MUSIC [3] in Figure 12. The proposed approach performs better than the MUSIC [3] for a segment duration of about 85 s. For shorter segment durations, the MUSIC [3] demonstrates a stable performance, outperforming the proposed SLIC+STFT. For different values of bandpass filter order, it is worth mentioning that by increasing segment duration, an increase in MCC is observed for all cases, as can be seen in Figure 13. The top MCC was achieved for a bandpass filter order of $\nu = 111$. The execution of the proposed approach was 572.5 s. The execution of the MUSIC [3] method required 639.5 s to conclude.

4.9. Assessment of MCC Differences

In order to assess whether the improvements in MCC of the proposed approach, employing SLIC and either STFT or ESPRIT against the MUSIC [3] is statistically significant, and hypothesis testing was applied to all six recordings. The null hypothesis, H_0: $c_1 = c_2$, indicates that MCCs are equal and the alternative one, H_1: $c_1 \neq c_2$ indicates the opposite.

For each video recording, the MCCs of the proposed approach and the MUSIC [3] undergo Fisher's z transformation [51]:

$$z = 0.5 \ln \frac{1+c}{1-c}. \tag{10}$$

The test statistic is given by:

$$q_F = \sqrt{K-3}\,(z_1 - z_2) \tag{11}$$

where K denotes the number of ENF samples. The test statistic q_F is distributed as Gaussian with zero mean value and unit variance, for large K.

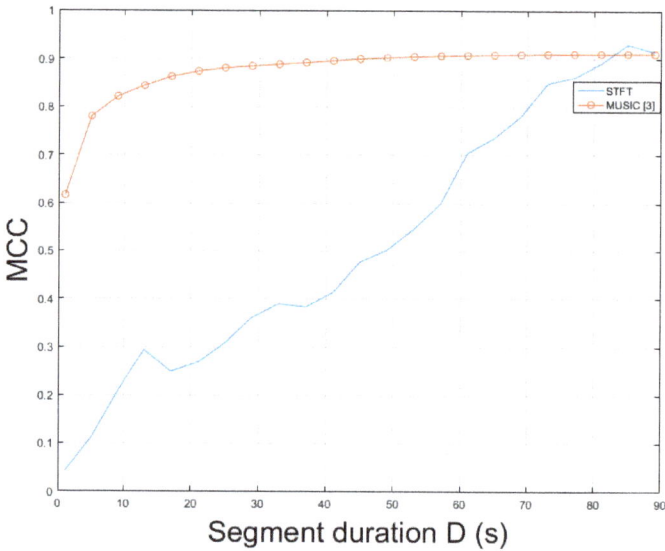

Figure 12. Maximum correlation coefficient of the proposed approach employing SLIC+STFT for various segment durations against the MUSIC [3] (mov6).

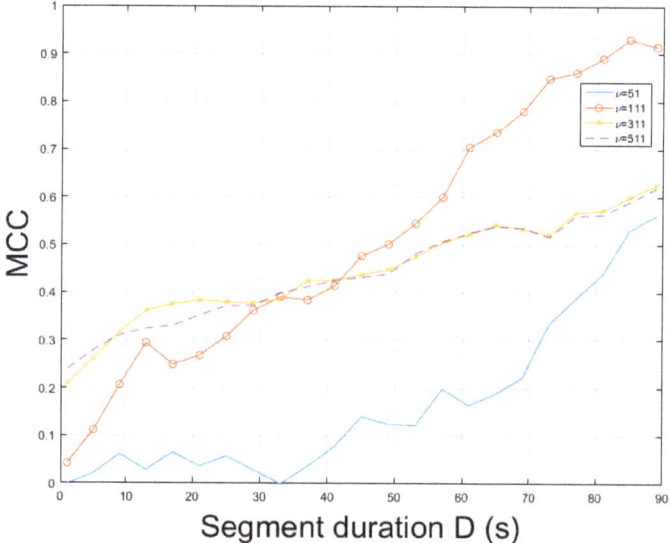

Figure 13. Maximum correlation coefficient of the proposed approach employing SLIC+STFT for various bandpass filter orders and segment durations (mov6).

It is checked whether the test statistic q_F falls within the region of acceptance for a significance level of 5%. If it does so, the null hypothesis H_0 is accepted and, thus, the differences between the MCC's are not statistically significant. On the other hand, if q_F falls outside the region of acceptance (i.e., $|q_F| > 1.965$), the alternative hypothesis H_1 is accepted, indicating that MCC differences are statistically significant. Statistical tests constitute an important contribution of the paper, offering a mechanism for making quantitative decisions, which can lead to accurate ENF estimation in practical forensic applications. The top MCC value of the proposed approach employing SLIC and either

STFT or ESPRIT and that of the MUSIC [3] for each recording and the filter order employed is summarized in Table 3.

Table 3. Maximum correlation coefficient of the proposed approach employing either STFT or ESPRIT and the MUSIC [3] for all recordings. The filter order employed is also quoted.

mov	MCC (here)	MCC [3]	Bandpass Filter Order ν	ENF Samples K
Mov_1	0.9926	0.9658	111	702
Mov_2	0.9704	0.9466	81	639
Mov_3	0.9877	0.9191	51	647
Mov_4	0.9837	0.8700	51	623
Mov_5	0.9432	0.8441	511	729
Mov_6	0.9309	0.9115	111	741

In all cases in Table 3, q_F was calculated and found to be outside the region of acceptance for significance level of 5%. Consequently, there is sufficient evidence to warrant the rejection of the null hypothesis. Therefore, the differences between the MCCs are statistically significant and the proposed approach yields statistically significant improvements in ENF estimation accuracy against the MUSIC [3].

5. Conclusions, Limitations, and Future Research

ENF estimation in static and non-static videos is a non-trivial task especially for complex environments comprising different objects, textures, and moving people. A novel automated approach has been proposed for ENF estimation in static and non-static videos recorded with CCD sensors. It is based on the SLIC algorithm for the generation of regions that share similar characteristics, especially luminance, where ENF variations can be precisely revealed. It has been demonstrated that the proposed approach, which applies either STFT or ESPRIT to a time-series created after SLIC, performs better than the MUSIC [3] in ENF estimation with respect to the maximum correlation coefficient. Moreover, the impact of two factors, namely, the segment duration and the bandpass filter order in ENF estimation accuracy, has been studied. Statistical tests have been conducted, attesting that the improvements in maximum correlation coefficient achieved by the proposed approach are statistically significant against the state-of-the-art approach, which employs the MUSIC method.

In this work, we have explored multiple videos recorded by a fixed camera. A scenario with a moving camera would possibly raise additional difficulties in finding areas of similar characteristics, which are employed in the proposed approach. Consequently, difficulties in accurately estimating the ENF estimate would be anticipated. In addition, although the recordings were of escalating difficulty, there was no more than one person present in the scene. It is difficult to predict whether the proposed approach would perform equally well in an unconstrained environment with a moving camera and scenes with many moving persons.

Future work will aim to extend this work by considering recordings that are captured by the rolling shutter mechanism of CMOS cameras. We are also interested in ENF estimation, when non-static cameras are employed. The latter scenario is very common in real-life applications due to the widespread use of mobile phones. Another challenging research direction is ENF estimation when multiple persons are recorded in the video.

Author Contributions: Conceptualization, G.K.; methodology, G.K.; software, G.K.; validation, G.K.; writing—original draft preparation, G.K.; writing—review and editing, C.K.; supervision, C.K. All authors have read and agreed to the published version of the manuscript.

Funding: This research was funded by the General Secretariat for Research and Technology (GSRT) and the Hellenic Foundation for Research and Innovation (HFRI) (Scholarship Code: 820).

Institutional Review Board Statement: Not applicable.

Informed Consent Statement: Not applicable.

Data Availability Statement: The data presented in this study are openly available in Zenodo at https://doi.org/10.5281/zenodo.3549379, accessed in 8 September 2021.

Acknowledgments: This research has been financially supported by the General Secretariat for Research and Technology (GSRT) and the Hellenic Foundation for Research and Innovation (HFRI) (Scholarship Code: 820). The authors would like to thank Fernando Pérez-González and Samuel Fernández Menduiña for having shared their dataset.

Conflicts of Interest: The authors declare no conflict of interest. The funders had no role in the design of the study; in the collection, analysis, or interpretation of data; in the writing of the manuscript, or in the decision to publish the results.

Abbreviations

f	ENF signal
Hz	Hertz
g	reference ENF signal
v	filter order
f_s	sampling frequency of camera (in frames per second (fps))
f_E	aliased frequency
f_l	frequency of light source illumination
I	identity matrix
γ	integer number
$x(t)$	mean intensity signal
$\hat{\phi}_l$	periodogram
D	segment duration (in s)
L	segment duration (in samples)
G	hop size (in samples)
m	order of the covariance matrix
τ	predefined threshold
S	segment shift (in s)
MV	median intensity value
N	number of superpixels
K	number of estimated ENF values
Λ	number of video frames
ζ_n	mean intensity value
V	overlapping segments
q_F	test statistic
W	principal eigenvectors
CCD	charge-coupled device
CMOS	complementary metal oxide semiconductor
ENF	electric network frequency
ESPRIT	estimation by rotational invariant techniques
MCC	maximum correlation coefficient
MUSIC	multiple signal classification
STFT	short-time Fourier transform
SLIC	simple linear iterative clustering

References

1. Castillo Camacho, I.; Wang, K. A Comprehensive Review of Deep-Learning-Based Methods for Image Forensics. *J. Imaging* **2021**, *7*, 69. [CrossRef] [PubMed]
2. Grigoras, C. Digital audio recording analysis: The electric network frequency (ENF) criterion. *Int. J. Speech Lang. Law* **2005**, *12*, 63–76. [CrossRef]
3. Garg, R.; Varna, A.L.; Hajj-Ahmad, A.; Wu, M. "Seeing" ENF: Power-Signature-Based Timestamp for Digital Multimedia via Optical Sensing and Signal Processing. *IEEE Trans. Inf. Forensics Secur.* **2013**, *8*, 1417–1432. [CrossRef]
4. Hua, G.; Liao, H.; Wang, Q.; Zhang, H.; Ye, D. Detection of Electric Network Frequency in Audio Recordings—From Theory to Practical Detectors. *IEEE Trans. Inf. Forensics Secur.* **2020**, *16*, 236–248. [CrossRef]
5. Ojowu, O.; Karlsson, J.; Li, J.; Liu, Y. ENF Extraction from Digital Recordings Using Adaptive Techniques and Frequency Tracking. *IEEE Trans. Inf. Forensics Secur.* **2012**, *7*, 1330–1338. [CrossRef]

6. Bykhovsky, D.; Cohen, A. Electrical Network Frequency (ENF) Maximum-Likelihood Estimation via a Multitone Harmonic Model. *IEEE Trans. Inf. Forensics Secur.* **2013**, *8*, 774–753. [CrossRef]
7. Hajj-Ahmad, A.; Garg, R.; Wu, M. Spectrum Combining for ENF Signal Estimation. *IEEE Signal Process. Lett.* **2013**, *20*, 885–888. [CrossRef]
8. Lin, X.; Kang, X. Robust Electric Network Frequency Estimation with Rank Reduction and Linear Prediction. *ACM Trans. Multimed. Com. Commun. Appl.* **2018**, *14*, 1–13. [CrossRef]
9. Karantaidis, G.; Kotropoulos, C. Blackman–Tukey spectral estimation and electric network frequency matching from power mains and speech recordings. *IET Signal Process.* **2021**, *15*, 396–409. [CrossRef]
10. Fu, L.; Markham, P.N.; Conners, R.W.; Liu, Y. An Improved Discrete Fourier Transform-Based Algorithm for Electric Network Frequency Extraction. *IEEE Trans. Inf. Forensics Secur.* **2013**, *8*, 1173–1181.
11. Karantaidis, G.; Kotropoulos, C. Assessing spectral estimation methods for Electric Network Frequency extraction. In Proceedings of the 22nd Pan-Hellenic Conference on Informatics, Athens, Greece, 29 November–1 December 2018; pp. 202–207.
12. Karantaidis, G.; Kotropoulos, C. Efficient Capon-Based Approach Exploiting Temporal Windowing for Electric Network Frequency Estimation. In Proceedings of the 2019 IEEE 29th International Workshop on Machine Learning for Signal Processing (MLSP), Pittsburgh, PA, USA, 13–16 October 2019.
13. Dosiek, L. Extracting Electrical Network Frequency From Digital Recordings Using Frequency Demodulation. *IEEE Signal Process. Lett.* **2015**, *22*, 691–695. [CrossRef]
14. Hajj-Ahmad, A.; Garg, R.; Wu, M. Instantaneous frequency estimation and localization for ENF signals. In Proceedings of the 2012 Asia Pacific Signal and Information Processing Association Annual Summit and Conference, Hollywood, CA, USA, 3–6 December 2012; pp. 1–10.
15. Cooper, A.J. The electric network frequency (ENF) as an aid to authenticating forensic digital audio recordings—An automated approach. In *Audio Engineering Society Conference: 33rd International Conference: Audio Forensics-Theory and Practice*; Audio Engineering Society: New York, NY, USA, 2008.
16. Hua, G.; Liao, H.; Zhang, H.; Ye, D.; Ma, J. Robust ENF Estimation Based on Harmonic Enhancement and Maximum Weight Clique. *IEEE Trans. Inf. Forensics Secur.* **2021**, *16*, 3874–3887. [CrossRef]
17. Zhu, Q.; Chen, M.; Wong, C.; Wu, M. Adaptive multi-trace carving for robust frequency tracking in forensic applications. *IEEE Trans. Inf. Forensics Secur.* **2020**, *16*, 1174–1189. [CrossRef]
18. Liao, H.; Hua, G.; Zhang, H. ENF Detection in Audio Recording via Multi-Harmonic Combining. *IEEE Signal Process. Lett.* **2021**, *28*, 1808–1812. [CrossRef]
19. Esquef, P.A.A.; Apolinario, J.A.; Biscainho, L.W.P. Edit Detection in Speech Recordings via Instantaneous Electric Network Frequency Variations. *IEEE Trans. Inf. Forensics Secur.* **2014**, *9*, 2314–2326. [CrossRef]
20. Rodriguez, D.P.N.; Apolinario, J.A.; Biscainho, L.W.P. Audio Authenticity: Detecting ENF Discontinuity With High Precision Phase Analysis. *IEEE Trans. Inf. Forensics Secur.* **2010**, *5*, 534–543. [CrossRef]
21. Hua, G.; Zhang, Y.; Goh, J.; Thing, V.L.L. Audio Authentication by Exploring the Absolute-Error-Map of ENF Signals. *IEEE Trans. Inf. Forensics Secur.* **2016**, *11*, 1003–1016. [CrossRef]
22. Reis, P.M.J.I.; Costa, J.P.C.L.; Miranda, R.K.; Galdo, G.D. ESPRIT-Hilbert-Based Audio Tampering Detection with SVM Classifier for Forensic Analysis via Electrical Network Frequency. *IEEE Trans. Inf. Forensics Secur.* **2017**, *12*, 853–864. [CrossRef]
23. Garg, R.; Hajj-Ahmad, A.; Wu, M. Geo-location estimation from electrical network frequency signals. In Proceedings of the 2013 IEEE International Conference on Acoustics, Speech and Signal Processing, Vancouver, BC, Canada, 26–31 May 2013; pp. 2862–2866.
24. Hajj-Ahmad, A.; Garg, R.; Wu, M. ENF-Based Region-of-Recording Identification for Media Signals. *IEEE Trans. Inf. Forensics Secur.* **2015**, *10*, 1125–1136. [CrossRef]
25. Lin, X.; Liu, J.; Kang, X. Audio Recapture Detection With Convolutional Neural Networks. *IEEE Trans. Multimed.* **2016**, *18*, 1480–1487. [CrossRef]
26. Hua, G.; Zhang, H. ENF Signal Enhancement in Audio Recordings. *IEEE Trans. Inf. Forensics Secur.* **2020**, *15*, 1868–1878. [CrossRef]
27. Elmesalawy, M.M.; Eissa, M.M. New Forensic ENF Reference Database for Media Recording Authentication Based on Harmony Search Technique Using GIS and Wide Area Frequency Measurements. *IEEE Trans. Inf. Forensics Secur.* **2014**, *9*, 633–644. [CrossRef]
28. Bykhovsky, D. Recording device identification by ENF harmonics power analysis. *Forensic Sci. Int.* **2020**, *307*, 110100. [CrossRef]
29. Hajj-Ahmad, A.; Wong, C.; Gambino, S.; Zhu, Q.; Yu, M.; Wu, M. Factors Affecting ENF Capture in Audio. *IEEE Trans. Inf. Forensics Secur.* **2019**, *14*, 277–288. [CrossRef]
30. Su, H.; Hajj-Ahmad, A.; Garg, R.; Wu, M. Exploiting rolling shutter for ENF signal extraction from video. In Proceedings of the 2014 IEEE International Conference on Image Processing (ICIP), Paris, France, 27–30 October 2014; pp. 5367–5371.
31. Vatansever, S.; Dirik, A.E.; Memon, N. Analysis of Rolling Shutter Effect on ENF-Based Video Forensics. *IEEE Trans. Inf. Forensics Secur.* **2019**, *14*, 2262–2275. [CrossRef]
32. Vatansever, S.; Dirik, A.E.; Memon, N. Detecting the Presence of ENF Signal in Digital Videos: A Superpixel-Based Approach. *IEEE Signal Process. Lett.* **2017**, *24*, 1463–1467. [CrossRef]

33. Fernández-Menduiña, S.; Pérez-González, F. Temporal Localization of Non-Static Digital Videos Using the Electrical Network Frequency. *IEEE Signal Process. Lett.* **2020**, *27*, 745–749. [CrossRef]
34. Hajj-Ahmad, A.; Berkovich, A.; Wu, M. Exploiting power signatures for camera forensics. *IEEE Signal Process. Lett.* **2016**, *23*, 713–717. [CrossRef]
35. Su, H.; Hajj-Ahmad, A.; Wong, C.; Garg, R.; Wu, M. ENF signal induced by power grid: A new modality for video synchronization. In Proceedings of the 2nd ACM International Workshop on Immersive Media Experiences, Orlando, FL, USA, 3–7 November 2014; pp. 13–18.
36. Su, H.; Hajj-Ahmad, A.; Wu, M.; Oard, D. Exploring the use of ENF for multimedia synchronization. In Proceedings of the 2014 IEEE International Conference on Acoustics, Speech and Signal Processing (ICASSP), Florence, Italy, 4–9 May 2014; pp. 4613–4617.
37. Wang, Y.; Hu, Y.; Liew, A.; Li, C.T. ENF Based Video Forgery Detection Algorithm. *Int. J. Digit. Crime Forensics* **2020**, *12*, 131–156. [CrossRef]
38. Nagothu, D.; Chen, Y.; Blasch, E.; Aved, A.; Zhu, S. Detecting malicious false frame injection attacks on surveillance systems at the edge using electrical network frequency signals. *Sensors* **2019**, *19*, 2424. [CrossRef]
39. Wong, C.W.; Hajj-Ahmad, A.; Wu, M. Invisible Geo-Location Signature in A Single Image. In Proceedings of the 2018 IEEE International Conference on Acoustics, Speech and Signal Processing (ICASSP), Calgary, AB, Canada, 15–20 April 2018; pp. 1987–1991.
40. Ferrara, P.; Sanchez, I.; Draper-Gil, G.; Junklewitz, H.; Beslay, L. A MUSIC Spectrum Combining Approach for ENF-based Video Timestamping. In Proceedings of the 2021 IEEE International Workshop on Biometrics and Forensics (IWBF), Rome, Italy, 6–7 May 2021; pp. 1–6.
41. Achanta, R.; Shaji, A.; Smith, K.; Lucchi, A.; Fua, P.; Süsstrunk, S. SLIC superpixels compared to state-of-the-art superpixel methods. *IEEE Trans. Pattern Anal. Mach. Intell.* **2012**, *34*, 2274–2282. [CrossRef] [PubMed]
42. Grigoras, C. Applications of ENF criterion in forensic audio, video, computer and telecommunication analysis. *Forensic Sci. Int.* **2007**, *167*, 136–145. [CrossRef] [PubMed]
43. Nicolalde-Rodríguez, D.P.; Apolinário, J.A.; Biscainho, L.W.P. Audio authenticity based on the discontinuity of ENF higher harmonics. In Proceedings of the 21st European Signal Processing Conference (EUSIPCO 2013), Marrakech, Morocco, 9–13 September 2013; pp. 1–5.
44. Hu, Y.; Li, C.T.; Lv, Z.; Liu, B.B. Audio forgery detection based on max offsets for cross correlation between ENF and reference signal. In *International Workshop on Digital Watermarking*; Springer: Berlin/Heidelberg, Germany, 2012; pp. 253–266.
45. Oppenheim, A.V.; Schafer, R.W. *Discrete-Time Signal Processing*, 3rd ed.; Prentice Hall Press: Upper Saddle River, NJ, USA, 2009.
46. Hajj-Ahmad, A.; Baudry, S.; Chupeau, B.; Doërr, G. Flicker forensics for pirate device identification. In Proceedings of the 3rd ACM Workshop on Information Hiding and Multimedia Security, Paris, France, 3–5 July 2019; pp. 75–84.
47. Allen, J.B.; Rabiner, L.R. A unified approach to short-time Fourier analysis and synthesis. *Proc. IEEE* **1977**, *65*, 1558–1564. [CrossRef]
48. Stoica, P.; Moses, R.L. *Spectral Analysis of Signals*; Pearson Prentice Hall: Upper Saddle River, NJ, USA, 2005.
49. Huijbregtse, M.; Geradts, Z. Using the ENF criterion for determining the time of recording of short digital audio recordings. In *International Workshop on Computational Forensics*; Springer: Berlin/Heidelberg, Germany, 2009; pp. 116–124.
50. Fernandez-Menduina, S.; Pérez-González, F. ENF Moving Video Database 2020. Available online: https://doi.org/https://doi.org/10.5281/zenodo.3549378 (accessed on 8 September 2021).
51. Papoulis, A. *Probability and Statistics*; Prentice-Hall, Inc.: Upper Saddle River, NJ, USA, 1990.

Review

A Survey on Anti-Spoofing Methods for Facial Recognition with RGB Cameras of Generic Consumer Devices

Zuheng Ming [1], Muriel Visani [1,2,*], Muhammad Muzzamil Luqman [1] and Jean-Christophe Burie [1]

1. L3i Laboratory, La Rochelle University, 17042 La Rochelle, France; zuheng.ming@univ-lr.fr (Z.M.); muhammad_muzzamil.luqman@univ-lr.fr (M.M.L.); jcburie@univ-lr.fr (J.-C.B.)
2. School of Information & Communication Technology, Hanoi University of Science and Technology, Hanoi 100000, Vietnam
* Correspondence: muriel.visani@univ-lr.fr; Tel.: +84-3-64-00-68-46

Received: 29 September 2020; Accepted: 3 December 2020; Published: 15 December 2020

Abstract: The widespread deployment of facial recognition-based biometric systems has made facial presentation attack detection (face anti-spoofing) an increasingly critical issue. This survey thoroughly investigates facial Presentation Attack Detection (PAD) methods that only require RGB cameras of generic consumer devices over the past two decades. We present an attack scenario-oriented typology of the existing facial PAD methods, and we provide a review of over 50 of the most influenced facial PAD methods over the past two decades till today and their related issues. We adopt a comprehensive presentation of the reviewed facial PAD methods following the proposed typology and in chronological order. By doing so, we depict the main challenges, evolutions and current trends in the field of facial PAD and provide insights on its future research. From an experimental point of view, this survey paper provides a summarized overview of the available public databases and an extensive comparison of the results reported in PAD-reviewed papers.

Keywords: biometrics; facial recognition; facial anti-spoofing; facial Presentation Attack Detection (PAD); RGB camera-based anti-spoofing methods; deep learning; survey; computer vision; pattern recognition

1. Introduction

1.1. Background

In the past two decades, the advancement of technology in electronics and computer science has provided access to top-level technology devices at affordable prices to an important proportion of the world population. Various biometric systems have been widely deployed in real-life applications, such as online payment and e-commerce security, smartphone-based authentication, secured access control, biometric passport and border checks. Facial recognition is among the most studied biometric technologies since the 90s [1], mainly for its numerous advantages compared to other biometrics. Indeed, faces are highly distinctive among individuals and facial recognition can be implemented even in nonintrusive acquisition scenarios or from a distance.

Recently, deep learning has dramatically improved the state-of-the-art performance of many computer vision tasks, such as image classification and object recognition [2–4]. With these significant progresses, facial recognition has also made great breakthroughs such as the success of DeepFace [5], DeepIDs [6], VGG Face [7], FaceNet [8], SphereFace [9] and ArcFace [10]. One of these spectacular breakthroughs occurred between 2014 and 2015, when multiple groups [5,8,11] approached and then surpassed human-level recognition accuracy on very challenging face benchmarks, such as

Labeled Faces in the Wild (LFW) [12] or YouTube Faces (YTF) [13]. Thanks to their convenience, excellent performances and great security levels, facial recognition systems are among the most widespread biometric systems in the market compared to other biometrics such as iris and fingerprint recognition [14].

However, given facial authentication systems' popularity, they became primary targets of Presentation Attacks (PAs) [15]. PAs are performed by malicious or ill-intentioned users who either aim at impersonating someone else's identity (impersonation attack) or at avoiding being recognized by the system (obfuscation attack). However, compared to face recognition performances, the vulnerabilities of facial authentication systems to PAs have been much less studied.

The main objective of this paper is to present a detailed review of face PAD methods that are crucial for assessing the vulnerability/robustness of current facial recognition-based systems towards ill-intentioned users. Given the prevalence of biometric applications based on facial authentication, such as online payment, it is crucial to protect genuine users against impersonation attacks in real-life scenarios. In this survey paper, we will focus more on impersonation detection. However, at the end of the paper, we will discuss obfuscation detection as well.

The next section provides a categorization of face PAs. Based on this categorization, we will present later in this paper a typology of existing facial PAD methods and then a comprehensive review of such methods, with an extensive comparison of these methods by considering the results reported in the reviewed works.

1.2. Categories of Facial Presentation Attacks

One can consider that there are basically two types of Presentation Attacks (PAs).

First, with the advent of internet and social medias where more and more people share photos or videos of their faces, such documents can be used by impostors to try and fool facial authentication systems for impersonation purposes. Such attacks are also called *impersonation* (*spoofing*) attacks.

Second, another (less studied) type of presentation attack is called an *obfuscation* attacks, where a person uses tricks to avoid being recognized by the system (but not necessarily by impersonating a legitimate user's identity).

In short, while impersonation (spoofing) attacks are generally performed by impostors who are willing to impersonate a legitimate user, obfuscation attacks aim at ensuring that the user remains under the radar of the facial recognition system. Despite their totally different objectives, both types of attacks are listed in the ISO standard [16] dedicated to biometric PAD.

In this survey paper, we focus on impersonation (spoofing) attacks, where the impostor might either use directly biometric data from a legitimate user to mount an attack or to create Presentation Attack Instruments (PAIs, usually spoofs or fakes) that will be used for attacking the face recognition system.

Common PAs/PAIs can generally be categorized as photo attacks, video replay attacks and 3D mask attacks (see Figure 1 for their categorization and Figure 2 for illustrations), whereas obfuscation attacks generally rely on tricks to hide the user's real identity, such as facial makeup, plastic surgery or face region occlusion.

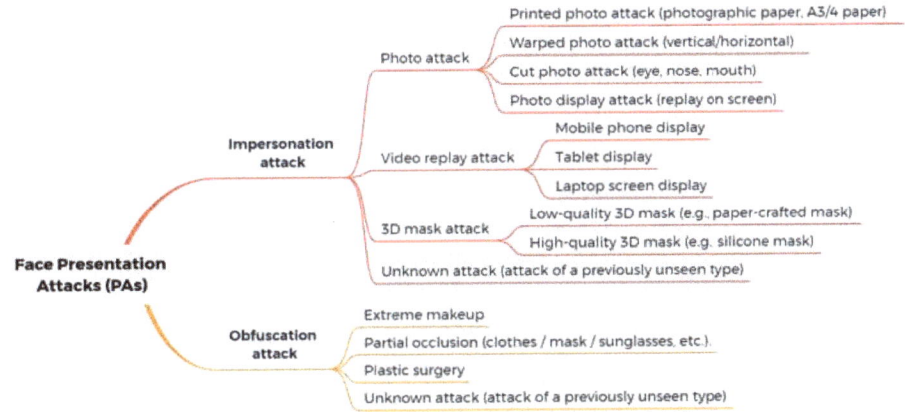

Figure 1. A typology of facial Presentation Attacks (PAs).

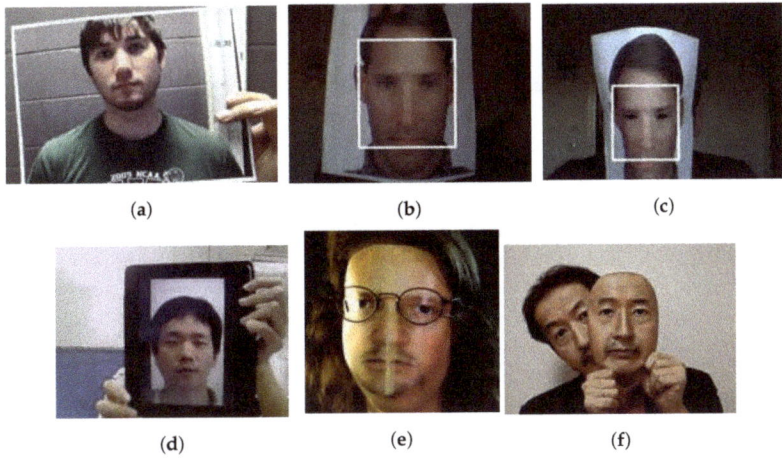

Figure 2. Examples of common facial presentation attacks: (**a**) a printed photo attack from the SiW dataset [17]; (**b**) an example of a warped photo attack extracted from [18]; (**c**) an example of a cut photo attack extracted from [18]; (**d**) a video replay attack from the CASIA-FASD dataset [19]; (**e**) a paper-crafted mask from UMRE [20]; and (**f**) a high-quality 3D mask attack from REAL-f [17].

Photo attacks (sometimes also called print attacks in the literature) and video replay attacks are the most common attacks due to the ever-increasing flow of face images available on the internet and the prevalence of low-cost but high-resolution digital devices. Impostors can simply collect and reuse face samples of genuine users. Photo attacks are carried out by presenting to the facial authentication system a picture of a genuine user. Several strategies are usually used by the impostors. Printed photo attacks (see Figure 2a) consist in presenting a picture printed on a paper (e.g., A3/A4 paper, copper paper or professional photographic paper). On the other hand, in photo display attacks, the picture is displayed on the screen of a digital device such as a smartphone, a tablet or a laptop and then presented to the system. Moreover, as illustrated in Figure 2b, printed photos can be warped (along a vertical and/or horizontal axis) to give some depth to the photo (this strategy is called a warped photo attack). Cut photo attacks consist in using the picture as a photo mask where the mouth, eyes and/or nose regions have been cut out to introduce some liveness cues from the impostor's face behind the photo, such as eye blinking or mouth movement (see Figure 2c).

Compared to static photo attacks, video replay attacks (see Figure 2d) are more sophisticated, as they introduce intrinsic dynamic information such as eye blinking, mouth movements and changes in facial expressions in order to mimic liveness [21].

Contrary to photo attacks or video replay attacks (that are generally 2D planar attacks, except for warped photo attacks), 3D mask attacks reconstruct 3D face artifacts. One can distinguish between low-quality 3D masks (e.g., crafted from a printed photo as illustrated in Figure 2e) and high-quality 3D masks (e.g., made out of silicone, see Figure 2f). The high realism of the "face-like" 3D structure and the vivid imitation of human skin texture in high-quality 3D masks makes it more challenging to detect 3D mask spoofing by traditional PAD methods (i.e., methods conceived to detect photo or video replay attacks [22,23]). Nowadays, manufacturing a high-quality 3D mask is still expensive [24] and complex and relies on complete 3D acquisition, generally requiring the user's cooperation [25]. Thus, 3D mask attacks are still far less frequent than photo or video replay attacks. However, with the popularization of 3D acquisition sensors, 3D mask attacks are expected to become more and more frequent in the coming years.

PAD methods for previously unseen attacks (unknown attacks) will be reviewed in Section 2.6, "New trends", as most of them are still under development and rely on recent approaches such as zero/few-shot learning.

Obfuscation attacks, in which the objective is quite different from impersonation attacks (as the aim for the attacker is to remain unrecognized by the system), generally rely on facial makeup, plastic surgery or face region occlusion (e.g., using accessories such as scarves or sunglasses). However, in some cases, obfuscation attacks can also rely on the use of another person's biometric data. It fundamentally differs from usual spoofing attacks in its primary objective. However, in some cases, the PAIs for obfuscation attacks can be similar to the ones used for impersonation attacks, e.g., the face mask of another person. While most of the PAD methods reviewed in this paper are usual anti-spoofing methods (for detecting impersonation attacks), obfuscation methods are specifically discussed in Section 5, "Discussion".

The objective of this paper is to give a review of the impersonation PAD (anti-spoofing) methods that do not require any specific hardware. In other words, we focus on methods that can be implemented with only RGB cameras from Generic Consumer Devices (GCDs). This obviously raises some difficulties and limitations, e.g., when it comes to distinguishing between 2D planar surfaces (photos and screens) and 3D facial surfaces. In the next section, we discuss the motivation for reviewing facial anti-spoofing methods using only GCDs.

1.3. Facial PAD Methods with Generic Consumer Devices (GCD)

To the best of our knowledge, there is still no agreed-upon PAD method that can tackle all types of attacks. Given the variety of possible PAs, many facial PAD approaches have been proposed in the past two decades. From a very general perspective, one can distinguish between the methods for facial PAD based on specific hardware/sensors and the approaches using only RGB cameras from GCDs.

Facial PAD methods using specific hardware may rely on structured-light 3D sensors, Time of Flight (ToF) sensors, Near-infrared (NIR) sensors, thermal sensors, etc. In general, such specific sensors considerably facilitate facial PAD. For instance, 3D sensors can discriminate between the 3D face and 2D planar attacks by detecting depth maps [26], while NIR sensors can easily detect video replay attacks (as electronic displays appear almost uniformly dark under NIR illumination) [27–30], and thermal sensors can detect the characteristic temperature distribution for living faces [31]. Even though such approaches tend to achieve higher performance, they are not yet broadly available to the general public. Indeed, such sensors are still expensive and rarely embedded on ordinary GCDs, with the exception of some costly devices. Therefore, the use of such specific sensors is limited to some applicative scenarios, such as physical access control to protected premises.

However, for most applicative scenarios, the user needs to be authenticated using their own device. In such scenarios, PAD methods that rely on specific hardware are therefore not usable. Thus, researchers and developers widely opt for methods based on RGB cameras that are embedded in most electronic GCDs (such as smartphones, tablets or laptops) [32–37].

This is the main reason why, in this work, we focus on the facial PAD approaches that do not require any specific hardware. More precisely, we present a comprehensive review of the research work in facial anti-spoofing methods for facial recognition systems using only the RGB cameras of GCDs. The major contributions of this paper are listed in the section below.

1.4. Main Contributions of This Paper

The major contributions of this survey paper are the following:

- We propose a typology of existing facial PAD methods based on the type of PAs they aim to detect and some specificities of the applicative scenario.
- We provide a comprehensive review of over 50 recent facial PAD methods that only require (as input) images captured by RGB cameras embedded in most GCDs.
- We provide a summarized overview of the available public databases for both 2D attacks and 3D mask attacks, which are of vital importance for both model training and testing.
- We report extensively the results detailed in the reviewed works and quantitatively compare the different PAD methods under uniform benchmarks, metrics and protocols.
- We discuss some less-studied topics in the field of facial PAD, such as unknown PAs and obfuscation attacks, and we provide some insights for future work.

1.5. Structure of This Paper

The remainder of this paper is structured as follows. In Section 2, we propose a typology for facial PAD methods based on RGB cameras from GCDs and review the most representative/recent approaches for each category. In Section 3, we present a summarized overview of the most used/interesting datasets together with their main advantages and limitations. Then, Section 4 presents a comparative evaluation of the reviewed PAD methods. Section 5 provides a discussion about current trends and some insights for future directions of research. Finally, we draw the conclusions in Section 6.

2. Overview of Facial PAD Methods Using Only RGB Cameras from GCDs

2.1. Typology of Facial PAD Methods

A variety of different typologies could be found in the literature. For instance, Chingovska et al. [37] proposed to group the facial PAD methods into three categories: motion-based, texture-based and image-quality based methods, while Costa-Pazo et al. [38] considered image quality-based facial PAD methods as a subclass of texture-based methods. Ramachandra and Busch [39] classified facial PAD methods into two more general categories: hardware-based and software-based methods. The different approaches are then hierarchically classified into subclasses of these two broad categories. Hernandez-Ortega et al. [40] divided the PAD methods as static or dynamic methods, depending on whether they take into account temporal information. Recently, Bhattacharjee et al. [41] considered the PAD methods as approaches based on visible light and extended-range imagery. The visible light here refers to the range of the electromagnetic spectrum which is typically perceptible by the human visual system such as by cameras from GCDs. Instead, in extended-range imagery, the subject is illuminated under a chosen wavelength band using NIR and SWIR-based cameras with appropriate filters to be able to capture data only in the chosen wavelength band.

Based on the type of attacks presented in Section 1.2 and inspired by [39,41], we categorize facail PAD methods into two broad categories: RGB camera-based PAD methods and PAD methods using specific hardware. As stated earlier, in this paper, we focus on the facial PAD approaches that use only RGB cameras embedded in most GCDs (smartphone, tablet, laptop, etc.). Inside this broad category, we distinguish between the following five different classes:

1. liveness cue-based methods;
2. texture cue-based methods;
3. 3D geometric cue-based methods;
4. multiple cues-based methods; and
5. methods using new trends.

As detailed in Figure 3, each of these five categories is then divided into several subclasses, depending on the applicative scenario or on the type of features/methods used. For each category/subcategory of PAD methods, Table 1 shows the type(s) of PAs that it aims to detect, whereas Figure 3 lists all the facial PAD methods that will be discussed in the remainder of this Section (over 50 methods in total).

Table 1. The type(s) of Presentation Attacks (PAs) each subtype that the PAD method aims to detect.

PAD Methods	Subtypes	PAs
Liveness cue-based	Nonintrusive motion-based	Photo attack (except cut photo attack)
	Intrusive motion-based	Photo attack (except cut photo attack) Video replay attacks (except sophisticated DeepFakes)
	rPPG-based	Photo attack "Low quality" video replay attacks 3D mask attack (low/high quality)
Texture cue-based	Static texture-based Dynamic texture-based	Photo attack Video replay attack 3D mask attack (low quality)
3D Geometry cue-based	3D shape-based Pseudo-depth map-based	Photo attack Video replay attack
Multiple cues-based	Liveness (Motion) + Texture	Photo attack Video replay attack
	Liveness + 3D Geometry (rPPG + Pseudo-depth map)	Photo attack Video replay attack 3D mask attack (low/high quality)
	Texture + 3D Geometry (Patched-base texture + Pseudo-depth map)	Photo attack Video replay attack

From a very general standpoint, we state the following:

1. Liveness cue-based methods aim to detect liveness cues in facial presentation or PAI. The most widely used liveness cues so far are motion (head movements, facial expressions, etc.) and micro-intensity changes corresponding to blood pulse. Thus, liveness cue-based methods can be classified into the following two subcategories:

   - Motion cue-based methods employ motion cues in video clips to discriminate between genuine (alive) faces and static photo attacks. Such methods can effectively in detecting static photo attacks but not video replay with motion/liveness cues and 3D mask attacks;
   - Remote PhotoPlethysmoGraphy (rPPG) is the most widely used technique for measuring facial micro-intensity changes corresponding to blood pulse. rPPG cue-based methods can detect photo and 3D mask attacks, as these PAIs do not show the periodic intensity changes that are characteristic of facial skin. They can also detect "low-quality" video replay attacks that are not able to display those subtle changes (due to the capture conditions and/or PAI characteristics). However, "high-quality" video replay attacks (displaying the dynamic changes of the genuine face's skin) cannot be detected by rPPG cue-based methods.

2. Texture cue-based methods use static or dynamic texture cues to detect facial PAs by analyzing the micro-texture of the surface presented to the camera. Static texture cues are generally spatial texture features that can be extracted from a single image. In contrast, dynamic texture cues usually consist of spatiotemporal texture features, extracted from an image sequence. Texture

cue-based facial PAD methods can detect all types of PAs. However, they might be fooled by "high-quality" 3D masks (masks with a surface texture that mimics good facial texture);
3. Three-dimensional geometric cue-based methods use 3D geometrical features, generally based on the 3D structure or depth information/map of the user's face or PAIs. Three-dimensional geometric cue-based PAD methods can detect planar photo and video replay attacks but not (in general) 3D mask attacks;
4. Multiple cues-based methods consider different cues (e.g., motion features with texture features) to detect a wider variety of face PAs;
5. Methods using new trends do not necessarily aim to detect specific types of PAs, but their common trait is that they rely on cutting-edge machine learning technology, such as Neural Architecture Search (NAS), zero-shot learning, domain adaption, etc.

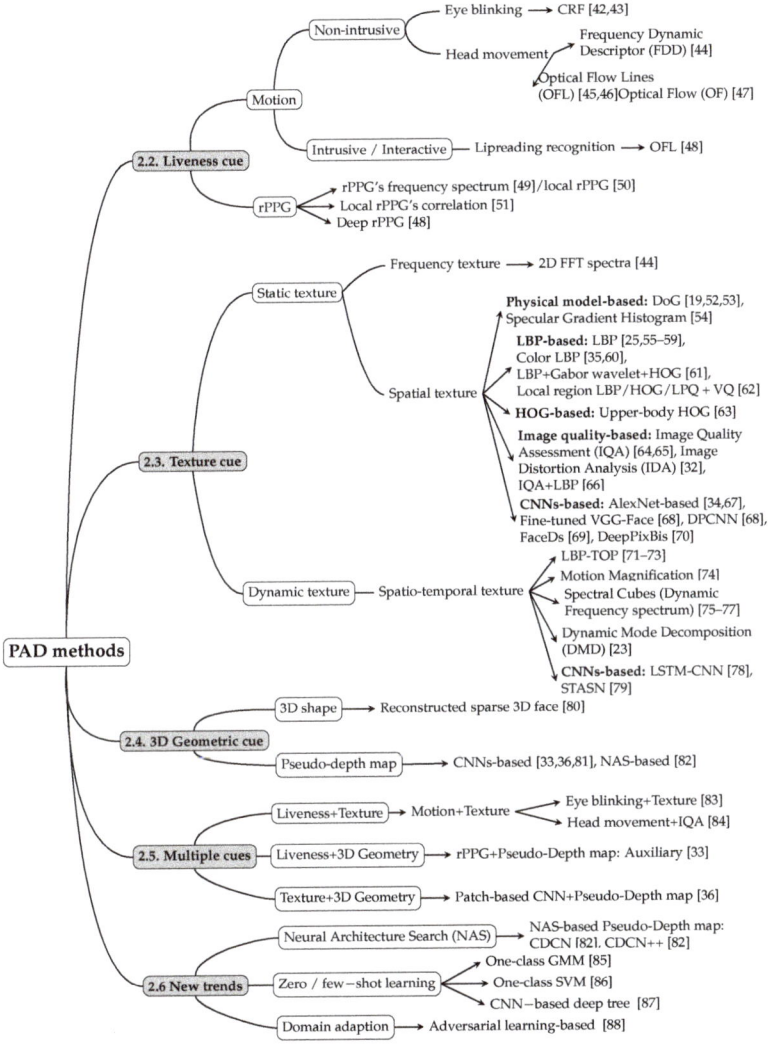

Figure 3. Our proposed typology for facial PAD methods [19,23,25,32–36,42–88]: the darkest nodes are numbered with their corresponding subsections in the remainder of Section 2.

In the remainder of this section, we present a detailed review of the over fifty recent PAD methods that are listed in Figure 3, structured using the above typology and in chronological order inside each category/subcategory. In each category, we elaborate both the "conventional" methods that have influenced facial PAD the most and their current evolutions in the deep learning era.

2.2. Liveness Cue-Based Methods

Liveness cue-based methods are the first attempt for facial PAD. Liveness cue-based methods aim to detect any dynamic physiological sign of life, such as eye blinking, mouth movement, facial expression changes and pulse beat. They can be categorized as motion-based methods (to detect the eye blinking, mouth movement and facial expression changes) and rPPG-based methods (to detect the pulse beat).

2.2.1. Motion-Based Methods

By detecting movements of the face/facial features, conventional motion-based methods can effectively detect static presentation attacks, such as most photo attacks (without dynamic information). However, they are generally not effective against video replay attacks that display liveness information such as eye blinking, head movements, facial expression changes, etc.

This is why interactive motion-based methods were later introduced, where the user is required to complete a specific (sequence of) movement(s) such as head rotation/tilting, mouth opening, etc. The latter methods are more effective for detecting video replay attacks, but they are intrusive for the user, unlike traditional methods that do not require the user's collaboration and are therefore nonintrusive.

The rest of this section is structured around two subcategories: (a) nonintrusive motion-based methods, that are more user-friendly and easier to implement, and (b) intrusive/interactive motion-based methods, that are more robust and can detect both static and dynamic PAs.

(a) Nonintrusive motion-based methods

Nonintrusive motion-based PAD methods aim to detect intrinsic liveness based on movement (head movement, eye blinking, facial expression changes, etc.).

In 2004, Li et al. [44] first used frequency-based features to detect photo attacks. More specifically, they proposed the Frequency Dynamic Descriptor (FDD), based on frequency components' energy, to estimate temporal changes due to movements. By setting an FDD threshold, genuine (alive) faces can be distinguished from photo PAs, even for relatively high-resolution photo attacks. This method is easier to implement and is less computationally expensive when compared to the previously proposed motion-based methods that used 3D depth maps to estimate head motions [89,90]. However, its main limitation is that it relies on the assumption that the illumination is invariant during video capture, which cannot always be satisfied in a real-life scenario. This can lead to the presence of a possibly large quantity of "noise" (coming from illumination variations) in the frequency component's variations, and the method is not conceived to deal with such noise.

Unlike the approach introduced in [44], the method proposed in 2005 by Kollreider et al. [45,46] works directly in the RGB representation space (and not in the frequency domain). More precisely, the authors try to detect the differences in motion patterns between 2D planar photographs and genuine (3D) faces using optical flows. The idea is the following: when a head has a small rotation (which is natural and unintentional), for a real face, the face parts that near the camera ("inner parts", e.g., nose) move differently from the parts further away from the camera ("outer parts", e.g., ears). In contrast, a translated photograph generates constant motion among all face regions [45].

More precisely, the authors proposed Optical Flow Lines (OFL), inspired from [91], to measure face motion in horizontal and vertical directions. As illustrated in Figure 4, the different greyscales obtained in the OFL from a genuine (alive face) with a subtle facial rotation reflect the motion differences in between different facial parts, whereas the OFL of a translated photo shows constant motion.

A liveness score in [0, 1] is then calculated from the OFLs of the different facial regions, where 1 indicates that the movement of the surface presented to the camera is coherent with facial movement and 0 indicates that this movement is not coherent with facial movement. By thresholding this liveness score, the method proposed in [45] can detect printed photo attacks, even if the photo is bent or even warped around a cylinder (as it is still far from the real 3D structure of a face). However, this method fails for most video replay attacks, and it can be disrupted by eyeglasses (because they partly cover outer parts of the face but are close to the camera) [46].

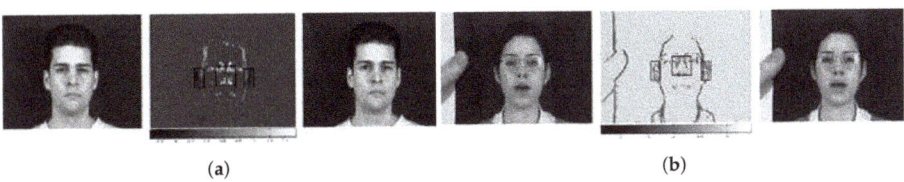

(a) (b)

Figure 4. The Optical Flow Lines (OFL) images obtained from (**a**) a genuine (alive face) presentation with a subtle facial rotation and (**b**) a printed photo attack with horizontal translation [46]: in (**a**), the inner parts are brighter than the outer parts of the face, which is characteristic of the motion differences between different face parts. In contrast, all parts of the planar photo in (**b**) display constant motion.

In 2009, Bao et al. [47] also leveraged optical flow to distinguish between 3D faces and planar photo attacks. Let us call O the object presented to the system (face or planar photo). By comparing the optical flow field of O deduced from its perspective projection to a predefined 2D object's reference optical flow field, the proposed method can determine if the given object is a really a 3D face or a planar photo.

However, like all other optical flow-based methods, the methods in [45–47] are not robust toward background and illumination changes.

In 2007, Pan et al. [42,43] chose to focus on eye blinking in order to distinguish between a face and a facial photo. Eye blinking is a physiological behavior that normally happens 15 to 30 times per minute [92]. Therefore, it is possible for GCD cameras having at least 15 frames per second (fps)—which is almost all GCD cameras—to capture two or more frames per blink [42]. Pan et al. [42,43] proposed to use Conditional Random Fields (CRFs) fed by temporally observed images x_i to model eye blinking with its different estimated (hidden) states y_i: Non-Closed (NC, including opened and half-opened eyes), then Closed (C) and then NC again, as illustrated in Figure 5. The authors showed that their CRF-based model (discriminative model) is more effective than Hidden Markov Model (HMM)-based methods [93] (generative model), as it takes into account longer-range dependencies in the data sequence. They also showed that their model is superior to another discriminative model: Viola and Jones' Adaboost cascade [94] (as the latter is not conceived for sequential data). This method, like all other methods based on eye blinking, can effectively detect printed photo attacks but not video replay attacks or eye-cut photo attacks that simulate blinking [19].

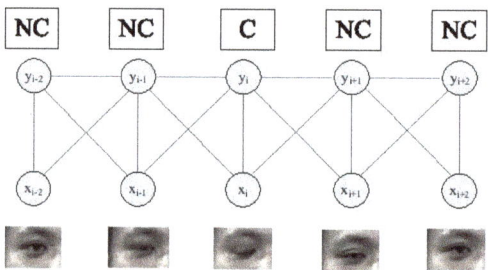

Figure 5. Conditional Random Field (CRF)-based eye-blinking model [42,43]: in this example, each hidden state y_i is conditioned by its corresponding observation (image) x_i and its two neighboring observations x_{i-1} and x_{i+1}.

(b) Intrusive motion-based methods

Intrusive methods (also called interactive methods) are usually based on a challenge–response mechanism that requires the users to satisfy the system's requirements. In this paragraph, we present methods where the challenge is based on some predefined head/facial movement (e.g., blinking the eyes, moving the head in a certain way, adopting a given facial expression or uttering a certain sequence of words).

In 2007, Kollreider et al. [48] first proposed an interactive method that can detect replay attacks as well as photo attacks by reading the presented face's lips when the user is prompted to utter a randomly determined sequence of digits. Like in their previous work [45] mentioned above, Kollreider et al. [48] used OFL to extract mouth motion. An interesting feature of this method is that it combines facial detection and facial PAD in a holistic system. Thus, the integrated facial detection module can also be used to detect the mouth region, and OFL is used for both facial detection and facial PAD.

Then, a 10-class Support Vector Machine (SVM) [95] is trained from 160-dimensional velocity vectors extracted from the mouth region's OFL to perform recognition of the 0–9 digits. This method detects effectively printed photo attacks and most video replay attacks. However, it is vulnerable to mouth-cut photo attacks, and even though this topic was not studied yet (at least, to the best of our knowledge), it certainly cannot detect sophisticated DeepFakes [96–98], where the impostor can "play" on-demand any digit. Another limitation of this method is that it is based on visual cues only, i.e., it does not consider audio together with images (unlike multi-modal audio-visual methods [99]). This makes it vulnerable to "visual-only" DeepFakes, which are of course easier to obtain than realistic audio-visual DeepFakes (with both the facial features and voice of the impersonated genuine user).

More generally, the emerging technology of DeepFakes [100] is a great challenge for interactive motion-based PAD methods. Indeed, based on deep learning models such as autoencoders and generative adversarial networks [101,102], DeepFakes can superimpose face images of a target person to a video of a source person in order to create a video of the target person doing or saying things that the source person does or says [96–98]. Impostors can therefore use DeepFake generation apps like FaceApp [103] or FakeApp [104] to easily create a video replay attack showing a genuine user's face satisfying the system requirements during the challenge–response authentication. Interactive motion-based methods generally have difficulties detecting DeepFakes-based video replay attacks.

However, recent works show that rPPG-based [105,106] and texture-based methods [107] can be used to detect video attacks generated using DeepFakes. rPPG-based methods are discussed in the next section.

2.2.2. Liveness Detection Based on Remote PhotoPlethysmoGraphy (rPPG)

Unlike head/facial movements that are relatively easy to detect, intensity changes in the facial skin that are characteristic of pulse/heartbeat are imperceptible for most human eyes. To detect these subtle changes automatically, remote PhotoPlethysmoGraphy (rPPG) was proposed [17,33,49]. rPPG can detect blood flow using only RGB images from a distance (in a nonintrusive way) based on the analysis of variations in the absorption and reflection of light passing through human skin. The idea behind rPGG is illustrated in Figure 6.

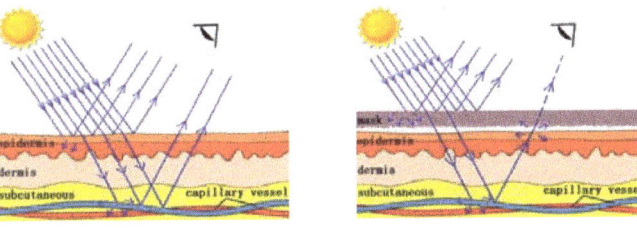

(a) Genuine (alive) face. (b) Masked (impostor's) face.

Figure 6. Illustration of how Remote PhotoPlethysmoGraphy (rPPG) can be used to detect blood flow for facial PAD [17]: (**a**) on a genuine (alive) face, the light penetrates the skin and illuminates capillary vessels in the subcutaneous layer. Blood oxygen saturation changes within each cardiac cycle, leading to periodic variations in the skin's absorption and reflection of the light. These variations are observable by RGB cameras. (**b**) On a masked face, the mask's material blocks light absorption and reflection, leading to no (or insignificant) variations in the reflected light.

Since photo-based PAs do not display any periodical variation in the rPPG signal, they can be detected easily by rPPG-based methods. Moreover, as illustrated in Figure 6, most kinds of 3D masks (including high-quality masks, except maybe extremely thin masks) can be detected by rPPG-based methods. However, "high-quality" video replay attacks (with good capture conditions and good-quality PAI) can also display periodic variation of the genuine face's skin light absorption/reflection. Thus, rPPG-based methods are only capable in detecting low-quality video replay attacks.

The first methods that applied rPPG to facial PAD were published in 2016. Li et al. [49] proposed a simple approach for which the framework is shown in Figure 7. The lower half of the face is detected and extracted as a Region of Interest (RoI). The rPPG signal is composed of the average RGB value of pixels in the ROI for each RGB channel of each video frame. This rPPG signal is then filtered (to remove noise and to extract the normal pulse range) and transformed into a frequency signal by Fast Fourier Transform (FFT). Two frequency features per channel (denoted as E_r, E_g and E_b and as Γ_r, Γ_g and Γ_b) in Figure 7) are extracted for each color channel based on the Power Spectral Density (PSD). Finally, these (concatenated) feature vectors are fed into an SVM to differentiate genuine facial presentation from PAs.

This rPPG-based method can effectively detect photo-based and 3D mask attacks—even high-quality 3D masks—but not (in general) video replay attacks. Because, on the other hand, texture-based methods (see Section 2.3) can detect video replay attacks but not realistic 3D masks [25,35,55], the authors also proposed a cascade system that uses first their rPPG-based method (to filter photo or 3D mask attacks) and then a texture-based method (to detect video replay attacks).

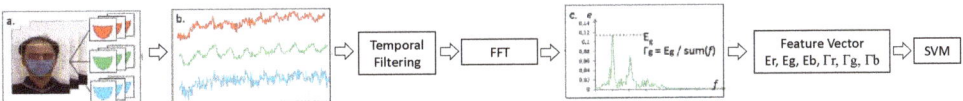

Figure 7. Framework of the rPPG-based method proposed in [49] (Figure extracted from [49]): (**a**) the ROI for extracting the rPPG signal; (**b**) the extracted rPPG signal for each RGB channel; (**c**) the frequence spectrum for calculating frequency features.

Also in 2016, Liu et al. [51] proposed another rPPG-based method for detecting 3D mask attacks. Its principle is illustrated in Figure 8. This method has three interesting features compared to the abovementioned approach proposed in [49] the same year. First, rPPG signals were extracted from multiple facial regions instead of just the lower half of the face. Secondly, the correlation of any two local rPPG signals was used as a discriminative feature (assuming they should all be consistent with the heartbeat's rhythm). Thirdly, a confidence map is learned, o weigh each region's contribution: robust regions that contain strong heartbeat signals are emphasized, whereas unreliable regions containing less heartbeat signals (or more noise) are weakened.

Finally, the weighted local correlation-based features are fed into an SVM (with Radial Basis Function (RBF) kernel) to detect photo and 3D mask PAs. This approach is more effective than the one proposed by Li et al. in [49].

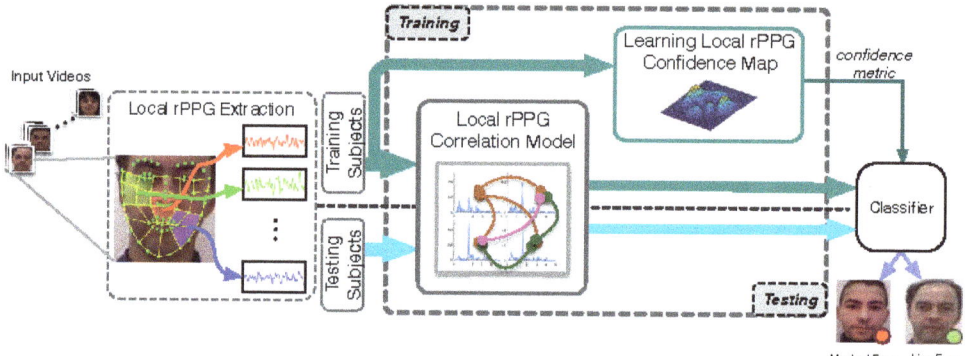

Figure 8. Framework of the local rPPG correlation-based method proposed in [51] (Figure extracted from [51]).

In 2017, Nowara et al. [50] proposed PPGSecure, a local rPPG-based approach within a framework that is very similar to the one in [49] (see Figure 7). The rPPG signals are extracted from three facial regions (forehead and left/right cheeks) and two background regions (on the left and right sides of the facial region). The use of background regions provides robustness against noise due to illumination fluctuations, as this noise can be subtracted from the facial regions after having been detected in the background regions. Finally, the Fourier spectrum's magnitudes of the filtered rPPG signals are fed into an SVM or a Random Forest Classifier [108]. The authors showed experimentally the interest of using background regions, and their method obtained better performances than the one in [51] on some dataset.

In 2018, Liu et al. [33] proposed a deep learning-based approach that can learn rPPG signals in a robust way (under different poses, illumination conditions and facial expression). In this approach, rPPG estimations (pseudo-rPPGs) were combined with the estimations of 3D geometric cues in order to tackle not only photo and 3D mask attacks (like all rPPG-based methods) but also video replay attacks. Therefore, this approach is detailed together with other multiple cue-based approaches, in Section 2.5.2, on page 25.

As mentioned in Section 2.2.1, recent studies show that, unlike motion-based PAD methods (e.g., the interactive motion-based PAD method, such as in Kollreider et al. [48], with better generalization based on challenge–response mechanism), rPPG-based PAD methods can be used to detect DeepFake videos.

Indeed, in 2019, Fernandes et al. [105] proposed to use Neural Ordinary Differential Equations (Neural-ODE) [109] for heart rate prediction. The model is trained on the heart rate extracted from the original videos. Then, the trained Neural-ODE is used to predict the heart rate of Deepfake videos generated from these original videos. The authors show that there is a significant difference between the original videos' heart rates and their predictions in the case of DeepFakes, implicitly showing that their method could discriminate between Deepfakes and genuine videos.

A more sophisticated method was proposed in 2020 by Ciftci et al. [106], in which several biological signals (including the rPPG signal) are fed into a specifically designed Convolutional Neural Network (CNN) to discriminate between genuine videos and DeepFakes. The reported evaluation results are very encouraging.

Either with the motion-based approaches or with the rPPG-based approaches, the liveness cue-based methods need a video clip accumulating enough numbers of video frames to detect dynamic biometric traits such as eye blinking, head movement or intensity changes in the facial skin. Thus, the duration of the videos needed to assess liveness makes liveness cue-based methods less user-friendly and hard to be applied in real-time scenarios.

2.3. Texture Cue-Based Methods

Texture feature-based methods are the most widely used for facial PAD so far. Indeed, they have several advantages compared to other kinds of methods. First, they are inherently nonintrusive. Second, they are capable to detect almost any kind of known attacks, e.g., photo-based attacks, video replay attacks and even some 3D mask attacks.

Unlike the liveness cue-based methods that rely on dynamic physiological signs of life, texture cue-based methods explore the texture properties of the object presented to the system (genuine face or PAI). With texture cue-based methods, PAD is usually formalized as a binary classification problem (real face/non-face) and these methods generally rely on a discriminative model.

Texture cue-based methods can be categorized as static texture-based and dynamic texture-based. Static texture-based methods extract spatial or frequential features, generally from a single image. In contrast, dynamic texture-based methods explore spatiotemporal features extracted from video sequences. The next two subsections present the most prominent approaches from these two types.

2.3.1. Static Texture-Based Methods

The first attempt to use static texture clues for facial PAD dates back to 2004 [44]. In this method, the difference of light reflectivity between a genuine (alive) face and its printed photo is analyzed using their frequency representations (and, more specifically, their 2D Fourier spectra). Indeed, as illustrated in Figure 9, the 2D Fourier spectrum of a face picture has much less high-frequency components than the 2D Fourier spectrum of a genuine (alive) facial image.

More specifically, the method relies on High-Frequency Descriptors (HFD), defined as the energy percentage explained by high-frequency components in the 2D Fourier spectrum. Then, printed photo attacks are detected by thresholding the HFD value (attacks being below the threshold). This method works well only for small images with poor resolution. For instance, it is vulnerable to photos of 124×84 mm or with 600 dpi resolution.

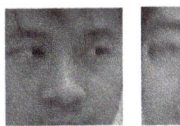
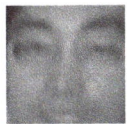

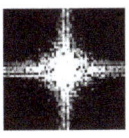

Figure 9. From left to right: a genuine (alive) face, a printed photo attack and their respective 2D Fourier spectra (Figure extracted from [44]).

In 2010, Tan et al. [52] first modeled the respective reflectivities of images of genuine (alive) faces and printed photos using physical models (here Lambertian models) [110], in which latent samples are derived using Difference of Gaussian (DoG) filtering [111]. The idea behind this method is that an image of a printed photo tends to be more distorted than an image of a real face because it has been captured twice (by possibly different sensors) and printed once (see Section 3.1 for more information about the capture process), whereas real faces are only captured once (by the biometric system only).

Several classifiers were tested, among which Sparse Nonlinear Logistic Regression (SNLR) and SVMs, with SNLR proving to be slightly more effective.

Since DoG filtering is sensitive to illumination variations and partial occlusion, Peixoto et al. [53] proposed in 2011 to apply Contrast-Limited Adaptive Histogram Equalization (CLAHE) [112] to preprocess all images, showing the superiority of CLAHE to a simple histogram equalization.

Similar to the work from Tan et al. [52] in 2010, Bai et al. [54] also used, in the same year, a physical model to analyze the images' micro-textures, using Bidirectional Reflectance Distribution Functions (BRDF). The original image's normalized specular component (called *specular ratio image*) is extracted [113], and then its gradient histogram (called *specular gradient histogram*) is calculated. As shown in Figure 10, the shapes of the specular gradient histograms of a genuine (alive) face and of a printed photo are quite different. To characterize the shape of a specular gradient histogram, a Rayleigh histogram model is fitted on the gradient histogram. Then, its two estimated parameters σ and β are used to feed an SVM. This SVM is trained to discriminate between genuine face images and planar PAs (in particular, printed photos and video replay attacks).

As shown in Figure 10, this method can detect planar attacks just from a small patch of the image. However, specular component extraction requires a highly contrasted image, and therefore, this method is vulnerable towards any kind of blur.

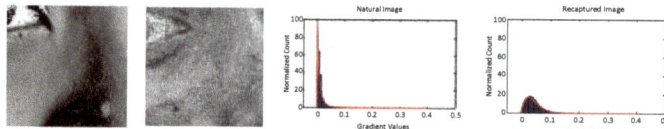

Figure 10. From **left** to **right**: patches extracted from a genuine face image and a printed photo, and their respective specular gradient histograms (Figure extracted from [54]).

Local Binary Pattern (LBP) [114] is one of the most widely used hand-crafted texture features in face analysis-related problems, such as face recognition [115], face detection [116] and facial expression recognition [117]. Indeed, it has several advantages, including a certain robustness toward illumination variations.

In 2011, Määttä et al. [55] first proposed to apply multi-scale LBP to face PAD. Unlike the previously described static texture-based approaches [52,54], LBP-based methods do not rely on any physical model; they just assume that the differences in surface properties and light reflection between a genuine face and a planar attack can be captured by LBP features.

Figure 11 illustrates this method. Three different LBPs were applied on a normalized 64 × 64 image in [55]: $LBP_{8,2}^{u2}$, a uniform circular LBP extracted from an 8-pixel neighbourhood with a 2-pixel radius; $LBP_{16,2}^{u2}$, a uniform circular LBP extracted from a 16-pixel neighbourhood with a 2-pixel radius; and $LBP_{8,1}^{u2}$, a uniform circular LBP extracted from a 8 pixel neighbourhood with a 1-pixel radius. Finally, a concatenation of all generated histograms formed a 833-bin/dimension histogram. This histogram is then used as a global micro-texture feature and fed to a nonlinear (RBF) SVM classifier for facial PAD.

In 2012, the authors extended their work in [61], adding two more texture features within the same framework: Gabor wavelets [118] (that can describe facial macroscopic information) and Histogram of Oriented Gradients (HOG) [119] (that can capture the face's edges or gradient structures). Each feature (LBP-based global micro-texture feature, Gabor wavelets and HOG) is transformed into a compact linear representation by using a homogeneous kernel map function [120]. Then, each transformed feature is separately fed into a fast linear SVM. Finally, late fusion between the scores of the three SVM output is applied to generate a final decision. The authors showed the superiority of this approach compared to the method they previously introduced in [55].

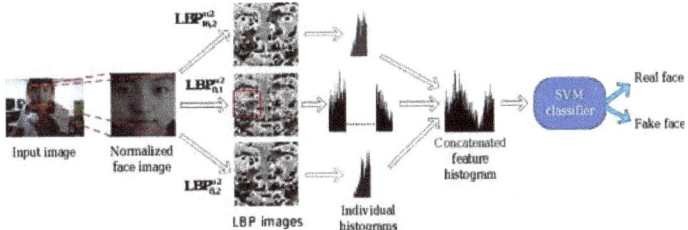

Figure 11. Illustration of the approach proposed in [55]: firstly, the face is detected, cropped and normalized into a 64 × 64 pixel image. Then, $LBP_{8,2}^{u2}$ and $LBP_{16,2}^{u2}$ are applied on the normalized face image, which generates a 59-bin histogram and a 243-bin histogram respectively. The obtained $LBP_{8,1}^{u2}$ image is also divided into 3 × 3 overlapping regions (as shown in the middle row). As each region generates a 59-bin histogram, a single 531-bin histogram is obtained by their concatenation. Then, all individual histograms are concatenated to obtain a 833-bin/dimension (59 + 243 + 531) histogram, which is fed to a nonlinear SVM classifier to detect photo/video replay attacks.

In 2013, the same authors continued to extend their work [63], using this time the upper-body region instead of the face region to detect spoofing attacks. As shown in Figure 12, the upper-body region includes more scenic cues of the context, which enables the detection of the boundaries of the PAI (e.g., video screen frame or photograph edge), and, possibly, the impostor's hand(s) holding the PAI. As a local shape feature, HOG is calculated from the upper-body region to capture the continuous edges of the PAI (see Figure 12d). Then, this HOG feature is fed to a linear SVM for detecting photo or video replay attacks. The upper-body region is detected using the method in [121], that can also be used to filter poor attacks (where the PAI is poorly positioned or with strong discontinuities between the face and shoulder regions), as shown in Figure 12c.

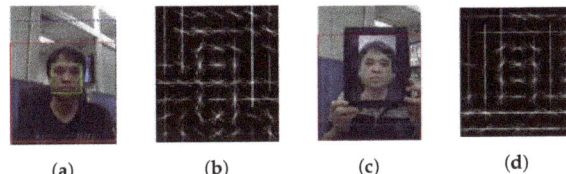

(a) (b) (c) (d)

Figure 12. Examples of upper-body images from the CASIA-FASD dataset [19] and their Histogram of Oriented Gradient (HOG) features [63]: (**a**) upper-body of a genuine face; (**b**) HOG feature of the blue dashed rectangle in (**a**); (**c**) video replay attack; and (**d**) HOG feature of the blue dashed rectangle in (**c**). The figure was extracted from [63].

In the same spirit of using the context surrounding a face, Yang et al. [62] proposed (also in 2013) to use a 1.6× enlarged face region, called Holistic-Face (H-Face), to perform PAD. In order to focus on the facial regions that play the most important role in facial PAD, the authors segmented four canonical facial regions: the left eye region, right eye region, nose region and mouth region, as shown in Figure 13. The rest of the face (mainly the facial contour region) and the original enlarged facial images were divided as 2 × 2 blocks to obtain another eight components. Thus, twelve face components are used in total. Then, different texture features such as LBP [55], HOG [119] and Local Phase Quantization (LPQ) [122] are extracted as low-level features from each component. Instead of directly feeding the low-level features to the classifier, a high-level descriptor is generated based on the low-level features by using spatial pyramids [123] with a 512-word codebook. Then, the high-level descriptors are weighted using average pooling to extract higher-level image representations. Finally, the histogram of these image representations are concatenated into a single feature vector fed into an SVM classifier to detect PAs.

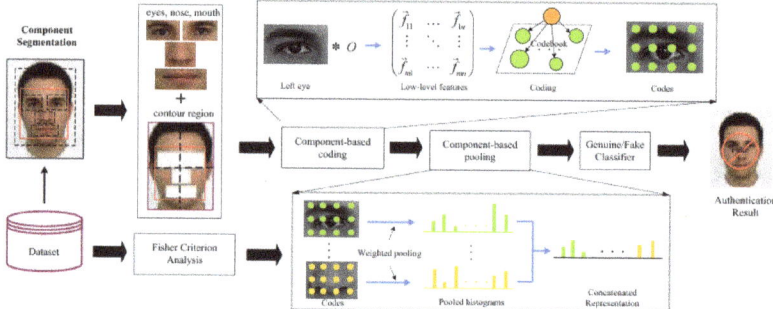

Figure 13. Illustration of the approach proposed in [62] (Figure extracted from [62]).

In 2013, Kose et al. [56] first proposed a static texture-based approach to detect 3D mask attacks. Due to the unavailability of public mask attack databases at that time, 3D mask PADs were much less studied than photo or video replay attacks. In this work, the LBP-based method in [55] is directly applied to detect 3D mask attacks by using the texture (original) image or depth image of the 3D mask attacks (from a self-constructed database), as shown in Figure 14. Note that all the texture images and the depth images were obtained by MORPHO (http://www.morpho.com/). This work showed that using the texture (original) image is better than using a depth image for detecting 3D mask attacks with LBP features. The authors also proposed in [57] to improve this method by fusing the LBP features of the texture image and depth image. They showed the superiority of this approach toward the previous method (using only texture images).

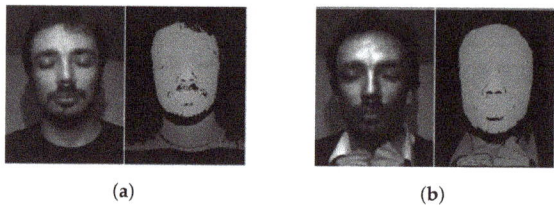

(a)   (b)

Figure 14. The texture image and its corresponding depth image for (**a**) a real access and (**b**) a 3D mask attack: the figure was extracted from [25].

Erdogmus et al. [25,58] also proposed in 2013 a method for 3D mask attack detection based on LBP. They used different classifiers, such as Linear Discriminant Analysis (LDA) and SVMs. On the proposed 3D Mask Attack Database (3DMAD), which is also the first public spoofing database for 3D mask attacks, LDA was proved to be best among the tested classifiers.

Galbally et al. [64,65] introduced in 2013 and 2014 new facial PAD methods based on Image Quality Assessment (IQA), assuming that a spoofing image captured in a photo or video replay PA should have a different quality than a real sample, as it was captured twice instead of once for genuine faces (this idea is similar to the underlying idea of the method in [52] presented above). The quality differences concern sharpness, colour and luminance levels, structural distortions, etc. Fourteen and twenty-five image quality measures were adopted in [64,65], respectively, to assess the image quality using scores extracted from single images. Then, the image-quality scores were combined as a single feature vector and fed into an LDA or Quadratic Discriminant Analysis (QDA) classifier to perform facial PAD. The major advantage of the IQA-based methods is that it is not a trait-specific method, i.e., it does not rely on a priori face/body region detection, so this is a "multi-biometric" method that can also be employed for iris or fingerprint-based liveness detection. However, the performance of the proposed IQA-based methods for PAD was limited compared to other texture-based methods, and the method is not conceived to detect 3D mask attacks.

In 2015, Wen et al. [32] also proposed an IQA-based method, using analysis of image distortion, for facial PAD. Unlike the methods from Tan et al. [111] and Bai et al. [54] presented above—methods that work in the RGB space—this method analyzes the image chromaticity and the colour diversity distortion in the HSV (Hue, Saturation and Value) space. Indeed, when the input image resolution is not enough, it is hard to tell the difference between a genuine face and a PA based only on the RGB image (or grey-scale image). The idea here is to detect imperfect/limited colour rendering of a printer or LCD screen. A 121-dimensional image distortion feature (which consists of a three-dimensional specular reflection feature [124], a two-dimensional no-reference blurriness feature [125,126], a 15-dimensional chromatic moment feature [127] and a 101-dimensional colour diversity feature) is fed into two SVMs corresponding respectively to photo attacks and video replay attacks. Finally, a score-level fusion based on the Min Rule [128] gives the final result. Unlike the IQA score-based features used in [65], this feature is face-specific. The proposed method has shown a promising generalization performance when compared with other texture-based PAD methods.

In 2015, Boulkenafet et al. [35,60] also proposed to extract LBP features in HSV or YCbCr colour spaces. Indeed, subtle differences between a genuine face and a PA can be captured by chroma characteristics, such as the Cr channel that is separated from the luminance in the YCbCr colour space (see Figure 15). By simply changing the colour space used, this LBP-based method achieved state-of-the-art performances when compared with some much more complicated PAD methods based on Component Dependent Descriptor (CDD) [62] and even the emerging deep CNNs [34]. This work showed the interest of using diverse colour spaces for facial PAD.

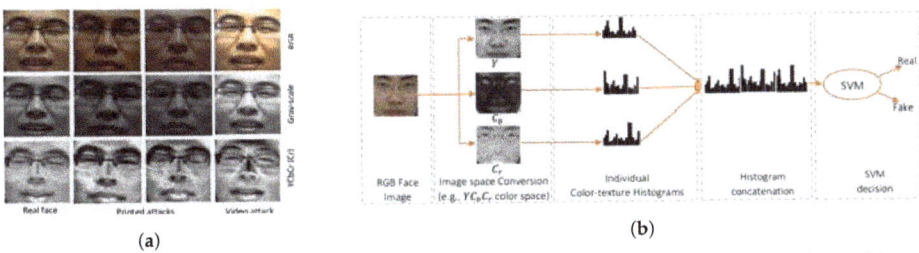

Figure 15. Illustration of the method in [60]: (**a**) an example of a genuine face presentation and its corresponding printed photo and video attacks in RGB, greyscale and YCbCr colour space and (**b**) the architecture of the method proposed in [60].

In 2016, Patel et al. [66] first proposed a spoof detection approach on a smartphone. They used a concatenation of multi-scale LBP [55] and image-quality-based colour moment features [32] as a single feature vector fed into an SVM for facial PAD. Like in [63], this work also introduced a strategy to prefilter poor attacks before employing the sophisticated SVM for facial PAD. For this purpose, the authors proposed to detect the bezel of PAI (e.g., the white bezel of photos or the screen's black bezel along the border) and the Inter-Pupillary Distance (IPD). For bezel detection, if the pixel intensity values remain fairly consistent (over 60 or 50 pixels) on any four sides (top, bottom, left and right sides), the region is considered as belonging to the bezel of a PAI. For IPD detection, if the IPD is too small (i.e., the PAI is too far from the acquisition camera) or too large (i.e., the PAI is too close to the acquisition camera), then the presentation is classified as a PA. The threshold is set to a difference exceeding two times the IPD's standard deviation observed for genuine faces with a smartphone. This strategy, relying on two simple countermeasures, can efficiently filter almost 95% of the poorest attacks. However, it may generate false rejections (e.g., if the genuine user is wearing a black t-shirt on a dark background).

More recently, deep learning-based methods are used to learn automatically the texture features. Researchers studying these techniques focus on designing an appropriate neural network so as to learn the best texture features rather than to design the texture features themselves (as is the case with most hand-crafted features presented above).

The first attempt to use Convolutional Neural Networks (CNNs) for detecting spoofing attacks was claimed by Yang et al. for their 2014 method [34]. In this method, a one-path AlexNet [2] is used for learning the texture features that best discriminate PAs (see Figure 16). The usual output of AlexNet (a 1000-way softmax) is replaced by an SVM with binary classes. The fully connected bottleneck layer, i.e., fc7, is extracted as the learned texture feature and fed into the binary SVM. Instead of being an end-to-end framework like many CNN frameworks used nowadays, the proposed approach was basically using a quite conventional SVM-based general framework, only replacing the hand-crafted features with the features learned by AlexNet. This method was shown to attain significant improvements when the input image was enlarged by a scale of 1.8 or 2.6. These results are consistent with the previous studies in [62,63] that had already shown that including more context information from the background can help facial PAD. It was the first time that CNNs were proven to be effective for automatically learning texture features for face PAD. This method has surpassed almost all the existing state-of-the-art methods for photo and video replay attacks. It showed the potential of deep CNNs for face PAD. Later, more and more CNN-based methods were explored for facial PAD.

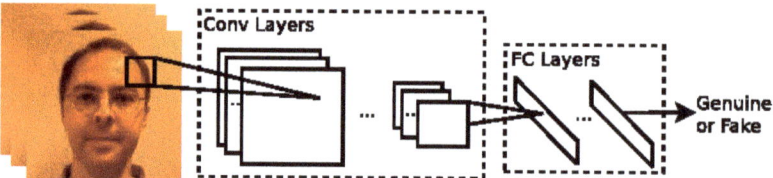

Figure 16. Illustration of the method proposed in [34] (Figure extracted from [34]).

In 2016, Patel et al. [67] first proposed an end-to-end framework based on one-path AlexNet [2], namely CaffeNet, for facial PAD. A two-way softmax replaced the original 1000-way softmax as a binary classifier. Given the small sizes of existing face spoof databases, especially at that time, such deep CNNs were likely to overfit [67] if trained on such datasets. Therefore, the proposed CNN was pretrained on ImageNet [129] and WebFace [130] to provide a reasonable initialization and fine-tuned using the existing face PAD databases. More specifically, two separate CNNs are trained, respectively from aligned face images and enlarged images including some background. Finally, a voting fusion is used to generate a final decision. Just like Yang et al.'s method [34], the proposed CNN-based method has surpassed the state-of-the-art methods based on hand-crafted features for photo and video replay attacks.

Also in 2016, Li et al. [68] proposed to train a deep CNN based on VGG-Face [7] for facial PAD. As in [67], the CNN was pretrained on massive datasets and fine-tuned on the (way smaller) facial spoofing database. Furthermore, the features extracted from the different layers of the CNN were fused to a single feature and fed into an SVM for facial PAD. However, as the dimension of the fused feature is much higher than the number of training samples, this approach is prone to overfitting. Principal component analysis (PCA) and the so-called *part features* are therefore used to reduce the feature dimension. To obtain part features, the mean feature map in a given layer is firstly calculated. Then, the critical positions in the mean feature map are selected, in which the values are higher than 0.9 times the maximum value in the mean feature map. Finally, the values of the critical positions on each feature map are selected to generate the part feature. The concatenation of all part features of all feature maps is used as the global part feature. Then, PCA is applied on the global part feature to further reduce the dimension. Finally, the condensed part feature is fed into an SVM to discriminate between genuine (real) faces and PAs. Benefitting from using a deeper CNN based on VGG-Face, the proposed method has achieved state-of-the-art performances in both intra-dataset and cross-dataset scenarios (see Section 4) for detecting photo and video replay attacks.

In 2018, Jourabloo et al. [69] proposed to estimate the noise of a given spoof face image to detect photo/video replay attacks (the authors also claimed that the proposed method could be applied to detect makeup attacks). In this work, the spoof image was regarded as the summation of the genuine image and image-dependent noise (e.g., blurring, reflection and moiré pattern) introduced when generating the spoof image. Since the noise of a genuine image was assumed as zero in this work, a spoof image can be detected by thresholding the estimated noise. A GAN framework based on CNNs, De-Spoof Net (DS Net), was proposed to estimate the noise. However, as there is no noise ground-truth, instead of assessing the quality of noise estimation, the authors de-noise the spoof images and assess the quality of the recovered (de-noised) image using Discriminative Quality Net (DQ Net) and Visual Quality Net (VQ Net). Besides, by fusing different losses for modelling different noise patterns in DS Net, the proposed method has shown a superior performance compared to other state-of-the-art deep facial PAD methods such as in [33].

In 2019, George et al. [70] proposed Deep Pixelwise Binary Supervision (DeepPixBiS), based on DenseNet [131], for facial PAD. Instead of only using the binary cross-entropy loss of the final output (denoted as Loss 2 in Figure 17) as in [67], DeepPixBiS also uses during training a pixel-wise binary cross-entropy loss based on the last feature map (denoted as Loss 1 in Figure 17). Each pixel in the feature map is annotated as 1 for a genuine face input and as 0 for a spoof face input. In the evaluation/test phase, only the mean value of pixels in the feature map is used as the score for facial PAD. Thanks to the powerful DenseNet and the proposed pixel-wise loss forcing the network to learn the patch-wise feature, DeepPixBiS showed a promising PAD performance for both photo and video replay attacks.

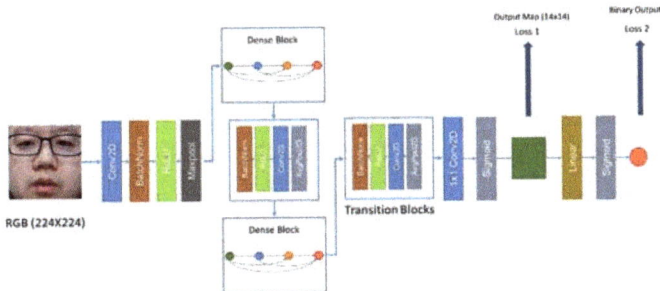

Figure 17. The diagram of Deep Pixelwise Binary Supervision (DeepPixBiS) as shown in [70].

2.3.2. Dynamic Texture-Based Methods

Unlike the static texture-based methods that extract spatial features usually based on a single image, dynamic texture-based methods extract spatiotemporal features using an image sequence.

Pereira et al. [71,72] first proposed in 2012 and 2014 the application of a dynamic texture based on LBP [114] for facial PAD. More precisely, they introduced the LBP from the Three Orthogonal Planes (LBP-TOP) feature [117]. LBP-TOP is a spatiotemporal texture feature extracted from an image sequence considering three orthogonal planes intersecting at the current pixel in the XY direction (as in traditional LBP) and in the XT and YT directions, where T is the time axis of the image sequence, as shown in Figure 18. The sizes of the XT and YT planes depend on the radii in the direction of time axis T, which is indeed the number of frames before or after the central frame in the image sequence. Then, the conventional LBP operation can be applied to each of the three planes. The concatenation of the three LBP features extracted from the three orthogonal planes generates the LBP-TOP feature of the current image. Similar to many static LBP-based facial PAD methods, LBP-TOP is then fed into a classifier such as SVM, LDA or χ^2 distance-based classifier to perform facial PAD.

In 2013, the same authors extended their work [73] by proposing two new training strategies to improve generalization. One strategy was to train the model with the combination of multiple datasets. The other was to use a score level fusion-based framework, in which the model was trained on each dataset, and a sum of the normalized score of each trained model was used as the final output. Despite the fact that these two strategies somehow ameliorate generalization, they have obvious drawbacks. First, even a combination of multiple databases cannot deal with new types of attacks that are not included in the current training datasets, so the model has to be retrained when a new attack type is added. Second, the fusion strategy relies on an assumption of statistical independence that is not necessarily verified in practice.

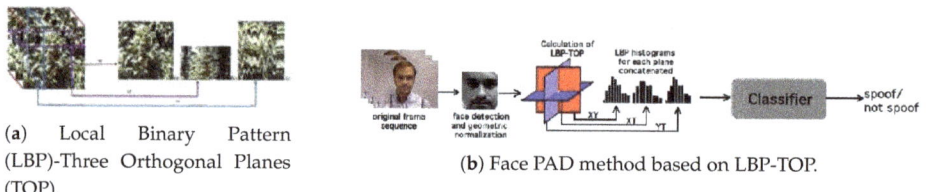

(a) Local Binary Pattern (LBP)-Three Orthogonal Planes (TOP).

(b) Face PAD method based on LBP-TOP.

Figure 18. Illustration of the LBP-TOP from [117] and LBP-TOP-based facial PAD method [71]: (a) the three orthogonal planes, i.e., XY plane, XT plane and YT plane, of LBP-TOP features extracted from an image sequence and (b) the framework of the approach based on LBP-TOP introduced in [71].

Also in 2013, Bharadwaj et al. [74] proposed to use motion magnification [132] as preprocessing to enhance the intensity value of motion in the video before extracting the texture features. The authors claimed that the motion magnification might enrich the texture of the magnified video. The authors proposed to apply Histogram of Oriented Optical Flows (HOOF) [133] on the enhanced video to conduct facial PAD. HOOF calculates the optical flow between frames at a fixed interval and collects the optical flow orientation angle weighted by its magnitude in a histogram. The histogram is computed from local blocks, and the resulting histograms for each block are concatenated to form a single feature vector as shown in Figure 19. HOOF is much computationally lighter than LBP-TOP. However, the proposed method based on motion magnification needs to accumulate a large number of video frames (>200 frames), which makes it hardly applicable real-time, resulting in solutions that are not very user-friendly.

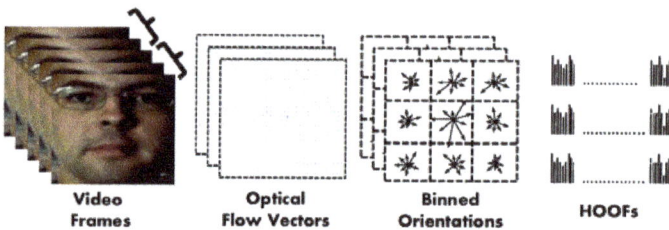

Figure 19. Illustration of the Histogram of Oriented Optical Flows (HOOF) feature proposed in [74].

In 2012 and 2015, Pinto et al. [75–77] proposed a PAD method based on the analysis of a video's Fourier spectrum. Instead of analyzing the Fourier spectra of the original video as in Li et al. [44], the proposed method analyzed the Fourier spectra of the residual noise videos, which only include noise information. The objective is to capture the effect of the noise introduced by the spoofing attack, e.g., the moiré pattern effect shown in Figure 20b,c. In order to obtain a residual noise video, the original video is first submitted to a filtering processing (e.g., Gaussian filter or Median filter). Then, a subtraction is performed between the original and the filtered video, resulting in the noise residual video. Given that the highest responses representing the noise are concentrated on the abscissa and ordinate axes of the logarithm of the Fourier spectrum, visual rhythms [134,135] are constructed to capture temporal information of the spectrum video sampling the central horizontal lines or central vertical lines of each frame and concatenating the sampling lines in a single image, called horizontal or vertical visual rhythm. Then, the grey-level cooccurrence matrices (GLCM) [136], LBP and HOG can be calculated on the visual rhythm as the texture features and can be fed into an SVM or Partial Least

Square (PLS). Furthermore, a more sophisticated method, based on the Bag-of-Visual-Word model [137], similar to the Vector Quantization (VQ) [123] used in [62], was also applied to extract the mid-level descriptor base on the low-level features, e.g., LBP and HoG, extracted from the Fourier spectrum.

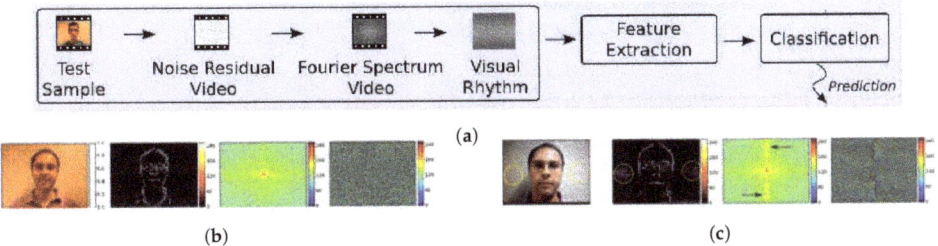

Figure 20. Illustration of the noise residual video and the visual rhythm-based approach as shown in [75,77]: (**a**) the framework of the visual rhythm-based approach, (**b**) example of valid access and (**c**) example of a frame from a video replay attack. For (**b**,**c**), from left to right: original frame, residual noise frame, magnitude spectrum and phase spectrum. In (**c**), the yellow circles in the original image and its corresponding residual noise frame highlight the Moiré effect. The black arrows in the magnitude spectrum show the impact of the Moiré effect on the Fourier spectrum.

Also in 2012 and 2015 [75,76], Tirunagari et al. [23] proposed to represent the dynamic characteristics of a video by a single image using Dynamic Mode Decomposition (DMD) [138]. Instead of sampling central lines of each frame in a video spectrum and concatenating them in a single frame (as in visual rhythms), the proposed approach selects the most representative frame in a video generated from the original video by applying DMD in the spatial space. DMD, similarly to Principal Component Analysis (PCA), is based on eigenvalues but, contrary to PCA, it can capture the motion in videos. The LBP feature of the DMD image is then calculated and fed into an SVM for facial PAD.

Xu et al. [78] first proposed to apply deep learning to learn the spatiotemporal features of a video for facial PAD in 2015. More specifically, they proposed an architecture based on Long Short-Term Memory (LSTM) and CNN networks. As shown in Figure 21, several CNN-based branches with only two convolutional layers are used. Each branch is used to extract the spatial texture features of one frame. These frames are sampled from the input video using a certain time step. Then, the LSTM units are connected at the end of each CNN branch to learn the temporal relations between frames. Finally, all the outputs of the LSTM units are connected to a softmax layer that gives the final classification of the input video for facial PAD. Like several researchers before them, the authors also observed that using the scaled image of an original detected face including more background information can help in facial PAD.

In 2019, Yang et al. [79] proposed a Spatiotemporal Anti-Spoofing Network (STASN) to detect photo and video replay PAs. STASN consists of three modules: Temporal Anti-Spoofing Module (TASM), Region Attention Module (RAM) and Spatial Anti-Spoofing Module (SASM). The proposed TASM is composed of CNN and LSTM units to learn the temporal features of the input video. One significant contribution is that, instead of using local regions with predefined locations as in [51,62], STASN uses *K* local regions of the image selected automatically by RAM and TASM based on attention mechanism. These regions are then fed into SASM (i.e., a CNN with *K* branches) for learning spatial texture features. STASN has significantly improved the performance for facial PAD, especially in terms of the generalization capacity shown in cross-database evaluation scenarios (see Section 4).

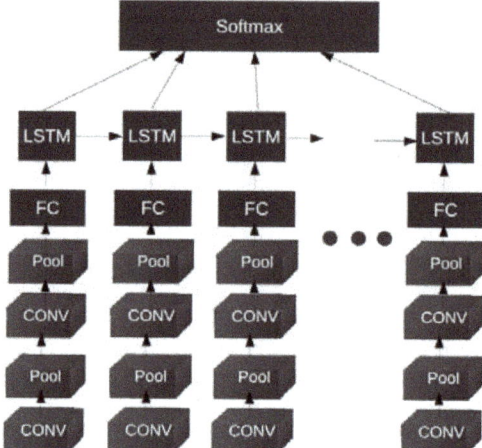

Figure 21. Long Short-Term Memory (LSTM)-Convolutional Neural Network (CNN) architecture used in [78] for facial PAD.

2.4. 3D Geometric Cue-Based Methods

Three-dimensional geometric cue-based PAD methods use 3D geometric features to discriminate between a genuine face with a 3D structure that is characteristic of a face and a 2D planar PA (e.g., a photo or video replay attack). The most widely used 3D geometric cues are the 3D shape reconstructed from the 2D image captured by the RGB camera and the facial depth map, i.e., the distance between the camera and each pixel in the facial region. The two following subsections discuss the approaches based on these two cues, respectively.

2.4.1. 3D Shape-Based Methods

In 2013, Wang et al. [80] proposed a 3D shape-based method to detect photo attacks, in which the 3D facial structure is reconstructed from 2D facial landmarks [139] detected using different viewpoints [54,140]. As shown in Figure 22, the reconstructed 3D structures of a real face and a planar photo are different. In particular, the reconstructed 3D structure from a real face profile preserves its 3D geometric structure. In contrast, the reconstructed structure of a planar photo in profile view is only a line showing the photo's edge. The concatenation of the 3D coordinates of the reconstructed sparse structure are used as 3D geometric features and fed into an SVM for face PAD. A drawback of this approach is that it requires multiple viewpoints and cannot be used from a single image; using not enough key frames can lead to inaccuracies in 3D structure reconstruction. Moreover, it is susceptible to inaccuracies in the detection of facial landmarks.

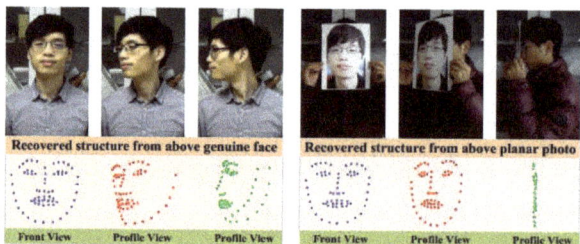

Figure 22. Illustration of reconstructed sparse 3D structures of genuine face (**left**) and photo attack (**right**) [80].

2.4.2. Pseudo-Depth Map-Based Methods

The depth map is defined as the distance of the face to the camera. Obviously, when using specific 3D sensors, the depth map can be captured directly. However, in this survey, we focus on approaches that can be applied using GCDs that do not usually embed 3D sensors. However, thanks to significant progress in the computer vision area, especially with the deep learning technology, it is possible to get a good reconstruction/estimation of a depth map from a single RGB image [141–143]. Such reconstructions are called *pseudo-depth maps*. Based on the pseudo-depth map of a given image, the different PAD methods can be designed to discriminate between genuine faces and planar PAs.

In 2017, Atoum et al. [36] first proposed a depth-map-based PAD method to detect planar face PADs, e.g., printed photo attack and video replay attacks. The idea is to use the fact that the depth map of an actual face has varying height values in the depth map, whereas planar attacks' depth maps are constant (see Figure 23) to distinguish between real 3D faces and planar PAs. In this work, an 11-layer fully connected CNN [144] for which the parameters are independent of the size of the input facial images is proposed to estimate the depth map of a given image. The ground truth of depth maps was estimated using a state-of-the-art 3D face model fitting algorithm [142,145,146] for real faces, while it was set to zero for planar PAs, as shown in Figure 23. Finally, the estimated depth maps are fed to a SVM (pretrained using the ground truth) to detect planar face PAs.

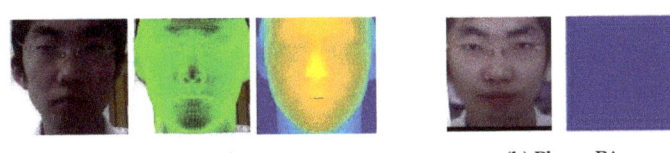

(a) Genuine face.   (b) Planar PA.

Figure 23. (a) A real face image, the fitted 3D face model and the depth map of the real 3D face, and (b) a planar PA and its ground-truth depth map: the yellow/blue colors in the depth map represent respectively a closer/further point to the camera. The figure was extracted from [36].

In 2018, Wang et al. [81] extended the single frame-based depth-map PAD method in [36] to videos by proposing Face Anti-Spoofing Temporal-Depth networks (FAS-TD). FAS-TD networks are used to capture the motion and depth information of a given video. By integrating Optical Flow guided Feature Block (OFFB) and Convolution Gated Recurrent Unit (ConvGRU) modules to a depth-supervised neural network architecture, the proposed FAS-TD can capture short-term and long-term motion patterns of real faces and planar PAs in videos well. The proposed FAS-TD further improved the performance of the depth-map-based PAD methods using a single frame as in [33,36] and achieved state-of-the-art performances.

Since pseudo-depth map approaches are very effective for detecting planar PAs, pseudo-depth maps are often used in conjunction with other cues in the multiple cues-based PAD method. Also, as pseudo-depth maps are among the most recently introduced cues for facial PAD, they are extensively used in the most recent approaches. These two points are further detailed in the following Sections 2.5 and 2.6, respectively.

2.5. Multiple Cue-Based Methods

Multi-modal systems are intrinsically more difficult to spoof than uni-modal systems [61,147]. Some attempts to counterfeit facial spoofing therefore combine methods based on different modalities, such as visible infrared [22], thermal infrared [148] or 3D [25] signals. However, the fact that such specific hardware is generally unavailable in most GCDs prevents these multi-modal solutions from being integrated into most existing facial recognition systems. In this work, we focus on the multiple cues-based methods that use only images acquired using RGB cameras.

Such multiple cues-based methods combine liveness cues, texture cues and/or 3D geometric cues to address the detection of various types of facial PAs. In general, late fusion is used to merge the scores obtained from the different cues to determine if the input image corresponds to a real face.

2.5.1. Fusion of Liveness Cue and Texture Cues

In this section, the motion cue is used as a liveness cue in conjunction with different texture cues.

In 2017, Pan et al. [83] proposed to jointly use eye-blinking detection and the texture-based scene context matching for facial PAD. The Conditional Random Field (CRF)-based eye-blinking model proposed by the same authors [42] (see page 9) is used to detect eye blinking. Then, a texture-based method is proposed to check the coherence between the background region and the actual background (reference image). The reference image is acquired by taking a picture of the background without the user being present. If the attempt is a real facial presentation, the background region around the face in the reference image and the input image should theoretically be identical. Contrarily, if a video or recaptured photo (printed or displayed on a screen) is presented before the camera, then the background region around the face should be different between the reference image and the input image. To perform a comparison between the input image's background and the reference image, LBP features are extracted from several fiducial points selected using the DoG function [149] and used to calculate the χ^2 distance as the scene matching score. If an imposter is detected by either the motion cue or the texture cue, then the system will refuse access. This method has some limitations for real-life applications, as the camera should be fixed and the background should not be monochrome.

The combination of motion and texture cues was widely used in competitions on countermeasures to 2D facial spoofing attacks [150] held respectively in 2011, 2013 and 2017. In the first competition [151] held in 2011, three of the six teams used multiple cues-based methods. The AMILAB team used jointly face motion detection, face texture analysis and eye-blinking detection in their solution (and the sum of weighted classification scores obtained by SVMs). The CASIA team also considered three different cues: motion cue, noise-based texture cue and face-background dependency cue. The UNICAMP team combined eye blinking, background-dependency and micro-texture of an image sequence. In the second competition [152] held in 2013, the two teams that obtained the best performances (CASIA and LNMIT) used multiple-cues based methods. CASIA proposed an approach based on the early (feature-based) fusion of motion and texture cues, whereas LNMIT combined LBP, 2D FFT and face–background consistency features [153] into a single feature vector, used as the input of Hidden Markov support vector machines (HM-SVMs) [154]. In the third competition [155] held in 2017, three teams used multiple cues-based methods. GRADIANT fused color [35], texture and motion information, exploiting both HSV and YCbCr color spaces. GRADIANT obtained the best performance on all protocols of the competition. Idiap proposed a score fusion method to fuse three cues (motion [147], texture (LBP) [37] and quality cue [32,64]) based on a Gaussian mixture model (GMM) to conduct face PAD. HKBU also proposed a multiple cue-based method fusing image quality [32], multi-scale LBP texture [55] and deep texture feature to give a robust presentation.

In 2016, Feng et al. [84] first integrated image-quality measures (see page 16) as a static texture cue and motion cues in a neural network. Three different cues, Shearlet-based image quality features (SBIQF) [156,157], a facial motion cue based on dense optical flow [158] and a scenic motion cue, were manually extracted and fed into the neural network (see Figure 24). The neural network had been pretrained and was then fine-tuned on the existing for face PAD datasets.

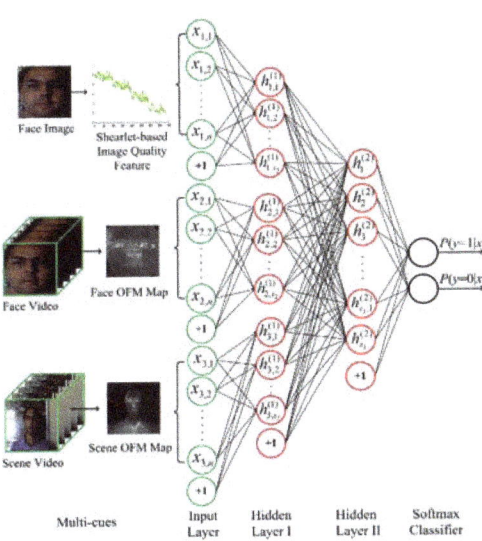

Figure 24. A flowchart of the multiple cues-based face PAD method using neural networks as shown in [84].

2.5.2. Fusion of Liveness and 3D Geometric Cues

In 2018, Liu et al. [33] proposed to use CNN-Recurrent Neural Network (RNN) architecture for fusing the remote PhotoPlethysmoGraphy (rPPG) cue and the pseudo-depth map cue for face PAD (see Figure 25). This approach uses the fully connected CNN proposed in [36] to estimate the depth map (see page 23). Besides, a bypass connection is used to fuse the features from different layers, as in ResNet [4]. This work was the first one to proposed using RNN with LSTM units to learn the rPPG signal features based on the feature maps learned using CNNs. The estimation of the depth maps was calculated in advance using CNNs, whereas the depth maps' ground truth was estimated in advance using [142,145,146] and the rPPG ground-truth was generated as described in Section 2.2.2. The authors also designed a non-registration layer to align the input face to a frontal face, as the input of the RNN, for estimating the rPPG signal features. Instead of designing a binary classifier, the face PAs are then detected by thresholding a score computed based on the weighted quadratic sum of the estimated depth map of the last frame of the video and the estimated rPPG signal features.

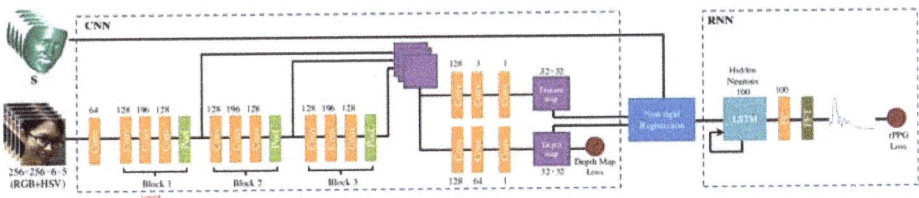

Figure 25. The proposed rPPG and depth-based CNN-RNN architecture for facial PAD as shown in [33].

2.5.3. Fusion of Texture and 3D Geometric Cues

In 2017, Atoum et al. [36] proposed to integrate patch-based texture cues and pseudo depth-map cues in two-stream CNNs for facial PAD as shown in Figure 26. The pseudo-depth map estimation, that aims at extracting the holistic features of an image, has been described in Section 2.4.2. The patch-based CNN stream (with 7 layers) focused on the image's local features. The local patches, with fixed size, are randomly extracted from the input image. The label of a patch extracted from a real face is set to 1, whereas the label of the patch of extracted from a PA is set 0. Then, the randomly extracted patches with their labels are used to train the patch-based CNN stream with the softmax loss. Using the patch-level input not only increases the number of training samples but also forces the CNNs to explore the spoof-specific local discriminative information spreading in the entire face region. Finally, the two streams' scores are weighed to sum up the final score to determine if the input image is a real face or a PA. As in [32,35,60], the authors also proposed to jointly use the HSV/YCbCr image with the RGB image as the input of the networks.

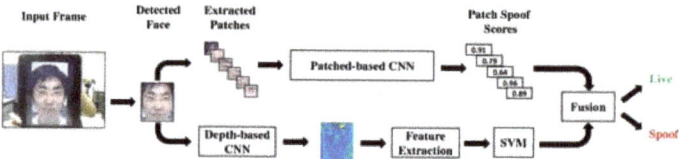

Figure 26. The architecture of the proposed patch-based and depth-based CNNs for facial PAD as shown in [36].

2.6. New Trends in PAD Methods

In this section, we describe the methods that constitute the leading edge of facial PAD methods based on RGB cameras. Thanks to the development of deep learning, especially in the computer vision domain, not only has face anti-spoofing detection performance been significantly boosted, but also many new ideas have been introduced. These new ideas relied on the following:

- the proposal of new cues to detect the face artifact (e.g., the pseudo-depth maps described in Section 2.4.2);
- learning the most appropriate neural networks architectures for facial PAD (e.g., using Neural Architecture Search (NAS) (see hereafter Section 2.6.1)); and
- address of the generalization issues, especially towards types of attacks that are not (or insufficiently) represented in the learning dataset. Generalization issues can be (at least partially) addressed using zero/few shot learning (see Section 2.6.2) and/or domain adaptation and adversarial learning (see Section 2.6.3).

The remainder of this section aims to present the two latter new trends more in details.

2.6.1. Neural Architecture Search (NAS)-Based PAD Methods

In the last few years, deep neural networks have gained great success in many areas, such as speech recognition [159], image recognition [2,160] and machine translation [161,162]. The high performance of deep neural networks is heavily dependent on the adequation between their architecture and the problem at hand. For instance, the success of models like Inception [163], ResNets [4] and DenseNets [131] demonstrate the benefits of intricate design patterns. However, even with expert knowledge, determining which design elements to weave together generally requires extensive experimental studies [164]. Since the neural networks are still hard to design *a priori*, Neural Architecture Search (NAS) has been proposed to design the neural networks automatically based on reinforcement learning [165,166], evolution algorithm [167,168] or gradient-based methods [169,170]. Recently, NAS has been applied to several challenging computer vision tasks, such as face recognition [171], action recognition [172], person reidentification [173], object detection [174] and segmentation [175]. However, NAS has just started being applied to facial PAD.

In 2020, Yu et al. [82] first proposed to use NAS to design a neural network for estimating the depth map of a given RGB image for facial PAD. The gradient-based DARTS [169] and Pc-DARTS [170] search methods were adopted to search the architecture of cells forming the network backbone for facial PAD. Three levels of cells (low-level, mid-level and high-level) from the three blocks of CNNs in [33] (see Figure 25) were used for the search space. Each block has four layers, including three convolutional layers and one max-pooling layer, and is represented as a Directed Acyclic Graph (DAG), with each layer as a node.

The DAG is used to present all the possible connections and operations between the layers in a block, as shown in Figure 27. Instead of directly using the original convolutional layers as in [33], the authors proposed to use Central Difference Convolutional (CDC) layers, in which the sample values in local receptive field regions are subtracted to the value of the central position, similar to LBP. Then, the convolution operation is based on the local receptive field region with gradient values.

A Multiscale Attention Fusion Module (MAFM) is also proposed for fusing low-, mid- and high-level CDC features via spatial attention [82]. Finally, the searched optimal architecture of the networks for estimating the depth map of a given image is shown in Figure 28. Rather than [33] fusing multiple cues in the CNNs, this work only estimated the depth map of an input image to employ facial PAD by thresholding the mean value of the predicted depth map.

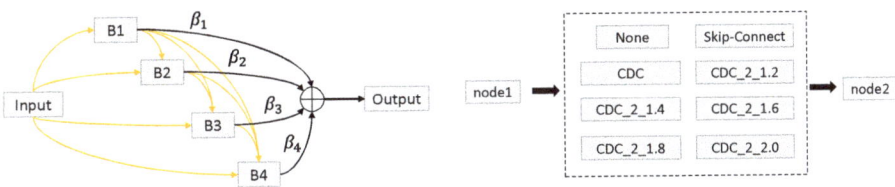

(a) Directed Acyclic Graph (DAG) of a block.   (b) Operation space.

Figure 27. The search space of Neural Architecture Search (NAS) for forming the network backbone for face PAD as shown in [82]: (a) Directed Acyclic Graph (DAG) of a block. Each node represents a layer in the block, and the edge is the possible information flow between layers. (b) Operation space, listing the possible operations between layers (8 operations were defined in [82]).

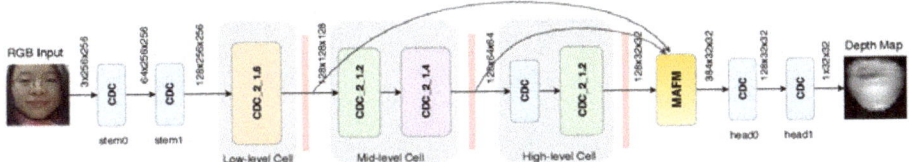

Figure 28. The architecture of the NAS-based backbone for depth map estimation as shown in [82].

2.6.2. Zero/Few-Shot Learning Based PAD Methods

Thanks to the significant development of deep learning, most state-of-the-art facial PAD methods show promising performance in intra-database tests on the existing public datasets [33,36,82] (see Section 4). Nevertheless, the generalization to cross-dataset scenarios is still challenging, in particular due to the possible presence in the test set of facial PAs that were not represented (or underrepresented) in the training dataset [32,65,155]. One possible solution is to collect a large-scale dataset to include as much diverse spoofing attack types as possible. However, as detailed below in Section 3, unlike other problems such as facial recognition where it is relatively easy to collect massive public dataset from the Internet, the images/videos of spoofing artifacts recaptured by a biometric system are quite rarely available on the Internet. Therefore, several research teams are currently investigating another solution that consists in leveraging zero/few-shot learning to detect the previously unseen face PAs. This problem has been named Zero-Shot Face Anti-spoofing (ZSFA) in [87].

In 2017, Arashloo et al. [86] first addressed unseen attack detection, as an anomaly detection problem where real faces constitute the positive class and are used to train a **one-class classifier** such as one-class SVM [176].

In the same spirit, in 2018, Nikisins et al. [85] also used one-class classification. However, they used one-class Gaussian Mixed Models (GMM) to model the distribution of the real faces in order to detect unseen attacks. Also, contrary to [86], they trained their model not only using one dataset but also aggregating three publicly available datasets (i.e., Replay-Attack [38], Replay-Mobile [38] and MSU MFSD [32], c.f. Section 3).

The abovementioned methods used only samples of genuine faces to train one-class classifiers, whereas in practice, known spoof attacks might also provide valuable information to detect previously unknown attacks.

This is why, in 2019, Liu et al. [87] proposed a CNN-based Deep Tree Network (DTN) in which 13 attack types covering both impersonation and obfuscation attacks were analyzed. First, they clustered the known PAs into eight semantic subgroups using unsupervised tree learning, and they used them as the eight leaf nodes of the DTN (see Figure 29). Then, Tree Routing Unit (TRU) was learned to route the known PAs to the appropriate tree leaf (i.e., subgroup) based on the features of known PAs learned by the tree nodes (i.e., Convolutional Residual Unit (CRU)). In each leaf node, a Supervised Feature Learning (SFL) module, consisting of a binary classifier and a mask estimator, was employed to discriminate between spoofing attacks. The mask estimation is similar to the depth map estimation as in the same authors' previous work [33] (see page 12). Unseen attacks can then be discriminated based on the estimated mask and the score of a binary softmax classifier.

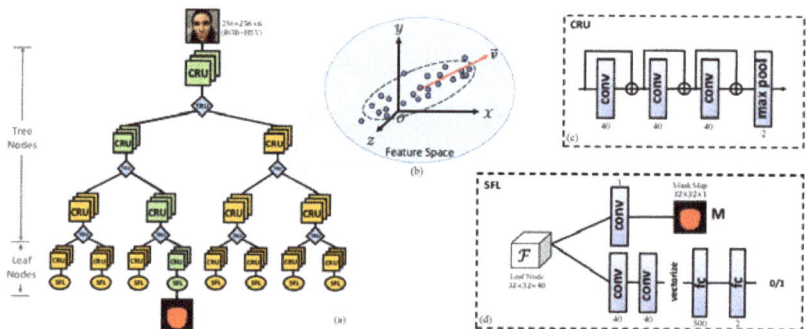

Figure 29. The proposed Deep Tree Network (DTN) architecture as shown in [87]: (**a**) overall structure of the DTN. A tree node consists of a Convolutional Residual Unit (CRU) and a Tree Routing Unit (TRU), whereas a leaf node consists of a CRU and a Supervised Feature Learning (SFL) module. (**b**) Tree Routing Unit (TRU) assigns the feature learned by CRU to a given child node based on an eigenvalue analysis similar to Principal component analysis (PCA). (**c**) Structure of each Convolutional Residual Unit (CRU). (**d**) Structure of the Supervised Feature Learning (SFL) in the leaf nodes.

2.6.3. Domain Adaption-Based PAD Methods

As detailed above, improving the generalization ability of existing facial PAD methods is one of the greatest challenges nowadays. To mitigate this problem, Pereira et al. [73] first proposed to combine multiple databases to train the model (see page 19). This is the most intuitive attempt towards improving generalization of the earned models. However, even by combining all the existing datasets, it is impossible to collect attacks from all possible domains (i.e., with every possible device and in all possible capture environments) to train the model. However, even though printed photo or video replay attacks from unseen domains may differ greatly from the source domain, they all are based on paper or video screens as PAI [88]. Thus, if there exists a generalized feature space underlying the observed multiple source domains and the (hidden but related) target domain, then domain adaptation can be applied [177,178].

In 2019, Shao et al. [88] first applied a domain adaption method based on adversarial learning [179,180] to tackle facial PAD. Under an adversarial learning schema, N discriminators were trained to help the feature generator produce generalized features for each of the N specific domains, as shown in Figure 30. Triplet loss is also used to enhance the learned generalized features to be even more discriminative, both within a database (intra-domain) and among different databases (inter-domain). To apply facial PAD, the learned generalized features are also trained to estimate the depth map of a given image as in [33] and to classify the image based on a binary classifier trained by softmax loss. This approach shows its superiority when increasing the number of source domains for learning generalized features. Indeed, in contrast, the previous methods without domain adaption such as LBP-TOP [71] or [33] cannot effectively improve the model's generalization capacity, even when using multiple source datasets for training.

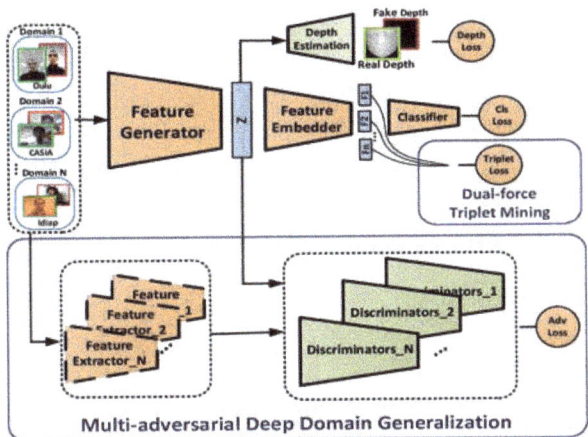

Figure 30. Overview of the domain adaption approach based on adversarial learning for facial anti-spoofing, as shown in [88]: each discriminator is trained to help the generalized features (learned by the generator from multiple source domains) to better generalize on their corresponding source domain. The depth loss, triplet loss and the classification loss ("Cls loss") are then used to enhance the ability to discriminate any kind of PA.

3. Existing Face Anti-Spoofing Datasets and Their Major Limitations

3.1. Some Useful Definitions

Facial PAD (anti-spoofing) datasets consist of two different kinds of documents (files) in the form of photos or videos:

- the set of "genuine faces", that contains photos or videos of the genuine users' faces (authentic faces of the alive genuine users), and
- the set of "PA documents", containing photos or videos of the PAI (printed photo, video replay, 3D mask, etc.)

Figure 31 illustrates the data collection procedure for constructing facial anti-spoofing databases.

In facial anti-spoofing datasets, genuine faces and PAIs (presented by imposters) are generally captured using the same device. This device plays the role of the biometric system's camera in real-life authentication applications; we therefore chose to call it the "biometric system acquisition device". For genuine faces and 3D mask attacks, only the biometric system acquisition device is used to capture the data.

However, for printed photo and video replay attacks, another device is used to create the PAI (photo or video) from a genuine face's data. We call this device the "PA acquisition device". It has to be noted that the PA acquisition device is in general different from the biometric system acquisition device.

Some authors use the term "recapture", as the original data is first collected using the PA acquisition device, then presented on a PAI and then recaptured using the biometric system acquisition device.

It has to be noted that, for photo display attacks and video replay attacks, the PAI itself can also be yet another electronic device. However, in general, only its screen is used, for displaying the PAI to the biometric system acquisition device. Of course, there could be datasets where the PAI also plays the role of the PA acquisition device, but this is not the case in general. Indeed, it is not the case in most real-life applications, where the imposter generally does not have control over the PA acquisition device (e.g., photos or videos found on the web).

For printed photo attacks, paper-crafted mask attacks and 3D mask attacks, yet another device is used: a printer. For photo attacks as well as paper-crafted mask attacks, usually (2D) printers are used. The printer's characteristics as well as the quality of the paper used can greatly affect the quality of the PAI and therefore the chances of success of the attack. For 3D mask attacks, a 3D printer is used; its characteristics as well as the material used (e.g., silicone or hard resin) and its thickness also have an impact on the attack's chances of success.

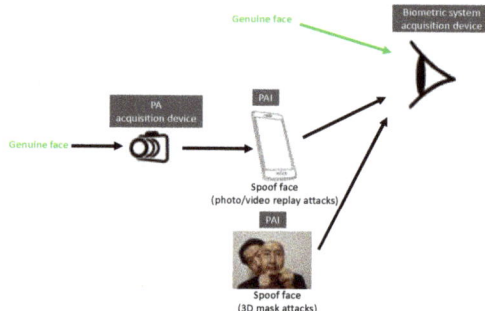

Figure 31. Diagram illustrating the data collection procedure for constructing facial anti-spoofing databases.

The devices used for each dataset's collection are detailed in Table 2 and Section 3.4, together with a detailed description of these datasets. However, before that, in the remainder of this section, we successively give a brief overview of the existing datasets (Section 3.2) and describe their main limitations (Section 3.3).

3.2. Brief Overview of the Existing Datasets

The early studies of facial PAD, such as [42,44–46,56,83], are mostly based on private datasets. Such private datasets being quite limited, both in volume and diversity of attack types, makes it very difficult to fairly compare the different approaches.

The first public dataset was proposed in 2008 by Tan et al. [52]. The dataset was named NUAA, and it contains examples of photo attacks. The NUAA dataset enabled researchers to compare the results of their methods on the same benchmark. Later on, respectively in 2011 and 2012, Anjos et al. publicly shared the datasets PRINT-ATTACK [147] (containing photo attacks) and its extended version REPLAY-ATTACK [37] (containing video replay attacks as well). Quickly, these two datasets were widely adopted by the research community and as was one of the most challenging datasets: CASIA-FASD [19], that has also been published in 2012 and contains photo/video replay attacks but with more diversity in the PAs, PAIs and video resolutions. Later on, several other similar datasets were shared publicly for photo and video replay attacks, such as MSU-MFSD [32], MSU-USSA [66], OULU-NPU [181], SiW [33] and the very recent multi-modal dataset CASIA-SURF [182]. These datasets contain more diverse spoofing scenarios, such as MSU-MFSD [32], which first introduced a mobile phone scenario; MSU-USSA [66], which used celebrities' photos from the Internet to increase the mass of data; OULU-NPU [181], which focused on attacks using mobile phones; and SiW [33], which contains faces with various poses, illumination and facial expressions.

The first public 3D mask attack dataset was 3DMAD [58], which includes texture maps, depth maps and point clouds together with the original images. Note that the depth maps and point clouds were collected by the Kinect 3D sensor rather than generic RGB cameras.

All the abovementioned datasets have been created under controlled environments, i.e., mostly indoors and with controlled illumination conditions, face poses, etc.

Although UAD [76] has collected videos from both indoors and outdoors and with a relatively large number of subjects, the dataset is no longer publicly available. Although MSU-USSA [66] contains a set of genuine faces captured under more diverse environments (including celebrities' images collected from the Internet by [183]), the PAs always took place in controlled indoor conditions. Even the latest CASIA-SURF dataset [182], which is so far the largest multi-modal facial anti-spoofing dataset with 1000 subjects, contains only images collected in the same well-controlled conditions.

Therefore, public datasets are still far from reproducing real-world applications in a realistic way. This is probably due to the difficulty of collecting impostors' PAs and PAIs in the wild. As a consequence, examples of PAs are generally acquired manually, which is a time-consuming and draining work. Creating a large-scale dataset for facial anti-spoofing in the wild, covering realistically various real-world applicative scenarios, is still a challenge. To circumvent these challenges, some researchers use data augmentation techniques to create synthetic (yet realistic) images of PAs [79].

A summarized overview of the existing public facial anti-spoofing datasets using only generic RGB cameras is provided in Table 2. More precisely, for each dataset, Table 2 gives (in columns) its release's year (*Year*); the number of subjects it contains (♯ *Subj*); the ethnicity of the subjects in the dataset (*Ethnicity*); the type of PA represented in the dataset (*PA type(s)*); the number and type(s) of documents provided in the dataset as the cumulated number of genuine attempts and PAs (*Document ♯ & type(s)*); the PAI(s) used (*PAI*); the head pose(s) in the set of genuine faces (*Pose*); whether there are facial expression variations in the genuine faces dataset (*Expressions*); the biometric system acquisition device(s) for capturing both the genuine attempts and, in case of an attack, the PAI (*Biometric system acquisition device*); and the PA acquisition device that is possibly used to create the PAI (*PA acquisition device*).

3.3. Major Limitations of the Existing Datasets

Given the acquisition difficulties mentioned above, the existing face PAD datasets are (compared to other face-related problems) still limited not only in terms of volume but also in terms of diversity regarding the types of PAs, PAIs and acquisition devices used for genuine faces, PAs and possibly PAIs. In particular, as of today, there is still no public large-scale facial PAD in the wild, whereas there are several such datasets for facial recognition.

This hinders the development of effective facial PAD methods. It partly explains why, compared to other face-related problems, such as facial recognition, the performances of the current facial PAD methods are still below the requirements of most real-world applications (especially in terms of their generalization ability).

Of course, this is not the only reason: as detailed earlier in this paper, facial PAD is a very challenging problem. However, because all data-driven (learning-based) methods' performances—including hand-crafted feature-based methods and more recent deep learning-based methods—are largely affected by the learning dataset's volume and diversity [129,130,184,185], the lack of diversity in the datasets contribute to the limited performances of the current facial PAD methods.

More details about these datasets, including discussions about their advantages and drawbacks, are provided in the remainder of this section.

Table 2. A summary of public facial anti-spoofing datasets based on generic RGB camera.

Database	Year	# Subj.	Ethnicity	PA Type(s)	Document # & Type(s) Images (I)/Videos (V)	PAI	Pose	Expression	Biometric System Acquisition Device	PA Acquisition Device
NUAA [52]	2010	15	Asian	Printed photos Warped photos	5105/7509 (I)	A4 paper	Frontal	No	Webcam (640 × 480)	Webcam (640 × 480)
PRINT-ATTACK [147]	2011	50	Caucasian	Printed photos	200/200 (V)	A4 paper	Frontal	No	Macbook Webcam (320 × 340)	Cannon PowerShot SX150 (12.1 MP)
CASIA-FASD [19]	2012	50	Asian	Printed photos Warped photos Cut photos Video replay	200/450 (V)	Copper paper iPad 1 (1024 × 768)	Frontal	No	Sony NEX-5 (1280 × 720) USB Camera (640 × 480)	Sony NEX-5 (1280 × 720) Webcam (640 × 480)
REPLAY-ATTACK [37]	2012	50	Caucasian 76% Asian 22% African 2%	Printed photos Photo display 2× video replays [a]	200/1000 (V)	A4 paper iPad 1 (1024 × 768) iPhone 3GS (480 × 320)	Frontal	No	Macbook Webcam (320 × 340)	Canon PowerShot SX 150 (12.1MP) iPhone 3GS
3DMAD [25,58]	2013	17	Caucasian	2× 3D masks [b]	170/85 (V)	Paper-crafted mask Hard resin mask (ThatsMyFace.com)	Frontal	No	Kinect (RGB camera) (Depth sensor)	—
MSU-MFSD [32]	2015	35	Caucasian 70% Asian 28% African 2%	Printed photos 2× video replays	110/330 (V)	A3 paper iPad Air (2048 × 1536) iPhone 5s (1136 × 640)	Frontal	No	Nexus 5 (built-in camera software 720 × 480) Macbook Air (640 × 480)	Cannon 550D (1920 × 1088) iPhone 5s (1920 × 1080)
MSU-RAFS [59]	2015	55	Caucasian 44% Asian 53% African 3%	Video replays	55/110 (V)	Macbook (1280 × 800)	Frontal	No	Nexus 5 (rear: 3264 × 2448) iPhone 6 (rear: 1920 × 1080)	The biometric system acquistion devices used in MSU-MFSD, CASIA-FASD, REPLAY-ATTACK.
UAD [76]	2015	404	Caucasian 44% Asian 53% African 3%	7× video replays	808/16,268 (V)	7 display devices	Frontal	No	6 different cameras (no moible phone) (1366 × 768)	6 different cameras (no moible phone) (1366 × 768)
MSU-USSA [66]	2016	1140	Diverse set (from web faces database from the [183])	Printed photos Photo display 3× video replays	1140/9120 (V)	White paper (11 × 8.5 paper) Macbook (2080 × 1800) Nexus 5 (1920 × 1080) Tablet (1920 × 1200)	Frontal	Yes	Nexus 5 (front: 1280 × 960) (rear: 3264 × 2448) iPhone 6 (rear: 1920 × 1080)	Same as MSU-RAFS Cameras used to capture celebrities' photos are unknown.

Table 2. Cont.

Database	Year	# Subj.	Ethnicity	PA Type(s)	Document # & Type(s) Images (I)/Videos (V)	PAI	Pose	Expression	Biometric System Acquisition Device	PA Acquisition Device
OULU-NPU [181]	2017	55	Caucasian 5% Asian 95%	Printed photos 2× video replays	1980/3960 (V)	A3 glossy paper Dell display (1280 × 1024) Macbook (2560 × 1600)	Frontal	No	Samsung Galaxy S6 (rear: 16 MP)	Samsung Galaxy S6 (front: 5 MP) HTC Desire EYE (front: 13 MP) MEIZU X5 (front: 5 MP) ASUS Zenfone Selfi (front: 13 MP) Sony XPERIA C5 (front: 13 MP) OPPO N3 (front: 16 MP)
SiW [33]	2018	165	Caucasian 35% Asian 35% African American 7% Indian 23%	Printed photos (high/low-quality photos) 4× video replays	1320/3300 (V)	Printed paper (High/low-quality) Samsung Galaxy S8 iPhone 7 iPad Pro PC screen(Asus MB168B)	[−90°, 90°]	Yes	Camera (1920 × 1080)	Camera (5184 × 3456)
CASIA-SURF [182]	2019	1000	Asian	Flat-cut/Warped-cut photos (eyes, nose, mouth)	3000/18,000 (V)	A4 paper	[−30°, 30°]	No	RealSense (RGB camera) (1280 × 720) (Depth sensor) (640 × 480) (IR sensor) (640 × 480)	RealSense (RGB camera) (1280 × 720) (Depth sensor) (640 × 480) (IR sensor) (640 × 480)

[a] x× video replays denotes x types of video replay attacks with different PAIs; [b] 2× 3D masks denotes two types of 3D masks attacks: paper-crafted masks and hard resin masks.

3.4. Detailed Description of the Existing Datasets

In this section, we provide a detailed description of all the datasets mentioned in Table 2.

NUAA Database [52] is the first publicly available facial PAD dataset for printed photo attacks. It includes some variability in the PAs, as the photos are moved/distorted in front of the PA acquisition device as follows:

- 4 kinds of translations: vertical, horizontal, toward the sensor and toward the background
- 2 kinds of rotations: along the horizontal axis and along the vertical axis (in-depth rotation)
- 2 kinds of bending: along the horizontal and vertical axis (inward and outward)

A generic webcam is used for recording the genuine face images. Fifteen subjects were enrolled in the database, and each subject was asked to avoid eye blinking and to keep a frontal pose, with neutral facial expression. The attacks are performed by using printed photographs (either on photographic paper or A4 paper printed by a usual color HP printer). The dataset is divided into two separate subsets: for training and testing. The training set contains 1743 genuine face images and 1748 PAs impersonating 9 genuine users. The test set contains 3362 genuine samples and 5761 PAs. Viola-Jones detector [186] was used to detect the faces in the images, and the detected faces were aligned/normalized according to the eyes locations detected by [187]. The facial images were then resized to 64×64 pixels. Extracts from the NUAA database are shown in Figure 32.

Figure 32. The NUAA Database (from left to right): five different photo attacks.

PRINT-ATTACK Database [147] is the second proposed public dataset, including photo-attacks impersonating 50 different genuine users. The data was collected in two different conditions: controlled and adverse. In controlled conditions, the scene background is uniform and the light of a fluorescent lamp illuminates the scene, while in adverse conditions, the scene background is nonuniform and daylight illuminates the scene. A MacBook is used to record video clips of the genuine faces and the PAs. To capture the photos used for the attack, a 12.1 megapixel *Canon PowerShot SX150 IS* camera was used. These photos were then printed on plain A4 paper using a *Triumph-Adler DCC 2520* color laser printer. Video clips of about 10 s were captured for each PA under two different scenarios: hand-based attacks and fixed-support attacks. In hand-based attacks, the impostor held the printed photos using their own hands, whereas in fixed-support attacks, the impostors stuck the printed photos to the wall so they do not move/shake during the PA. Finally, 200 genuine attempts and 200 PA video clips were recorded. The 400 video clips were then divided into three subsets: training, validation and testing. Genuine identities (real identities or impersonated identities) in each subset were chosen randomly but with no overlap. Extracts of the PRINT-ATTACK dataset are shown in Figure 33.

Figure 33. PRINT-ATTACK (from **left** to **right**): photo attack under controlled and adverse scenarios.

CASIA-FASD Database [19] is the first publicly available face PAD dataset that provides both printed photo and video replay attacks. The CASIA-FASD database is a spoofing attack database which consists of three types of attacks: warped printed photos (which simulates paper mask attacks), printed photos with cut eyes and video attacks (motion cue such as eye blinking is also included). Each real face video and spoofing attack video is collected in three different qualities: low, normal and high quality. The high-quality video has a high resolution 1280 × 720, and the low/normal quality video has the same resolution 640 × 480. However, the low and normal quality is defined empirically by the perceptual feeling rather than strict quantitative measures. The whole database is split into a training set (containing 20 subjects) and a testing set (containing 30 subjects). Seven test scenarios are designed considering three different image qualities, three different attacks (warped/cut photo attack and video replay attack) and the overall test combining all the data. Examples of CASIA-FASD database are shown in Figure 34.

Figure 34. CASIA-FASD (from **left** to **right**): real face, two warped/cut photo attacks and a video replay attack.

REPLAY-ATTACK Database [37] is an addendum of the abovementioned PRINT-ATTACK database [147] proposed by the same team. Compared to the PRINT-ATTACK database, REPLAY-ATTACK adds two more attacks, which are Phone-Attack and Tablet-Attack. The Phone-Attack uses an iPhone screen to display the video or photo attack, and the Tablet-Attack uses an iPad screen to display high-resolution (1024 × 768) digital photos or videos. Thus, the REPLAY-ATTACK database can be used to evaluate photo attacks using printed photo or screens, and video replay attacks. The number of video clips for spoof attacks is increased from 200 to 1000 for 50 identities (subjects). The dataset is divided into training, validation and test sets. REPLAY-ATTACK database also offers an extra subset as the enrollment videos for 50 genuine clients to be used for evaluating the vulnerabilities of a facial recognition system without facial PAD is vulnerable towards various types of attacks. Examples of REPLAY-ATTACK database are shown in Figure 35.

Figure 35. REPLAY-ATTACK (from **left** to **right**): real face, video replay attack, photo displayed on screen and printed photo attack.

3DMAD Database [25,58] is the first public facial anti-spoofing database for 3D mask attacks. Previous databases contain attacks performed with 2D artifacts (i.e., photo or video) that are in general unable to fool facial PAD systems relying on 3D cues. In this database, the attackers wear customized 3D facial masks made out of a hard resin (manufactured by ThatsMyFace.com) of a valid user to impersonate the real access. It is worth mentioning that paper-craft mask files are also provided in this dataset. The dataset contains a total of 255 videos of 17 subjects. For each access attempt, a video was captured using the *Microsoft Kinect for Xbox 360*, which provides RGB data and depth information of size 640 × 480 at 30 frames per second. This dataset allows for the evaluation of both 2D and 3D PAD techniques, and their fusion. It is divided into three sessions: two real access sessions recorded with a time delay and one attack session captured by a single operator (attacker). Examples of the 3DMAD database are shown in Figure 36.

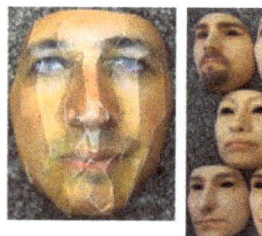
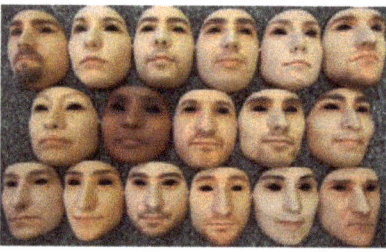

Figure 36. 3DMAD (from **left** to **right**): paper-craft mask and 17 hard resin masks.

MSU-MFSD Database [32] is the first publicly available database to use mobile phones to capture real accesses. This database includes real access and attack videos for 55 subjects (among which 35 subjects are in the public version: 15 subjects in the training set and 20 subjects in test set). The genuine faces were captured using two devices: a Google Nexus 5 phone using its front camera (720 × 480 pixels) and a MacBook Air using its built-in camera (640 × 480 pixels). The Canon 550D SLR camera (1920 × 1088) and iPhone 5S (rear camera 1920 × 1080) are used to capture high-resolution pictures or videos (for photo attacks and video replay attacks). The printed high-resolution photo is played back using an iPhone 5S as PAI, and high definition (HD) (1920 × 1088) video-replays (captured on a Canon 550D SLR) are played back using an iPad Air. Examples of MSU-MFSD database are shown in Figure 37.

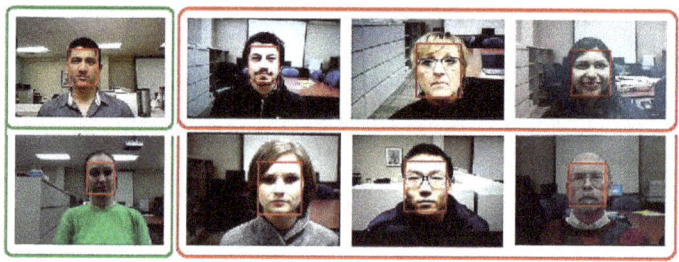

Figure 37. MSU-MFSD (from **left** to **right**): genuine face, video replay attacks respectively displayed on iPad and iPhone, and printed photo attack.

MSU-RAFS Database [59] is an extension of MSU-MFSD [32], CASIA-FASD [19] and REPLAY-ATTACK [37], where the video replay attacks are generated by replaying (on a MacBook) the genuine face videos in MSU-MFSD, CASIA-FASD and REPLAY-ATTACK. Fifty-five videos are genuine face videos from MSU-MFSD (captured by using the front camera of a Google Nexus 5), while 110 (2 × 55) videos are video replay attacks, captured using the built-in rear camera of a Google Nexus 5 and the built-in rear camera of an iPhone 6 and replayed using a MacBook as a PAI. In addition, 100 genuine face videos from CASIA-FASD and REPLAY-ATTACK were both used as genuine face videos and used to generate 200 video replay attacks by replaying these genuine face videos using a MacBook as a PAI. During the attack, the average standoff of the smartphone camera (used by the biometric system) from the screen of the MacBook was 15 cm, which assured that replay videos do not contain the bezels (edges) of the MacBook screen. Unlike the previously described databases, MSU-RAFS is constructed using existing genuine face videos (without having control over the biometric system acquisition devices used). Therefore, in this dataset, the biometric system acquisition devices used for capturing genuine face videos generally differ from the devices used for capturing the PAs. Thus, there is a risk of introducing bias when evaluating methods based on this dataset only.

Examples of MSU-RAFS database are shown in Figure 38.

Figure 38. MSU-RAFS (from **left** to **right**): genuine face and PAs from MSU-MFSD (attacks using a MacBook (as a PAI) to replay the genuine attempts from MSU-MFSD captured by different devices (respectively Google Nexus 5 and iPhone 6)).

UAD Database [76] is the first database to collect data both indoors and outdoors. It is also much bigger than the previous databases, both in terms of the number of subjects (440 subjects) and the number of videos (808 for training/16,268 for testing). All videos have been recorded at full-HD resolution, but subsequently cropped and resized to 1366 × 768 pixels. The dataset includes real access videos collected using six different cameras. For each subject, two videos are provided, both using the same camera but under different ambient conditions. Spoof attack videos corresponding to a given subject have also been captured using the same camera as for his/her real access videos. The video replay attacks have been displayed using seven different electronic monitors. However, this database seems to be no longer publicly available nowadays. Examples of UAD database are shown in Figure 39.

Figure 39. UAD (from **left** to **right**): video replay attacks, captured outdoors (first and second images) and indoors (last three images).

MSU-USSA Database [66] can be regarded as an extension of the MSU-RAFS [59], proposed by the same authors. There are two subsets in the database: (1) following the same idea as for MSU-RAFS, the first subset consists of 140 subjects from REPLAY-ATTACK [37] (50 subjects), CASIA-FASD [19] (50 subjects) and MSU-MFSD [32] (40 subjects); (2) the second subset consists of 1000 subjects taken from the web faces database collected in [183], containing images of celebrities taken under a variety of backgrounds, illumination conditions and resolutions. Only a single frontal facial image of each celebrity is retained. Thus, the MSU-USSA database contains color facial images of 1140 subjects, where the average resolution of genuine face images is 705 × 865. Two cameras (front and rear cameras of a Google Nexus 5 smartphone) have been used to collect 2D attacks using four different PAIs (laptop, tablet, smartphone and printed photos), resulting in a total of 1140 genuine faces and 9120 PAs. Just like MSU-RAFS, MSU-USSA has not captured genuine face videos with the same device used for capturing the PAs. Thus, there is a risk of introducing bias when evaluating methods based on this dataset only. Examples of MSU-USSA database are shown in Figure 40.

Figure 40. MSU-USSA (from **left** to **right**): spoof faces recaptured from the celebrity dataset [183].

OULU-NPU Database [181] is a more recent dataset (introduced in 2017) that contains PAD attacks acquired with mobile devices. In most previous datasets, the images were acquired in constrained conditions. On the other hand, this database contains a variety of motion, blur, illumination conditions, backgrounds and head poses. The database includes data corresponding to 55 subjects.

The front cameras of 6 different mobile devices have been used to capture the images included in this dataset. The images have been collected under three separate conditions (environment/face artifacts/ acquisition devices), each corresponding to a different combination of illumination and background. Presentation attacks include printed photo attacks created using two printers as well as video replay attacks using two different display devices. Four protocols are proposed for methods benchmarking (see Section 4.3 for more details). In total, the dataset is composed of 4950 real accesses and attack videos. Examples of the OULU-NPU database are shown in Figure 41.

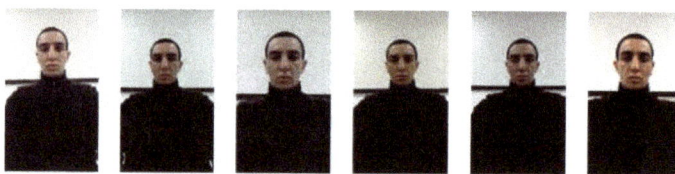

Figure 41. Extracts of the OULU-NPU dataset.

SiW Database [33] is the first database to include facial spoofing attacks with both various labelled poses and facial expressions. This database consists of 1320 genuine access videos captured from 165 subjects and 3300 attack videos. Compared to the abovementioned databases, it includes subjects from a wider variety of ethnicities, i.e., Caucasian (35%), Indian (23%), African American (7%) and Asian (35%). Two kinds of print (photo) attacks and four kinds of video replay attacks have been included in this dataset. Video replay attacks have been created using four spoof mediums (PAIs): two smartphones, a tablet and a laptop. Four different sessions corresponding to different head poses/camera distances, facial expressions and illumination conditions were collected, and three protocols were proposed for benchmarking (see Section 4.3 for more details). Examples of the SiW database are shown in Figure 42.

Figure 42. SiW: genuine access (**top**) and PA (**bottom**) videos with different poses, facial expressions and illumination conditions for genuine accesses and PAI devices for PAs.

CASIA-SURF Database [182] is currently the largest facial anti-spoofing dataset containing multi-modal images, i.e., RGB (1280 × 720), depth (640 × 480) and Infrared (IR) (640 × 480) images, of 1000 subjects in 21,000 videos. Each sample includes one live (genuine) video clip and six spoof (PA) video clips under different types of attacks. Six different photo attacks are included in this database: flat/warped printed photos where different regions are cut from the printed face. During the dataset capture, genuine users and imposters were required to turn left or right, to move up or down and to walk towards or away from the camera (imposters holding the printed color photo on an A4 paper). The face angle was only limited to 300 degrees. Imposters stood within a range of 0.3 to 1.0 m from the camera. The RealSense SR300 camera was used to capture the RGB, depth and Infrared (IR) images. The database is divided into three subsets for training, validation and testing. In total, there are 300 subjects and 6300 videos (2100 for each modality) in the training set, 100 subjects and 2100 videos

(700 for each modality) in the validation set, and 600 subjects and 12,600 videos (4200 for each modality) in the testing set. Examples of the CASIA-SURF database are shown in Figure 43.

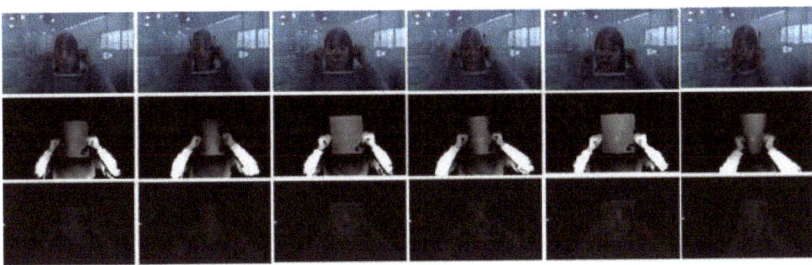

Figure 43. Extract from CASIA-SURF showing six photo attacks in each 3 modalities: RGB (**top**), depth (**middle**) and IR (**bottom**).

4. Evaluation

In this section, we present a comprehensive evaluation of the approaches for facial PAD detailed in Section 2. By doing so, our objective is to investigate the strengths and weaknesses of the different types of methods in order to draw future research directions for facial PAD to make facial authentication less vulnerable to imposters. We first present (in Section 4.1) the evaluation protocol, then (in Section 4.2) the evaluation metrics, and finally (in Section 4.3) the comparison of the results reported in the reviewed works.

4.1. Evaluation Protocol

In this section, we present the protocol we used to compare experimentally the different facial PAD methods. In the early studies of facial anti-spoofing detection, there was no uniform protocol to train and evaluate the facial PAD methods. In 2011, a first standard protocol was proposed by Anjos et al. [147] in order to fairly compare the different methods. In 2017, a second standard protocol was proposed by Boulkenaf et al. [181] based on an ISO/IEC standard. On top of the evaluation metrics to be used, these protocols address mainly two aspects: (1) how to divide the database and (2) what kinds of tests should be conducted for evaluation, e.g., intra-database and inter (cross)-database tests.

(a) Dataset division

The protocol proposed by Anjos et al. [147] is widely used when the evaluation is based on PRINT-ATTACK [147], REPLAY-ATTACK [37], OULU-NPU [181], 3DMAD [25,58] and/or CASIA-SURF [182]. This protocol relies on the division of the dataset into three subsets: training, validation set and test sets (respectively for training, tuning the model's parameters and assessing the performances of the tuned model).

Other databases, such as CASIA-FASD [19], MSU-MFSD [32] and SiW [33], only consist of two independent subsets: training and test subsets. In this case, either a small part of the training set is used as a validation set or cross-validation is used to tune the model's parameters. In some datasets (such as OULU-NPU and SiW), the existence of different sessions explicitly containing different capture conditions allowed the authors to propose refined protocols for evaluation (as detailed above in Section 3.4) and can also be used for dataset division.

(b) Intra-database vs. inter-database evaluation

An intra-database evaluation protocol uses only a single database to both train and evaluate the PAD methods. However, as the current databases are still limited in terms of variability, intra-database evaluations can be subject to overfitting, and therefore, report biased (optimistic) results.

The inter-database test, proposed by Pereira et al. [73] for evaluating the generalization abilities of a model, consists in training the model on a certain database and then evaluating it on a separate database. Although inter-database tests (or cross-database tests) aim to evaluate the model's generalization abilities, it is important to note that the evaluation performances are still affected by the distribution of the two datasets. Indeed, if the two datasets' distribution is close (e.g., if the same PAIs or spoof acquisition devices were used), the inter-database test will also report optimistic results. For instance, for a given model, inter-database evaluations between PRINT-ATTACK and MSU-MFSD (using the same MacBook camera to acquire the images) result in much better performances than inter-database evaluations between CASIA-FASD and MSU-MFSD (where CASIA-FASD uses a USB camera with very differentfrom a MacBook), as reported in [32].

4.2. Evaluation Metric

To compare different PAD methods, Anjos et al. [147] proposed in 2011 to use Half Total Error Rate (*HTER*) as an evaluation metric. As a PAD system is subject to two types of errors, either the real accesses are rejected (false rejection) or the attacks are accepted (false acceptance); *HTER* combines the False Rejection Rate (*FRR*) and the False Acceptance Rate (*FAR*) to measure the PAD performance as follows:

$$HTER = \frac{FRR + FAR}{2} \quad (1)$$

where the *FAR* and *FRR* are respectively defined as

$$FAR = \frac{FP}{FP + TN} \quad (2)$$

$$FRR = \frac{FN}{FN + TP} \quad (3)$$

with *TP*, *FP*, *TN* and *FN* respectively corresponding to the numbers of true positives (the accepted real accesses), false positives (the accepted attacks), true negatives (the rejected attacks) and false negatives (the rejected real accesses). *TP*, *FP*, *TN* and *FN* are calculated using model parameters based on a selected threshold achieving Equal Error Rate (EER) on the validation set (the selected threshold for which FRR = FAR). It can be noted that EER is also often used for assessing the model's performance on the validation and training subsets.

However, since 2017 and the work proposed in [181], the performance is most often reported using the metrics defined in the standardized ISO/IEC 30107-3 metrics [16]: Attack Presentation Classification Error Rate (*APCER*) and Bona Fide Classification Error Rate (*BPCER*) (also called Normal Presentation Classification Error Rate (*NPCER*) in some research papers). These two metrics correspond respectively to the False Acceptance Rate (*FAR*) and the False Rejection Rate (*FRR*), but for obtaining *APCER*, the *FAR* is computed separately for each PAI/type of attack and *APCER* is defined as the highest *FAR* (i.e., the *FAR* of the most successful type of attack). Similar to *HTER*, the Average Classification Error Rate (*ACER*) is then defined as the mean of *APCER* and *BPCER* using the model parameters achieving EER on the validation set:

$$ACER = \frac{APCER + NPCER}{2} \quad (4)$$

On top of the *HTER* and *ACER* scalar values, the Receiver Operating Characteristic (ROC) curve and the Area Under the Curve (AUC) are also commonly used to evaluate the PAD method's performance. The latter two have the advantage that they can provide a global evaluation of the model's performances over different values of the parameter set.

4.3. Comparison and Evaluation of the Results

In this part, we compare some of the facial PAD methods detailed in Section 2 on the public benchmarks presented in Section 3 following the intra-database and inter/cross-database protocols described above. Among the more than 50 methods presented in Section 2, we selected here the most influential methods and/or the ones that are among the most characteristic of their type of approach (following the typology presented in Section 2.1 and Figure 3, page 7 and used for the methods presentation in Section 2). To compare the performances of the different methods, we used the metrics EER, HETR, APCER, BPCER and ACER described above. The results we report are extracted from the original papers introducing the methods, i.e., we did not redevelop all these methods to perform the evaluation ourselves. As a consequence, some values might be missing (and are then noted as "–") in the following tables. Another point that is important to note is that we chose to focus our analysis on the type of features used. Of course, depending on the method, the type of classifier used (or the neural network architecture, for end-to-end deep learning methods) might also have an impact on the overall performance. However, we consider that, for each method, the authors have chosen to use the most effective classifier/architecture and that therefore the overall performances they report are largely representative of the descriptive and discriminative capabilities of the features they use.

4.3.1. Intra-Database Evaluation on Public Benchmarks

Tables 3 and 4 respectively show the results of the intra-database evaluation on the CASIA-FASD and REPLAY-ATTACK datasets. Compared to static texture feature-based methods such as DoG, LBP-based methods, dynamic texture-based methods such as LBP-TOP, Spectral Cubes [77] and DMD [23] are more effective on both benchmarks. However, the static features learned using CNNs can boost the performance significantly and sometimes even outperform dynamic texture hand-crafted features. For instance, even the earliest CNN-based method with static texture feature [34] has shown a superior performance in terms of HTER than almost all previously introduced state-of-the-art methods based on hand-crafted features. It was the first time that deep CNNs showed potential for facial PAD. Later, researchers proposed more and more models learning static or dynamic features based on deep CNNs such as LSTM-CNN [78], DPCNN [68] and Patch-based CNN [36], that has achieved the state-of-the-art performances on both the CASIA-FASD and REPLAY-ATTACK datasets. Besides, we can see both in Tables 3 and 4 that Patch-Depth CNN [36], fusing different cues (i.e., texture cue and 3D geometric cue (depth map)), has shown its superiority over single cue-based methods using the same CNN, such as Patch cue-based CNN [36] or Depth cue-based CNN [36]. Indeed, their HTERs are respectively 2.27%, 2.85% and 2.52% on CASIA-FASD and 0.72%, 0.86% and 0.75% on REPLAY-ATTACK. These results show the effectiveness of multiple cues-based methods that, by leveraging different cues, are able to effectively detect a wider variety of PA types.

As explained earlier in Section 3.4, on OULU-NPU and SiW, the different protocols corresponding to different applicative scenarios were proposed.

More specifically, for the benchmark OULU-NPU, four protocols were proposed in [181]:

- Protocol 1 aims to test the PAD methods under different environmental conditions (illumination and background);
- Protocol 2's objective is to test the generalization abilities of the methods learnt using different PAIs;
- Protocol 3 aims to test the generalization across the different acquisition devices (i.e., using Leave One Camera Out (LOCO) protocol to test the method over six smartphones); and
- Protocol 4 is the most challenging scenario, as it combines the three previous protocols to simulate real-world operational conditions.

For SiW, three different protocols were proposed in [33]:

- Protocol 1 deals with variations in facial pose and expression;
- Protocol 2 tests the model over different spoof mediums (PAIs) for video replay; and

- Protocol 3 tests the methods over different PAs, e.g., learning from photo attacks and testing on video attacks and vice versa.

From Tables 5 and 6, one can see that, both for OULU-NPU and SiW and for all the evaluation protocols, the best methods are the 3D geometric cue methods using depth estimation. Furthermore, the architectures obtained using NAS with depth maps (e.g., CDCN++ [82]) has achieved state-of-the-art performances both on OULU-NPU and SiW .

Moreover, we can see that the protocols used on OULU-NPU for testing generalization abilities (protocols 2 and 3) are especially challenging. When considering the protocol defined to evaluate the performances in near real-worldapplicative conditions (protocol 4), the model's performance can degrade up to 25 times compared to "easier" protocols (e.g., CDCN++'s ACER arises from 0.2% for protocol 1 to 5.0% for protocol 4). Similar results can be observed on SiW.

It indicates that the generalization across scenarios is still a challenge for facial PAD methods, even within the same dataset.

Table 3. Evaluation of various facial PAD methods on CASIA-FASD.

Method	Year	Feature	Cues	EER (%)	HTER (%)
DoG [19]	2012	DoG	Texture (static)	17.00	-
LBP [37]	2012	LBP	Texture (static)	-	18.21
LBP-TOP [72]	2014	LBP	Texture (dynamic)	10.00	-
Yang et al. [34]	2014	CNN	Texture (static)	4.92	4.95
Spectrual Cubes [77]	2015	FourrierSpectrum +codebook	Texture (dynamic)	14.00	-
DMD [23]	2015	LBP	Texture (dynamic)	21.80	-
Color texture [35]	2015	LBP	Texture (HSV/static)	6.20	-
LSTM-CNN [78]	2015	CNN	Texture (dynamic)	5.17	5.93
Color LBP [60]	2016	LBP	Texture (HSV/static)	3.20	-
Fine-tuned VGG-Face [68]	2016	CNN	Texture (static)	5.20	-
DPCNN [68]	2016	CNN	Texture (static)	4.50	-
Patch-based CNN [36]	2017	CNN	Texture (static)	4.44	3.78
Depth-based CNN [36]	2017	CNN	Depth	2.85	2.52
Patch-Depth CNN [36]	2017	CNN	Texture+Depth	2.67	2.27

Table 4. Evaluation of various facial PAD methods on REPLAY-ATTACK.

Method	Year	Feature	Cues	EER (%)	HTER (%)
LBP [37]	2012	LBP	Texture (static)	13.90	13.87
Motion Mag [74]	2013	HOOF	Texture (dynamic)	-	1.25
LBP-TOP [72]	2014	LBP	Texture (dynamic)	7.88	7.60
Yang et al. [34]	2014	CNN	Texture (static)	2.54	2.14
Spectral Cubes [77]	2015	Fourier Spectrum +codebook	Texture (dynamic)	-	2.80
DMD [23]	2015	LBP	Texture (dynamic)	5.30	3.80
Color texture [35]	2015	LBP	Texture (HSV/static)	0.40	2.90
Moire pattern [59]	2015	LBP+SIFT	Texture (static)	-	3.30
Color LBP [60]	2016	LBP	Texture (HSV/static)	0.10	2.20
Fine-tuned VGG-Face [68]	2016	CNN	Texture (static)	8.40	4.30
DPCNN [68]	2016	CNN	Texture (static)	2.90	6.10
Patch-based CNN [36]	2017	CNN	Texture (static)	2.50	1.25
Depth-based CNN [36]	2017	CNN	Depth	0.86	0.75
Patch-Depth CNN [36]	2017	CNN	Texture+Depth	0.79	0.72

Table 5. Evaluation of various facial PAD methods on OULU-NPU.

Protocol	Method	Year	Feature	Cues	APCER (%)	BPCER (%)	ACER (%)
1	CPqD [155]	2017	Inception-v3 [188]	Texture (static)	2.9	10.8	6.9
1	GRADIANT [155]	2017	LBP	Texture (HSV/dynamic)	1.3	12.5	6.9
1	Auxiliary [33]	2018	CNN+LSTM	Depth+rPPG	1.6	1.6	1.6
1	FaceDs [69]	2018	CNN	Texture (Quality/static)	1.2	1.7	1.5
1	STASN [79]	2019	CNN+Attention	Texture (dynamic)	1.2	2.5	1.9
1	FAS_TD [81]	2019	CNN+LSTM	Depth	2.5	0.0	1.3
1	DeepPixBis [70]	2019	DenseNet [131]	Texture	0.8	0.0	0.4
1	CDCN [82]	2020	CNN	Depth	0.4	1.7	1.0
1	CDCN++ [82]	2020	NAS+Attention	Depth	0.4	0.0	0.2
2	MixedFASNet [155]	2017	DNN	Texture (HSV/static)	9.7	2.5	6.1
2	GRADIANT [155]	2017	LBP	Texture (HSV/dynamic)	3.1	1.9	2.5
2	Auxiliary [33]	2018	CNN+LSTM	Depth+rPPG	2.7	2.7	2.7
2	FaceDs [69]	2018	CNN	Texture (Quality/static)	4.2	4.4	4.3
2	STASN [79]	2019	CNN+Attention	Texture (dynamic)	4.2	0.3	2.2
2	FAS_TD [81]	2019	CNN+LSTM	Depth	1.7	2.0	1.9
2	DeepPixBis [70]	2019	DenseNet [131]	Texture (static)	11.4	0.6	6.0
2	CDCN [82]	2020	CNN	Depth	1.5	1.4	1.5
2	CDCN++ [82]	2020	NAS+Attention	Depth	1.8	0.8	1.3
3	MixedFASNet [155]	2017	DNN	Texture (HSV/static)	5.3 ± 6.7	5.30 ± 6.7	5.3 ± 6.7
3	GRADIANT [155]	2017	LBP	Texture (HSV/dynamic)	2.6 ± 3.9	5.0 ± 5.3	3.8 ± 2.4
3	Auxiliary [33]	2018	CNN+LSTM	Depth+rPPG	2.7 ± 1.3	3.1 ± 1.7	2.9 ± 1.5
3	FaceDs [69]	2018	CNN	Texture (Quality/static)	4.0 ± 1.8	3.8 ± 1.2	3.6 ± 1.6
3	STASN [79]	2019	CNN+Attention	Texture (dynamic)	4.7 ± 3.9	0.9 ± 1.2	2.8 ± 1.6
3	FAS_TD [81]	2019	CNN+LSTM	Depth	5.9 ± 1.9	5.9 ± 3.0	5.9 ± 1.0
3	DeepPixBis [70]	2019	DenseNet [131]	Texture	11.7 ± 19.6	10.6 ± 14.1	11.1 ± 9.4
3	CDCN [82]	2020	CNN	Depth	2.4 ± 1.3	2.2 ± 2.0	2.3 ± 1.4
3	CDCN++ [82]	2020	NAS+Attention	Depth	1.7 ± 1.5	2.0 ± 1.2	1.8 ± 0.7
4	Massy_HNU [155]	2017	LBP	Texture (HSV+YCbCr)	35.8 ± 35.3	8.3 ± 4.1	22.1 ± 17.6
4	GRADIANT [155]	2017	LBP	Texture (HSV/dynamic)	5.0 ± 4.5	15.0 ± 7.1	10.0 ± 5.0
4	Auxiliary [33]	2018	CNN+LSTM	Depth+rPPG	9.3 ± 5.6	10.4 ± 6.0	9.5 ± 6.0
4	FaceDs [69]	2018	CNN	Texture (Quality/static)	1.2 ± 6.3	6.1 ± 5.1	5.6 ± 5.7
4	STASN [79]	2019	CNN+Attention	Texture (dynamic)	6.7 ± 10.6	8.3 ± 8.4	7.5 ± 4.7
4	FAS_TD [81]	2019	CNN+LSTM	Depth	14.2 ± 8.7	4.2 ± 3.8	9.2 ± 3.4
4	DeepPixBis [70]	2019	DenseNet [131]	Texture (static)	36.7 ± 29.7	13.3 ± 14.1	25.0 ± 12.7
4	CDCN [82]	2020	CNN	Depth	4.6 ± 4.6	9.2 ± 8.0	6.9 ± 2.9
4	CDCN++ [82]	2020	NAS+Attention	Depth	4.2 ± 3.4	5.8 ± 4.9	5.0 ± 2.9

Table 6. Evaluation of various facial PAD methods on SiW.

Protocol	Method	Year	Feature	Cues	APCER (%)	BPCER (%)	ACER (%)
1	Auxiliary [33]	2018	CNN+LSTM	Depth+rPPG	3.58	3.58	3.58
1	STASN [79]	2019	CNN+Attention	Texture (dynamic)	-	-	1.0
1	FAS_TD [81]	2019	CNN+LSTM	Depth	0.96	0.50	0.73
1	CDCN [82]	2020	CNN	Depth	0.07	0.17	0.12
1	CDCN++ [82]	2020	NAS+Attention	Depth	*0.07	0.17	0.12
2	Auxiliary [33]	2018	CNN+LSTM	Depth+rPPG	0.57 ± 0.69	0.57 ± 0.69	0.57 ± 0.69
2	STASN [79]	2019	CNN+Attention	Texture (dynamic)	-	-	0.28 ± 0.05
2	FAS_TD [81]	2019	CNN+LSTM	Depth	0.08 ± 0.14	0.21 ± 0.14	0.14 ± 0.14
2	CDCN [82]	2020	CNN	Depth	0.00 ± 0.00	0.13 ± 0.09	0.06 ± 0.04
2	CDCN++ [82]	2020	NAS+Attention	Depth	0.00 ± 0.00	0.09 ± 0.10	0.04 ± 0.05
3	Auxiliary [33]	2018	CNN+LSTM	Depth+rPPG	8.31 ± 3.81	8.31 ± 3.80	8.3 ± 3.81
3	STASN [79]	2019	CNN+Attention	Texture (dynamic)	-	-	12.10 ± 1.50
3	FAS_TD [81]	2019	CNN+LSTM	Depth	3.10 ± 0.81	3.09 ± 0.81	3.10 ± 0.81
3	CDCN [82]	2020	CNN	Depth	1.67 ± 0.11	1.76 ± 0.12	1.71 ± 0.11
3	CDCN++ [82]	2020	NAS+Attention	Depth	1.97 ± 0.33	1.77 ± 0.10	1.90 ± 0.15

4.3.2. Cross-Database Evaluation on Public Benchmarks

Compared to the promising results shown in the intra-database test, the inter/cross-database test results are still way worse than most real-world applications requirements. Several databases have been adopted to perform cross (inter)-database evaluation, such as CASIA-FASD vs. MSU-MFSD [32] and MSU-USSA vs. REPLAY-ATTACK/CASIA-FASD/MSU-MFSD [66]. However, most researchers have reported their cross-database evaluation results using REPLAY-ATTACK vs. CASIA-FASD [33,69,73,79,81,82], since the important differences between these two databases introduce a great challenge for cross-database testing.

Table 7 reports the results of cross-database tests between REPLAY-ATTACK and CASIA-FASD. Although the use of deep learning methods significantly improves the generalization between different databasets, there is still a large gap compared to the intra-database results. Especially if we train the model on REPLAY-ATTACK and then test the trained model on CASIA-FASD, even the best methods can only achieve at best a 29.8% HTER.

Moreover, all the PAD methods based on hand-crafted features show weak generalization abilities. For instance, the HTER of LBP-based methods based on RGB image (such as basic LBP [37] and LBP-TOP [73]) are about 60%. However, the LBP in HSV/YCbCr color space shows a comparable or even better generalization ability than some deep learning-based methods (e.g., the method in [60] achieves 30.3% and 37.7% HTER when trained on CASI-FASD and REPLAY-ATTACK, respectively). It is noteworthy that the multiple cues-based method Auxiliary [33], by fusing depth map and rPPG cues, achieves a good generalization even in the most difficult cross-database tests. For instance, when trained on REPLAY-ATTACK and tested on CASIA-FASD, it achieves slightly better HTER (28.4%) than the latest method CDCN++ [82] based on NAS (29.8%, see Table 7). This demonstrates that the multiple cues-based methods, when using different cues that are inherently complementary to each other, can achieve better generalization than facial PAD models based on single cues. However, from a very general perspective, improving the generalization abilities of the current face PAD methods is still a great challenge for facial anti-spoofing.

Table 7. Cross-database testing between CASIA-FASD and REPLAY-ATTACK: the reported evaluation metric is Half Total Error Rate (HTER) (%).

Method	Year	Feature	Cues	Train CASIA-FASD	Test REPLAY-ATTACK	Train REPLAY-ATTACK	Test CASIA-FASD
LBP [37] [a]	2012	LBP	Texture (static)	55.9		57.6	
Correlation 19 [189]	2013	MLP	Motion	50.2		47.9	
LBP-TOP [73]	2013	LBP	Texture (dynamic)	49.7		60.6	
Motion Mag [74]	2013	HOOF	Texture+Motion	50.1		47.0	
Yang et al. [34]	2014	CNN	Texture (static)	48.5		45.5	
Spectral cubes [77]	2015	Fourier Spectrum +codebook	Texture (dynamic)	34.4		50.0	
Color texture [35]	2015	LBP	Texture (HSV/static)	47.0		39.6	
Color LBP [60]	2016	LBP	Texture (HSV/static)	30.3		37.7	
Auxiliary [33]	2018	CNN+LSTM	Depth+rPPG	27.6		28.4	
FaceDs [69]	2018	CNN	Texture (Quality/static)	28.5		41.1	
STASN [79]	2019	CNN+Attention	Texture (dynamic)	31.5		30.9	
FAS_TD [81]	2019	CNN+LSTM	Depth	17.5		24.0	
CDCN [82]	2020	CNN	Depth	15.5		32.6	
CDCN++ [82]	2020	NAS+Attention	Depth	6.5		29.8	

[a] Results taken from [73].

5. Discussion

From the evaluation results presented in the previous Section 4.3, we can see that facial PAD is still a very challenging problem. In particular, the performances of the current facial PAD methods are still below the requirements of most real-world applications (especially in terms of generalization ability).

More precisely, the performances are acceptable when there is not too much variation between the conditions of the genuine faces capture for enrollment and the genuine face/PA presentation for authentication (intra-database evaluation).

However,

- all hand-crafted features show a limited generalization ability, as they are not powerful enough to capture all the possible variations in the acquisition conditions; and
- the features learned by deep/wide neural networks are of very high dimensions, compared to the limited size of the training data.

Thus, both types of features suffer from overfitting and therefore poor generalization capacity.

Therefore, learning features that are able to discriminate between a genuine face and any kind of PA, possibly under very different capture conditions, is still an open issue. This issue will be discussed in Section 5.1. Then, in Section 5.2, we discuss a less studied topic in the field of facial PAD: how to detect obfuscation attacks.

5.1. Current Trends and Perspectives

As stated earlier, learning features that are distinctive enough to discriminate between genuine faces and various PAs, possibly in very different environments, is still an open issue. Of course, this kind of issue (related to the generalization abilities of data-driven models) are common in the field of computer vision, way beyond facial PAD.

However, as collecting impostors' PAs and PAIs is nearly impossible in the wild, collecting/creating a face PAD dataset with sufficient samples and variability (not only regarding the capture conditions but also regarding the different types of PA/PAIs) is still very time-consuming and costly (see Section 3.2). It is indeed much easier to create a dataset for most object recognition tasks (e.g., face authentication).

In order to tackle all previously seen PAs, a current trend is to combine multiple cues (see Section 2.5). However, due to the abovementioned challenges in the dataset creation as well as the technological advances that ill-intentioned users can access to deploy increasingly sophisticated attacks, the PAD method might have to detect PAs that were not included in its training dataset. This problem, called "Unknown attack" previously, is especially challenging.

Beyond the current methods that try and use zero/few-shot learning approaches to tackle this problem, the question of learning features that are representative enough of "real" faces, so that they can discriminate between genuine faces and any kind of PAs under any type of capture condition, is still an open issue. This issue, for which some researchers have recently proposed solutions based on domain adaptation, will very probably raise a lot of attention from researchers in the coming years, especially with the emergence of ever more sophisticated DeepFakes.

5.2. Obfuscation Face PAD

As stated in Section 1.2, two types of PAs are defined in the relevant ISO standard [16]: impersonation (spoofing) attacks, i.e., attempts of impostors to impersonate a genuine user, and obfuscation attacks, i.e., attempts for the impostor to hide her own identity.

Most current facial PAD research focuses on the former type, i.e., impersonation spoofing, as it is the most frequent attack for biometric systems based on facial recognition/authentication.

However, there are some applicative scenarios where obfuscation attacks are very important to detect. For instance, in law-enforcement applications based on video surveillance, one of the main objectives is to be able to detect criminals, whereas the goals of criminals using obfuscation attacks is to remain unrecognized by the system.

As detailed in Figure 1 on page 3, obfuscation attacks may entail (possibly extreme) facial makeup or occluding significant portions of the face using scarves, sunglasses, face masks, hats, etc. In some cases, the person deploying obfuscation attack may also use tricks that are usually used for impersonation attacks, e.g., by using a mask showing the face of a noncriminal. As well as impersonation attacks, obfuscation attacks also include previously unseen attacks/unknown attacks. The detection of unseen/unknown obfuscation attacks is still an open issue which needs to be further studied.

To the best of our knowledge, so far, the only dataset containing examples of obfuscation attacks is SiW-M. This dataset has been introduced in [87], where the authors have shown the effectiveness of extreme makeup for facial obfuscation. One solution is to process the facial image so as to synthetically "remove" the makeup, as in [190,191].

More generally, given that compared to impersonation attacks obfuscation attacks are still less frequent, several research groups consider obfuscation attacks as a zero/few-shot PAD problem [87].

Even though obfuscation attack detection has been so far much less studied than impersonation attack detection, it is very likely that this topic will become more and more studied in the future, given the conjunction of several factors, such as the generalization of video surveillance in public places, geo-political issues including risks of terrorist attacks in some regions of the world and recent technological developments that allow researchers to tackle this problem.

6. Conclusions

In this survey paper, we have thoroughly investigated over 50 of the most influential face PAD methods that can work in scenarios where the user only has access to RGB cameras of Generic Consumer Devices. By structuring our paper according to a typology of facial PAD methods based on the types of PA that they are aiming to thwart and in chronological order, we have shown the evolution in the facial PAD during the last two decades. This evolution covers a large variety of methods, from hand-crafted features to the most recent deep learning-based technologies such as Neural Architecture Search (NAS). Benefiting from the recent breakthroughs obtained by researchers in computer vision, thanks to the advent of deep learning, facial PAD methods are getting ever more effective and efficient. We have also gathered, summarized and detailed the most relevant information about a dozen of the most widespread public datasets for facial PAD.

Using these datasets as benchmarks, we have extensively compared different types of facial PAD methods using common experimental protocol and evaluation metrics. This comparative evaluation allows us to point out which types of approaches are most effective, depending on the type of PA. More specifically, according to our investigation, texture-based methods which are also the most widely used PAD methods, and especially dynamic texture-based methods, are able to detect almost all types of PAs. Furthermore, the methods based on texture features learned using deep learning have significantly improved the state-of-the-art facial PAD performances compared to methods based on hand-crafted texture features. However, in general, high-quality 3D mask attacks are still a great challenge for texture-based approaches. On the other hand, liveness-based methods or 3D geometric-based methods can achieve relatively better generalization capabilities, even though they are still vulnerable to video replay attacks or complex illumination conditions. Multiple cues-based methods, by leveraging different cues for facial PAD, are in general more effective for detecting various PAs. Nevertheless, the computational complexity of multiple-cues based methods is an issue that needs to be considered for real-time applications. Partly because of the complexity of the facial PAD problem, the huge variability in the possible attacks and the lack of dataset that contains enough samples with sufficient variability, all current approaches are still limited in terms of generalization.

We have also identified some of the most prominent current trends in facial PAD, such as combining approaches that aim to thwart various kinds of attacks or to tackle previously unseen attacks. We have also provided some insights for future research and have listed the still open issues, such as learning features that are able to discriminate between genuine faces and all kinds of PAs.

Author Contributions: All authors contributed to the study conceptualisation and design. The first draft of the manuscript was written by Z.M., supervised by M.V., J.-C.B. and M.M.L. All authors provided critical feedback, brought amendments and helped shape the manuscript. All authors have read and agreed to the published version of the manuscript.

Funding: This research was funded by Project IDECYS+.

Conflicts of Interest: The authors declare no conflict of interest. The funders had no role in the design of the study; in the collection, analyses, or interpretation of data; in the writing of the manuscript, or in the decision to publish the results.

References

1. Turk, M.; Pentland, A. Eigenfaces for recognition. *J. Cogn. Neurosci.* **1991**, *3*, 71–86. [CrossRef] [PubMed]
2. Krizhevsky, A.; Sutskever, I.; Hinton, G.E. Imagenet classification with deep convolutional neural networks. In Proceedings of the NIPS, Lake Tahoe, NV, USA, 3–6 December 2012; pp. 1097–1105.
3. Szegedy, C.; Liu, W.; Jia, Y.; Sermanet, P.; Reed, S.; Anguelov, D.; Erhan, D.; Vanhoucke, V.; Rabinovich, A. Going deeper with convolutions. In Proceedings of the CVPR, Boston, MA, USA, 7–12 June 2015; pp. 1–9.
4. He, K.; Zhang, X.; Ren, S.; Sun, J. Deep residual learning for image recognition. In Proceedings of the CVPR, Las Vegas, NV, USA, 27–30 June 2016; pp. 770–778.
5. Taigman, Y.; Yang, M.; Ranzato, M.; Wolf, L. Deepface: Closing the gap to human-level performance in face verification. In Proceedings of the CVPR, Columbus, OH, USA , 23–28 June 2014; pp. 1701–1708.
6. Sun, Y.; Wang, X.; Tang, X. Deeply learned face representations are sparse, selective, and robust. In Proceedings of the CVPR, Boston, MA, USA, 8–10 June 2015; pp. 2892–2900.
7. Parkhi, O.M.; Vedaldi, A.; Zisserman, A. Deep Face Recognition. In Proceedings of the BMVC, Swansea, UK, 7–10 September 2015; Volume 1, p. 6.
8. Schroff, F.; Kalenichenko, D.; Philbin, J. Facenet: A unified embedding for face recognition and clustering. In Proceedings of the CVPR, Boston, MA, USA, 8–10 June 2015; pp. 815–823.
9. Liu, W.; Wen, Y.; Yu, Z.; Li, M.; Raj, B.; Song, L. Sphereface: Deep hypersphere embedding for face recognition. In Proceedings of the the CVPR, Honolulu, HI, USA, 21–26 June 2017; Volume 1, p. 1.
10. Deng, J.; Guo, J.; Xue, N.; Zafeiriou, S. Arcface: Additive angular margin loss for deep face recognition. In Proceedings of the CVPR, Long Beach, CA, USA, 16–20 June 2019; pp. 4690–4699.

11. Sun, Y.; Wang, X.; Tang, X. Deep learning face representation from predicting 10,000 classes. In Proceedings of the CVPR, Columbus, OH, USA, 24–27 June 2014; pp. 1891–1898.
12. Huang, G.B.; Ramesh, M.; Berg, T.; Learned-Miller, E. *Labeled Faces in the Wild: A Database for Studying Face Recognition in Unconstrained Environments*; Technical Report, Technical Report 07-49; University of Massachusetts: Amherst, MA, USA, 2007.
13. Wolf, L.; Hassner, T.; Maoz, I. Face recognition in unconstrained videos with matched background similarity. In Proceedings of the CVPR, Colorado Springs, CO, USA, 20–25 June 2011; pp. 529–534.
14. de Luis-García, R.; Alberola-López, C.; Aghzout, O.; Ruiz-Alzola, J. Biometric identification systems. *Signal Process.* **2003**, *83*, 2539–2557. [CrossRef]
15. Souza, L.; Oliveira, L.; Pamplona, M.; Papa, J. How far did we get in face spoofing detection? *Eng. Appl. Artif. Intell.* **2018**, *72*, 368–381. [CrossRef]
16. ISO/IEC JTC 1/SC 37 Biometrics. *Information Technology—Biometric Presentation Attack Detection—Part 1: Frame-Work*; International Organization for Standardization: Geneva, Switzerland, 2016.
17. Liu, S.; Yang, B.; Yuen, P.C.; Zhao, G. A 3D mask face anti-spoofing database with real world variations. In Proceedings of the CVPR Workshops, LasVegas, NV, USA, 27–30 June 2016; pp. 100–106.
18. Kollreider, K.; Fronthaler, H.; Bigun, J. Verifying liveness by multiple experts in face biometrics. In Proceedings of the CVPR Workshops, Anchorage, AK, USA, 23–28 June 2008; pp. 1–6.
19. Zhang, Z.; Yan, J. A face antispoofing database with diverse attacks. In Proceedings of the International Conference on Biometrics, New Delhi, India, 30 March–1 April 2012; pp. 26–31.
20. Available online: http://www.urmesurveillance.com (accessed on 29 September 2020).
21. Marcel, S.; Nixon, M.S.; Li, S.Z. *Handbook of Biometric Anti-Spoofing*; Springer: Berlin/Heisenberg, Germany, 2014; Volume 1.
22. Zhang, Z.; Yi, D.; Lei, Z.; Li, S.Z. Face liveness detection by learning multispectral reflectance distributions. In Proceedings of the Face and Gesture 2011, Santa Barbara, CA, USA, 21–24 March 2011; pp. 436–441.
23. Tirunagari, S.; Poh, N.; Windridge, D.; Iorliam, A.; Suki, N.; Ho, A.T. Detection of face spoofing using visual dynamics. *IEEE Trans. Inf. Forensics Secur.* **2015**, *10*, 762–777. [CrossRef]
24. Galbally, J.; Satta, R. Three-dimensional and two-and-a-half-dimensional face recognition spoofing using three-dimensional printed models. *IET Biom.* **2016**, *5*, 83–91. [CrossRef]
25. Erdogmus, N.; Marcel, S. Spoofing face recognition with 3D masks. *IEEE Trans. Inf. Forensics Secur.* **2014**, *9*, 1084–1097. [CrossRef]
26. Lagorio, A.; Tistarelli, M.; Cadoni, M.; Fookes, C.; Sridharan, S. Liveness detection based on 3D face shape analysis. In Proceedings of the 2013 International Workshop on Biometrics and Forensics (IWBF), Lisbon, Portugal, 4–5 April 2013; pp. 1–4.
27. Li, S.; Yi, D.; Lei, Z.; Liao, S. The casia nir-vis 2.0 face database. In Proceedings of the IEEE Conference on Computer Vision and Pattern Recognition Workshops, Portland, OR, USA, 25–27 June 2013; pp. 348–353.
28. Bhattacharjee, S.; Marcel, S. What you can't see can help you-extended-range imaging for 3d-mask presentation attack detection. In Proceedings of the 2017 International Conference of the Biometrics Special Interest Group (BIOSIG), Darmstadt, Germany, 20–22 September 2017; pp. 1–7.
29. Hernandez-Ortega, J.; Fierrez, J.; Morales, A.; Tome, P. Time analysis of pulse-based face anti-spoofing in visible and NIR. In Proceedings of the IEEE Conference on Computer Vision and Pattern Recognition Workshops, Salt Lake City, UT, USA, 18–22 June 2018; pp. 544–552.
30. Yi, D.; Lei, Z.; Zhang, Z.; Li, S.Z. Face anti-spoofing: Multi-spectral approach . In *Handbook of Biometric Anti-Spoofing*; Springer: Berlin/Heisenberg, Germany, 2014; pp. 83–102.
31. Sun, L.; Huang, W.; Wu, M. TIR/VIS correlation for liveness detection in face recognition. In Proceedings of the International Conference on Computer Analysis of Images and Patterns, Seville, Spain, 29–31 August 2011; Springer: Berlin/Heisenberg, Germany, 2011; pp. 114–121.
32. Wen, D.; Han, H.; Jain, A.K. Face spoof detection with image distortion analysis. *IEEE Trans. Inf. Forensics Secur.* **2015**, *10*, 746–761. [CrossRef]
33. Liu, Y.; Jourabloo, A.; Liu, X. Learning Deep Models for Face Anti-Spoofing: Binary or Auxiliary Supervision. In Proceedings of the CVPR, Salt Lake City, UT, USA, 18–22 June 2018; pp. 389–398.
34. Yang, J.; Lei, Z.; Li, S.Z. Learn convolutional neural network for face anti-spoofing. *arXiv* **2014**, arXiv:1408.5601

35. Boulkenafet, Z.; Komulainen, J.; Hadid, A. Face anti-spoofing based on color texture analysis. In Proceedings of the 2015 IEEE international conference on image processing (ICIP), Quebec City, QC, Canada, 27–30 September 2015; pp. 2636–2640.
36. Atoum, Y.; Liu, Y.; Jourabloo, A.; Liu, X. Face anti-spoofing using patch and depth-based CNNs. In Proceedings of the 2017 IEEE International Joint Conference on Biometrics (IJCB), Denver, CO, USA, 1–4 October 2017; pp. 319–328.
37. Chingovska, I.; Anjos, A.; Marcel, S. On the effectiveness of local binary patterns in face anti-spoofing. In Proceedings of the International Conference of the Biometrics Special Interest Group (BIOSIG), Darmstadt, Germany, 6–7 September 2012; pp. 1–7.
38. Costa-Pazo, A.; Bhattacharjee, S.; Vazquez-Fernandez, E.; Marcel, S. The replay-mobile face presentation-attack database. In Proceedings of the 2016 International Conference of the Biometrics Special Interest Group (BIOSIG), Darmstadt, Germany, 21–23 September 2016; pp. 1–7.
39. Ramachandra, R.; Busch, C. Presentation attack detection methods for face recognition systems: A comprehensive survey. *ACM Comput. Surv. (CSUR)* **2017**, *50*, 1–37. [CrossRef]
40. Hernandez-Ortega, J.; Fierrez, J.; Morales, A.; Galbally, J. Introduction to face presentation attack detection. In *Handbook of Biometric Anti-Spoofing*; Springer: Berlin/Heisenberg, Germany, 2019; pp. 187–206.
41. Bhattacharjee, S.; Mohammadi, A.; Anjos, A.; Marcel, S. Recent advances in face presentation attack detection. In *Handbook of Biometric Anti-Spoofing*; Springer: Berlin/Heisenberg, Germany, 2019; pp. 207–228.
42. Pan, G.; Sun, L.; Wu, Z.; Lao, S. Eyeblink-based anti-spoofing in face recognition from a generic webcamera. In Proceedings of the ICCV, Rio de Janeiro, Brazil, 14–20 October 2007; pp. 1–8.
43. Sun, L.; Pan, G.; Wu, Z.; Lao, S. Blinking-based live face detection using conditional random fields. In Proceedings of the International Conference on Biometrics, Seoul, Korea, 27–29 August 2007; Springer: Berlin/Heisenberg, Germany, 2007; pp. 252–260.
44. Li, J.; Wang, Y.; Tan, T.; Jain, A.K. Live face detection based on the analysis of fourier spectra. *Biometric technology for human identification. Int. Soc. Opt. Photonics* **2004**, *5404*, 296–303.
45. Kollreider, K.; Fronthaler, H.; Bigun, J. Evaluating liveness by face images and the structure tensor. In Proceedings of the Fourth IEEE Workshop on Automatic Identification Advanced Technologies (AutoID'05), Buffalo, NY, USA, USA, 17–18 October 2005; pp. 75–80.
46. Kollreider, K.; Fronthaler, H.; Bigun, J. Non-intrusive liveness detection by face images. *Image Vis. Comput.* **2009**, *27*, 233–244. [CrossRef]
47. Bao, W.; Li, H.; Li, N.; Jiang, W. A liveness detection method for face recognition based on optical flow field. In Proceedings of the 2009 International Conference on Image Analysis and Signal Processing, Kuala Lumpur, Malaysia, 18–19 November 2009; pp. 233–236.
48. Kollreider, K.; Fronthaler, H.; Faraj, M.I.; Bigun, J. Real-time face detection and motion analysis with application in "liveness" assessment. *IEEE Trans. Inf. Forensics Secur.* **2007**, *2*, 548–558. [CrossRef]
49. Li, X.; Komulainen, J.; Zhao, G.; Yuen, P.C.; Pietikäinen, M. Generalized face anti-spoofing by detecting pulse from face videos. In Proceedings of the 2016 23rd International Conference on Pattern Recognition (ICPR), Cancun, Mexico, 4–8 December 2016; pp. 4244–4249.
50. Nowara, E.M.; Sabharwal, A.; Veeraraghavan, A. Ppgsecure: Biometric presentation attack detection using photopletysmograms. In Proceedings of the 2017 12th IEEE International Conference on Automatic Face & Gesture Recognition (FG 2017), Washington, DC, USA, 30 May–3 June 2017; pp. 56–62.
51. Liu, S.; Yuen, P.C.; Zhang, S.; Zhao, G. 3D mask face anti-spoofing with remote photoplethysmography. In Proceedings of the European Conference on Computer Vision, Amsterdam, The Netherlands, 10–16 October 2016; Springer: Berlin/Heisenberg, Germany, 2016; pp. 85–100.
52. Tan, X.; Li, Y.; Liu, J.; Jiang, L. Face liveness detection from a single image with sparse low rank bilinear discriminative model. In Proceedings of the Computer Vision–ECCV 2010, Crete, Greece, 5–11 September 2010; pp. 504–517.
53. Peixoto, B.; Michelassi, C.; Rocha, A. Face liveness detection under bad illumination conditions. In Proceedings of the 2011 18th IEEE International Conference on Image Processing, Brussels, Belgium, 11–14 September 2011; pp. 3557–3560.
54. Bai, J.; Ng, T.T.; Gao, X.; Shi, Y.Q. Is physics-based liveness detection truly possible with a single image? In Proceedings of the 2010 IEEE International Symposium on Circuits and Systems, Paris, France, 30 May–2 June 2010; pp. 3425–3428.

55. Määttä, J.; Hadid, A.; Pietikäinen, M. Face spoofing detection from single images using micro-texture analysis. In Proceedings of the Biometrics (IJCB), 2011 International Joint Conference on Biometrics, Washington, DC, USA, 11–13 October 2011; pp. 1–7.
56. Kose, N.; Dugelay, J.L. Countermeasure for the protection of face recognition systems against mask attacks. In Proceedings of the 2013 10th IEEE International Conference and Workshops on Automatic Face and Gesture Recognition (FG), Shanghai, China, 22–26 April 2013; pp. 1–6.
57. Kose, N.; Dugelay, J.L. Shape and texture based countermeasure to protect face recognition systems against mask attacks. In Proceedings of the IEEE Conference on Computer Vision and Pattern Recognition Workshops, Portland, OR, USA, 23–28 June 2013; pp. 111–116.
58. Erdogmus, N.; Marcel, S. Spoofing 2D face recognition systems with 3D masks. In Proceedings of the 2013 International Conference of the BIOSIG Special Interest Group (BIOSIG), Darmstadt, Germany, 4–6 September 2013; pp. 1–8.
59. Patel, K.; Han, H.; Jain, A.K.; Ott, G. Live face video vs. spoof face video: Use of moiré patterns to detect replay video attacks. In Proceedings of the 2015 International Conference on Biometrics (ICB), Phuket, Thailand, 19–22 May 2015; pp. 98–105.
60. Boulkenafet, Z.; Komulainen, J.; Hadid, A. Face spoofing detection using colour texture analysis. *IEEE Trans. Inf. Forensics Secur.* **2016**, *11*, 1818–1830. [CrossRef]
61. Määttä, J.; Hadid, A.; Pietikäinen, M. Face spoofing detection from single images using texture and local shape analysis. *IET Biom.* **2012**, *1*, 3–10. [CrossRef]
62. Yang, J.; Lei, Z.; Liao, S.; Li, S.Z. Face liveness detection with component dependent descriptor. In Proceedings of the 2013 International Conference on Biometrics (ICB), Madrid, Spain, 4–7 June 2013; pp. 1–6.
63. Komulainen, J.; Hadid, A.; Pietikainen, M. Context based face anti-spoofing. In Proceedings of the 2013 IEEE Sixth International Conference on Biometrics: Theory, Applications and Systems (BTAS), Arlington, VA, USA, 29 September–2 October 2013; pp. 1–8.
64. Galbally, J.; Marcel, S. Face Anti-spoofing Based on General Image Quality Assessment. In Proceedings of the 2014 22nd International Conference on Pattern Recognition (ICPR '14), Stockholm, Sweden, 24–28 August 2014; pp. 1173–1178.
65. Galbally, J.; Marcel, S.; Fierrez, J. Image quality assessment for fake biometric detection: Application to iris, fingerprint, and face recognition. *IEEE Trans. Image Process.* **2013**, *23*, 710–724. [CrossRef] [PubMed]
66. Patel, K.; Han, H.; Jain, A.K. Secure face unlock: Spoof detection on smartphones. *IEEE Trans. Inf. Forensics Secur.* **2016**, *11*, 2268–2283. [CrossRef]
67. Patel, K.; Han, H.; Jain, A.K. Cross-database face antispoofing with robust feature representation. In Proceedings of the Chinese Conference on Biometric Recognition, Shenyang, China, 7–9 November 2014; Springer: Berlin/Heisenberg, Germany, 2016; pp. 611–619.
68. Li, L.; Feng, X.; Boulkenafet, Z.; Xia, Z.; Li, M.; Hadid, A. An original face anti-spoofing approach using partial convolutional neural network. In Proceedings of the 2016 Sixth International Conference on Image Processing Theory, Tools and Applications (IPTA), Oulu, Finland, 12–15 December 2016; pp. 1–6.
69. Jourabloo, A.; Liu, Y.; Liu, X. Face de-spoofing: Anti-spoofing via noise modeling. In Proceedings of the European Conference on Computer Vision (ECCV), Munich, Germany, 8–14 September 2018; pp. 290–306.
70. George, A.; Marcel, S. Deep pixel-wise binary supervision for face presentation attack detection. In Proceedings of the 2019 International Conference on Biometrics (ICB), Crete, Greece, 4–7 June 2019; pp. 1–8.
71. de Freitas Pereira, T.; Anjos, A.; De Martino, J.M.; Marcel, S. LBP-TOP based countermeasure against face spoofing attacks. In Proceedings of the ACCV, Daejeon, Korea, 5–9 November 2012; pp. 121–132.
72. de Freitas Pereira, T.; Komulainen, J.; Anjos, A.; De Martino, J.M.; Hadid, A.; Pietikäinen, M.; Marcel, S. Face liveness detection using dynamic texture. *EURASIP J. Image Video Process.* **2014**, *2014*, 2. [CrossRef]
73. de Freitas Pereira, T.; Anjos, A.; De Martino, J.M.; Marcel, S. Can face anti-spoofing countermeasures work in a real world scenario? In Proceedings of the 2013 international conference on biometrics (ICB), Madrid, Spain, 4–7 June 2013; pp. 1–8.
74. Bharadwaj, S.; Dhamecha, T.I.; Vatsa, M.; Singh, R. Computationally efficient face spoofing detection with motion magnification. In Proceedings of the CVPR Workshops, Portland, OR, USA, 23–24 June 2013; pp. 105–110.

75. da Silva Pinto, A.; Pedrini, H.; Schwartz, W.; Rocha, A. Video-based face spoofing detection through visual rhythm analysis. In Proceedings of the 2012 25th SIBGRAPI Conference on Graphics, Patterns and Images, Ouro Preto, Brazil, 22–25 August 2012; pp. 221–228.
76. Pinto, A.; Schwartz, W.R.; Pedrini, H.; de Rezende Rocha, A. Using visual rhythms for detecting video-based facial spoof attacks. *IEEE Trans. Inf. Forensics Secur.* **2015**, *10*, 1025–1038. [CrossRef]
77. Pinto, A.; Pedrini, H.; Schwartz, W.R.; Rocha, A. Face spoofing detection through visual codebooks of spectral temporal cubes. *IEEE Trans. Image Process.* **2015**, *24*, 4726–4740. [CrossRef]
78. Xu, Z.; Li, S.; Deng, W. Learning temporal features using LSTM-CNN architecture for face anti-spoofing. In Proceedings of the 2015 3rd IAPR Asian Conference on Pattern Recognition (ACPR), Kuala Lumpur, Malaysia, 3–6 November 2015; pp. 141–145.
79. Yang, X.; Luo, W.; Bao, L.; Gao, Y.; Gong, D.; Zheng, S.; Li, Z.; Liu, W. Face anti-spoofing: Model matters, so does data. In Proceedings of the IEEE Conference on Computer Vision and Pattern Recognition, Long Beach, CA, USA, 16–20 June 2019; pp. 3507–3516.
80. Wang, T.; Yang, J.; Lei, Z.; Liao, S.; Li, S.Z. Face liveness detection using 3D structure recovered from a single camera. In Proceedings of the 2013 international conference on biometrics (ICB), Crete, Greece, 4–7 June 2013; pp. 1–6.
81. Wang, Z.; Zhao, C.; Qin, Y.; Zhou, Q.; Qi, G.; Wan, J.; Lei, Z. Exploiting temporal and depth information for multi-frame face anti-spoofing. *arXiv* **2018**, arXiv:1811.05118.
82. Yu, Z.; Zhao, C.; Wang, Z.; Qin, Y.; Su, Z.; Li, X.; Zhou, F.; Zhao, G. Searching central difference convolutional networks for face anti-spoofing. In Proceedings of the IEEE/CVF Conference on Computer Vision and Pattern Recognition, Seattle, WA, USA, 14–19 June 2020; pp. 5295–5305.
83. Pan, G.; Sun, L.; Wu, Z.; Wang, Y. Monocular camera-based face liveness detection by combining eyeblink and scene context. *Telecommun. Syst.* **2011**, *47*, 215–225. [CrossRef]
84. Feng, L.; Po, L.M.; Li, Y.; Xu, X.; Yuan, F.; Cheung, T.C.H.; Cheung, K.W. Integration of image quality and motion cues for face anti-spoofing: A neural network approach. *J. Vis. Commun. Image Represent.* **2016**, *38*, 451–460. [CrossRef]
85. Nikisins, O.; Mohammadi, A.; Anjos, A.; Marcel, S. On effectiveness of anomaly detection approaches against unseen presentation attacks in face anti-spoofing. In Proceedings of the 2018 International Conference on Biometrics (ICB), Crete, Greece, 4–7 June 2018; pp. 75–81.
86. Arashloo, S.R.; Kittler, J.; Christmas, W. An anomaly detection approach to face spoofing detection: A new formulation and evaluation protocol. *IEEE Access* **2017**, *5*, 13868–13882. [CrossRef]
87. Liu, Y.; Stehouwer, J.; Jourabloo, A.; Liu, X. Deep tree learning for zero-shot face anti-spoofing. In Proceedings of the IEEE Conference on Computer Vision and Pattern Recognition, Long Beach, CA, USA, 16–20 June 2019; pp. 4680–4689.
88. Shao, R.; Lan, X.; Li, J.; Yuen, P. Multi-Adversarial Discriminative Deep Domain Generalization for Face Presentation Attack Detection. In Proceedings of the 2019 IEEE/CVF Conference on Computer Vision and Pattern Recognition (CVPR), Long Beach, CA, USA, 16–20 June 2019; pp. 10015–10023.
89. Aggarwal, J.; Nandhakumar, N. On the computation of motion from sequences of images—A review. *Proc. IEEE* **1988**, *76*, 917–935. [CrossRef]
90. Azarbayejani, A.; Starner, T.; Horowitz, B.; Pentland, A. Visually controlled graphics. *IEEE Trans. Pattern Anal. Mach. Intell.* **1993**, *15*, 602–605. [CrossRef]
91. Bigün, J.; Granlund, G.H.; Wiklund, J. Multidimensional orientation estimation with applications to texture analysis and optical flow. *IEEE Trans. Pattern Anal. Mach. Intell.* **1991**, *13*, 775–790. [CrossRef]
92. Karson, C.N. Spontaneous eye-blink rates and dopaminergic systems. *Brain* **1983**, *106*, 643–653. [CrossRef]
93. Rabiner, L.R. A tutorial on hidden Markov models and selected applications in speech recognition. *Proc. IEEE* **1989**, *77*, 257–286. [CrossRef]
94. Viola, P.; Jones, M. Rapid object detection using a boosted cascade of simple features. In Proceedings of the 2001 IEEE Computer Society Conference on Computer Vision and Pattern Recognition, CVPR 2001, Kauai, HI, USA, 8–14 December 2001; Volume 1, p. I.
95. Vapnik, V. *The Nature of Statistical Learning Theory*; Springer: Berlin/Heisenberg, Germany, 2013.
96. Howcroft, E. *How Faking Videos Became Easy and Why That's So Scary*; Bloomberg: New York, NY, USA, 2018.
97. Chesney, R.; Citron, D. Deepfakes and the new disinformation war: The coming age of post-truth geopolitics. *Foreign Aff.* **2019**, *98*, 147.

98. Nguyen, T.T.; Nguyen, C.M.; Nguyen, D.T.; Nguyen, D.T.; Nahavandi, S. Deep learning for deepfakes creation and detection. *arXiv* **2019**, arXiv:1909.11573.
99. Dupont, S.; Luettin, J. Audio-visual speech modeling for continuous speech recognition. *IEEE Trans. Multimed.* **2000**, *2*, 141–151. [CrossRef]
100. Deepfakes Web. Available online: https://deepfakesweb.com/ (accessed on 15 September 2020).
101. Badrinarayanan, V.; Kendall, A.; Cipolla, R. Segnet: A deep convolutional encoder-decoder architecture for image segmentation. *IEEE Trans. Pattern Anal. Mach. Intell.* **2017**, *39*, 2481–2495. [CrossRef] [PubMed]
102. Zhang, H.; Xu, T.; Li, H.; Zhang, S.; Wang, X.; Huang, X.; Metaxas, D.N. Stackgan++: Realistic image synthesis with stacked generative adversarial networks. *IEEE Trans. Pattern Anal. Mach. Intell.* **2018**, *41*, 1947–1962. [CrossRef] [PubMed]
103. FaceApp. Available online: https://www.faceapp.com/ (accessed on 15 September 2020).
104. FakeApp. Available online: https://www.fakeapp.org/ (accessed on 15 September 2020).
105. Fernandes, S.; Raj, S.; Ortiz, E.; Vintila, I.; Salter, M.; Urosevic, G.; Jha, S. Predicting Heart Rate Variations of Deepfake Videos using Neural ODE. In Proceedings of the IEEE International Conference on Computer Vision Workshops, Seoul, Korea, 27 October–2 November 2019.
106. Ciftci, U.A.; Demir, I.; Yin, L. Fakecatcher: Detection of synthetic portrait videos using biological signals. *IEEE Trans. Pattern Anal. Mach. Intell.* **2020**. [CrossRef]
107. Li, L.; Bao, J.; Zhang, T.; Yang, H.; Chen, D.; Wen, F.; Guo, B. Face x-ray for more general face forgery detection. In Proceedings of the IEEE/CVF Conference on Computer Vision and Pattern Recognition, Seattle, WA, USA, 14–19 June 2020; pp. 5001–5010.
108. Ho, T.K. Random decision forests. In Proceedings of the 3rd International Conference on Document Analysis and Recognition, Montreal, QC, Canada, 14–16 August 1995; Volume 1, pp. 278–282.
109. Chen, R.T.; Rubanova, Y.; Bettencourt, J.; Duvenaud, D.K. Neural ordinary differential equations. In Proceedings of the Advances in Neural Information Processing Systems, Montreal, QC, Canada, 3–8 December 2018; pp. 6571–6583.
110. Oren, M.; Nayar, S.K. Generalization of the Lambertian model and implications for machine vision. *Int. J. Comput. Vis.* **1995**, *14*, 227–251. [CrossRef]
111. Tan, X.; Triggs, B. Enhanced local texture feature sets for face recognition under difficult lighting conditions. *IEEE Trans. Image Process.* **2010**, *19*, 1635–1650.
112. Zuiderveld, K. Contrast limited adaptive histogram equalization. In *Graphics Gems*; Elsevier: San Diego, CA, USA, 1994; pp. 474–485.
113. Tan, R.T.; Ikeuchi, K. Separating reflection components of textured surfaces using a single image. In *Digitally Archiving Cultural Objects*; Springer: Berlin/Heisenberg, Germany, 2008; pp. 353–384.
114. Ojala, T.; Pietikainen, M.; Maenpaa, T. Multiresolution gray-scale and rotation invariant texture classification with local binary patterns. *IEEE Trans. Pattern Anal. Mach. Intell.* **2002**, *24*, 971–987. [CrossRef]
115. Ahonen, T.; Hadid, A.; Pietikainen, M. Face description with local binary patterns: Application to face recognition. *IEEE Trans. Pattern Anal. Mach. Intell.* **2006**, *28*, 2037–2041. [CrossRef]
116. Zhang, L.; Chu, R.; Xiang, S.; Liao, S.; Li, S.Z. Face detection based on multi-block lbp representation. In Proceedings of the International Conference on Biometrics, Gold Coast, Australia, 20–23 February 2007; pp. 11–18.
117. Zhao, G.; Pietikainen, M. Dynamic texture recognition using local binary patterns with an application to facial expressions. *IEEE Trans. Pattern Anal. Mach. Intell.* **2007**, *29*, 915–928. [CrossRef]
118. Manjunath, B.S.; Ma, W.Y. Texture features for browsing and retrieval of image data. *IEEE Trans. Pattern Anal. Mach. Intell.* **1996**, *18*, 837–842. [CrossRef]
119. Dalal, N.; Triggs, B. Histograms of oriented gradients for human detection. In Proceedings of the 2005 IEEE Computer Society Conference on Computer Vision and Pattern Recognition (CVPR'05), San Diego, CA, USA, 20–26 June 2005; Volume 1, pp. 886–893.
120. Vedaldi, A.; Zisserman, A. Efficient additive kernels via explicit feature maps. *IEEE Trans. Pattern Anal. Mach. Intell.* **2012**, *34*, 480–492. [CrossRef] [PubMed]
121. Ferrari, V.; Marin-Jimenez, M.; Zisserman, A. Progressive search space reduction for human pose estimation. In Proceedings of the 2008 IEEE Conference on Computer Vision and Pattern Recognition, Anchorage, AK, USA, 24–26 June 2008; pp. 1–8.

122. Ojansivu, V.; Heikkilä, J. Blur insensitive texture classification using local phase quantization. In Proceedings of the International Conference on Image and Signal Processing, Cherbourg-Octeville, France, 1–3 July 2008; pp. 236–243.
123. Lazebnik, S.; Schmid, C.; Ponce, J. Beyond bags of features: Spatial pyramid matching for recognizing natural scene categories. In Proceedings of the 2006 IEEE Computer Society Conference on Computer Vision and Pattern Recognition (CVPR'06), New York, NY, USA, 17–22 June 2006; Volume 2, pp. 2169–2178.
124. Gao, X.; Ng, T.T.; Qiu, B.; Chang, S.F. Single-view recaptured image detection based on physics-based features. In Proceedings of the 2010 IEEE International Conference on Multimedia and Expo, Singapore, 19–23 July 2010; pp. 1469–1474.
125. Crete, F.; Dolmiere, T.; Ladret, P.; Nicolas, M. The blur effect: Perception and estimation with a new no-reference perceptual blur metric. In Proceedings of the Human Vision and Electronic Imaging XII. International Society for Optics and Photonics, San Jose, CA, USA, 29 January–1 February 2007; Volume 6492, p. 64920I.
126. Marziliano, P.; Dufaux, F.; Winkler, S.; Ebrahimi, T. A no-reference perceptual blur metric. In Proceedings of the International Conference on Image Processing, New York, NY, USA, 22–25 September 2002; Volume 3, p. III.
127. Chen, Y.; Li, Z.; Li, M.; Ma, W.Y. Automatic classification of photographs and graphics. In Proceedings of the 2006 IEEE International Conference on Multimedia and Expo, Toronto, ON, Canada, 9–12 July 2006; pp. 973–976.
128. Jain, A.; Nandakumar, K.; Ross, A. Score normalization in multimodal biometric systems. *Pattern Recognit.* **2005**, *38*, 2270–2285. [CrossRef]
129. Deng, J.; Dong, W.; Socher, R.; Li, L.J.; Li, K.; Li, F.-F. Imagenet: A large-scale hierarchical image database. In Proceedings of the 2009 IEEE Conference on Computer Vision and Pattern Recognition, Miami, FL, USA, 20–25 June 2009; pp. 248–255.
130. Yi, D.; Lei, Z.; Liao, S.; Li, S.Z. Learning face representation from scratch. *arXiv* **2014**, arXiv:1411.7923.
131. Huang, G.; Liu, Z.; Van Der Maaten, L.; Weinberger, K.Q. Densely connected convolutional networks. In Proceedings of the IEEE Conference on Computer Vision and Pattern Recognition, Honolulu, HI, USA, 21–26 July 2017; pp. 4700–4708.
132. Wu, H.Y.; Rubinstein, M.; Shih, E.; Guttag, J.; Durand, F.; Freeman, W. Eulerian video magnification for revealing subtle changes in the world. *ACM Trans. Graph. (TOG)* **2012**, *31*, 1–8. [CrossRef]
133. Chaudhry, R.; Ravichandran, A.; Hager, G.; Vidal, R. Histograms of oriented optical flow and binet-cauchy kernels on nonlinear dynamical systems for the recognition of human actions. In Proceedings of the 2009 IEEE Conference on Computer Vision and Pattern Recognition, Miami, FL, USA, 20–25 June 2009; pp. 1932–1939.
134. Chun, S.S.; Kim, H.; Jung-Rim, K.; Oh, S.; Sull, S. Fast text caption localization on video using visual rhythm. In *Proceedings of the International Conference on Advances in Visual Information Systems*; Springer: Berlin/Heisenberg, Germany, 2002; pp. 259–268.
135. Guimar, S.J.F.; Couprie, M.; Leite, N.J.; Araujo, D.A. A method for cut detection based on visual rhythm. In Proceedings of the XIV Brazilian Symposium on Computer Graphics and Image, Florianopolis, Brazil, 15–18 October 2001; pp. 297–304.
136. Haralick, R.M.; Shanmugam, K.S.; Dinstein, I. Textural Features for Image Classification. *IEEE Trans. Syst. Man Cybern.* **1973**, *3*, 610–621. [CrossRef]
137. Sivic, J.; Zisserman, A. Video Google: A text retrieval approach to object matching in videos. In Proceedings of the 9th IEEE International Conference on Computer Vision, Nice, France, 14–17 October 2003; p. 1470.
138. Schmid, P.J.; Li, L.; Juniper, M.P.; Pust, O. Applications of the dynamic mode decomposition. *Theor. Comput. Fluid Dyn.* **2011**, *25*, 249–259. [CrossRef]
139. Saragih, J.M.; Lucey, S.; Cohn, J.F. Deformable model fitting by regularized landmark mean-shift. *Int. J. Comput. Vis.* **2011**, *91*, 200–215. [CrossRef]
140. Hartley, R.I.; Sturm, P. Triangulation. *Comput. Vis. Image Underst.* **1997**, *68*, 146–157. [CrossRef]
141. Jourabloo, A.; Liu, X. Large-pose face alignment via CNN-based dense 3D model fitting. In Proceedings of the IEEE Conference on Computer Vision and Pattern Recognition, Las Vegas, NV, USA, 27–30 June 2016; pp. 4188–4196.

142. Jourabloo, A.; Liu, X. Pose-invariant face alignment via CNN-based dense 3D model fitting. *Int. J. Comput. Vis.* **2017**, *124*, 187–203. [CrossRef]
143. Feng, Y.; Wu, F.; Shao, X.; Wang, Y.; Zhou, X. Joint 3d face reconstruction and dense alignment with position map regression network. In Proceedings of the European Conference on Computer Vision (ECCV), Munich, Germany, 8–14 September 2018; pp. 534–551.
144. Long, J.; Shelhamer, E.; Darrell, T. Fully convolutional networks for semantic segmentation. In Proceedings of the IEEE Conference on Computer Vision and Pattern Recognition, Boston, MA, USA, 7–12 June 2015; pp. 3431–3440.
145. Blanz, V.; Vetter, T. Face recognition based on fitting a 3d morphable model. *IEEE Trans. Pattern Anal. Mach. Intell.* **2003**, *25*, 1063–1074. [CrossRef]
146. Matsumoto, T. Graphics System Shadow Generation Using a Depth Buffer. U.S. Patent 5043922, 27 August 1991.
147. Anjos, A.; Marcel, S. Counter-measures to photo attacks in face recognition: A public database and a baseline. In Proceedings of the 2011 International Joint Conference on Biometrics (IJCB), Washington, DC, USA, 11–13 October 2011; pp. 1–7.
148. Socolinsky, D.A.; Selinger, A.; Neuheisel, J.D. Face recognition with visible and thermal infrared imagery. *Comput. Vis. Image Underst.* **2003**, *91*, 72–114. [CrossRef]
149. Lowe, D.G. Distinctive image features from scale-invariant keypoints. *Int. J. Comput. Vis.* **2004**, *60*, 91–110. [CrossRef]
150. Komulainen, J.; Boulkenafet, Z.; Akhtar, Z. Review of face presentation attack detection competitions. In *Handbook of Biometric Anti-Spoofing*; Springer: Berlin/Heisenberg, Germany, 2019; pp. 291–317.
151. Chakka, M.M.; Anjos, A.; Marcel, S.; Tronci, R.; Muntoni, D.; Fadda, G.; Pili, M.; Sirena, N.; Murgia, G.; Ristori, M.; et al. Competition on counter measures to 2-d facial spoofing attacks. In Proceedings of the 2011 International Joint Conference on Biometrics (IJCB), Washington, DC, USA, 11–13 October 2011; pp. 1–6.
152. Chingovska, I.; Yang, J.; Lei, Z.; Yi, D.; Li, S.Z.; Kahm, O.; Glaser, C.; Damer, N.; Kuijper, A.; Nouak, A.; et al. The 2nd competition on counter measures to 2D face spoofing attacks. In Proceedings of the 2013 International Conference on Biometrics (ICB), Madrid, Spain, 4–7 June 2013; pp. 1–6.
153. Yan, J.; Zhang, Z.; Lei, Z.; Yi, D.; Li, S.Z. Face liveness detection by exploring multiple scenic clues. In Proceedings of the 2012 12th International Conference on Control Automation Robotics & Vision (ICARCV), Guangzhou, China, 5–7 December 2012; pp. 188–193.
154. Altun, Y.; Tsochantaridis, I.; Hofmann, T. Hidden Markov support vector machines. In Proceedings of the 20th International Conference on Machine Learning (ICML-03), Washington, DC, USA, 21–24 August 2003; pp. 3–10.
155. Boulkenafet, Z.; Komulainen, J.; Akhtar, Z.; Benlamoudi, A.; Samai, D.; Bekhouche, S.E.; Ouafi, A.; Dornaika, F.; Taleb-Ahmed, A.; Qin, L. A competition on generalized software-based face presentation attack detection in mobile scenarios. In Proceedings of the 2017 IEEE International Joint Conference on Biometrics (IJCB), Denver, CO, USA, 1–4 October 2017; pp. 688–696.
156. Easley, G.; Labate, D.; Lim, W.Q. Sparse directional image representations using the discrete shearlet transform. *Appl. Comput. Harmon. Anal.* **2008**, *25*, 25–46. [CrossRef]
157. Li, Y.; Po, L.M.; Xu, X.; Feng, L. No-reference image quality assessment using statistical characterization in the shearlet domain. *Signal Process. Image Commun.* **2014**, *29*, 748–759. [CrossRef]
158. Liu, C. Beyond Pixels: Exploring New Representations and Applications for Motion Analysis. Ph.D. Thesis, Massachusetts Institute of Technology, Cambridge, MA, USA, 2009.
159. Hinton, G.; Deng, L.; Yu, D.; Dahl, G.E.; Mohamed, A.R.; Jaitly, N.; Senior, A.; Vanhoucke, V.; Nguyen, P.; Sainath, T.N.; et al. Deep neural networks for acoustic modeling in speech recognition: The shared views of four research groups. *IEEE Signal Process. Mag.* **2012**, *29*, 82–97. [CrossRef]
160. LeCun, Y.; Boser, B.; Denker, J.; Henderson, D.; Howard, R.; Hubbard, W.; Jackel, L Backpropagation applied to handwritten zip code recognition. *Neural Comput.* **1989**, *1*, 541–551. [CrossRef]
161. Sutskever, I.; Martens, J.; Dahl, G.; Hinton, G. On the importance of initialization and momentum in deep learning. In Proceedings of the International Conference on Machine Learning, Atlanta, GA, USA, 16–21 June 2013; pp. 1139–1147.
162. Bahdanau, D.; Cho, K.; Bengio, Y. Neural machine translation by jointly learning to align and translate. *arXiv* **2014**, arXiv:1409.0473.

163. Szegedy, C.; Ioffe, S.; Vanhoucke, V.; Alemi, A. Inception-v4, inception-resnet and the impact of residual connections on learning. *arXiv* **2016**, arXiv:1602.07261.
164. Brock, A.; Lim, T.; Ritchie, J.M.; Weston, N. Smash: One-shot model architecture search through hypernetworks. *arXiv* **2017**, arXiv:1708.05344.
165. Zoph, B.; Le, Q.V. Neural architecture search with reinforcement learning. *arXiv* **2016**, arXiv:1611.01578.
166. Zoph, B.; Vasudevan, V.; Shlens, J.; Le, Q.V. Learning transferable architectures for scalable image recognition. In Proceedings of the IEEE Conference on Computer Vision and Pattern Recognition, Salt Lake City, UT, USA, 18–22 June 2018; pp. 8697–8710.
167. Real, E.; Moore, S.; Selle, A.; Saxena, S.; Suematsu, Y.L.; Tan, J.; Le, Q.; Kurakin, A. Large-scale evolution of image classifiers. *arXiv* **2017**, arXiv:1703.01041.
168. Real, E.; Aggarwal, A.; Huang, Y.; Le, Q.V. Regularized evolution for image classifier architecture search. In Proceedings of the aaai Conference on Artificial Intelligence, Honolulu, HI, USA, 27 January–1 February 2019; Volume 33, pp. 4780–4789.
169. Liu, H.; Simonyan, K.; Yang, Y. Darts: Differentiable architecture search. *arXiv* **2018**, arXiv:1806.09055.
170. Xu, Y.; Xie, L.; Zhang, X.; Chen, X.; Qi, G.J.; Tian, Q.; Xiong, H. Pc-darts: Partial channel connections for memory-efficient differentiable architecture search. *arXiv* **2019**, arXiv:1907.05737.
171. Zhu, N. Neural architecture search for deep face recognition. *arXiv* **2019**, arXiv:1904.09523.
172. Peng, W.; Hong, X.; Zhao, G. Video action recognition via neural architecture searching. In Proceedings of the 2019 IEEE International Conference on Image Processing (ICIP), Taipei, Taiwan, 22–25 September 2019; pp. 11–15.
173. Quan, R.; Dong, X.; Wu, Y.; Zhu, L.; Yang, Y. Auto-reid: Searching for a part-aware convnet for person re-identification. In Proceedings of the IEEE International Conference on Computer Vision, Seoul, Korea, 27 October–2 November 2019; pp. 3750–3759.
174. Ghiasi, G.; Lin, T.Y.; Le, Q.V. Nas-fpn: Learning scalable feature pyramid architecture for object detection. In Proceedings of the IEEE Conference on Computer Vision and Pattern Recognition, Seoul, Korea, 27 October–2 November 2019; pp. 7036–7045.
175. Zhang, Y.; Qiu, Z.; Liu, J.; Yao, T.; Liu, D.; Mei, T. Customizable architecture search for semantic segmentation. In Proceedings of the IEEE Conference on Computer Vision and Pattern Recognition, Long Beach, CA, USA, 16–20 June 2019; pp. 11641–11650.
176. Tax, D.M.J. One-Class Classification: Concept Learning in the Absence of Counter-examples. Ph.D. thesis, Delft University of Technology, Delf, The Netherlands, 2002.
177. Saenko, K.; Kulis, B.; Fritz, M.; Darrell, T. Adapting visual category models to new domains. In Proceedings of the European Conference on Computer Vision, Heraklion, Greece, 5–11 September 2010; pp.213–226.
178. Torralba, A.; Efros, A.A. Unbiased look at dataset bias. In Proceedings of the CVPR 2011, Colorado Springs, CO, USA, 20–25 June 2011; pp. 1521–1528.
179. Li, D.; Yang, Y.; Song, Y.Z.; Hospedales, T.M. Deeper, broader and artier domain generalization. In Proceedings of the IEEE International Conference on Computer Vision, Venice, Italy, 22–29 October 2017; pp. 5542–5550.
180. Li, H.; Jialin Pan, S.; Wang, S.; Kot, A.C. Domain generalization with adversarial feature learning. In Proceedings of the IEEE Conference on Computer Vision and Pattern Recognition, Salt Lake City, UT, USA, 18–22 June 2018; pp. 5400–5409.
181. Boulkenafet, Z.; Komulainen, J.; Li, L.; Feng, X.; Hadid, A. OULU-NPU: A mobile face presentation attack database with real-world variations. In Proceedings of the International Conference on Automatic Face & Gesture Recognition, Washington, DC, USA, 30 May–3 June 2017; pp. 612–618.
182. Zhang, S.; Wang, X.; Liu, A.; Zhao, C.; Wan, J.; Escalera, S.; Shi, H.; Wang, Z.; Li, S.Z. A dataset and benchmark for large-scale multi-modal face anti-spoofing. In Proceedings of the IEEE Conference on Computer Vision and Pattern Recognition, Long Beach, CA, USA, 16–20 June 2019; pp. 919–928.
183. Wang, D.; Hoi, S.C.; He, Y.; Zhu, J.; Mei, T.; Luo, J. Retrieval-based face annotation by weak label regularized local coordinate coding. *IEEE Trans. Pattern Anal. Mach. Intell.* **2013**, *36*, 550–563. [CrossRef] [PubMed]
184. Kemelmacher-Shlizerman, I.; Seitz, S.M.; Miller, D.; Brossard, E. The megaface benchmark: 1 million faces for recognition at scale. In Proceedings of the IEEE Conference on Computer Vision and Pattern Recognition, Las Vegas, NV, USA, 27–30 June 2016; pp. 4873–4882.

185. Lin, T.Y.; Maire, M.; Belongie, S.; Hays, J.; Perona, P.; Ramanan, D.; Dollár, P.; Zitnick, C.L. Microsoft coco: Common objects in context. In Proceedings of the European Conference on Computer Vision, Zurich, Switzerland, 6–12 September 2014; pp. 740–755.
186. Viola, P.; Jones, M.J. Robust real-time face detection. *Int. J. Comput. Vis.* **2004**, *57*, 137–154. [CrossRef]
187. Tan, X.; Song, F.; Zhou, Z.H.; Chen, S. Enhanced pictorial structures for precise eye localization under incontrolled conditions. In Proceedings of the 2009 IEEE Conference on Computer Vision and Pattern Recognition, Miami, FL, USA, 20–25 June 2009; pp. 1621–1628.
188. Szegedy, C.; Vanhoucke, V.; Ioffe, S.; Shlens, J.; Wojna, Z. Rethinking the inception architecture for computer vision. In Proceedings of the CVPR, Las Vegas, NV, USA, 27–30 June 2016; pp. 2818–2826.
189. Anjos, A.; Chakka, M.M.; Marcel, S. Motion-based counter-measures to photo attacks in face recognition. *IET Biom.* **2013**, *3*, 147–158. [CrossRef]
190. Chen, C.; Dantcheva, A.; Ross, A. Automatic facial makeup detection with application in face recognition. In Proceedings of the 2013 International Conference on Biometrics (ICB), Madrid, Spain, 4–7 June 2013; pp. 1–8.
191. Chang, H.; Lu, J.; Yu, F.; Finkelstein, A. Pairedcyclegan: Asymmetric style transfer for applying and removing makeup. In Proceedings of the IEEE Conference on Computer Vision and Pattern Recognition, Salt Lake City, UT, USA, 18–22 June 2018; pp. 40–48.

Publisher's Note: MDPI stays neutral with regard to jurisdictional claims in published maps and institutional affiliations.

© 2020 by the authors. Licensee MDPI, Basel, Switzerland. This article is an open access article distributed under the terms and conditions of the Creative Commons Attribution (CC BY) license (http://creativecommons.org/licenses/by/4.0/).

Journal of Imaging

Review

A Comprehensive Review of Deep-Learning-Based Methods for Image Forensics

Ivan Castillo Camacho and Kai Wang *

GIPSA-Lab, Grenoble INP, CNRS, Université Grenoble Alpes, 38000 Grenoble, France;
ivan.castillo-camacho@gipsa-lab.grenoble-inp.fr
* Correspondence: kai.wang@gipsa-lab.grenoble-inp.fr

Abstract: Seeing is not believing anymore. Different techniques have brought to our fingertips the ability to modify an image. As the difficulty of using such techniques decreases, lowering the necessity of specialized knowledge has been the focus for companies who create and sell these tools. Furthermore, image forgeries are presently so realistic that it becomes difficult for the naked eye to differentiate between fake and real media. This can bring different problems, from misleading public opinion to the usage of doctored proof in court. For these reasons, it is important to have tools that can help us discern the truth. This paper presents a comprehensive literature review of the image forensics techniques with a special focus on deep-learning-based methods. In this review, we cover a broad range of image forensics problems including the detection of routine image manipulations, detection of intentional image falsifications, camera identification, classification of computer graphics images and detection of emerging Deepfake images. With this review it can be observed that even if image forgeries are becoming easy to create, there are several options to detect each kind of them. A review of different image databases and an overview of anti-forensic methods are also presented. Finally, we suggest some future working directions that the research community could consider to tackle in a more effective way the spread of doctored images.

Keywords: image forensics; fake image detection; deep learning; neural network; Deepfake

Citation: Castillo Camacho, I.; Wang, K. A Comprehensive Review of Deep-Learning-Based Methods for Image Forensics. *J. Imaging* **2021**, *7*, 69. https://doi.org/10.3390/jimaging7040069

Academic Editor: Irene Amerini

Received: 11 March 2021
Accepted: 1 April 2021
Published: 3 April 2021

Publisher's Note: MDPI stays neutral with regard to jurisdictional claims in published maps and institutional affiliations.

Copyright: © 2021 by the authors. Licensee MDPI, Basel, Switzerland. This article is an open access article distributed under the terms and conditions of the Creative Commons Attribution (CC BY) license (https://creativecommons.org/licenses/by/4.0/).

1. Introduction

Given our era of advanced technology and the high availability of image-editing tools that make it extremely easy and fast to alter and create fake but realistic images, the trust of digital images has diminished. We can no longer easily accept an image as proof of an event without asking ourselves if the image has been modified. This has been in a continuous development together with the easy accessibility of tools used to create tampered-with content and with the deep-learning advancements which have led to an increase in the realism of fake images or videos [1].

During recent years, an evolution of disinformation has appeared to manipulate and disrupt public opinion. This disinformation comprises sophisticated campaigns aided by doctored images with the goal of influencing economic and societal events around the world. Different kinds of problems related to the usage of tampered-with images have appeared in different fields and will get worse as both digital cameras and software editing tools become more and more sophisticated.

In July 2010, British Petroleum (BP) came under public outcry over several doctored images of its Gulf of Mexico oil spill response, as images were tampered with to indicate that BP staff were busier than they actually were. Figure 1 shows two pairs of the original (first column) and the tampered-with (second column) images. A spokesperson for the company eventually admitted that in one image (first row of Figure 1) two screens were actually blank in the original picture. On the second row of Figure 1, we see a photo taken inside a company helicopter which appeared to show it flying off the coast. It was later shown to be fake after Internet bloggers identified several problems, which suggested that the helicopter was not even flying. The problems included part of a control tower appearing in the top left of the picture, its pilot holding a pre-flight checklist, and the control gauges showing the helicopter's door and ramp open and its parking brake engaged (Please refer to details presented at the following webpage: https://metro.co.uk/2010/07/22/bp-admits-to-doctoring-another-deepwater-horizon-oil-spill-image-456246/ accessed on 2 April 2021).

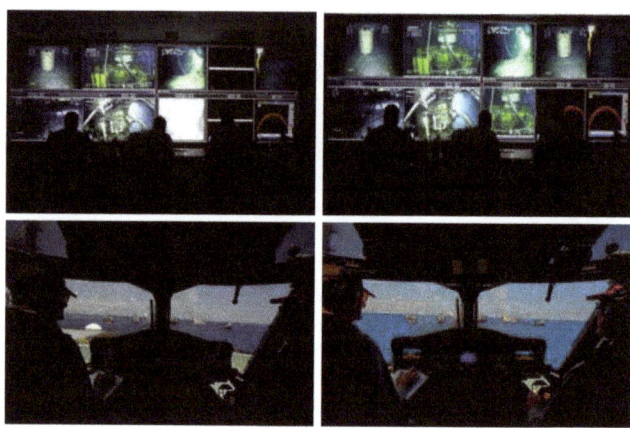

Figure 1. Examples of image forgery during the BP oil spill. First row shows how the original image was modified by copying some screens over the initially blank ones. On the second row, the helipad was removed in the tampered-with version. Images were obtained from the following webpage: https://www.cbsnews.com/news/bp-and-the-gulf-oil-spill-misadventures-in-photoshop/ accessed on 2 April 2021 .

From this context, it is necessary to develop strategies and methods to allow the verification of the authenticity of digital images. Image forensics [2] is the science that can help us to know if the image was acquired by the claimed device or if the current state corresponds to the original captured image, with the objective of detecting and locating image forgeries. Image forensics techniques depend on the assumption that each stage of the image acquiring and processing, from the raw image to its compression, storage and post-processing, holds some inherent statistics and leaves a particular trace. It is then possible to infer the source of the image or decide whether it is authentic or tampered with by identifying the existence, lack or inconsistency of forensic traces that are inherent to the image itself.

The research on this field started around 20 years ago and has recently seen a boost with the latest deep-learning tools. The deep-learning framework [3] usually uses a hierarchical structure of artificial neural networks, which are built in a similar way to the neural structure of the human brain, with the neuron nodes connected to simulate a neural network. This architecture can approach data analysis in a non-linear way. The striking advantage of deep learning is its ability to automatically learn useful features from available data, allowing us to bypass the tedious procedure of handcrafted feature design. Regardless of the big progress in the computer vision field using deep-learning tools, the same strategies cannot be applied directly to the image forensics domain as the traces or fingerprints that we are looking for are normally not present in the visible domain. Most of the traces that we search are hardly perceptible by the human eyes. Therefore, as we can see later in this paper certain strategies have been proposed to cope with this difference.

Early surveys on image forensics [2,4–7] naturally focused mainly on conventional feature-based methods. Recent surveys [8,9] consider both conventional and deep-learning methods yet with a different focus or coverage from ours. For instance, ref. [8] mainly considers the detection of copy-move, splicing and inpainting, while we cover more image forensics problems including also the detection of routine image processing operations, the detection of synthetic images, etc.; Ref. [9] classifies existing methods from a machine learning perspective (e.g., supervised, unsupervised and anomaly detection) with a special and timely focus on Deepfake detection, while we classify with a rather comprehensive list of image forensics problems and focus on the particularities of deep network design for different problems. Other existing surveys have dedicated their reviews to presenting and analyzing the methods for one or several specific issues such as copy-move (and splicing) detection [10,11], computer-generated image detection [12], camera identification [13] and image source identification [14], while we attempt to have a broader coverage.

In this paper, we review existing deep-learning-based methods for a variety of image forensics problems. The research works presented in this survey are classified into three large groups: the detection of image *manipulations* (i.e., routine image processing operations such as median filtering and contrast enhancement), the detection of image *falsifications* which intentionally alter the semantic meaning of the image (e.g., copy-move, splicing and inpainting) and other specific forensic problems. We pay attention to special designs of the deep models and special features used on the network input. Considering the rapid advancement in the image forensics field and the difference between our review and existing ones as discussed in the last paragraph, we believe that our survey can be helpful for the research community and is complementary to previous reviews. Our classification of research works on image forensics is illustrated in Figure 2.

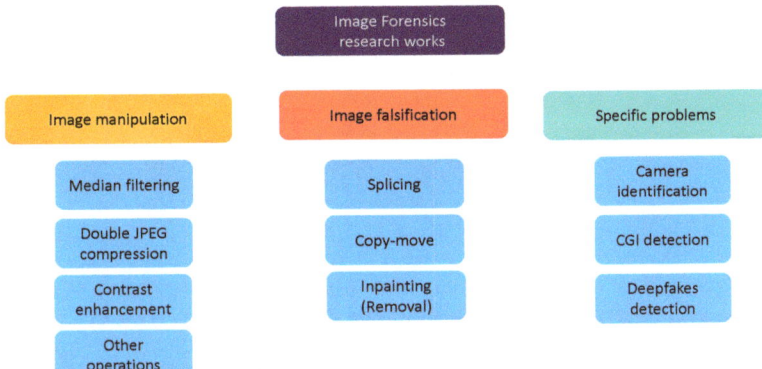

Figure 2. Classification diagram for deep-learning-based image forensics works. "CGI" means computer graphics image.

The remainder of this paper is organized as follows. We first present in Section 2 the datasets used for image forensics research which are vital for data-driven methods based on deep learning. Sections 3–5 are dedicated respectively to the presentation of deep-learning-based methods for the detection of routine image manipulations, the detection of intentional image falsifications and other specific forensic problems, in accordance with the classification mentioned above and shown in Figure 2. We present in Section 6 a brief review of anti-forensic methods which aim at defeating the analysis of forensic detectors. We conclude and suggest some future working directions in Section 7.

2. Datasets

Aside from the different models and different approaches, the access to a proper dataset is the first step and has a crucial role in the deep-learning paradigm to make it work properly. This means using a dataset that corresponds to the results a researcher wants to predict. The dataset should match the problem context including the acquiring and any processing steps. Constructing a dataset is a time-consuming task which requires problem and context knowledge of the procedure to collect compatible data. If the dataset contains sufficient and adequate data and information, problems such as overfitting and underfitting could be mitigated. Furthermore, the usage of multiple available datasets is of paramount importance to obtain a more reliable benchmarking of existing and new methods. In this section, the publicly available datasets for different categories of image forensics tasks will be introduced. Different datasets are grouped according to the different image forensics categories for which they are used.

2.1. Original Data

Datasets of pristine data used in the image forensics field (e.g., in the manipulation detection area) often contain original uncompressed image data. In this way, researchers can recreate different manipulation operations and conduct experiments on an adequate and customized dataset. Some of these databases were originally designed for the purpose of benchmarking camera identification techniques.

One of the first works in this field is the UCID dataset [15] with 1338 uncompressed images (version 2) in TIFF format stemming from a single camera. The BOSSBase 1.01 dataset [16] contains 10,000 grayscale uncompressed images, originally designed for research in the steganalysis field. In the Dresden image dataset [17], 73 digital cameras with 25 different models were used to create 14,000 Joint Photographic Experts Group (JPEG) images. The RAISE dataset [18] contains 8156 uncompressed high-resolution images of different categories such as landscape or indoor scenes. It comprises 4 subsets called RAISE-1K, RAISE-2K, RAISE-3K and RAISE-4K.

Some recent datasets introduced cell phone cameras to their catalogue. A small number of devices was considered in the MICHE-I dataset [19] comprising 3732 iris images from 3 different smartphones using both front and back cameras. The IEEE and Kaggle [20] organized a camera identification challenge in 2018 with a dataset captured from 10 different camera models (9 of 10 being smartphone cameras) with 275 images from each device.

The Vision dataset [21] also purposed for camera model identification and contained 34,427 images and 1914 videos from 35 portable devices of 11 major brands, both in the native format and in their social platform version including Facebook, YouTube and WhatsApp. Some datasets like [22,23] are designed for a specific domain. For instance [23] is an ongoing collection of satellite images of all land on Earth produced by the LandSat 8 satellite. Other proposals like [24–28], initially designed for object and scene detection, segmentation and recognition, were used in the image forensics field to create synthetic data. For example, the Microsoft COCO dataset [25], originally constructed for object and scene analysis and comprising more than 300,000 images in JPEG format, has been used to create different image forgeries. Another example is the SUN2012 dataset [28], composed of 130,519 images of different outdoor and indoor scenes, has been employed to create synthetic data for image forensics purposes.

Regarding the creation of Deepfakes (i.e., fake images generated by deep neural networks), some well-known datasets of human faces have been used for network training, for instance the CelebA dataset [29] which contains around 200,000 faces with different annotations originally designed for facial image analysis. Stemming from CelebA dataset, CelebAHQ [30] is a set of high-resolution face images and is one of the first datasets used for training and evaluation of Generative Adversarial Network (GAN) models for face generation and editing.

2.2. Falsified Data

To our knowledge, the first public datasets for detection of *splicing* (i.e., a common image falsification in which one copies a part of an image and pastes it to another image) were the Columbia gray DVMM dataset [31] and the Columbia color splicing dataset [32]. The two datasets comprise respectively 1845 grayscale images for the first one and 180 color spliced images for the second one, both with rather non-realistic random-like splicing falsifications. Two other well-known splicing datasets are the CASIA V1 and V2 [33] with more realistic forgeries and post-processing operations on the V2 to cover the traces of splicing. In 2013, the IEEE Information Forensics and Security Technical Committee (IFS-TC) organized an image forensics challenge and released a dataset of pristine and forged images [34] with a set of different falsification techniques such as splicing and *copy-move* (i.e., another common falsification in which one copies a part of an image and pastes it in the same image). Each fake image had an associated ground-truth binary map showing the regions that were falsified. As a small sub-dataset from the IFS-TC proposal, the DS0-1 dataset (also known as Carvalho dataset) [35] contains forgeries created in a careful and realistic manner.

The National Institute of Standards and Technology (NIST) developed the Nimble [36] and MFC [37] datasets. The first one, often called NIST Nimble 2016, included three types of falsifications including splicing, copy-move and *inpainting* (i.e., a third type of common falsification in which a part of an image is replaced and filled with realistic synthetic content), with different levels of compression and post-processing. Figure 3 shows some example images from this dataset. The NIST MFC17 dataset [37] included more challenging image forgeries but did not contain the different compressed versions.

Figure 3. Sample images from the NIST Nimble 2016 Dataset [36]. Top row shows the original images, and bottom row shows from left to right falsifications of inpainting-based removal, copy-move and splicing.

The Realistic Tampered Dataset [38], also known as Korus dataset, comprises 220 splicing and copy-move forgeries of a realistic level. The authors included PRNU signatures and ground-truth maps. Other datasets have been created with a specific purpose in mind. Regarding the double compression scenario, the VIPP dataset [39] was created to evaluate the detection of double JPEG compression artifacts which may be present for instance in the splicing falsification.

The use of datasets specific for copy-move falsification, such as [40,41], is not very common for the deep-learning-based detection methods. The main reason is that existing datasets are relatively small. Therefore, majority of research on deep-learning-based copy-move detection has created customized synthetic datasets which are derived from dataset of original images and which contain much more samples.

Table 1 shows a list of popular datasets for image forensics research including datasets of original data and falsified data. In the case of falsified data, we provide the number ratio of pristine and tampered-with images. Regarding the "Operations" columns we mention the main operations (mostly falsifications) contained in the dataset and the "Others" case mainly includes double JPEG compression.

Table 1. Summary of datasets of original image data and falsified image data. In the "Format" column we show the compression type of images by using the first character, with "U" for uncompressed, "C" for lossless compression, and "L" for lossy compression. "Grayscale/color and bit depth" is color coded as follows: **G** grayscale, **C** color, followed by the number of bits of the grayscale or color information. "GT" stands for "Ground-truth". The "Content ratio" column shows the number of pristine/tampered-with images.

Type	Name	Size	Format	Grayscale/Color and Bit Depth	Content Ratio	Copy-Move	Splicing	Inpainting	Others	GT Mask
Original data	BossBase [16]	512 × 512	U-PGM	G 8-bit	10K					N/A
	UCID [15]	512 × 384, 384 × 512	U-TIFF	C 24-bit	1338					N/A
	Landsat [23]	650 × 650; 5312 × 2988	C-TIFF	C 48-bit	Ongoing					N/A
	MIT SUN [28]	200 × 200	L-JPEG	C 24-bit	130,519					N/A
	NRCS [42]	1500 × 2100	U-TIFF, L-JPEG	C 24-bit G 8-bit	11,036					N/A
	MS COCO [25]	Various	L-JPEG	C 24-bit	328K					N/A
	CelebA [29]	64 × 64; 512 × 512	L-JPEG	C 24-bit	200K					N/A
	CelebAHQ [30]	512 × 512	L-JPEG	C 24-bit	30K					N/A
	RAISE [18]	4288 × 2848	C-TIFF, U-NEF	C 36-bit	8156					N/A
	Dresden [17]	3039 × 2014; 3900 × 2616	L-JPEG, U-NEF	C 24-bit, 36-bit	14K					N/A
	MICHE-I [19]	640 × 480; 2322 × 4128	L-JPEG	C 24-bit	3732					N/A
	Kaggle Camera [20]	1520 × 2688; 4160 × 3120	L-JPEG, C-TIFF	C 24-bit	2750					N/A
	Vision [21]	960 × 720; 5248 × 3696	L-JPEG	C 24-bit	34427					N/A
Falsified data	Columbia gray [31]	128 × 128	U-BMP	G 8-bit	1845/912		●			No
	IEEE IFS-TC [34]	1024 × 768; 3000 × 2500	C-PNG	C 24-bit	1050/1150	●	●			Yes
	CASIA v1 [33]	384 × 256	L-JPEG	C 24-bit	1725/925		●			No
	CASIA v2 [33]	240 × 160; 900 × 600	L-JPEG, U-BMP, U-TIFF	C 24-bit	7491/5123	●	●			No
	NIST Nimble 16 [36]	500 × 500; 5616 × 3744	L-JPEG	C 24-bit	560/564	●	●	●		No
	NIST Nimble 17 [37]	60 × 120; 8000 × 5320	U-NEF, C-PNG, U-BMP, L-JPEG, U-TIFF	C 36-bit, 24-bit	2667/1410	●	●	●		No
	Coverage [40]	400 × 486	C-TIFF	C 24-bit	100/100	●				Yes
	Columbia color [32]	757 × 568; 1152 × 768	U-TIFF	C 24-bit	183/180		●			Yes
	Carvalho [35]	2048 × 1536	C-PNG	C 24-bit	100/100		●			Yes
	Realistic (Korus) [38]	1920 × 1080	C-TIFF	C 24-bit	220/220	●	●			Yes
	CoMoFoD [41]	512 × 512; 3000 × 2000	C-PNG	C 24-bit	260/260	●				Yes
	VIPP [39]	300 × 300; 3456 × 5184	U-TIFF	C 24-bit	68/69		●		●	Yes

2.3. Artificially Generated Data

In the case of artificially generated data, it is important to use datasets that contain realistic examples. Existing datasets considered different scenes of authentic images taken by a camera and artificially generated fake images either with conventional Computer-Generated Image (CGI) creation algorithms or recent GAN architectures.

One of the first popular dataset of CGIs is the Columbia dataset [43] with 1600 photorealistic computer graphics images. Afchar et al. [44] created a dataset with 5100 fake images generated from videos downloaded from the Internet. Rahmouni et al. created a dataset of CGIs coming from high-resolution video game screenshots. There are several online repositories for CGI [45–48] that have been used as datasets for different detection approaches.

A small dataset of 49 Deepfake and 49 original videos was created by Yang et al. [49] using the FakeApp application. A bigger one is the FaceForensics dataset [50] comprising about 1000 videos and their corresponding forged versions focused on expression swap created with the Face2Face model. The same authors extended the dataset [51] with 4000 forged videos. Li et al. [52] created a dataset of 590 original videos and 5639 Deepfake videos. In comparison to other face datasets [29,30], the diversity among genders, ages and ethnic groups is bigger. The IDIAP institute created DeepfakeTIMIT [53] also known as DF-TIMIT containing 620 videos where faces were swapped. This dataset was generated using the faceswap-GAN [54] with 32 subjects and 2 subsets of different resolutions: low quality with 64 × 64 and high quality with 128 × 128.

Recently, Google in collaboration with Jigsaw and Facebook have created a Deepfake dataset to contribute to the relevant research. In 2019, Facebook created the DFDC dataset [55] for the Deepfake detection challenge with 4113 Deepfake and 1131 original videos from 66 subjects of diverse origins who gave their consent for the relevant data. Finally, the DFD dataset [56] contains 3068 Deepfake videos and 363 original ones from 28 individuals who consented to the data.

Table 2 summarizes the artificially generated datasets presented above. The "Content ratio" column shows the number of pristine/fake images.

Table 2. Datasets of artificially generated data.

Type	Name	Size	Format	Codec	Content Ratio	Media Video	Media Image
CGI	Columbia [43]	700 × 500; 3000 × 2000	JPEG	-	1600/1600		●
CGI	Rahmouni [57]	1920 × 1080; 4900 × 3200	JPEG	-	1800/1800		●
CGI and Deepfakes	Faceforensics [50]	480p	MP4	H.264	1000/1000	●	
Deepfakes	UADFV [49]	294 × 500	MP4	H.264	49/49	●	
Deepfakes	Faceforensics++ [51]	480p, 720p, 1080p	MP4	H.264	1000/4000	●	
Deepfakes	Afchar [44]	854 × 480	JPEG	-	7250/5100		●
Deepfakes	PGGAN [30]	64 × 64; 1024 × 1024	JPEG	-	-/100 K		●
Deepfakes	Deepfake TIMIT [53]	64 × 64; 128 × 128	AVI	H.264	-/620	●	
Deepfakes	CelebDF [52]	Various	MP4	H.264	509/5639	●	
Deepfakes	DFDC [55]	180p; 2160p	MP4	H.264	1131/4113	●	
Deepfakes	DFD [56]	1080p	MP4	H.264	363/3068	●	

From the next section, we present different kinds of deep-learning-based image forensics methods, starting by the detection of routine image manipulations.

3. Manipulation Detection

We consider image manipulation as routine operations modifying or improving digital images with basic and benign image processing such as median filtering, JPEG compression or contrast enhancement. These operations may be used to enhance the visual quality of tampered-with images or to hide the traces of falsification operations that may leave an apparent fingerprint if used alone. In this subsection we introduce the most relevant strategies to detect some of the most common manipulation operations using deep learning as the core technique. We present both *targeted* (i.e., aiming at a specific manipulation operation) and *general-purpose* (i.e., aiming at various operations) detectors.

3.1. Median Filtering Detection

The early deep-learning proposals in the literature of image forensics were focused on designing a specific strategy to cope with each forensic challenge individually. The goal of one of the first methods proposed in 2015 by Chen et al. [58] was to detect median filtering manipulation.

In their paper, Chen et al. [58] used a tailored Convolutional Neural Network (CNN) to detect median filtering with JPEG post-processing. The JPEG compression after median filtering made the forensic problem more challenging because the compression can partially remove the forensic traces of medial filtering. The tailored CNN took the Median Filtering Residual (MFR) rather than the raw pixel values as input for the first layer in the CNN. The MFR is the difference between a given image and its median filtered version. The authors found that using this special input, the network achieved a better forensic classification performance, with a better detection accuracy when compared with handcrafted-feature-based strategies on small patches of 64×64 and 32×32.

More recently, Tang et al. [59] proposed to upscale the input with nearest neighbor interpolation in an attempt to enlarge the difference between manipulated and original patches. After this upscaling, the first two layers in the network are mlpconv layers introduced in [60]. An mlpconv consists of a special layer for deep-learning architectures that defines a group of convolutional layers with activation functions that can enhance the non-linear ability of the network. Specifically, it proposes to replace a traditional convolutional layer followed by a Rectified Linear Unit (ReLU) activation function with a convolutional layer, ReLU activation function, convolutional layer with filters of shape 1×1 and a final ReLU activation function. In the case of median filtering detection, Tang et al. [59] made use of mlpconv to enhance the network's non-linearity to deal with the detection of median filtering non-linearity.

Both the above proposals [58,59] rely heavily on having a special input for the network being either the MFR or an upscaled version, regardless of their differences in the network architecture.

3.2. Double JPEG Compression Detection

JPEG images are widely used in daily life as one of the most common image formats. Hence, most of the forensic tasks are related to JPEG images. Typically, inside a normal forgery creation process, an image is decompressed from JPEG to the spatial domain for falsification, and later recompressed again in JPEG format for storage and further use. For this reason, the image forensics community has dedicated important research efforts to the detection of double JPEG compression through the years. Detection and localization of double JPEG compression provides valuable information towards image authenticity assessment.

In double JPEG compression, double quantization of Discrete Cosine Transform (DCT) coefficients leaves special artifacts in the DCT domain, in particular, on histograms of block-DCT coefficients [61]. In [62,63] authors proposed to use as input the concatenation of DCT histograms for their CNNs. These approaches outperformed non-deep-learning methods, especially on small-sized images up to 64 × 64 pixels. Afterwards, Barni et al. [64] found that CNN architectures could detect double JPEG compression with high accuracy when the input of the network was noise residuals or histogram features; this was tested on double compression with both different and same quantization matrix.

In [65], Amerini et al. designed a multi-domain convolutional network to detect and localize double JPEG compression. They proposed to use both DCT coefficients and spatial features for the localization. The architecture achieved a better detection accuracy when compared to using only pixel values or DCT coefficients. In their implementation, two branches were used as inputs for the network, one receiving the image patches and the other the DCT coefficients. After several convolutional blocks (convolutional layer, activation function and pooling layer), both outputs are concatenated and fed to a final fully connected layer followed by the classification layer for detecting different JPEG quality factors. Figure 4 shows the proposed multi-domain neural network. The architecture of the sub-network with the frequency-domain input has some similarities to the one in [62], while the range of the bins in the DCT histogram is augmented.

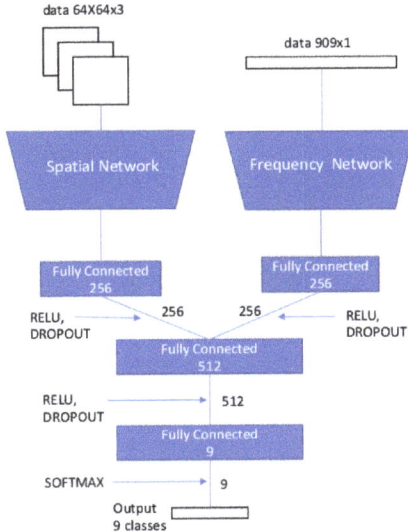

Figure 4. Architecture of the multi-domain convolutional neural network proposed in [65] for double JPEG compression detection.

The method proposed in [66] extracted block-wise histogram-related statistical features under mixed quality factor conditions to achieve better accuracy and localization capability. The proposed CNN takes a multi-branch approach using histogram features and quantization tables as inputs. The quantization branch is directly concatenated to the last max-pooling layer output and two fully connected layers. The authors reported that the ability of the network to distinguish between single and double JPEG compressed blocks was dramatically improved by including quantization table branch.

The above presentation suggests that using special features as input for the first layer of CNN can achieve good detection performance and that in the case of using multiple inputs the multi-branch approach can combine them properly.

3.3. Contrast Enhancement Detection

Like median filtering, contrast enhancement is one of the routine image manipulations commonly applied to conceal the traces of tampering. In the case of a falsified image, it is common to have contrast differences between the background and the forged region, which may be caused by different lightning conditions. In this scenario, contrast enhancement is broadly used to remove or alleviate visual clues that would give away the forgery. Consequently, detecting the application of this operation has drawn researchers' attention in the image forensics field [67].

In [68] authors proposed a 9-layer CNN that is directly fed with 64 × 64 image pixel values with no special features, making the discriminative features self-learned by the network. The authors showed good robustness against JPEG compression post-processing over a wide range of quality factors by training the network with different contrast adjustments. The proposed architecture also generalized well to unseen tonal adjustments.

Sun et al. [69] proposed to use the Gray Level Co-occurrence Matrix (GLCM) which is computed by accumulating the occurrence of the pixel intensity pairs between each pixel and its neighboring pixels. The GLCM was used as input for a shallow CNN of three convolutional groups for detecting contrast enhancement. The authors reported good results when an image is JPEG compressed after the contrast enhancement on 256 × 256 image patches. The proposed method outperformed the conventional ones in terms of the manipulation detection accuracy.

Using the GLCM as input of the network in a similar way, Shan et al. [70] also proposed a JPEG-robust forensic technique based on CNN to detect both local and global contrast enhancement. The adopted network architecture is one convolutional block (4 layers in one block) deeper than the one proposed in [69]. Experimental results showed that Shan et al.'s method could efficiently detect both local and global contrast enhancement in compressed images regardless of the order of contrast enhancement and JPEG compression.

3.4. General-Purpose Manipulations Detection

The manipulation detection methods presented until now focus on the detection of a specific and targeted manipulation. This limits the application range of such methods because for creating a doctored image, several different processing operations can be applied to obtain a visually convincing result. For instance, in the case of splicing falsification, the forged part of the image can go through one or several basic operations such as rescaling, contrast enhancement and median filtering. Therefore, it is of great importance to develop general-purpose strategies that can detect different kinds of image manipulation operations.

As mentioned in previous subsections, the usage of special features in the CNN input in general leads to a better performance for image forensics problems. Following this approach, Bayar and Stamm [71] proposed a new constrained filter for the first layer of a CNN to suppress the image content for detecting various image processing operations. Their constrained network is forced to learn a set of high-pass filters by imposing a constraint on the weights of all the K first-layer filters in each forward pass of the learning process. This filter constraint enforcement is shown in the following Equation (1) as proposed in Bayar and Stamm's original paper [71]:

$$\begin{cases} w_k^{(1)}(0,0) = -1, \\ \sum_{m,n \neq 0} w_k^{(1)}(m,n) = 1, \end{cases} \quad (1)$$

where $w_k^{(1)}(m,n)$ denotes the weight at position (m,n) of the kth filter in the first layer (the indices m and n can be negative or positive), and $w_k^{(1)}(0,0)$ denotes the weight at the center of the corresponding filter kernel. In this manner the sum of all filter elements in each filter is 0, and the constrained first-layer filter operates like a high-pass one by effectively removing image content. This prediction error layer extracts and highlights the local dependency of pixels with its neighbors, which is an important piece of information from the forensics point of view. Experimental results in [71] also showed that the usage of tanh as activation function outperforms the more common functions such as ReLU. The reason may be that tanh tends to preserve more information related to the sign of the values at the function input, without setting all negative values to be 0 as in ReLU. The sign information may be important for image forensics tasks.

Recently, Castillo Camacho and Wang [72] proposed a different initialization method for the first layer of a CNN to cope with a challenging setting of general-purpose image manipulation detection. It is challenging because the considered manipulations are of small amplitude. Taking advantage of the milestone work of the famous Xavier initialization [73], they proposed a way to create random high-pass filters that could operate without constrains. The method had a high detection rate for manipulations such as median filtering, Additive White Gaussian Noise (AWGN) and resampling. Recently, the same authors [74] proposed a data-dependent scaling approach for first-layer filters initialized by different algorithms. The proposed approach considered natural image statistics and could ensure the stability of the amplitude (i.e., the variance) of data flow in a CNN, which was beneficial for general-purpose image manipulation detection.

3.5. Summary and Comparisons of Manipulation Detection Methods

Besides qualitative comparisons between different forensic methods (in particular special network design and special input features), we have also made efforts to carry out quantitative comparisons of forensic performance for each category of methods. In order to ensure as much as possible a fair comparison, performances are extracted from the original papers and reported for the most commonly used databases whenever possible. Concerning the cases where the results for several patch sizes are available, we share the results for the most common size among the compared methods.

Regarding the metric used for evaluating the forensic performance, we have endeavored to select the most common one among each category of methods. We mention the metric used for each method when we are forced to use different metrics for different methods even on a same database. Indeed, given the heterogeneous experimental settings adopted in the original papers, it is in general difficult to carry out performance comparison that can cover all methods with a same setting of tested database and used metric.

The most commonly used metrics in this review are accuracy, precision (mainly the average precision as defined later in this paper), and Area Under the Curve (AUC) score. Accuracy is the percentage of correctly classified samples among all samples, as calculated with the following equation:

$$\text{Acc} = \frac{\text{TP} + \text{TN}}{\text{TP} + \text{TN} + \text{FN} + \text{FP}}, \qquad (2)$$

where TP, TN, FP, and FN stand for respectively true positive, true negative, false positive and false negative numbers of classified samples.

The precision represents the fraction of correctly classified positive samples among all samples classified as positive, which is computed as

$$\text{Prec} = \frac{\text{TP}}{\text{TP} + \text{FP}}. \qquad (3)$$

Theoretically, the AUC score is equal to the probability that a model ranks a randomly selected positive sample higher than a randomly selected negative one. It is defined by the following formula

$$\text{AUC} = \int_0^1 \text{TPR}\left(\text{FPR}^{-1}(x)\right) dx, \qquad (4)$$

where the true positive rate is defined as $\text{TPR} = \text{TP}/(\text{TP} + \text{FN})$ and the false positive rate is defined as $\text{FPR} = \text{FP}/(\text{TN} + \text{FP})$. In practice, in order to obtain the AUC score which lies between 0 and 1, we first draw the Receiver Operating Characteristic (ROC) curve of TPR against FPR for a classifier by varying the decision threshold, and then we compute the area under this curve.

The choice of metric depends on many factors, including the forensic problem at hand, experimental setting, a kind of tradition among researchers working on a same problem, preference of authors of a forensic method, and technical or even legal requirements when a forensic detector is deployed in real-world applications. For instance, in an experimental setting with imbalanced data from different classes, the accuracy metric in general results in biased value and thus is not preferred; in certain application scenarios, we need to consider a decision threshold corresponding to a certain level of false positive rate; etc. Nevertheless, in academic papers, authors often consider a simplified and controlled laboratory experimental setting and accordingly attempt to achieve good performance in terms of an appropriate metric of their choice. As mentioned earlier, in this review for a fair comparison we extract and report results from the original papers of forensic methods. When comparing a category of methods, we try to use the most commonly adopted metric among different papers and intuitively explain why this metric is used. However, in many cases we are forced to report results in terms of different metrics as adopted in the original papers of compared methods. Indeed, it would be important that the research community could build high-quality benchmarking datasets with a unified metric for each dataset (e.g., with instructions on how to choose decision threshold).

Table 3 summarizes existing deep-learning-based image manipulation detection methods, by considering different technical aspects in particular the input feature of the network and the specificity of CNN design. Listed methods created an ad-hoc dataset of manipulated images/patches from pristine images. We show in the table the original datasets of pristine images used to create manipulated samples for each method. Meanwhile, every method may also have its own parameters of manipulation operations, e.g., different JPEG compression quality factors. Consequently, performance of each method is shown on an ad-hoc dataset, except for the comparison of general-purpose manipulation detection methods (i.e., the group of methods named GIPO in Table 3). For the comparison of GIPO methods, we report the performance results extracted from [74] where a fair comparison was conducted by using same datasets of pristine and manipulated images/patches and same manipulation operations with same parameters. We can observe from Table 3 that the most commonly used metric is the accuracy. This is mainly because of the fact that for image manipulation detection researchers almost always consider a controlled laboratory experimental setting with balanced data from each class. Therefore, in this case the accuracy is a simple and adequate metric that has been widely used by researchers working on manipulation detection. In the following, we present and analyze each group of methods.

Median filtering comparison results were taken for a patch size of 64×64 with a median filter kernel of size 3. Slightly different datasets of pristine images were used in the two compared methods [58,59]. From the results in Table 3 we can see that Tang et al.'s method [59] obtained better results, which implies that upscaling can be an effective pre-processing for the detection of median filtering by using CNN. This pre-processing would make the traces of median filtering more prominent and easier to be detected by a neural network.

The double JPEG compression detection methods used different datasets and settings for their experiments. In some methods the quality factor for each compression was taken randomly from a uniform distribution while other methods used pre-defined fixed factors. Additionally, in some cases aligned double JPEG compression was considered while this point was omitted or not clearly presented in some other methods. Nevertheless, we present the best case shared by each method when tested on patches of size 64×64. The best case varies for different methods, for example for the method in [65] the best case was obtained with a first compression with quality factor of 55 followed by a second compression with quality factor of 85, while for the method of [62] it was achieved with quality factor of 70 and 80 for respectively the first and the second compression. We are aware that the results are not directly comparable, and our purpose here is to give a rough idea on the performance of forensic methods designed to detect double JPEG compression. From the results in Table 3, we can observe that the performances of all methods in the best case are quite satisfactory, all higher than 90%. Interestingly, all methods considered DCT features as network input. These features appeared to be effective in detecting double JPEG compression manipulation, and this may intuitively explain the good performance of all compared methods.

The papers on contrast enhancement detection also used different databases and experimental settings for the validation of their methods. In Table 3, results are provided for gamma correction with factor 0.6 and a random value taken from $\{0.6, 0.8, 1.2, 1.4\}$, on patches of size 64×64 and 256×256, respectively for the methods proposed in [68,70]. The experimental setting of [69] was more complicated: the result shown in the table was obtained on a dataset of 256×256 patches manipulated with a combination of three different contrast enhancement techniques being histogram stretching, gamma correction (with a factor randomly taken from $\{0.5, 0.8, 1.2, 1.5\}$), and S-curve mapping. Though it is not easy and not our purpose to rank the performance of the three methods mainly due to different experimental settings, all of them achieved very good results close to a perfect detection of 100%. This may imply that CNN is able to extract discriminative information from both pixel values [67] and GLCM features [68,69] for detecting contrast enhancement.

The comparison of general-purpose manipulation detection methods is made for 64×64 patches with results taken from [74]. A challenging experimental setting with five different manipulations (median filtering, Gaussian blurring, additive white Gaussian noise, resizing, and JPEG compression) was tested for the three methods under comparisons [71,72,74]. As mentioned above, same datasets and same manipulations with same parameters were used for each method to ensure a fair comparison. From the results in Table 3, we can see that the method in [74] outperforms the two other methods. This is because [74] attempts to keep a stable data flow for the first convolutional layer which normally has a special design. This means that a combination of an appropriate design of first-layer filters (e.g., high-pass filters) and a proper scaling of these filters can lead to a better performance.

Table 3. Image manipulation detection methods. Network depth describes the number of convolutional blocks with C for a convolutional layer, or M for mlpconv layer, followed by an activation function and pooling layer, as well as the number of fully connected blocks denoted by an F (fully connected layer and activation function). MF stands for median filtering, DJPEG for double JPEG, CE for contrast enhancement, GIPO for general-purpose image processing operations, and approach is color coded as: (D) detection, (L) localization. Dataset is color coded as follows: (U) UCID [15], (B) BOSSBase [16], (D) Dresden [17], (K) RAISE [18], (F) MS COCO [25], (N) NRCS [42], and (S) when it is an ad-hoc dataset created by authors of the original paper. In the column of "Patch performance", Acc. stands for accuracy, TPR stands for true positive rate, and AUC stands for area under the curve (all in %).

Problem	Method	Network Depth	Input Feature	Special CNN Design	Input Size	Approach	Dataset	Patch Performance
MF	[58]	5C-2F	MFR	N/A	64×64, 32×32	(D)	(B)(D)(N)(U)	Acc. 85.14
	[59]	2M-3C	Upscaled values	mlpconv	64×64, 32×32	(D)	(B)(N)(U)	Acc. 89.96
DJPEG	[63]	4C-3F	DCT features	N/A	128×128	(D)	(U)	Acc. 99.48
	[62]	2C-2F	DCT features	Customized 3×1 kernels	64×64, 128×128, ..., 1024×1024	(D)	(U)	AUC 100.00
	[64]	3C-2F	Noise residuals or DCT features	N/A	64×64, 256×256	(D)	(K)	Acc. 96.30
	[65]	2C-2F, 3C-1F	DCT features, pixel values	Two-branch CNN	64×64	(D)(L)	(U)	Acc. 99.60
	[66]	4C-3F, 3F	DCT features, quantization tables	Two-branch CNN	256×256	(D)(L)	(S)	Acc. 92.76

Table 3. Cont.

CE	[68]	9C-1F	Pixel values	N/A	64 × 64	D	K	AUC 99.7
	[69]	3C-2F	GLCM	N/A	256 × 256	D	F	TPR 99.80
	[70]	4C-2F	GLCM	N/A	256 × 256	D	B	AUC 99.40
GIPO	[71]	5C-2F	Pixel values	Constrained 1st layer	256 × 256, 64 × 64	D	D	Acc. 94.19
	[72]	5C-2F	Pixel values	Special init. for 1st layer	64 × 64	D	D	Acc. 93.71
	[74]	5C-2F, 6C	Pixel values	Scaling for 1st layer	64 × 64	D	D	Acc. 96.02

4. Falsification Detection

We consider image falsification as the creation of fake content in some part of the image to deceive viewers about the facts happened in the past. In contrast to routine image manipulation, image falsification is conducted intentionally to change the image's semantic meaning, often by inserting or removing certain content.

The most common image falsification techniques can be roughly divided into three broad categories: copy-move forgery where one part of the image (the source region) is copied and pasted into the same image as the fake part (the target region); splicing forgery where the tampered-with region in a host image was originally from a different image; and inpainting forgery which is sometimes considered to be a subgroup of copy-move with the difference that the fake region in inpainting falsification is often constructed by using and combining small motifs at different locations of the same image. It is worth mentioning that the inpainting technique is traditionally used to reconstruct a lost or corrupted part of the image and that inpainting falsification is often applied for carrying out object removal in an image. Research on splicing detection is in general more active than copy-move and inpainting. This is probably because it is more convenient to create diverse splicing forgeries from a large pool of publicly available pristine images. Figure 3 shows, from left to right, examples of inpainting, copy-move and splicing forgeries. In the following, we will organize the presentation of deep-learning-based falsification detection methods into two groups: (1) *multipurpose* detectors which can detect different kinds of image forgeries among the above three categories and (2) *targeted* detectors which are focused on the detection of one specific falsification.

4.1. Multipurpose Detectors

Multipurpose detectors are usually based on the general assumption that any image falsification introduces statistical deviation with respect to the authentic part, i.e., within the fake region, around the fake region boundary, or both.

Zhang et al. [75] proposed to use an autoencoder [76] which is a type of neural network taking an image as input and reconstructing it using fewer number of bits. Wavelet features were used as input for the network to detect and localize in a patch-wise manner the tampered-with regions. Besides wavelet features, local noise features originally proposed for steganalysis, such as Spatial Rich Model (SRM) [77], have been largely used to solve image forensics problems with encouraging results. In SRM, a group of handcrafted filters was designed to extract local noise from neighboring pixels, and this often allows us to obtain disparities between forged and original areas. SRM filters have been used for creating a special input for CNNs. This is one important difference from CNNs used in computer vision tasks: it is considered beneficial for CNNs of image forensics tasks to use SRM filters as initialization for the first layer, instead of the random weights conventionally used in CNNs from the computer vision community. In [78], Rao and Ni proposed to use the 30 SRM filters as initialization for the first layer in a CNN to detect splicing and copy-move forgeries. The results from the pre-trained CNN were used in a Support Vector

Machine (SVM) classifier for solving a binary problem (authentic/forged). In a similar approach based on steganalysis features, Cozzolino et al. [79] proposed to use a shallow or short CNN to detect image forgeries on small patches.

In [80,81], authors made use of a Long Short-Term Memory (LSTM) architecture for localizing at pixel level the tampered-with regions. An LSTM as proposed in [82] is a special type of Recurrent Neural Network (RNN) designed for sequences or time series data. An LSTM layer consists of a set of recurrently connected blocks, known as memory blocks. Each block contains one or more recurrently connected memory cells and three multiplicative units—the input (sigmoid and tanh functions), output (sigmoid and tanh functions) and forget (a sigmoid function) gates—that regulate the flow of information into and out of the cell. Figure 5 shows an unrolled example of an LSTM block. The core strength of using LSTM in the image forensics field is to acquire from previous blocks the boundary information, which is decisive to obtain particular features to classify between original and tampered-with regions. In [80] experiments showed that both CNNs with Radon transform as input and LSTM-based strategies were effective in exploiting resampling features to detect and localize tampered-with regions. Bappy et al. [81] proposed an LSTM and an encoder–decoder network to semantically segment falsified regions in a tampered-with image.

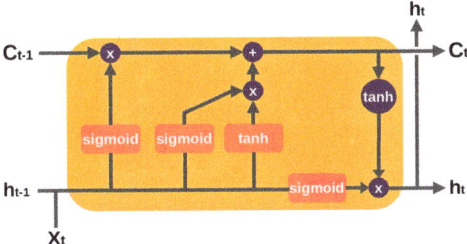

Figure 5. An LSTM cell. X_t is the input, h_{t-1} and h_t are the output of the previous and current block, C_{t-1} and C_t are the cell state of the previous and current block. An LSTM block can help to correlate neighboring blocks and search for inconsistencies when a forgery is present. This is achieved via gates of activation functions to determine if certain data is relevant for forwarding it or forgetting it.

Some researchers suggested that a CNN trained for detecting camera traces could be used to detect and localize image splicing. If an analyzed image contains patches of different sources, then the blocks can be clustered in different groups separating the suspicious area. Works in [83,84] made use of camera-specific features obtained by a CNN that focuses on them. Both methods analyzed patches and looked for traces of different cameras in the same image. Bondi et al. [83] used a clustering algorithm to create different groups of the authentic and suspicious areas. In [84] a noise residual called *Noiseprint* was extracted and used to check inconsistencies within a single image.

Yarlagadda et al. [85] used a GAN that included an adversarial feedback loop to learn how to generate some information in a realistic manner, with the objective to detect satellite image forgeries. There are two major components within GANs: the *generator* that takes a noise vector as input and outputs an image improved at each step with the knowledge of what a valid input should be, and the *discriminator* that tries to classify between real and fake (i.e., created by generator) content. Their proposed architecture was followed by an SVM to detect whether feature vectors come from pristine images or forgeries.

Recently, refs. [86,87] proposed the multi-branch CNNs to tackle the challenge of image forgery detection. Specifically, Zhou et al. [86] proposed a multi-branch Region-Convolutional Neural Network (R-CNN) which is a type of CNN typically used for object detection to coarsely locate the tampered-with regions in bounding boxes. The authors used pixel values in one branch with ResNet-101 architecture [88] and noise features obtained by SRM filters in the second branch. Wu et al. [87] suggested a multi-branch CNN joined with an LSTM trained with a set of 385 different image manipulations. Their architecture named Mantra-Net generates a pixel-level detection mask reflecting the probability of a falsification. In the three input branches of Mantra-Net the first layers are initialized with SRM filters, high-pass constrained filters of Bayar and Stamm [71], and normal random weights. Figure 6 shows example results of bounding-box localization of falsifications produced by Zhou et al.'s detector [86].

Figure 6. Bounding-box localization results generated by using the implementation of [86] on NIST 16 dataset [36]. Top and bottom rows show copy-move and splicing examples, respectively. (**A**) is the original image, (**B**) is the falsified image, (**C**) is the ground-truth mask, and (**D**) is the localization result.

Very recently, Mara et al. [89] worked on a full-image CNN based on Xception architecture [90] to detect and localize image falsifications. The proposed end-to-end network used the *Noiseprint* [84] as features extracted from the image input. Meanwhile, in [91] a GAN was proposed to generate falsified images avoiding the burdensome task of creating and labeling image forgery examples in a conventional way. With this big number of synthetic examples, the proposed algorithm was able to segment and refine the focus on boundary artifacts around falsified regions during the training process.

Table 4 provides a summary of the various multipurpose falsification detection techniques. The summary includes the method reference, input for the network, initialization used in the first layer, input size, localization level, considered databases, and network type. We also show in the last two columns of the table the performance comparisons on the two most common datasets used among all methods, i.e., CASIA [33] and NIST 16 [36]. Besides the accuracy metric and the AUC metric, respectively introduced in Equations (2) and (4) in Section 3.5, in the table we also use a new metric of F-1 score which is defined by the following equation:

$$F1 = \frac{2TP}{2TP + FP + FN}. \qquad (5)$$

In Table 4, the reported results correspond to patch size of 64 × 64 and 256 × 256 for [80,87], respectively. For the other methods, the performance corresponds to the only patch size given in the column of "Input size". It is worthwhile mentioning that the performance is reported at image level for [78] and at patch level for [75], while for all other methods the metric is pixel-level localization performance which is naturally a more challenging metric than image-level and patch-level counterparts. We can observe from Table 4 that besides the accuracy, the AUC and the F1-score have also been used as performance evaluation metrics. This is probably because for falsification detection researchers usually have imbalanced classes of authentic and falsified samples, with the falsified samples being fewer than the authentic ones. In this case of imbalanced classes, the AUC and the F1-score are more appropriate metrics than the accuracy. On the CASIA dataset the methods of [86,87] achieve satisfying performance of pixel-level localization results. We notice that both methods have either a special input of noise features [86] or a special design of first-layer filters [87]. It appears that both options can be effective in detecting and locating falsifications which may leave traces in the high-frequency component of images. On the NIST 16 dataset, methods of [80,81] share comparable and very good results. These two methods consider resampling traces as one of the discriminative features for the falsification localization task. This technical choice seems quite adequate for exposing forgery traces on falsified images in the NIST 16 dataset.

Table 4. Multipurpose image falsification detection methods. Loc. level describes whether the localization is performed in a pixel-, block- or bounding-box-wise manner. Dataset is color coded as follows: **U** UCID [15], **D** Dresden [17], **K** Kaggle Camera Challenge [20], **O** Vision [21], **A** Landsat on AWS [23], **F** MS COCO [25], **L** Columbia gray [31], **B** Columbia color [32], **C** CASIA [33], **I** IEEE Forensics Challenge [34], **H** Carvalho [35], **N** NIST 16 [36], **V** Coverage [40], and **S** when it is an ad-hoc dataset created by authors of the original paper. In the last two columns of performance (Perf.) on respectively CASIA [33] dataset and NIST 16 [36] dataset, F1 stands for F-1 score, Acc. stands for accuracy, and AUC stands for area under the curve (all in %).

Method	Input Feature	Init. First Layer	Input Size	Loc. Level	Dataset	Network Type	Perf. on CASIA	Perf. on NIST 16
[78]	Pixel values	SRM filters	128 × 128	pixel	C L	CNN - SVM	Acc. 97.8	-
[75]	Wavelet features	Random init.	32 × 32	block	C	Autoencoder	Acc. 91.1	-
[79]	Steganalysis features	Random init.	128 × 128	pixel	S	CNN - SVM	-	-
[83]	Pixel values	Random init.	64 × 64	block	S D	CNN	-	-
[80]	Radon features	Random init.	64 × 64, 128 × 128	pixel	N	LSTM	-	Acc. 94.9
[92]	Resampling features	Random init.	64 × 64	pixel	S I N V	CNN	-	Acc. 89.4
[86]	Pixel values, noise features	Random init.	224 × 224	bbox	S C F N V	Multi-branch	AUC 79.5	AUC 93.7
[85]	Pixel values	Random init.	64 × 64	block	S A	GAN-SVM	-	-
[84]	Pixel values, Noiseprints	Random init.	44 × 44, 64 × 64	pixel	S D	CNN	-	-
[81]	Resampling features	Random init.	Resized 256 × 256	pixel	S I N V	LSTM	-	Acc. 94.8
[87]	Pixel values	SRM filters, Bayar filters, Random init.	256 × 256, 512 × 512	pixel	S B C D K N V	Multi-branch	AUC 81.7	AUC 79.5
[89]	Pixel values, Noiseprints	Random init.	960 × 720; 4640 × 3480	pixel	S O U	CNN incremental learning	-	-
[91]	Pixel values	Random init.	224 × 224	pixel	S C H V	GAN-CNN	F1 57.4	-

4.2. Targeted Detectors

Targeted detectors, which are designed to detect only one type of image falsification, have been developed in parallel with multipurpose ones.

4.2.1. Splicing Detection

Some early works dealing with splicing detection and localization were based on autoencoders. In [93], authors used SRM features as input for their autoencoder model. The method in [94] used the steganalysis features from SRM to analyze frames in a video with autoencoder and LSTM to detect splicing forgeries.

Wu et al. [95] proposed a framework of Constrained Image Splicing Detection and Localization (CISDL) based on the well-known VGG-16 architecture [96]. Using two input branches they calculated the probability that one image had been partially spliced to another one and localized the spliced region. Meanwhile, in [97,98], a CNN without fully connected layers known as Fully Convolutional Network (FCN) [99] was used to predict a tampering map for a given image. In [97], the proposed architecture has two exit localization branches. The first one was used for localizing the inner part of the spliced area and the second one for detecting the boundary between pristine and spliced regions. Concurrently, Liu et al. [98] made use of three FCNs to deal with different scales; moreover, conditional random field was used to combine the results of different scales.

Some approaches [100,101] attempted to detect anomalies or inconsistencies within tampered-with images. In [100], a Siamese CNN with a self-consistency approach to determine if contents had been produced by a single device was proposed. The proposed model could predict the probability that two patches had similar EXchangeable Image File (EXIF) attributes and output a "self-consistency" heatmap, highlighting image regions that had undergone possible forgery. In [101] authors used transfer learning from a pre-trained residual network (ResNet-50) with illumination maps taken from input images to find hints of forgeries.

Recent strategies [102,103] made use of U-Net [104] architectures. In a U-Net, the features are captured by a size-reducing way of consecutive layers, then upsampled and concatenated with the first path in a U-shaped symmetric path, attempting to reduce loss and improve localization capability. In [102], authors took advantage of U-Net architecture for the training of a GAN with image retouching generator, which helped a splicing localization model to learn a wide range of image falsifications. Meanwhile Bi et al. [103] proposed a method mainly based on U-Net as a segmentation network for splicing forgery detection.

Given the popularity of GANs in the computer vision field, some researchers have also started to use them for image forensics purposes. This is the case of [105] where the authors made use of a conditional GAN for the training of a detector to locate forgeries in satellite images. Liu et al. [106] proposed a deep matching CNN together with a GAN to generate probability maps in a CISDL scenario.

Special initialization of first layer was also considered for splicing detector. For example, Rao et al. [107] designed and implemented a CNN with the first layer of the network initialized with 30 SRM filters to locate splicing forgeries.

Table 5 summarizes the targeted detectors of splicing falsification. The considered properties of the detection methods are similar to those in Table 4. A performance comparison on the two most common datasets used among all methods (i.e., Carvalho [35] and CASIA [33]) is provided, in terms of pixel-level falsification localization performance. Besides the accuracy and F-1 score metrics which were introduced previously, in the table we use a new metric of mean average precision (mAP). In order to define this new metric, we first introduce the definition of the average precision (AP) metric as shown in the following equation:

$$AP = \int_0^1 \text{Prec}(r) dr, \qquad (6)$$

where Prec is the precision metric as given in Equation (3) and r is the recall metric defined as $r = \text{Recall} = \frac{TP}{TP+FN}$. In practice, the precision can be regarded as a function of the recall when varying the decision threshold, and vice versa. The AP metric calculates the average precision value $\text{Prec}(r)$ for recall value r varying from 0 to 1. Consequently, the mAP metric is defined as the mean average precision over all classes, as given by:

$$\text{mAP} = \frac{1}{C} \sum_{i=1}^{C} AP(i), \qquad (7)$$

where C is the number of classes and i represents a particular class. In Table 5, forensic performance is reported in terms of F1-score and mean average precision, mainly for two reasons: (1) these two metrics are well suited for the classification problem of imbalanced classes of authentic and falsified samples; (2) the mean average precision has been introduced probably by researchers who have worked for long time in the computer vision field where the mAP is a widely used metric.

We notice from Table 5 that performance on Carvalho dataset is rather limited for existing methods. As mentioned in Section 2.2, falsified images in Carvalho dataset were carefully created. This limited performance implies that forensic analysis of high-quality falsified images is still a challenging task, and future efforts shall be devoted to this research problem. By contrast, falsified images in CASIA dataset are less difficult to handle. Recent methods achieved good results on this dataset, either by leveraging adversarial learning [106] or by using special forensic features as network input [107].

Table 5. Targeted splicing detection methods. AE stands for autoencoder. Dataset is color coded as follows: (A) Landsat on AWS [23], (F) MS COCO [25], (T) SUN 2012 [28], (L) Columbia gray [31], (B) Columbia color [32], (C) CASIA [33], (H) Carvalho [35], (N) NIST 16 [36], (R) Realistic (Korus) [38], (W) On-the-wild websites, and (S) when it is an ad-hoc dataset created by authors of the method (information of source images used for dataset creation may be provided in the original paper). In the last two columns of performance (Perf.) on respectively Carvalho [35] and CASIA [33], F1 stands for F-1 score, mAP stands for mean average precision, and Acc. stands for accuracy (all in %).

Method	Input Feature	Input Size	Dataset	Network Type	Backbone Architecture	Perf. on Carvalho	Perf. on CASIA
[93]	SRM features	768 × 1024	S	AE	Own	-	-
[95]	Pixel values	256 × 256	S F T	CNN	VGG-16	-	-
[94]	SRM features	720 × 1280	S	AE-LSTM	Own	-	-
[97]	Pixel values	224 × 224	S C H L N	FCN	VGG-16	F1 47.9	F1 54.1
[100]	EXIF metadata, pixel values	128 × 128	S H L R W	CNN	ResNet-v2	mAP 51.0	-
[101]	Illuminant maps	224 × 224	S L	CNN-SVM	ResNet-v1	-	-
[98]	Pixel values	224 × 224	S B	FCN	VGG-16	-	-
[103]	Pixel values	384 × 384	S B C	CNN (U-Net)	ResNet-v1	-	F1 84.1
[102]	Pixel values	512 × 512	S H	GAN (U-Net)	VGG-16	mAP 48.0	mAP 74.0
[106]	Pixel values	256 × 256	C F	GAN	VGG-16	-	F1 90.8
[105]	Pixel values	70 × 70	A	GAN	Pix2Pix	-	-
[107]	SRM features for 1st layer init.	128 × 128	S C L	CNN-SVM	Own	-	Acc. 97.0

4.2.2. Copy-Move Detection

Copy-move detection is one of the forensic techniques that have been studied with more balance between conventional and deep-learning approaches. As mentioned before, in a copy-move forgery, a part of the original image (source area) is copied and pasted at a different place (target area) of the same image. Before pasting, the target area can be transformed (rotation, scaling, shearing, etc.) to make the forgery visually realistic. Routine image manipulation (smoothing, contrast adjustment, etc.) can be applied locally or globally to enhance the visual quality. Copy-move is mainly used for falsifications where certain content needs to be disguised or cloned.

Probably the first proposal using a deep-learning approach to solve the copy-move detection problem was the method from Ouyang et al. [108], which was based on the famous pre-trained AlexNet [109] originally designed for image recognition. The authors generated forged images by choosing a random square from the upper left corner and copying it to the center. Although this method obtained decent results in this artificial scenario, the performance was diminished for realistic forgeries.

Wu et al. [110] proposed a CNN-based method which first divided the input image into blocks, then extracted special features, correlated features between blocks, localized matches between blocks and finally predicted a copy-move forgery mask. Furthermore, routine image manipulation operations to hide the forgery traces such as JPEG compression, blurring and AWGN were applied to training data as a means of data augmentation. The objective was to easily detect these manipulations as possible telltales of copy-move falsification. Very shortly after this piece of work, the same authors [111] proposed to use a different architecture with two exit branches to deal with the problem of source-target disambiguation where it is necessary to discern between source (original) and target (falsified) regions in a copy-move forgery. Another deep-learning method for source-target disambiguation was proposed in [112] where CNN with multi-exit branches was also used to identify source and target regions. This method was shown to be capable of learning special features focusing on the presence of interpolation artifacts and boundary inconsistencies. Figure 7 shows two examples of source-target disambiguation localization results generated by Wu et al.'s detector [111].

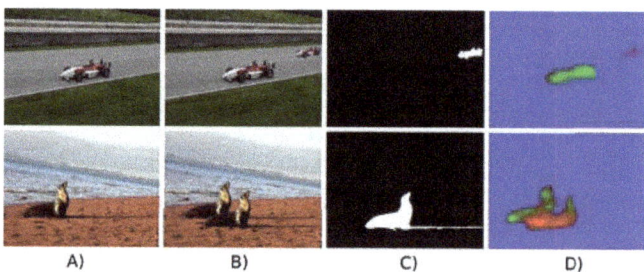

Figure 7. Source-target disambiguation results generated by using the implementation of [111] on images from the NIST 16 dataset [36]. (**A**) is the original image, (**B**) is the falsified image, (**C**) is the ground-truth mask, and (**D**) is the localization result in which green and red color represents respectively the source (original) and target (falsified) region in a copy-move forgery.

In [113] Liu et al. proposed one of the first copy-move detectors that used a CNN approach. Their proposal was partially based on conventional methods, by taking keypoints features such as Scale-Invariant Feature Transform (SIFT) or Speeded-Up Robust Features (SURF) as input for their network. One limitation was that this method had low performance when duplicated areas have a homogeneous content, because the keypoints could be hardly identified within such areas.

Very recently, Zhu et al. [114] proposed an adaptive attention and residual-based CNN to localize copy-move forgeries. The self-attention module allowed neurons to interact with each other to find out which neurons should receive more attention. Experiments showed comparable results with previous deep-learning approaches, but the problem of source-target disambiguation was not addressed.

Illumination direction, contrast and noise are usually inconsistent in splicing forgery, so the tampering traces could be found rather easily by the CNN. However, the source and target regions are derived from the same image in copy-move, accordingly the illumination and contrast would be highly consistent, which raises a greater challenge for copy-move detection based on CNN. This may be one reason for the fewer published papers focused on copy-move when compared with splicing.

The first part of Table 6 summarizes the existing deep-learning methods targeted at copy-move detection and localization. We show in the second-last column a comparison of localization performance of methods that reports results on both of the popular datasets of CoMoFoD [41] and CASIA [33]. Here CASIA means a specific subset of CASIA images with only copy-move falsification, which were properly selected and shared by the authors of the copy-move detection method of [111]. On CoMoFoD and CASIA datasets the comparison is fair with same set of images, evaluation protocol and metric. It is worth mentioning that the F1-score has become a commonly used evaluation metric of copy-move detection methods in part owing to Wu et al.'s paper [111], where the authors proposed a detailed evaluation protocol of copy-move localization performance with the F1-score as the metric. The proposed evaluation protocol and metric in [111] are later widely accepted and used by researchers in the community. From Table 6 we can see that methods of [111,114] have competitive results on both datasets of CoMoFoD and CASIA. Nevertheless, the method in [111] provides the additional capability of source-target disambiguation which may bring more information for the forensic analysis. Moreover, having a dedicated architecture for the copy-move forensic problem is helpful to achieve satisfying performance, in particular the block correlation module of [111] and the self-attention module of [114]. Finally, it can be observed that the performance is not high and there is still much room for improvement of copy-move localization results.

Table 6. Targeted detectors of copy-move and inpainting falsifications. S-T disam. means source-target disambiguation. Dataset is color coded as follows: ⓤ UCID [15], ⓓ Dresden [17], ⓚ RAISE [18], ⓞ Vision [21], ⓥ MvTec [22], ⓧ Oxford [24], ⓕ MS COCO [25], ⓖ ImageNet [26], ⓛ MIT Place [27], ⓣ SUN 2012 [28], ⓒ CASIA [33], ⓥ Coverage [40], ⓜ CoMoFoD [41], ⓟ ROME patches [115], ⓕ CMFD [116], and ⓢ when it is an ad-hoc dataset. We show in the second-last column performances of F-1 scores (in %) for copy-move detectors on respectively CoMoFoD [41] and CASIA [33] datasets with the following format: F1CoMoFoD / F1CASIA. For inpainting forensic methods, we show in the last column the localization performance (mean average precision (mAP), F-1 score (F1), area under the curve (AUC) or accuracy (Acc.), all in %) for one typical setting of inpainted images with 10% of pixels tampered with by inpainting.

Method	Input Features	Input Size	Localization Level	Dataset	Backbone Architecture	Performance Copy-Move	Performance Inpainting
			Copy-move				
[108]	Pixel values	256 × 256	Detection	ⓢⓕⓤⓧ	AlexNet	-	N.A.
[110]	Pixel values	256 × 256	Image	ⓢⓒⓕⓜⓣ	VGG-16	31.3 / 14.6	N.A.
[113]	Keypoints	51 × 51	Pixel	ⓢⓜⓟ	Own	-	N.A.
[111]	Pixel values	256 × 256	Pixel, S-T disam.	ⓢⓒⓕⓜⓣ	VGG-16	49.3 / 45.6	N.A.
[112]	Pixel values	64 × 64	Pixel, S-T disam.	ⓢⓒⓓⓚⓞ	ResNet-V1	-	N.A.
[114]	Pixel values	256 × 256	Pixel	ⓢⓒⓜⓥ	VGG-16	50.1 / 45.5	N.A.
			Inpainting				
[117]	High-pass residuals	256 × 256	Pixel	ⓢⓛ	Own	N.A.	mAP 97.8
[118]	Pixel values	128 × 128	bbox	ⓢⓖ	ResNet-V1	N.A.	F1 91.5
[119]	High-pass residuals	Various	Pixel	ⓢⓖ	ResNet-V1	N.A.	F1 97.3
[120]	LBP, pixel values	256 × 256	Pixel & bbox	ⓢⓕⓖ	Own	N.A.	mAP 97.8
[121]	Pixel values	256 × 256	Pixel	ⓢⓥ	Own	N.A.	AUC 94.2
[122]	Pixel values	256 × 256	Pixel & bbox	ⓢⓤ	Own	N.A.	Acc. 93.6

4.2.3. Inpainting Detection

The inpainting technique can create plausible image forgeries which are difficult to spot by the naked eye. In contrast to copy-move where an image area is copied and pasted, in inpainting the falsified area is often filled with micro components (e.g., blocks of 7 by 7 pixels) extracted from different places of the image. These small blocks usually represent a kind of micro-texture and are combined in inpainting in a visually convincing way. Although the inpainting method can be used for inoffensive purposes such as repairing partially deteriorated images, it is used likewise in forgery creation, for instance for object removal to falsify an image or for erasing visible watermarks. Some splicing or copy-move detection algorithms could be exploited to detect inpainting forgeries, but in general they do not consider the particularity of inpainting and their performance remains not as good as expected.

To our knowledge the first method targeted at inpainting detection was proposed by Zhu et al. [117], where authors used an encoder–decoder network to predict the inpainting probability on each patch. Li and Huang [119] focused on detecting inpainting forgeries made by deep-learning methods (also known as deep-inpainting). Image high-pass residuals were fed to an FCN in which transpose convolutional layers were initialized with bilinear kernel.

Wang et al. [118] used a R-CNN, originally designed for object detection, to output a bounding box of the inpainted region along with a probability score. Very recently, the same authors [120] designed a multi-task CNN with two inputs, i.e., a Local Binary Pattern (LBP) image as the first input and the pixel values as the second one, for inpainting detection. This new network could produce a bounding box of inpainted area together with an estimated mask of forgery.

In [121] authors proposed an anomaly detection method by randomly removing partial image regions and reconstructing them with inpainting methods to detect a forgery. The authors used a U-Net-based encoder–decoder network to reconstruct the removed regions and output a tampering map in which each image is assigned an anomaly score according to the region with the poorest reconstruction quality. Meanwhile, Lu and Niu [122] published an object removal detection method by combining CNN and LSTM to detect inpainting with single and combined post-processing operations such as JPEG compression and Gaussian noise addition.

The second part of Table 6 provides a summary of the deep-learning-based forensic methods targeted at inpainting falsification. For experimental studies, the listed methods created an ad-hoc dataset from different databases of pristine images with different inpainting techniques and experimental protocols. This makes very difficult to carry out a fair comparison. We have made efforts and decided to report performances of compared methods under one typical experimental setting where in falsified images 10% of pixels were tampered with by inpainting falsification. We can see from the last column of Table 6 that methods in [117,119,120] achieved good inpainting localization performance. This may imply that the special inputs of high-pass residuals in [117,119] and of LBP features in [120] are effective in exposing traces left by inpainting techniques. We also observe that different methods tend to use different evaluation metrics, in part because authors of each method tested their method on an ad-hoc dataset created by themselves. This makes difficult to carry out easy and fair comparisons between different methods. The development of a high-quality open benchmarking dataset is desirable and will be beneficial for the advancement of the relevant research. Finally, it can be observed that localization performance is better for inpainting than copy-move (please compare the last two columns of Table 6). A possible reason is that in copy-move the falsified region is originally from the pristine part of the same image, while in inpainting the falsified region is a kind of new content created by inpainting algorithm though with attempt to mimic the pristine areas.

5. Other Specific Forensic Problems

This subsection is dedicated to the presentation about some other specific problems on which the image forensics research community has conducted extensive work. We divide them into three groups: (1) camera identification, (2) computer graphics image detection, and (3) detection of Deepfake images.

5.1. Camera Identification

A typical image acquiring process is shown in Figure 8. First, the light rays are redirected by the lens, then different filters such as anti-aliasing can be applied before the

Color Filter Array (CFA) divides the light into one of the red (R), green (G) and blue (B) components per pixel. A demosaicing step is performed afterwards to reconstruct the full-color scene from the input samples taken by the previous step. Depending on the camera model and software, several post-processing operations such as white balancing, gamma correction and JPEG compression can take place. These post-processing steps contribute with important and distinctive clues to the image forensics field. When the final output image of camera is falsified to create a forgery, additional traces unique for each falsification are usually left behind.

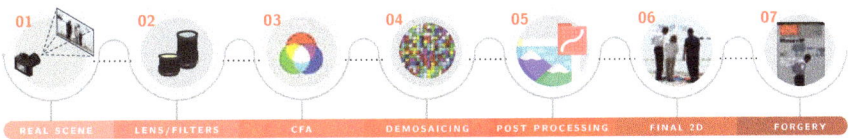

Figure 8. Illustration of typical pipeline of image acquisition and forgery creation.

The challenge of verifying the authenticity of an image can be tackled from different perspectives. One of them is approached by answering the following question: given an image, is it possible to find out the model of the camera with which the image was taken? Even though camera model, date and time, and other information can be found in the EXIF or in the JPEG header, in general it is not possible to consider such information as reliable and legitimate because image metadata can be easily modified. By contrast and as mentioned before, the traces of the post-processing steps carried out by each camera constitute important source of information that can be used to authenticate the image provenance in the image forensics field.

First deep-learning methods for camera identification were mainly dedicated to classifying patches produced by different cameras. Bondi et al. [123] used a CNN followed by an SVM to classify patches coming from different unknown cameras. In addition, with the output of their CNN they looked for anomalies in an image to search for forgeries. Tuama et al. [124] applied a high-pass filter in the first layer to suppress image content and obtain image residuals as input for a shallow CNN that was trained to learn to classify among different camera models. Due to the release of new camera models and the difficulty to keep an updated database, Bayar and Stamm [125] suggested an open-set scenario which aimed to predict an unseen camera device. The authors used a constrained initialization for the first layer of a CNN to infer whether the image was taken by an unknown device.

Ding et al. [126] proposed a multi-task CNN to predict information about brand, modes and devices from a patch. The authors used ResNet [88] blocks together with high-pass filter residuals as input for the network and with inputs of different sizes. In [127], authors used a shallow CNN for mobile camera identification in a multi-class challenging scenario. Experiments showed good forensic performance, but the performance diminished when devices came from a same manufacturer.

Methods in [128,129] both used Siamese network for this camera classification problem. There are multiple inputs in a Siamese network with the same architecture and same initial weights for each sub-network. Parameter updating is mirrored across all sub-networks. The purpose of this architecture is to learn the similarity of inputs. In [128], authors proposed a Siamese CNN to extract the camera unique fixed-pattern noise from an image's Photo Response Non-Uniformity (PRNU) to classify camera devices and furthermore trace device fingerprints for image forgery detection. Sameer and Naska [129] worked on the scenario where annotated data (i.e., in this case image samples) were not available in big quantities and training had to be performed using a limited number of samples per class. This approach is called *few-shot* learning and refers to learning and understanding a new model based on a few examples. For this few-shot learning approach, a Siamese network was used to enhance classification accuracy of camera models. The intuition behind the

Siamese network for this challenge is to form pairs of image patches coming from the same camera models to improve the training.

Table 7 gives a summary of the deep-learning-based camera identification techniques. In the table, we include the accuracy performance mainly on the Dresden dataset [17]. Even in cases where the same number of camera models was considered, the size of the patches was not the same, which makes difficult to deliver a fair comparison. Nevertheless, it must be mentioned that methods using smaller patch sizes such as 64 × 64 or smaller, combined with a bigger number of camera models present a bigger challenge due to the less information available on each patch and the bigger number of classes for the classification task. In addition, similar to the evaluation of image manipulation detection methods in Section 3.5, the experiments for evaluating camera model identification methods are usually conducted in a controlled laboratory setting with balanced classes. Therefore, in this case the simple accuracy metric has been widely used for the performance evaluation. It can be observed once again from Table 7 that special input features of high-pass residuals [124–126] and/or special first-layer design [125] appear to be effective in highlighting the subtle differences between the traces of different camera models, leading to a satisfying identification accuracy. Finally, we would like to mention our observations of two interesting trends regarding the research on camera model identification: (1) techniques such as few-shot learning would be helpful in realistic scenarios in which we have a limited number of annotated samples, and (2) the deep-learning methods are promising techniques to deliver a good camera model classification performance and may further help in the search of anomalies for image forgery detection.

Table 7. Camera identification methods. ET means extremely randomized trees. Dataset is color coded as follows: (D) Dresden [17], (I) MICHE-I [19], (O) Vision [21], and (S) when it is an ad-hoc dataset. In the last column we show the accuracy performance on the Dresden dataset [17], except for two methods for which the dataset icon is given in the corresponding rows in the last column. We provide information about the number of tested camera models and the accuracy (in %) with the format Number of Camera Models : Accuracy.

Method	Input Features	Initialization	Input Size	Dataset	Network Type	Performance
[124]	High-pass residuals	Random init.	256 × 256	(D)	CNN	12: 98.0
[123]	Pixel values	Random init.	64 × 64	(S)(D)	CNN-SVM	18: 93.0
[125]	High-pass residuals	Bayar's constrained	256 × 256	(D)	CNN-SVM CNN-ET	10: 93.9
[127]	Pixel values	Random init.	32 × 32	(I)	CNN-SVM	(I) 3: 91.1
[128]	Pixel values	Random init.	48 × 48	(S)	Siamese	(S) 3: 100.0
[126]	High-pass residuals	Random init.	48 × 48	(S)(D)	Multi-scale CNN	14: 97.1
[129]	Pixel values	Random init.	64 × 64	(D)(O)	Siamese	10: 87.3

5.2. Detection of Computer Graphics Images

Computer graphics techniques produce visually plausible images of fictive scenes. Despite the benefits of CGI in virtual reality and 3D animation, it can also be used as false information thus affecting real-life decisions, and this situation is augmented with the fast dissemination of content enabled by the Internet. Consequently, the challenge of discerning between a real photograph and CGI has been explored by image forensics researchers. Figure 9 shows how challenging it is to distinguish between CGI and an image taken by a camera.

Figure 9. Examples to show the difficulty of visually differentiating between CGI (on the **left**) and an image taken by a camera (on the **right**). The CGI is from Tumblr forum (https://hyperrealcg.tumblr.com/post/112323738189/title-a-land-where-dreams-take-wings-artist accessed on 2 April 2021) and the camera image is from Reddit forum (https://www.reddit.com/r/EarthPorn/comments/4o9u03/no_filter_needed_grand_tetons_national_park_wy_oc/ accessed on 2 April 2021).

Rezende et al. [130] proposed a deep CNN taking advantage of transfer learning from ResNet-50 model to classify small patches of computer graphics images and real photographic images. Yu et al. [131] investigated for this CGI forensics problem the usage of a CNN without pooling layers. The authors of [57,132] proposed to use shallow CNNs in a patch-based manner. Rahmouni et al. [57] used a CNN with a customized pooling layer that computed statistics such as mean and variance followed by an SVM to detect CGI patches. In order to classify a whole image, a weighted voting strategy was applied to combine the local probabilities on patches of sliding windows to produce a final label. Quan et al. [132] proposed an end-to-end approach that used a Maximal Poisson-disk Sampling (MPS) method to crop patches in a lossless manner from a full-sized image. Nguyen et al. [133] continued with the sliding window approach to deal with high-resolution images using VGG-19 followed by multi-layer perceptron-based CNN as classifier. In [134], authors proposed an approach for discriminating CGI using high-pass residuals as input for a CNN.

He et al. [135] designed a two-input CNN-RNN taking the color and texture from YCbCr color space on each input to detect CGIs. In [136] authors investigated the usage of an Attention-Recurrent Neural Network (A-RNN) to classify CGIs in a local-to-global approach following the sliding window strategy and using the simple majority voting rule to produce a decision on a whole image. Nguyen et al. [137] studied the application of dynamic routing capsule networks [138] based on the VGG-19 model for detecting CGI. Capsule networks were able to identify objects that hold spatial relationship between features.

More recently, Zhang et al. [139] proposed a CNN containing a special block at input called hybrid correlation module composed of a 1×1 convolution layer followed by three blocks of convolutional layers, which would correlate channels and pixels in an attempt to detect CGIs. Meena and Tyagi [140] used the transfer learning approach from DenseNet-201 [141] followed by an SVM as classifier. In [142] authors made use of a shallow A-CNN with two inputs for CGI classification. Interestingly, the inputs for this network were preprocessed by a Gaussian low-pass filter as the authors wanted to focus on general patterns rather than local details. Quan et al. [143] designed a CNN combining SRM filters and Gaussian random weights as initializations for the first layer on a two-branch architecture. The authors also proposed to use the so-called negative samples created via gradient-based distortion to achieve a better generalization on test images created by unknown graphics rendering engines.

Table 8 summarizes the deep-learning-based CGI forensic techniques. In the last column of the table, we provide a performance comparison mainly for the Rahmouni dataset [57] and the He dataset [135]. The accuracy at patch level is used as the performance metric on these two datasets. This is mainly because similar to manipulation detection (Section 3.5) and camera model identification (Section 5.1), researchers consider a controlled experimental setting with balanced classes of natural image patches and CGI patches in the experiments; therefore in such cases the patch-level accuracy is a simple and appropriate metric. For the results in Table 8, the patch size is 60 × 60, 60 × 60 and 64 × 64 for method in [132,136,142], respectively. For other methods, results are reported for the only patch size listed in the column of "Input size". In the case of the Rahmouni [57] dataset, we can see that in general accuracy improves as forensic method uses larger patches, with the two highest accuracy values achieved by [134,137] respectively on patches of 650 × 650 and 128 × 128. Regarding the performance on the He [135] dataset, we still have the same trend with better results achieved by [135,139] both on 96 × 96 patches, when compared to method [142] on 64 × 64 patches. In all, a larger patch size generally results in a better forensic performance of CGI detection but also leads to a higher computational cost. Future efforts could be devoted to the performance improvement on small patches and the aggregation strategy from patch-level results to image-level decision.

Table 8. CGI detection methods. Dataset is color coded as follows: (K) RAISE [18], (O) Vision [21], (G) ImageNet [26], (C) Columbia CGI [43], (F) MesoNet [44], (T) Artlantis [45], (B) Corona [46], (Y) VRay [47], (K) Autodesk [48], (N) FaceForensics [50], (R) Rahmouni [57], (H) He [135], (T) Tokuda [144], (W) Web images, and (S) when it is an ad-hoc dataset. In the last column we show the performance in terms of patch-level accuracy (in %), except for method [143] for which HTER (half total error rate, in %) is used, on the Rahmouni [57] dataset (R), the He [135] dataset (H), and ad-hoc dataset (S) constructed or considered by authors of the corresponding method. In many cases the ad-hoc dataset (S) is a customized combination of the image sets listed in the third column of "Dataset".

Method	Input Size	Dataset	Network Type	Backbone Architecture	Performance
[130]	224 × 224	G T	CNN-SVM	ResNet-50	S Acc. 94.1
[131]	32 × 32	S C W	CNN	VGG-16	S Acc. 98.0
[57]	100 × 100	R	CNN-SVM	Own	R Acc. 84.8
[132]	30 × 30, ..., 240 × 240	C R	CNN	Own	R Acc. 94.8
[134]	650 × 650	R	CNN	Own	R Acc. 99.9
[133]	100 × 100	K R	Two-input CNN-RNN	VGG-19	R Acc. 96.5
[135]	96 × 96	H W	CNN-RNN	ResNet-50	H Acc. 93.9
[136]	30 × 30,..., 240 × 240	C K	A-RNN	Own	S Acc. 94.9
[137]	128 × 128	F N R	Capsule	VGG-19	R Acc. 97.0
[139]	96 × 96	H	CNN	Own	H Acc. 94.2
[140]	224 × 224	C T	CNN	DenseNet-201	S Acc. 94.1
[142]	32 × 32, 64 × 64	H	Two-input A-CNN	Inception	H Acc. 87.8
[143]	233 × 233	B K K O T Y	Two-branch CNN	Own	S HTER 1.31

5.3. Deepfake Detection

Lately, GAN models have been used in various applications and have transformed a time-consuming task previously reserved to high-skilled experts now to a simple and fast operation. One of such applications is to create synthetic yet visually realistic images and videos. GAN-generated multimedia contents are commonly known as *Deepfakes*, referring to the usage of a deep-learning model and the fabricated synthetic results. Majority of cases have been used to replace a person (or a person's face) in an existing image or video with another person (or the face of this other person). Figure 10 illustrates the synthesis process realized by a GAN which replaces the face in the target (image on the left) by using a source (image in the middle) to generate the resulting frame (image on the right). Although benign material has been created for the illustrated example, this technique can have more serious impact in other situations, e.g., to create political distress. Recently a big amount of research activities has been dedicated to detecting GAN-generated fake content, mainly due to the easiness and impact of Deepfakes. In comparison with images, videos contain more information and different approaches have been proposed based on different kinds of clues for the detection of Deepfake videos.

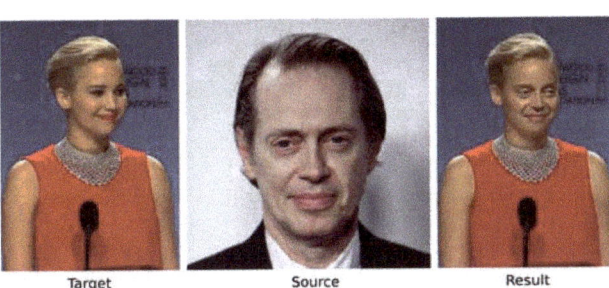

Figure 10. Example frame of a Deepfake video. The tool used to generate this video is available at the following webpage: https://faceswap.dev/ accessed on 2 April 2021, and the full resulting video can be viewed at https://www.youtube.com/watch?v=r1jng79a5xc accessed on 2 April 2021.

First proposals in the literature [44,145–147] focused on the detection of GAN-generated images created by a specific GAN model. In [145], authors searched for statistical artifacts introduced by GAN with a pre-processing layer that extracted high-pass residuals. Marra et al. [146] tested the performance of some popular CNN-based image forensics methods for the detection of images created by GANs and shared in social networks. In [44], authors used a shallow CNN to detect Deepfakes and Face2Face [50] videos. Interestingly, Chan et al. [147] developed as first objective a GAN for video-to-video translation in dancing poses. Additionally, they developed a detector that would detect videos coming from their own model. In [148], authors compared several popular sophisticated architectures and a shallow CNN. Experiments showed that the shallow CNN had better performance in detecting Deepfakes.

Güera and Delp [149] proposed to use a CNN for frame feature extraction and an LSTM for temporal sequence analysis to detect Deepfake videos which contained inconsistent frames. Amerini et al. [150] investigated the use of optical flow vectors to detect discrepancies in motion across several frames using the PWC-Net model [151]. Optical flow is a vector computed on two consecutive frames to extract apparent motion between the observer and the scene itself. In a follow-up work [152], an LSTM was used in a sequence-based approach which exploited the dissimilarities between consecutive frames of Deepfake videos.

Other proposals like [53,153–156] focused on the spatial coherence and temporal consistency among different physiological features. In [153], authors designed a CNN to detect variations of heart rate extracted from face regions on different frames. Li et al.'s method [154] was based on the observation that faces in Deepfake videos had a lower rate of blinking in comparison with real videos. This occurred in early GAN-generated videos for which the GAN was trained on faces with open eyes. The authors carried out a couple of pre-processing steps to locate the eyes and used this feature as input for an LSTM to detect a lower or higher rate of blinking as a telltale of Deepfake videos. Korshunov et al. [53] proposed an LSTM to search for anomalies between the audio and mouth movements. The method in [155] went in the same direction by comparing mouth shapes with the sound associated with M, B an P phonemes which required complete mouth closure and were in many cases incorrectly synthesized. Recently, Mittal et al. [156] went a step forward using a Siamese network to look for anomalies between the audio and video and combined it with the affective cues of both inputs to learn the differences between real and Deepfake videos.

The signal-level artifacts introduced during the synthesis were investigated for the detection of fake content. Li et al. [157] focused on artifacts at face boundaries by exploiting the fact that most existing face tampering methods shared a common blending operation. Meanwhile in [158], authors exploited the inconsistencies between warped face area and the surrounding background. The method in [159] adopted Gaussian noise extraction as a pre-processing step for a CNN, enforcing the network to learn more meaningful features about GAN traces.

In [160] a multi-task CNN was proposed to detect fake faces and to segment tampered-with areas. Dang et al. [161] investigated the use of attention mechanism for the detection and segmentation of tampered-with faces. In [162], authors used deep transfer learning for face swapping detection. Hsu et al. [163] made use of a so-called Common Fake Feature Network (CFFN) consisting of several dense units and a Siamese network for Deepfake detection. One limitation was that the CFFN may fail when the fake features of the results of a new GAN were significantly different from most of those used in the training phase.

To overcome data scarcity, refs. [164,165] proposed some solutions. Fernandes et al. [164] used a Attribution Based Confidence (ABC) metric to detect Deepfake videos with a deep model only trained on original videos. Khalid and Woo [165] formulated the challenge as a one-class anomaly detection problem by using a Variational Autoencoder trained only on real face images and subsequently detected Deepfakes as anomalies.

More recently, Wang et al. [166] used the well-known ResNet50 with careful data preparation to study the artifacts left by GANs. Their method demonstrated good generalization performance on unseen Deepfake content. In [167], authors designed a two-branch CNN to exploit the distribution differences between pixels in the face region and the background. Masi et al. [168] proposed a two-branch LSTM to combine color and frequency information. A multi-scale Laplacian-of-Gaussian operator was used in their method, which acted as a band-pass filter to amplify the artifacts.

Table 9 provides a summary of Deepfake detection methods presented above. In particular, in the table we present the main cue used by each method, by grouping cues into several categories as spatial context, generator traces, physiology-inspired, inter-frame consistency, and anomaly classification. We show performance comparison mainly on the two most common datasets used among all methods, i.e., FaceForensics [50] and FaceForensics++ [51]. The simple accuracy metric is the most commonly used evaluation metric for Deepfake detection methods, still because researchers mainly consider a controlled experimental setting with balanced classes of real and fake samples. Other metrics, e.g., mAP and AUC, have also been used for instances by researchers originally coming from the computer vision field. Even though accuracy is the most common metric, different settings were used for each method. Specifically, video compression levels were not the same for methods that conducted tests on a same dataset. H.264 compression was sometimes applied on the testing set providing different subsets with different compression levels. Additionally, lossless compression was used in some cases. Given the fact that Deepfake traces can get lost after lossy compression, uncompressed settings may present better results than scenarios with compression. Finally, compression level was not specified in all methods. Therefore, a direct and fair comparison is difficult. Nevertheless, we discuss some interesting points on these methods. We can see that most methods achieved a good performance on a binary classification for GAN-generated images. In the case of videos as input (cf., column of "Video") and using FaceForensics++ as dataset, the use of an architecture that can track changes among frames, such as LSTM in the method of [168], leads to very good performance. On images (cf., column of "Image"), results from [166] show that traces of current GANs are easy to detect. In addition, with data augmentation techniques detectors can achieve a good generalization on unseen data created by unknown Deepfake generation tools. A final remark is that the different metrics, e.g., accuracy, AUC and mAP, are not directly comparable. First, there is a clear difference between the threshold-dependent accuracy metric and the more comprehensive AUC and mAP metrics which in theory consider all possible threshold values. Second, although under certain conditions and with additional information of the classification system AUC and mAP can have an approximate relationship [169], in general these two metrics are not easily convertible to each other. This highlights the importance of open-source policy of forensic methods and free availability of high-quality datasets. With open implementations and datasets, it will be possible to carry out reliable evaluation of existing and future methods even on new datasets and with new metrics.

Table 9. Deepfake detection methods. Dataset is color coded as follows: (A) CelebA [29], (H) CelebAHQ [30], (F) MesoNet [44], (U) UADFV [49], (N) FaceForensics [50], (M) FaceForensics++ [51], (V) CelebDF [52], (T) DeepfakeTIMIT [53], (D) DFDC [55], (G) DFD [56], (Y) CycleGAN [170], and (S) when it is an ad-hoc dataset. We show in the last column performance mainly on FaceForensics [50] dataset (N) and FaceForensics++ [51] dataset (M), as well as on other datasets considered or constructed by authors of the corresponding method. In some cases, ad-hoc dataset (S) used for performance evaluation comprises fake samples generated by authors of the corresponding method with existing Deepfake generation tools. Acc. stands for accuracy, AUC for area under the curve, EER for equal error rate, TPR for true positive rate, Prec. for precision, and AP for average precision (all in %).

Method	Input Size	Dataset	Network Type	Backbone Architecture	Image	Video	Cue Spatial	GAN Trace	Physiology	Inter-Frame	Anomaly	Performance
[145]	256 × 256	S H	CNN	Own	●			●				S Acc. 99.4
[146]	256 × 256	S Y	CNN	XceptionNet	●			●				S Acc. 94.5
[154]	224 × 224	S	CNN-LSTM	VGG16		●			●			S AUC 99.0
[149]	299 × 299	S	CNN-LSTM	Inception V3		●				●		S Acc. 97.1
[44]	256 × 256	N	CNN	Inception	●		●					N Acc. 95.3
[148]	1024 × 1024	S A H	CNN	VGG16, ResNet110, etc.	●			●				S AUC 94.0
[158]	224 × 224	T U	CNN	VGG16, ResNet50,101	●		●	●				U AUC 97.4
[147]	256 × 256	S	CNN	Own	●		●					S Acc. 97.0
[150]	224 × 224	M	CNN	PWC-Net		●				●		M Acc. 81.6
[153]	128 × 128	S M N U V	CNN	Own	●				●			N Acc. 82.5 / M Acc. 80.6
[53]	720 × 576, 512 × 384	S	CNN-LSTM	Own		●			●			S EER 9.8
[160]	256 × 256	M N	AE-CNN	Own	●		●	●				N Acc. 90.3 / M Acc. 84.9
[159]	128 × 128	S H	CNN	Own	●			●				S Acc. 95.5
[162]	224 × 224	S	CNN	ResNet18	●		●					S Acc. 99.9
[135]	128 × 128	S	CNN	XceptionNet	●				●			S TPR 97.8
[157]	64 × 64	D G M V	CNN	XceptionNet	●		●					M AUC 98.5
[161]	299 × 299	S	CNN	XceptionNet, VGG16	●		●	●				S AUC 99.7
[152]	256 × 256	M	LSTM	Inception V3		●				●		M Acc. 94.3
[164]	224 × 224	S A M V	ABC-CNN	ResNet50	●				●			S Acc. 96.0
[163]	64 × 64	S A	Siamese-CNN	Own	●			●				S Prec. 98.8
[165]	100 × 100	M	VAE	One-Class VAE	●						●	M Acc. 98.2
[167]	224 × 224	S F N T	CNN	ResNet18	●			●				N Acc. 99.4
[168]	224 × 224	M V	LSTM	Own		●			●			M Acc. 96.4
[156]	Unknown	D T	CNN	Own		●				●		T AUC 96.3
[166]	224 × 224	M	CNN	ResNet50	●		●					M AP 98.2

6. Anti-Forensics

Anti-forensics also called counter-forensics aims at defeating the analysis and examination of forensic methods. Different techniques can be adopted by a smart and determined adversary to modify an image while attempting to prevent image forensics tools from getting useful clues on manipulations, falsifications, source devices, etc.

Early research [171,172] showed that CNN models are vulnerable to adversarial attacks. In the deep-learning-based anti-forensics field this has been translated to the use of GANs to recreate or hide different cues with visually imperceptible distortions.

Güera et al. [173] proposed a method to slightly modify images to alter their estimated camera model when analyzed by a CNN. The authors showed that adversarial-attack-based approaches such as Jacobian-based Saliency Map Attack (JSMA) and Fast Gradient Sign Method (FGSM) are capable of misleading CNN models that have been trained to perform camera model identification.

In [174], Chen et al. proposed a white-box scenario where information on the forensic tool and camera model is known. A GAN was proposed to modify traces used to identify a camera model. Additionally, they introduced a new loss function focused on both fooling a CNN-based detector of camera models and introducing minimum distortion into the image. Later, the same authors proposed in [175] the usage of GAN for two scenarios: a data-dependent scenario where camera model is known and a data-independent one where no information is available. In both cases a generative model was used to fool CNN-based camera model identification methods.

An anti-forensic method for recaptured image detection was proposed by Zhao et al. [176]. The authors proposed to employ Cycle-GANs typically used for image translation to accomplish this anti-forensic task of hiding traces of image recapturing. In their work, high-pass filters were used within the model to improve the anti-forensic performance. Moreover, the loss function was also adapted to ensure that the image content would not be changed too drastically.

Other proposals focused on concealing the traces left by routine image manipulations. Kim et al. [177] proposed a GAN model which was able to reproduce and hide the cues left by median filtering operation. Meanwhile, Wu and Sun [178] investigated the use of GANs and a tuned loss function to hide the traces left by multiple image manipulation operations. Uddin et al. [179] proposed a GAN-base anti-forensic method against double JPEG compression detection. Results showed that detection accuracy could be reduced from 98% to 85% by using the proposed method.

In [180], authors designed a small GAN architecture to prevent CGIs from being correctly detected. In this approach, the first layer of the discriminator was initialized with 2 *Sobel* filters to guide the network to concentrate more on the texture information of the input image.

Barni et al. [181] presented an analysis on the transferability of anti-forensic attacks. Their results showed that in most cases, attacks are not transferable, which facilitates the design of appropriate counter measures against anti-forensics. This is particularly true when an anti-forensic adversary does not have full knowledge of the targeted forensic method.

Table 10 provides a summary of deep-learning-based anti-forensic methods presented above. In particular, in the table we present the main component used by each method and the targeted forensic problem. We can see that the current trend is to design GAN-based anti-forensic algorithms against camera model identification methods and detectors of routine image manipulations. We expect to see in the near future interesting anti-forensic works considering more advanced tampering operations.

Table 10. Anti-forensic methods. The column of "Backbone strategy" shows the main technical component used in each method. Dataset is color coded as follows: **B** BOSSBase [16], **D** Dresden [17], **K** RAISE [18], **O** Vision [21], **A** CelebA [29], **C** Cao [182], **U** Agustsson [183], and **S** when it is an ad-hoc dataset created by authors of the original paper.

Method	Problem	Backbone Strategy	Input Size	Dataset
[173]	Camera identification	JSMA, FGSM	32 × 32	**S**
[174]		GAN	256 × 256	**D**
[175]		GAN	64 × 64, 227 × 227	**D**
[176]	Recaptured image detection	Cycle-GAN	256 × 256	**C**
[177]	Median filtering	GAN	64 × 64, 227 × 227	**K**
[178]	Multiple image manipulations	GAN	256 × 256	**B**
[179]	Double JPEG compression	GAN	512 × 384	**U**
[180]	CGI detection	GAN	178 × 218	**A**
[181]	Attack transferability	GAN	128 × 128	**K** **O**

7. Concluding Remarks

Through this review, we provide a general understanding of the detection methods in the image forensics field. We collected and presented many deep-learning-based methods divided into three broad categories, with a focus on the different characteristics that are particular for the image forensics approaches. It can be observed that a pre-processing step to obtain a certain feature or a special initialization on the network's first layer have been used in many pioneer works and still exist in recent ones. It is interesting to see that these characteristics are mainly present in the manipulation, falsification, camera identification and CGI detection methods but scarcely seen in the Deepfake detection works. We have not found clear reasons to explain this observation, and it would be interesting to carry out theoretical studies and practical comparisons with and without the use of pre-processing step and with different initializations of the first layer, for various forensic problems. This is a research opportunity to be explored in our future work. As any arms race scenario where two opponents, in this case a forger and a forensic investigator, try to make their respective actions successful, both sides will keep evolving with new technologies and challenges. Deep learning has brought a tremendous advance due to its ability to automatically learn useful features from available data and this strength has been used on both sides and their competition will be continued in the future.

One promising working direction is that it is beneficial to gain access to real-life forgery datasets that include ground-truth masks with a vast number of samples. Currently, depending on the forensic problem we want to study, existing datasets may have a limited number of examples or focus on a small range of devices or subjects. Although data scarcity has been tackled with the few-shot learning approach, the generalization problem may still be in game. In the case of Deepfake detection, a very popular research topic as we see from the large number of recent works collected in this review, high-quality datasets are becoming more and more available because of the involvement and commitment of big companies.

We also believe that although single works can obtain good performance, the combination of several domains or features will be of huge importance in the future. We have listed some works that combine the usage of image and audio features to detect Deepfakes, and probably these works would benefit from other features or strategies if properly combined. To this end, the availability of open-source implementation of existing methods is of paramount importance.

Another interesting future research topic is the development of different counter-forensic methods which we believe have a right of existence. Indeed, the creation of tools to deceive forensic detectors adds another interesting and important player in the game who challenges the detectors of fake multimedia content. As we saw in Section 6, almost all existing deep-learning-based anti-forensic methods make use of a GAN model which has proved to show good results. Nevertheless, different strategies could be explored to realize the objective of removing forensic cues, from the design of appropriate network architectures to the explicit analysis and removal of forensic traces with customized layers and loss function. Additionally, it is interesting to notice that special initializations on the first layer of a network architecture have also been used in the anti-forensics field. The resilience of forensic detectors would be improved by considering the attacks of anti-forensic methods. We believe that the competition between the two sides of forensics and anti-forensics would be beneficial for the advancement of both subjects and is an interesting topic to follow.

In all, we think that the image forensics research presents big challenges and opportunities for the future in which we hope to see more deep-learning-based methods to take better account of the particularities of the image forensics field.

Author Contributions: All authors contributed to the study conceptualisation and methodology for this manuscript. The first draft of the manuscript was written by I.C.C. and supervised and reviewed by K.W. All authors have read and agreed to the submitted version of the manuscript.

Funding: This work is partially funded by the French National Research Agency (DEFALS ANR-16-DEFA-0003, ANR-15-IDEX-02) and the Mexican National Council of Science and Technology (CONACYT).

Institutional Review Board Statement: Not applicable.

Informed Consent Statement: Not applicable.

Data Availability Statement: Not applicable.

Conflicts of Interest: The authors declare no conflict of interest. The founding sponsors had no role in the design of the study; in the collection, analyses, or interpretation of data; in the writing of the manuscript, and in the decision to publish the results.

References

1. Agarwal, S.; Farid, H.; Gu, Y. Protecting world leaders against deep fakes. In Proceedings of the IEEE/CVF Conference on Computer Vision and Pattern Recognition Workshops, Long Beach, CA, USA, 16–17 June 2019; pp. 38–45.
2. Piva, A. An overview on image forensics. *ISRN Signal Process.* **2013**, *2013*, 1–22. [CrossRef]
3. Goodfellow, I.J.; Bengio, Y.; Courville, A.C. *Deep Learning*; MIT Press: Cambridge, MA, USA, 2016.
4. Farid, H. A survey of image forgery detection. *IEEE Signal Process. Mag.* **2009**, *2*, 16–25. [CrossRef]
5. Rocha, A.; Scheirer, W.; Boult, T.; Goldenstein, S. Vision of the unseen: Current trends and challenges in digital image and video forensics. *ACM Comput. Surv.* **2011**, *43*, 1–42. [CrossRef]
6. Stamm, M.C.; Wu, M.; Liu, K.R. Information forensics: An overview of the first decade. *IEEE Access* **2013**, *1*, 167–200. [CrossRef]
7. Birajdar, G.K.; Mankar, V.H. Digital image forgery detection using passive techniques: A survey. *Digit. Investig.* **2013**, *10*, 226–245. [CrossRef]
8. Zheng, L.; Zhang, Y.; Thing, V.L. A survey on image tampering and its detection in real-world photos. *J. Vis. Commun. Image Represent.* **2019**, *58*, 380–399. [CrossRef]
9. Verdoliva, L. Media forensics and deepfakes: An overview. *IEEE J. Sel. Top. Signal Process.* **2020**, *14*, 910–932. [CrossRef]
10. Asghar, K.; Habib, Z.; Hussain, M. Copy-move and splicing image forgery detection and localization techniques: A review. *Aust. J. Forensic Sci.* **2017**, *49*, 281–307. [CrossRef]
11. Zhang, Z.; Wang, C.; Zhou, X. A survey on passive image copy-move forgery detection. *J. Inf. Process. Syst.* **2018**, *14*, 6–31.
12. Ni, X.; Chen, L.; Yao, Y. An evaluation of deep learning-based computer generated image detection approaches. *IEEE Access* **2019**, *7*, 130830–130840. [CrossRef]
13. Wu, J.; Feng, K.; Tian, M. Review of imaging device identification based on machine learning. In Proceedings of the International Conference on Machine Learning and Computing, Shenzhen, China, 15–17 February 2020; pp. 105–110.

14. Yang, P.; Baracchi, D.; Ni, R.; Zhao, Y.; Argenti, F.; Piva, A. A survey of deep learning-based source image forensics. *J. Imaging* **2020**, *6*, 9. [CrossRef]
15. Schaefer, G.; Stich, M. UCID—An uncompressed colour image database. In Proceedings of the SPIE: Storage and Retrieval Methods and Applications for Multimedia, San Jose, CA, USA, 20–22 January 2004; pp. 472–480.
16. Bas, P.; Filler, T.; Pevny, T. Break our steganographic system: The ins and outs of organizing BOSS. In Proceedings of the International Workshop on Information Hiding, Prague, Czech Republic, 18–20 May 2011; pp. 59–70.
17. Gloe, T.; Bohme, R. The Dresden image database for benchmarking digital image forensics. In Proceedings of the ACM Symposium on Applied Computing, Sierre, Switzerland, 22–26 March 2010; pp. 1584–1590.
18. Dang-Nguyen, D.T.; Pasquini, C.; Conotter, V.; Boato, G. RAISE: A raw images dataset for digital image forensics. In Proceedings of the ACM Multimedia Systems Conference, Portland, OR, USA, 18–20 March 2015; pp. 219–224.
19. De Marsico, M.; Nappi, M.; Riccio, D.; Wechsler, H. Mobile iris challenge evaluation (MICHE)-I, biometric iris dataset and protocols. *Pattern Recognit. Lett.* **2015**, *57*, 17–23. [CrossRef]
20. IEEE Signal Processing Society. IEEE's Signal Processing Society—Camera Model Identification Competition. 2018. Available online: https://www.kaggle.com/c/sp-society-camera-model-identification (accessed on 2 April 2021).
21. Shullani, D.; Fontani, M.; Iuliani, M.; Shaya, O.A.; Piva, A. VISION: A video and image dataset for source identification. *EURASIP J. Inf. Secur.* **2017**, *2017*, 15. [CrossRef]
22. Bergmann, P.; Fauser, M.; Sattlegger, D.; Steger, C. MVTec AD–A comprehensive real-world dataset for unsupervised anomaly detection. In Proceedings of the IEEE/CVF Conference on Computer Vision and Pattern Recognition, Long Beach, CA, USA, 15–20 June 2019; pp. 9592–9600.
23. Amazon Web Services Inc. Landsat on AWS. 2018. Available online: https://aws.amazon.com/public-datasets/landsat (accessed on 2 April 2021).
24. Nilsback, M.; Zisserman, A. Automated flower classification over a large number of classes. In Proceedings of the Indian Conference on Computer Vision, Graphics & Image Processing, Assam, India, 18–22 December 2008; pp. 722–729.
25. Lin, T.; Maire, M.; Belongie, S.; Hays, J.; Perona, P.; Ramanan, D.; Dollár, P.; Zitnick, C.L. Microsoft COCO: Common objects in context. In Proceedings of the European Conference on Computer Vision, Zurich, Switzerland, 6–12 September 2014; pp. 740–755.
26. Deng, J.; Dong, W.; Socher, R.; Li, L.; Li, K.; Fei-Fei, L. ImageNet: A large-scale hierarchical image database. In Proceedings of the IEEE/CVF Conference on Computer Vision and Pattern Recognition, Miami, FL, USA, 20–25 June 2009; pp. 248–255.
27. Zhou, B.; Lapedriza, A.; Xiao, J.; Torralba, A.; Oliva, A. Learning deep features for scene recognition using places database. In Proceedings of the Advances in Neural Information Processing Systems, Montreal, QC, Canada, 8–13 December 2014; pp. 487–495.
28. Xiao, J.; Hays, J.; Ehinger, K.; Oliva, A.; Torralba, A. Sun database: Large-scale scene recognition from abbey to zoo. In Proceedings of the IEEE/CVF Conference on Computer Vision and Pattern Recognition, San Francisco, CA, USA, 13–18 June 2010; pp. 3485–3492.
29. Liu, Z.; Luo, P.; Wang, X.; Tang, X. Deep learning face attributes in the wild. In Proceedings of the IEEE International Conference on Computer Vision, Santiago, Chile, 7–13 December 2015; pp. 3730–3738.
30. Karras, T.; Aila, T.; Laine, S.; Lehtinen, J. Progressive growing of GANs for improved quality, stability, and variation. *arXiv* **2017**, arXiv:1710.10196.
31. Ng, T.; Hsu, J.; Chang, S. A Data Set of Authentic and Spliced Image Blocks. 2004. Available online: http://www.ee.columbia.edu/ln/dvmm/downloads/AuthSplicedDataSet/AuthSplicedDataSet.htm (accessed on 2 April 2021).
32. Hsu, Y.F.; Chang, S.F. Detecting image splicing using geometry invariants and camera characteristics consistency. In Proceedings of the International Conference on Multimedia and Expo, Toronto, ON, Canada, 9–12 July 2006.
33. Dong, J.; Wang, W. CASIA image tampering detection evaluation database. In Proceedings of the IEEE China Summit and International Conference on Signal and Information Processing, Beijing, China, 6–10 July 2013; pp. 1–5.
34. IEEE IFS-TC. IEEE IFS-TC Image Forensics Challenge Dataset. 2014. Available online: http://ifc.recod.ic.unicamp.br/fc.website/index.py (accessed on 2 April 2021).
35. Carvalho, T.D.; Riess, C.; Angelopoulou, E.; Pedrini, H.; de Rezende Rocha, A. Exposing digital image forgeries by illumination color classification. *IEEE Trans. Inf. Forensics Secur.* **2013**, *8*, 1182–1194. [CrossRef]
36. Guan, H.; Kozak, M.; Robertson, E.; Lee, Y.; Yates, A.N.; Delgado, A.; Zhou, D.; Kheyrkhah, T.; Smith, J.; Fiscus, J. MFC datasets: Large-scale benchmark datasets for media forensic challenge evaluation. In Proceedings of the 2019 IEEE Winter Applications of Computer Vision Workshops (WACVW), Waikoloa Village, HI, USA, 7–11 January 2019; pp. 63–72.
37. NIST. Nimble Datasets. 2017. Available online: https://www.nist.gov/itl/iad/mig/nimble-challenge-2017-evaluation (accessed on 2 April 2021).
38. Korus, P.; Huang, J. Multi-scale analysis strategies in PRNU-based tampering localization. *IEEE Trans. Inf. Forensics Secur.* **2017**, *12*, 809–824. [CrossRef]
39. Bianchi, T.; Piva, A. Image forgery localization via block-grained analysis of JPEG artifacts. *IEEE Trans. Inf. Forensics Secur.* **2012**, *7*, 1003–1017. [CrossRef]
40. Wen, B.; Zhu, Y.; Subramanian, R.; Ng, T.; Shen, X.; Winkler, S. COVERAGE—A novel database for copy-move forgery detection. In Proceedings of the IEEE International Conference on Image Processing, Phoenix, AZ, USA, 25–28 September 2016; pp. 161–165.

41. Tralic, D.; Zupancic, I.; Grgic, S.; Grgic, M. CoMoFoD—New database for copy-move forgery detection. In Proceedings of the International Symposium on Electronics in Marine, Zadar, Croatia, 25–27 September 2013; pp. 49–54.
42. Macdonald, H. NRCS Photo Gallery. 2004. Available online: http://serc.carleton.edu/introgeo/interactive/examples/morrisonpuzzle.html (accessed on 2 April 2021).
43. Ng, T.; Chang, S.; Hsu, J.; Pepeljugoski, M. *Columbia Photographic Images and Photorealistic Computer Graphics Dataset*; ADVENT Technical Report; Columbia University: New York, NY, USA, 2005; pp. 205–2004.
44. Afchar, D.; Nozick, V.; Yamagishi, J.; Echizen, I. Mesonet: A compact facial video forgery detection network. In Proceedings of the IEEE International Workshop on Information Forensics and Security, Hong Kong, China, 11–13 December 2018; pp. 1–7.
45. ABVENT. Artlantis Gallery. 2005. Available online: https://artlantis.com/en/gallery/ (accessed on 2 April 2021).
46. Chaos Czech a.s. Corona Renderer Gallery. 2020. Available online: https://corona-renderer.com/gallery (accessed on 2 April 2021).
47. Ltd, C.P. Learn V-Ray Gallery. 2020. Available online: https://www.learnvray.com/fotogallery/ (accessed on 21 January 2021).
48. Autodesk Inc. Autodesk A360 Rendering Gallery. 2020. Available online: https://gallery.autodesk.com/a360rendering/ (accessed on 2 April 2021).
49. Yang, X.; Li, Y.; Lyu, S. Exposing deep fakes using inconsistent head poses. In Proceedings of the IEEE International Conference on Acoustics, Speech and Signal Processing, Brighton, UK, 12–17 May 2019; pp. 8261–8265.
50. Rössler, A.; Cozzolino, D.; Verdoliva, L.; Riess, C.; Thies, J.; Nießner, M. Faceforensics: A large-scale video dataset for forgery detection in human faces. *arXiv* **2018**, arXiv:1803.09179.
51. Rössler, A.; Cozzolino, D.; Verdoliva, L.; Riess, C.; Thies, J.; Nießner, M. Faceforensics++: Learning to detect manipulated facial images. In Proceedings of the IEEE International Conference on Computer Vision, Seoul, Korea, 27–28 October 2019; pp. 1–11.
52. Li, Y.; Yang, X.; Sun, P.; Qi, H.; Lyu, S. Celeb-DF: A large-scale challenging dataset for DeepFake forensics. In Proceedings of the IEEE/CVF Conference on Computer Vision and Pattern Recognition, Seattle, WA, USA, 14–19 June 2020; pp. 3207–3216.
53. Korshunov, P.; Halstead, M.; Castan, D.; Graciarena, M.; McLaren, M.; Burns, B.; Lawson, A.; Marcel, S. Tampered speaker inconsistency detection with phonetically aware audio-visual features. In Proceedings of the International Conference on Machine Learning, Long Beach, CA, USA, 10–15 June 2019; pp. 1–5.
54. deepfakes@Github. Faceswap Github. 2020. Available online: https://github.com/deepfakes/faceswap (accessed on 2 April 2021).
55. Dolhansky, B.; Howes, R.; Pflaum, B.; Baram, N.; Ferrer, C.C. The deepfake detection challenge (DFDC) preview dataset. *arXiv* **2019**, arXiv:1910.08854.
56. Google AI. Deepfakes Detection Dataset. 2019. Available online: https://ai.googleblog.com/2019/09/contributing-data-to-deepfake-detection.html (accessed on 2 April 2021).
57. Rahmouni, N.; Nozick, V.; Yamagishi, J.; Echizen, I. Distinguishing computer graphics from natural images using convolution neural networks. In Proceedings of the IEEE Workshop on Information Forensics and Security, Rennes, France, 4–7 December 2017; pp. 1–6.
58. Chen, J.; Kang, X.; Liu, Y. Median filtering forensics based on convolutional neural networks. *IEEE Signal Process. Lett.* **2015**, *22*, 1849–1853. [CrossRef]
59. Tang, H.; Ni, R.; Zhao, Y.; Li, X. Median filtering detection of small-size image based on CNN. *J. Vis. Commun. Image Represent.* **2018**, *51*, 162–168. [CrossRef]
60. Lin, M.; Chen, Q.; Yan, S. Network in network. *arXiv* **2013**, arXiv:1312.4400.
61. Popescu, A.; Farid, H. Statistical tools for digital forensics. In Proceedings of the International Workshop on Information Hiding, Toronto, ON, Canada, 23–25 May 2004; pp. 128–147.
62. Wang, Q.; Zhang, R. Double JPEG compression forensics based on a convolutional neural network. *EURASIP J. Inf. Secur.* **2016**, *2016*, 23. [CrossRef]
63. Verma, V.; Agarwal, N.; Khanna, N. DCT-domain deep convolutional neural networks for multiple JPEG compression classification. *Signal Process. Image Commun.* **2018**, *67*, 22–33. [CrossRef]
64. Barni, M.; Bondi, L.; Bonettini, N. Aligned and non-aligned double JPEG detection using convolutional neural networks. *J. Vis. Commun. Image Represent.* **2017**, *49*, 153–163. [CrossRef]
65. Amerini, I.; Uricchio, T.; Ballan, L.; Caldelli, R. Localization of JPEG double compression through multi-domain convolutional neural networks. In Proceedings of the IEEE/CVF Conference on Computer Vision and Pattern Recognition Workshops, Honolulu, HI, USA, 21–16 July 2017; pp. 1865–1871.
66. Park, J.; Cho, D.; Ahn, W.; Lee, H. Double JPEG detection in mixed JPEG quality factors using deep convolutional neural network. In Proceedings of the European Conference on Computer Vision, Munich, Germany, 8–14 September 2018; pp. 636–652.
67. Stamm, M.C.; Liu, K.R. Forensic detection of image manipulation using statistical intrinsic fingerprints. *IEEE Trans. Inf. Forensics Secur.* **2010**, *5*, 492–506. [CrossRef]
68. Barni, M.; Costanzo, A.; Nowroozi, E.; Tondi, B. CNN-based detection of generic contrast adjustment with JPEG post-processing. In Proceedings of the IEEE International Conference on Image Processing, Athens, Greece, 7–10 October 2018; pp. 3803–3807.
69. Sun, J.; Seung-Wook, K.; Sang-Won, L.; Sung-Jea, K. A novel contrast enhancement forensics based on convolutional neural networks. *Signal Process. Image Commun.* **2018**, *63*, 149–160. [CrossRef]

70. Shan, W.; Yi, Y.; Huang, R.; Xie, Y. Robust contrast enhancement forensics based on convolutional neural networks. *Signal Process. Image Commun.* **2019**, *71*, 138–146. [CrossRef]
71. Bayar, B.; Stamm, M.C. Constrained convolutional neural networks: A new approach towards general purpose image manipulation detection. *IEEE Trans. Inf. Forensics Secur.* **2018**, *13*, 2691–2706. [CrossRef]
72. Camacho, I.C.; Wang, K. A simple and effective initialization of CNN for forensics of image processing operations. In Proceedings of the ACM Workshop on Information Hiding and Multimedia Security, Paris, France, 3–5 July 2019; pp. 107–112.
73. Glorot, X.; Bengio, Y. Understanding the difficulty of training deep feedforward neural networks. In Proceedings of the International Conference on Artificial Intelligence and Statistics, Sardinia, Italy, 13–15 May 2010; pp. 249–256.
74. Camacho, I.C.; Wang, K. Data-dependent scaling of CNN's first layer for improved image manipulation detection. In Proceedings of the International Workshop on Digital-forensics and Watermarking, New York, NY, USA, 6–11 December 2020; pp. 1–15.
75. Zhang, Y.; Goh, J.; Win, L.; Thing, V. Image region forgery detection: A deep learning approach. In Proceedings of the Singapore Cyber-Security Conference, Singapore, 14–15 January 2016; pp. 1–11.
76. Kramer, M.A. Nonlinear principal component analysis using autoassociative neural networks. *AIChE J.* **1991**, *37*, 233–243. [CrossRef]
77. Fridrich, J.; Kodovsky, J. Rich models for steganalysis of digital images. *IEEE Trans. Inf. Forensics Secur.* **2012**, *7*, 868–882. [CrossRef]
78. Rao, Y.; Ni, J. A deep learning approach to detection of splicing and copy-move forgeries in images. In Proceedings of the IEEE International Workshop on Information Forensics and Security, Abu Dhabi, United Arab Emirates, 4–7 December 2016; pp. 1–6.
79. Cozzolino, D.; Poggi, G.; Verdoliva, L. Recasting residual-based local descriptors as convolutional neural networks: An application to image forgery detection. In Proceedings of the ACM Workshop on Information Hiding and Multimedia Security, Philadelphia, PA, USA, 20–21 June 2017; pp. 159–164.
80. Bunk, J.; Bappy, J.; Mohammed, T.M.; Nataraj, L.; Flenner, A.; Manjunath, B.; Chandrasekaran, S.; Roy-Chowdhury, A.K.; Peterson, L. Detection and localization of image forgeries using resampling features and deep learning. In Proceedings of the IEEE/CVF Conference on Computer Vision and Pattern Recognition Workshops, Honolulu, HI, USA, 21–16 July 2017; pp. 1881–1889.
81. Bappy, J.; Simons, C.; Nataraj, L.; Manjunath, B.; Roy-Chowdhury, A.K. Hybrid LSTM and encoder–decoder architecture for detection of image forgeries. *IEEE Trans. Image Process.* **2019**, *28*, 3286–3300. [CrossRef] [PubMed]
82. Hochreiter, S.; Schmidhuber, J. Long short-term memory. *Neural Comput.* **1997**, *9*, 1735–1780. [CrossRef] [PubMed]
83. Bondi, L.; Lameri, S.; Güera, D.; Bestagini, P.; Delp, E.J.; Tubaro, S. Tampering detection and localization through clustering of camera-based CNN features. In Proceedings of the IEEE/CVF Conference on Computer Vision and Pattern Recognition Workshops, Honolulu, HI, USA, 21–16 July 2017; pp. 1855–1864.
84. Cozzolino, D.; Verdoliva, L. Camera-based image forgery localization using convolutional neural networks. In Proceedings of the European Signal Processing Conference, Rome, Italy, 3–7 September 2018; pp. 1372–1376.
85. Yarlagadda, S.K.; Güera, D.; Bestagini, P.; Zhu, F.M.; Tubaro, S.; Delp, E.J. Satellite image forgery detection and localization using gan and one-class classifier. *Electron. Imaging* **2018**, *2018*, 241-1–241-9. [CrossRef]
86. Zhou, P.; Han, X.; Morariu, V.; Davis, L.S. Learning rich features for image manipulation detection. In Proceedings of the IEEE/CVF Conference on Computer Vision and Pattern Recognition, Salt Lake City, UT, USA, 18–22 June 2018; pp. 1053–1061.
87. Wu, Y.; AbdAlmageed, W.; Natarajan, P. ManTra-Net: Manipulation tracing network for detection and localization of image forgeries with anomalous features. In Proceedings of the IEEE/CVF Conference on Computer Vision and Pattern Recognition, Long Beach, CA, USA, 16–20 June 2019; pp. 9543–9552.
88. He, K.; Zhang, X.; Ren, S.; Sun, J. Deep residual learning for image recognition. In Proceedings of the IEEE/CVG Conference on Computer Vision and Pattern Recognition, Las Vegas, NV, USA, 27–30 June 2016; pp. 770–778.
89. Marra, F.; Gragnaniello, D.; Verdoliva, L.; Poggi, G. A full-image full-resolution end-to-end-trainable CNN framework for image forgery detection. *IEEE Access* **2020**, *8*, 133488–133502. [CrossRef]
90. Chollet, F. Xception: Deep learning with depthwise separable convolutions. In Proceedings of the IEEE/CVF Conference on Computer Vision and Pattern Recognition, Honolulu, HI, USA, 21–16 July 2017; pp. 1251–1258.
91. Zhou, P.; Chen, B.; Han, X.; Najibi, M.; Shrivastava, A.; Lim, S.; Davis, L. Generate, Segment, and Refine: Towards Generic Manipulation Segmentation. In Proceedings of the Association for the Advancement of Artificial Intelligence Conference, New York, NY, USA, 7–12 February 2020; pp. 13058–13065.
92. Bappy, J.; Roy-Chowdhury, A.K.; Bunk, J.; Nataraj, L.; Manjunath, B. Exploiting spatial structure for localizing manipulated image regions. In Proceedings of the IEEE/CVF International Conference on Computer Vision, Venice, Italy, 22–29 October 2017; pp. 4970–4979.
93. Cozzolino, D.; Verdoliva, L. Single-image splicing localization through autoencoder-based anomaly detection. In Proceedings of the IEEE International Workshop on Information Forensics and Security, Abu Dhabi, United Arab Emirates, 4–7 December 2016; pp. 1–6.
94. D'Avino, D.; Cozzolino, D.; Poggi, G.; Verdoliva, L. Autoencoder with recurrent neural networks for video forgery detection. *Electron. Imaging* **2017**, *2017*, 92–99. [CrossRef]
95. Wu, Y.; Abd-Almageed, W.; Natarajan, P. Deep matching and validation network: An end-to-end solution to constrained image splicing localization and detection. In Proceedings of the ACM international conference on Multimedia, Mountain View, CA, USA, 23–27 October 2017; pp. 1480–1502.

96. Simonyan, K.; Zisserman, A. Very deep convolutional networks for large-scale image recognition. *arXiv* **2014**, arXiv:1409.1556.
97. Salloum, R.; Ren, Y.; Kuo, C.C.K. Image splicing localization using a multi-task fully convolutional network (MFCN). *J. Vis. Commun. Image Represent.* **2018**, *51*, 201–209. [CrossRef]
98. Liu, B.; Pun, C. Locating splicing forgery by fully convolutional networks and conditional random field. *Signal Process. Image Commun.* **2018**, *66*, 103–112. [CrossRef]
99. Long, J.; Shelhamer, E.; Darrell, T. Fully convolutional networks for semantic segmentation. In Proceedings of the IEEE/CVF Conference on Computer Vision and Pattern Recognition, Boston, MA, USA, 7–12 June 2015; pp. 3431–3440.
100. Huh, M.; Liu, A.; Owens, A.; Efros, A.A. Fighting fake news: Image splice detection via learned self-consistency. In Proceedings of the European Conference on Computer Vision, Munich, Germany, 8–14 September 2018; pp. 101–117.
101. Pomari, T.; Ruppert, G.; Rezende, E.; Rocha, A.; Carvalho, T. Image splicing detection through illumination inconsistencies and deep learning. In Proceedings of the IEEE International Conference on Image Processing, Athens, Greece, 7–10 October 2018; pp. 3788–3792.
102. Kniaz, V.V.; Knyaz, V.; Remondino, F. The point where reality meets fantasy: Mixed adversarial generators for image splice detection. In Proceedings of the Advances in Neural Information Processing Systems, Vancouver, BC, Canada, 8–14 December 2019; pp. 215–226.
103. Bi, X.; Wei, Y.; Xiao, B.; Li, W. RRU-Net: The ringed residual U-Net for image splicing forgery detection. In Proceedings of the IEEE/CVF Conference on Computer Vision and Pattern Recognition Workshops, Long Beach, CA, USA, 16–17 June 2019; pp. 1–10.
104. Ronneberger, O.; Fischer, P.; Brox, T. U-Net: Convolutional networks for biomedical image segmentation. In Proceedings of the International Conference on Medical Image Computing and Computer-Assisted Intervention, Munich, Germany, 5–9 October 2015; pp. 234–241.
105. Bartusiak, E.; Yarlagadda, S.; Güera, D.; Bestagini, P.; Tubaro, S.; Zhu, F.; Delp, E.J. Splicing detection and localization in satellite imagery using conditional gans. In Proceedings of the IEEE Conference on Multimedia Information Processing and Retrieval, San Jose, CA, USA, 28–30 March 2019; pp. 91–96.
106. Liu, Y.; Zhu, X.; Zhao, X.; Cao, Y. Adversarial learning for constrained image splicing detection and localization based on atrous convolution. *IEEE Trans. Inf. Forensics Secur.* **2019**, *14*, 2551–2566. [CrossRef]
107. Rao, Y.; Ni, J.; Zhao, H. Deep learning local descriptor for image splicing detection and localization. *IEEE Access* **2020**, *8*, 25611–25625. [CrossRef]
108. Ouyang, J.; Liu, Y.; Liao, M. Copy-move forgery detection based on deep learning. In Proceedings of the International Congress on Image and Signal Processing, BioMedical Engineering and Informatics, Shanghai, China, 14–16 October 2017; pp. 1–5.
109. Krizhevsky, A.; Sutskever, I.; Hinton, G. ImageNet classification with deep convolutional neural networks. In Proceedings of the Advances in Neural Information Processing Systems, Lake Tahoe, NV, USA, 3–6 December 2012; pp. 1097–1105.
110. Wu, Y.; Abd-Almageed, W.; Natarajan, P. Image copy-move forgery detection via an end-to-end deep neural network. In Proceedings of the IEEE Winter Conference on Applications of Computer Vision, Lake Tahoe, NV, USA, 12–15 March 2018; pp. 1907–1915.
111. Wu, Y.; Abd-Almageed, W.; Natarajan, P. Busternet: Detecting copy-move image forgery with source/target localization. In Proceedings of the European Conference on Computer Vision, Munich, Germany, 8–14 September 2018; pp. 168–184.
112. Barni, M.; Phan, Q.; Tondi, B. Copy move source-target disambiguation through multi-branch CNNs. *arXiv* **2019**, arXiv:1912.12640.
113. Liu, Y.; Guan, Q.; Zhao, X. Copy-move forgery detection based on convolutional kernel network. *Multimed. Tools Appl.* **2018**, *77*, 18269–18293. [CrossRef]
114. Zhu, Y.; Chen, C.; Yan, G.; Guo, Y.; Dong, Y. AR-Net: Adaptive attention and residual refinement network for copy-move forgery detection. *IEEE Trans. Ind. Inform.* **2020**, *16*, 6714–6723. [CrossRef]
115. Mattis, P.; Douze, M.; Harchaoui, Z.; Mairal, J.; Perronin, F.; Schmid, C. Local convolutional features with unsupervised training for image retrieval. In Proceedings of the IEEE International Conference on Computer Vision, Santiago, Chile, 1–13 December 2015; pp. 91–99.
116. Christlein, V.; Riess, C.; Jordan, J.; Riess, C.; Angelopoulou, E. An evaluation of popular copy-move forgery detection approaches. *IEEE Trans. Inf. Forensics Secur.* **2012**, *7*, 1841–1854. [CrossRef]
117. Zhu, X.; Qian, Y.; Zhao, X.; Sun, B.; Sun, Y. A deep learning approach to patch-based image inpainting forensics. *Signal Process. Image Commun.* **2018**, *67*, 90–99. [CrossRef]
118. Wang, X.; Wang, H.; Niu, S. An image forensic method for AI inpainting using faster R-CNN. In Proceedings of the International Conference on Artificial Intelligence and Security, Okinawa, Japan, 16–18 April 2019; pp. 476–487.
119. Li, H.; Huang, J. Localization of deep inpainting using high-pass fully convolutional network. In Proceedings of the IEEE International Conference on Computer Vision, Seoul, Korea, 27–28 October 2019; pp. 8301–8310.
120. Wang, X.; Niu, S.; Wang, H. Image inpainting detection based on multi-task deep learning network. *IETE Tech. Rev.* **2020**, *38*, 1–9. [CrossRef]
121. Zavrtanik, V.; Kristan, M.; Skčaj, D. Reconstruction by inpainting for visual anomaly detection. *Pattern Recognit.* **2021**, *112*, 107706. [CrossRef]
122. Lu, M.; Niu, S. A detection approach using LSTM-CNN for object removal caused by exemplar-based image inpainting. *Electronics* **2020**, *9*, 858. [CrossRef]

123. Bondi, L.; Baroffio, L.; Güera, D.; Bestagini, P.; Delp, E.J.; Tubaro, S. First steps toward camera model identification with convolutional neural networks. *IEEE Signal Process. Lett.* **2016**, *24*, 259–263. [CrossRef]
124. Tuama, A.; Comby, F.; Chaumont, M. Camera model identification with the use of deep convolutional neural networks. In Proceedings of the IEEE International Workshop on Information Forensics and Security, Abu Dhabi, United Arab Emirates, 4–7 December 2016; pp. 1–6.
125. Bayar, B.; Stamm, M.C. Towards open set camera model identification using a deep learning framework. In Proceedings of the IEEE International Conference on Acoustics, Speech and Signal Processing, Calgary, AB, Canada, 15–20 April 2018; pp. 2007–2011.
126. Ding, X.; Chen, Y.; Tang, Z.; Huang, Y. Camera identification based on domain knowledge-driven deep multi-task learning. *IEEE Access* **2019**, *7*, 25878–25890. [CrossRef]
127. Freire-Obregón, D.; Narducci, F.; Barra, S.; Castrillón-Santana, M. Deep learning for source camera identification on mobile devices. *Pattern Recognit. Lett.* **2019**, *126*, 86–91. [CrossRef]
128. Cozzolino, D.; Verdoliva, L. Noiseprint: A CNN-based camera model fingerprint. *IEEE Trans. Inf. Forensics Secur.* **2019**, *15*, 144–159. [CrossRef]
129. Sameer, V.U.; Naskar, R. Deep siamese network for limited labels classification in source camera identification. *Multimed. Tools Appl.* **2020**, *79*, 28079–28104. [CrossRef]
130. De Rezende, E.; Ruppert, G.; Carvalho, T. Detecting computer generated images with deep convolutional neural networks. In Proceedings of the SIBGRAPI Conference on Graphics, Patterns and Images, Niteroi, Brazil, 17–20 October 2017; pp. 71–78.
131. Yu, I.J.; Kim, D.G.; Park, J.S.; Hou, J.U.; Choi, S.; Lee, H.K. Identifying photorealistic computer graphics using convolutional neural networks. In Proceedings of the IEEE International Conference on Image Processing, Beijing, China, 17–20 September 2017; pp. 4093–4097.
132. Quan, W.; Wang, K.; Yan, D.M.; Zhang, X. Distinguishing between natural and computer-generated images using convolutional neural networks. *IEEE Trans. Inf. Forensics Secur.* **2018**, *13*, 2772–2787. [CrossRef]
133. Nguyen, H.H.; Tieu, T.N.D.; Nguyen-Son, H.Q.; Nozick, V.; Yamagishi, J.; Echizen, I. Modular convolutional neural network for discriminating between computer-generated images and photographic images. In Proceedings of the International Conference on Availability, Reliability and Security, Hamburg, Germany, 27–30 August 2018; pp. 1–10.
134. Yao, Y.; Hu, W.; Zhang, W.; Wu, T.; Shi, Y.Q. Distinguishing computer-generated graphics from natural images based on sensor pattern noise and deep learning. *Sensors* **2018**, *18*, 1296. [CrossRef]
135. He, P.; Jiang, X.; Sun, T.; Li, H. Computer graphics identification combining convolutional and recurrent neural networks. *IEEE Signal Process. Lett.* **2018**, *25*, 1369–1373. [CrossRef]
136. Tariang, D.B.; Senguptab, P.; Roy, A.; Chakraborty, R.S.; Naskar, R. Classification of computer generated and natural images based on efficient deep convolutional recurrent attention model. In Proceedings of the IEEE/CVF Conference on Computer Vision and Pattern Recognition Workshops, Long Beach, CA, USA, 16–17 June 2019; pp. 146–152.
137. Nguyen, H.H.; Yamagishi, J.; Echizen, I. Capsule-forensics: Using capsule networks to detect forged images and videos. In Proceedings of the IEEE International Conference on Acoustics, Speech and Signal Processing, Brighton, UK, 12–17 May 2019; pp. 2307–2311.
138. Sabour, S.; Frosst, N.; Hinton, G. Dynamic routing between capsules. In Proceedings of the Advances in Neural Information Processing Systems, Long Beach, CA, USA, 4–9 December 2017; pp. 3856–3866.
139. Zhang, R.; Quan, W.; Fan, L.; Hu, L.; Yan, D.M. Distinguishing Computer-Generated Images from Natural Images Using Channel and Pixel Correlation. *J. Comput. Sci. Technol.* **2020**, *35*, 592–602. [CrossRef]
140. Meena, K.B.; Tyagi, V. A deep learning based method to discriminate between photorealistic computer generated images and photographic images. In Proceedings of the International Conference on Advances in Computing and Data Sciences, Valletta, Malta, 24–25 April 2020; pp. 212–223.
141. Huang, G.; Liu, Z.; Van Der Maaten, L.; Weinberger, K.Q. Densely connected convolutional networks. In Proceedings of the IEEE/CVF Conference on Computer Vision and Pattern Recognition, Honolulu, HI, USA, 21–16 July 2017; pp. 4700–4708.
142. He, P.; Li, H.; Wang, H.; Zhang, R. Detection of Computer Graphics Using Attention-Based Dual-Branch Convolutional Neural Network from Fused Color Components. *Sensors* **2020**, *20*, 4743. [CrossRef]
143. Quan, W.; Wang, K.; Yan, D.M.; Zhang, X.; Pellerin, D. Learn with diversity and from harder samples: Improving the generalization of CNN-Based detection of computer-generated images. *Forensic Sci. Int. Digit. Investig.* **2020**, *35*, 301023. [CrossRef]
144. Tokuda, E.; Pedrini, H.; Rocha, A. Computer generated images vs. digital photographs: A synergetic feature and classifier combination approach. *J. Vis. Commun. Image Represent.* **2013**, *24*, 1276–1292. [CrossRef]
145. Mo, H.; Chen, B.; Luo, W. Fake faces identification via convolutional neural network. In Proceedings of the ACM Workshop on Information Hiding and Multimedia Security, Innsbruck, Austria, 20–22 June 2018; pp. 43–47.
146. Marra, F.; Gragnaniello, D.; Cozzolino, D.; Verdoliva, L. Detection of GAN-generated fake images over social networks. In Proceedings of the IEEE Conference on Multimedia Information Processing and Retrieval, Miami, FL, USA, 10–12 April 2018; pp. 384–389.
147. Chan, C.; Ginosar, S.; Zhou, T.; Efros, A.A. Everybody dance now. In Proceedings of the IEEE International Conference on Computer Vision, Seoul, Korea, 27–28 October 2019; pp. 5933–5942.

148. Tariq, S.; Lee, S.; Kim, H.; Shin, Y.; Woo, S.S. Detecting both machine and human created fake face images in the wild. In Proceedings of the International Workshop on Multimedia Privacy and Security, Toronto, ON, Canada, 15 October 2018; pp. 81–87.
149. Güera, D.; Delp, E.J. Deepfake video detection using recurrent neural networks. In Proceedings of the IEEE International Conference on Advanced Video and Signal Based Surveillance, Auckland, New Zealand, 27–30 November 2018; pp. 1–6.
150. Amerini, I.; Galteri, L.; Caldelli, R.; Del Bimbo, A. Deepfake video detection through optical flow based CNN. In Proceedings of the IEEE/CVF International Conference on Computer Vision Workshops, Seoul, Korea, 27–28 October 2019; pp. 1–3.
151. Sun, D.; Yang, X.; Liu, M.Y.; Kautz, J. PWC-Net: CNNs for optical flow using pyramid, warping, and cost volume. In Proceedings of the IEEE/CVF Conference on Computer Vision and Pattern Recognition, Salt Lake City, UT, USA, 18–22 June 2018; pp. 8934–8943.
152. Amerini, I.; Caldelli, R. Exploiting prediction error inconsistencies through LSTM-based classifiers to detect deepfake videos. In Proceedings of the ACM Workshop on Information Hiding and Multimedia Security, Denver, CO, USA, 22–24 June 2020; pp. 97–102.
153. Ciftci, U.A.; Demir, I.; Yin, L. Fakecatcher: Detection of synthetic portrait videos using biological signals. *IEEE Trans. Pattern Anal. Mach. Intell.* **2020**, 1–17. [CrossRef]
154. Li, Y.; Chang, M.C.; Lyu, S. In ictu oculi: Exposing AI created fake videos by detecting eye blinking. In Proceedings of the IEEE International Workshop on Information Forensics and Security, Hong Kong, China, 11–13 December 2018; pp. 1–7.
155. Agarwal, S.; Farid, H.; Fried, O.; Agrawala, M. Detecting deep-fake videos from phoneme-viseme mismatches. In Proceedings of the IEEE/CVF Conference on Computer Vision and Pattern Recognition Workshops, Seattle, WA, USA, 14–19 June 2020; pp. 1–9.
156. Mittal, T.; Bhattacharya, U.; Chandra, R.; Bera, A.; Manocha, D. Emotions don't lie: A deepfake detection method using audio-visual affective cues. *arXiv* **2020**, arXiv:2003.06711.
157. Li, L.; Bao, J.; Zhang, T.; Yang, H.; Chen, D.; Wen, F.; Guo, B. Face X-ray for more general face forgery detection. In Proceedings of the IEEE/CVF Conference on Computer Vision and Pattern Recognition, Seattle, WA, USA, 14–19 June 2020; pp. 5001–5010.
158. Li, Y.; Lyu, S. Exposing deepFake videos by detecting face warping artifacts. In Proceedings of the IEEE Conference on Computer Vision and Pattern Recognition Workshops, Salt Lake City, UT, USA, 18–22 June 2018; pp. 46–52.
159. Xuan, X.; Peng, B.; Wang, W.; Dong, J. On the generalization of GAN image forensics. In Proceedings of the Chinese Conference on Biometric Recognition, Zhuzhou, China, 12–13 October 2019; pp. 134–141.
160. Nguyen, H.H.; Fang, F.; Yamagishi, J.; Echizen, I. Multi-task learning for detecting and segmenting manipulated facial images and videos. In Proceedings of the IEEE International Conference on Biometrics Theory, Applications and Systems, Tampa, FL, USA, 23–26 September 2019; pp. 1–8.
161. Dang, H.; Liu, F.; Stehouwer, J.; Liu, X.; Jain, A.K. On the detection of digital face manipulation. In Proceedings of the IEEE/CVF Conference on Computer Vision and Pattern Recognition, Seattle, WA, USA, 14–19 June 2020; pp. 5781–5790.
162. Ding, X.; Raziei, Z.; Larson, E.C.; Olinick, E.V.; Krueger, P.; Hahsler, M. Swapped face detection using deep learning and subjective assessment. *EURASIP J. Inf. Secur.* **2020**, *2020*, 6. [CrossRef]
163. Hsu, C.C.; Zhuang, Y.X.; Lee, C.Y. Deep fake image detection based on pairwise learning. *Appl. Sci.* **2020**, *10*, 370. [CrossRef]
164. Fernandes, S.; Raj, S.; Ewetz, R.; Singh Pannu, J.; Kumar Jha, S.; Ortiz, E.; Vintila, I.; Salter, M. Detecting deepfake videos using attribution-based confidence metric. In Proceedings of the IEEE/CVF Conference on Computer Vision and Pattern Recognition Workshops, Seattle, WA, USA, 14–19 June 2020; pp. 308–309.
165. Khalid, H.; Woo, S.S. OC-FakeDect: Classifying deepfakes using one-class variational autoencoder. In Proceedings of the IEEE/CVF Conference on Computer Vision and Pattern Recognition Workshops, Seattle, WA, USA, 14–19 June 2020; pp. 656–657.
166. Wang, S.Y.; Wang, O.; Zhang, R.; Owens, A.; Efros, A.A. CNN-generated images are surprisingly easy to spot . . . for now. In Proceedings of the IEEE/CVF Conference on Computer Vision and Pattern Recognition, Seattle, WA, USA, 14–19 June 2020; pp. 8695–8704.
167. Li, X.; Yu, K.; Ji, S.; Wang, Y.; Wu, C.; Xue, H. Fighting against deepfake: Patch&pair convolutional neural networks (PPCNN). In Proceedings of the Web Conference 2020, Ljubljana, Slovenia, 19–23 April 2020; pp. 88–89.
168. Masi, I.; Killekar, A.; Mascarenhas, R.M.; Gurudatt, S.P.; AbdAlmageed, W. Two-branch recurrent network for isolating deepfakes in videos. *arXiv* **2020**, arXiv:2008.03412.
169. Su, W.; Yuan, Y.; Zhu, M. A relationship between the average precision and the area under the ROC curve. In Proceedings of the International Conference on the Theory of Information Retrieval, Northampton, MA, USA, 27–30 September 2015; pp. 349–352.
170. Zhu, J.Y.; Park, T.; Isola, P.; Efros, A.A. Unpaired image-to-image translation using cycle-consistent adversarial networks. In Proceedings of the IEEE International Conference on Computer Vision, Venice, Italy, 22–29 October 2017; pp. 2223–2232.
171. Nguyen, A.; Yosinski, J.; Clune, J. Deep neural networks are easily fooled: High confidence predictions for unrecognizable images. In Proceedings of the IEEE/CVF Conference on Computer Vision and Pattern Recognition, Boston, MA, USA, 7–12 June 2015; pp. 427–436.
172. Szegedy, C.; Zaremba, W.; Sutskever, I.; Bruna, J.; Erhan, D.; Goodfellow, I.; Fergus, R. Intriguing properties of neural networks. *arXiv* **2013**, arXiv:1312.6199.
173. Güera, D.; Wang, Y.; Bondi, L.; Bestagini, P.; Tubaro, S.; Delp, E.J. A counter-forensic method for CNN-based camera model identification. In Proceedings of the IEEE/CVF Conference on Computer Vision and Pattern Recognition Workshops, Honolulu, HI, USA, 21–16 July 2017; pp. 1840–1847.

174. Chen, C.; Zhao, X.; Stamm, M.C. MISLGAN: An anti-forensic camera model falsification framework using a generative adversarial network. In Proceedings of the IEEE International Conference on Image Processing, Athens, Greece, 7–10 October 2018; pp. 535–539.
175. Chen, C.; Zhao, X.; Stamm, M.C. Generative adversarial attacks against deep-learning-based camera model identification. *IEEE Trans. Inf. Forensics Secur.* **2019**, 1–16. [CrossRef]
176. Zhao, W.; Yang, P.; Ni, R.; Zhao, Y.; Li, W. Cycle GAN-based attack on recaptured images to fool both human and machine. In Proceedings of the International Workshop on Digital-Forensics and Watermarking, Hong Kong, China, 11–13 December 2018; pp. 83–92.
177. Kim, D.; Jang, H.U.; Mun, S.M.; Choi, S.; Lee, H.K. Median filtered image restoration and anti-forensics using adversarial networks. *IEEE Signal Process. Lett.* **2017**, *25*, 278–282. [CrossRef]
178. Wu, J.; Sun, W. Towards multi-operation image anti-forensics with generative adversarial networks. *Comput. Secur.* **2021**, *100*, 102083. [CrossRef]
179. Uddin, K.; Yang, Y.; Oh, B.T. Anti-forensic against double JPEG compression detection using adversarial generative network. In Proceedings of the Korean Society of Broadcast Engineers Conference: Korea Institute of Science and Technology Information, Daejeon, Korea, 2019; pp. 58–60.
180. Cui, Q.; Meng, R.; Zhou, Z.; Sun, X.; Zhu, K. An anti-forensic scheme on computer graphic images and natural images using generative adversarial networks. *Math. Biosci. Eng.* **2019**, *16*, 4923–4935. [CrossRef]
181. Barni, M.; Kallas, K.; Nowroozi, E.; Tondi, B. On the transferability of adversarial examples against CNN-based image forensics. In Proceedings of the IEEE International Conference on Acoustics, Speech and Signal Processing, Brighton, UK, 12–17 May 2019; pp. 8286–8290.
182. Cao, H.; Kot, A.C. Identification of recaptured photographs on LCD screens. In Proceedings of the IEEE International Conference on Acoustics, Speech and Signal Processing, Dallas, TX, USA, 15–19 March 2010; pp. 1790–1793.
183. Agustsson, E.; Timofte, R. Ntire 2017 challenge on single image super-resolution: Dataset and study. In Proceedings of the IEEE/CVF Conference on Computer Vision and Pattern Recognition Workshops, Honolulu, HI, USA, 21–16 July 2017; pp. 126–135.

MDPI
St. Alban-Anlage 66
4052 Basel
Switzerland
Tel. +41 61 683 77 34
Fax +41 61 302 89 18
www.mdpi.com

Journal of Imaging Editorial Office
E-mail: jimaging@mdpi.com
www.mdpi.com/journal/jimaging

www.ingramcontent.com/pod-product-compliance
Lightning Source LLC
LaVergne TN
LVHW070122100526
838202LV00016B/2215